Standards	Chapters									
	1	2	3	4	5	6	7	8	9	10
Life Science Standards										
Characteristics of organisms		•				•			•	
Organisms and environments		•				•				•
Earth and Space Science Standards										
Properties of earth materials			•							
Objects in the sky				•						•
Changes in earth and sky		•		•				•		•
Science and Technology Standards										
Abilities of technological design	•									•
Understanding about science and technology	•									•
Science in Personal and Social Perspectives Standards										
Science and technology in society	•				•					•
History and Nature of Science Standards										
Science as a human endeavor	•									
Nature of science	•									
History of science	•									
NSES Science Education Program Standards										
The program of study in science should connect to other school subjects	•	•	•					•		•
Science content must be embedded in a variety of curriculum programs that are developmentally appropriate, interesting, and relevant to students' lives			•						•	
The science program should be coordinated with the mathematics program		•						•		•
Collaborative inquiry requires adequate and safe space							•			
The most important resource is professional teachers	•		•	•	•	•			•	

TENTH EDITION

PEARSON

Merrill
Prentice Hall

Upper Saddle River, New Jersey
Columbus, Ohio

Teaching Science as Inquiry

ARTHUR A. CARIN (DECEASED)
Professor Emeritus Queens College

JOEL E. BASS
Professor Emeritus, Sam Houston State University

TERRY L. CONTANT
Sam Houston State University

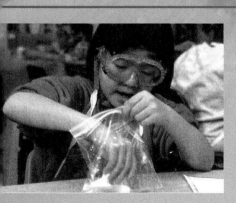

Library of Congress Cataloging in Publication Data b25091144x

Carin, Arthur A.
    Teaching science as inquiry/Arthur A. Carin, Joel E. Bass, Terry L. Contant.—10th ed.
        p. cm.
    Includes bibliographical references and index.
    ISBN 0-13-118165-3
    1. Science—Study and teaching (Elementary) I. Bass, Joel E. II. Contant, Terry L. III. Title.
    LB1585.C28 2005
    372.3'5044—dc22   2004003375

Vice President and Executive Publisher: Jeffery W. Johnston
Editor: Linda Ashe Montgomery
Editorial Assistant: Laura Weaver
Development Editor: Hope Madden
Production Editor: Mary M. Irvin
Production Coordination: Carlisle Publishers Services
Design Coordinator: Diane C. Lorenzo
Cover Designer: Ali Mohrman
Cover Images: Index Stock
Photo Coordinator: Kathy Kirtland
Production Manager: Pamela D. Bennett
Director of Marketing: Ann Castel Davis
Marketing Manager: Darcy Betts Prybella
Marketing Coordinator: Tyra Poole

Additional Credits: The *National Science Education Standards* boxes throughout the text were reprinted with permission from *National Science Education Standards* by the National Academy of Sciences, courtesy of the National Academies Press, Washington, DC; Quote on p. 126 reprinted by permission of Nekia Communications from Kober, Nancy, EDTALK, *What We Know About Science Teaching and Learning*, p. 44, 1993. Washington, DC: Council for Educational Development and Research; Quote on p. 308 reprinted with permission from *National Education Technology Standards for Students—Connecting Curriculum and Technology*, copyright © 2000, ISTE (International Society for Technology in Education), 800.336.5191 (U.S. & Canada) or 541.302.3777 (International), iste@iste.org. All rights reserved. Permission does not constitute an endorsement by ISTE.

This book was set in Goudy by Carlisle Communications, Ltd. It was printed and bound by Courier Kendallville, Inc. The cover was printed by Coral Graphic, Inc.

Photo Credits: Kenneth P. Davis/PH College: ii; Anthony Magnacca/Merrill: iii (top), 4, 9, 30 (top left and right), 36, 47, 73, 81, 86, 98, 101, 126, 130, 145, 154, 157, 210, 217, 231, 250, 260, 308, 314 (top and bottom); Arthur A. Carin: 8, 88 (top); Siede Preis/Getty Images, Inc.–PhotoDisc: 17 (top left); National Oceanic and Atmospheric Administration: 17 (top right); NASA Headquarters: 17 (bottom); Silver Burdett Ginn: 30 (bottom left and right); Anne Vega/Merrill: 40; Barbara Schwartz/Merrill: 68; Scott Cunningham/Merrill: iii (bottom), 88 (bottom left and right), 113, 276, 294; David Young-Wolff/PhotoEdit: 108; David Napravnik/Merrill: 244; John Morrell and Company: 270 (top left); Portland Chamber of Commerce: 270 (top right); Helen Bass: 270 (bottom) A-232; Richard Haynes/Prentice Hall School Division: 297. Color insert: Anthony Magnacca/Merrill: between pp. 38–39; Robert Brenner/PhotoEdit: between pp. 260–261.

372.35044
'C35
2005

Pearson Prentice Hall™ is a trademark of Pearson Education, Inc.
Pearson® is a registered trademark of Pearson plc
Prentice Hall® is a registered trademark of Pearson Education, Inc.
Merrill® is a registered trademark of Pearson Education, Inc.

Pearson Education Ltd.
Pearson Education Singapore Pte. Ltd.
Pearson Education Canada, Ltd.
Pearson Education–Japan

Pearson Education Australia Pty. Limited
Pearson Education North Asia Ltd.
Pearson Educación de Mexico, S.A. de C.V.
Pearson Education Malaysia Pte. Ltd.

10 9 8 7 6 5 4 3
ISBN: 0-13-118165-3

Arthur A. Carin
1928–2003

I was first introduced to Arthur Carin while planning the revision of the seventh edition of this book. Awed by his longstanding reputation as a leading science educator, I wondered what kind of author I would find Dr. Carin to be—open to suggestions or resistant to change. Art was always open to new ideas and always excited to begin a new revision and improve the text. During our tenure together, I developed a great respect for Dr. Carin, knowing him to remain informed about science education research, still hungry to make a difference in the lives of teachers, and forever excited to be the one who turned a child's natural curiosity about the world into scientific adventure. He leaves this message.

> "I wish you much success as you experience the joy of seeing your students construct and broaden their science knowledge and grow in their appreciation of this marvelous world."

A few years before his death, we recognized Arthur Carin as one of our most highly esteemed and successful authors, a great presence for Merrill Education for over forty years. Even as it is hard to say good-bye, we who worked with Art continue to be humbled by his knowledge and leadership in the field of science education and are immensely grateful to have worked with such a giant. We miss you, Art.

Linda Montgomery
Senior Editor

Educator Learning Center:
An Invaluable Online Resource

Merrill Education and the Association for Supervision and Curriculum Development (ASCD) invite you to take advantage of a new online resource, one that provides access to the top research and proven strategies associated with ASCD and Merrill—the Educator Learning Center. At **www.EducatorLearningCenter.com** you will find resources that will enhance your students' understanding of course topics and of current educational issues, in addition to being invaluable for further research.

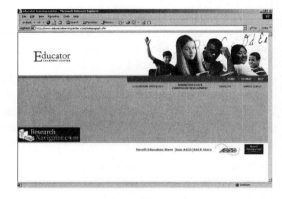

How the Educator Learning Center will help your students become better teachers

With the combined resources of Merrill Education and ASCD, you and your students will find a wealth of tools and materials to better prepare them for the classroom.

Research

- More than 600 articles from the ASCD journal *Educational Leadership* discuss everyday issues faced by practicing teachers.
- A direct link on the site to Research Navigator™ gives students access to many of the leading education journals, as well as extensive content detailing the research process.
- Excerpts from Merrill Education texts give your students insights on important topics of instructional methods, diverse populations, assessment, classroom management, technology, and refining classroom practice.

Classroom Practice

- Hundreds of lesson plans and teaching strategies are categorized by content area and age range.
- Case studies and classroom video footage provide virtual field experience for student reflection.
- Computer simulations and other electronic tools keep your students abreast of today's classrooms and current technologies.

Look into the value of Educator Learning Center yourself

A four-month subscription to Educator Learning Center is $25 but is FREE when used in conjuction with this text. To obtain free passcodes for your students, simply contact your local Merrill/Prentice Hall sales representative, and your representative will give you a special ISBN to give your bookstore when ordering your textbooks. To preview the value of this website to you and your students, please go to **www.EducatorLearningCenter.com** and click on "Demo."

Preface

THE RAPID ADVANCE of cognitive learning theories in the past few years has led educators to realize the need for students to be more actively engaged in their own construction of knowledge. This research tells us that an inquiry approach to science teaching motivates and engages every type of student, helping them understand science's relevance to their lives, as well as the nature of science itself.

Inquiry is both a way for scientists and students to investigate the world, and a way to teach. In this instructional environment, teachers act as facilitators of learning, guiding students in asking simple but thoughtful questions about the world and finding ways to engage them in answering their questions.

Inquiry incorporates the use of hands-on and process-oriented activities for the benefit of knowledge construction, while building investigation skills and habits of mind in students. Inquiry encourages students to connect their prior knowledge to observations and to use their observations as evidence to increase personal scientific knowledge and explain how the world works.

But is there a manageable way for new and experienced teachers to bring inquiry into their science classrooms?

Drawing on a solid understanding of inquiry with a teaching framework that builds in accountability for science content learning, and using inquiry-based activities, teachers can create and manage an engaging, productive science classroom. By integrating an inquiry approach, science content, teaching methods, standards, and a bank of inquiry activities, the tenth edition of *Teaching Science as Inquiry* demonstrates a manageable way for new and experienced teachers to bring inquiry successfully into the science classroom.

The Inquiry Framework

In this edition we have taken the *National Science Education Standards* (NSES) and the 5-E Learning Cycle model of instruction to create an inquiry framework for science teaching. *Teaching Science as Inquiry* models this effective approach to science teaching with a two-part structure. *Part 1: Methods for Teaching Science as Inquiry* lays the foundation for teaching standards-based elementary science, scaffolding an understanding of an inquiry lesson model and how to use it to teach science.

Part 2: Activities for Teaching Science as Inquiry utilizes the 5-E instructional model, clarified in Part 1 of the text, as a framework for all inquiry activities. By keying each activity

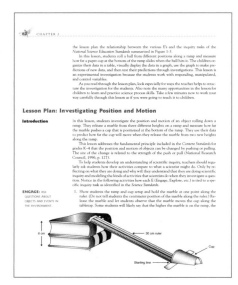

to the *National Science Education Standards*, the text further provides new and experienced teachers with a solid foundation for science teaching.

National Science Education Standards

Many years of work and research in the science education community have provided a coherent, research-based vision for a new era of science education. As a result, the *National Science Education Standards* (NSES) were created to coordinate the goals and objectives for science instruction.

Throughout this edition, you will have an opportunity to become familiar with the *National Science Education Standards* through margin notes and lengthier features quoting from the *Standards* document, showing the *Standards'* relationship to chapter content and specifically connecting activities to the *Standards*. This integrated coverage in all chapters and activities highlights the importance of using the *National Science Education Standards* to inform instruction.

5-E Model

The *Activities* portion of the text follows the 5-E model of instruction, which frames each activity in terms of engaging, exploring, explaining, elaborating, and evaluating. This Learning Cycle model, introduced early in the text, reflects the NSES *Science as Inquiry Standards*, seamlessly integrating inquiry and the *Standards* to create a science teaching framework best suited for engaging students in meaningful science learning while providing accountability opportunities for teachers.

Methods for Teaching Science as Inquiry

The *Methods* portion of this edition scaffolds the understanding of science concepts; investigation procedures; concepts of teaching, learning, and assessment; and the 5-E and other instructional models to help readers understand the inquiry approach to teaching. Among the many highlights of this revision, you will find

- a strong focus throughout the book on the 5-E model of instruction;
- a more comprehensive discussion of conceptual change and how to use conceptual change strategies within the 5-E model of instruction;
- margin notes that link readers to activities that model standards-based inquiry and developmentally appropriate science content;
- a reorganization of the chapter on assessment based on the new revision of Bloom's taxonomy of educational objectives;
- more suggestions on how to construct and use performance assessments, and how to use traditional assessments in new ways;
- an expanded, research-based focus on using hands-on, inquiry-oriented activities with learners who have special learning needs;
- the presentation of exciting new advancements and trends in educational technology and how they apply to the science classroom;
- clarification of various ideas important to inquiry, including aspects of the nature of science and constructivist principles of learning;

- the addition of classroom scenarios to illustrate strategies of inquiry instruction and introduce readers to important science concepts; and
- an expanded view of descriptive investigations, classificatory investigations, and experimental investigations, three main ways children can learn to investigate the world.

Video Case Studies

The process of observing and reflecting on teachers' actions, and on students' learning and thinking, can lead to changes in the knowledge, beliefs, attitudes, and ultimately the practice of pre-service and in-service teachers.

Use classroom discussions about the Video Case Studies to

- extend and apply knowledge presented in the chapters,
- formulate questions and ideas,
- learn from one another,
- become aware of alternative perspectives and strategies,
- reflect on real problems faced by practicing teachers, and
- increase your science knowledge, as more than 30 science topics are taught in the case studies.

The Video Case Study features in the chapters focus on each teacher's growth over time and look specifically at the inquiry approach in each classroom. The features provide *Questions for Reflection* to help you and others increase your involvement with the Video Case Study and look for changes in the knowledge, beliefs, and instructional plans and approaches of the featured teacher. Also included in most of the chapter video guides are examples of strategies you may want to implement in your own science teaching practice.

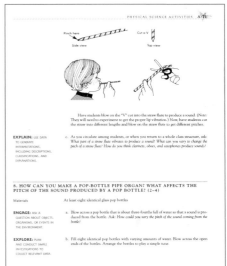

Activities for Teaching Science as Inquiry

A very significant change in the tenth edition is the complete revision of *Part 2: Activities for Teaching Science as Inquiry*. The activities have been reorganized to follow the NSES *Content Standards*, further developing new and experienced teachers' fluency with a *Standards*-based science classroom, and have been restructured to follow the 5-E instructional model, creating a manageable way to engage students in inquiry activities.

Using Activities for Teaching Science as Inquiry

The Activities for Teaching Science as Inquiry

- can be used to illustrate and expand on the science content, and model the 5-E lesson procedures, engaging students in constructivist inquiry;
- provide a comprehensive view of how the NSES *Science Content Standards* can be used to organize curriculum and inform instruction in elementary and middle school science;
- provide an interesting way for methods students to learn significant science content that will be important for them to know in teaching science;
- provide a way for students to prepare for the science portion of state certification exams; and

    • become a bank of activities students can draw on in developing lesson plans to teach during their science methods courses and when they move into the schools as professional teachers.

Collectively, the changes made to this edition help to present a more coherent picture of teaching science as inquiry and practical methods for implementing an inquiry approach to science teaching and learning.

Supplements

Videos by Annenberg

The Video Case Studies that accompany this text are free to professors who use this text and are part of the professional library developed by Annenberg. Chosen for their value in illustrating professional development, ten video cases depict nine different teachers in three videos from Annenberg's Case Studies in Science Education series. Each video case has three modules: Introducing the Case, Trying New Ideas, and Reflecting and Building on Change. The three parts of each video case enable you to look in on a teacher and his or her students at intervals throughout the school year. From one segment to the next, you will see how the teacher undergoes professional changes in approaching science teaching. The changes reflect the real-life experiences of teachers who see a need to improve the way they teach, meet with a teaching mentor to gather ideas, and implement ways to improve their science teaching practice. As a result of this work, you will witness not only a teacher's growing confidence and capability in science teaching but also a growing involvement of students in their own science learning.

Instructor's Manual

Free to adopters, this manual provides chapter-by-chapter supplements to enrich each class meeting. You find an extensive test bank, as well as suggested activities, objectives and overviews, suggested readings, and other tools for teaching.

The Companion Website

A Virtual Learning Environment

Built on and enhancing this edition's content, the Companion Website offers many valuable tools for broadening and deepening the reader's feel for inquiry science teaching.

For the Student—

- **Chapter Objectives**—serve to overview each chapter's main points.
- **Interactive self-quizzes**—both multiple choice and essay, these quizzes help students gauge their understanding of chapter concepts.

    After students submit their answers for the interactive self-quizzes, the Companion Website **Results Reporter** computes a percentage grade, provides a graphic representation of how many questions were answered correctly and incorrectly, and gives a question by question analysis of the quiz. Students are given the option to send their quiz to up to four email addresses (professor, teaching assistant, study partner, etc.).

- **Virtual Classrooms**—provide classroom video clips and questions for reflection, ideal ways to observe, assess, and reflect on inquiry teaching.
- **Web Destinations**—links to www sites including national and state standards sites, as well as other sites providing meaningful tools to pre-service science teachers.
- **Glossary**—this chapter-by-chapter glossary of terms will be helpful as students study and review each chapter's content.
- **Message Board**—serves as a virtual bulletin board to post—or respond to—questions or comments to/from a national audience.

For the Professor—

Every Companion Website integrates **Syllabus Manager™,** an online syllabus creation and management utility.

- **Syllabus Manager™** provides you, the instructor, with an easy, step-by-step process to create and revise syllabi, with direct links into Companion Website and other online content without having to learn HTML.
- Students may logon to your syllabus during any study session. All they need to know is the web address for the Companion Website and the password you've assigned to your syllabus.
- After you have created a syllabus using **Syllabus Manager™,** students may enter the syllabus for their course section from any point in the Companion Website.
- Clicking on a date, the student is shown the list of activities for the assignment. The activities for each assignment are linked directly to actual content, saving time for students.
- Adding assignments consists of clicking on the desired due date, then filling in the details of the assignment—name of the assignment, instructions, and whether or not it is a one-time or repeating assignment.
- In addition, links to other activities can be created easily. If the activity is online, a URL can be entered in the space provided, and it will be linked automatically in the final syllabus.
- Your completed syllabus is hosted on our servers, allowing convenient updates from any computer on the Internet. Changes you make to your syllabus are immediately available to your students at their next logon.

To take advantage of the many available resources, please visit the *Teaching Science as Inquiry* Companion Website at

www.prenhall.com/carin

Acknowledgments

To be meaningful, educational visions have to be practically implemented in teacher education and staff development programs, and most important, in our nation's classrooms. Our goal in writing and revising this textbook has been to present the new vision of science education and provide you with specific help, guidelines, and examples as you prepare to teach science in a new millennium.

The reviewers for the tenth edition of this text, as well as those who read and commented on the chapters in the ninth edition, have been very perceptive and insightful and have offered many comments and suggestions that, hopefully, have led to significant improvements. We acknowledge and express our gratitude to the following reviewers: Kerri M. Skinner, University of Nebraska at Kearney; Carol Brewer, The University of Montana; Rosemarie Kolstad, East Texas State University; Mark R. Malone, The University of Colorado; Richard H. Moyer, The University of Michigan—Dearborn; Michael Odell, The University of Idaho; William A. Rieck, The University of Southwestern Louisiana; Joseph D. Sharpe, Tennessee Technological University; Leone E. Snyder, Northwestern College; M. Dale Streigle, Iowa State University; and Dana L. Zeidler, The University of South Florida–Tampa. A special thanks to Dr. Phil Swicegood of Sam Houston State University for his helpful review of Chapter 9.

We thank editor Linda Montgomery at Merrill/Prentice Hall, who has provided substantive as well as editorial assistance throughout the writing and revision efforts. She has a great sensitivity to education issues, not only in science but in other specialized fields as well. We wish to acknowledge her contributions to this text and convey our appreciation to her.

We also wish to thank Hope Madden, our diligent and amenable development editor; Joan Lyon, copyeditor; Carlisle Communications, designer; Mary Irvin, production editor; and Emily Hatteberg, project coordinator at Carlisle Publishers Services.

From Art Carin

I am certain you will find this text a valuable resource as you become an even more competent, confident decision maker. I strongly encourage you to adapt the strategies in this text and appeal to you to apply the concepts in ways that are meaningful to you and your students. It is my hope that it will empower you confidently to teach science to your students in your unique classroom situations. I wish you much success as you experience the joy of seeing your students construct and broaden their science knowledge and grow in their appreciation of this marvelous world.

For their continued support and encouragement, I wish to personally thank my wife, Doris Terry, a former classroom teacher; my adult children, Jill, Amy, and Jon; and their respective spouses, Kevin, Rich, and Oberon. I appreciate the love and inspiration I continually get from my three wonderful grandchildren: Andy, a fine young man in high school; Becky, a beautiful, delightful student in first grade; and our newest addition, preschooler Scarlett who enjoys nature and learning about the world around her.

From Joel Bass

Congratulations on your choice of teaching children as a career. The real rewards for teachers come from the satisfaction of watching our students grow and change. But teaching is a two-way street. The pages in this book reflect a great deal that my own students have taught me about science, children, and teaching. Thanks to each and every one of you. Thanks also to my own teachers and colleagues for their guidance and friendship.

I would like to express my special appreciation for the support and encouragement of my wife, Helen, and our sons Randy and Ricky. I am grateful to Helen for enlarging my own view of science and culture, particularly as it relates to American history. In our mutual quest to understand the first Americans, we have trudged down canyons, explored ancient ruins, gazed in wonder at rock art, meditated at sacred sites, and danced in tribal powwows. Our experiences in following the Lewis and Clark trail from Missouri to Oregon are reflected in Chapter 8 discussions. Helen, thanks for your continued love and care in the day-to-day life of balancing family, professional, and other concerns and responsibilities.

From Terry Contant

As a science educator, my favorite phrase is "I don't know, let's find out!" These words describe the fundamental nature of scientific endeavors, encourage the mutual learning that should take place in an ideal science classroom, and concisely sum up the essence of inquiry. I hope they also express your lifelong quest to understand how to be a great teacher. Inquiry is about questioning, planning, evaluating data, making connections, and communicating ideas. These activities are vital in both science and teaching. I encourage you to use this book as a resource as you apply inquiry approaches in your classroom and to your professional growth.

I want to thank my husband, Charlie, and my daughter, Heather, for helping me explore and discover the world around me as I grow personally and professionally. Whether stargazing, strolling on the beach, or petting the cats, sharing nature with my family is tremendously rewarding. Dinner discussions about current science discoveries on the news or what happened at school that day have stimulated my thinking about science education. Finding "good science fair projects" in everyday life is common in our home. I am also grateful to my parents and many teachers, colleagues, and students who have encouraged me to continue to "find out" throughout my life.

With sincere gratitude to all,

Art Carin
Joel Bass
Terry Contant

Brief Contents

Contents

Video Case Study: Jennie 10

Video Case Study: Linda, following p. 38

Video Case
Study: Patricia 90

Video Case
Study: Sarah,
following p. 102

Video Case
Study: Donna,
following p. 262

Video Case
Study: Jean 278

IV Earth and Space Science Activities A-219

Structure of the Earth A-219

The Atmosphere, Weather, and Climate of the Earth A-236

The Earth's Oceans A-257

Viewing the Sky from Earth A-267

APPENDIXES

Science Topics Covered in the Video Case Studies

Chapter	Teacher	Grade	Science Topics
1	Jennie	K	Leaves ◆ Seasons ◆ Solids and Liquids ◆ Heat and Changes of State ◆ Seeds and Plants
2	Linda	2, 4	Cartesian Diver ◆ Snails and Controlled Investigations ◆ Forces and Inclined Planes ◆ Mealworms and Controlled Investigations
3	Patricia	1	Fish ◆ Human Heart ◆ Seeds and Plants
4	Sarah	5	Compound Pendulums ◆ Food Chemistry: Testing for Sugar, Starch, Proteins, and Fat
5	Erien (1)	5	Wetlands Investigations ◆ Soil Profiles ◆ Science, Technology, and Society: Considering Wetlands Issues
6	Tom	5	Digestion ◆ Electrical Circuits ◆ Motors ◆ Electromagnetism
7	Erien (2)	7	Excretory and Respiratory Systems ◆ Immune System ◆ Spread of Infectious Diseases ◆ Ecology of Wetlands Areas
8	Donna	5	Knowledge of the Natural World in Native American Myths ◆ Middens, Excavation, Archaeological Evidence, and Inferences About the Lives of Ancient People ◆ Food, Shelter, Medicine, and Transportation of People in Ancient Cultures
9	Jean	3	Properties of Solids, Liquids, and Gases ◆ Properties of Mystery Powders ◆ Frog Life Cycle
10	Dotty	6	Science, Technology, Society: Environment Issues ◆ Water Quality and Pollution ◆ Electrical Energy Production and Use ◆ Telecommunications

Methods for Teaching
Science as Inquiry

"Messing about in Science"

An Introduction

THE DEVELOPERS of the Elementary Science Study (ESS) program drew on the adventures of Rat and Mole in The Wind in the Willows *to express the spirit of "fun" they wanted to incorporate into science for children. Rat and Mole found pure joy in "messing about in boats." The ESS developers sought to design science activities that would create similar feelings in young learners. Thus, they adopted "messing about in science" as a metaphor for their program activities. Written by Kenneth Grahame in the early 1900s,* The Wind in the Willows *still enchants young readers today. We want you too to feel a sense of enchantment when you "mess about" in science. Read this delightful excerpt from Mole's first river adventure and see how Rat and Mole can serve as models for you and your students as you freely engage in scientific inquiry and encounter, once again, the wonders of science.*

As the narrative begins, Mole and Water Rat are eyeing each other cautiously across a great river.

"Hullo, Mole!" said the Water Rat.

"Hullo, Rat!" said the Mole.

"Would you like to come over?" inquired the Rat presently.

"Oh, it's all very well to *talk*," said the Mole, rather pettishly, he being new to a river and riverside life and its ways.

The Rat said nothing, but stooped and unfastened a rope and hauled on it; then lightly stepped into a little boat which the Mole had not observed. It was painted blue outside and white within, and was just the size for the two animals; and the Mole's whole heart went out to it at once, even though he did not yet fully understand its uses.

The Rat sculled smartly across and made fast. Then he held up his fore-paw as the Mole stepped gingerly down. "Lean on that!" he said. "Now then, step lively!" and the Mole to his surprise and rapture found himself actually seated in the stern of a real boat.

"This has been a wonderful day!" said he, as the Rat shoved off and took to the sculls again. "Do you know, I've never been in a boat before in all my life."

"What?" cried the Rat, open-mouthed. "Never been in a—you never—well I—what have you been doing, then?"

"Is it so nice as all that?" asked the Mole shyly, though he was quite prepared to believe it as he leant back in his seat and surveyed the cushions, the oars, the rowlocks, and all the fascinating fittings, and felt the boat sway lightly under him.

"Nice? It's the *only* thing" said the Water Rat solemnly, as he leant forward for his stroke. "Believe me, my young friend, there is *nothing*—absolutely *nothing*—half so much worth doing as simply messing about in boats. Simply messing," he went on dreamily: "messing—about—in—boats: messing—"

"Look ahead, Rat!" cried the Mole suddenly.

It was too late. The boat struck the bank full tilt. The dreamer, the joyous oarsman, lay on his back at the bottom of the boat, his heels in the air.

"—about in boats—or *with* boats," the Rat went on composedly, picking himself up with a pleasant laugh. "In or out of 'em, it doesn't matter. Nothing seems to matter, that's the charm of it. Whether you get away, or whether you don't, whether you arrive at your destination or whether you reach somewhere else, or whether you never get anywhere at all, you're always busy, and you never do anything in particular; and when you've done it there's always something else to do, and you can do it if you like, but you'd much better not. Look here! If you've really nothing else on hand this morning, supposing we drop down the river together, and have a long day of it?"

The Mole waggled his toes from sheer happiness, spread his chest with a sigh of full contentment, and leaned back blissfully into the soft cushions. "What a day I'm having!" he said. "Let us start at once!"

Source: From *The Wind in the Willows* (pp. 3–5), by Kenneth Grahame, 1908/1981, E. Shepard, illus. New York: Charles Scribner's Sons.

1

F*rom the earliest grades, students should experience science in a form that engages them in the active construction of ideas and explanations and enhances their opportunities to develop the abilities of doing science. Teaching science as inquiry provides teachers with the opportunity to develop student abilities and to enrich student understanding of science.*

(*National Science Education Standards*, National Research Council, 1996, p. 121. Emphasis added.)

Children, Science, and Inquiry

CHILDHOOD IS A SPECIAL TIME of questioning, exploring, and finding out about this fascinating world that surrounds us. See the wonder and joy on the faces of the children in the picture (opposite page) as they encounter a new organism for the first time. We recognize the questions forming in their minds even before they speak: *What is this thing? Is it alive? Where did it come from? What does it do? Will it bite me?*

How we as teachers view science and the learning of science is critically important to the ways we respond to children's questions and how we build on and nurture their inborn curiosity. If the meaning teachers attach to science is "finding the right answer," they will probably focus on providing factual answers to children through a direct instruction and reading approach to science (Rowe, 1996, p. 164). Taught in this way, however, students are not likely to remain interested in questioning, collecting information, and generating explanations, because that is not the approach to science they encounter. On the other hand, if teachers view science as inquiry and children as constructive learners, they will want to teach science in a way that engages students in the active construction of ideas and explanations and enhances their abilities to inquire.

The vision of science education we present in this book is one in which *all* children have the opportunity to engage in science as inquiry—to explore and construct ideas and explanations of the natural world within a supportive community of learners (Loucks-Horsley, Hewson, Love, & Stiles, 1998). The realization of this vision for each of your students depends on what you choose to teach in science, the ways you teach and assess it, and how you arrange your classroom environment for learning. Solid scientific knowledge is necessary, yet you do not need to be a science major to teach science effectively in this way. What you do need is contagious curiosity, a willingness to explore with your students, and a commitment to personal excellence and continued learning. Your own science knowledge will grow as you teach.

This chapter provides background and guidance as you begin to explore the *what, why,* and *how* of teaching science as inquiry to children and adolescents. When you have finished studying this chapter, you should be able to answer these questions:

- *Why should children learn science?*

- *Where have we been, where are we now, and where are we going in elementary and middle school science education in the United States?*

- *What is science? What does it mean to approach a question scientifically?*

Collect responses to these questions as you find them in the chapter. The focus questions also appear on the Companion Website at http://www.prenhall.com/carin.

What is the nature of science, scientific inquiry, and science knowledge?

What attitudes and values characterize the doing of science?

What is the connection between science, technology, and society?

What are science education goals for children and youth today?

Why Should Children Learn Science?

There are many reasons children should begin to learn science in elementary school. Science provides children opportunity to exercise their innate curiosity, learn about the natural world, and develop their problem-solving skills. Children wonder about many things. Why does it rain? What happens to the water when puddles dry up? How do fish breathe? What are the underground homes of ants like? Why does the moon appear to change its shape? Science is a way for children to find answers to their questions.

Children ask questions to gain new insights that help them understand and adapt to their surroundings, but they are often not equipped to deal with the verbal explanations that are provided (Keil & Wilson, 2000). However, young students can be led to use their abilities to observe objects, to act on them and see the results of their actions, and to talk with one another and their teachers about what they are doing, and thus learn a great deal about the world around them (Lowery, 1997). As an example of children's inquiry, consider this second grade lesson on magnets.

Museums, science discovery centers, aquariums, arboretums, botanical gardens, and so on, appeal to the sense of wonder of children and adults. The next time you visit such a place, notice the children's excitement as they observe, explore, and talk about the various exhibits.

Julie Clark arranged her second grade class in cooperative learning groups and gave each group sets of materials consisting of magnets and an assortment of metal and nonmetal objects. She challenged the children to find out how the magnets interacted with each other and with the various objects and to sort the objects in some way based on how they interacted with the magnets.

Driven by curiosity, the children eagerly explored the materials. Holding up two magnets, one surprised child said, "Look, Ms. Clark, these push apart and they are not even touching." Another child noted, "Put them like this and they come together." "It won't pick this thing up," a third child observed. Touching base with prior knowledge and familiar experiences, a fourth child reported, "We have some of these at home on the refrigerator."

Ms. Clark circulated among the small groups, asking and answering questions, supplying terms, and suggesting some procedures. As she went about the room, she asked each group to explain how they had sorted the objects. Some children had grouped the objects by color or size. After some prompting, these children began to understand how to classify the objects, not by their more obvious attributes, but by the ways the objects interacted with the magnets. Most children ended up with two piles: things that were attracted to a magnet and things that were not attracted to a magnet.

Ms. Clark brought the children back together as a whole class and asked them to talk about what they had done and what they had learned. Through discussion and writing on the chalkboard, she helped the children verbalize these principles about magnetism and use them to summarize their activities:

Many interesting activities on magnetism that you can use to involve your students in inquiry can be found on pages A-110–A-120 in *Activities for Teaching Science as Inquiry*, the companion volume to this text.

- Two magnets can *attract* each other.
- Two magnets can also *repel* each other.
- Magnets will *not attract* nonmetal objects.
- Magnets *attract* some metal objects.

Science Teaching Methods

Inquiry is one of several approaches teachers use to teach science. As illustrated in the magnets lesson, in an inquiry approach to science, children focus on questions about the natural world, collect data through their own investigation activities, and, with teacher assistance, use their data as evidence to answer their questions. In this approach, children not only construct science knowledge but also learn how to investigate and solve problems.

Inquiry is sometimes contrasted with a textbook approach. In the textbook approach, teachers present information, and students read text materials, examine pictures (such as of magnets and magnetic interactions), and engage in independent and guided practice activities using worksheets and end-of-chapter questions. Students acquire science knowledge through this approach, but they are not likely to be able to apply it well to new problem situations.

The *National Science Education Standards* call for inquiry approaches to teaching and learning science. In direct comparisons with other methods, students learn and retain more through inquiry and enjoy this method much more. In this book, we emphasize teaching science through inquiry methods, but also provide guidelines to help you use expository and other methods effectively.

In an application of their new knowledge, the young inquirers went around the room, excitedly testing to see how the magnets interacted with additional objects. They found that the magnets would stick to the metal filing cabinet, but not to the teacher's wooden desk. Surprisingly for most children, they found that the magnets did not attract a cola can. One child explained, "The cola can is not made of iron." Ms. Clark noted the comment, but said nothing, as she planned to introduce this concept later.

In addition to gaining new knowledge about how the world works, the children in this classroom had opportunities to practice and improve essential inquiry skills as they investigated and gathered evidence to answer the questions posed. Through engaging in inquiry, the children were learning approaches to problem solving that would serve them well in school, as well as in everyday life.

Another reason children should study science is to begin to build scientific literacy. As a teacher in a new millennium, you must prepare children for an ever-changing world. Advances in science and technology have dramatically changed our understanding of the universe. New products and procedures, invented or discovered almost daily, promise important benefits for humankind but also make new demands on society. Problems and issues affecting people—health and aging, biotechnology, energy use, conservation of natural resources, environmental quality, population dynamics, computer technology, transportation, communications, and equity in access to benefits—increasingly require innovative thinking and caring attitudes.

In the 21st century, this country will need many more people with special training in science, health care, and technology. *Some* of your students will likely choose to work in a scientific, technical, or health-care profession, but *all* of them will need to be scientifically literate to take an active role in recognizing problems, contributing solutions, and making informed decisions about local, state, national, and global issues.

The *National Science Education Standards* (National Research Council, 1996) define **scientific literacy** as

the knowledge and understanding of scientific concepts and processes required for personal decision-making, participation in civic and cultural affairs, and economic productivity. (p. 22)

Because magnets can damage computer monitors and television screens, before this activity the teacher put stickers announcing "NO MAGNETS HERE!" on all the classroom computers and the television.

Learning Science Is Also Essential

"Obviously, reading/language arts and mathematics are bedrocks of what our children should know and be able to do, but they're not the only ones. To understand science is to understand how the world works, and that is just as essential to full participation in society as being able to read or compute. A science lesson can be a good opportunity for students to practice and deepen skills gained in language arts and math. Keeping lab notes affords the chance to practice expository writing, and charting the growth of a plant, for instance, puts to work what may be newly learned skills in measurement."

Judith Opert Sandler

Education Week, (Vol. XXII, Number 29, April 2, 2003). Vice President and Director of Center for Science Education. Education Development Center, Inc. Newton, MA.

Scientific literacy requires that people have an enduring interest in the natural and human-constructed worlds and some conceptual understanding of science. It demands that people understand how science knowledge is generated, tested, and used. And it necessitates that people have an abiding concern with how science impacts society. According to the *National Science Education Standards* (National Research Council, 1996, p. 114), "Lifelong scientific literacy begins with understandings, attitudes, and values established in the earliest years."

Science can be highly interesting and motivational for children, especially if it is activity-oriented and deals with everyday things. Thus, connecting science to other subjects can enrich the entire curriculum for both children and teachers. For example, science provides many opportunities for children to develop their language arts skills. Reading about the lives of scientists, including the scientific achievements of women and ethnic minorities, can be highly inspirational for students. There are trade books on special topics, such as magnets and

Chapter 8 provides many examples of ways to connect science with other subjects.

"Lifelong scientific literacy begins with understandings, attitudes, and values established in the earliest years." (National Science Education Standards, *National Research Council, 1996, p. 114)*

Children's Literature and Science

There are many wonderful books that connect science and literacy. For example, when studying *astronomy* in science, read some of the following books during language arts time.

A cricket looks for another insect that is just like himself. This and other Eric Carle books, The Very Hungry Caterpillar, The Very Busy Spider, *and* The Very Clumsy Click Beetle, *delight children with surprising interactive elements. All of these stories launch children into wanting to find out more about insects, patterns, and the natural environments where survival is dependent on interdependency.*

- *Follow the Drinking Gourd* by Jeanette Winter (Grades K–6). Runaway slaves followed the "Drinking Gourd," another name for the Big Dipper, north to Canada and freedom. In science, children can learn how to use the Big Dipper to tell time and find the North Star.
- *The Magic School Bus Lost in the Solar System* by Joanna Cole (Grades K–6). A fantasy trip to the moon, sun, and planets, noting their colors, sizes, and unique features. In science, construct scale models of the solar system and charts of planetary features.
- *Sky Songs* by Myra Cohn Livingston (Grades 5–12). Poems about various aspects of the sky.
- *To Space and Back* by Sallie Ride with Susan Okie (Grades 4–7). An astronaut's fascinating description of what it's like to travel in space—to live and work in conditions unlike anything we know on earth. In science, students can access and study NASA's web site, including real-time data.
- *The Way to Start a Day* by Byrd Baylor (Grades 3–7). The many ways peoples of the world have celebrated the dawn. In science, construct models of the earth-sun system that explain why the sun rises each morning. Also, observe the changing positions of sunrise and sunset throughout the seasons.

Figure 1-1 Children's literature connections to science.
Source: "Children's literature connections to science" is based on material in the Great Explorations in Math and Science (GEMS) teacher's handbook entitled *Once Upon a GEMS Guide: Connecting Young People's Literature to Great Explorations in Math and Science,* copyright by The Regents of the University of California, and is used with permission. The GEMS series includes more than 70 teacher's guides and handbooks for preschool through eighth grade, available from: LHS GEMS, Lawrence Hall of Science, University of California, Berkeley, CA 94720–5200. (510) 642–7771. For more information, visit our web site at www.lhsgems.org

weather and how things work, that are interesting, informative, and meaningful. There are also many interesting treatments of science topics in children's literature (see Figure 1-1).

Writing, editing collaboratively, refining investigation procedures, and rewriting at each stage of the inquiry process can be an effective way to enhance inquiry and to improve writing skills (Champagne & Kouba, 2000). Keeping science journals, recording data, and constructing charts are other natural ways to connect science and writing.

Science can also provide a context in which children can apply and practice their math skills—such as measuring, counting, estimating, putting data into tables, and constructing and interpreting graphs.

Science can also be connected closely to social studies, art, music, and other subjects within the curriculum. The Annenberg Video Case Studies in Science Education that accompany this book provide numerous examples of such connections. In one video, Jennie combines various subjects in a kindergarten lesson on the seasons. The lesson is built around a nature walk on a cold winter day to an area the children had visited earlier in the year.

Jennie and her kindergarten children are featured in the Annenberg Video Case Study entitled, appropriately, "Jennie." This and other Annenberg videos are provided by Merrill Education to science methods instructors using this book. You will find a viewing guide for the Annenberg video featuring Jennie in this chapter.

VIDEO CASE STUDY: *JENNIE*

As you watch this case study, use the Questions for Reflection for each of the three modules to guide your note taking, analysis, and discussion. For group discussions, choose a facilitator to solicit various perspectives and keep the discussion on track.

Introducing the Case

Jennie teaches an ethnically diverse group of kindergarten children in an urban elementary school. She says her children are curious, eager, and natural scientists— descriptors teachers commonly use to tell about children ages 5 and 6. Jennie wants to engage her children in science experiences that capture their enthusiasm and prepare them for future science learning. However, she wants to ensure that the science activities that she designs for her students are developmentally appropriate but do not intrude on activities they will do in first grade.

Questions for Reflection

1. What do you think Jennie's instructional objectives are for her lesson on fall leaves?

   ◆ *The leaves on some trees do not change color in the fall.*

   ◆ *The leaves on different trees are different from one another.*

   ◆ *Leaves from the same tree can be different from one another.*

   ◆ *You can observe changes in leaves.*

   ◆ *You can compare leaves and classify them by their differences.*

2. How does Jennie use a chart like the one illustrated to facilitate children's use of the science skills of observing and classifying in their leaf activity?

3. What misunderstandings are revealed in these examples of children's thinking?

   ◆ *One child responds to why his maple leaf is green. . . . "No, it is just a 'regular.' . . . Regular means it (the leaf) is just from a regular tree that doesn't change to all different colors."*

   ◆ *Another child determines to place a maple leaf under the category for aspens.*

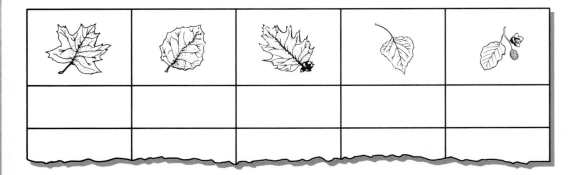

"We want children to be able to exchange ideas with each other, work together in analyzing their scientific experiences."

Dr. Anita Greenwood, University of Massachusetts-Lowell

4. How does Jennie respond to the children's misconceptions? When do you think it is appropriate for teachers to attempt to replace young children's misconceptions with exact science knowledge?

Trying New Ideas
Jennie doesn't think there is a clear-cut science curriculum for her kindergartners. She wants to give her students a sense of inquiry—observing, predicting, interpreting, verifying, and formulating ideas about their science experiences. Further, she wants them to be able to record what they discover and to know what to do if they find discrepancies in their information.

Questions for Reflection

1. What does developmentally appropriate mean for science teaching and science curriculum?
2. How is Jennie's snow activity developmentally appropriate and valid science?
3. How can different documents help Jennie further develop age appropriate science lessons?
4. What connections to reading and mathematics might Jennie make in her snow, leaves, and seeds lessons?

Reflecting and Building on Change
In the spring, Jennie provides her students a number of experiences with seeds. Before she decides what concepts to focus on she meets with a first grade teacher and her teaching mentor, Dr. Anita Greenwood of the University of Massachusetts-Lowell. Dr. Greenwood shares with Jennie that how far she should go with these ideas, what she should teach in her science lessons, and how her ideas link up with students' future science experiences will become clearer to Jennie over time.

Questions for Reflection

1. Why might it be important to work with other grade level teachers to plan the teaching of science concepts?
2. What objectives does Jennie want her students to learn in the seed activity?
3. What are some of the activities Jennie uses to have students learn about seeds?
4. What questions does Jennie use to assess her students' understanding that like seeds produce like plants?
5. What fundamental skills did Jennie's students begin to use in kindergarten to help prepare them for the science concepts and processes they will learn more about in future grades?

NSES   *The* National Science Education Standards *include these fundamental concepts and principles about seasonal changes and matter to be learned by children in grades K–4:*

- Weather changes from day to day and over the seasons.
- Materials can exist in different states—solid, liquid, and gas. Some common materials, such as water, can be changed from one state to another by heating or cooling.

In the video of Jennie's classroom, we watch the children put on warm clothing and begin to parade out into the cold. They march out singing this song, which Jennie has skillfully woven into the seasons lesson:

Put on our mittens,
Button up our coats,
Wrap our scarves so snugly,
Around our throats.
Put our boots and hats on,
Now we're ready for the snow.
Open up the door and out we go.

The little song and their activities outside help the children understand the important social studies idea that one way people adapt to seasonal changes in the environment is by dressing differently.

One of the activities the children engage in while outside is to gather snow and put it into several containers. On returning to the classroom, the children investigate the snow they have collected—learning, for example, that when snow becomes warm it can change into water. Jennie explained the science goals of the activity this way: "I was hoping that the children would be able to predict and understand that if you take snow and heat it, it will turn into water. Also, we were introducing terms such as *solid* and *liquid*. When you heat a solid, you can turn it into a liquid."

So, why should children learn science? In summary, children are innately curious and highly interested in the phenomena of their everyday lives. From the earliest grades, science provides an opportunity for children to exercise their natural curiosity, learn critical content, and develop essential skills for investigating and understanding the world around them. Additionally, an early introduction to science is very important for the development of scientific literacy, an increasingly important goal in the 21st century. Finally, science supports learning in reading and language arts, mathematics, social studies, and other important subjects in the school curriculum.

What do you think? Do you agree that early experiences in science are essential for children today?

U.S. Science Education: Where Have We Been, Where Are We Now, Where Are We Going?

Off and on since the 1950s, there has been national concern about the quality of U.S. science education. (See Appendix A for a graphic display of 50 years of science education efforts.) The initial stimulus to these concerns was the successful launching of an earth-orbiting satellite, *Sputnik*, by the Russians in 1957. In response to *Sputnik*, the federal government began to commit more and more tax money to the development of exemplary science programs in the United States.

The "Alphabet Soup" Programs

Most of the newly developed science programs were widely known by acronyms. At the elementary school level, the most successful programs funded by the National Science Foundation (NSF) were SAPA (Science—A Process Approach), SCIS (Science Curriculum Improvement Study), and ESS (Elementary Science Study). These programs, which were all developed beginning in the 1960s, represent three very different approaches to science education. SAPA focused on the processes involved in doing science, SCIS on broad concepts for organizing scientific ideas, and ESS on investigation as a way to develop science knowledge.

The various "alphabet soup" programs were widely used in school districts across the nation. But it was the common, hands-on spirit of these new approaches to learning science that most influenced science education in the 1960s, 1970s, and 1980s. In federally funded programs in science, students did not just read about science, they did science. Science was more than a noun; it was also a verb—*sciencing*.

Integrating Processes and Content

By the 1980s, in accord with the new cognitive psychology, the integration of content knowledge and ways of processing information permeated all academic disciplines. Content and processes were seen as acting together. In science, the phrase "hands-on, minds-on" was coined to emphasize the interactive nature of discovery, prior knowledge, and science processes in the construction of new scientific knowledge and understanding.

Despite the new perspective on learning, the U.S. Department of Education, in an influential report called *A Nation at Risk* (National Commission on Excellence in Education, 1983), indicated that U.S. children were academically behind children in Japan and other countries, particularly in science and math. Although there are certainly flaws in this report and other international comparisons (Bracey, 1998; Wang, 2001), the evidence suggested that all was not right with U.S. science education. The late 1980s thus saw national movements toward establishing standards of excellence for science and other subjects.

Developing National Science Education Standards

Before setting national standards in science, the American Association for the Advancement of Science (AAAS) established **Project 2061** to begin to arrive at a consensus on what all U.S. students should know and be able to do in science in the 21st century. The year 2061 marks the next return of Halley's comet to our region of the solar system. By including the distant date in the project title, AAAS implied that it intended to take a very long view in determining what students will need to know and be able to do to be scientifically literate throughout a new century.

Project 2061 published two pivotal documents, *Science for All Americans* (Rutherford & Ahlgren, 1990) and *Benchmarks for Science Literacy* (American Association for the Advancement of Science, 1993), which laid the foundation for developing national standards for science education. These two documents effectively expressed and clarified ideas about the nature and importance of science and science teaching held by leading scientists, science teachers, science educators, historians and philosophers of science, and other concerned citizens.

A distinguished panel, coordinated by the National Research Council (NRC), worked on standards for science education throughout the early 1990s. In 1996, the *National Science Education Standards* were published. The *Science Standards* offer the U.S. public a coherent vision of what it means to be scientifically literate. The document does not

NSES   *The* National Science Education Standards *provide six types of standards or expectations for U.S. science education:*

- *Science Teaching Standards* describe what teachers of science at all grade levels should know and be able to do.
- *Professional Development Standards* present a vision for the development of professional knowledge and skill among teachers.
- *Assessment Standards* provide criteria against which to judge the quality of assessment practices.
- *Science Content Standards* outline what students should know, understand, and be able to do in the natural sciences over the course of K-12 education.
- *Science Education Program Standards* describe the conditions necessary for quality school science programs.
- *Science Education System Standards* consist of criteria for judging the performance of the overall science education system.

prescribe curriculum; that is a state and local responsibility. Rather, it describes what all students must understand and be able to do in science as a result of their cumulative learning experiences. Through the *Science Standards*, criteria are provided for judging science programs, teaching approaches, science assessments, the professional development of teachers, and administrative policies and initiatives that can establish enhanced opportunities for all students to learn science.

The central message that the *National Science Education Standards* convey is that students should be engaged in an *inquiry* approach to science that basically parallels the procedures scientists use and the attitudes they display in doing science. Through engaging in inquiry, students learn how science knowledge is generated, they learn how to investigate on their own and to work cooperatively with others, and they construct meaningful knowledge that they can use in understanding the objects, organisms, and events in their environments. It is clear why the *Science Standards* have declared that "inquiry into authentic questions generated from student experience is the central strategy for teaching science" (National Research Council, 1996, p. 31).

Local schools and districts, state departments of education, and national curriculum groups are using the *National Science Education Standards* to form the backbone for curriculum frameworks, programs, and assessment systems to guide science education. Table 1-1 briefly describes some reform programs and documents that can impact the "whats and hows" of your science education program. For additional information, you are invited to access the Internet sites given in Table 1-1.

"Science teaching must involve students in inquiry oriented investigations in which they interact with their teachers and peers. . . . Hands-on activities are not enough—students must also have 'minds on' experiences."

(National Research Council, 1996, p. 20)

No Child Left Behind

At the dawn of the 21st century, the federal *No Child Left Behind Act* was passed. This legislation takes very seriously the responsibility of providing for the optimum education of all children in the nation. Education in science is an important part of this act. The act requires that all states receiving federal education funds must have their own science standards developed by the 2005–2006 school year. Further, states must administer an assessment in science beginning in 2007 in at least one grade level in each of three grade spans: 3–5, 6–9, and 10–12. Schools must show annual progress toward the goal of 100% student proficiency on this test or face severe sanctions. There are many decisions to be made in preparing for these "high stakes" tests which will greatly affect students, teachers, and schools (Anderson & Krathwohl, 2000, pp. 247–250).

In Chapter 9 we offer specific suggestions and teaching guidelines for you to consider as you work in the classroom to ensure that science is, indeed, for all children and that no child is left behind in science education.

TABLE 1-1   NATIONAL SCIENCE EDUCATION REFORM PROJECTS

Project	Description
Science for All Americans Project 2061 http://www.project2061.org/	• describes the nature of science and technology, including historical perspectives and their impact on society • describes understandings and ways of thinking that are essential for all citizens in a world shaped by science and technology
Benchmarks for Science Literacy* Project 2061 http://www.project2061.org/	• builds on *Science for All Americans* • states what all students should know or be able to do in science by the end of grades 2, 5, 8, and 12
How People Learn: Brain, Mind, Experience, and School* Edited by John D. Bransford, Ann L. Brown, and Rodney Cocking http://www.nap.edu	• provides a learning research foundation for the *Science Standards* • sponsored by the National Research Council
National Science Education Standards* National Research Council http://www.nap.edu/readingroom/books/nses/html/	• draws on efforts of Project 2061 and other national groups • defines science education standards for teaching, professional development, assessment, science content, programs, and systems • emphasizes scientific literacy, inquiry approaches to teaching, more time on fewer topics to encourage deeper understanding
NSTA Pathways to the Science Standards: Elementary School Ed. National Science Teachers Association Available from NSTA Science Store: http://www.nsta.org/scistore	• a practical guidebook for elementary science teachers • demonstrates how you can carry the vision of the *Standards* into your own classroom and school • contains more than 20 examples describing standards-based classrooms in action
Texas Essential Knowledge and Skills for Science* Texas Assessment of Knowledge and Skills Texas Education Agency http://www.tea.state.tx.us	• shows how one state's science teaching framework and assessment program builds on the *Standards*
Science and Technology for Children (STC) Science Resources Center http://www.si.edu/nsrc	• demonstrates how one national group has built on the *National Standards* in developing a science program • includes 24 tested units for science in grades 1–6 • units are correlated with the *Standards*
Full Option Science System (FOSS) Lawrence Hall of Science Preview this program at http://www.fossweb.com	• demonstrates how another national group has built on the *Standards* in developing a science program • includes a complete science program for grades 1–6, correlated with the *National Science Education Standards*
Federal No Child Left Behind Act of 2002* http://www.ed.gov	• requires that states have science standards in place by 2005–2006 • requires that states must administer science assessments by 2007

*The complete document is available on the Internet at the given address.

What Is the Nature of Science?

For children, an important part of learning science is learning about its nature (American Association for the Advancement of Science, 1993, pp. 3–7). Simply, science is an attempt to understand the world by

- questioning, investigating, and observing what happens;
- trying to make sense of our observations;
- using our new knowledge to make predictions about what might happen in the future; and
- testing our predictions to see if our understanding is correct (Paulu & Martin, 1991).

Doing science can be as simple as one individual conducting field studies or as complex as hundreds of people across the world working on a major scientific problem. Whatever the circumstances or level of complexity, scientists are likely to work from some common assumptions, have some common goals, and use some common procedures.

Order and Organization

Regardless of the methods scientists use, their goal is to understand the natural world by finding, describing, and explaining its patterns, order, and organization. Scientists assume that the behavior of the universe is not capricious, that nature is the same everywhere, and that it is understandable and predictable (National Research Council, 1996, p. 116). Matter, for example, can take billions of forms, from a crystal of salt to a galaxy, from a single-celled amoeba to a complex human being. There is a hidden order, unseen unless searched for, that connects these diverse forms of matter. Science is possible precisely because we live in an orderly and predictable world.

While watching a science demonstration, one fourth grader said, "Science is like magic." When his teacher asked what he meant, he replied, "There is always a reason in science too, isn't there?" Perhaps he could not yet fully explain the teacher's demonstration, but he was beginning to understand that the world is orderly, and he believed that there was a reasonable, scientific basis for what he saw happen—in the demonstrations of the teacher and in the magic tricks of a magician.

Evidence and Explanations

Scientific understanding begins with *questions* that can be empirically investigated. Scientists' questions pertain to such things as the properties of objects and organisms, how properties are organized and structured, how structures function and how they change over time, and how and why different natural events might occur. In elementary school science, questions should come from the activities of learners. Children need ample time to simply watch and wander about their world—to observe and compare leaves, tend to mealworms, watch fish in classroom aquariums, find out about air, study the properties of minerals, explore the causes of floating and sinking, observe weather changes, and on and on. It is from such experiences that interesting and productive questions about the natural world can be generated.

Scientific questions lead to investigations that produce data that can be used as **evidence** for answering the questions. In their investigations, scientists and children might observe what things are like or what is happening within a system, collect specimens for analysis, or do experiments (American Association for the Advancement of Science, 1993, p. 11).

"Evidence consists of observations and data on which to base scientific explanations."

(National Research Council, 1996, p. 117)

"The spiral is the most versatile of nature's patterns. It is found in the smallest virus and the largest galaxy" (Judson, 1980, p. 36). (Top) chambered nautilus, (right) the eye of a hurricane, (bottom) Andromeda, a spiral galaxy.

Scientists use the evidence of investigation to answer their questions. They arrive at (1) descriptions of objects, organisms, and events; (2) classifications that suggest which properties might be most significant; (3) inferences, predictions, and relationships; and (4) explanations of how and why things work. Explanations require creative insight and imagination, as well as some prior knowledge of concepts and principles. Explanations must be logically sound, must be consistent with currently accepted scientific principles, and must incorporate valid observations.

The essence of science is validation of claims by observational evidence. Explanations should not only fit available observations, they should also lead to predictions about additional observations not yet made (American Association for the Advancement of Science, 1993, p. 11).

The interplay between evidence, scientific knowledge, and explanations provides the stimulus for most activities in the world of science (see Figure 1-2). Observations are exploratory experiences in search of understanding. New observations can stimulate the formation of new theories and alternative explanations. New explanations, in turn, motivate the quest for additional supporting evidence.

Science Is Dynamic

Science is dynamic and continually changing. Because all scientific ideas depend on experimental and observational confirmation, all scientific knowledge is subject to change as new evidence becomes available (National Research Council, 1996, p. 201). Even in the best of circumstances, the conclusions of scientists must be considered tentative. In science, as in all other human endeavors, we know only in part. Science knowledge is never fixed, never complete, and always subject to revision with new evidence.

All students should come to understand that no matter how well a widely accepted theory fits observations, a new theory might fit them just as well or better, or might fit a wider range of observations (American Association for the Advancement of Science, 1993, p. 8). Paralleling the tentativeness of knowledge in science and the necessity of testing all scientific ideas must be a willingness by scientists and children to modify or let go of their own ideas when evidence does not support them.

To better appreciate the nature of science, consider the following example of science in action.

Science in Action

A supernova is an exploding star that typically shines very brightly when it first appears, slowly decays in magnitude, and disappears from view within a period of time varying from

The *Benchmarks for Science Literacy* (American Association for the Advancement of Science, 1993, p. 8) remind us that even though science knowledge is subject to change, students should understand that it also has an enduring quality. Some science knowledge is very old and yet is still applicable today.

Figure 1-2 Scientific explanations make sense of puzzling observations by connecting them to scientific knowledge about the world.

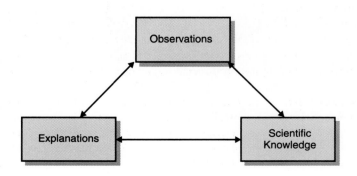

a few months to 2 or more years. Supernovae are very dramatic, but very rare phenomena. Indeed, only eight supernovae have been seen within our own Milky Way galaxy in the last 2,000 years, none since the early 1600s.

In 1987 a new supernova, designated SN1987A, was discovered, not in our own galaxy, but in a nearby galaxy called the Large Magellanic Cloud (Wheeler, 2000). Since supernovae provide important clues to the origin and evolution of stars and the universe as a whole, astronomers from all over the world rallied to investigate the new supernova. Craig Wheeler (2000), a renowned astronomer from the University of Texas at Austin, wrote of his own experiences with the supernova.

Dr. Wheeler thought that SN1987A might emit X-rays, but the details of the mechanism or timing of X-ray emission from supernovae were not well understood. X-rays are absorbed by the atmosphere and cannot be detected by ordinary ground-based instruments. They can be detected, however, with instruments carried aboard satellites that orbit the earth above the atmosphere. The Japanese had just launched a new X-ray satellite, called *Ginga* (meaning galaxy in Japanese), so Wheeler called the head of the Japanese *Ginga* group to alert the team to look for X-rays from the new supernova. It turned out that there were no X-rays to be seen in the first few days of SN1987A.

Wheeler related that at an international meeting in Tokyo 6 months after SN1987A was first seen, theoretical astronomers, drawing on existing models of supernovae, presented their predictions that a stream of X-rays from the supernova should be seen in about another year. Japanese astronomers then calmly stood up and reported that they had already detected the X-rays with their new *Ginga* satellite.

In the complicated interaction of evidence, theory, and explanation that characterizes modern science, theoreticians began to alter their models and theories of supernova explosions to fit this new observational data. Wheeler (2000) summed it up succinctly: "We learn from our mistakes" (p. 125).

As this example shows, doing science means raising questions, searching for evidence, forming explanations, making and testing predictions, and revising scientific understanding. It is these types of activities that should form the heart of your own science lessons with children.

Science begins with questions about the natural world. What questions about supernovae did Dr. Wheeler ask?

Scientists find ways to gather evidence to answer their questions. How did Dr. Wheeler propose to gather evidence to answer his supernova questions?

Forming and testing predictions is the primary way of judging the validity of a scientific theory. How did astronomers test their theories of X-ray emission from supernovae?

Scientific knowledge is always tentative; if a prediction fails, theories must be modified to fit new evidence.

Science as a Human Endeavor

Science is a human endeavor and always has a human quality that should not be overlooked when we emphasize its formal characteristics. For scientists, like those in the supernova example, there are fascinating puzzles to be solved, innovative methods and instruments to be developed, contacts with colleagues to keep up, reports to write, and scientific meetings to attend. The pursuit of science is, for most scientists, sheer *fun* (Judson, 1980). "And," as the science writer Gary Zukav (1979) observed, "the clever rascals get paid for doing it" (p. 3).

For children, too, noted the American Association for the Advancement of Science's Commission on Science Education (Sears & Kessen, 1964), "there is joy in the search for knowledge" and "excitement in seeing, however partially, into the workings of the physical and biological world" (p. 4). Awakening and nurturing this sense of joy and excitement in doing science should be an important part of science education at every level.

The Limitations of Science.   It is not too early for children to begin to understand the limitations of science. Science is a critically important way of thinking in the modern world, but it should be remembered that science is only one way humans seek understanding and answers to their questions. Science is concerned with questions about the objects, organisms, and events in the environment that can be investigated empirically. There is a pervasive

NSES   **Content Standard C**

Science as a Human Endeavor

As a result of their science activities, students should develop an understanding that:

- Science and technology have been practiced by people for a long time.
- Men and women have made a variety of contributions throughout the history of science and technology.
- Although much has been learned about nature, much more remains to be understood.
- Many people choose science as a career and devote their entire lives to studying it. Many people derive great pleasure from doing science.

mystery to the universe, our place within it, the joys and sorrows of relationships between people, and the ultimate meaning of our lives that lies beyond the precise and objective ways of knowing that characterize science. Human beings have sought to express this complex and elusive mystery in poetry, literature, art, music, and religion. Our scientific culture educates us to focus our attention on the physical and material world. This method of looking at the world has achieved great results. We must take care, however, that we do not edit out of young people and out of ourselves a sense of the mystery of life in an unfathomable universe.

What Shall We Teach in Science?

The *Benchmarks for Science Literacy* (American Association for the Advancement of Science, 1993) and the *National Science Education Standards* (National Research Council, 1996) were developed by a large number of scientists, educators, and others who were concerned with science education in the United States. Ronald Good (2000), a noted science educator, points out that the recommendations of the *Benchmarks* and *Standards* panels on what should be taught in science are about as close as we will ever get to national consensus. There is general agreement among these groups that four main themes should be emphasized in elementary and middle school science:

1. Scientific inquiry
2. Scientific knowledge
3. Attitudes and values that characterize science
4. Science, technology, and society

Let us consider each of these themes in turn.

Scientific Inquiry

Humans are innate inquirers (National Research Council, 2000, p. 5). From birth, we learn to employ trial-and-error techniques to learn about our surroundings. As children and adults, we reflect on the world around us by gathering, organizing, and interpreting information. People have used trial-and-error and reflective approaches to the solution of problems since prehistory. In recent centuries, this problem-solving capacity has been refined to the strategies and understandings of *scientific inquiry*. Though developed and applied in science, scientific inquiry procedures have also proven valuable in solving many types of problems in the home, in the workplace, in the community, and throughout the world.

"The thrust of a scientific approach to problem solving is to answer questions about the world through observational evidence."

(American Association for the Advancement of Science, 1993, p. 286)

According to the *National Science Education Standards* (National Research Council, 1996, pp. 122, 145), when children engage in scientific inquiry they:

- *Ask a question about objects, organisms, and events in the environment.* The *Science Standards* emphasize that questions asked by children should be ones they can answer through their own investigations.
- *Plan and conduct a simple investigation.* Children investigate and gather evidence to use in answering their questions. They make observations, collect and analyze specimens, and design and conduct simple experiments.
- *Use appropriate tools and techniques to gather and interpret data.* As students investigate they use simple tools such as thermometers, metersticks, and magnifying lenses and practice simple skills such as observing, measuring, recording data, graphing, inferring, and predicting.
- *Use evidence and scientific knowledge to develop explanations.* As they develop descriptions, classifications, and explanations to answer their questions, children should draw on scientific knowledge and the evidence they obtained to support their thinking. Students should learn to determine what constitutes evidence and to judge the merits and strengths of the data they collect. They should also check their explanations against the scientific knowledge, experiences, and observations of others.
- *Communicate investigations, data, and explanations to others.* Throughout the inquiry process, students engage in discourse with one another and their teachers about problems, investigations, findings, and explanations. Students should use different means, including writing, speaking, and drawing, to communicate their procedures, observations and data, and explanations to others.

> *"Full inquiry involves asking a simple question, completing an investigation, answering the question, and presenting the results to others."*
>
> (National Research Council, 1996, p. 122)

Figure 1-3 graphically depicts these inquiry tasks.

According to the *Science Standards* (National Research Council, 1996, p. 121), these tasks should not be interpreted as the "scientific method." The tasks suggest some common characteristics of scientists' investigations and a logical progression, but they do not imply a rigid approach to solving problems. Inquiry in elementary and middle school science classes, like inquiry in scientists' studies of the natural world, can take many forms, but

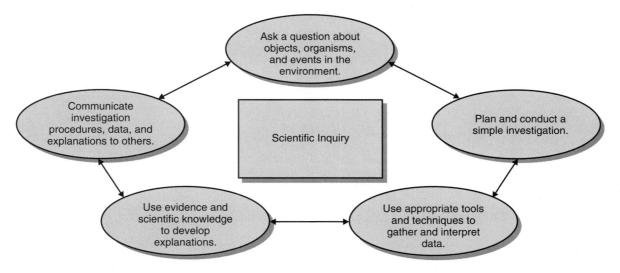

Figure 1-3 Tasks of scientific inquiry.

A variety of interesting activities for children on light can be found in *Activities for Teaching Science as Inquiry*, the companion volume to this text.

each form generally involves some level of use of each of these inquiry tasks. As an example of children's inquiry, consider the following lesson activity on light.

In the course of a series of inquiry lessons on properties of light, Don Roach's fifth grade students pointed out one morning that they could see their "reflections" in a plate glass door. Don had investigated children's ideas about light in an in-service workshop and knew that his students would have a variety of conceptions and misconceptions about reflection and images. He thought that these different ideas would form the basis for a good inquiry activity.

Through class discussion, Mr. Roach led his students to think about where the image is in mirrors and other reflecting surfaces, such as glass doors. Most of the students thought that the image was on the surface of a mirror or just behind it (Shapiro, 1994). A few thought it might be deeper in the mirror. From this discussion, Don helped the students form a simple question that might be investigated: "Where is my image in a mirror?"

Don led the children to search for evidence to answer the question by investigating their own images in the glass door. In the investigation, students worked in small groups. One student, called the *object* partner, stood on one side of the glass door so she could see her image in it (see Figure 1-4). Another student, the *image* partner, went to the other side of the door and, after some direction, stood right on top of the image of the partner's shoes.

Don was quite pleased when one group decided to use the classroom metersticks to measure each partner's distance from the door. They placed the object partner 200 cm in front of the door and found that the image partner was also about 200 cm on the other side of the door. Soon other groups were also using the metersticks to make measurements of object and image distances.

The different cooperative groups entered their measurements in a data table (see Figure 1-5) that Don prepared on a classroom computer and projected onto a wall with an LCD projector. After analyzing and discussing the data, all the children agreed, "The image is not on the surface; it seems to be on the other side of the door. It is about as far on the other side of the door as the object is in front of it." Through engaging in this inquiry lesson, the children gained a better knowledge of reflection and of how science is done.

Essential Features of Classroom Inquiry. Figure 1-6 presents five essential features of classroom inquiry identified in *Inquiry and the National Science Education Standards* (National Research Council, 2000), a follow-up volume to the *Science Standards* that examines more fully the nature of inquiry and inquiry instruction.

Notice how the lesson on reflection and images incorporates these five essential features of classroom inquiry. The lesson is initiated by a question that comes out of the experiences of the children. The students are involved in planning and conducting an

NSES   **Concepts and Principles That Support the Science Standards Related to Light**

- Light travels in straight lines until it strikes an object (grades K–4).
- Light can be reflected by a mirror, refracted by a lens, or absorbed by an object (grades K–4).
- Light interacts with matter by transmission (including refraction), absorption, or scattering (including reflection) (grades 5–8).
- To see an object, light from that object—emitted by or scattered from it—must enter the eye (grades 5–8).

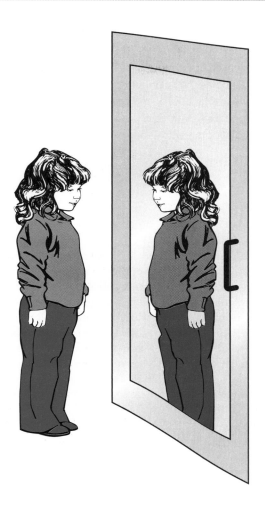

Figure 1-4 A child examines the image of herself formed in a glass door.

Group Name	Distance of Image from Door (cm)	Distance of Object from Door (cm)
Elves	200	190
Dwarves	350	365
Hobbits	250	238
Ents	225	225
Wizards	300	320

Figure 1-5 Data table for mirror images activity. What are some things you might conclude from the data?

investigation to gather relevant evidence. The data collected is applied in arriving at an explanation that proposes an answer to the initial question. The children's new findings and interpretations enhance their knowledge of reflection. The students post their results in a class data table, compare and analyze class results, and discuss the problem, investigation, and solution with one another and the teacher.

Figure 1-6 Essential features of classroom inquiry.
Source: Reprinted with permission from *Inquiry and the* National Science Education Standards: *A Guide for Teaching and Learning* (2000) by the National Academy of Sciences, courtesy of the National Academies Press, Washington, DC.

> When learning science through inquiry learners,
>
> 1. are engaged by scientific questions;
> 2. give priority to evidence as they plan and conduct investigations;
> 3. develop descriptions, explanations, and predictions using collected evidence;
> 4. connect evidence and explanations to their developing scientific knowledge; and
> 5. engage in critical discourse with others about procedures, evidence, and explanations.

Although what scientists do is a model for inquiry instruction, because of developmental differences children are not able to engage in inquiry in the same ways scientists do in professional communities. Thus, elementary and middle school inquiry science must occur in a simplified form that enables children to participate with understanding (Lee, 2002). The key ingredient in accommodating scientific inquiry to the level of children is the teacher, who plans, prepares, presents, hints, prompts, questions, informs, guides, directs, tells, and explains—all in the context of children's hands-on engagement with the objects and organisms of the real world. Are you beginning to understand your responsibilities in teaching children science as inquiry?

The inquiry activities of scientists and children generally lead to new scientific knowledge about the world.

Scientific Knowledge

Scientific knowledge is a human construction that can be used in describing, predicting, explaining, and adapting to the phenomena of the natural world. It has been accumulating for centuries as the result of the investigations of scientists—inquisitive men and women from all races and cultures. In teaching science, it is useful to think in terms of two main types of scientific knowledge: factual knowledge (facts) and conceptual knowledge (concepts, principles, and theories).

Factual Knowledge. **Facts** are objectively confirmed statements about observable objects and events. Facts in science are not mere collections of random observations. We make observations and generate facts selectively, based on prior knowledge and assumptions about what is valuable and what might be disregarded (Shapiro, 1994, p. 5).

In elementary science, children should be engaged in many activities that simply allow them to learn new facts about the world. Examine Activity 1-1. What facts about water can children discover from this activity?

It is a fact, for example, that water drops bead up on wax paper but spread out on aluminum foil. Also, when water is added drop by drop to a small plastic medicine cup, the water will tend to heap up a surprising amount before it starts to spill over the edge. Even then, as many as 30 paper clips can be gently slid along the edge into the cup without the water overflowing. Such facts are the data or products of our observations that we organize and attempt to explain. Facts, however, begin to make sense only as they are attached to concepts and principles and placed into explanatory frameworks.

A glossary containing definitions of important terms used in this chapter is included in the Companion Website at http://www.prenhall.com/carin.

See *Activities for Teaching Science as Inquiry* for a variety of interesting activities for children on properties of water.

Activity 1-1: Facts about Water

1. Fill a 30 ml medicine cup all the way to the top with water. How many drops of water from a dropper do you think you can add to the small cup before it overflows? Make a prediction. Try it and see.
2. Add some water back into the cup so that it is completely filled again. How many paper clips do you think you can add to the filled medicine cup before it overflows? Make a prediction. Now, gently slide paper clips into the cup, one at a time down the edge of the cup. How many paper clips could you put in the water?
3. Using a dropper, put drops of water on wax paper. Make large drops and small drops. What do the drops look like? Can you lead a drop around with a toothpick? Compare drops of water on wax paper with those on aluminum foil.

Conceptual Knowledge. Factual knowledge is based on direct sensory experience with things in the world. Conceptual knowledge, in contrast, consists of ideas people have formed in making sense of the world. There are three main types of conceptual knowledge that are constructed.

Concepts. In general, **concepts** are ideas derived from experience around which new experiences may be organized. By reducing many observations to fewer categories, concepts bring a measure of coherence and simplicity to the world. Concepts encountered in elementary science include magnets, magnetic poles, birds, minerals, air, heat conduction, light reflection, and so on. Each of these concepts is a class in which the members have some common attributes (Vitale & Romance, 2000). Birds, for example, have two legs, wings, and feathers. They fly, lay eggs in nests, and live in trees (Murphy, 2000).

Concepts enable us to use past experiences to make sense of new experiences (Ausubel, 2000, p. 2). Suppose we encounter a creature that has two legs, wings, and feathers, but cannot fly (an ostrich, for instance). Guided by our previous experiences with birds, we might make sense of this new creature by assuming that it is a bird, but one with wings that are too short to support its weight in flight. Further observations would be needed to answer the question about whether the creature can be validly classified as a bird.

Principles. **Principles** are generalizations about relationships among concepts. They are formed from investigations and observations of a few situations and generalized to all similar events and situations. An example of a principle is that *water particles* (a concept) tend to *bond* (another concept) or stick to one another when they are very close. Children say, more simply, that water is "sticky" or "grabby." Principles are applied in making scientific

Why are the four statements about magnets given on page 6 in this chapter rightfully considered to be principles?

explanations. Children from about grade 3 might use the "grabby water" principle to explain, for instance, why water tends to heap up in cups. Drops of water in a medicine cup that is already heaping full grab onto new drops to keep them from falling over the edge.

As another example, consider a science principle related to how things change with heat. Expanding (getting larger), contracting (getting smaller), hot (having a high temperature), and cold (having a low temperature) are all concepts in science (Vitale & Romance, 2000). These concepts are combined in the principle, "objects expand when heated and contract when cooled." The principle that objects expand when heated can be used to explain, for example, why concrete sidewalks are poured in sections with "expansion gaps" between the sections.

Theories. Children and scientists hold theories about the world. Scientific **theories** are imaginative networks of facts, concepts, principles, and assumptions that serve to explain observations. Because of the tentative nature of science, theories must always be considered to be *best guesses*—proposals about the way things may be.

A theory of the nature of water, for example, might be built around

- *facts* about the behavior of water in different situations,
- *concepts* related to water particles and bonding forces, and
- *principles* that *cohesive* forces bind water particles together, while *adhesive* forces bind water drops to different surfaces, such as plastic surfaces.

Incorporating facts, concepts, and principles of water into a simple, but tentative, theory can enable students (with appropriate cues, hints, and prompts from teachers) to come up with their own ideas of the causes of different water phenomena. For example, applying a theory of water, students might conclude the following:

- Because of attractive forces, water acts like its outer surface is a skin that holds the water drops in.
- Water heaps up in cups because the skinlike effect due to attractive forces is stronger than gravity forces that also act on the drops—until the water heaps up too much.
- Water spreads out on aluminum foil because the adhesive forces between water drops and the aluminum are greater than the cohesive bonds within the drops.
- Water beads up on wax paper because the cohesive forces within drops are greater than the adhesive forces between the drops and the wax paper.

Scientists call the skinlike effect of liquids "surface tension," implying that the particles at the surface of the liquid are in dynamic tension with one another.

All of these explanations about the behavior of water should be thought of as tentative hypotheses about causes that must be supported through further investigations.

Table 1-2 summarizes how scientific knowledge about water can be analyzed in terms of facts, concepts, principles, and theories. Seeing these aspects of scientific knowledge in a connected way leads to scientific understanding.

Constructing Scientific Understanding. It is always important in science to challenge students to go beyond knowledge to understanding. Understanding is based in scientific knowledge, yet it involves more than mere recall. What does it mean for a student to understand an idea? Contemporary researchers suggest that when students understand, they are able to

- integrate new knowledge and connect it to their prior knowledge, including prior knowledge about other science topics and other subject areas;
- use their knowledge to interpret what they learn; and
- apply their knowledge in making predictions, constructing explanations, and solving novel problems (Wiggins & McTighe, 1998; Wiske, 1998).

TABLE 1-2 ANALYZING SCIENCE TOPICS IN TERMS OF FACTS, CONCEPTS, PRINCIPLES, AND THEORIES		
Knowledge Component	**Definition**	**Examples Related to Water**
Facts	objectively confirmed statements about observable objects or events	water heaps in medicine cups and beads up on wax paper
Concepts	classes of things or ideas that serve in the organization of experiences	bonds between particles, adhesion, cohesion
Principles	generalizations about the relationships among concepts	the closer the water particles, the stronger the bonds
Theories	networks of terms, assumptions, concepts, principles, and inferences that can be used to form tentative explanations of observations	at the surface of water the particles bond, forming a skinlike effect that can be applied to explain heaping and beading

For example, if students truly understand the nature of water, they should be able to interpret in their own ways the causes of its heaping and beading effects, apply their knowledge in explaining events such as "floating" paper clips, and predict from prior knowledge whether drops will bead up on new kinds of surfaces. Whenever you challenge and guide students to interpret, apply, explain, and make new connections, you are teaching for understanding. Teaching for understanding also implies helping students confront, modify, and sometimes abandon their misconceptions.

Scientific Attitudes and Human Values

Science and its applications in the world are social activities that incorporate certain human attitudes and values (Rutherford & Ahlgren, 1990, p. 190). There are many important attitudes, values, and habits of mind for children to learn and display in doing science, such as accepting ambiguity, being willing to change, withholding judgment, keeping an open mind, being honest in observing and reporting observations, having a positive approach to failure, avoiding superstitions, and recognizing beauty in the world and in scientific descriptions and explanations of it.

Let us look in more detail at several attitudes that are particularly important when engaging in inquiry science:

1. *Being Curious.* Young children enjoy finding out about the world. They explore the texture, size, weight, color, and even taste of sand at the seashore or in the sandbox simply because sand intrigues them. Similarly, scientists study the marvels of nature because they delight in them. This dynamic, almost compulsive involvement of children and adults in searching for answers provides the fuel for investigation.

   Nurturing, sustaining, and, if necessary, rekindling interest in the natural world is essential in contemporary science education. Teachers should continually relate classroom science to familiar circumstances and real-world issues, reveal the human side of science and scientists, and link science to themes in literature, art, music, mathematics, and social studies. Ultimately, your own curiosity and interest can be the model for your students to follow. As an old proverb teaches: If you would kindle others, you must yourself glow.

2. *Insisting on Evidence.* Scientists insist on evidence to support conclusions and claims. This means rigorous testing of ideas and respecting the facts as they are accrued. In teaching science, frequently ask: "Why do you think so?" and "What is your evidence?" Gradually lead children to ask themselves these questions.

3. *Being Willing to Reflect on and Change Ideas.* Scientists must maintain an attitude of skepticism about their own conclusions and those of others. As evidence suggests different explanations of objects or events, scientists must be willing to change even their own original explanations. Questions such as "How could we test this idea?" and "Might there be another explanation?" should be standard fare from science teachers and students.

Lee (2002, p. 38) points out that the attitudes of skepticism and critiquing others' viewpoints may be incongruent with attitudes and values of cultures that favor cooperation, social and emotional support, and acceptance of the authority of teachers and elders. Teachers can help students recognize that, in science, authoritarian statements can be challenged and tested, but there is an appropriate time and place to question people's conclusions.

4. *Being Predisposed to Apply Science Knowledge.* According to Mary Budd Rowe (1973), "Teaching students how to make better use of concepts they already know probably represents the major task to be accomplished in inquiry training" (p. 347). Children may have relevant knowledge but do not think to use it in problem-solving situations. Students must be ready to think of their knowledge not only as information to recall, but also as procedures to apply. One way we can help children learn to apply their knowledge is by monitoring and assessing the *processes* involved in explaining and solving problems rather than just the *outcomes.*

5. *Working Cooperatively.* Scientists generally work as a team, raising and answering questions, analyzing data, solving problems, and publishing reports. Success in collaboration requires a substantial amount of interdependence among team members and a willingness to accept and learn from the insights and criticisms of others. Cooperative small group work can stimulate much conversation within and between groups that makes members aware of different perspectives and stimulates further inquiry as the group seeks clarification (Rowe, 1996).

6. *Caring for Others, for the Natural Environment, and for the Human-Made World.* Knowledge that is constructed through science and applied through technology can be used for the benefit of society, but there are always negative side effects. Increasingly, scientists, politicians, educators, and other concerned citizens are trying to educate the public about problems such as pollution and the depletion of natural resources. You must be prepared to help your students to recognize and care about the impact of science on their everyday lives and on society.

Caring involves the ways individuals and communities protect the rights, interests, and well-being of others and invest in their ongoing development (Chaskin & Rauner, 1995). Care is conveyed in many ways. Group activities in science can be organized to provide support for relationships of cooperation, care, and trust (Noddings, 1995). Studies of issues and problems related to our environment may lead to new appreciation of people who work daily to keep the environment clean. They may also lead to expressions of care—for example, in reducing or recycling trash in the home, classroom, and school.

A checklist for use in assessing children's science attitudes and habits of mind is given in Figure 6-27 in Chapter 6 on assessing inquiry learning. The checklist is keyed to the attitudes and habits of mind described in this section.

Science and Technology

An important part of elementary and middle school science is learning about the relationship between science and technology and the applications of science and technology in the everyday world. As emphasized in the *Science Standards*, science and technology are closely related, but they differ in goals. The goal of science is to understand the natural world; the goal of technology is to make modifications in the world to meet human needs (National Research Council, 1996, p. 24).

Computers are one example of the many technological advances we enjoy today. Bicycles and airplanes, satellites and cellular phones, electrical power plants and household appliances, and modern medicines and medical treatments, as well as the myriad applications of computer hardware, peripherals, and software are other technologies that serve human needs and aspirations.

The goal of including technology in the science curriculum is to connect students to the designed world, offer them experiences in making models of useful things, and introduce them to laws of nature through their understanding of how technological objects and systems work (National Research Council, 1996, p. 135). The *National Science Education Standards* emphasize developing students' abilities to design a solution to a problem, understand the relationship of science and technology, and recognize and appreciate the way people are involved in both.

As an example of a technology lesson, have children study different types of clothes fasteners, such as buttons, zippers, and hooks. Then challenge them to design a different type of fastener. In a lesson that integrates science and social studies, present an old technology mystery object, such as an apple peeler. Have students investigate to figure out what it does, how it helps people, and what problems it might solve and cause. As another example, have children design, construct, and test a way to use mirrors to see over barriers or around corners—that is, to reinvent the periscope.

Stages of Technological Design. Paralleling the components of scientific inquiry, the *National Science Education Standards* (National Research Council, 1996, p. 137) identify five tasks of technological design (see Figure 1-7). The five components of technological design are described next.

Identify a Simple Problem. In problem identification, children identify a specific need, problem, or task and explain it in their own words.

Propose a Solution. Students should make proposals to build something or to make something work better. They should use different forms of communication to describe their solutions to others. Also, students should recognize constraints such as cost, materials, time, space, and safety.

Implement a Proposed Solution. Children should work individually and collaboratively, and use simple materials, tools, techniques, and appropriate quantitative measurements when solving the problem. They should balance various constraints in problem solving.

Evaluate a Product or a Design. Students should evaluate their own results or solutions as well as those of other children by considering how well a product or design met the challenge to solve a problem. When possible, students should use measurements and include constraints in their evaluations. Designs should be modified based on the results of evaluations.

Inventing with simple machines: Pulley and lever.

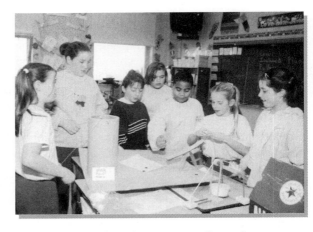

Inventing with simple machines: Lever, pulley, and screw.

Making the Invention Convention: The "Flippomatic."

Making the Invention Convention: Automatic Dog Washer.

Given encouragement and opportunity, children think "out-of-the box" and create original, innovative designs.

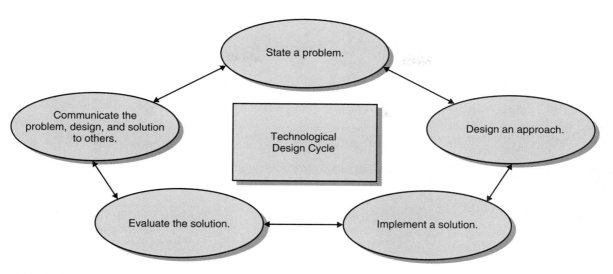

Figure 1-7   Tasks in designing a technological solution to a problem.

Communicate a Problem Design and Solution. Students should prepare oral, written, and pictorial communication of the design process and products. Depending on the students' abilities and the design product, the communication might be show-and-tell, group discussions, short written reports, pictures, or multimedia computer presentations.

As an example of implementing the technological design cycle, one third grader learned in health class that people should change their toothbrushes periodically. To meet this need, he designed and built a toothpaste tube joined to a toothbrush. When the toothpaste tube was empty, brush and tube were discarded in favor of new ones. Another child feared for her father, who jogged at night. She designed and made a vest for him with battery-powered flashing lights that announced to all his neighbors that he was coming.

Awards for Young Inventors.   The National Science Teachers Association (NSTA) and Craftsman sponsor an annual Young Inventors Awards Program. In one competition (Schafer, 2001), there were 3,400 entries nationwide from students in grades 2–8. One award-winning student attached a small bicycle to a push mower to create a pedal-powered lawn mower. Another student created the Mail-O-Matic, providing an easy way to retrieve mail from a mailbox. He assembled a wooden box, put rollers on it, placed it in the mailbox, and attached it to the mailbox door. When the mailbox door was opened, the mail rolled out. National winners as well as first, second, and third place winners at the regional level for grades 2–5 and 6–8 received awards of savings bonds. In each of these examples, the children identified a problem, proposed and developed a solution, and presented their new product to others for use or suggested revisions.

NSTA maintains a great Website with information on the Young Inventors Awards Program and many other resources for teachers and students. The Web address is http://www.nsta.org.

Science, Technology, and Society.   The acronym STS has been used to express the connectedness of science, technology, and society in contemporary life. You can readily see these relationships—and their implications for your teaching—in Figure 1-8. By helping your students to link science to technology to society, you facilitate their learning in all three fields.

Problems dealt with in STS lessons should come from issues that are meaningful to the students. Researching the concepts and issues relevant to the problem might involve many different kinds of activities, including hands-on science investigations, reading, library

Figure 1-8 The
relationship between
science, technology, and
society—and their
connections to
educational goals.
Source: From *Elementary School
Science for the 90s,* by Susan Loucks-
Horlsey, et al., 1989, Andover, MA: The
NETWORK, Inc. Reproduced with
permission of the National Center for
Improving Science Education/The
NETWORK, Inc. Copyright © 1990.
Reprinted by permission.

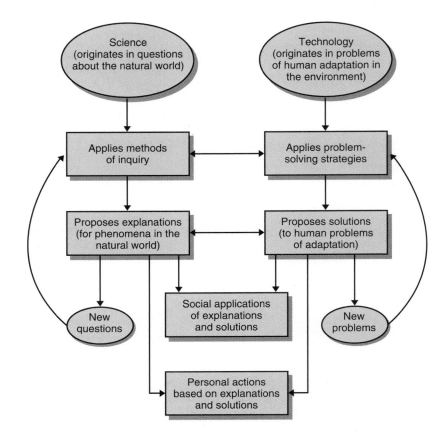

research, searching Websites, and consulting the teacher or outside experts. Proposing various solutions to STS problems provides opportunities for students to produce unusual ideas, combine objects in new ways, design new devices, suggest innovative policies, and find alternate and unusual uses for things (McCormack & Yager, 1989). Creativity is called for as students act on proposed solutions and communicate in various ways with other people, trying to convince them of the value of the solutions. Here is an example of an STS project.

Students in a Florida middle school studied local water resource issues and created public service announcements (PSAs) to convey the message of water conservation to their community (Stokes & Hull, 2002). In preparation for developing their PSAs, different groups of students went to the library, the Internet, and other sources to research water use issues, such as aquifer storage and recovery, desalination, water treatment, and water quality. Students also examined the various ways their community used water, classifying uses as essential and nonessential. As a class, the students brainstormed ways to reduce both essential and nonessential uses of water.

In creating the PSAs, students were required to list objectives and develop scripts and storyboards to convey their messages. Selected PSAs were produced and aired by a local television station. This innovative project served to motivate students, to engage them in researching significant STS topics, and to connect their learning to the community. Of course, students thought the whole project was "cool!"

It is clear from the ways students engaged in this project and their reactions to it that they were beginning to understand, appreciate, and care about the real-world interactions of science, technology, and society.

Goals for Elementary and Middle School Science

Statements of goals for elementary and middle school science have been developed by a number of prominent groups, including the *National Science Education Standards* panels and the National Center for Improving Science Education (Bybee et al., 1989). In general, descriptions of science goals draw on themes of scientific inquiry, scientific knowledge, scientific habits of mind, and the interactions of science, technology, and society. Here is a synthesis of goals for elementary and middle school science and some suggestions about what teachers can do to help students reach these goals.

I. *Skills for Inquiring.* Children should develop an understanding of and abilities to engage in scientific inquiry. To promote the development of skills for inquiring, teachers should

  - provide many opportunities for children to explore the natural world;
  - develop children's abilities to ask simple questions about the natural world, plan scientific investigations, collect and organize data, and coordinate evidence and science knowledge to form explanations; and
  - develop children's understanding of the nature of science as inquiry and the tentativeness of scientific knowledge.

II. *Scientific Knowledge.* Children should have a developing base of factual and conceptual knowledge of the world. To help children construct scientific knowledge, teachers should

  - help children learn and interrelate scientific facts, concepts, principles, and theories by building on their own investigations;
  - assist children to use their scientific knowledge in improving descriptions and explanations of their world and how it works; and
  - help children to go beyond knowledge to understanding—that is, guide them to personally apply their knowledge in new situations.

III. *Scientific Attitudes and Habits of Mind.* Children should recognize and apply scientific attitudes and habits of mind. To guide children in developing scientific attitudes and habits of mind, teachers should

  - model scientific attitudes and habits of mind;
  - guide children to develop and exercise their curiosity;
  - encourage children to always insist on evidence to support claims; and
  - guide children to be fair and cooperative as they work with others in doing science.

IV. *Science, Technology, and Society.* Children should begin to understand the connections between science and technology and recognize how science and technology affect people. To promote an understanding of the connections of science, technology, and society, teachers should

  - increase children's understanding of science and technology as major human achievements;
  - help children to become more aware of, interested in, and caring about the benefits and challenges of science and technology for people; and
  - help children recognize that the solution to one problem can create new problems.

Our focus throughout this book is on how you can use an inquiry/constructivist approach to guide and challenge learners to develop a scientific view of the natural world and the attitudes and abilities to inquire on their own.

Welcome to the exciting world of teaching science to children.

Use the self-assessment questions for Chapter 1 at http://www.prenhall.com/carin to assess how well you understand this chapter and how prepared you are for a test over its content.

SUMMARY

● Science in the elementary and middle school is important for numerous reasons. It can build on children's natural curiosity and help them gain new insights into how the world works. Science is a natural place for children to develop inquiry abilities, and it provides entry to other areas of the curriculum. To become scientifically literate in this ever-changing world, children should begin to learn science in the earliest grades.

● The *National Science Education Standards,* which were developed in the 1990s, describe what all students must understand and be able to do in science as a result of their cumulative learning experiences. An essential message conveyed by the *Standards* is that students should be engaged in an inquiry approach to science that basically parallels the procedures scientists use and the attitudes they display in doing science.

● Scientific inquiry and scientific knowledge are inextricably linked. Inquiry involves asking questions, planning investigations, gathering data, using scientific knowledge to make sense of observational data, and communicating results to others. Scientific knowledge must always be considered tentative. Scientists must adjust their ideas when investigations produce new evidence that no longer supports old conclusions.

● The study of science can build and reinforce certain attitudes, values, and habits of mind. Curiosity—the urge, even rage, to know—is the driving force for science. Scientists are skeptical of new ideas; they always insist on examining evidence offered in support of conclusions. Caring for others and for the natural and human-made environment is a value that should be emphasized in science, as well as all other school subjects.

● Science is closely connected to technology and society. It is important for students to be interested in and appreciate the achievements of people engaged in science and technology, and for them to care about the benefits and risks of science and technology.

REFERENCES

American Association for the Advancement of Science. (1993). *Benchmarks for science literacy.* New York: Oxford University Press.

Anderson, L. W., & Krathwohl, D. R. (Eds.). (2000). *A taxonomy for learning and teaching: A revision of Bloom's taxonomy of educational objectives.* New York: Longman.

Ausubel, D. P. (2000). *The acquisition and retention of knowledge; a cognitive approach.* Boston: Kluwer.

Bracey, G. (1998). Tinkering with TIMSS. *Phi Delta Kappan, 79*(2), 32–36.

Bransford, J. D., Brown, A. L., & Cocking, R. R. (Eds.). (1999). *How people learn: Brain, mind, experience, and school.* Washington, DC: National Academy Press. (Also available at http://www.nap.edu)

Bybee, R. W., Buchwald, C. E., Crissman, S., Heil, D. R., Kuerbis, P. J., Matsumoto, C., McInerney, J. P. (1989). *Science and technology education for the elementary years: Frameworks for curriculum and instruction.* Washington, DC: National Center for Improving Science Education.

Champagne, A. L., & Kouba, V. L. (2000). Writing to inquire: Written products as performance measures. In J. J. Mintzes, J. H. Wandersee, & J. D. Novak (Eds.), *Assessing science understanding: A human constructivist view* (pp. 223–248). New York: Academic Press.

Chaskin, R. J., & Rauner, D. M. (1995). Youth and caring: An introduction. *Phi Delta Kappan, 76*(9), 667–674.

Good, R. G. (2000). Cautionary notes on assessment of understanding science concepts and nature of science. In J. J. Mintzes, J. H. Wandersee, & J. D. Novak (Eds.), *Assessing science understanding: A human constructivist view* (pp. 343–354). New York: Academic Press.

Judson, H. F. (1980). *The search for solutions.* New York: Holt, Rinehart & Winston.

Keil, F. C., & Wilson, R. A. (2000). Explaining explanation. In F. C. Keil & R. A. Wilson (Eds.), *Explanation and cognition* (pp. 1–18). Cambridge, MA: The MIT Press.

Lee, O. (2002). Promoting scientific inquiry with elementary students from diverse cultures and languages. In W. C. Secada (Ed.), *Review of research in education* (Vol. 26, pp. 23–69). Washington, DC: American Education Research Association.

Loucks-Horsley, S., Hewson, P., Love, N., & Stiles, K. (1998). *Designing professional development for teachers of science and mathematics.* Thousand Oaks, CA: Corwin Press.

Lowery, L. F. (Ed.). (1997). *Pathways to the science standards: Elementary edition.* Arlington, VA: National Science Teachers Association.

McCormack, A. J., & Yager, R. E. (1989). A new taxonomy of science education. *The Science Teacher, 56*(2), 47–48.

Murphy, G. L. (2000). Explanatory concepts. In F. C. Keil & R. A. Wilson (Eds.), *Explanation and cognition* (pp. 361–392). Cambridge, MA: The MIT Press.

National Commission on Excellence in Education. (1983). *A nation at risk. The imperatives for educational reform.* Washington, DC: U.S. Government Printing Office.

National Research Council. (1996). *National science education standards.* Washington, DC: National Academy Press.

National Research Council. (2000). *Inquiry and the national science education standards: A guide for teaching and learning.* Washington DC: National Academies Press.

Noddings, N. (1995). Teaching themes of care. *Phi Delta Kappan, 76*(9), 675–679.

Paulu, N., & Martin, M. (1991). *Helping your child learn science.* Washington, DC: U.S. Department of Education, Office of Educational Improvement.

Pizzini, E. L., Bell, S. A., & Shepardson, D. P. (1988). Rethinking thinking in the science classroom. *The Science Teacher, 55*(9), 22–25.

Rowe, M. B. (1973). *Teaching science as continuous inquiry.* New York: McGraw-Hill.

Rowe, M. B. (1996). Mounting and maintaining an elementary science program: What supervisors can learn from research. In J. Rhoton & P. Bowers (Eds.), *Issues in science education* (pp. 162–166). Arlington, VA: National Science Teachers Association.

Rutherford, F. J., & Ahlgren, A. (1990). *Science for all Americans.* New York: Oxford University Press.

Schafer, M. (2001, October). Those amazing inventions. *Science and Children, 39*(2), 34–37.

Sears, P. B., & Kessen, W. (1964). Statement of purposes and objectives of science education in school. *Journal of Research in Science Teaching 2*(1), 3–6.

Shapiro, B. (1994). *What children bring to light: A constructivist perspective on children's learning in science.* New York: Teachers College Press.

Stokes, N. C., & Hull, M. M. (2002, May). Every drop counts. *The Science Teacher, 69*(5), 40–41.

Vitale, M. R., & Romance, N. R. (2000). Portfolios in science assessment: A knowledge-based model for classroom practice. In J. J. Mintzes, J. H. Wandersee, & J. D. Novak (Eds.), *Assessing science understanding: A human constructivist view* (pp. 167–196). New York: Academic Press.

Wang, J. (2001). TIMSS primary and middle school data: Some technical concerns. *Educational Researcher, 30*(6), 16–21.

Wheeler, J. C. (2000). *Cosmic catastrophes: Supernovae, gamma-ray bursts, and adventures in hyperspace.* New York: Cambridge University Press.

Wiggins, G., & McTighe, J. (1998). *Understanding by design.* Alexandria, VA: Association for Supervision and Curriculum Development.

Wiske, M. S. (Ed.). (1998). *Teaching for understanding.* San Francisco: Jossey-Bass.

Zukav, G. (1979). *The Dancing Wu Li Masters:* New York: Bantam Books.

2

I n the vision presented by the Standards, *inquiry is a step beyond "science as process," in which students learn skills, such as observation, inference, and experimentation. The new vision includes the "processes of science" and requires that students combine processes and scientific knowledge as they use scientific reasoning and critical thinking to develop their understanding of science.*

(National Research Council, 1996, p. 105)

Processes of Science and Scientific Inquiry

Processes of science are mental and physical skills for collecting information, organizing it in various ways, and using it to make predictions, explain phenomena, and solve problems. Scientists employ a variety of scientific processes, including *observing, measuring, inferring, experimenting,* and *communicating,* as they investigate the mysteries of our universe.

Because students need practice to become proficient in using scientific processes, it makes sense to emphasize individual processes in teaching science. But the real value of a process approach to science comes as students learn to incorporate processes of science into scientific inquiry.

To guide you in planning to teach science process skills, both individually and within the context of inquiry, this chapter is organized around the following questions:

 What specific processes of science are featured in elementary and middle school classrooms? What activities might be useful in teaching children how to apply specific processes of science?

 How can processes of science be learned and used as tools within a context of scientific inquiry?

 What is meant by descriptive, classificatory, and experimental investigations? What are the main characteristics of each of these forms of investigation? How are processes of science used in these different ways of investigating?

 Collect responses to these questions as you find them in the chapter. The focus questions also appear on the Companion Website at http://www.prenhall.com/carin.

Processes of Science

Although the processes of science are especially characteristic of the work of professional scientists, everyone can exercise them in thinking about various matters of interest in everyday life (Rutherford & Ahlgren, 1990). The value of developing sciencing skills in our students has been summarized by Mechling and Oliver (1983) in this way:

> Competence in using process skills provides children with the ability to apply knowledge, not only to science and other subjects in the classroom, but outside the classroom in their everyday lives as well. They are the same skills that will serve them as adults, when they measure their floor for a carpet, try to figure out why their automobile didn't start, or decide which presidential candidate to vote for. These are the thinking skills they will use when separating evidence from opinion while listening to someone's side of a story, or when looking for

Teaching science processes parallels a well-known proverb: Give a man a fish and he eats for a day. Teach him how to fish and he eats for a lifetime.

Many good activities on science process skills can be found in Rezba, Sprague, Fiel, and Funk (2003) and Ostlund and Mercier (1999).

evidence and contradictions in written or spoken opinions. They are the science processes children will use as adults to separate inferences from evidence in a systematic way. (p. 8)

Process skills similar to those used in science are also important in other areas of the curriculum. Consider language arts, for example. As Santa and Alvermann (1991) have emphasized, "Science and reading teachers have very similar goals for their students. Foremost is the pursuit of meaning" (p. vi). In science, students construct meaning from the natural world; in reading, they construct meaning from text. Although investigative processes in science and comprehension processes in reading are quite different, processing strategies remain at the heart of both disciplines. For example, both science and reading teachers want their students to be able to describe events, make inferences, interpret information, draw conclusions, and make and test predictions (Padilla, Muth, & Padilla, 1991; Tompkins & Hoskisson, 1994). These types of skills can be emphasized in both disciplines.

A process approach is also integral to social studies. *Observations* about such things as geographical regions, natural resources, and people in different cultures make up the facts to be considered in social studies. *Comparison and contrast* of facts and *generalizations* about patterns lead to organizing concepts such as interdependence, cooperation, and cultural change. *Application* of these concepts helps students to understand what is happening in cultural interactions and to make *predictions* about future events.

You can build on process similarities to help your students strengthen their skills and integrate their understandings across the curriculum.

A variety of science processes that are emphasized in elementary and middle school science classes are described in Table 2-1 and in the following sections. We will look first at the process of observing.

Observing

Observation is the process of gathering information using all appropriate senses and instruments that extend the senses, such as magnifying glasses, telescopes, microphones and speakers, and the various instruments used in medical diagnosis. Children use their senses to explore the world from the day they are born—or perhaps earlier. In preschool and kindergarten, they begin to discover the part each of their senses plays in making their observations. "What can you tell me about this?" a kindergarten teacher asks her class as she holds up a flower. "Yes, it is a flower. But can you tell me more about it? What color is it? What part of your body tells you that?" Then she asks the children to touch and smell the flower and to identify which sense they use to acquire their information (Minnesota Mathematics and Science Teaching Project, 1970).

Young children tend to observe globally and, thus, to miss potentially relevant details. They often see what they expect to see, and they may focus more on differences than similarities. As they develop skills in observing, children learn to observe for detail, to see what is actually there, and to pay attention to both similarities and differences (Harlen & Jelly, 1990).

Science provides children many opportunities to observe, to wonder, and to seek their own answers to questions through discovery and testing. Almost any objects, organisms, or events are suitable as a base for developing observing skills. For example, observing popcorn—including observing characteristics of the uncooked kernels, observing the popcorn as it is being popped, and observing the cooked popcorn—provides an excellent context for children to consider how each of their senses provides different information.

Take a moment to examine Activity 2-1. This activity can be used to test your own observation skills or as an activity to help your students develop their observation skills. Do this activity on observing candy before reading further.

VIDEO CASE STUDY: *Linda*

Previewing the Video
As you watch this case study, use the *Questions for Reflection* to guide your note taking, thoughts, and discussion. For group discussion, choose a group facilitator to solicit various perspectives and keep the discussion on track.

Introducing the Case

Linda, after spending 15 years as a classroom teacher, begins her first year as a K–4 science specialist in an urban school district. Linda rotates among 600 students in 26 classrooms. An innovative science teacher, Linda works in cooperation with classroom teachers to supply them with resources and initiate the teaching of core concepts, or helps develop concepts first introduced by the classroom teacher. Most often, though, she works directly with a class of students as they engage in inquiry. Early in the year, after working with students on activities such as the Cartesian diver, Linda decides she needs to promote scientific processes appropriate for different grade levels. She asks one class of students to use certain materials to design a "fair" experiment using land snails.

Questions for Reflection

1. What question are students asked to use in designing their land snail experiment? Why did Linda ask students to investigate this question? What designs do the students use to set up their investigation?

2. What student actions and answers indicate to Linda that this teaching and learning experience is not very successful?

Close observations allow students to wonder and appreciate how snails react to light and touch.

Students find that land snails like carrots, moist lettuce, and oatmeal sopped with water or milk.

Safety Precaution:
Be sure that students wash their hands before and after handling any animals you bring into the classroom.

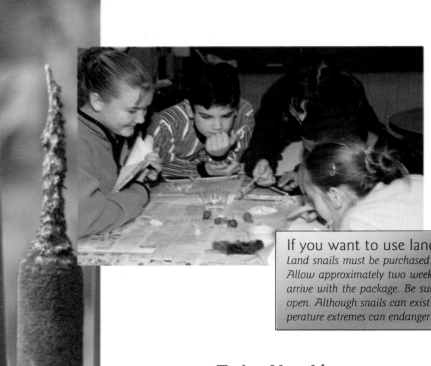

Students enjoy observing land snails when they first emerge from their shells.

If you want to use land snails . . .

Land snails must be purchased from a biological supply house (see Appendix C). Allow approximately two weeks for shipping. Directions for caring for snails will arrive with the package. Be sure the snails are delivered on a day your school is open. Although snails can exist in a somewhat dormant state for a few days, temperature extremes can endanger their survival.

Trying New Ideas *In a later lesson, Linda works with a fourth-grade teacher, Mrs. Nelson, to follow up on concepts about simple machines. For an inquiry activity in which students experiment with the use of an inclined plane, Linda and Mrs. Nelson provide students with specific materials to test. The teachers give the students a number of choices to make in the use of the materials to design their investigation.*

Questions for Reflection

1. Based on previous lessons and Linda's discussion with her teaching mentor, what does Linda realize she could do differently to plan a process-oriented lesson?

2. What did Linda choose to structure for the inclined plane experiment? What choices were given to students to test their first experiment with the inclined plane?

3. How did some of the choices students made in their experiment cause some confusion in their results?

4. In which tasks of scientific inquiry described in Chapter 1 (Figure 1-3) do the students in Linda's class engage? What kind of guidance could Linda have given to involve the students more in each of the tasks of inquiry?

5. What different answers did students give to the inquiry question between the first and second experiment? What student answers indicate to you that students "got it" after the second experiment? Do you think all students in this class now understand the concept? Why or why not?

6. When do you think reteaching an inquiry lesson would be appropriate? What significant differences would need to be in place to warrant reteaching a lesson?

A Rubber-Band Force Scale

Materials:

- *Stiff piece of cardboard about 4" x 6"*
- *Flexible rubber band*
- *Paper clips*
- *Centimeter ruler*

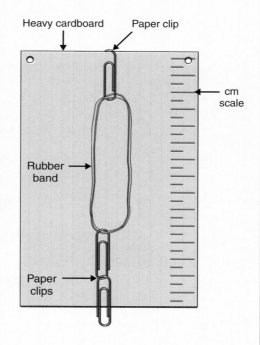

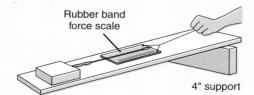

Instructions:

- *Using the ruler, mark a scale along one long edge of the cardboard strip, with marks 0.5 centimeters apart.*
- *Hook a paper clip over one end of the cardboard strip and hang a rubber band from it.*
- *Hang a chain of two or three paper clips from the other end of the rubber band so that the chain extends beyond the edge of the card.*
- *Hook the end of the paper clip chain over the object to be moved; hold the cardboard rubber band scale firmly and move the object.*
- *Record how much the rubber band stretches (in cm.). The amount of stretch is a nonstandard measure of the amount of force applied by the rubber band to the object moved.*

"The ultimate goal in science education is no longer just amassing a body of knowledge, but it's also developing the skills to go about answering questions independently. It is not possible for any one individual to learn that whole body of knowledge. Perhaps equally as important is to be able to generate ways of thinking about questions that we have and how we might go about exploring those questions on our own."

—Dr. Anita Greenwood, University of Massachusetts–Lowell

Reflecting and Building on Change *Linda has numerous opportunities to meet and talk with a teaching mentor, Dr. Anita Greenwood at the University of Massachusetts–Lowell. Through their discussions and Linda's implementation of ideas, Linda recognizes how to better structure her inquiry activities to guide students toward limiting their choices to extract fair test results and thus better understand experimental design.*

A bed of oatmeal on newspaper provides a good environment for students to observe mealworms.

If you need mealworms . . .
Mealworms are the larval stage of various beetles. They can usually be purchased from a local pet store. Talk to your pet store about how to feed, care for, and humanely dispose of mealworms.

To observe mealworms, student groups will need newspaper, oatmeal, crackers, plastic forceps, petri dish (for water), hand lenses, and their journals.

Questions for Reflection

1. What do students do during the mealworm experiment that indicates this inquiry lesson is effective? What student answers indicate that they understand what constitutes a "fair test"? Why is the process students use more important to Linda than the results students get from their experiment?

2. What does the teaching mentor identify as reasons some inquiry lessons can result in confusion for students? What can teachers do to help avoid confusion during process-oriented lessons.

3. What insight throughout these three modules does Linda give you that can help you plan more effective inquiry activities for your students?

**TABLE 2-1   SOME PROCESSES OF SCIENCE EMPHASIZED IN
ELEMENTARY AND MIDDLE SCHOOLS**

Process of Science	Method	Example
Observing	Gather information using all appropriate senses and instruments that extend the senses.	Look at a melting ice cube to determine its changing shape, feel the water to determine its coldness, or use a thermometer to measure its temperature.
Measuring	Quantify variables using a variety of instruments and standard or nonstandard units.	Use a clock to count the number of minutes for an ice cube to melt; weigh ice cubes and water before and after the ice cube melts.
Classifying	Group objects or organisms according to one or more common properties.	Place objects, such as solids and liquids, in groups according to their properties.
Inferring	Draw a tentative conclusion about observations based on prior knowledge.	Infer that heat caused the disappearance of the ice cube.
Hypothesizing	Make a statement about a possible relationship in the natural world that might be found through investigations.	Make a statement that might be used to guide an experiment: "The larger the ice cube, the more time it will take to melt in water."
Controlled Investigating	Investigate by deliberately manipulating one variable at a time and observing the effect on a responding variable, while holding all other variables constant.	Conduct an experiment to determine the effect of a mass of ice cubes on the time it takes them to melt in water, while keeping the amount of water, the temperature of the water, and the shape of the ice cubes the same.
Predicting	Make a forecast of a possible outcome of an investigation based on known patterns in data.	Use data from an investigation and state: "Based on this investigation data, I think the 30 gram ice cube will melt in 10 minutes."
Explaining	Logically link evidence and scientific knowledge to make sense of puzzling events.	Explain why ice-cream salt placed in ice water can lower the temperature of the water below its freezing point of 0°C.
Communicating	Record and present the results of investigations to others in multiple ways.	Record data on melting ice in a data table; give an oral report on how ice cream is made.

Activity 2-1: Observing Candy

Obtain two pieces of hard candy. The pieces should be similar, but different in some ways. Write down as many qualitative and quantitative observations of the candy as you can make.

Under your guidance as a sensitive teacher, students can develop effective observation skills.

TABLE 2-2   COMPONENTS OF GOOD SCIENTIFIC OBSERVING

Component	Description
Senses	Use all appropriate senses as well as instruments that extend the senses in gathering extensive and clear information.
Measurements	Make quantitative observations, that is, measurements, to supplement qualitative observations when it matters.
Changes	Observe natural changes occuring in the objects or system of interest; whenever appropriate, make deliberate alterations in a system and observe the responding changes.
Questions	Be curious and keep an open mind while observing; be alert to discrepancies; raise questions that can lead to new observations and new information.
Communication	Report your observations clearly, using verbal descriptions, charts, diagrams, drawings, and other methods as appropriate.

Did you make a variety of observations about the candy in Activity 2-1? Use the components of good scientific observing shown in Table 2-2 as a checklist to see how comprehensive your list of observations is.

- Did you use all appropriate *senses*, and perhaps a magnifying lens in observing your candy? Did you note both similarities and differences in the two pieces of candy?
- Did you make quantitative observations? For example, did you measure the diameter or circumference and the weight of the candy, in nonstandard or standard units?
- What *changes* did you make to the candy? For example, did you crush it or place a piece in water and observe changes?

- Did you raise *questions* about the candy that might be investigated through further observations or experiments?
- How did you *communicate* your observations? Did you make a written list, or perhaps a chart that might facilitate comparisons? Did you include drawings?

Science and Children, one of several excellent journals of the National Science Teachers Association (NSTA), offers many useful articles for teachers. See the article titled "Inspired Inquiry" by Elizabeth Wafler (2001) for another activity on using candy and containers of water to improve students' observational skills and spark their interest in investigating. In another article, "Oh Say Can You See," Checkovich and Sterling (2001) offer a valuable classroom perspective on helping children learn to be better observers. Included in this article is an observation guide for use with elementary students that incorporates many of the elements of Table 2-2.

Learning to be a good observer is a lifelong task. Under your guidance as a sensitive teacher, students can develop effective observation skills.

Several good activities using a variety of materials to teach and assess observation skills are available on the PALS (Performance Assessment Links in Science) Website at http://pals.sri.com/index.html.

Measuring

Measurement is another main process used in doing science. As suggested in Activity 2-1, it is often important in science to quantify observations through measurement. For example, knowing the length of the roots and stems of developing plants and how these variables change from day to day can be important for understanding plant growth. Accurate measurements not only enhance descriptions, they can improve the quality of predictions and explanations of natural phenomena.

A shared emphasis on measurement is an important way to connect science and mathematics in elementary and middle schools. Through their experiences in both science and mathematics, by the end of middle school, students should begin to understand

- the meaning of each property that is being measured, such as volume or temperature;
- how to use a variety of measuring instruments;
- the meaning and use of various standard units of measurement;
- the meaning and relationships among the various prefixes used with metric measurement units, such as *milli-, centi-,* and *kilo-;*
- how to interpolate between numbers in reading thermometers, rulers, and other instruments;
- how to express measurements in terms of decimals when appropriate; and
- how to estimate measurements and determine when estimation is appropriate.

In elementary and middle school science, children should be afforded a great deal of practice in using and reading metric rulers, metersticks, thermometers, balances, spring scales, timers of various kinds, graduated cylinders, measuring cups, and other measuring instruments.

Appendix H describes important tools and skills for measuring length, area, volume, mass, weight, and temperature at the elementary and middle school level.

Classifying

Classification is an important way to organize information in science. In classifying, people sort objects according to their properties. Two special ways of classifying often introduced in elementary science are binary and multistage classification.

In a *binary classification system,* a set of objects is divided into two groups on the basis of whether each object has a particular property. For example, a set of buttons might be

Figure 2-1 A multistage classification of button properties.

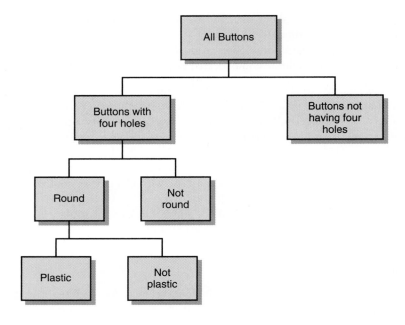

classified into two groups based on the number of holes they have. One group might consist of all the buttons that have four holes; the other group would be made up of all buttons that do not have four holes.

In the magnets lesson described in Chapter 1, children organized information gathered about magnets and material objects in a binary way by separating the objects into two piles based on whether they were attracted to magnets. As another example, living things in a terrarium habitat might be classified as plants and animals (that is, organisms that are not plants). In a *multistage classification system*, the objects in the original set are sorted again and again so that a hierarchy of sets and subsets is formed. For example, the four-hole buttons in our example of binary classification might be further classified as being round and not round. Four-hole, round buttons might then be classified as being plastic or not plastic.

Figure 2-1 shows an example of a multistage classification of button properties. What might a multistage classification of living things in a terrarium look like?

Focusing on similar properties in classifying can lead to understandings about the most significant properties of objects and about their functions. For example, a focus on the four-hole property of buttons might lead to a question about why some buttons have holes and others do not. What is the function of the holes? Do buttons without holes have some characteristic that substitutes for the holes (such as another means to attach them to garments)?

A variety of activities on observing and describing the properties of objects, such as buttons, and developing classifications of them are provided in *Activities for Teaching Science as Inquiry,* the companion volume to this book.

Inferring

Observations are statements about information that is available directly through the five senses; inferences are interpretations of these observations. In inferring, we use experiences and knowledge to fill in gaps about observed events and information.

An **inference,** then, is an *interpretation* of observations that is based on prior knowledge and experiences. Children should be especially encouraged to make explicit the observations, assumptions, concepts, and principles on which their inferences are based.

When they draw inferences, students should routinely be asked: "What is your evidence?" and "Why do you think so?"

In one popular activity designed to teach the skill of inferring, students are supplied with closed boxes in which mystery objects have been placed. They lift, shake, and tilt the boxes to gain information about the mystery objects. A student might note, for instance, that the object rolls when the box is tilted one way and slides when it is tilted differently. What is the shape of the object? A good inference is that the shape is cylindrical. The goal of this activity is not just for children to find out what is in the box, but to help them learn to distinguish between observations and inferences and to use the skill of inferring in probing the unknown.

To better understand the process of inferring, spend some time now doing Activity 2-2.

Have you drawn some inferences about where the moisture on the outside of the glass of ice water in Activity 2-2 comes from? If you had appropriate prior experiences and scientific knowledge (such as is given in Figure 2-2) you might have inferred that the moisture on the glass came from water vapor in the air surrounding the glass. Some students

Activity 2-2: Why Does Moisture Collect on a Glass of Ice Water?

Moisture is often seen collected on the outside of a glass of ice water. Before reading on, make some inferences about where the moisture that formed on the glass came from.

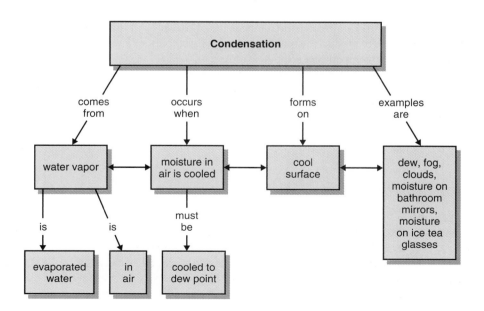

Figure 2-2 To be useful, scientific knowledge must be well structured and interconnected.

 A glossary containing definitions of important terms used in this chapter can be found on the Companion Website for Chapter 2 at http://www. prenhall.com/carin.

infer, in contrast, that the moisture came from inside the glass, gradually seeping through its walls. Even adults often say a glass of ice water is *sweating,* implying that the moisture comes from inside the glass.

Inferences in science need to be checked out through further investigation. What kinds of investigations might be carried out to help students decide between these two inferences? (*Hint:* Students might be led to put red food dye in the water and then be guided to see that the water on the outside of the glass is clear, with no hint of red.)

The ability to infer is also a key component of reading comprehension. Many reading tests, including statewide reading competency tests, have sections on inferring meanings from written text. Developing inferring skills through science investigations can benefit children in reading, because in science they have opportunities to work with concrete materials rather than just with abstract text. What they learn in science, they can apply analogously in reading.

Predicting

It is often important in science to predict future occurrences. A **prediction** is a forecast of a possible outcome based on knowledge of patterns in data. Predictions look forward—to what might happen. Inferences, in contrast, look backward; inferences are types of explanations of what has already happened.

It is important for children to learn to state the reasons supporting their predictions. By asking "Why do you think so?" the teacher can help the children learn to elaborate on their reasoning and to think of data, relationships, and patterns as dynamic and useful knowledge.

Predictions are greatly enhanced when measurement data is organized into graphs to illustrate a trend. For example, suppose students wished to investigate the rate of cooling of a sample of hot water contained in a plastic cup. Specifically, how does the temperature of the water vary with time? In gathering data to answer this question, students might measure the initial temperature of the water and then measure the temperature every few minutes as the water cools.

Figure 2-3 shows a graph for an investigation of temperature versus time for water as it cools. The graph indicates that the temperature decreases in a regular way with time. Using the graph, students can predict the temperature of the water at different times. For example, use the graph to predict the temperature of the water after 25 minutes. What do you predict would be the temperature after 40 minutes?

Figure 2-3 Graph of how the temperature of water changes with time as the water cools.

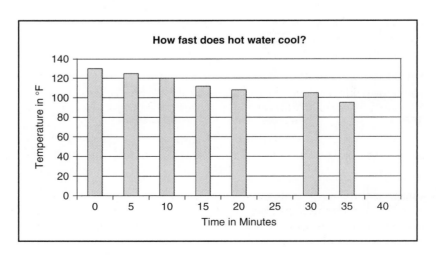

To make these predictions, determine what temperature would continue the trend already established by the data. A good prediction for the first case (after 25 minutes) is about 104°F, while a good prediction for the second case is about 95°F. Some estimation from the graph is necessary in both cases. The first prediction in the water temperature example is called an *interpolation* because it is between (*inter-*) available data points; the second prediction is called an *extrapolation* because it is outside (*extra-*) the collected data points.

A discussion of different kinds of graphs and how they might be used to connect science and mathematics in the classroom is included in Chapter 8.

Experimenting

Sometimes scientists or students can control circumstances deliberately and precisely in an experiment to obtain evidence. Scientists may, for example, control the temperature while changing the concentration of chemicals in an experiment. In a variation of the experiment on water cooling, students may keep the room temperature and size and type of the cup the same, while varying the volume of water to see if volume affects the rate of cooling. By controlling all other conditions and varying just one condition in the experiment, they can hope to identify its effects on what happens, uncomplicated by changes in other conditions (Rutherford & Ahlgren, 1990).

Controlled experiments involve (1) deliberately changing one variable at a time, (2) observing the effect on another variable, while (3) holding all other variables constant. A controlled investigation might be used to answer questions such as these:

- What factors affect the rate of swing of a pendulum?
- How does milk in a hamster's diet affect its health and growth?
- Which brand of paper towel is the best buy, considering such factors as absorbency, wet strength, quality, and cost per sheet?

Elementary and middle school students seem to understand controlled experiments better when they think of them as **fair tests**. If an experimental test is a fair one, the conditions are exactly the same for an experimental situation and a controlled situation, except that one variable is changed for the experimental situation. In carrying out fair tests, students must identify relevant variables, formulate hypotheses, conduct a controlled experiment, interpret data, and communicate conclusions to others.

Research suggests that children in grades K–5 may not be able to plan, conduct, and interpret the results of controlled investigations on their own. Children need many investigative experiences, with a great deal of assistance from their teachers, to learn to identify variables and design and carry out controlled tests.

Manipulated, Responding, and Control Variables. Working with variables is a particularly important part of controlled investigations. A **variable** is a property of objects or events that can change and have differing amounts. The height and weight of a growing child, the time a candle can burn under a glass jar, and the amount of rainfall in a day are all examples of variables.

Three types of variables are important in scientific investigations:

- A **manipulated variable** (also called an **independent variable**) is a variable that the experimenter deliberately changes or manipulates in an investigation.
- A **responding variable** (also called a **dependent variable**) is a variable that changes in an investigation in response to changes in the manipulated variable.
- **Control variables** are variables that are deliberately kept constant or unchanged in an investigation in order not to confound the results, that is, so the investigation is a "fair test."

To illustrate the three types of variables, suppose a team of children was investigating the effect of water temperature on the time it takes for an effervescent antacid tablet to dissolve in water. Before reading on, identify the manipulated variable, the responding variable, and possible control variables for this investigation.

TABLE 2-3   DEFINITIONS AND EXAMPLES OF MANIPULATED, RESPONDING, AND CONTROL VARIABLES

Variable Type	Definition	Example from Dissolving Antacid Tablets Investigation
Manipulated variable	variable that is deliberately changed	temperature of water
Responding variable	variable that responds to manipulated changes	time for tablet to dissolve
Control variables	variables that are carefully held constant	type of container; amount of water; tablet size; form of tablet, whether solid or powder

The manipulated variable in the tablets investigation would be the temperature of the water; temperature is the variable that the investigator would deliberately change. The responding variable would be the time it takes for the tablet to dissolve; time is the outcome variable the investigator would measure for each trial. To make the temperature test a fair one, in each investigation trial, the team would have to control such variables as the size of the tablets, the amount of water, and possibly the kind of container for the water.

Did you correctly identify the responding and manipulated variables and name some possible control variables for this investigation? The three types of variables are defined and examples from the dissolving tablets investigation are given in Table 2-3.

Hypothesizing

The process of formulating and testing hypotheses is one of the core activities of scientific investigations. A **hypothesis** is a statement about a possible relationship that might be identified through investigations. Hypotheses guide scientists in choosing what available data to pay attention to, what additional data to seek, and how to interpret the data in an investigation. To be useful, a hypothesis should suggest what observational evidence would support it and what evidence would refute it.

According to Rutherford and Ahlgren (1990), "Inventing hypotheses or theories to imagine how the world works and then figuring out how they can be put to the test of reality is as creative as writing poetry, composing music, or designing skyscrapers" (p. 7).

Hypotheses are often stated in a form such as "the greater the manipulated variable, the greater (or less) the responding variable will be." Through brainstorming, children might come up with this hypothesis for the dissolving tablets investigation: The warmer the water, the faster the tablet will dissolve in it.

To test this hypothesis, students would need to conduct a controlled experiment in which the temperature of the water is systematically varied. For example, water temperatures of 40°F, 60°F, and 80°F might be used. Then, the time for the tablet to completely dissolve would be measured for each temperature. All other variables, such as the volume of water and the size and type of tablet, remain fixed. The data would be examined to see whether or not the hypothesis is supported.

Children can learn to observe, measure, classify, and perform fair tests as part of isolated exercises, but these science processes become more meaningful when utilized together as

See the *Science and Children* article by Louise Baxter and Martha Kurtz (2001) for an interesting perspective on teaching children the similarities and differences among predictions, hypotheses, and theories.

Children investigate the effects of temperature on the rate at which an effervescent tablet dissolves in water.

intellectual tools in the context of full scientific inquiry. In the following sections, we will look more closely at how children can learn processes of science through inquiry activities.

Incorporating Science Processes in Scientific Investigations

Although recognizing the value of students knowing how to use individual processes of science, the authors of the *National Science Education Standards* (National Research Council, 1996) have called for "more than 'science as process'" (p. 2). The *Standards* stress that children should learn to use science processes within a framework of inquiry.

Consider, for example, how observation is used in inquiry in the process of generating scientific understanding. Kathleen Roth (1993), an educational researcher who has drawn much of her research data from teaching fifth graders in science and social studies, has suggested that:

> A scientist who observes well . . . is not one who spends endless hours documenting and describing every possible detail that can be observed about a particular phenomenon. . . . In contrast, a good scientific observation focuses on key features in ways that will contribute new knowledge, increase the explanatory power of a particular conceptual framework, generate new understandings of relationships among concepts, or raise significant questions about accepted conceptual frameworks. . . . The importance of the observations is not how accurately the scientists can detail and describe all facets of the observed phenomenon, but how the scientists use the observed phenomenon to develop more powerful and complete explanations. (pp. 31–32)

All of the processes of science are essential to inquiry into the natural world.

	TABLE 2-4 WAYS OF INVESTIGATING		
Ways of Investigating	**Investigative Procedures**	**Example Science Topics**	**Example Focusing Questions**
Descriptive Investigations	Gather observational and measurement data to answer questions about the properties and actions of objects, events, and systems.	States of matter	What happens to snow when it is heated?
		Light phenomena	Where is the image in a mirror?
		Ants and ant homes	What are the body parts of ants? What do ants eat? What are ant homes like?
		Seeds and plants	What is the sequence of germination and growth for a bean seed?
Classificatory Investigations	Organize collected information by sorting and grouping it according to one or more properties in order to identify relationships and define properties.	Magnetic interactions	How do magnets interact with different kinds of things?
		Properties of matter	What are the defining physical and chemical properties of common white powders?
Experimental Investigations	Conduct experiments, including controlled experiments, to determine how variables are related and to isolate causal factors in natural phenomena.	Color and heat absorption	Do different colored materials absorb heat differently?
		Seeds and plants	Do seeds need light to grow? Do plants take in water through their leaves or through their roots?
		Position and motion on a ramp	How does the position a ball is released from on a ramp affect the motion of the ball?

There is no fixed set of steps that scientists always follow in doing science, no one path that leads them unerringly to scientific knowledge (Rutherford & Ahlgren, 1990, p. 5). However, there are some specific forms of investigation that children should experience. These include

- descriptive investigations;
- classificatory investigations; and
- experimental investigations.

In *descriptive investigations*, students gather observational and measurement data to answer questions about the properties and actions of objects, events, and systems. *Classificatory investigations* focus on using classification processes to organize collected information by sorting and grouping it according to one or more properties. Organizing data through classification and other procedures is an important step in identifying the defining properties of the objects and organisms of interest and in answering questions. *Experimental investigations* use experimental procedures, including controlled experiments, to determine how variables are related and to isolate causal factors in natural phenomena. Table 2-4 identifies the main characteristics of each of these ways of investigating.

The *Science Standards* emphasize that "different kinds of questions suggest different kinds of scientific investigations" (National Research Council, 1996, p. 148). Table 2-4 provides sample questions that might initiate each of the types of investigation. These initiating ques-

In actual classroom investigations, students are often required to use the various forms of investigations together, rather than separately, in collecting and organizing data to answer questions.

Good questions for initiating inquiry:

* lead to interesting new knowledge about the world;
* lead to a deeper understanding of the nature of science and scientific inquiry;
* require students to gather observable evidence and use it with developing knowledge to generate answers;
* require a variety of science processes to answer them;
* may require students to observe, compare, and classify objects and organisms;
* may require students to infer and predict;
* may require students to identify and measure variables;
* may require controlled experiments;
* may relate to the form and function of parts of objects and organisms.

Figure 2-4
Characteristics of good questions for initiating inquiry.

tions are drawn from the many inquiries described in the first two chapters of this text. Figure 2-4 describes some characteristics of good questions for initiating scientific inquiry.

The three main approaches to investigating involve the application of processes of observing, measuring, classifying, inferring, predicting, and so on. By making processes of science explicit to students during scientific investigations, you help them to develop skills for doing science, better understand how science is done, and appreciate more fully the real-world basis of all scientific knowledge.

Let us examine the various forms of scientific investigation in more detail.

Descriptive Investigations

Questions leading to descriptive investigations are often "what" questions, such as, "What are different animals like?" To investigate this question, children might begin by observing and identifying defining characteristics of animals they encounter in the backyard, at the zoo, or in the classroom. In thinking about and communicating their observations, young children might use creative art and role-playing (Barrett et al., 1991). For example, what defining characteristics of opossums and ladybugs are modeled in the art and play of the children in Figure 2-5?

Finding Out about Ants: A Descriptive Investigation. In the early grades, children's investigations are largely based on systematic description and classification of material objects and organisms (Lowery, 1997). Young children's natural curiosity motivates them to explore the world by manipulating and observing, comparing and contrasting, and sorting simple objects in their environment.

Finding out about ants and other little "creatures" can be an especially fascinating venture for preschool and primary grade children. As in other types of science investigations, descriptive investigations of ants begin with the children's questions, proceed to observations that can be used to answer the questions, and include appropriate communications of questions, findings, and conclusions.

On a nature walk near the classroom, Elena Orosco's first grade children watched with wonder as a long line of ants, carrying what looked like food, disappeared into a hole in the ground. Many of the children had seen ants at picnics and watched them along ant trails and near ant hills, but they had little specific knowledge about them. The children were

The PEACHES (Preschool Explorations for Adults, Children, and Educators in Science) program from Lawrence Hall of Science has developed a number of activity guides for leading young children in exploring animal characteristics, animals and their babies, and animal homes. For the PEACHES address, see Appendix K.

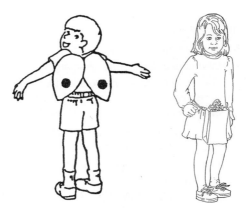

Figure 2-5 What characteristics of ladybugs and opossums are modeled in the art and play of the children shown here?
Source: The illustration "boy with ladybug wings" was reprinted from the Great Explorations in Math and Science (GEMS) teacher's guide entitled *Ladybugs.* The illustration "girl with sack around waist" was reprinted from the Great Explorations in Math and Science (GEMS) teacher's guide entitled *Mother Opossum and Her Babies.* Both guides are copyright by The Regents of the University of California, and the illustrations are used with permission. The GEMS series includes more than 70 teacher's guides and handbooks for preschool through eighth grade, available from: LHS GEMS, Lawrence Hall of Science, University of California, Berkeley, CA 94720-5200. (510) 642-7771. For more information, visit our web site at www.lhsgems.org.

full of questions: "What are they carrying?" "Is that their food?" "How do they live underground?" "Do they have tunnels?" Ms. Orosco encouraged the children to talk and to ask questions, but because she wanted them to learn how to answer their own questions through investigating, she did not answer the questions yet.

Back in the classroom, Ms. Orosco used a KWL approach to structure a discussion about ants. She asked first what the children already **K**new and what they **W**anted to know about ants. Throughout the study of ants, she would assess and discuss with them what they had **L**earned. Many more questions about ants arose in the discussion. With some assistance from their teacher, the class decided to focus on three questions that might be investigated through observing:

- • What do ants do underground?
- • What are the body parts of ants?
- • What foods do ants eat?

The use of journals in science provides an opportunity for students from primary grades through middle school to improve their writing skills, while they explore content and enhance their science learning.

To facilitate the investigation of ants, Ms. Orosco helped the children set up ant homes in large jars (see Figure 2-6 and the accompanying lesson activities). The children observed the ants in the jars over several days, including observing with magnifying lenses. In a version of experimental inquiry, they also put a paper plate with different foods on it outside near an ant trail to investigate what ants eat. Ms. Orosco helped the children steer a course between noticing as much detail as possible and selectively observing for what was relevant to answering their questions. Using drawings and words, the students recorded what they observed in their nature journals for later reference.

The *Benchmarks for Science Literacy* (American Association for the Advancement of Science, 1993), emphasize that

An important part of students' explorations is telling others what they see, what they think and what it makes them wonder about. Children should have lots of time to talk about what they observe and to compare their observations with others. (p. 10)

Figure 2-6   A classroom ant home made from a large jar.

Ms. Orosco provided ample opportunities for the children to talk about their observations of the ants, to learn from one another, and to ask questions that lead to further observations and learning. Through discussion among themselves and with their teacher, and through using their journals, the children decided that

- ants live underground and make tunnels to reach their homes;
- all ants have the same body parts: head, body, and six legs—with the legs attached to the body; and
- ants tend to eat foods with sugar.

In follow-up activities, the children listened as their teacher read from a children's book on ants, learned some new songs about ants, constructed a giant ant hill out of butcher paper, and role-played ants dragging food through a tunnel-like structure. These activities helped the children to integrate observations, facts, and concepts about ants.

Through engaging in descriptive investigations, children not only develop their observation skills, they begin to learn how to raise questions and answer them. At the same time, they begin to acquire significant knowledge about their surroundings and begin to see how scientific knowledge is generated.

Lesson Activities: Investigating Ants

Caution children to watch, but not to handle the ants. As a defense, ants bite and sting. Sometimes after biting an enemy, ants will spray a chemical into the open wound. Some children will be allergic to ant stings. You will need to assist children as they introduce ants into their jar ant homes. Also, help the children secure the covering over the jars to prevent the ants from escaping.

Activities on building an ant home and observing ants can be found in *Activities for Teaching Science as Inquiry*. Also you will find many sites on the Internet with lesson activities on ants that integrate content and processes across the curriculum.

A great source for ideas to help young children investigate ants is the PEACHES guide *Ant Homes Under the Ground* by Jean C. Echols, Kimi Hosoume, and Jaine Kopp. See Appendix K for the PEACHES Website address.

Safety

Where Do Ants Live?

Place a small juice can, open end down, in the center of a large glass jar. Fill the jar with loose soil, and add ants. Use a rubber band to secure an old stocking on the top of the jar, and cut off the excess, leaving a good amount left to cover the ant home and keep the ants from escaping. Tape black paper around the outside of the jar so the ants will build tunnels on the sides of the jar around the juice can. After a couple of hours, take off the paper and see what is happening.

What Are Ants Like?

Use a magnifier to observe your ants. Are they all alike? What body parts do you notice? What do you think each body part is for? How many legs do they have? Where are the legs attached? Draw a large picture of an ant.

Do not forget to feed and water your ants. What do you think the ants will eat?

What Do Ants Eat?

Divide a paper plate into sections with a black marker. Place various food items on the plate (e.g., crackers, small seeds, sugar, lettuce). Set the plate outside near an ant trail on a nice warm day. Check back after 1 hour to see what has happened. Check back after 2 hours. What food have the ants taken? What appears to be their favorite food?

Source: Adapted from The Activity Idea Place, http://www.123child.com/animals/ants.html. Reprinted with permission.

A study guide for the Video Case Study featuring Jean and her third grade class can be found in Chapter 9 of this text. Watch the video to see more activities children can do to learn about matter and other science concepts.

Instructions for making class-sized quantities of oobleck and suggested activities for investigating it are given on pages A-30–A-31 in *Activities for Teaching Science as Inquiry,* the companion volume for this text. Also, you may wish to examine the GEMS guide on oobleck (Sneider, 1985), produced by the Lawrence Hall of Science at Berkeley.

Classificatory Inquiries

In classificatory inquiries, students find out more about objects and organisms by discovering ways of grouping them according to their properties or traits. By focusing on properties, classificatory investigations tend to incorporate descriptive inquiry procedures. Investigating the physical and chemical properties of white powders forms the basis for an exciting descriptive and classificatory inquiry for children.

Mystery Powders: A Descriptive and Classificatory Investigation. In one of the Video Case Studies in Science Education, the children in Jean's third grade classroom are investigating the properties of a substance that has been called *oobleck* (Sneider, 1985). A sample of oobleck can be made by adding a small amount of water to a tablespoon of cornstarch, mixing until a bloblike consistency develops. This substance seems solid when you press on it but is gooey and drippy when it is handled.

In the video, one boy picks up some oobleck, watches and feels it dripping through his fingers, and says with a grimace, "Ooh! It's dis-gust-ing!" Two other children, working as a pair, try to classify the substance.

> *Student 1: It's a liquid.*
> *Student 2: It's mostly liquid.*
> *Student 1: It's both.*
> *Student 2: We need to do the shape test (to determine if it's a solid).*

The children look at and feel the substance to see if it maintains its shape. But the oobleck seems to flow when it is picked up and to keep its shape when on the table. It simply does not conform to a shape test. By examining something that has the characteristic properties of both a solid and a liquid, the children learn more about the nature of matter and enhance their ability to use the process of classifying.

A few days later, Jean's third grade children continue their studies of matter by investigating common white powders, including sugar, table salt, baking soda, and cornstarch

| TABLE 2-5   PROPERTIES OF WHITE POWDERS | | | | |
Observations	Powder 1 Granulated Sugar	Powder 2 Table Salt	Powder 3 Baking Soda	Powder 4 Cornstarch
Visual (Magnifying Glass)	White crystals	White box-shaped crystals	Fine white powder	Fine yellowish white powder
Water Test	Dissolves in water	Dissolves in water	Forms milky mix	Makes water cloudy
Vinegar Test	Dissolves in vinegar	Has no reaction with vinegar	Fizzes with vinegar	Gets thick, then hard with vinegar
Iodine Test	Turns yellow with iodine	Has no reaction with iodine	Turns yellow-orange with iodine	Turns red, then black with iodine

(see the accompanying Lesson Activities: Investigating White Powders). The powders are similar in color but differ in other properties. The children have already learned several indicator tests they can use to identify properties of the powders. For example, they have learned that salt dissolves in water and baking soda fizzes in vinegar. Table 2-5 shows a chart of the properties of some common white powders.

Now the children are preparing to investigate "mystery powders" consisting of mixtures of *two* powders. Jean says that her goal in this activity is to assess whether the children understand the different properties of powders and what different indicators do.

A comprehensive set of activities on investigating chemical and physical properties of powders can be found on pages A-32–A-35 in *Activities for Teaching Science as Inquiry*, the companion volume to this book.

Lesson Activities: Investigating White Powders

- *Materials:* Salt, sugar, baking soda, and cornstarch; containers of water, vinegar, and iodine; medicine droppers; plastic spoons; toothpicks; plastic wrap to use as an investigation tray; magnifying lenses; safety goggles.
- *Safety Precautions:* Wear safety goggles for these investigations with powders. Do not taste any of the powders or liquids. Wash your hands after you test each powder.
- *Initiating Question:* What are the identifying properties of some common white powders?
- *Investigating Procedures*
    1. *Preparation.* Make an investigation tray by smoothing a sheet of plastic wrap onto your table.
    2. *Visual Observations.* Use a plastic spoon to place a small amount of each powder in a row on your plastic wrap investigation tray. Use a magnifying glass to observe each powder. Write down your observations on a second copy of the investigation record.
    3. *Water Test.* Use a clean plastic spoon to place a small amount of each powder in a row on your investigation tray. Add several drops of water and mix with a toothpick to see what happens. Record your observations in your data table.
    4. *Iodine Test.* Use a clean plastic spoon to place a small amount of each powder in a row on your tray. Add a drop or two of iodine to each powder. Write down the results in your data table. Be careful! Iodine can stain your hands and clothing.

5. *Vinegar Test.*   Use a clean plastic spoon to place a small amount of each powder in a row on your tray. Add several drops of vinegar to each powder. Write down the results in your data table.

• *Conclusions:* How are the four powders alike? How are the powders different? What is the best test for each powder? Write down your conclusions on your record sheet.

• *Clean Up:* Throw away plastic wrap and toothpicks. Return powders and test supplies to teacher-designated spot. Clean and dry anything dirty including your hands. Do not put powders in the sink as they might harden and clog the drain.

DATA TABLE AND CONCLUSIONS FOR INVESTIGATING WHITE POWDERS

Observations	Powder 1 Sugar	Powder 2 Table Salt	Powder 3 Baking Soda	Powder 4 Cornstarch
Visual (Magnifying Glass)				
Water Test				
Iodine Test				
Vinegar Test				
Conclusions:				

Note: Good references for this activity can be found at these web sites: http://www.csulb.edu/~lhenriqu/mysterypowder.htm, http://etc.sccoe.k12.ca.us/i98/ii98Units/Cross/Mystery/test/powders.html, and http://eduref.org/cgi-bin/printlessons.cgi/Virtual/Lessons/Science/Chemistry/CHM0200.html.

Study Jean's introduction to this lesson:

We are going to have a grand adventure with a very mysterious mixture of powders. And what you're going to do is use all of the information about powders you have acquired so far. Now you are each going to get a powder, and we are going to see how many scientists figure out what their powders are.

In this model introduction to an inquiry lesson, Jean

• piques the children's curiosity by describing the activity as a *grand adventure* with a *mysterious mixture*;
• alludes to information the children already know, helping them access their relevant, prior knowledge;
• gives general directions about what the children are to do, yet leaves the investigation open-ended by not telling precisely what steps to follow; and
• encourages the children by comparing their task to that of scientists.

To connect science and social studies, you might ask children in social studies to investigate which white powders pioneer settlers would have carried with them on wagon trains and why they would need them.

Working as pairs, the children take their role as scientists very seriously. They are thoughtful, respectful of one another, but excited. Here is what some of the children do and say in their mystery powders investigations:

Student 1: *Put a little bit here.*

Student 2: *(Student 2 pours some of the mystery powder on a piece of white paper, and the pair look at it and feel it.)*

Student 3: *You do the water (test); I'll do the vinegar. (One of the partners in this pair drops water from a small bottle on a bit of the mystery powder. The other one puts a few drops of vinegar on another small amount of the powder. The children observe the resulting reactions.)*

Student 4: *It's fizzing a little!*

Student 3: *Fizzing, yeah! Try one more time. (The partner puts more drops of vinegar on the powder.)*

Student 4: *There's definitely baking soda in there.*

Student 3: *Big time!*

Student 5: *I think it's not salt.*

Student 6: *I don't know. What would be the best way to find out if it is not salt? (Pauses and ponders for a moment.) All right, let's try water.*

Student 7: *We thought it was cornstarch. We did the iodine test and we're positive that it is cornstarch. We want to move on to a really, really, hard one, a challenge. We want to put four (powders) in.*

Jean: *Do you think you can solve that?*

Students: *Yes!*

Jean's lessons on matter align well with the *National Science Education Standards* for grades K–4 (see the concepts and principles related to the standards on material objects in Figure 7-1, page 213, in this book).

Through these lessons, the child-scientists develop well-structured and grade-level-appropriate knowledge about matter. They also have many opportunities to practice and extend their science process skills—but always within a context of significant concepts and principles. Roth's (1993) description of scientific observations fits the children well:

> To make … observations, the scientist draws from existing conceptual knowledge, asks questions about important pieces of the [knowledge] …, develops hypotheses, and designs experiments that will permit the critical and relevant observations to be made. (p. 31)

Engaging in inquiry is a powerful learning strategy for students at every level.

In the white powders lesson, the inquiries are primarily descriptive and classificatory. Now, let us see what happens in experimental investigations.

Experimental Investigations

Experimental investigations focus on how variables might be related and on what happens in a system when one variable is manipulated. Although controlled investigations are difficult for students in the elementary grades, with appropriate teacher assistance, young children can engage in experimental inquiry. In the ant investigation described previously, the teacher helped first graders find a way to vary the foods available to ants while controlling other conditions so they could observe which foods the ants tended to eat.

Questions for experimental investigations can arise in many different contexts. During class discussion, one group of fifth grade students wondered why NASA chose white as the color for astronauts' space suits. Challenged and guided by their teacher, they reformulated their question to: Do different colored containers absorb sunlight differently? The students then designed and carried out a controlled investigation to help answer their question.

Working in cooperative groups, the students took two identical, empty vegetable cans and covered one with black construction paper and the other with white construction paper. They then filled the two cans with the same amount of water, placed a Styrofoam lid on each can, and placed them in the sunlight, side by side, for a specific length of time. They measured the initial and final temperatures of the water in the two cans and calculated the temperature change for each. Noting that the dark can got warmer, the children concluded it had absorbed more sunlight.

Returning to their initial question, they reasoned that NASA chose white for astronauts' suits because white suits absorb less heat in sunlight than darker-colored suits. Follow-up reading activities confirmed this inference.

Let us look at a classroom investigation of seeds and plants that enables children to learn many science concepts and practice their science process skills. This project involves descriptive and experimental investigation procedures.

Germinating Seeds and Growing Plants: A Descriptive and Experimental Inquiry Project. There is nothing like being around children to rekindle our own interest in the natural world. Children love to study living things. They especially enjoy planting seeds and watching and caring for plants as they grow. Teachers can capitalize on and nurture the natural curiosity of children through inquiry units like seed germination and plant growth.

Investigations about seeds, seed germination, and plant growth utilize many science processes. Through investigating the nature of seeds, children can develop facility in observing, measuring, classifying, inferring, predicting, communicating, and other processes of science.

Questions for Inquiry about Seeds and Plants. Forming good questions that can be empirically investigated and that lead to significant knowledge is the first step in scientific inquiry. Some questions, such as "Will my seeds grow?" or "What will the color of the roots be?", are too narrow to provoke much inquiry. Good inquiry questions should be open-ended, suggest possible investigations, and lead to interesting knowledge (see Figure 2-4).

Some interesting questions about seeds can come from wondering about their form and function. A seed contains the ingredients of life. For children, the parts of a seed can represent its *form*. "What are the parts of a seed?" can be a productive question for elementary students. Activity 2-3 reveals that once bean seeds are soaked and broken into two halves, three main parts can be observed: a seed coat, a pulpy mass, which children learn to call the cotyledon, and a small plantlike structure—the embryo plant or "beanie baby." The beginnings of a leaf and root are clearly observable in the embryo plant (see Figure 2-7). Take some time to do Activity 2-3. Be sure to use a magnifying lens to see details of seed parts for yourself.

Figure 2-7   A bean seed has three main parts: a seed covering, the cotyledon, and an embryo plant.

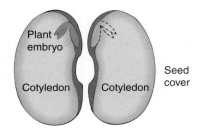

Plant embryo

Cotyledon   Cotyledon

Seed cover

Activity 2-3: How Are Seeds Alike and Different?

Obtain several lima bean seeds and at least one other kind of seed. Soak some of the seeds for at least 48 hours. Write down as many observations, including measurements, of the soaked and unsoaked seeds as you can make. Carefully break a lima bean seed open into its two halves, observe them using a magnifying lens, and compare your observations with those of another student.

Once children identify the parts of a seed, they might engage in brainstorming and raise their own questions about the functions of the seed parts, such as "What is the seed coat for?" or "What does the cotyledon do?" Children can answer their questions from observations and investigations of the seed and the plant as it grows and changes.

Questions about the role of external conditions in germination and growth can also be raised. For example, "Do seeds need light during the germination process?" "Will seeds germinate in the dark?" There are, thus, many questions that could be asked about seeds. In addition, there are a variety of questions that might be asked about the developing plant. In our example of inquiry for children, let us focus on three questions:

- What is the sequence of germination and growth for a bean seed?
- Is light needed for seed germination? That is, will a seed germinate in the dark?
- Do plants get water through their roots or through their leaves?

Investigating questions such as these can be instrumental in helping children attain the K–4 NSES Content Standards related to organisms (see Table 2-6).

In inquiry, children must plan investigations carefully and use their science process skills selectively in collecting data. The investigation procedures and the science processes used depend on the inquiry questions asked. Let us examine some possible approaches to answering the first inquiry question.

TABLE 2-6 CONCEPTS AND PRINCIPLES ABOUT ORGANISMS AND THEIR LIFE CYCLES EMPHASIZED FOR GRADES K–4

Standards for Grades K–4	Concepts and Principles Children Should Learn
Characteristics of Organisms	• Organisms have basic needs. For example, organisms need air, water, and food; plants require air, water, nutrients, and light. Organisms can survive only in environments in which their needs can be met.
	• Each plant or animal has different structures that serve different functions in growth, survival, and reproduction.
Life Cycles of Organisms	• Plants and animals have life cycles that include being born, developing into adults, reproducing, and eventually dying. The details of this life cycle are different for different organisms.

Source: Reprinted with permission from *National Science Education Standards* by The National Academy of Sciences, courtesy of the National Academies Press, Washington DC.

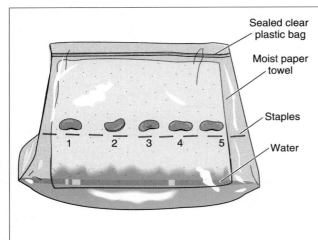

Sealed clear plastic bag

Moist paper towel

Staples

Water

1   2   3   4   5

- Line a 7 inch × 8 inch (quart size) sealable, transparent storage bag with a moist paper towel.
- Place six staples across the bag about 4 to 5 cm from the bottom, as shown in the diagram.
- Position each seed to be germinated above one of the staples.
- The seeds may be presoaked for about 24 hours.
- Gently pour water from a small container into the bag, being careful not to dislodge the seeds (the water should bulge slightly at the bottom of the bag to about a finger's thickness).

The water will soak the paper towel and keep the seeds moist. The staples keep the seeds from lying in the water at the bottom of the bag. The transparent bag allows the seeds and roots to be observed.

Figure 2-8   How to construct a seed germination bag.

What Is the Sequence of Germination and Growth for Bean Seeds? Answering this "what" question calls for a descriptive investigation. Children cannot just place the seeds underground in moist soil, because then they would not be able to see them germinate. However, they can use a transparent germination bag like the one shown in Figure 2-8. The germination bags should be attached to a bulletin board or some other flat, vertical surface.

To answer their questions about the progression of changes, children should observe their germinating seeds and developing plants regularly for 2 or 3 weeks. They should record on a data sheet or in a journal any changes in color, length, and other features that might occur in the seeds and in the emerging roots, stems, and leaves. Figure 2-9 illustrates a sample data sheet for communicating investigative data about seed growth.

Records of measurement data should show the date measured, what was measured, the units used, and the measured data for each variable. Students should routinely be expected to use metric units in science investigations—millimeters or centimeters in the case of measuring plant growth. Graphs can be constructed from data to facilitate comparisons and predictions. The process of constructing and using different kinds of graphs in science is discussed in some detail in Chapter 8.

Younger children might make measurements by placing a colored paper strip next to the plant and cutting the strip to the length of the plant stem. These nonstandard measurements of stem length can be displayed on a daily/weekly time line made from a calendar showing days of the week and month.

In investigating the process of germination, children might observe first that the seed becomes moist and softens. Early in the process, a "sprout" begins to emerge from the bean seed near where the embryo plant is located. As children observe further, they can see that the tip of this initial protrusion becomes the root. The stem grows upward from the root. Because the root has emerged from near the location of the embryo plant, children might infer that the growing plant develops from the embryo.

At some point in the germination process, the seed coat comes off. Although they cannot know for sure from observation alone, children might infer that the seed coat protected the seed to ensure that it did not become moist earlier than desired.

A variety of activities on seeds and plants can be found on pages A-139–A-167 in the companion volume to this text, *Activities for Teaching Science as Inquiry.* Also, see the delightful activity book *GrowLab: Activities for Growing Minds* (1992), published by the National Gardening Association (see Appendix C for address).

	Descriptions			Measurements		
Date	Changes in seeds	Changes in roots	Changes in stems	Length of roots	Length of stems	Drawing
Monday March 5						
Wednesday March 7						
Friday March 9						
Monday March 12						

Figure 2-9 Sample data sheet for recording seed germination data.

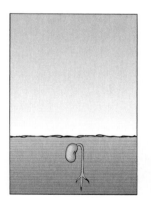

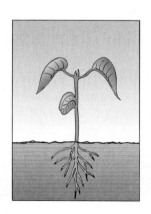
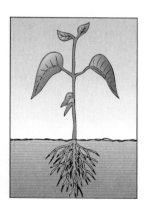

Figure 2-10 The developmental sequence of a bean seed and young bean plant.

As the plant develops, the cotyledon shrivels and sometimes falls off the stem. Building on this observation, children might infer that it is a food or energy source and is used by the young plant as it is germinating. Your students can investigate further by trying to germinate the two halves of a cotyledon, one with the embryo plant and one without.

Eventually in the development of the bean plant, green leaves begin to grow. Figure 2-10 summarizes the developmental sequence of a bean seed and young bean plant.

Is Light Needed for Seed Germination? Exploring the role of light in seed germination requires that the children conduct a controlled experiment or fair test. In their experiment, children could set up two transparent bag germinators that are alike for every condition except that one of the germination bags is kept in a dark place and one is kept in ordinary classroom light. This makes the experimental test a fair one: temperatures and other conditions are kept the same, so that one bag will not have an unfair advantage over the other.

The children will observe that the bean seeds germinate equally in the dark and the light. This is evidence that light is not needed for germination. However, elementary school students are likely to have difficulty linking evidence and explanations (Kuhn, Amsel, & O'Loughlin, 1988) and, despite their observational evidence, may still think that light is needed for germination. In one classroom, children resisted the conclusion that light is not necessary for seeds to germinate, until one student pointed out that seeds germinate underground, in the dark. Then, the children realized that seeds must not need light to germinate.

Some of the children may know terms such as *photosynthesis*, but it is not just terminology that we want children to learn. In inquiry, we want them to bring their textual learning alive by connecting it to real-world observations. At the same time, we want children to interpret their real-world observations through application of their text knowledge. In this way, both their observations and their acquired knowledge begin to make sense for them.

Do Plants Get Water Through Roots or Leaves? To gather evidence to use in answering this question, children might set up a controlled investigation like the one illustrated in Figure 2-11. This investigation involves two plants. The manipulated variable is how the plants are watered. The responding variable is the resulting condition of each plant. The variables that are controlled and kept constant are the amount of water each plant gets, and environmental conditions such as temperature and light exposure. In the investigation, water is added to the soil of one plant so that it can reach the roots. Water is sprinkled on the leaves of the second plant, with a plastic bib keeping the water from reaching the soil and roots (National Gardening Association, 1992).

Children would keep daily records of their observations. After about 2 weeks, the teacher would guide the children as they reviewed their observations and discussed their findings. For example, the teacher might ask:

What did you do in the investigation? What did you observe? How did your findings compare with your predictions? What can you infer about the role of leaves in taking in water? Did you

Figure 2-11 Do plants get water through their roots or their leaves?

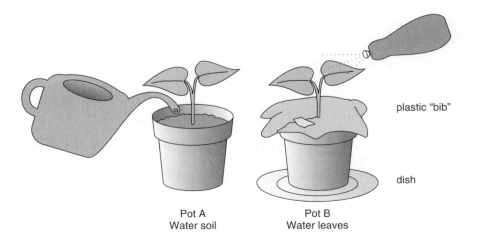

plastic "bib"

dish

Pot A
Water soil

Pot B
Water leaves

actually see roots taking in water? What makes you confident in your inference that water is taken in by roots? What factors might have affected the results of your investigation? (National Gardening Association, 1992)

Communicating Investigations and Conclusions. Full inquiry involves asking a simple question, completing an investigation, answering the question, and communicating the results to others. Abilities to communicate grow with age, experience, and cognitive development. In one kindergarten class, at the conclusion of a unit in which they planted seeds and investigated plant growth, the children acted out seed germination and plant growth. As the teacher read aloud from a children's book about seeds and life, the children solemnly played the roles of seeds, moisture, and sunlight. At first, each seed-child rolled into a tight ball close to the floor. As the water-child went about, sprinkling blue crepe-paper "rain-water" on the seed-children, they began, one by one, to shake themselves and gradually spring to life. When the seed-children popped up through the "ground," they looked around for the sun-child, who held a large yellow circle with rays drawn on it. With the warming rays of the sun, the seed-children began to stretch and grow to their full heights. The children's understanding of seed germination and plant growth could be inferred from the seriousness of their role-playing, the ways their actions paralleled the teacher's reading, and how each seed-child's actions followed on cue the actions of the growth factors of moisture and sunlight.

In the upper elementary grades and in middle schools, students produce oral and written reports that present the results of their inquiries. According to the *National Science Education Standards* (National Research Council, 1996, p. 144), such reports and discussions should occur frequently in science classes.

Reports for investigations might be organized into four parts as described in the following list:

I. *Purposes: What I wanted to find out*
   (The focus question for investigation is given here.)
II. *Procedures: What I did to answer my questions*
   (Investigation procedures are described.)
III. *Findings: What I found out from my observations and measurements*
   (Data sheets, verbal information, measurement data, graphs, and pictures, perhaps from digital cameras, would be included here.)
IV. *Conclusions: What I concluded*
   (In drawing conclusions, children should use their observational data as evidence to support their answers to the questions raised in the Purposes section of the report.)

Learning to communicate effectively is a major goal of education at all levels. Working to improve children's skills of communicating investigative questions, procedures, results, and conclusions is an important way to link science and writing. Language arts time might even be used to compose journals and to develop and present reports.

Position and Motion on a Ramp: A Structured Inquiry Lesson. Students can often go further when they have examples of personal, structured inquiries on which to build. Thus, we have included a well-structured lesson plan on position and motion (appropriate for grade 3 or 4) for you to review and use.

The position and motion lesson plan follows an instructional model called the 5-E model: *Engagement, Exploration, Explanation, Elaboration,* and *Evaluation.* Notice in

Watch the Video Case Study featuring Erien, Year Two, for ideas on the use of journals as an important communication tool. A guide for this case study is provided in Chapter 7.

Encourage your students to use computer presentation packages, such as *HyperStudio, Kid Pix,* and *PowerPoint,* to present their investigations, evidence, and conclusions.

the lesson plan the relationship between the various E's and the inquiry tasks of the *National Science Education Standards* summarized in Figure 1-3.

In this lesson, students roll a ball from different positions along a ramp and measure how far a paper cup at the bottom of the ramp slides when the ball hits it. The children organize their data in a table, visually display the data in a graph, use the graph to make predictions of new data, and then test their predictions through investigations. This lesson is an experimental investigation because the students work with responding, manipulated, and control variables.

As you read through the lesson plan, look especially for ways the teacher helps to structure the investigation for the students. Also note the many opportunities in the lesson for children to learn and practice science process skills. Take a few minutes now to work your way carefully through this lesson as if you were going to teach it to children.

Lesson Plan: Investigating Position and Motion

Introduction

In this lesson, students investigate the position and motion of an object rolling down a ramp. They release a marble from three different heights on a ramp and measure how far the marble pushes a cup that is positioned at the bottom of the ramp. They use their data to predict how far the cup will move when they release the marble from two new heights along the ramp.

This lesson addresses the fundamental principle included in the *Content Standards* for grades K–4 that the position and motion of objects can be changed by pushing or pulling. The size of the change is related to the strength of the push or pull (National Research Council, 1996, p. 127).

To help students develop an understanding of scientific inquiry, teachers should regularly ask students how their activities compare to what a scientist might do. Only by reflecting on what they are doing and why will they understand that they are doing scientific inquiry and modeling the kinds of activities that scientists do when they investigate a question. Notice in the following activities how each E (Engage, Explore, etc.) is tied to a specific inquiry task as identified in the *Science Standards*.

ENGAGE: ASK QUESTIONS ABOUT OBJECTS AND EVENTS IN THE ENVIRONMENT.

1. Show students the ramp and cup setup and hold the marble at one point along the ruler. (Do not tell students the centimeter position of the marble along the ruler.) Release the marble and let students observe that the marble moves the cup along the tabletop. Some students will likely say that the higher the marble is on the ramp, the

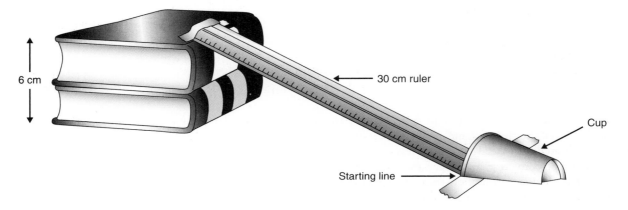

6 cm

30 cm ruler

Cup

Starting line

farther the cup will move. Ask the students, "Why do you think so?" Encourage them to relate the marble and ramp to experiences they have had sledding down a hill, skateboarding down a ramp, or sliding down a slide.

2. Show students the release points of 10 cm and 20 cm from the bottom of the ramp. Ask, "When I release the marble from the 10 cm mark, how far will the cup move?" Then ask, "When I release the marble from the 20 cm mark, how far will the cup move?" After each question, record student responses on the chalkboard.

3. Ask students to suggest ways that they could predict more accurately how far the cup will move from a point without actually releasing the marble from that point. Guide students to suggest collecting data to show a pattern and then using the pattern to make a prediction.

4. Give each student a copy of the Making Predictions Data Table. Review with students the questions they are trying to answer by doing this investigation.

   A. How can we make accurate predictions of how far the cup will move without actually releasing the marble from every point along the ruler? (This question relates to scientists' use of data or evidence to make predictions or draw conclusions.)

   B. How is this investigation like what a scientist might do? (This question helps students develop their understanding of inquiry. In this investigation, students are asking questions about an event, using simple tools to gather data, and basing their predictions on the data they gather.)

MAKING PREDICTIONS DATA TABLE

Release point on ramp	Distance cup usually moves
5 cm	
15 cm	
25 cm	

1. Instruct teams to set up their equipment and show them again how to release the marble and measure the distance the cup moves. Have them begin the investigation by releasing the marble from the 5 cm point. How far did the cup usually move? Tell them to release the marble from the same point at least three times and then record the most typical (average) distance the cup moved.

2. Stop and compare the results from all teams. Discuss any differences in the teams' data. Ask students what might account for the differences. Help them determine a uniform way to set up the ramps and make their measurements so they can compare their data.

3. Have teams complete the investigation by releasing the marble from the 5, 15, and 25 cm points on the ramp. Make sure they record their results in their data tables.

EXPLORE: CONDUCT AN INVESTIGATION AND EMPLOY SIMPLE EQUIPMENT TO GATHER DATA.

1. Distribute copies of Graphing the Results.

2. Help students transfer the data from their data tables onto their graphs. Instruct them to color in the appropriate spaces on their graph outline.

3. Using the data from their graph, ask students to predict how far they think the cup would move if they released the marble from 10 cm and 20 cm. First, ask the students

EXPLAIN: USE DATA TO CONSTRUCT A REASONABLE EXPLANATION.

to record their predictions on paper. Have students compare their predictions with their earlier guesses. The range of predictions should not be as wide as the range of guesses.

4. Ask students to explain their predictions. How do they know how far the cup should move? (They should base their predictions on their data, or evidence, from the investigation.) Is there a pattern on their graph that they can use to help them make predictions? (The graph should show a sloping pattern.)

5. Invite teams to test their predictions by releasing the marble from the 10 cm and 20 cm points. Compare their results with their predictions. If their results did not confirm their predictions, ask them to suggest why.

ELABORATE: DESIGN NEW INVESTIGATIONS.

1. Encourage students to ask a question of interest to them, such as: "What will happen if we change the height of the books that support the ramp?", "Will the cup move farther?", or "How much farther?"

2. After they have predicted in writing what they think will happen and why, ask them to conduct their new investigation.

3. Ask them to explain their results in terms of the position and motion of the marble and cup.

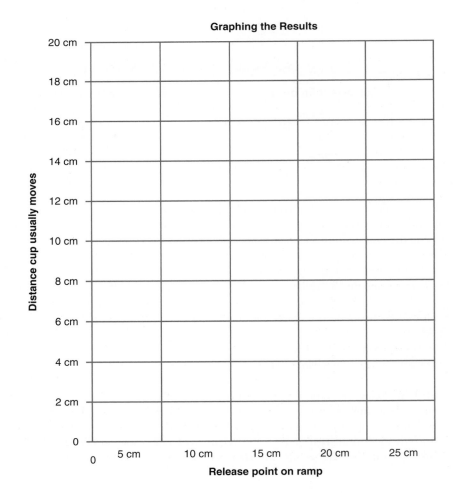

Graphing the Results

1. As students design and conduct their independent investigation, use this opportunity to assess students' abilities to do scientific inquiry. Can they ask a question about an object or event? Can they plan and conduct an investigation? Can they use a tape measure to gather accurate data? Can they use their data to explain their results? Can they tell you about their investigation and compare it with the original investigation?

2. To evaluate students' understanding of the position and motion of objects rolling down a ramp, set up a marble and ramp system and ask students to predict how far the cup will move if you release the marble from 30 cm. (Allow students to use their data and graphs from their investigation to make their prediction.) Instruct students to write an explanation of why they think this will happen. (You can use this to evaluate whether students base their predictions on the previous evidence.)

3. To assess students' understanding of scientific inquiry, ask them to describe their investigation in terms of what they think scientists do. In other words, how did they act like a scientist in learning about the position and motion of objects that roll down a ramp?

Source: Adapted from *Science for Life and Living: Integrating Science, Technology, and Health*, Level 3, by Biological Sciences Curriculum Study, 1992, Dubuque, IA: Kendall/Hunt. Reprinted with permission.

Did you note how many science processes children have the opportunity to practice in the position and motion lesson? For example, children are called on to observe, measure, explain, predict, and communicate. They also conduct a controlled experiment. What are the responding and manipulated variables in this experiment? What variables should be controlled?

Notice how much more structured this lesson is than the seed germination lessons. In the position and motion lesson, the teacher structures each of the inquiry tasks, providing the question to be investigated, giving instructions on experimental procedures, providing a table to record the data, and giving guidance in interpreting the data. Structuring the lesson helps to provide children a model of inquiry they can later begin to follow on their own.

Did you note in the position and motion lesson plan that the teacher is asked to discuss with the children how their inquiry activities are like those that scientists use? In teaching science to children, you should take the opportunity often to discuss what scientists do as they investigate a question or try to solve a problem. In addition, it is important to discuss how the various processes of inquiry used in science are like those we use in our everyday lives.

Teachers and Children's Inquiry

Scientific inquiry is a special way of knowing the world. Through all stages of inquiry, according to the *National Science Education Standards* (National Research Council, 1996, p. 33), effective teachers must be skilled observers of students, as well as knowledgeable about science and how it is learned.

The starting place for inquiry is well-formed questions about the natural world that arise from students' own experiences. Inquiry continues as students use processes of science such as observing, measuring, inferring, and predicting as they gather and interpret information about the real world to answer their questions.

Some children may learn the ways and attitudes of inquiry on their own, but most depend on sensitive teachers who can match their teaching actions to the particular needs of students, deciding when and how to guide, when to encourage more exploration, when to demand more rigorous grappling by the students, when to provide information, and when to connect students to other sources (National Research Council, 1996, p. 3).

Teaching and learning through an inquiry approach is challenging, but well worth the effort!

Use the self-assessment questions for Chapter 2 at http://www.prenhall.com/carin to assess how well you understand this chapter and how prepared you are for a test over its content.

SUMMARY

- Processes of science are skills that scientists and children apply in collecting, organizing, and using data to interpret and make sense of the world. Specific processes emphasized in elementary and middle school science include observing, measuring, classifying, inferring, hypothesizing, conducting controlled investigations, predicting, explaining, and communicating. These science processes are not so very different from the mental processes we all use in solving everyday problems.

- Sometimes processes of science are taught in elementary classrooms primarily through isolated activities. But the *National Science Education Standards* have called for more than science as process, emphasizing that processes should be embedded and integrated in inquiry.

- Elementary and middle school students can be expected to engage in descriptive, classificatory, and experimental inquiries. In the early grades, investigations are largely based on systematic description and classification of material objects and organisms. Young children's natural curiosity motivates them to explore the world by manipulating and observing, comparing and contrasting, and sorting and classifying simple objects and organisms in their environment.

- By grade 5 or 6, and even earlier with a great deal of teacher guidance, children begin to engage in experimental inquiries. In controlled investigations, students work to understand some phenomenon by determining the effect of a manipulated variable on a responding variable, while controlling all other relevant variables.

- Participating in investigations that incorporate processes of science is very important to the science learning and cognitive development of elementary and middle grade students. All of these ways of investigating involve the application of processes of observing, measuring, classifying, inferring, predicting, and so on. By making processes of science explicit to students during scientific investigations, you help them to develop skills for doing science, to better understand the nature of scientific inquiry, and to appreciate more fully the real-world basis of all scientific knowledge.

REFERENCES

American Association for the Advancement of Science. (1993). *Benchmarks for science literacy.* New York: Oxford University Press.

Barrett, K., Blinderman, E., Boffen, B., Echols, J., Hosoume, K., House, P. A., & Kopp, J. (1991). *Preschool science and math explorations: The PEACHES handbook for educators.* Berkeley: University of California, Lawrence Hall of Science.

Baxter, L. M., & Kurtz, M. J. (2001, April). When a hypothesis is not an educated guess. *Science and Children, 38*(7), 18–20.

Biological Sciences Curriculum Study. (1992). *Science for life and living: Integrating science, technology, and health.* Dubuque, IA: Kendall/Hunt.

Checkovich, B. H., & Sterling, D. R. (2001, January). Oh say can you see. *Science and Children, 38*(4), 32–35.

Harlen, W., & Jelly, S. (1990). *Developing science in the primary classroom.* Portsmouth, NH: Heinemann.

Kuhn, D., Amsel, E., & O'Loughlin, M. (1988). *The development of scientific thinking skills.* New York: Academic Press.

Lowery, L. F. (Ed.). (1997). *Pathways to the science standards: Elementary school edition.* Arlington, VA: National Science Teachers Association.

Mechling, K. R., & Oliver, D. L. (1983). *Handbook 1: Science teaches basic skills.* Arlington, VA: National Science Teachers Association.

Minnesota Mathematics and Science Teaching Project. (1970). *Overview: Minnesota mathematics and science teaching project.* Minneapolis: Minnemast Project, University of Minnesota.

National Gardening Association. (1992). *GrowLab: Activities for growing minds.* Burlington, VT: National Gardening Association.

National Research Council. (1996). *National science education standards.* Washington, DC: National Academy Press.

Ostlund, K., & Mercier, S. (1999). *Rising to the challenge of the national science education standards: The processes of science inquiry.* Squaw Valley, CA: S&K Associates.

Padilla, M. J., Muth, K. D., & Padilla, R. K. (1991). Science and reading: Many process skills in common? In C. M. Santa & D. E. Alvermann (Eds.), *Science learning: Processes and applications* (pp. 14–19). Newark, DE: International Reading Association.

Rezba, R. J., Sprague, C., Fiel, R. L., & Funk, H. J. (2003). *Learning and assessing science process skills.* Dubuque, IA: Kendall/Hunt.

Roth, K. (1993). *What does it mean to understand science? Changing perspectives from a teacher and her students.* East Lansing, MI: Center for the Learning and Teaching of Elementary Subjects, Institute for Research on Teaching, Michigan State University.

Rutherford, F. J., & Ahlgren, A. (1990). *Science for all Americans*. New York: Oxford University Press.

Santa, C. M., & Alvermann, D. E. (Eds.). (1991). *Science learning: Processes and applications*. Newark, DE: International Reading Association.

Sneider, C. (1985). *Oobleck: What do scientists do?* Berkeley, CA: Lawrence Hall of Science (Great Explorations in Math and Science).

Tompkins, G. E., & Hoskisson, K. (1994). *Language arts: Content and teaching strategies* (3rd ed., p. 521). Upper Saddle River, NJ: Merrill/Prentice Hall.

Wafler, E. S. (2001, January). Inspired inquiry. *Science and Children, 38* (4), 28–31.

3

L earning science is something students do, not something that is done to them.

(*National Science Education Standards*,
National Research Council, 1996, p. 20)

Learning Science with Understanding

THE *NATIONAL SCIENCE EDUCATION STANDARDS* emphasize an active approach to learning where students have an opportunity to learn science with understanding. Understanding is based in knowledge, but it goes beyond mere recall. When students understand, they are able to do something with their knowledge. They can use it to guide inquiry and to interpret, explain, and make sense of the world.

To facilitate understanding, teachers need to know how children learn so they can adjust instruction to meet the cognitive and developmental capabilities of learners (Lowery, 1997). Fortunately, there is a growing body of research on learning and cognitive development that can provide a strong theory base for you in guiding student learning.

Theories of learning are important in teaching, but they do not inform teachers specifically about what to do in instruction. As John Dewey suggested in the 1929 Kappa Delta Pi lecture series, knowing and applying learning theories can help teachers to make observations and interpretations about learners that might otherwise go unnoticed. The instructional practices of teachers can thus be rendered more intelligent and flexible, and better adapted to deal effectively with what is happening in the classroom. In short, a theoretical perspective can lead to teaching as a truly professional activity and improved learning by all students.

In this chapter, we present some research-based information and theories on learning and cognitive development that can be helpful as you teach science to children. The chapter is organized around the following questions:

- *How do children and adolescents learn science?*

- *How do children process information and construct knowledge when they learn about the world? What are discovery learning and acquisition learning?*

- *What is meant by learning with understanding? How can inquiry teaching approaches facilitate the construction of understanding by students?*

- *How do students' naive theories and alternative conceptions affect their science learning?*

- *How do children and adolescents develop cognitively?*

- *What kinds of science activities are developmentally appropriate for students at different grade levels?*

Collect responses to these questions as you find them in the chapter. The focus questions also appear on the Companion Website at http://www.prenhall. com/carin.

Let us begin by sketching a cognitive theory of learning and then examine its importance in teaching science.

How Do Children Learn?

Motivated by curiosity, equipped with a marvelous array of sensory windows upon the world, and having a fantastic capability of processing and making sense of whatever they encounter, children are born learners. Although endowed with a great learning capacity, children "don't learn simply by listening to someone talk or by reading a book. Students have to take an active role in their own learning" (Lowery, 1997, p. 7).

Contemporary cognitive theorists view learning as a constructive process in which learners, in concert with their peers and their teachers, construct their own knowledge.

A Constructivist Model of Learning

In constructing new knowledge, learners

1. *select* specific aspects of incoming information to consider;
2. *organize* the selected information in various ways such as by sequencing, classifying, connecting, and relating to form new factual and conceptual knowledge; and
3. *integrate* new knowledge with prior knowledge, thus expanding the knowledge base.

The processes and structures involved in constructing knowledge of the world are illustrated in Figure 3-1. The arrows represent mental *processes*; the boxes represent *knowledge*. The processes of selection, organization, and integration of information are automatic, but they become more effective as children learn to monitor and regulate their own learning, and as they build up a bank of knowledge and experiences (Mayer, 1998).

The Role of Prior Knowledge

The construction of new knowledge is always guided and enabled by the learner's prior knowledge. What learners already know influences what they attend to, how they organize input, and how they are able to integrate new constructions to expand their knowledge base. According to educational psychologist David Ausubel (1968), the most important thing to do in teaching is to ascertain the prior knowledge of learners and teach them accordingly. Understanding what children know, then, is a critical aspect of teaching.

Figure 3-1 A cognitive model of knowledge construction.
Source: Modified from R. E. Mayer. (1992). Guiding Students' Cognitive Processing of Scientific Information. In M. Pressley, K. Harris, and J. Guthrie (Eds.), *Promoting Academic Competence and Literacy: Cognitive Research and Innovation.* San Diego: Academic Press (p. 246), Used with permission from Elsevier.

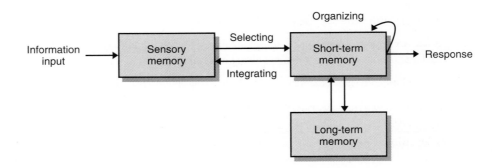

Concept Mapping. Researchers theorize that knowledge is organized in memory in some structured way, for example, as networks, webs, or maps. Rowe (1973) described knowledge organization this way:

> Concepts, principles, and generalizations are the markers on a conceptual map. These markers become connected into a complex network of mental highways over which the student travels during problem solving. (p. 305)

Linking learning theory to instructional practice, Rowe added,

> Such networks are unlikely to develop in instructional programs which fail to give students direct access to phenomena, time to investigate, and opportunity to discuss their work. (p. 366)

A variety of graphic organizers have been used to portray and facilitate the organization of knowledge in memory (Jones, Palincsar, Ogle, & Carr, 1987, pp. 37–40). You might already be familiar with different kinds of *graphic organizers* such as spider maps and Venn diagrams.

Joseph Novak and his colleagues (Mintzes, Wandersee, & Novak, 1998; Novak, 1995) have advocated the use of **concept maps** to represent the science knowledge of students. In constructing concept maps, teachers and students enclose specific concepts in circles or boxes. They draw lines between these concepts to indicate connections and hierarchical relationships. Words or phrases written on or near the connecting lines specify the type of relationship that might exist between two concepts. Bigger ideas are generally placed near the top of the concept map and more specific concepts below.

Ideal concept maps represent the knowledge of experts in a discipline. Teachers can generate maps of students' current knowledge and understanding from classroom observations and careful questioning. Students can also construct their own concept maps to indicate their understanding of science ideas. Figure 3-2 shows concept maps that illustrate the differences of two students' conceptual understanding of the heart and circulatory system.

Concept maps can be used in planning and teaching science lessons to ensure that concepts and relationships needed in learning are emphasized. Student concept maps can be compared with ideal concept maps in assessing the progress of learners and matching instruction to students' developing knowledge levels.

To learn more about how to construct and use concept maps, go to http://cmap.coginst.uwf.edu/. This Website contains descriptions of how concept maps are used by research groups, an informative article by Joseph Novak, and free software that you can download to make your own concept maps.

The use of concept maps in assessing student knowledge attainment is treated in Chapter 6.

Assimilation and Accommodation. The knowledge base of learners grows and changes in the process of integrating new knowledge with existing knowledge. Integration takes place as learners *assimilate* new information to existing knowledge structures and *accommodate* or modify structures to fit reality. In assimilation, learners draw upon relevant prior knowledge to assist them as they organize new information. Assimilation is like fitting a new animal, such as an aardvark or a koala, into an existing animal classification scheme. Accommodation requires altering existing knowledge in some way, such as altering an animal classification scheme to include insects, birds, and fish, as well as mammals.

Accommodation might involve tuning or refining prior knowledge or restructuring existing knowledge in some way. Accommodation might even require discarding old knowledge structures in favor of completely new ones that serve to correct misconceptions and make sense of novel situations (Shuell, 1986).

Advance Organizers. A teaching strategy advocated by Ausubel (2000) to facilitate the linking of new material with prior knowledge is the use of advance organizers. An **advance**

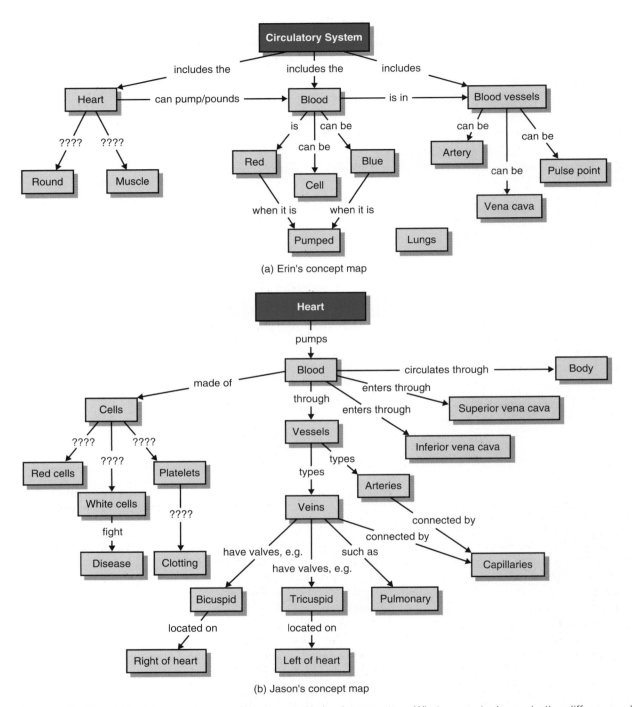

Figure 3-2 Two students' concept maps of the heart and circulatory system. What conceptual organization differences do you note between Erin and Jason?

Source: Figures from Joel J. Mintzes, James H. Wandersee, and Joseph D. Novak, in J. Mintzes, J. Wandersee, and J. Novak (Eds.), *Teaching Science for Understanding: A Human Constructivist View,* copyright © 1998 by Academic Press. Used with permission from Elsevier.

organizer is an abstract, general introduction to a new body of information or subject matter content to be learned. Organizers that have been learned in advance provide a framework for the assimilation of new ideas.

As an example, suppose students were going to learn about electrical circuits, and they had already learned about the human circulatory system. The teacher might use concepts related to circulation and the circulatory system, such as those mapped in Figure 3-2, as an advance organizer for electrical circuits. In studying electrical circuits, students may compare the battery to the heart, the wires to the blood vessels, and the electrical current to the blood. Through these comparisons, they can better understand that a complete circuit is necessary for electrical components, such as bulbs and motors, to work.

Information that forms the raw material in the construction of science knowledge comes from a combination of two main sources of input: discovery and acquisition. Children learn science from information they discover through direct encounters with the world and from information they acquire from teachers, books, videos, computers, and other sources. Let us examine the nature of discovery and acquisition learning.

Discovery Learning

Children learn many things from exploring their surroundings. They discover, for example, that fire is hot, ice is cold, water can change into ice, and ice into water. From concrete experiences they also learn that water heaps up in medicine cups, magnets can attract and repel other magnets, some objects float and others do not, seeds have distinct characteristics, and so on. A major goal of science education at every level is for students to discover for themselves what the world is made of and how it works. Thus, when we go into kindergarten, elementary, and middle school science classrooms, we expect to see students actively involved with a rich variety of material objects and organisms.

In learning science from discovery activities, children do not simply make copies of the world; rather, they construct their own meanings of it. The phrase "hands-on, minds-on" science emphasizes the interaction of discovery, prior knowledge, and mental processes in the construction of scientific knowledge.

Children's discovered knowledge becomes more personally meaningful when they have a chance to organize it in some way.

In the process of constructing meaningful knowledge, children impose some *organization* or order on their observations, as is suggested in the cognitive learning model shown in Figure 3-1. Young students may impose order on the world through sorting, grouping, and arranging objects based on observed attributes (Lowery, 1997). Older students organize the world in more complex ways, such as by classifying, sequencing, or relating information. Here are some examples of how students organize discovered information in science.

In an Elementary Science Study (ESS) investigation called *Rocks and Charts* (Rowe, 1993), students are asked to describe a rock in a set in sufficient detail for another student to pick it out. Children might initially describe a rock according to color, but this property is not sufficient because there may be other rocks in the set that have a similar color. Gradually, the children learn to add other properties, such as texture, hardness, and streak, to describe and classify the rocks. A rock might then be described, for instance, as smooth and glassy, harder than a penny, and leaving a dark-colored streak on a streak plate. In this case, the children's knowledge is made more meaningful as they combine properties of rocks in arriving at more complex systems for describing, classifying, and identifying them.

Students also impose order on the world as they generalize about objects, events, and relationships. For example, while investigating homemade musical instruments, students may recognize that all of them produce sound via some vibrating part. Strings, drumheads, and air columns are all parts of instruments that produce musical sounds as they vibrate. Students observe a few cases and generalize to a relationship fitting all possible cases: *if* a sound is heard, *then* it must have been caused by a vibrating object.

Through processes such as generalizing, classifying, and relating, discovered information becomes organized into knowledge that can be applicable to new learning, thinking, and problem-solving situations.

As shown in Figure 3-1, learning involves *integrating* newly constructed knowledge with existing knowledge. Initially, discovery knowledge is tied to very specific circumstances. For example, in Chapter 1 we described activities in which children learned through discovery and acquisition that water heaps up in a medicine cup when added drop by drop to the cup *because* water is "grabby." That is, cohesive forces between water particles keep water from flowing over the rim of the cup as it heaps up. When children first discover that water drops "bead" up on wax paper (see Activity 1-1, p. 25), they may initially think of it as a totally new phenomenon. Their initial knowledge of beading is fragmented and not connected to their prior knowledge. When children connect the beading of water to their prior knowledge of heaping, they are able to explain beading as a consequence of the grabbiness of water. Connecting new knowledge to existing knowledge results in knowledge that is better understood and more broadly useful.

Discovery learning typically involves many experiences, ample time on relevant tasks, learner insight, and, especially, teacher guidance. Teachers are an indispensable component of children's discovery learning. Hints, cues, prompts, information, and questions (such as "How is it like . . . ?", "How is it different from . . . ?", or "How is it related to . . . ?") can help children make concrete discoveries and use them to bridge to more abstract ways of knowing the world.

Discovering how to sort rocks and identify new samples by their properties is a classificatory investigation.

Acquisition Learning

According to a panel of distinguished researchers on "how people learn,"

A common misconception regarding "constructivist" theories of knowing (that existing knowledge is used to build new knowledge) is that teachers should never tell students anything directly but, instead, should always allow them to construct knowledge for themselves. This perspective confuses a theory of pedagogy (teaching) with a theory of knowing. (Bransford, Brown, & Cocking, 1999, p. 11)

Thus, acquisition learning need not be inconsistent with constructivist theories of learning. Children can and do acquire new knowledge from information presented directly to them from teachers, books, videos, and other sources.

However, learners often have a difficult time transforming presented information into personally meaningful and useful knowledge. The most important thing teachers can do to facilitate acquisition learning is to ensure that students have a base of prior hands-on (discovery) experiences that can be used to make sense of transmitted information. In the 1960s, Robert Karplus (Karplus & Thier, 1974) and his colleagues developed a teaching model for the SCIS (Science Curriculum Improvement Study) elementary science program that combines elements of discovery and acquisition learning. The model, called the Learning Cycle, has been widely used by science teachers since that time. As is shown in Figure 3-3, the Learning Cycle consists of three phases of instruction:

- *Exploration*, in which children explore materials and discover new knowledge
- *Concept invention*, in which teachers formally present information, concepts, and principles that help students make sense of their discoveries
- *Concept application*, in which students construct new understandings by applying their discovered and acquired knowledge in new situations

As an example, the second grade lesson on magnets presented in Chapter 1 essentially follows the Learning Cycle. In that lesson, the children first *explored* the interactions between magnets and different materials. The teacher then built on the children's activities to *invent* four conceptual ideas to help the children organize and make sense of their discovery experiences.

Having relevant prior experiences and knowledge is critical for learners, but for real understanding, more is needed. If transmitted information, such as information on magnets, is to be truly meaningful and useful to students, they need to be active rather than passive in learning. Learners, continually guided and encouraged by their teachers, need to actively

- relate presented terms to their prior, real-world experiences;
- fill in gaps in presentations through inferences based on the applications of their prior experiences and knowledge; and
- organize presented information and integrate it with prior knowledge.

The phases of the Learning Cycle have acquired different designations across the years (see Tobin, Tippins, & Gallard, 1994), but we choose to refer to them as exploration, concept invention, and concept application.

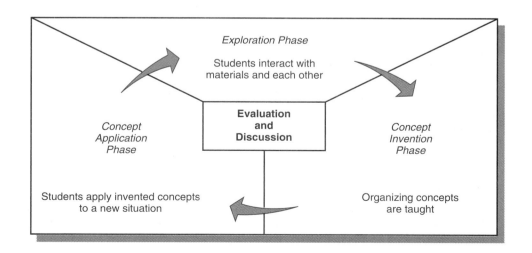

Figure 3-3 The Karplus and Thier SCIS Learning Cycle.
Source: Modified with permission from Charles R. Barman, "An Expanded View of the Learning Cycle: New Ideas About an Effective Teaching Strategy." Monograph and Occasional Paper Series, no. 4 (Washington, DC: Council for Elementary Science International, 1990), 5.

Exploration Phase
Students interact with materials and each other

Evaluation and Discussion

Concept Application Phase

Concept Invention Phase

Students apply invented concepts to a new situation

Organizing concepts are taught

To facilitate understanding, learners must also try out their new knowledge in new situations. This is the third phase of the Learning Cycle, *concept application*. In the magnets example, in an application of their new conceptual knowledge, children went about the room testing many different materials to see how they interacted with magnets. Discoveries of discrepant objects that do not seem to follow the general magnet rules open up the possibility of new learning and instruction. When children discover that some metal objects, such as aluminum cola cans, do not interact with magnets, they must modify or accommodate their old magnet rules.

Another way teachers can assist learners to construct meaning from presented information is to attend to certain instructional guidelines. According to Rosenshine (1986), to teach effectively by direct, verbal means, teachers should do the following:

- Present information and ideas in small steps, checking for understanding before going to the next step.
- Focus on one thought at a time before beginning another.
- Organize material so one point is mastered before the next is given.
- Avoid digressions.
- Provide ample opportunity for practice and review.

To further help students to retain and apply acquired knowledge, the teacher should also provide for vocabulary enhancement and provide opportunities for learners to encounter transmitted information in multiple ways (Mastropieri, Scruggs, & Magnusen, 1999).

Reading is a special type of acquisition learning. A constructivist approach to reading comprehension emphasizes the learner's active role in the reading process. Asking students questions about new content and teaching them to generate their own questions are critical strategies for fostering comprehension (Rosenshine, Meister, & Chapman, 1996). Questions help students to activate prior knowledge, concentrate on main ideas, search for supporting details, and try different ways of organizing content. Questions can also help students generate explanations and apply knowledge in new ways.

Here is an example of how reading might be used to enhance science learning.

Generating Meaning from Science Text. Figure 3-4 shows a page from a FOSS (Full Option Science System) "science stories" book that is part of a third or fourth grade investigation of magnetism. Consistent with the theory of the SCIS Learning Cycle, reading materials in FOSS are designed to be used after hands-on activities. Lawrence Lowery (1998), director of the FOSS program, has explained that new, meaningful knowledge acquired from text materials is actually a construction based on prior knowledge and linguistic input. With something to work with, an author can help readers understand abstract ideas and make difficult connections. But if readers have inadequate prior knowledge related to the content, they will gain little from reading. Thus, reading is more powerful in science when it *follows* experience and is based on prior knowledge.

Take a moment to study Figure 3-4. Write down some questions you could ask to help your students comprehend this textual information more completely. Here are some examples:

1. What do you already know about magnets?
2. How do N and S poles of bar magnets interact?
3. Do doughnut-shaped magnets have N and S poles?
4. How could you make one doughnut magnet "float" above a second doughnut magnet?
5. How does a magnetic compass work?
6. How could you use a bar magnet to make a compass?

HOW MAGNETS INTERACT

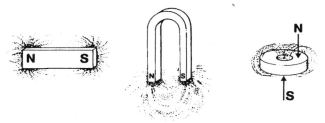

Figure 3-4 A sample page of text from a *FOSS Science Stories* reader. Students study this book after engaging in discovery and inquiry activities on electricity and magnetism. *Source:* From Magnetism and Electricity FOSS® (Full Option Science System®) Science Stories. ©The Regents of the University of California and published by Delta Education. Used with permission.

Every magnet has two ends that behave differently. One end is called the north pole and the other is the south pole.

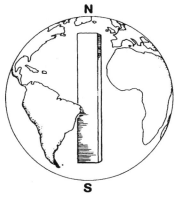

The Earth has two poles very much like a magnet's poles. It has a north pole and a south pole.

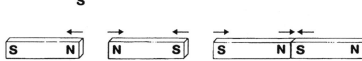

Two north poles always repel each other. Two south poles also repel each other. But north and south poles attract each other.

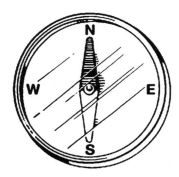

A compass needle is a magnet. One end points to the Earth's magnetic north pole. The other points to the Earth's magnetic south pole. Because the Earth behaves like a magnet, a small magnet like a compass needle can help us determine directions on Earth.

Are some of these questions like the ones you formulated? Each of the example questions relates to some aspect of comprehending the text.

- Question 1 calls for students to recall prior activities with magnets; accessing available knowledge is a critical step in reading comprehension.
- Question 2 requires the students to note a relationship between N and S poles.
- Questions 3 and 4 relate to a later FOSS activity in which children place several doughnut-shaped magnets over a pencil, alternating S and N poles. Due to magnetic repulsion, all but the bottom magnet on the pencil "float."
- Questions 5 and 6 call for students to note that the earth has a magnetic field and to consider how compasses might be designed to interact with it and indicate magnetic north.

Acquisition learning can be a useful learning strategy when teachers ensure that learners have essential prior knowledge and provide appropriate assistance. The problem with acquisition learning in most science classes, however, is that it is relied on far too much and is often isolated from real-world activities. Reading and lecture are important in elementary and middle school science education, not so much as primary sources of information, but to summarize, supplement, and extend knowledge and understanding constructed through hands-on, minds-on discovery and inquiry.

Learning with Understanding

Reading, writing, and arithmetic are critically important subjects in elementary schools, but these basic skills must be recognized as tools for the advancement of knowledge and understanding. Howard Gardner, who is best known for his theory of *multiple intelligences*, has noted that neither basics nor skills will be worthwhile unless they can be mobilized in the service of understanding. "Education for understanding," according to Gardner (1998), "puts the focus of education where it should be: on people's ever-increasing grasp of the world" (p. 350).

As emphasized in Chapter 1, when students *understand* a concept, principle, or idea in science, they can do something with it (Perkins, 1998; Wiggins & McTighe, 1998). For example, they can relate concepts to real-world experiences, connect new ideas to other ideas, and apply principles to new situations as they construct inferences, predictions, and explanations. Students who *understand* a thing are confident in "what they know" and "how they know it," and are able to critically examine their own knowledge and that of others (Kuhn, 1999).

Students often have limited opportunity to develop understanding because the curriculum, textbooks, and tests emphasize memory and recall. Too much emphasis on memory results in knowledge that is fragmented, incomplete, and tied to specific situations. In contrast, understanding in science is based in knowledge that is integrated, growing in completeness, and applicable in a wide range of contexts and situations. Inquiry investigations, such as the investigations of ants, common powders, and seeds described in Chapter 2, provide an excellent context in which to foster children's science understanding.

When used insightfully, existing knowledge can guide the construction and application of new knowledge. Unfortunately, existing knowledge not only facilitates understanding, it can also interfere with it. In the next section, we will examine the effect of children's existing alternative conceptions on their understanding of new concepts.

Children's Alternative Conceptions and Science Learning

Children are busy learning every day, processing and organizing information from many sources (Rutherford & Ahlgren, 1990). They learn from their own explorations of the environment and from their parents, siblings, classmates, teachers, and others. They learn from movies, television, books, computers, churches, and a variety of other sources. They also learn from the school environment in general, from formal instruction and school textbooks, and from personal reconstructions of discovered and acquired knowledge.

Consequently, when they come to science classes, children already have formed many ideas about the world from their daily experiences. The knowledge children bring to new learning situations is often fragmented, incomplete, and naive, and their ideas are generally not congruent with accepted scientific views. Children's partial understandings, naive theories, and alternative conceptions must be recognized and dealt with by teachers if students are to learn science with understanding.

Children's ideas about the world have received a great deal of attention by researchers (see Table 3-1). Here are two humorous examples of students' spontaneous notions (Paulu & Martin, 1991):

- "Fossils are bones that animals are through wearing."
- "Some people can tell what time it is by looking at the sun, but I have never been able to make out the numbers."

TABLE 3-1 SOME ALTERNATIVE CONCEPTIONS CHILDREN HAVE ABOUT SCIENTIFIC TOPICS	
Science Topics	**Students' Conceptions**
Biology	• Things that are active and move (including cars and the sun) are alive. (ages 4–7) • Animals are living because they move, but plants are nonliving. (ages 4–7)
Physical Science	• Weight and density are not differentiated but are included in the idea of "heaviness." (ages 7–11) • Weight and volume are not differentiated but are included in the ideas of size or how big something is. (ages 7–11 and many older children) • Stiff materials are solids, whereas pliable or soft materials are somewhere between solids and liquids. (ages 5 and 6) • Anything that pours is a liquid, including powders. (ages 5 and 6) • When liquids evaporate, they just disappear. (ages 5 and 6) • Electric current is used up in bulbs and there is less current going back to a battery than coming out of it. (up to age 12) • Light rays move out from the eye in order to illuminate objects. (as old as 10 or 11)

Source: From *Learning to Teach Science: A Model for the 21st Century* (pp. 86–87), by Jazlin Ebenezer and Sylvia Connor, © 1998. Reprinted by permission of Prentice Hall, Inc., Upper Saddle River, NJ.

Kathleen Roth (1991) described an interesting example of children's alternative conception from her research with fifth grade students. Children may know the word *photosynthesis*, but they have a lot of alternative ideas about where plants get their energy for growth. They may have the conception, for instance, that plants get their food from the soil through their roots. Plants do absorb nutrients from the soil, but this alternative conception conflicts in critical ways with the scientific view that plants use sunlight to make food from carbon dioxide and water. But students have arrived at their explanations through their own experience with plants, and the explanations work for them. Furthermore, common language usage about "plant food" that is mixed with the soil to "feed" plants reinforces erroneous beliefs. Personal theories are not easy to give up, especially when they are so commonly reinforced.

Research shows clearly that what learners already know and believe is a powerful determiner of what they observe from experience, what they select and represent for processing, how they organize new information, and how they make sense of what they encounter.

For example, in a lesson presented on a Merrill video, a group of seventh grade children were studying the factors that affect the rate of swing of a pendulum. They thought of three possible variables that might make a difference: the weight of the pendulum bob, the length of the pendulum string, and the angle of swing. After some false starts and assistance from their teacher, the students devised a plan—a fair test or controlled experiment—to determine how these factors might make a pendulum swing faster or slower. In their experiment, they deliberately changed each variable while keeping the other two variables the same and measured the number of complete back-and-forth swings in a fixed time. They entered all of their data in a chart.

The data clearly showed that changes in the angle had no effect on the rate of swing; the students got about the same number of swings for three different angles. Yet the student leading the group said, "It swings slower when you increase the angle." The rest of the group agreed.

Research indicates that when students' observations do not fit their predictions, they sometimes forget or choose not to use the measurements that are contrary to their own beliefs or predictions. In other words, they fail to check the validity of their own theories by comparing their predictions with available evidence.

The Soda Straw: A Persistent Alternative Conception

Learners tend to hold fast to some naive conceptions, even into adulthood. These alternative conceptions must be challenged and changed before more accurate concepts and explanations can be built. The influence of a persistent alternative theory can be seen in this example of the workings of a soda straw. How does liquid in a glass get up a soda straw and into a person's mouth?

Many people explain this event in terms of **suction.** According to this explanation, when someone sucks on a straw, they create a vacuum that pulls the liquid up into the straw. The notion of suction is a naive theory that is reinforced by common usage of the term. Even dictionaries define suction in terms of "to pull or draw a liquid in." However, the scientific explanation for how a soda straw works is more coherent and powerful than the suction explanation.

From a scientific point of view, the operation of a soda straw is related to atmospheric pressure. From this theoretical perspective, we live at the bottom of an ocean of air—the atmosphere—that extends upward a hundred miles or so above the earth. The weight of the atmosphere presses down on us and everything else on earth, much like the weight of

This lesson on pendulums can be seen in the Merrill video *Insights Into Learning: Designing Experiments in Seventh Grade*. It is in the set of videos provided by Merrill to instructors using this book.

water in an ocean pushes down on a submarine or scuba diver. Air pressure tends to move objects from regions of high pressure to regions of low pressure. Objects in the earth's atmosphere, even very big objects, can be moved by air pressure, as perhaps you have experienced or seen in films of violent storms.

Here is a scientific explanation of what happens when a person drinks through a soda straw:

- In drinking through a straw, a person first expands the lungs.
- Some air moves out of the straw into the expanded space in the lungs.
- The air pressure in the straw is now reduced, because some of the air has gone into the lungs.
- When the air pressure inside the straw is reduced, the atmospheric pressure pushing down on the surface of the liquid forces some liquid to move through the straw and into the person's mouth.

Simply presenting accurate scientific explanations to students is not enough, though. They must be challenged to critically examine alternative explanations and deliberately discard misconceptions when they are found wanting.

Conceptual Change

For conceptual change to occur, students must recognize that their personal theories and explanations are in conflict with accepted scientific views. As Roth (1991) concluded,

> They need to be convinced that their own theories are inadequate, incomplete, or inconsistent with experimental evidence, and that the scientific explanations provide a more convincing alternative to their own notions. (p. 49)

Convincing children that they should change their conceptions does not come from "telling" or threats. Roth proposed that to change their beliefs, students need repeated opportunities to struggle with the inconsistencies between their own ideas and scientific explanations, to reorganize their ways of thinking, and to make appropriate links between their own ideas and scientific concepts.

Students' misconceptions and alternative theories can be a major barrier to their building understanding of verbally presented ideas. Consequently, Roth (1991) advised that students should be guided to recognize and think about statements that conflict with their personal ideas and to pay attention to and work to resolve conceptual confusion while reading or listening.

Teaching for conceptual change requires that teachers have adequate content knowledge. They also need to understand how students' alternative thinking can affect their learning. Further, teachers must be aware that naive theories are often very difficult to change; students may need many learning opportunities to confront their alternative, inaccurate, and naive ideas before they are able to let go of them.

Learning and development are closely related terms but convey different meanings. In the next section we consider what is meant by development and how it relates to learning.

Chapter 4 presents more ideas on how to teach for conceptual change.

Learning and Cognitive Development

The term *learning* refers to the construction of knowledge or performance capabilities in specific situations. *Development*, in contrast, refers to the extension of knowledge and performance capabilities from specific to general states, rather than particular ones (Brown,

Bransford, Ferrara, & Campione, 1983). Development occurs over time and requires abundant learning experiences as well as maturation.

The period of time from age 5 to 13, encompassing grades K–8, is marked by very dramatic developments in children's cognitive capabilities. These changes greatly affect what is appropriate to teach in science at the various grade levels.

According to the *Benchmarks for Science Literacy* (American Association for the Advancement of Science, 1993),

> Overestimation of what students can learn at a given age results in student frustration, lack of confidence, and unproductive learning strategies, such as memorization without understanding. Underestimation of what students can learn results in boredom, overconfidence, and poor study habits, and a needlessly diluted education. So it is important to make decisions about what to expect of students and when on the basis of as much good information as possible. (p. 327)

It is essential, then, for teachers to pay attention to the level of development of students.

Piaget's theory of cognitive development is a rich source of details about children's cognitive development, as well as about their theories of the world.

Piaget, Cognitive Development, and Knowledge Construction in Science

Through many years of research, stretching from the 1920s through the 1970s, Jean Piaget developed a complex theory of cognitive development. Though not all of Piaget's findings and theoretical formulations have been supported by more recent research (e.g., see Ormrod, 1999, pp.159–160), certain of his ideas have stood the test of time and continue to be important for education.

From his studies, Piaget concluded that there are four main factors that influence the development of children's thinking:

- **Physical maturation:** biological growth, including age-related growth in brain capacity and cognitive capabilities (see Ausubel, 2000, pp. 12–14)
- **Physical experience:** experiences with the physical world, including manipulation of material objects, leading to the discovery of physical knowledge
- **Social interaction:** interactions with other people, including peers, teachers, and mentors, leading to the acquisition of transmitted knowledge
- **Equilibration:** a self-regulated learning process involving the recognition of and persistent determination to resolve discrepancies between physical reality and personal ideas

The first three factors—maturation, experience, and social interaction—are important in most cognitive development theories. Equilibration is unique to Piaget's system and emphasizes the importance to children's development of their habits of mind related to curiosity, risk taking, effort, and persistence. For Piaget, it is equilibration that drives the knowledge construction process.

As a teacher, you can certainly attend to the physical experience and social interaction needs of developing children and adolescents. You may also be able to help ensure that needed conditions for physical maturation are present. But your greatest contribution to their development may be to encourage the curiosity, persistence, and effort that characterize equilibration. Of course, hands-on inquiry science is an excellent way to promote equilibration processes.

Cognitive development theories, like other theories in science, should be considered tentative and subject to change with new research evidence.

Cognitive Stages and Approximate Age Spans	The Child at This Stage
TABLE 3-2 CHARACTERISTICS OF CHILDREN'S THINKING IN PIAGET'S FOUR COGNITIVE STAGES	
Sensorimotor (0–2 years)	• adapts to the external world through actions • coordinates actions related to substance, space, time, and causality
Preoperational (2–7 years)	• maintains sensorimotor capabilities • develops extensive physical knowledge of objects, organisms, and events • begins to represent objects and actions with words and sentences • does not think "reversibly" • makes judgments on the basis of perceptions, not conceptual considerations
Concrete Operational (5–11 years)	• maintains capabilities of previous stages • thinks reversibly • groups elements into coherent wholes • conserves substance, liquid volume, length, and area • identifies *variables* and measures them • forms *classes* and uses them to organize perceptions and experiences • forms and uses *relationships,* including simple scientific principles and cause-and-effect relationships
Formal Operational (12+ years)	• maintains capabilities of previous stages • engages in higher-order thinking • forms hypotheses, carries out controlled experiments, and relates evidence to theories • deals with ratios, proportions, and probabilities • constructs and understands complex explanations

A main focus of Piaget was on the development of children's logical thinking capabilities. Piaget theorized that the development of thinking takes place across four age-related stages: the sensorimotor, preoperational, concrete operational, and formal operational stages. Progress within stages and from one stage to the next takes place as children *assimilate* new information to existing knowledge structures, and *accommodate* existing structures to fit reality.

The four stages are characterized by different ways children perceive and organize information about the world. Children do not just pass through lower-level stages, leaving them behind as they develop more advanced capabilities. Rather, the abilities of lower stages are incorporated into higher stages. Table 3-2 provides a synopsis of children's capabilities in Piaget's four stages. The age spans given in the table are approximations. Individual children may show characteristics of a given stage at earlier or later ages than their peers.

Let us examine some of the characteristics of knowing and thinking in the different stages and how they affect the learning of science.

Sensorimotor Actions. According to Piaget, logical thinking capabilities, as well as conceptions of space, time, substance, and causality, are grounded in the sensory explorations and motor actions of infants and toddlers. Toddlers develop preliminary notions of space as they maneuver around and sometimes over barriers trying to reach a goal. They develop notions of time as they remember and use past occurrences to anticipate future happenings, even if their thinking carries them only a few seconds into the past or future. And they learn about cause and effect as they act on the world and see how it responds to their actions. The role of physical actions in the development of thinking is one reason concrete experiences are so important for children in science, mathematics, and other subjects.

Preoperational Thinking. The word "*pre*operational" implies "*before* operations." In Piaget's theory, an **operation** is a reversible grouping of elements of thought into a logical whole (Piaget & Inhelder, 1969). As indicated by this definition, operations have two main characteristics. First, an operation involves *combining* mental elements into a whole, such as a class or a relationship. Second, the connection must be *reversible*. When connections are reversible, children can move back and forth flexibly between two mental aspects of a situation, for example, between the elements of a relationship and the relationship itself.

At the *pre*operational level, as the term implies, children do not yet form operations. That is, they do not form reversible combinations. Difficulty with reversible thinking is a challenge for preoperational children in doing science, because this type of thinking is essential in such processes as measuring, classifying, inferring, predicting, and constructing concepts and principles.

One way that science teachers can assess whether children are thinking operationally is through the use of **conservation** tasks. When children conserve, they recognize that when an object or system of objects is transformed in some way, there is an aspect of the object or system that remains unchanged. In a conservation of liquid volume task, for example, children are shown two identical containers filled with equal amounts of liquid (see Figure 3-5). After the children agree that the amounts of liquid are the same, the liquid in one of the containers is poured into a slimmer, taller glass. Preoperational children do not tend to consider the heights and widths of the containers reversibly. Thus, they may focus on the heights of the containers while ignoring the widths. Noting that the new container is taller, they conclude that there is more liquid in it. They think that the amount of liquid changed when it was transformed in shape. Failure to conserve length, area, volume, and weight serves to restrict preoperational children's understanding of variables and measurement processes.

As development continues, the thinking of children changes, so that sometime after about age 6 or 7 they become able to deal with the world in a different way.

A glossary containing definitions of important terms used in this chapter is included in the Companion Website at http://www.prenhall.com/carin.

Concrete Operational Thinking. At the concrete operational level, children combine factors reversibly rather than just sequentially. This new flexibility in thinking allows them to deal with more than one factor at a time. Reversible thinking leads to success in many tasks, including the conservation of length, area, and liquid volume. In conserving length, for example, concrete operational learners are able to coordinate perceptions about the two endpoints of a string and the pathway joining the endpoints (whether straight or curved) and, thus, to reason that a piece of string has a constant length, regardless of how it is configured.

The ability to combine elements reversibly into logical, holistic groups enables concrete operational thinkers to build some new types of knowledge. Three important types

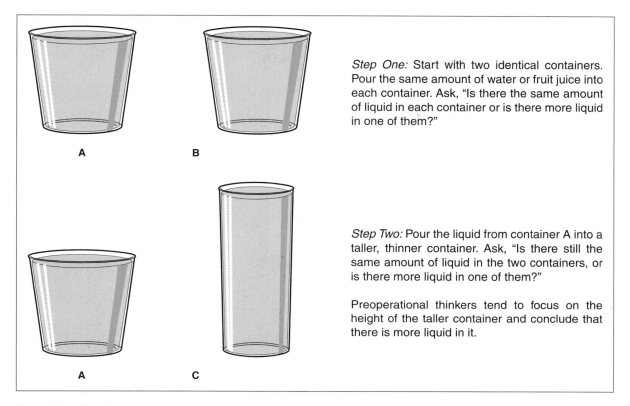

Step One: Start with two identical containers. Pour the same amount of water or fruit juice into each container. Ask, "Is there the same amount of liquid in each container or is there more liquid in one of them?"

Step Two: Pour the liquid from container A into a taller, thinner container. Ask, "Is there still the same amount of liquid in the two containers, or is there more liquid in one of them?"

Preoperational thinkers tend to focus on the height of the taller container and conclude that there is more liquid in it.

Figure 3-5 Task for assessing conservation of liquid volume.

of logical combinations constructed at this stage are *classes*, *series*, and *relationships*. These three special ways of combining information are critical tools for the construction of knowledge and understanding in elementary science.

The ability to form classes enables children to sort through complex information and events and to form logical concepts. The ability to form series (coupled with the development of conservation abilities) enables children to measure and to work with measurable variables, such as length, volume, weight, and temperature. The ability to construct and use relationships (or principles) enables children to understand and explain, if incompletely, the wide range of phenomena they are likely to encounter in doing science.

Given the chance through hands-on inquiry activities and teacher guidance, concrete operational thinkers begin to organize investigations in terms of concepts and variables, measure variables meaningfully, and arrange data in tables and graphs. They can also form and understand simple principles, use what they know to make inferences and predictions, and generalize from common experiences. The concrete operational years can be especially exciting times in science for children and their teachers.

Formal Operational Thinking. The formal operational level is characterized by higher-order thinking with the concepts, variables, and principles formed at the concrete operational level. The cognitive advances at the formal operational level are revealed as adolescents engage more independently in thinking tasks such as

An *Inquiry in Virtual Classrooms* link illustrating concrete and formal operational thinking of seventh graders in a video lesson on designing pendulum investigations can be found on the Companion Website for Chapter 3 at http://www. prenhall.com/carin.

- planning and conducting controlled experiments or fair tests that involve responding (dependent), manipulated (independent), and control variables—as described in Chapter 2;
- organizing and thinking about complex numerical data sets in terms of ratios, proportions, and equations;
- constructing theories and models that coordinate facts, concepts, and principles; and
- coordinating evidence and knowledge in forming explanations of puzzling phenomena.

These advances enable learners to seek answers to their questions through designing and carrying out more complicated investigations involving variables and controls.

For a closer look at how scientific concepts and principles develop, we will examine Piagetian research on children's developing understanding of concepts of floating and sinking.

Children's Theories of Floating and Sinking. When young children are given an array of objects and asked to predict whether the objects will float or sink, the children rely primarily on past experiences. When asked *why* they think something will float or sink, they tend to focus on salient characteristics of the objects. Their answers are generally inconsistent. For instance, they may say one object floats because it is large and a second thing floats because it is small.

A lesson plan on floating and sinking is featured in Chapter 7. This lesson was developed for concrete operational learners.

As children mature, their thinking about floating and sinking becomes more consistent. By grades 3–5, many children realize that both weight and volume (size) of objects make a difference in whether they float or sink. The children describe the weight of objects as heavy or light; they also describe the volume of objects as large or small. Crossing these two descriptions, they come up with a system of four classifications:

- *Heavy* objects that are *small* in size, such as pennies, which generally sink
- *Light* objects that are *large* in size, such as wooden blocks, which generally float
- *Heavy* objects that are *large* in size, such as ships, which may either float or sink

Although preoperational thinkers tend to focus on salient characteristics of objects, the descriptions they use to explain their observations will likely be inconsistent.

- *Light* objects that are *small* in size, such as paper clips and wooden dowels, which may either float or sink

At this level, this system of classifications is implicit and is evident in the children's actions, rather than explicitly explained.

Although children in grades 3–5 can classify the objects and reason about the classifications, some of their judgments are still indeterminate. For example, some large heavy objects, such as bowling balls, sink; but some even larger and heavier objects, such as boats, float.

It is not until adolescence that students can add numerical considerations about weight and volume to their judgments. Some learners at grades 6–8 (though by no means a large percent) learn to deal with the weight and volume of things in terms of ratios (weight divided by volume). The ratio of weight to volume is called **density.** Quantitatively, the dividing line for whether an object sinks or floats is the density of water, which is 1 gram per cubic centimeter (or 1 g/cc).

Centimeter-gram cubes—small cubes that are 1 cm on each side and have a mass of 1 g—are often used in elementary and middle school math and science. The volume of each of these cubes is exactly 1 cc; the density of the cubes is then 1 g/cc. Thus, these cubes float just under the surface of fresh water because their density is exactly the same as the density of water. If a small bit of clay is added to a cube, its density goes above 1 g/cc and the cube sinks in water.

In addition to studying how children's thinking about floating and sinking develops, Piaget investigated children's ideas of length, area, volume, time, speed, equal-arm balances, inclined planes, pendulums, and many other topics. Research studies by Piaget and other investigators have been greatly supplemented by the collective research and practical experiences of many educators, as we shall see in the next section.

Additional discussion of the measurement of volume and weight is included in Appendix H.

Developmentally Appropriate Science

The very useful NSTA publication, *Pathways to the Science Standards: Elementary School Edition* (Lowery, 1997), presents a great deal of wisdom for teachers on how children's scientific thinking develops and what this information suggests for science teaching. Lawrence Lowery, author of the volume, reminds us that all children have the capacity to inquire, but that capacity changes and becomes more sophisticated as children mature, gain experience, and construct more complex knowledge.

Children in grades K–2 tend to explore the answer to a question through trial and error. Descriptive investigations are especially suitable for this age group. Around grades 3–4, children begin to explore through simple tests conducted in descriptive and classificatory investigations. Students in grades 5–6 begin to seek answers to their questions through designing and carrying out more complicated experimental investigations involving variables and controls.

Figure 3-6 provides a summary of some characteristics of learners that impact inquiry learning in different grade spans. Keep in mind that children are unique, and the grade placements of the learning characteristics in Figure 3-6 are only approximations.

Vygotsky's Theory of Instruction and Development

Piaget was concerned primarily with mapping the spontaneous development of children's concepts. The importance of educational intervention in children's learning and development has been especially emphasized in the psychological theories of Lev Vygotsky.

Grades K–2 Learners

- Have a natural interest in almost everything around them.
- Observe the world using all of their senses, but do not construct consistent explanations of it.
- Push, pull, and transform objects by acting on them.
- Explore the world by watching and mimicking others.
- Carry out simple descriptive investigations.
- Make inquiries by guessing how things work and behave.
- Observe, sort, group, and order objects.
- Have difficulty classifying objects using several characteristics.
- Initially have difficulty thinking "reversibly"; later begin to retrace steps in thinking, with assistance.
- Make simple inferences and predictions, with assistance.
- Can solve complex problems through trial and error, if allowed to work step by step.
- Learn best by building understanding from their own actions and telling stories about what they did and what they found out.

Grades 3–4 Learners

- Retain the learning capabilities they developed at the primary level and begin to experience a broad view of the world.
- Tend to create large, complex organizations, instead of being satisfied with grouping and ordering objects by limited attributes.
- Discover and understand simple rules of classification.
- Carry out simple classificatory investigations.
- Design simple comparative tests (not controlled experiments), carry out the tests, analyze the results, and communicate their findings.
- Take simple notes, record data, and keep simple journals.
- Use data and knowledge to make inferences, predictions, and simple explanations.
- Construct and use simple principles and cause-and-effect relationships.
- Understand cycles (life cycles, seasons, water cycles) as continuous, repeatable chains of events.

Grades 5–6 Learners

- Continue to be good observers, and retain all the abilities developed in previous years.
- Use cause-and-effect relationships in constructing explanations.
- Engage in experimental inquiries that are more advanced than simple descriptive and classificatory investigations.
- Generate simple hypotheses, conduct "fair" tests, and record and analyze data to find evidence to support or not support the original hypotheses.
- Can keep extensive journals, diaries, and records of information over time, and prepare written reports based on these records.
- Have difficulty controlling all the variables in an experiment.
- Have preconceptions and expectations that can influence interpretation of data, even in a fair test.
- Generate, interpret, and make predictions from graphs; understand that graphs describe two variables at the same time.

Figure 3-6 Characteristics of learners in different grade spans.
Source: Adapted from Lawrence F. Lowery (Ed.). (1997). *Pathways to the Science Standards: Elementary School Edition.* Arlington, VA: National Science Teachers Association.

Vygotsky was a Russian psychologist who translated Piaget's early works into Russian. He accepted the developmental nature of knowledge as proposed by Piaget but especially emphasized social interaction, including discourse between children, and between children and adults, as a main factor in development. According to Vygotsky, the acquisition of knowledge through instruction is essential in short-term learning and is a critical factor in long-term development. "What the child can do in cooperation today," Vygotsky wrote (1962, p. 104), "he can do alone tomorrow."

Vygotsky believed that instruction needs to be challenging, running ahead of the learner's actual level of development. He used the term **zone of proximal development** to describe the region between the learner's spontaneous level of knowing and thinking, and the level the learner can reach in problem solving with assistance. An important goal of instruction is to discover this "construction zone" and help the learner attain optimal levels of thought.

Scaffolding. Scaffolding is an important technique of instruction that is derived from Vygotsky's ideas on education. In **scaffolding,** the teacher supplies external support that helps children to be successful with the various learning tasks. Deciding how much and what kind of support to give is an art that can be enhanced through understanding of research and practical experience related to child development.

Teachers may provide scaffolding support for either knowledge or mental processing. An example of scaffolding knowledge development is simply to remind learners to use the knowledge they already have. Scaffolding support for processing might involve providing more structure for inquiry tasks.

To scaffold inquiry learning, the teacher might provide assistance to learners in formulating the focus question for an investigation, determining the procedures for data collection and analysis, and accessing and using prior knowledge to make sense of the data and answer the question posed. The younger the children and the less experience they have with scientific inquiry, the more scaffolding assistance they will probably need—that is, the more structured the inquiry lessons will need to be.

Just as scaffolds in a building project are designed to be taken down when the building walls are strong, scaffolding support in teaching should be gradually removed or "faded" (Ormrod, 1999) as students gain more facility with developing science knowledge and inquiry processes.

To scaffold the learning process for students, teachers can (Grigorenko, 1998; Roehler & Cantlon, 1997):

- start by making the learning task one that is challenging and interesting with an appropriate degree of novelty;
- simplify the task so that the learner can manage it if necessary;
- facilitate student talk in small group and large group settings;
- ask meaningful questions at just the right time;
- lead students to clarify, elaborate, or justify their responses;
- supply necessary information or direct learners to appropriate sources;
- provide verbal instruction on concepts and principles as needed;
- provide models of thinking processes; and
- provide external support, such as diagrams and concept maps, to aid students in making difficult connections.

An important task in the art of teaching is to know when to scaffold or support a student's learning and when to allow it to take its own course. In the long run, students should develop their own self-regulated strategies to guide learning.

Scaffolding is a key concept in inquiry learning and instruction. Teachers add varying amounts of structure to inquiry lessons by making different levels of scaffolding available to students, as is shown in Table 4-1 in Chapter 4.

As we will show in Chapter 6, scaffolding is a key part of balanced classroom assessment strategies. Formative assessment information provides teachers a concrete basis for developing scaffolds to improve student learning.

VIDEO CASE STUDY: *PATRICIA*

Previewing the Video

As you watch the three modules for this case study, use the "Questions for Reflection" to guide your thoughts and notes for any group discussion or individual feedback. If you watch the video as a group and then participate in a group discussion, choose a group facilitator to solicit various perspectives and keep the discussion on track.

Introducing the Case

At the first of the year, Patricia, a first grade teacher in a suburban town, teaches from a very structured approach. Her approach may have been developed out of her desire to ensure that her classroom is managed well or it may have come from her teaching background that focused on direct instruction. For whatever reason, Patricia is reticent about letting go of her control as she leads her students through studies on fish, the human heart, and seeds. After working with a science educator, she tries to increase students' roles in their own learning by using more student exploration and cooperative learning structures.

Questions for Reflection

1. What words would you use to describe the teaching approach Patricia uses to discuss characteristics about fish with her students?

2. What is Patricia's philosophy about young children's attitude about science? How is her teaching method somewhat contradictory to her philosophy about learning science?

Trying New Ideas *Science educator Dr. Anita Greenwood talks to Patricia about having students work in cooperative groups to make science instruction more student-centered. Patricia uses student pairs to have students exchange their observations and ideas about the human heart.*

Questions for Reflection

1. How does Patricia respond to having students work in small groups versus students working alone? What does Dr. Greenwood say to help Patricia understand the value of students working together?

> "We want children to be able to exchange ideas so that they are listening and learning from one another, thinking about their observation and comparing it to somebody else's observation."
>
> *Dr. Anita Greenwood, University of Massachusetts-Lowell*

2. What activities does Patricia have students do to measure their pulse and to listen to one another's heartbeat? How does she have them record their data?
3. What part of Patricia's heart lesson is probably less meaningful for student learning? What makes you think so?

Building and Reflecting on Change

Three months later, Patricia has students work in groups of three to categorize seeds. Then, she has two student groups choose one property of seeds and sort them by that property. Patricia says activities in science should be patterned after the way students think.

Questions for Reflection

1. In your opinion, what are the most significant changes evident in Patricia's classroom with regard to making science teaching and learning more student-centered? What do you think are challenges teachers face to do inquiry-oriented lessons?
2. What challenges do teachers undertake when using cooperative group work in science? How would you address these challenges?
3. In the Introducing the Case module, Patricia is the center of learning. What evidence do you see in Modules 2 and 3 that she is beginning to establish a classroom community of learners as described in this chapter on page 92?
4. How does Patricia sum up her own professional development from the beginning to the end of the year?

Patricia sums up her own professional development in science teaching in this way:

At the beginning of the year as a science teacher, I found myself at the front of the room teaching all of the students at once, dealing out information to the whole group. Now, I've tried to step away from the front of the room and involve myself with the children, either as a group or individually. I try to let the children ask me questions based on their experiences, rather than me questioning them about what I had taught.

Learning Communities.   In a **social constructivist** model of learning, which draws on perspectives of both Vygotsky and Piaget, teachers work to establish a shared understanding of a learning task among a "community of learners" (Hogan & Pressley, 1997). According to Brown and Campione (1998),

> A community of learners reflects a classroom ethos different from that found in traditional classrooms. In the traditional classroom, students are perceived as relatively passive learners who receive wisdom from teachers, textbooks, or other media. In the community of learners classroom, students are encouraged to engage in self-reflective learning and critical inquiry. . . . In the community of learners classroom, teachers are expected to serve as active role models of learning and as responsive guides to students' discovery processes. (p. 153)

The teacher's role within a community of inquirers is to organize the learning environment in order to establish an underlying culture that centers around thinking. Just as communication among scientists is central in the construction of scientific knowledge, students learn by talking among themselves and writing about and formally presenting their ideas. Teachers, as part of the classroom community of learners, make students' ideas more meaningful by commenting and elaborating on them and asking students to clarify, expand, and justify their own emerging conceptions and those of others. Conversational partnerships with the teacher allow students to build on and use the teacher's thinking processes to support their own efforts to think in more flexible and mature ways. In addition, the give and take among learners in a learning community enables them to scaffold one another's learning.

This description of the classroom for thinking reflects the type of environment envisioned in the *National Science Education Standards* as one that promotes inquiry.

Learning, Development, and Instruction: The Case of the Cartesian Diver

To illustrate the interaction among learning, developmental levels, and instructional interventions, let us examine the Cartesian diver lesson from the Annenberg Video Case Study featuring Linda (see a study guide for this Video Case Study in Chapter 2). Take time now to read through Activity 3-1, which describes the Cartesian diver activity. We strongly urge you to try this activity before reading the explanation of it in Figure 3-7.

In this lesson, Linda works with a second grade class. She holds up a Cartesian diver apparatus and begins her lesson.

> *Linda: What do you think will happen when I squeeze the middle of the bottle?*
> *Student: That little screw (the bottle cap) might twist and come off.*

Linda gives groups of children the bottles with the diving medicine droppers inside and says, "I want you to find out what happens when you squeeze it. Then, you need to figure out why it happens. Why . . . that's the tough part. You need to collaborate and talk with your group and find out why what happens does happen."

Linda is inviting the children to work together to find out about the apparatus. Excitedly, the children squeeze the bottle and observe that the dropper descends to the bottom; when they release the bottle, the dropper comes back up. In their small groups and in later large group discussions, the children offer a variety of statements about the phenomenon.

> *Student 1: It's like a parachute going up and down.*
> *Student 2: I think when the water goes in, then the air pushes it up with the metal thing.*

Activity 3-1: The Cartesian Diver

1. To make a Cartesian diver, obtain a glass medicine dropper with a rubber bulb. Squeeze the bulb, place the glass dropper in a container of water to which some food coloring has been added, and release the bulb, letting water come into the dropper. Try to fill the dropper about one-half full of water. Test that the dropper floats almost under water by placing it in a beaker or jar full of water. If the dropper sinks to the bottom, release some water from it. If it floats too high in the water, add a bit of oil-based modeling clay to the glass dropper near the rubber bulb, until the dropper just floats with a small part of the bulb above the surface.
2. Next, fill a plastic, two-liter soda bottle within about 5 or 6 cm from the top. Put the medicine dropper in the water, making sure that the dropper still floats near the surface of the water.
3. Now, squeeze the bottle gently. Watch carefully. What do you observe? (The dropper should sink to the bottom of the bottle. When you release the pressure on the bottle, the dropper should rise to the surface again.) Why do you think this happened? Write down your answer.

Student 3: When you squeeze it, the water goes in the eye dropper and when you let it go, some water goes out of it.
Student 4: It gets heavier when it goes down and then it gets lighter and then it goes up.

As teachers, we need to listen carefully to what children say, filter their ideas through theories of learning and development and our own experiences, and decide how we should respond. Let us use the theories introduced in this chapter to analyze these second grade children's thinking on the diving dropper.

Student 1 provides a *description* of the actions of the dropper. Focusing on descriptions without attempting explanations is a general learning characteristic of K–2 students, as is shown in Figure 3-6.

Student 2, the child who had earlier talked about the bottle cap, gives a somewhat confused explanation of the event. He brings in the role of the push of air and the water going into the dropper, but no cause and effect seems to be implied. Because the child fails to give clear statements of relationships between causes and effects, we might judge that he is not yet thinking at Piaget's concrete operational level.

Student 3 observes the event more closely, noting that water goes into and then comes out of the dropper. These observations relate to steps 2 and 4 in Figure 3-7. Thus, part of the basis of the explanation is present, but the child does not use these ideas further in explaining the event. Similarly, Student 4 gives a combination of steps 2 and 5 of the explanation (the dropper gets heavier and then gets lighter), but does not say why the weight of the dropper changes or what the effect of the weight changes might be. Both of these children have provided some accurate cause-and-effect statements about floating and sinking that are consistent with the thinking of learners at grades 3 and 4 (see Figure 3-6). The thinking of these children is somewhat advanced, but they still do not recognize and connect the three key factors of the explanation: (1) the actions on the bottle, (2) the resulting changes in the air pressure in the bottle, and (3) the consequent changes in the weight of the dropper.

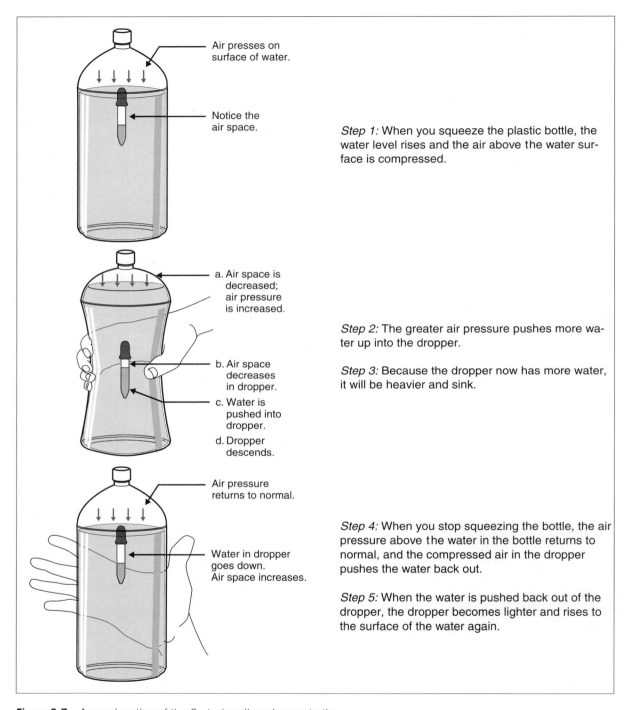

Air presses on surface of water.

Notice the air space.

Step 1: When you squeeze the plastic bottle, the water level rises and the air above the water surface is compressed.

a. Air space is decreased; air pressure is increased.

b. Air space decreases in dropper.

c. Water is pushed into dropper.

d. Dropper descends.

Step 2: The greater air pressure pushes more water up into the dropper.

Step 3: Because the dropper now has more water, it will be heavier and sink.

Air pressure returns to normal.

Water in dropper goes down. Air space increases.

Step 4: When you stop squeezing the bottle, the air pressure above the water in the bottle returns to normal, and the compressed air in the dropper pushes the water back out.

Step 5: When the water is pushed back out of the dropper, the dropper becomes lighter and rises to the surface of the water again.

Figure 3-7 An explanation of the Cartesian diver demonstration.

According to Vygotsky (1962), a primary distinguishing characteristic of children's spontaneous concepts learned through discovery is the absence of a system that holds the concepts together. Similarly, Ebenezer and Connor (1998) have described children's initial knowledge about the world as fragmented, made up not of organized theories but of a large number of fragments. This is just what we see with Students 3 and 4. Taken together, the partial explanations of these two students come close to explaining the diving dropper. However, neither student appears to have an underlying framework that leads them to systematically connect the various causes and effects into a more adequate explanation. From the perspective of Piaget, the underlying *structures of thought* that would enable the children to construct the explanation as a whole do not develop until somewhat later than second grade.

Next, consider how you might provide scaffolds to advance the children's explanations. You could, for example, provide assistance through questioning. Hearing Student 3's explanation, you might ask what causes the dropper to get heavier and then get lighter. Hearing Student 4's explanation, you might ask why the water goes into the dropper and what happens to the dropper when the water does go into it. Even if students do not form complete scientific explanations initially, you can help them to make better connections between the various links and to think about them more flexibly.

However, because second grade children generally have difficulties in constructing consistent explanations, the Cartesian diver is not a developmentally appropriate activity for most learners at this grade level. In Vygotskian terms, the explanation of the Cartesian diver is not within the *zone of proximal development* for second grade children. It is not a phenomenon that children at this level are likely to understand well, even with good scaffolding assistance. Thus, it would be more appropriate to provide second graders with other experiences on the properties of air and on floating and sinking and to wait until later grades to introduce the Cartesian diver.

Look at the list of scaffolding actions given on page 89 again. What are some other ways teachers could use the various suggestions in the list to help children understand the Cartesian diver activity more completely?

 Use the self-assessment questions for Chapter 3 at http://www.prenhall.com/carin to assess how well you understand this chapter and how prepared you are for a test over its content.

SUMMARY

● In the process of learning, learners *select* input information to consider, *organize* the selected information in various ways to form new knowledge, and *integrate* new knowledge with prior knowledge to expand the knowledge base. Two main types of learning in science are discovery learning and acquisition learning. Inquiry instruction combines discovery and acquisition learning to enable learners to generate understanding, which entails the ability to apply knowledge in novel situations.

● Students often come to science classes with pervasive alternative conceptions about how the world works. Teachers must help students recognize and deal with their incomplete and erroneous ideas.

● Jean Piaget proposed a stage theory of cognitive development. By looking closely at Piaget's theory, science teachers get an idea of the developmental appropriateness of specific concepts and principles.

● Building on the work of Lev Vygotsky, contemporary science educators emphasize the importance of enhancing learning through instructional interaction, communities of inquirers, cooperative group structures, and well-planned scaffolding by teachers. To scaffold student learning, teachers set challenging and interesting learning tasks; simplify tasks for students; facilitate student talk in different settings; ask meaningful questions; lead students to clarify, elaborate, or justify their responses; and supply necessary information for learners.

● Learning to understand characteristics of student learning and cognitive development, and applying this knowledge in planning developmentally appropriate science lessons is a career-long venture. Continual professional development to be able to better assist learners is part of the challenge and fun of teaching.

REFERENCES

American Association for the Advancement of Science. (1993). *Benchmarks for science literacy*. New York: Oxford University Press.

Ausubel, D. (1968). *Educational psychology: A cognitive view*. New York: Holt, Rinehart and Winston.

Ausubel, D. (2000). *The acquisition and retention of knowledge; a cognitive approach*. Boston: Kluwer.

Bransford, J. D., Brown, A. L., & Cocking, R. R. (Eds.). (1999). *How people learn: Brain, mind, experience, and school*. Washington, DC: National Academy Press. (Also available at http://www.nap.edu)

Brown, A. L., Bransford, J. D., Ferrara, R., & Campione, J. C. (1983). Learning, remembering, and understanding. In J. H. Flavell & E. M. Markman (Eds.), *Carmichael's manual of child psychology* (Vol. 3). New York: Wiley.

Brown, A. L., & Campione, J. C. (1998). Designing a community of young learners: Theoretical and practical lessons. In N. L. Lambert & B. L. McCombs (Eds.), *How students learn: Reforming schools through learner-centered education*. Washington, DC: American Psychological Association.

Dewey, J. (1929). *The sources of a science of education*. New York: Liveright Publishing Co.

Ebenezer, J., & Connor, S. (1998). *Learning to teach science: A model for the 21st century*. Upper Saddle River, NJ: Merrill/Prentice Hall.

Gardner, H. (1998). Conclusion: Melding progressive and traditional perspectives. In M. S. Wiske (Ed.), *Teaching for understanding*. San Francisco: Jossey-Bass.

Grigorenko, E. L. (1998). Mastering tools of the mind in school (Trying out Vygotsky's ideas in classrooms). In R. J. Sternberg & W. M. Williams (Eds.), *Intelligence, instruction, and assessment*. Mahwah, NJ: Erlbaum.

Hogan, K., & Pressley, M. (1997). Scaffolding scientific competencies within classroom communities of inquiry. In K. Hogan & M. Pressley (Eds.), *Scaffolding student learning: Instructional approaches and issues*. Cambridge, MA: Brookline Books.

Jones, B. F., Palincsar, A. S., Ogle, D. S., & Carr, E. G. (Eds.). (1987). *Strategic teaching and learning: Cognitive instruction in the content areas*. Alexandria, VA: Association for Supervision and Curriculum Development.

Karplus, R. & Thier, H. (1974). *SCIS Teacher's Handbook*. Berkeley, CA: Science Curriculum Improvement Study.

Kuhn, D. (1999). A developmental model of critical thinking. *Educational Researcher, 28*(2), 16–25.

Kuhn, D., Amsel, E., & O'Loughlin, M. (1988). *The development of scientific thinking skills*. New York: Academic Press.

Lowery, L. (1998, November). How new science curriculums reflect brain research. *Educational Leadership, 56*(3), 26–30.

Lowery, L. F. (Ed.). (1997). *Pathways to the science standards: Elementary school edition*. Arlington, VA: National Science Teachers Association.

Mastropieri, M. A., Scruggs, T. F., & Magnusen, M. (1999, Fall). Activities-oriented science instruction for learners with disabilities. *Learning Disability Quarterly, 22*, 240–249.

Mayer, R. E. (1992). Guiding students' cognitive processing of scientific information. In M. Pressley, J. Harris, and J. Guthrie (Eds.), *Promoting academic competence and literacy: cognitive research and innnovation*. San Diego, CA: Academic Press.

Mayer, R. E. (1998). Cognitive theory. In N. L. Lambert & B. L. McCombs (Eds.), *How students learn: Reforming schools through learner-centered education*. Washington, DC: American Psychological Association.

Merrill Education. (1999). *Insights into learning: Designing experiments in seventh grade* (video). Upper Saddle River, NJ: Merrill/Prentice Hall.

Mintzes, J., Wandersee, J., & Novak, J. (1998). *Teaching science for understanding: A human constructivist view*. San Diego, CA: Academic Press.

National Research Council. (1996). *National science education standards*. Washington, DC: National Academy Press.

Novak, J. (1995). Concept mapping: A strategy for organizing knowledge. In S. Glynn & R. Duit (Eds.), *Learning science in the schools: Research reforming practice*. Mahwah, NJ: Erlbaum.

Ormrod, J. (1999). *Human learning*. Upper Saddle River, NJ: Merrill/Prentice Hall.

Paulu, N., & Martin, M. (1991). *Helping your child learn science*. Washington, DC: U.S. Department of Education, Office of Educational Research and Improvement.

Perkins, D. (1998). What is understanding? In M. S. Wiske (Ed.), *Teaching for understanding*. San Francisco: Jossey-Bass.

Piaget, J., & Inhelder, B. (1969). *The psychology of the child*. New York: Basic Books.

Roehler, L. R., & Cantlon, D. J. (1997). Scaffolding: A powerful tool in social constructivist classrooms. In K. Hogan & M. Pressley (Eds.), *Scaffolding student learning: Instructional approaches and issues*. Cambridge, MA: Brookline Books.

Rosenshine, B. (1986). Synthesis of research on direct instruction. *Educational Leadership, 43*(7, 9), 60–69.

Rosenshine, B., Meister, C., & Chapman, S. (1996). Teaching students to generate questions: A review of intervention studies. *Review of Educational Research, 66*(2), 181–221.

Roth, K. (1991). Reading science texts for conceptual change. In C. M. Santa & D. V. Alverson (Eds.), *Science learning: Processes and applications*. Newark, DE: International Reading Association.

Rowe, M. B. (1973). *Teaching science as continuous inquiry*. New York: McGraw-Hill.

Rowe, M. B. (1993). *Science helper K–8: A CD-ROM with over 900 science and math lessons*. Armonk, NY: The Learning Team.

Rutherford, F. J., & Ahlgren, A. (1990). *Science for all Americans*. New York: Oxford University Press.

Shuell, T. J. (1986). Cognitive conceptions of learning. *Reviews of Educational Research, 56*(4), 411–436.

Tobin, K., Tippins, D., & Gallard, A. (1994). Research on instructional strategies for teaching science. In D. L. Gabel (Ed.), *Handbook of research on science teaching and learning*. New York: Macmillan.

Vygotsky, L. S. (1962). *Thought and language*. Cambridge, MA: The MIT Press.

Wiggins, G., & McTighe, J. (1998). *Understanding by design*. Alexandria, VA: Association for Supervision and Curriculum Development.

4

As a consequence of the pronouncements in the AAAS *Benchmarks* and the NRC *Standards*, science teachers face the challenge of using inquiry, a highly complex activity, as an effective method of developing their students' understanding of the natural world, while simultaneously developing their students' understanding of the nature of scientific inquiry and ability to inquire.

(Champagne & Kouba, 2000, p. 224)

Teaching Science Through Inquiry

IN THE TEACHING-LEARNING APPROACH EMPHASIZED in the *National Science Education Standards*, children build science knowledge, investigation skills, and scientific habits of mind through inquiry procedures that mirror methods used by scientists. As inquirers, learners assume major responsibility for constructing their own knowledge and understanding. Teachers share in and facilitate this process, guiding children as they ask questions, conduct investigations, and use observational evidence and scientific knowledge to develop explanations.

Teaching science through inquiry is effective and rewarding, but it can also be complex, as is suggested in the chapter-opening quote. To help you simplify the process, we discuss in this chapter some essential features of inquiry instruction and some instructional models that you can use to facilitate inquiry and guide children to go beyond surface knowledge and achieve greater depths of scientific understanding.

As you study this chapter, consider these questions:

- *What are the essential features of classroom inquiry?*

- *What do teachers do when they teach science through inquiry?*

- *What are the guided discovery and 5-E models for teaching science? What are the advantages of each model and how are they related?*

- *How can you use inquiry methods to promote conceptual change and deeper understanding of science?*

 Collect responses to these questions as you find them in the chapter. The focus questions also appear on the Companion Website at http://www.prenhall. com/carin.

Essential Features of Inquiry Instruction

Think of *inquiry* in two ways. First, inquiry refers to the diverse ways scientists investigate nature. Second, inquiry is also a teaching-learning method in which students "develop knowledge and understanding of scientific ideas, as well as an understanding of how scientists study the natural world" (National Research Council, 1996, p. 23). What do we mean when we talk about inquiry as a teaching-learning method? What are the essential features of inquiry instruction?

A special committee convened to study inquiry and the *National Science Education Standards* (National Research Council, 2000) identified five essential features that characterize classroom inquiry. We introduced these features in Chapter 1. Now let us examine them in more detail.

NSES   *According to* Teaching Standard B *of the* National Science Education Standards, *to guide and facilitate learning, teachers should*

- focus and support inquiries while interacting with students;
- orchestrate discourse among students about scientific ideas;
- challenge students to accept and share responsibility for their own learning;
- recognize and respond to student diversity and encourage all students to participate fully in science learning; and
- encourage and model the skills of scientific inquiry, as well as the curiosity, openness to new ideas and data, and skepticism that characterize science.

1. Learners Are Engaged by Scientific Questions

Ideally, inquiry in the classroom should begin with authentic questions generated by students from their own experiences (American Association for the Advancement of Science, 1993, pp. 9–12). In actual practice, students may need assistance in formulating questions to be investigated. Students learn from teachers how to ask good questions. If teachers' questions are open-ended, with no one right answer, students can learn to ask open-ended questions. Teachers should ask and encourage questions such as "What would happen if . . . ?", "What will happen next?", and "Why did that happen?"

Student inquiry can be initiated from a wide range of activities (National Research Council, 1996, p. 33):

- Something puzzling that children may notice in their everyday experiences may trigger inquiry.
- Some questions for inquiry grow out of hands-on activities involving observations, data collection, data organization, and reflection.
- Questions may come from the critical analysis of information gathered from books, CD-ROMs, the Internet, and other sources.
- Discrepant events demonstrated by the teacher or presented through pictures, slides, films, and videos may also generate questions for inquiry.
- It is even possible for inquiry to begin with lecture, if the questions raised are authentic and relate to the students' own experiences.

Additional suggestions for helping students form good questions for inquiry are given in Chapter 2 and Chapter 5.

2. Learners Give Priority to Evidence as They Plan and Conduct Investigations

In inquiry approaches, teachers guide students as they devise ways to gather evidence to answer their questions. With varying degrees of assistance, students determine what data might be relevant, decide how to collect it, represent collected data in some form, and organize it in useful ways. Students use a variety of investigational approaches to gather evidence, including descriptive, classificatory, and experimental investigations. They also gather information from articles, textbooks, encyclopedias, databases, the Internet, and so on, placing an emphasis on understanding the natural world rather than acquiring terminology and facts.

In the process of gathering data, students develop simple skills such as how to observe, measure, cut, connect, switch, pour, tie, hold, and hook. Beginning with simple instru-

Encourage students to collect, organize, and interpret data.

ments, students learn to use rulers, thermometers, watches, spring scales, and balance beams to measure important variables. They learn to use magnifiers and microscopes to see finer details of objects and organisms. Students also begin to develop skills in the use of computers and calculators in investigations (National Research Council, 2000).

3. Learners Develop Descriptions, Explanations, and Predictions Using Evidence

Continuing in inquiry, students describe, classify, and explain their observations, and clarify and justify their work to themselves and to one another. Children gradually learn that explanations must always be based on evidence. As they develop cognitive skills, students should learn to distinguish between explanations, which are ideas about *why* something happens, and descriptions, which are based on observations of *what* has happened.

4. Learners Connect Evidence and Explanations to Developing Scientific Knowledge

As they form explanations, children coordinate evidence and their developing concepts, relationships, and theories. Students should be encouraged to continually connect abstract ideas and observational evidence. They should reflect on their observations often, reexamining them, using prior knowledge to draw inferences from their observations, and collecting more data if necessary.

5. Learners Engage in Critical Discourse with Others about Procedures, Evidence, and Explanations

Children love to talk about their experiences. Inquiry science provides a rich context in which to develop language and thought (Rowe, 1973). Confronted with puzzling phenomena, and given some freedom to investigate, children work hard at expressing their experiences in language.

Communicating and justifying scientific procedures, collected evidence, and interpretations focuses the students on *what* they know, *how* they know it, and *how* their knowledge connects to the knowledge of other people, to other subjects, and to the world beyond the classroom (National Research Council, 1996, p. 36).

Teachers can support student discourse in many ways, such as

- promoting multiple forms of communication, including the use of spoken, written, pictorial, graphic, mathematical, and physical representations;
- requiring students to write about their work in journals and to record their inquiry questions, observations, data, explanations, and justifications in reports; and
- using small group and whole class discussion strategies that encourage children to interact, assist one another, present their ideas, recognize the ideas of others, and work toward common meanings.

The use of cooperative learning groups promotes peer interaction and discourse in inquiry learning (Johnson & Johnson, 1987; Slavin, 1990). Peers within small cooperative groups help each other overcome deficiencies through scaffolding—providing terms, explanations, hints, and questions that enable understanding of new situations and construction of new knowledge.

Jones and Carter (1997) described a verbal interaction between two fifth grade boys, in which one of the boys assisted the other in understanding written directions about a lever activity. The goal of the activity was to formulate a generalization about how to get a crossbar to balance. Larry was confused about the task:

> Larry: *Do we place the three blocks on the same side of this thing?*
> Billy: *No, we are supposed to figure out how to balance these two blocks using this other block.*
> Larry: *How do we know when it is balanced?*
> Billy: *The lever will be straight out. Neither side of the lever will be touching the table. That means it's balanced.* (p. 265)

In this exchange, Billy provided Larry with an interpretation of the problem and the meaning of the term *balance*, which enabled Larry to proceed toward constructing generalizations.

Teachers can also enhance student learning by bringing the whole class back together and giving groups opportunities to make presentations of their work. Deeper understanding is attained when students explain, clarify, and justify what they have learned (National Research Council, 1996, p. 30). As the students communicate their findings and explanations, they should be encouraged to accept and react to the constructive criticism of others.

Teachers: The Key Ingredient in Inquiry Instruction

The five essential features of inquiry described in the previous sections are based on a model of what scientists do in the real world. To mirror the activities of scientists, children in an inquiry classroom are provided the opportunity to participate in scientific practices

Strategies for forming and working with cooperative groups are discussed in Chapter 7.

Children might use word processors, spreadsheets, graphing programs, and multimedia presentation software, such as *PowerPoint*, *HyperStudio*, and *Kid Pix*, to plan and make their class presentations.

VIDEO CASE STUDY: *Sarah*

Annenberg/CPB

Previewing the Video
As you watch this case study, use the *Questions for Reflection* to guide your note taking and analysis. For group discussion, choose a group facilitator to solicit various perspectives and keep the discussion on track.

Introducing the Case

Sarah has been teaching school for five years. As a fifth-grade teacher she is responsible for teaching some sophisticated science concepts. Although she does not have a strong science background, she conscientiously tries to set up inquiry experiences that challenge her students. One such experience required students to use a compound pendulum to create a patterned design. The science experience was not very successful for either Sarah or her students until she called in a friend who had taught this lesson at a local museum.

Questions for Reflection

1. What did Sarah want her students to learn by doing this experiment? Why do you think most students encountered problems doing the compound pendulum experiment?

2. How did Sarah handle the students' frustrations?

3. Comment on what Sarah says: "I think that students are going to make discoveries through open-ended activities that I may not have even planned for them to make or expected them to make, and those type of discoveries or those thoughts you can only get if you give them the space to do it." How does open-ended inquiry differ from closed investigation?

4. What did Sarah and her students learn from this teaching experiment?

Trying New Ideas *As part of Sarah's fifth-grade science curriculum, she was responsible for introducing students to a unit on food chemistry. After reviewing the materials she needed to conduct this twelve-week unit, Sarah felt a little overwhelmed. How would she be able to manage students' inquiry to test for protein, glucose, starch, and fats? How would she keep students from contaminating the food samples? How would she get students to record their findings?*

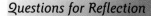

1. What did Sarah learn about data collection that might make working with student groups and the handling of materials more manageable?

2. Look at the observation datasheet shown below. How might this datasheet help keep students on task? How might this datasheet be improved?

3. Review the glucose datasheet (on the facing page) and record sheet (on the following page). What elements of the record sheet and the glucose datasheet would be valuable for collecting individual or group data for this food chemistry lesson?

4. Sarah's science mentor, Dr. Rick Duschl, discussed the value of data collection. What does Duschl mean by "data manipulation" and "data interpretation"? How would you create a class summary sheet to facilitate data manipulation and interpretation?

5. The 5-E model of instruction is a teaching tool that incorporates the tasks of scientific inquiry (Figure 1-3) and the learning cycle (Figure 3-3). Do you think that Sarah's lessons on compound pendulums and food chemistry reflect the use of each of the five phases of the 5-E model of instruction? How might the lessons be changed to better reflect the phases of the 5-E model?

Reflecting and Building on Change *In a culminating activity Sarah asks students to use their knowledge and skills for food testing and act as chemists to test marshmallows for their nutrient value. Such real life, relevant activities engage Sarah's students once again in meaningful science inquiry.*

Observation Data Sheet

Students in group:

Date of inquiry:

Purpose of inquiry:

Observations generally require the use of all of your senses. Do not use your sense of taste, however, unless your teacher indicates it is safe to do so in this inquiry. Use this checklist to record your observations.

Use your eyes without a hand lens. What do you see?

Use your eyes with a hand lens. What do you see?

Use your nose. What do you smell?

Use your tongue. What do you taste? *SAFETY PRECAUTIONS. DO THIS ONLY IF YOUR TEACHER TELLS YOU TO.*

Use your hands. What do you feel?

Name: _____

Date: _____

Glucose Test for Foods

Pre-Lab Questions

1. What nutrient are you testing for? _____
_____

2. What test material are you using to identify the nutrient? _____
_____

3. What color is the test material before it is used? _____
_____

Lab

Now test each liquid for glucose. As you complete each test, record your results on the table on the next page. When the table is completed, answer the questions below.

Post-Lab Questions

1. Using your results, how can you identify a positive test (+) for glucose?
_____
_____

2. Using your results, how can you identify a negative test (–) for glucose?
_____
_____

3. Describe the results of this test on any food for which the result was not clearly positive or negative. _____
_____

Source: Copyright 1994 National Academy of Sciences. Reproduced with permission from Science and Technology for Children™ *Food Chemistry*, National Science Resource Center.

Name: _____

Date: _____

Glucose Test for Foods Table

Test Foods	Prediction: Present: (+) Not present: (−) Don't know: (dk)	Observation of Glucose Test Paper After Test	First Test Results: +, −, dk	Second Test Results: +, −, dk

Questions for Reflection

1. How did the class data summary table hold student groups accountable for their findings?

2. Sarah thinks students engage in more meaningful discussion when they use a class summary table. How does the information in such a table help the class draw conclusions to an inquiry lesson?

3. How does requiring each student group to find unique data facilitate class inquiry?

that offer experiences and tools to explore and construct knowledge. But there are funda-mental differences in what scientists do and what developing children can do. "Thus," as Lee (2002) explained, "science instruction occurs in a simplified form that children can participate in, comprehend, and communicate" (p. 42). The key ingredient in this simpli-fied form of science instruction is the teacher.

When planning and guiding inquiry, the teacher's role is not unlike a juggling act. Teachers must determine how to focus, challenge, and encourage student learning, using their own knowledge of students, as well as their knowledge of science and how it is learned.

Teachers in inquiry classrooms constantly make decisions such as how to initiate in-quiry, how to encourage student discourse, when to shift from small group activities to whole class discussions, when and how to confront misconceptions, when to directly teach needed scientific knowledge, and how to best model scientific skills and attitudes. Throughout the learning process, teachers must struggle with the tension between em-phasizing content knowledge and focusing on inquiry procedures. Similarly, teachers face difficult choices between staying on schedule and providing ample time for students to ex-plore. The realities of classroom life mean that even the best-planned lessons have to be modified, continued the next day, and sometimes cut short or abandoned.

A crucial decision teachers must make in teaching science by inquiry is how much guidance (or scaffolding) they will supply to students. Table 4-1 shows the variation in teacher input that might be present in each of the essential features of classroom inquiry. The amount of teacher guidance might vary from little in independent investigations to almost total in structured inquiry lessons.

In deciding how much guidance to give, you should consider the purpose of the lesson. You may provide less guidance when you wish to promote independent thought. It may be appropriate to give more guidance at every stage of a lesson intended to provide students with a model of how to investigate, such as the lesson on position and motion described in Chapter 2. Also, the younger the learners or the less experience they have in investigat-ing, the more guidance they will need.

How and when to assist students in acquiring content knowledge needed to answer initiating questions is a special problem in inquiry instruction. Although students should be provided every opportunity to construct relevant knowledge, they are not able to dis-cover many scientific concepts, principles, and theories on their own (American Associ-ation for the Advancement of Science, 1993, p. 12). Thus, teachers must be ready to build on student activities to present new knowledge by direct or expository teaching methods. Direct presentation of science knowledge should always build on the hands-on activities of children.

Regardless of the amount of assistance you provide, your goal is for the students to be-come engaged with scientific questions, explore ideas on their own, construct relevant knowledge, actively build and test explanations, and begin to understand the inquiry process itself (National Research Council, 2000, pp. 21–33).

Research on the Effectiveness of Inquiry Instruction

Inquiry approaches to science model the inquiry procedures of scientists and are founded on contemporary understandings of how people learn (Bransford, Brown, & Cocking, 1999). Research data from science classrooms also support the effectiveness of inquiry instruction.

Although definitions of inquiry vary from study to study, data from various research studies indicate that inquiry instruction is effective in fostering problem solving, creativ-ity, and independent learning (Shymansky, Hedges, & Woodworth, 1990), as well as im-proving reasoning, observing, and logical analysis (Minstrell, 1989; Rosebery, Warren, &

TABLE 4-1   ESSENTIAL FEATURES OF STUDENT INQUIRY AND THEIR VARIATIONS IN THE SCIENCE CLASSROOM

Essential Features of Classroom Inquiry	Level of Student Self-Direction		
	Level 3 High	Level 2 Moderate	Level 1 Low
1. Learners are engaged by scientific questions.	Learners pose scientific questions for themselves.	Learners clarify and select from among questions suggested by the teacher.	Learners use questions provided by the teacher or other source.
2. Learners give priority to evidence as they plan and conduct investigations.	Learners carry out investigations and information searches on their own.	Learners are guided by the teacher in carrying out investigations and searches.	Learners perform investigations and search sources following directions provided.
3. Learners develop descriptions, explanations, and predictions using evidence.	Learners formulate descriptions, explanations, and predictions from their collected evidence.	Learners are guided by the teacher in formulating appropriate descriptions, explanations, and predictions.	Learners draw from descriptions, explanations, and predictions presented by the teacher.
4. Learners connect evidence and explanations to developing scientific knowledge.	Learners take the lead in connecting evidence and explanations to their developing knowledge.	Learners are guided by the teacher in connecting evidence and explanations to scientific knowledge.	Learners are shown how evidence and explanations link to scientific knowledge.
5. Learners engage in critical discourse with others about procedures, evidence, and explanations.	Learners take the lead in presenting, discussing, and challenging questions, evidence, and explanations.	Learners are guided in communicating procedures, evidence, and explanations.	Learners follow procedures for communication given to them by the teacher.
	Less Teacher Direction	←——————→	More Teacher Direction

Source: Reprinted with permission from *Inquiry and the* National Science Education Standards: *A Guide for Teaching and Learning* (2000) by the National Academy of Sciences, courtesy of the National Academies Press, Washington, DC.

Conant, 1992). Students exposed to inquiry methods in science typically perform better than peers in more traditional classes on measures of general science achievement, process skills, analytical skills, and related skills such as language arts and mathematics (Shymansky, 1983; Shymansky, Kyle, & Alpert, 1982).

Based on a review of research, Haury (1993) concluded that hands-on, inquiry-oriented instruction can result in scientific literacy, familiarity with science processes, conceptual understanding, critical thinking, and positive attitudes toward science.

Studies indicate that the advantages of inquiry-oriented instruction also extend to special student populations. Research by Rosebery et al. (1992) indicated that students learning English can successfully engage in inquiry and learn science concepts as they learn the language. In research on students with learning disabilities, Scruggs, Mastropieri, Bakken, and Brigham (1993) found significantly higher learning with an inquiry-oriented approach than with a textbook-oriented approach.

The Science Curriculum Improvement Study (SCIS) program uses an inquiry approach to science instruction built around the Learning Cycle introduced in Chapter 3. Studies of this program have shown that—when compared with students in more traditional, textbook-oriented science programs—students engaged in SCIS activities

- found science more exciting and interesting,
- wished they had more science,
- felt that science was more useful in their everyday lives,
- had greater feelings of success, and
- had a more positive view of science and scientists than non-SCIS students (Kyle, Bonnstetter, & Gadsen, 1986).

Research data on measurable cognitive and affective variables support the advantages of inquiry instruction over other methods. Yet, intangible achievements may outweigh tangible ones, as students learn through an inquiry approach to ask questions, place a priority on evidence, and use observable data and knowledge to arrive at explanations and evaluate claims.

As you juggle the various factors involved in teaching science through inquiry, you will have many decisions to make. As in any complex task involving human interactions, you need some tools to simplify the process.

Models for Inquiry Instruction

Various instructional models and strategies have been designed for teaching science. Instructional models involve some arrangement of phases, steps, actions, or decision points for teaching and learning. Different instructional models build on different points of view about the nature of inquiry, processes of science, scientific knowledge, and the goals and dimensions of learning. They also incorporate different principles from research on learning and development.

According to Brown and Campione (1994), teachers cannot just import an instructional model, follow prescribed procedures, and expect to attain student understanding of complex subject matter. A teacher's use of a model must reflect the viewpoints and principles on which it is based.

Two models of instruction, the guided discovery and 5-E models, are particularly relevant for inquiry teaching. In the following sections, we develop these two models of science instruction for you.

Guided Discovery

In guided discovery learning, children begin with interesting questions and concrete materials. Learners work individually or in small groups to explore materials, make observations, and discover answers to their questions about the natural world. The teacher serves as a facilitator and guide through the discovery process.

Discovery lessons are highly motivational. There is joy for children—as well as for adults—in probing into and finding out about the unknown (Sears & Kessen, 1964). As children start to explore, they seem to suddenly awaken to exciting possibilities in the natural world and in themselves. Discovery allows students to find their own meanings and organize their own ideas. In discovery learning, children's imagination, hunches, and insight precede proof and instruction by teachers (Wiggins & McTighe, 1998). As young students engage in probing interesting questions, much open inquiry can take place if teachers allow students to explore. Students do not have to be scientifically mature, merely curious.

In one Annenberg Video Case Study in Science Education, Sarah, a fifth grade teacher, reminds herself and other teachers that "students are going to make discoveries through open-ended activities that I may not have planned for them to make. You can only get these types of activities if you give them the space to do it." A guide to this video is included in this chapter.

Science Helper includes nearly a thousand lessons developed in federally funded programs. This CD-ROM is available from The Learning Team, 10 Long Pond Road, Armonk, NY 10504–0217. Telephone: (914) 223–2226.

To appreciate Mole's fascination with the natural world and his openness to new discoveries, read all of Chapter 1 of *The Wind in the Willows.*

The Elementary Science Study (ESS) program developed in the 1960s with federal funds was one of the pioneers in the use of discovery approaches to learning. The ESS group devised many activities and units and tested them in classrooms across the nation. Dozens of lessons from ESS modules such as Kitchen Physics, Bones, Mealworms, Gases and Airs, Rocks and Minerals, Mystery Powders, and Small Things are reproduced for teachers' use today on the CD-ROM called *Science Helper* (Rowe, 1988).

The ESS philosophy was captured in the phrase "messing about in science," which was based on an expression in Kenneth Grahame's (1981) children's book *The Wind in the Willows*. In this delightful tale, Water Rat explained to Mole the joys of simply "messing about in boats" on a lazy afternoon. If you have not already done so, read the account of Mole and Water Rat's river adventure in the introduction to this book (page 2) and think about why it inspired the developers of ESS. As you read, consider how Water Rat's little speech at the end of the selection can also fit some of the purposes of discovery learning.

Through discovery learning, children enjoy simply messing about in science. But well-planned discovery activities also give children opportunities and time to observe, explain, and appreciate the order and diversity of the world.

Preparing for Guided Discovery. Although it is the students who engage in the discovery work, careful teacher planning is necessary for successful discovery lessons. Teachers must consider the kinds of introductory questions to ask or lead the students to ask to begin exploration. Here are some sample questions:

- What are some things you notice about butterflies? What colors are they and what patterns do you see? Can you discover ways that different color patterns might serve to protect butterflies?
- How do mealworms respond to environmental conditions, such as moisture, light, and heat? What foods do mealworms prefer?
- What things live on the edge of the pond? How do they interact with one another? Why do they live on the edge of the pond and not in it?
- Do magnets attract through different materials? What factors affect the strength of electromagnets?

Teachers must also plan for activities that will enable students to discover or lay a foundation for intended concepts and principles. The planned activities then determine the types of material that teachers must obtain, prepare, and arrange into sets for use by small groups of students.

Strategies for Guided Discovery. To teach by guided discovery, you should introduce the problem, distribute materials in an orderly way, and let the discoveries begin as soon as possible. Circulate among the children as they engage in discovery activities, spending no more than about 30 to 60 seconds with each student or small group. You should give only enough assistance to ensure that students do not become overly frustrated, experience undue failure, and give up.

Rather than telling the students what to do while investigating, teachers can scaffold children's discoveries by asking questions or giving hints that help them sense the direction for solving problems. You must be careful to respect the discovery process and not to supply too much information. Do not rob the children of the opportunities they have for thought and creativity in their investigations. Thus, in discovery lessons, you might choose to answer children's questions with "What do you think?" or "What are your ideas?" Deciding when to give assistance and when to withhold it is an important part of the art of discovery teaching.

At different points in the discovery process, you will want to hear from and talk with the class as a whole about their procedures and discoveries. You will be tempted to give students the "right" answer. However, a skillful discovery teacher listens to and uses the ideas of children in questioning and discussion to help them organize their thoughts and build more scientifically accurate understandings of the world.

Guided Discovery in a Nutshell. We can summarize the teaching approach to discovery learning in the following way:

- Engage children in activities.
- Encourage them to explore concrete materials and reflect on what they find out.
- Engage children in conversations, listen to their ideas, and provide guidance to help them build and test their own explanations of what is happening (Koch, 1999, p. 12).

Following is a classroom example of a guided discovery lesson.

Discovery Activities with Batteries and Bulbs. Joyce Jackson guided her fourth grade class in a series of discovery activities on electricity. (The activities are shown in the accompanying lesson plan.) Many of the activities were selected from an ESS unit called *Batteries and Bulbs*. When children learn about batteries and bulbs through discovery, they explore electrical circuits, form generalizations about them, and use the generalizations to explain why bulbs in different circuit arrangements do or do not light.

Joyce arranged her class in cooperative groups. She began with an improbable little story about three campers who had strayed deep into the woods, far from their campsite. Night had fallen and they had no flashlight to find their way back in the darkness. However, one camper had a spare battery in his backpack, another had a flashlight bulb, and a third had a piece of copper wire. Unfortunately, they did not know how to connect the battery, bulb, and wire to light the bulb. As she talked, Joyce quietly placed a 1.5 volt flashlight cell, a small bulb, and a piece of wire before each child. Then she asked her class: "Can you use the materials in front of you to light a bulb and help the campers get back to their campsite safely?"

The story helped the young learners comprehend and maintain focus on the task. Initially, the students worked individually to light the bulb (see Activity 1 in the batteries and bulbs lesson activities). Many students lit the bulb within a few minutes; others took considerably longer. During the discovery process, Joyce resisted the temptation to give too much help. As individuals successfully lit their bulbs, they moved into their small groups for subsequent activities. Children freely exchanged information and ideas as they worked in their groups.

In the process of discovery, students thought about possibilities, made hypotheses and predictions, and tried out their ideas. Each cooperative group moved through the batteries and bulbs activities at their own pace, with the teacher giving hints, adding information, posing questions, or providing additional activities as needed. Most of the groups were able to complete Activities 1–3 on day one.

To start the next science time, Ms. Jackson turned out the lights in the classroom and asked the children to individually make a bulb light and hold it aloft to light the room. As she walked about the room watching what the children were doing, she was able to quickly assess the knowledge and skills of each child, to note who needed help, and to either supply assistance or ask someone in a cooperative group to help.

Next, she directed the children's attention to Activities 4 and 5. Children individually drew pictures of the different ways they had found to light a bulb. This activity was designed to lift thought from a kinesthetic, hands-on level to an iconic, imaging level. As she assessed each child's drawings, she noted that some had not perceived exactly what it was they did to light a bulb. Again, she either provided assistance or asked another child in the group to assist.

Joyce next passed out Prediction Sheet 1 and gave directions for it (see Activity 6). Circulating among the students, she supplied scaffolding assistance as needed. When all

Chapter 5 provides a number of strategies for questioning and leading inquiry discussions.

You may need to study circuit ideas yourself before teaching batteries and bulbs activities. Good presentations on electricity and electrical circuits at an elementary level are available in many curriculum sources. Especially good treatments can be found in the teachers' guides for STC (Science and Technology for Children) and FOSS (Full Option Science System) modules on electricity.

The Annenberg Video Case Study in Science Education featuring Tom shows fifth grade students involved in guided discovery activities on batteries and bulbs. A study guide for this case study is provided in Chapter 6.

groups had finished the prediction sheet she went over each frame with the class, probing student answers to assess and enhance understanding.

Ms. Jackson began the third class day with Activity 7. She posed the question for this activity by saying,

"Suppose one of the campers lost in the woods had a cell phone and called you to find out how to light a bulb. What would you tell her? Write out your answer."

Children worked individually, then as groups to answer the question. The "reporter" in each cooperative group read the group's answer to the class while children in other groups listened and critiqued. Most groups succeeded at this task with varying amounts of teacher scaffolding. Later, the students under Ms. Jackson's guidance, decided on these rules:

To light a bulb with one wire:

1. Touch the tip of the bulb to one end of the battery.
2. Touch a wire to the metal on the side of a bulb.
3. Make a complete pathway for the electricity to flow by touching the other end of the wire to the other end of the battery.

For the rest of the science time that day and for the next two days in science, children worked on Activities 8–13. Although all of the children enjoyed these activities and were able to learn a good deal more factual and conceptual information about electrical circuits, few of the children spontaneously applied the rules of Activity 7 to understand what happened in each case.

Lesson Plan: Discovery Activities with Batteries and Bulbs

Safety

- Respect electricity! Do not touch or go near frayed or broken wires. Do not insert anything but an electrical plug into an electrical outlet.
- Never try these activities with any battery larger than a 1.5 volt "D" cell.
- Wear goggles when you work with batteries, bulbs, and wires to protect your eyes from the sharp points of wires.

Objectives

- For students to perform some simple investigations with batteries and bulbs and explain their observations using the concept of circuits and circuit rules.

Encourage children to discover new knowledge through exploration.

Processes

Activities

Discover What Happens

1. Light a bulb using one wire and one battery.
2. Find several ways to light the bulb.
3. Light a bulb using two wires, without the bulb touching the battery.

Show What You Observe

4. Draw pictures to represent the bulb-battery-wire arrangements for Activities 1 and 2.
5. Draw a picture to represent the arrangement of the bulb, wires, and battery in Activity 3.

Predict and Test

6. Complete Prediction Sheet 1. Work frame by frame, using what you learn to move from one to another.
   • Make a prediction.
   • Test your prediction.
   • Learn from your test.
   • Apply what you have learned.

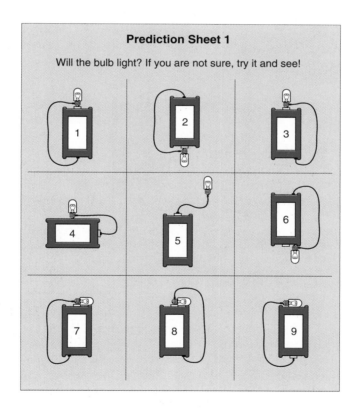

Prediction Sheet 1

Will the bulb light? If you are not sure, try it and see!

Generalize

7. Where must a bulb be touched in order for it to light? Where must a battery be touched? Write a general rule for what must be done to make a bulb light. Apply your generalizations or rule to explain each frame in Prediction Sheet 1.

Use Knowledge to Infer and Explain

8. Examine a bulb with a magnifying glass. The coiled wire across the top of the bulb is called a filament. That is what uses electrical energy to produce light. Do you see the two wires that disappear into the base of the bulb? How do you think they are connected internally within the base of the bulb? Use your rules from Activity 7 in making your inference.

9. Examine a bulb holder. What are its parts? How is a bulb holder designed to touch the tip and metal side of a bulb?

Apply Knowledge to New Situations

10. Light a bulb using two batteries.
11. Find several ways to light two bulbs.

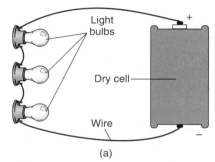

(a)

12. Make the circuit shown in Diagram A.
    • How many wires are needed?
    • Remove one of the bulbs from its holder. What happens? Why?
    • Replace the bulb. Remove another bulb. What happens? Why?
    • Add one or two more batteries. What happens? Why?
    • What would the label "series circuit" describe about the circuit in Diagram A?

13. Make the circuit shown in Diagram B.
    • How many wires are needed?
    • Remove one of the bulbs from its holder. What happens? Why?
    • Replace the bulb. Remove another bulb. What happens? Why?
    • Add one or two more batteries. What happens? Why?
    • What would the label "parallel circuit" describe about the circuit in Diagram B?

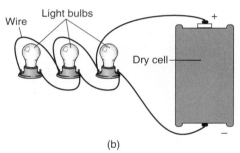

(b)

Diagram A. A series circuit.
Diagram B. A parallel circuit.

Source: Adapted from discovery activities in *Batteries and Bulbs*, Elementary Science Study, 1968, Cambridge, MA: Educational Development Center.

Guided discovery is a wonderful approach to learning science that students and teachers have enjoyed for many years. Nothing raises the sense of wonder and joy of learning about the natural world like discovery. Yet, often missing in guided discovery teaching are careful attention to constructing and applying specific scientific knowledge, and a planned development of specific abilities of inquiry. The 5-E instructional model, described in the next section, begins with guided discovery but adds an explicit focus on developing scientific knowledge and inquiry abilities.

The 5-E Model of Instruction

The 5-E model of instruction was developed by the BSCS group (Biological Sciences Curriculum Study, 1989). There are five phases in the 5-E model:

- *Engagement.* Teachers engage students in questions about objects, organisms, and events in the environment, and probe background knowledge and conceptions.
- *Exploration.* Students plan and conduct investigations to gather evidence to answer the questions.
- *Explanation.* Building on students' explorations and explanations, teachers formally present labels, concepts, and principles; students, guided by the teacher, use new knowledge to construct scientific explanations and answer initiating questions.
- *Elaboration.* Students apply new understandings to new problems.
- *Evaluation.* Teachers and students use formal and informal means to assess new knowledge, understandings, appreciations, and abilities.

The 5-E model builds on the tasks of inquiry identified in the *National Science Education Standards* and utilizes the essential features of inquiry described previously in the chapter.

The 5-E model of instruction represents a second generation of the Learning Cycle that we described in Chapter 3 (see Figure 3-3). The Learning Cycle consists of three phases: *exploration, concept invention,* and *concept application* (Jacobson & Kondo, 1968; Karplus & Thier, 1974). The middle three phases of the 5-E model, exploration, explanation, and elaboration, are similar to the three phases of the Learning Cycle. The engagement phase of the 5-E model is intended to provide a focus for the lesson and to allow the teacher to probe students' initial conceptions. The evaluation phase reflects contemporary ideas about ongoing assessment of children's performance and learning.

The 5-E model shares many similarities with guided discovery, especially at the engagement and exploration phases. For example, the same batteries and bulbs activities we discussed with guided discovery might be organized according to a 5-E format, as shown in Figure 4-1. However, there are essential differences in the two models.

Guided discovery emphasizes more open inquiry; with 5-E, there are clear objectives and specific concepts and explanations you want children to learn. With guided discovery, teachers supply assistance only as needed; in the 5-E model, teachers prepare in advance to provide expository instruction on specific concepts and explanations. Instruction with 5-E proceeds in a more step-by-step fashion than with guided discovery, with each step providing focus, data, or concepts for the next step. Still, both models engage children in inquiry and develop understanding of the world as well as problem-solving abilities.

Now, let us examine each of the 5-E components.

Engagement. The first component in the 5-E instructional model, engagement, is intended to pique curiosity and provide focus for the ensuing activities. At this stage, the question for investigation is formulated. Further, teachers probe students' conceptions and misconceptions about the topic to be investigated, help students make connections with prior knowledge, establish rules and procedures, and provide safety precautions.

You might engage children in the problem for inquiry in ways similar to that used with the guided discovery lessons. In a 5-E batteries and bulbs lesson, for instance, the scenario about some campers needing to know how to put a battery, bulb, and wire together to light the bulb would work well. Plan the engagement activities so that once the problem is introduced and curiosity is high, students can begin to work immediately, manipulating materials and making observations.

Exploration. Once students are engaged in the learning tasks, exploration activities follow. The exploration phase of the 5-E model proceeds much like guided discovery. As they

All of the activities in *Activities for Teaching Science as Inquiry,* the companion volume to this book, are organized according to the 5-E format.

Figure 4-1 Organizing batteries and bulbs activities according to the 5-E instructional model.

NSES *Science Standards*

• Electricity in circuits can produce light, heat, sound, and mechanical motion (K–4).

Concepts and Principles That Support the Standards on Electricity:

• Electrical circuits require a complete conducting loop through which an electric current can pass (K–4).

Objectives

1. Construct circuits in which bulbs light.
2. Use the concept of complete circuits to explain why bulbs do or do not light in various simple circuits.
3. Apply the notion of complete circuits in the construction and explanations of more complex circuits.

Phases of the 5-E Model	Activities with Batteries and Bulbs
Engage. Ask a question about objects, organisms, and events in the environment.	Present a scenario about people needing to find a way to use a bulb, battery, and wire to make a bulb light.
Explore. Plan and conduct investigations to gather evidence to answer the question posed.	Conduct Activities 1–6 from Discovery Activities with Batteries and Bulbs.
Explain. Use new knowledge and observable evidence to construct scientific explanations and answer initiating questions.	Conduct Activities 7–9 from Discovery Activities with Batteries and Bulbs; provide explicit instruction as needed on the concept of *complete circuits* and its application.
Elaborate. Apply new understandings to new problems.	Conduct Activities 10–13 from Discovery Activities with Batteries and Bulbs.
Evaluate. Assess developing understandings and inquiry skills.	Use continuous (formative) assessment; assess performance on a new prediction sheet, including written explanations of predictions.

---

explore, students spontaneously handle and freely manipulate materials, make discoveries, and talk about them with one another and the teacher. The teacher plays an indirect role as observer, question poser, and guide to students.

The teacher allows the students to explore on their own, providing scaffolding assistance as needed. This phase of the model gives students a concrete basis of physical experience for forming concepts, generalizations, and explanations at the next level.

Explanation. In the explanation phase of the 5-E strategy, teachers help students make sense of their observations and the questions that arise from them. First, the teacher asks children to describe what they see and give their own explanations of why it happened (Biological Sciences Curriculum Study, 1989). Building on the activities and discussion of students, the teacher then formally introduces scientific concepts needed to make sense of the event. The teacher introduces the new concepts and guides students to link the con-

Young girls are as curious as boys about science and inquiry. Sensitive teachers nurture that interest.

cepts back to the real-world experiences they had in the exploration phase of learning. The teacher then assists students to use the new concepts along with the evidence from investigations to build descriptions and scientific explanations that help to answer the initiating question.

Here is an example of how you might teach a concept needed by students. Suppose in a 5-E approach to batteries and bulbs you have given children the task of building on their exploration activities to write out procedures for lighting a bulb. As you interact with and listen to students, you decide that to complete the task appropriately they need to understand the concept of *circuits*. In formally presenting this new concept, follow these simple guidelines:

- Group your students near you so they can all see anything you demonstrate or write on the chalkboard or overhead, hear your questions, and communicate with each other.
- Refer to an activity the students have done themselves during exploration, such as their activities with the prediction sheet.
- As you discuss the activity, introduce the label (word or words) for the concept you want to develop. For example, you might say
    "A *circuit* is an arrangement of bulbs, batteries, and wires. A circuit is a complete circuit if the bulb lights. If the circuit is complete, there is an unbroken path around the circuit from the terminal of a battery, along the wires, through the bulb, and back to the other terminal of the battery."
- Write the word *circuit* on the board for all the children to see. (Writing the word gives visual as well as oral introduction of the new word.)
- Through questioning and verbal instruction, lead the class to apply their new knowledge of circuits to the circuit arrangements they have already encountered. For example, work with students to trace and describe the electricity pathway for each case in Prediction Sheet 1.

This instructional sequence repeats an activity your students have already done or observed, but adds a new word for the concept.

Once they have been introduced, concepts, principles, and theories must be linked to one another and to real-world experiences. An important way to do this is through their application to new problem situations.

Elaboration. Elaboration activities provide opportunity for students to apply newly learned concepts and skills in new situations. Mary Budd Rowe (1973, pp. 367–372) has suggested that concept application is too often the neglected ingredient in inquiry teaching. It is through concept application that understanding is generated. Rowe emphasized that children need to learn to view knowledge as procedures to be applied rather than just as information to be memorized and recalled.

Thus, in this phase of the 5-E model, the teacher guides the students to apply the new knowledge acquired through the exploration and explanation phases to new problem-solving situations. In learning to apply new knowledge of electricity and electrical circuits to everyday experiences, students might

- construct and investigate series and parallel circuits (Activities 12 and 13);
- wire the lights in a model house (built from a cardboard box); and
- consider how the electric lights might be wired in their own classroom.

Students might also apply their new knowledge to decide whether holiday lights should be wired in series or parallel circuits, examine and design switches and fuses, and so on. Small group and whole class discussions furnish students opportunities to present and defend their own understandings and explanations of the new activities.

The novelty of new problem situations makes understanding them challenging, yet they yield to the application of concepts developed in earlier activities.

Evaluation. Evaluation is intended to emphasize contemporary ideas about assessment. Part of the art of teaching is to decide when and how to give students feedback on the adequacy of their ideas and inquiry procedures. Assessment used for feedback can occur at any point in the teaching sequence. The goal of informal assessment is to confirm the direction students are moving or to encourage them to examine their ideas and to look again at their procedures. More formal means of assessment, including paper-and-pencil tests and performance tasks, may also be used to provide feedback to students and the teacher. Based on formal and informal assessment evidence, teachers may decide to have students repeat one or more activities from the different phases of the 5-E instructional model.

Self-assessment is an important aspect of the evaluation process. Brown and Campione (1994) argued that students should be taught metacognition strategies for planning, executing, monitoring, and adjusting one's own efforts on a cognitive task.

To better help you in planning and implementing the 5-E model of inquiry instruction, we include a detailed lesson plan on moon watching. The lesson plan follows.

A variety of strategies for assessing science learning through traditional and performance assessment means are discussed in Chapter 6.

Lesson Plan: Moon Watching (Grades 5–6)

Lesson Overview   In this lesson, students watch the moon each night or day for at least one month.

Objectives   Students should be able to describe, record, and explain the changing position of the moon in the sky and the apparent change in the shape of the moon as it progresses through the lunar cycle.

Begin the lesson when the moon is visible in the daytime sky (after the third quarter or before the first quarter). You will need to make advance observations yourself to make sure the moon is visible during the day. Ask the following questions:

ENGAGE: ASK A QUESTION ABOUT OBJECTS AND EVENTS IN THE ENVIRONMENT.

- Who has seen the moon in the last few days or nights?
- What did it look like?
- When did you see it?
- Where did you see it?

If no one suggests it, ask: "Can we ever see the moon in the daytime?" Allow students to discuss their ideas. Take students outside and observe the moon in the daytime. Invite them to record their observations.

On the next class day, ask: "Will you be able to see the moon again today?" "Do you think it will be in the same place?" "How will we know if it is in the same place?" Encourage the students to use landmarks to note the position of the moon. Wait a few hours and bring the students outside again to observe the moon. Have them record the position of the moon and its appearance. Has the moon's position changed? Has the appearance of the moon changed?

Start the exploration when the moon is in its new moon phase. Encourage students to look for the moon every night just after dark and before bedtime and to observe its position and appearance.

EXPLORE: CONDUCT A SIMPLE INVESTIGATION.

Students should draw in the appearance of the moon and describe its position on the Weekly Moon Calendar. Some parents might be willing to assist children in their observations. Continue to make observations and record the position and appearance of the moon every day for a month. The moon's cycle actually lasts 29 1/2; days from one new moon to the next new moon.

Do not supply the names for the phases yet, but allow students to describe the phases in a way that makes sense to them.

Weekly Moon Calendar

Sunday	Monday	Tuesday	Wednesday	Thursday	Friday	Saturday
◯	◯	◯	◯	◯	◯	◯
Date _____ Time _____ Position _____ _____ _____	Date _____ Time _____ Position _____ _____ _____	Date _____ Time _____ Position _____ _____ _____	Date _____ Time _____ Position _____ _____ _____	Date _____ Time _____ Position _____ _____ _____	Date _____ Time _____ Position _____ _____ _____	Date _____ Time _____ Position _____ _____ _____

Invite students to use their data to describe the pattern of the phases and movement of the moon in the sky. Make a class chart of the data. Beginning about 2 days after the new moon, a thin crescent is seen on the western horizon just after sunset. Over the next 2 weeks, the moon waxes in size, growing toward a full moon, and is seen in the sky further and further toward the east each day. After 14 or 15 days from new moon, the moon is full and at sunset is all the way across the sky on the eastern horizon. During the next 2 weeks, the moon rises later and later after sunset each night and wanes toward a thin crescent rising just before sunrise. Students will probably describe the moon as "getting bigger" as it grows toward the full moon and "getting smaller" from the full moon to the crescent moon.

EXPLAIN: USE DATA TO CONSTRUCT A REASONABLE EXPLANATION.

After students describe the phases of the moon in order, introduce the names that scientists use for the phases: new moon, waxing crescent, first quarter, waxing gibbous, full moon, waning gibbous, third quarter, waning crescent, and back to new moon again.

Knowledge of the patterns of the moon's phases and positions in the sky is next extended to an explanation of the causes of the phases. Through discussion and expository instruction as needed, help students to build on their observations of the moon to understand these prerequisite facts and concepts:

- The moon is round at all times; it does not really change its shape but only appears to do so.
- Clouds and eclipses have nothing to do with the phases of the moon.
- Half of the moon is lighted by the sun at all times.
- We see only a portion of the lighted side except during the full moon.

Building on the students' moon observations, explicitly teach a scientific explanation for moon phases: *Light from the distant sun strikes the moon, but only a portion of that sunlight is reflected to the earth, resulting in the appearance of moon phases.* Guide students to make sense of the explanation through diagrams, physical models, computer planetarium displays, and discussion. The explanation is only introduced at this point; it is developed in the elaboration phase.

ELABORATE: EXTEND THE CONCEPT.

Introduce a physical model of the sun-earth-moon system. Instruct students to stand facing a light source, but caution them not to look directly at the light. Provide each student with a Styrofoam ball. Give these instructions:

1. Imagine that the Styrofoam ball is the moon, that the light source is the sun, and that your head is the earth.
2. Place your Styrofoam ball on a stick or pencil. Hold your Styrofoam ball away from you at arm's length, slightly above your head, with the ball between you and the light. Look at the ball. Notice how much of the ball is lighted from where you are standing. Does it look like any of the phases of the moon you have observed?
3. Stay in one spot. With your arm extended, slowly move your arm and the ball 90 degrees to your left. Look at the ball again. How much of the ball's visible surface is lighted from where you stand? Is this like another phase of the moon you have seen?
4. Rotate another 90 degrees to the left and look at the ball. How much of the visible surface of the ball is lighted now? Is this like another phase of the moon you have observed?
5. Rotate your arm 90 degrees more to the left and look at the ball. Compare what you see to the phases of the moon you have seen in the sky.
6. Can you see some of the phases of the moon? When is the Styrofoam "moon" full? What position creates the new moon? Why can't you see the new moon? (The new moon occurs when the lighted side of the moon is turned away from the earth.)
7. Try to identify the positions of the moon relative to the earth and sun when you see the waxing crescent moon, the first quarter moon, the waxing gibbous moon, the full moon, and the waning phases.

EVALUATE: DEMONSTRATE UNDERSTANDING OF CONCEPTS AND ABILITY TO USE INQUIRY SKILLS.

Cut the moon phase cards into sets of eight pictures of phases. Distribute one set of the eight cards to each student. Make sure the cards are in random order. Instruct students to put the moon phases in order, beginning with the new moon, and to glue them in place on a piece of paper. Because you want to know what each student understands, allow students to use their personal records.

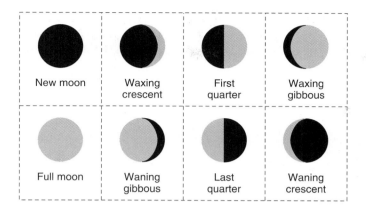

Ask students to write a few sentences beneath their diagrams that describe the changes in the phases of the moon. Students should explain that the visible part of the moon gets larger, or waxes, from the new moon through the full moon, and then gets smaller, or wanes, from the full moon through the new moon. Then the cycle begins again.

Source: Adapted from *Investigating Objects in the Sky*, BSCS Science T.R.A.C.S., and *Patterns of Change*, BSCS Science & Technology, Biological Sciences Curriculum Study, 1999. Dubuque, IA: Kendall-Hunt. Used with permission.

Engagement in the moon-watching lesson comes through teacher-led observations of the daytime moon and class discussion. In the exploration phase of the moon-watching lesson, students observe and record the appearance and position of the moon each day or night for one month. Explanation activities add organization to student's moon-watching records and provide a preliminary explanation of phases. In the elaboration phase, students use a physical model to develop the explanation of the moon's phases. Informal evaluation takes place throughout the lesson; in a more formal performance assessment task, students show their understanding by ordering moon phase cards and writing about what they have learned of the moon's phases.

As a summary view of the 5-E instructional model, Table 4-2 provides a chart that identifies teacher actions and student behaviors consistent with each phase of the model.

Conceptual Change and the 5-E Model of Inquiry Teaching

Students come to science classes with a variety of conceptions and misconceptions about the topics studied. Anderson (1987) pointed out that when asked to provide facts, rules, and definitions, it often appears that students have little knowledge about new topics to be studied. But a different picture emerges when they are asked to explain something. Students do have explanations, but not the ones scientists have generated.

As discussed in Chapter 3, initial explanations of students are likely to be laden with naive ideas, misconceptions, and alternative theories. An inquiry approach to science is especially compatible with *conceptual change strategies*. In teaching through inquiry, teachers have many opportunities to interact with students, observe and listen to them, and

TABLE 4-2 APPLYING THE 5-E INSTRUCTIONAL MODEL

Stage of the Instructional Model	What the teacher does	
	that is consistent with this model	that is inconsistent with this model
Engage	• Creates interest • Generates curiosity • Raises questions • Elicits responses that uncover what the students know or think about the concept/topic	• Explains concepts • Provides definitions and answers • States conclusions • Provides closure • Lectures
Explore	• Encourages students to work together without direct instruction from the teacher • Observes and listens to students as they interact • Asks probing questions to redirect students' investigations when necessary • Provides time for students to puzzle through problems • Acts as a consultant for students	• Provides answers • Tells or explains how to work through the problem • Provides closure • Tells students that they are wrong • Gives information or facts that solve the problem • Leads students step-by-step to a solution
Explain	• Encourages students to explain concepts and definitions in their own words • Asks for justification (evidence) and clarification from students • Formally provides definitions, explanations, and new labels • Uses students' previous experiences as the basis for explaining concepts	• Accepts explanations that have no justification • Neglects to solicit students' explanations • Introduces unrelated concepts or skills
Elaborate	• Expects students to use formal labels, definitions, and explanations provided previously • Encourages students to apply or extend the concepts and skills in new situations • Reminds students of alternative explanations • Refers students to existing data and evidence and asks: "What do you already know?" "Why do you think . . . ?" (Strategies from Explore apply here also.)	• Provides definitive answers • Tells students that they are wrong • Lectures • Leads students step-by-step to a solution • Explains how to work through the problem
Evaluate	• Observes students as they apply new concepts and skills • Assesses students' knowledge and/or skills • Looks for evidence that students have changed their thinking or behaviors • Allows students to assess their own learning and group-process skills • Asks open-ended questions, such as: "Why do you think . . . ?", "What evidence do you have?", "What do you know about x?", "How would you explain x?"	• Tests vocabulary words, terms, and isolated facts • Introduces new ideas or concepts • Creates ambiguity • Promotes open-ended discussion unrelated to the concept or skill

TABLE 4-2 APPLYING THE 5-E INSTRUCTIONAL MODEL		
Stage of the Instructional Model	**What the student does**	
	that is consistent with this model	**that is inconsistent with this model**
Engage	• Asks questions, such as: "Why did this happen?", "What do I already know about this?", "What can I find out about this?" • Shows interest in the topic	• Asks for the "right" answer • Offers the "right" answer • Insists on answers or explanations • Seeks one solution
Explore	• Thinks freely, but within the limits of the activity • Tests predictions and hypotheses • Forms new predictions and hypotheses • Tries alternatives and discusses them with others • Records observations and ideas • Suspends judgment	• Lets others do the thinking and exploring (passive involvement) • Works quietly with little or no interaction with others (only appropriate when exploring ideas or feelings) • Plays around indiscriminately with no goal in mind • Stops with one solution
Explain	• Explains possible solutions or answers to others • Listens critically to one another's explanations • Questions one another's explanations • Listens to and tries to comprehend explanations offered by the teacher • Refers to previous activities • Uses recorded observations in explanations	• Proposes explanations from thin air with no relationship to previous experiences • Brings up irrelevant experiences and examples • Accepts explanations without justification • Does not attend to other plausible explanations
Elaborate	• Applies new labels, definitions, explanations, and skills in new, but similar, situations • Uses previous information to ask questions, propose solutions, make decisions, and design experiments • Draws reasonable conclusions from evidence • Records observations and explanations • Checks for understanding among peers	• Plays around with no goal in mind • Ignores previous information or evidence • Draws conclusions from thin air • Uses in discussions only those labels that the teacher provided
Evaluate	• Answers open-ended questions by using observations, evidence, and previously accepted explanations • Demonstrates an understanding or knowledge of the concept or skill • Evaluates her own progress and knowledge • Asks related questions that would encourage future investigations	• Draws conclusions, not using evidence or previously accepted explanations • Offers only yes-or-no answers, memorized definitions, or explanations an answers • Fails to express satisfactory explanations in own words • Introduces new, irrelevant topics

Source: Teaching Secondary School Science, 6th ed. (pp. 218–219), by Leslie Trowbridge and Rodger Bybee, 1996, © Reprinted by permission of Pearson Education, Inc., Upper Saddle River, NJ.

recognize their conceptions that are inadequate and need further development. In learning through inquiry, students encounter problematic situations that cannot be resolved with their current conceptions. Through inquiry instruction, "Teachers . . . structure learning experiences that assist the reconstruction of core concepts. New constructions can then be applied to different situations and tested against other conceptions of the world" (Trowbridge & Bybee, 1996, p. 214).

For conceptual change to occur, Anderson (1987) suggested that teachers must identify alternative conceptions, promote dissatisfaction with them, introduce scientific conceptions, and provide for application and integration of new conceptions.

Identify Alternative Conceptions

One function of the engagement, exploration, and explanation phases of the 5-E model is to uncover what students already know or think about a topic. In all phases of 5-E inquiry lessons, students are encouraged to talk and frequently write about their understandings of the natural world and to illustrate them through drawing pictures and diagrams. By paying close attention to student ideas, you can begin to gain some insight into their prior knowledge, including their misconceptions (Anderson, 1987).

For example, consider the 5-E lesson on moon watching. Early in the lesson, students might be asked to explain why they think there are phases of the moon. Research and experience suggest that children and adolescents ages 9–16 are likely to give these explanations about why lunar phases appear:

- Clouds cover part of the moon so that we cannot see all of it (cloud viewpoint).
- The shadow of the earth falls on the moon so that we cannot see all of the moon (eclipse viewpoint).
- The shadow of the sun falls on the moon.
- Planets cast shadows on the moon.
- Only a portion of the sunlight illuminating the moon is reflected to earth (scientific viewpoint) (Stahly, Krockover, & Shepardson, 1999).

In various studies, up to 70% of subjects explained the phases of the moon from the "eclipse viewpoint." A large percentage of preservice teachers also held the eclipse view of lunar phases.

Promote Dissatisfaction with Alternative Conceptions

In teaching for conceptual change, it is not enough to just discredit misconceptions; nor is it sufficient to merely provide correct explanations. Rather, teachers should encourage students to test their own ideas through observation and investigation.

For example, if children think that lunar phases are caused by clouds, you might lead them to add information on "cloud conditions" to the daily and weekly moon-watching charts they keep.

Students can then examine their data and see if there is evidence to support the hypotheses of a connection between clouds and moon phases. This process can help students develop awareness of and dissatisfaction with their own inaccurate and incomplete explanations.

Sometimes students have inadequate conceptions simply because they lack relevant information. For example, students may have difficulty in explaining lunar phases due to their lack of knowledge about earth-moon-sun distance relationships. On the National Assessment of Educational Progress (NAEP) for 2000, eighth grade students were given this item:

The earth's moon is

a. always much closer to the sun than it is to the earth. (8%)
b. always much closer to the earth than it is to the sun. (49%)
c. about the same distance from the sun as it is from the earth. (9%)
d. sometimes closer to the sun than it is to the earth and sometimes closer to the earth than it is to the sun. (33%)

The percentage of students choosing each response for this item is shown after the response choices. Learner difficulties with the arrangement of the sun-earth-moon system is shown by the fact that only 49% of the eighth grade students chose the correct answer, B, while 33% chose answer D.

"Most students are told by teachers what causes the seasons and the phases of the moon, and they read about them without understanding. Moon phases are difficult because of students' unfamiliarity with the geometry of light and 'seeing.' To help figure out the geometry, students act out the sun-moon-earth relationships and make physical models."

(American Association for the Advancement of Science, 1993, p. 66)

The NAEP test results for science are available at http://nces.ed.gov/nationsreportcard/naepdata/.

Most models of the sun-earth-moon system that are illustrated in science texts or assembled by students for science projects do not show relative sizes and distances on the same scale. One way for students to begin to understand the size and distance relationships of the earth, moon, and sun is to do the math involved in the relationships and build a scale model. If a basketball were used to represent the earth, the moon would be a Styrofoam ball about 4 inches in diameter placed about 30 feet away. On this scale, the sun would be represented by a 10-story building about 2 miles away from the basketball and Styrofoam ball. Such a model can help students realize that the earth and moon are near neighbors that orbit the distant sun together.

Introduce Scientific Conceptions

According to Anderson (1987), exploratory activities are useful but do not in themselves lead to conceptual change. Left to their own devices, children may learn many interesting things about the moon, but they will develop scientific ideas about phases "about as rapidly as the human race: in other words, not in a single lifetime. Therefore," Anderson asserted, "scientific concepts need to be explicitly introduced and taught to students" (p. 86).

When students have become dissatisfied with their own conceptions and have collected a great deal of data and information at the exploration phase, it is time to formally teach key scientific concepts, principles, and explanations related to the topic. Build on exploratory activities in ways that can be meaningfully understood by students. Examine and contrast misconceptions with scientific conceptions (Anderson, 1987). At each point in instruction, assist students to modify, restructure, or abandon their existing conceptions in building new understandings of scientific concepts and explanations.

Realizing that clouds and eclipses are not satisfactory explanations for moon phases and that the earth and moon are near neighbors that are a great distance from the sun can help prepare children for a scientific explanation. Then, through expository instruction, diagrams, physical models, computer planetarium displays, and discussion, the scientific explanation for phases is presented. According to this explanation, light from the distant sun strikes the moon, but only a portion of that sunlight is reflected to the earth, resulting in the appearance of moon phases.

Provide for Application of New Conceptions

It is through applying new conceptions in new situations that students integrate and make sense of the new conceptions. Thus, when students examine how light reflects off a Styrofoam ball in the elaboration phase of the 5-E lesson on moon watching, they have an opportunity to think more deeply about the scientific explanation of lunar phases.

For all students to attain real understanding of scientific conceptions remains a challenging ideal. Nevertheless, as Anderson (1987) reported from his studies, when teachers utilize conceptual change approaches with inquiry methods the percentage of students attaining real understanding jumps from the 0 to 20% range to the 50 to 80% range. This is clearly a great improvement, helping to close the performance gap that so often exists among groups of learners.

Teaching Science Through Direct Instruction

This chapter has focused on the use of inquiry instruction models to help students construct conceptual understanding in science while developing their abilities to do scientific inquiry. The emphasis on inquiry, however, does not imply that teachers should pursue a single approach to teaching. According to the *Science Standards* (National Research Council, 1996), "Just as inquiry has many different facets, so teachers need to use many different strategies to develop the understandings and abilities described in the *Standards*" (p. 2).

Traditionally, one of the most popular approaches to teaching science has been direct instruction. Although the term has been employed to designate some specific teaching models, we will use *direct instruction* to refer to any teaching approach in which information, concepts, or strategies are presented directly to students through oral or visual means.

Direct instruction methods can be useful and effective for teaching well-defined performance skills or specific facts, concepts, and information to be remembered (Rosenshine, 1986). Even within inquiry contexts, direct, expository methods can be important, such as for providing background knowledge, giving directions, teaching specific skills, inventing concepts and applying them in new situations, and summarizing investigations (Wolfinger, 2000). Arbitrary conventions such as stoplight colors, measurement equivalencies, and vocabulary labels that cannot be logically deduced, as well as concepts and procedures that may be invented by some students but not by others, are better taught by direct methods (Scruggs et al., 1993). Finally, direct instruction is more appropriate for content that we do not want students to learn by trial and error, such as safety precautions or how to focus a microscope.

Hunter (1984) incorporated principles of learning into a strategy called "Lesson Design" which can serve as a model for planning and implementing direct instruction. The instructional steps in Hunter's Lesson Design include the following:

- *Anticipatory Set.* In this phase, focusing activities are carried out that orient students to the lesson and lead them to access relevant prior knowledge.
- *Objectives and Purpose.* Here, the students are informed of the objectives for the day. The teacher also explains how and why the ideas of the lesson are useful and important.
- *Instructional Input.* The teacher uses a wide variety of methods—including lecture, media presentations, role-playing, simulations, demonstrations, and even laboratory investigations—to help the students achieve the objectives. The specific content and processes to be learned are contained explicity in the instructional input.
- *Modeling.* Through modeling, the teacher provides examples of the content knowledge and procedures to be learned.
- *Monitoring Understanding and Adjusting Instruction.* The teacher elicits active response from each student and assesses the response for evidence of understanding. The teacher adjusts instruction as necessary to improve understanding.
- *Independent and Guided Practice.* Because practice is essential to learning and retention, ample opportunity is afforded for students to practice the new content and processes.

A research study on the comparative effectiveness of inquiry and direct presentation methods of teaching science to junior high school students with learning disabilities is discussed in Chapter 9. Students understood concepts better and retained more with the inquiry approach. Also, students enjoyed the inquiry approach much more.

Well-structured lessons, whether they involve inquiry, direct instruction, or another approach, should involve daily review, clear presentation of objectives, active engagement by students, a variety of practice activities, regular evaluation of student products, and teacher questioning. Regardless of the instructional approach, effective teachers should also pay attention to such presentation variables as structure, clarity, redundancy, enthusiasm, appropriate rate of presentation, and maximum engagement through questioning and feedback. "If these variables are considered along with the specific needs of students during instruction," conclude Mastropieri and Scruggs (2004, p. 181), ". . . overall achievement will improve."

Selecting Instructional Approaches for Teaching Science

In addition to inquiry and direct instruction methods, a variety of other strategies available for use in science are presented in this book. The use of advance organizers in expository instruction is discussed in Chapter 3. Some of the questioning strategies of Chapter 5 work well with demonstrations. Projects as a strategy for learning science and assessing understanding is presented in Chapter 6. Learning centers and outdoor classrooms are discussed in Chapter 7. Reading as a strategy for learning science is discussed in Chapter 8. Web-based lessons are also presented in Chapter 8. Computer simulations and virtual field trips as teaching methods are introduced in Chapter 10. Role-playing as a teaching method is shown in the first Video Case Study featuring Erien. A study guide for this video is included in Chapter 5.

There is not one best way to teach all science concepts to all children. You cannot predict or guarantee how effective any individual method will be. Students differ in prior knowledge, experiences, learning abilities, preferred learning approaches, and the amount of structure they need in learning. Classroom and environmental factors vary and can affect teaching and learning. That is why you need to use a variety of teaching techniques.

What conclusions are you beginning to form about science teaching models and strategies? Although there are many valuable methods for teaching science, all children should experience the joy and satisfaction of asking questions about the natural world, finding ways to investigate and gather evidence, and, with their teachers' assistance, using their evidence to arrive at explanations that provide answers to their questions. In short, all children should have the opportunity to learn science through inquiry.

 Self-assessment questions for Chapter 4 are available at http://www.prenhall.com/carin. Use the questions to assess how well you understand this chapter and how prepared you are for a test over its content.

SUMMARY

- Inquiry instruction refers to any teaching procedure focused on developing science understanding *and* inquiry abilities. Student inquiry can be initiated from a wide range of activities. In answering their questions through inquiry, students devise ways to collect data and decide how to represent and organize the data. They coordinate data and prior or acquired scientific knowledge to explain and clarify their work to themselves and to one another. Throughout the inquiry process, teachers guide, focus, challenge, and encourage student learning, using their knowledge of students as well as their knowledge of science and how it is learned.

- Several different instructional strategies have been developed for guiding students in inquiry. In guided discovery approaches, children are presented with interesting questions and concrete materials. They work individually or in small groups to explore materials, make observations, and discover answers to their questions about the natural world. The teacher serves as facilitator and guide of the discovery process. For most children, there is joy in probing into and finding out about the unknown through discovery.

- The 5-E model of instruction is a second-generation version of the Learning Cycle model. The five E's in the model are engagement, exploration, explanation, elaboration, and evaluation. The 5-E model provides a specific focus on the NSES *Science as Inquiry Standards*. It also extends guided discovery strategies through the use of direct teaching of core concepts.

- Inquiry approaches to instruction are very compatible with conceptual change strategies. For example, in the 5-E instructional model, students are provided with specific opportunities to confront and deal with their naive theories and alternative conceptions, and to arrive at deeper understandings of scientific concepts, principles, and explanations of natural phenomena.

- No one method of teaching science is best for all teachers and all students, all the time, under all circumstances. Inquiry models of instruction mirror inquiry procedures of science, are consistent with constructivist approaches to learning, and are motivational and effective in teaching science to children. All children should have the opportunity to learn science through inquiry.

REFERENCES

American Association for the Advancement of Science. (1993). *Benchmarks for science literacy*. New York: Oxford University Press.

Anderson, C. W. (1987). Strategic teaching in science. In B. F. Jones et al. (Eds.), *Strategic teaching and learning: Cognitive instruction in the content areas*. Alexandria, VA: Association for Supervision and Curriculum Development.

Barman, C. R. (1990). *An expanded view of the learning cycle: New ideas about an effective teaching strategy* (p. 5). Monograph and Occasional Paper Series, no. 4. Washington, DC: Council for Elementary Science International.

Biological Sciences Curriculum Study. (1989). *New designs for elementary school science and health: A cooperative project of Biological Sciences Curriculum Study (BSCS) and International Business Machines (IBM)*. Dubuque, IA: Kendall/Hunt.

Biological Sciences Curriculum Study. (1999). *BSCS middle school science and technology*. Dubuque, IA: Kendall/Hunt.

Bransford, J. D., Brown, A. L., & Cocking, R. R. (Eds.). (1999). *How people learn: Brain, mind, experience, and school*. Washington, DC: National Academy Press. (Also available at http://www.nap.edu)

Brown, A. L., & Campione, J. (1994). Guided discovery in a community of learners. In K. McGilly (Ed.), *Classroom lessons: Integrating cognitive theory and classroom practice*. Cambridge, MA: The MIT Press.

Champagne, A. L., & Kouba, V. L. (2000). Writing to inquire: Written products as performance measures. In J. J. Mintzes, J. H. Wandersee, & J. D. Novak (Eds.), *Assessing science understanding: A human constructivist view* (pp. 223–248). New York: Academic Press.

Elementary Science Study. (1968). *Batteries and bulbs*. Cambridge, MA: Education Development Center.

Grahame, K. (1981). E. Shepard, Illus. *The wind in the willows*. New York: Charles Scribner's Sons.

Haury, D. L. (1993). Teaching science through inquiry. *ERIC CSMEE Digest* (March Ed 359 048).

Hunter, M. (1984). Knowing, teaching, and supervising. In P. A. Hosford (Ed.), *Using what we know about teaching* (pp. 169–192). Alexandria, VA: Association for Supervision and Curriculum Development.

Jacobson, W., & Kondo, A. (1968). *SCIS elementary science sourcebook*. Berkeley, CA: Science Curriculum Improvement Study.

Johnson, D. W., & Johnson, R. T. (1987). *Learning together and alone: Cooperation, competition, and individualization*. Upper Saddle River, NJ: Prentice Hall.

Jones, M. G., & Carter, G. (1997). Small groups and shared constructions. In J. J. Mintzes, J. H. Wandersee, & J. D. Novak (Eds.), *Teaching science for understanding: A human constructivist view*. New York: Academic Press.

Karplus, R., & Thier, H. (1974). *SCIS teacher's handbook*. Berkeley, CA: Science Curriculum Improvement Study.

Koch, J. (1999). *Science stories: Teachers and children as science learners*. Boston: Houghton Mifflin.

Kyle, W. C., Jr., Bonnstetter, R. J., & Gadsen, T., Jr. (1986). An analysis of elementary students' and teachers' attitudes toward science in process-approach vs. traditional science classes. *Journal of Research in Science Teaching, 25*, 103–120.

Lee, O. (2002). Promoting scientific inquiry with elementary students from diverse cultures and languages. In W. C. Secada (Ed.), *Review of research in education* (Vol. 26, pp. 23–69). Washington, DC: American Education Research Association.

Mastropieri, M. A., & Scruggs, T. E. (2004). *The inclusive classroom: Strategies for effective instruction*. Upper Saddle River, NJ: Merrill/Prentice Hall.

Minstrell, J. (1989). Teaching science for understanding. In L. B. Resnick & L. E. Klopfer (Eds.), *Toward the thinking curriculum: Current cognitive research* (pp. 129–149). Alexandria, VA: Association for Supervision and Curriculum Development.

Mintzes, J., & Wandersee, J. (1998). Research in science teaching and learning. In J. Mintzes, J. Wandersee, & J. Novak (Eds.), *Teaching science for understanding: A human constructivist view*. San Diego, CA: Academic Press.

National Research Council. (1996). *National science education standards*. Washington, DC: National Academy Press.

National Research Council. (2000). *Inquiry and the national science education standards: A guide for teaching and learning*. Washington DC: National Academies Press.

Rosebery, A. S., Warren, B., & Conant, F. R. (1992). Appropriating science discourse: Findings from language minority classrooms. *Journal of Learning Sciences, 2*(1), 61–94.

Rosenshine, B. V. (1986). Synthesis of research on explicit teaching. *Educational Leadership, 43*(7), 50–69.

Rowe, M. B. (1973). *Teaching science as continuous inquiry*. New York: McGraw-Hill.

Rowe, M. B. (1988). *Science helper K–8, Version 3.0*. Armonk, NY: The Learning Team.

Scruggs, T. E., Mastropieri, M. A., Bakken, J. P., & Brigham, F. J. (1993). Reading versus doing: The relative effects of textbook-based and inquiry-oriented approaches to science learning in special education classrooms. *Journal of Special Education, 27*(1), 1–15.

Sears, P. B., & Kessen, W. (1964). Statement of purposes and objectives of science education in school. *Journal of Research in Science Teaching, 2*(1), 3–6.

Shymansky, J. A. (1983). The effects of new science curricula on student performance. *Journal of Research in Science Teaching, 20*, 387–404.

Shymansky, J. A., Hedges, L. V., & Woodworth, G. (1990). A reassessment of the effects of inquiry-based science curricula of the '60s on student performance. *Journal of Research in Science Teaching, 27*, 127–144.

Shymansky, J. A., Kyle, W. C., Jr., & Alpert, J. M. (1982). How effective were hands-on science programs of yesterday? *Science and Children, 20*(3), 14–15.

Slavin, R. E.(1990). *Cooperative learning: Theory, research, and practice*. Upper Saddle River, NJ: Prentice Hall.

Stahly, L. L., Krockoveer, G. H., & Shepardson, D. P. (1999). Third grade students' ideas about the lunar phases. *Journal of Research in Science Teaching, 36*(2), 159–177.

Trowbridge, L., & Bybee, R. (1996). *Teaching secondary school science* (6th ed.). Upper Saddle River, NJ: Merrill/Prentice Hall.

Wiggins, G., & McTighe, J. (1998). *Understanding by design.* Alexandria, VA: Association for Supervision and Curriculum Development.

Wolfinger, D. M. (2000). *Science in the elementary and middle school.* New York: Longman.

5

In a science classroom that encourages students to construct understanding through scientific inquiry, questioning plays different roles during distinct phases of the learning process. An initial question posed by the teacher or raised by a student—Why are there waves in the ocean?—can set learning in motion and induce the class to conduct an experiment. . . . In the investigation stage, additional questions from the teacher and classmates—What would happen if you changed this?—help students see different routes to a solution and propose subsequent explorations and new hypotheses. When students are ready to propose explanations, questions help clarify, justify, and in some cases alter thinking. Did anything you discover surprise you? . . . A concluding round of questions—Where could you get more information on this topic?—can stimulate students to act on what they have learned.

(Kober, 1993, p. 44)

Questioning Strategies for Inquiry Teaching

ASKING THE RIGHT QUESTION is at the heart of doing science. John Dalton was a Quaker schoolmaster in Manchester, England, in the late 18th and early 19th centuries (Bronowski, 1974). Dalton took long walks in the English countryside every day. As he walked, he thought. The things he was interested in were the things of nature—the weather, the water, and the marsh gas that still characterize the Manchester environment today. Dalton particularly wondered about the patterns in the weather. For 57 years, day after day, he measured and recorded Manchester's temperature and rainfall. Of all that mass of data he gathered, *nothing whatsoever came.*

But Dalton also asked searching, almost childlike questions about the composition of water, of carbon dioxide, and of marsh gas (methane). He wondered how different chemical elements combine in the formation of these substances, for example, the way hydrogen and oxygen combine to form water. Dalton asked his questions in a way that they could be investigated. For instance, *Why is the ratio of the weight of oxygen to the weight of hydrogen always the same when water is formed?* Out of John Dalton's penetrating investigations of such questions came modern atomic theory. Jacob Bronowski (1974) said of Dalton's experience, "That is the essence of science: ask an impertinent question, and you are on the way to the pertinent answer" (p. 153).

Asking the right questions is also at the heart of learning and teaching science as inquiry. This chapter is intended to provide some guidelines as you help children learn how to form "impertinent" questions and as you form your own questions to guide their inquiry.

Here are our questions to guide your study of this chapter:

- *What is meant by open-ended and closed questions, and what are their functions in teaching science?*

- *How can you help children formulate productive questions to initiate investigation?*

- *What types of questions can teachers ask to guide children's inquiry and facilitate understanding?*

- *How can you strategically listen and respond to children to promote their science learning?*

Keep these questions in mind as you work your way through the chapter and lay a background for developing your own and children's questioning skills.

Collect responses to these questions as you find them in the chapter. The focus questions also appear on the Companion Website at http://www.prenhall.com/carin.

Questioning: An Essential Tool for Teachers

Questions are among the most important tools teachers have. Science teachers use questions for many purposes: to manage classroom activities, discourage inattentiveness, and cut down on disruptive behavior; to initiate inquiry; to focus and stimulate reflective thinking and encourage creativity; to structure a discussion, assess students' prior knowledge, and develop student understanding; and so on. To accomplish your instructional purposes, you need to use questions strategically—choosing the right type of question for the task at hand.

Strategic questioning involves selecting and using specific types of questions with well-defined functions (Gilbert, 1992). A specific questioning skill, such as asking open-ended questions, is like a tool used by a master carpenter. Tools have unique purposes. Different tools are needed by carpenters to drive a nail, to cut a board, or to square off the end of a piece of lumber. The master carpenter plans ahead by keeping a well-stocked toolbox and becoming proficient in using each tool. Similarly, different questioning tools are needed by master teachers, for example, to set the cognitive level of inquiry, to promote discussion by each class member, to stimulate deeper thought on the part of students, and to build meaningful explanations that connect investigative evidence to what students already know. Teachers, like carpenters, need well-honed tools that they know when and how to use.

Closed and Open-Ended Questions

One important tool in your questioning toolbox is the skill of knowing how and when to ask open-ended and closed questions. Both types of questions are important for assessing prior knowledge and promoting new learning, but in very different ways. A **closed question** has a single correct answer. Closed questions require students to think *convergently*, that is, to focus on a single fact, define a particular term, or attend to specific objects or specific aspects of events. Children's responses to closed questions help you assess their factual recall and observation skills and allow you to adjust your teaching accordingly.

An **open-ended question** is a question that can be answered in a number of ways. Open-ended questions enable all students to make useful contributions to a discussion (Cliatt & Shaw, 1985). Open-ended questions require children to engage broad portions of their schemas. They also trigger *divergent* thinking. In thinking divergently, children consider a wide array of possibilities.

Figure 5-1 provides a series of closed and open-ended questions about a pictorial riddle. The closed questions focus on specific observations and recall of prior knowledge and experience. The open-ended questions are broader questions that can engage students reflectively and build toward understanding.

In typical classrooms in every subject, the large majority of teachers' questions are closed, calling for factual knowledge and convergent thinking. Research indicates that even a slight increase in the percentage of open-ended questions by teachers yields a significant increase in divergent productivity by students; that is, a larger number of students respond, and their responses are more thoughtful and exhibit higher levels of thinking. These types of responses, in turn, stimulate further discussion among students (Carin & Sund, 1978).

In the following sections we describe some questioning strategies for engaging children in inquiry and guiding them as they discuss their observations, explanations, and applications of new ideas. Although the questioning strategies are organized around the 5-E model of instruction, as is shown in Table 5-1, it is often appropriate to apply the different types of questions in any phase. For example, observation questions might be asked in the exploration phase or to initiate the explanation phase of 5-E instruction. Similarly, observation, explanation, and application questions might all be used in the elaboration phase.

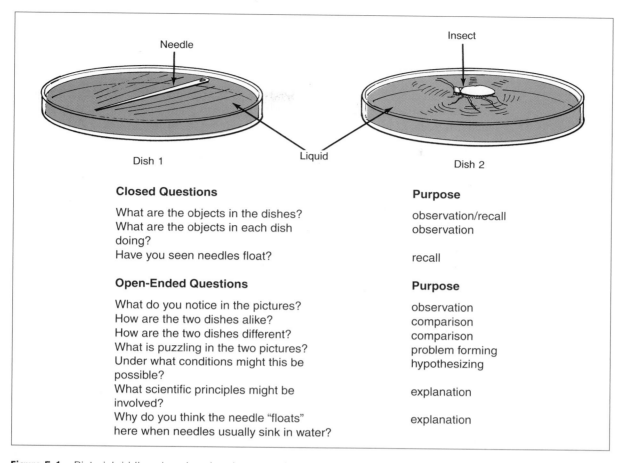

Figure 5-1 Pictorial riddle using closed and open-ended questions.

TABLE 5-1 STRATEGIC QUESTIONING FOR TEACHING SCIENCE AS INQUIRY	
Phases of 5-E Inquiry Instruction	**Description of Questions to Promote Inquiry**
Engage	*Prior Knowledge*. Ask questions to assess students' prior knowledge and conceptions. *Initiate Inquiry*. Ask questions that lead students to formulate simple questions to guide inquiry about objects, organisms, and events.
Explore	*Observation*. Ask questions to focus students' thought on their observations and data.
Explain	*Patterns and Relationships*. Ask questions that require students to identify patterns and relationships from their data; *Explanations*. Ask questions that require students to offer explanations of why an event took place.
Elaborate	*Application*. Ask questions that require students to apply new knowledge in new situations.
Evaluate	*Continual Assessment*. Ask questions that assess students' knowledge, understanding, and inquiry processes.

Using Questions to Engage Students in Inquiry

Engaging students in inquiry involves creating interest, generating curiosity, assessing what students know or think about the topic to be investigated, and raising questions to initiate and focus inquiry activities. Let us see how questioning can be used to facilitate these tasks.

Creating Motivation and Interest

Nothing creates intrinsic motivation in students more than presenting them with novel events and asking for explanations. With extrinsic motivation, the source of motivation lies outside the task. Grades and teacher approval are examples of outside sources of motivation. With intrinsic motivation, the source of learning is within the learner and the task itself. When individuals are intrinsically motivated, they engage in activities for their own sake and out of interest in and curiosity about the activity (Wigfield, Eccles, & Rodriguez, 1998).

Novel or discrepant events that provoke interest and reflection might be presented through hands-on student investigations, or you might present a demonstration using science materials. If time and resources are constrained, you could show a film segment or use a pictorial riddle instead.

To create a novel event with a surprising outcome for students,

- select a scientific concept or principle from the topic to be learned;
- present an activity or situation that involves the concept or principle in an unusual or surprising way; and
- formulate questions to stimulate students' thinking about the subject and set the intellectual stage for further scientific investigations.

Activity 5-1 shows a discrepant event that is sure to be interesting and puzzling to children. Try this activity yourself before reading further.

Have you formed an explanation about the phenomenon in Activity 5-1? Did you observe that the raisins initially sink to the bottom, and then rise to the top of the liquid, stay

Teaching for scientific literacy includes helping students "ask, find, or determine answers to questions derived from curiosity about everyday experiences."

(National Research Council, 1996, p. 22)

A few raisins placed in a glass of clear, carbonated soda water create a "raisin elevator."

Activity 5-1: A Raisin Elevator

- Place a few raisins in a glass of clear, carbonated soda water.
- Wait a minute or so.
- What do you observe?
- How would you explain the "raisin elevator" phenomenon?
- What scientific concepts and principles did you use in your explanation?

a moment, then descend once more, only to rise again? How did you explain this phenomenon? If you had appropriate prior experiences and scientific knowledge about floating and sinking, you might have inferred that the raisins were initially too heavy to float and, thus, sank. You might also have inferred that when the raisins rose in the liquid, somehow they had gotten lighter.

Explanations in science need to be checked out through further investigation. By looking very carefully, perhaps with a magnifying lens, children can watch the bubbles attaching themselves to the raisins when they are at the bottom of the carbonated drink and popping when the raisins reach the surface.

Novel events also provide an excellent context in which to assess students' prior knowledge and conceptions about a topic.

Questioning to Assess Prior Knowledge

To help your students build and strengthen their scientific concepts, you must be aware of what they know or do not know at the start of any study. You might assess children's prior knowledge by simply asking them what they already know about a topic. However, it is often better to provide a concrete activity so that students are called on to observe an object or event, form a question about why something happens, and recall relevant knowledge to be used in explaining the event. As children conduct an investigation or watch a demonstration, they typically talk about what they observe and think. By listening and interacting with the students, you will be better able to assess their prior knowledge and conceptions.

For example, in the raisin elevator activity, children display their prior knowledge of floating and sinking as they describe their observations, make predictions, draw inferences, and propose explanations about this discrepant event. In probing children's prior knowledge (as well as in generating interest and raising curiosity) you might ask:

What is happening in the glass?
What have you seen that is like this?
What is puzzling here? What needs explaining?
What might cause the raisins to rise? Why did they then sink in the water?

Students' responses to questions like these provide you with information about what they may already know and help you decide what you should do next in the teaching sequence.

Questioning to Initiate Inquiry

The very first task in inquiry, according to the *National Science Education Standards*, is to ask a simple question about objects, organisms, and events in the environment. There are dozens of things children wonder about and many questions they can ask. But which ones can be investigated through their hands-on activities? And what questions are most likely

The raisin elevator is used as an initiating activity to engage fourth graders and ascertain their prior conceptions in a floating and sinking lesson that is presented in Chapter 7.

to lead to significant results—from the perspective of young learners? How can we teach children to form simple questions that can guide their empirical investigations and lead to pertinent answers?

Questions requiring students to describe, classify, discover relationships, and form explanations can lead to productive investigations. Questions that can be investigated empirically can also come from considering unifying themes such as systems and interactions, change, and form and function (National Research Council, 1996, pp. 115–119).

Questions about Systems and Interactions. Asking questions about systems and interactions within them is often productive. Scientists define small portions, called "systems," for the convenience of investigating and describing the order and organization of the world (National Research Council, 1996, p. 116). A **system** is a group of objects or components that interact and form a whole. Some examples are solar systems, nervous systems, circulatory systems, and ecosystems.

Children tend to think of objects, their properties, and the ways the objects might change individually rather than in terms of a system. Thus, they need many opportunities to recognize and talk about the parts and interactions within small-scale systems. A small aquarium, for example, can provide a fascinating context for children to investigate interdependencies in aquatic life. They might be guided to ask:

How do fish interact with the plants in an aquarium?
What do the snails do in the aquarium?

These questions can lead to interesting descriptive investigations of aquariums and aquatic life.

Children might also be asked:

What are the essential parts of an aquarium?

They might decide initially that fish, snails, plants, and water are the essential components of the system. But what about air? Should the air above the surface of the water and the air pump also be a part of the system? These considerations might lead to a question about how fish breathe. Such a question can be investigated through observation and reading.

Focusing on the parts of the aquarium system, asking specific questions about the interactions of the parts, and observing over a period of days or weeks will allow students to explore how the various components in the system are interdependent.

Questions about Change. The natural world is characterized by change. Changes might occur, for example, in properties of materials, behaviors of organisms, and positions and motions of objects. Children can ask many questions about changes, for instance, about the changing appearance of the moon (as in Chapter 4's moon-watching lesson):

How does the moon change?
What is its rate of change?
Is there a pattern in the moon's changes?

Sometimes it is useful to measure changes. In investigating the nature of ice, for example, children might ask:

What happens to the temperature of water when ice is added?
Does the amount of water make a difference in the final temperature? Does the amount of ice make a difference?

These are kinds of questions that could be answered through experiments.

Questions about Form and Function. Asking questions about the form or parts of an object or organism and how these parts function can lead to productive descriptive, classificatory, and experimental investigations. In Chapter 2, we asked questions about the structure of seeds and plants and the functions of their various parts:

What are the parts of a seed?
What happens to the cotyledon as the young plant develops?
Do plants get water through their leaves or roots?

What questions about the structure of fish and the function of their different body parts might children ask to initiate investigations?

Questioning to Guide Discussion of Observations

One way children seek answers to their questions is through using the senses or instruments that extend the senses to observe what happens in an investigation or demonstration activity. Observing what happens familiarizes children with the natural world and provides the evidence for understanding it.

You can guide children in reflecting on their observations through the questions you ask. In general, observation questions should be open-ended. An open-ended question such as "What are some of the things you noticed during the demonstration?" allows many students to contribute useful information during inquiry.

Following are some suggestions you might follow and some sample questions you might ask or train students to ask to focus their attention on observing and describing.

1. In discussion with a group or a class as a whole, if you seek *descriptions of events* in an investigation, ask such questions as:
    *   What did you do?
    *   What happened in the experiment (activity, situation, investigation, demonstration)?
    *   What are some of the changes you noticed in the . . . ?
    *   What did you see that surprised you? (that you liked? that startled you?)

    By focusing on the aspect of an event that is puzzling, the last question begins to lay the groundwork for explanations.
2. Often discussion about observations occurs when children report their observations and data to the class. When groups report, train them to consider two kinds of questions about observational information (Rowe, 1973, p. 347):
    *   What was observed?
    *   In what sequence did events happen?

    Then, ask students to compare their observations:
    *   Were the observations of all groups the same? Are the reported sequences the same? How are they alike? How are the observations different?

    Differences among groups in reports of what they observed or the sequence of events observed can lead to disagreements. To resolve these disagreements, students must think more carefully about their data and sometimes repeat an activity. If students are unclear about what happened in an investigation, they will not have adequate evidence for constructing explanations for why it happened.
3. If the observations reported by groups represent numerical data, and you want children to consider and compare measurements (quantitative observations), you might ask:
    *   Which of the reported measurements is highest? Which is lowest?
    *   Why do you think there is variation in the class's measurements?

Organizing initiating questions around systems, change, and form and function draws on these *unifying concepts and processes* from the *Science Standards*: systems, order, and organization; change, constancy, and measurement; and form and function.

Discussing differences in the data reported by groups gives you an opportunity to discuss the nature of science with your students. According to the *Benchmarks for Science Literacy* (American Association for the Advancement of Science, 1993, pp. 6, 10), by the end of second grade, students should know that

- science investigations generally work the same way in different places; and
- when people give different descriptions of the same thing, it is usually a good idea to make some fresh observations instead of just arguing who is right.

Sometimes you want children to compare measurements and notice changes that occurred:

- What changes in the temperature of the water did you notice?

4. Novel or discrepant events offer excellent contexts for students to observe and later use their observations as evidence to develop explanations. If you seek descriptions of objects in a discrepant event or investigation, ask such questions as:
What objects do you see here?
What are some things you noticed about . . . in the investigation?
What was the sequence of events?

When working with small groups or the class as a whole, do not seek closure on a question until a number of responses have accumulated. Such a strategy not only gives more students a chance to enter into the discussion but also ensures that all students will have a variety of descriptive information from which to later build explanations. Observational information from students might be recorded on the chalkboard or on an overhead transparency.

When getting responses from several students on the same question, it is generally not necessary to repeat or rephrase the question. After one student has supplied an answer, you may *redirect* the question to another student by asking a question such as, "Juan, would you like to add anything else?"

It is important that children spend considerable time at the *observation* level before beginning to search for problem *explanations*. Unless sufficient time is spent in developing an adequate foundation at the lower cognitive level, students are often not able to sustain discussion at higher levels of thought.

Questioning to Guide Discussion of Explanations

Explaining is the counterpart of observing. In observing, students are directly involved with objects and events. Explanations require students to reason about their experiences and to make up and test interpretations of them. Careful observations determine *what* happens. Explanation is concerned with *why* it happened.

The *Science Standards* (National Research Council, 1996, p. 145) emphasize that in constructing explanations, students must think critically about evidence, considering which of their observations constitute evidence and which are irrelevant. They must also have adequate subject matter knowledge. Finally, they must be able to link their evidence with their knowledge in a reasonable way to explain why something happened.

In Chapter 3, we suggested that learners in grades K–2 observe the world using all of their senses, but typically do not construct consistent explanations of it. It is not until around grade 3 or 4 that children begin to distinguish between observations and interpretations of an event, and to construct simple explanations involving effects and their causes. Complex explanations involving chains of causes and effects are not formed until the formal operational period (see Table 3-2). Yet learners at every grade level can profit from considering why an event happened and how the world works.

When you are ready to shift instruction from an observation or exploration phase to explanation, let children help you decide which aspects of an investigation might need explaining. Find out what *they* want to know about the results of an investigation or why a puzzling event occurred. List the children's questions where they can see and think about them. Make sure that all children have a chance to frame their own questions.

In leading students to identify problems, you might ask:

What do you think needs explaining here?
What surprised you?
What is puzzling?

When attempting to focus thought on interpreting and explaining, a good approach is to start with the simpler problems that have been identified, gradually gather interpretative ideas, and build toward the more difficult problems.

A first step in developing explanations is for students to organize their data or observations in some way. To *organize* means to fit individual parts into an organic whole. Discussion of data and organization might take place as groups report their findings to the class, or perhaps in a whole class discussion.

Research suggests that understanding is enhanced when students actively integrate information in various ways (King, 1994). To help students see their data holistically rather than as fragmented parts, teachers might ask them to

* describe to others what they did and what they found out;
* summarize their data;
* organize their data/information into tables and graphs;
* elaborate information by adding details;
* generate relationships between the new material and information already in memory; and
* develop patterns from observational data.

For example, in developing ideas on *patterns*, ask such questions as:

How is this situation like (different from) the other one?
What similarities (differences) do you see in these situations?
Do you notice any pattern in your data (in your moon observations)?

Viewing data holistically is not enough, however. Kuhn, Amsel, and O'Loughlin (1988) found that children and adolescents had particular problems in coordinating evidence and theories. Through strategic use of questions, science teachers can help children reflect on and represent evidence more completely, think at deeper levels, and connect evidence and knowledge more logically in explaining events in the natural world.

Students may need considerable assistance in accessing prior knowledge to make sense of observations. Sometimes, as is emphasized in the Learning Cycle model of instruction, relevant scientific knowledge must be taught directly to students.

Here are some sample questions that focus on accessing knowledge and constructing explanation.

1. If you seek suggestions on *scientific knowledge* that might be involved in an explanation, ask such questions as:
   * What principles that we have learned do you think may come into play here?
   * What principles (rules, laws, concepts) do you think are needed in solving this problem?

- How do you think that (a particular principle) applies to this problem?
- What do we already know that might help us here?

2. If you seek ideas on the possible *cause of an event*, ask questions such as:
   - Why do you think (the event) happened?
   - What ideas do you have on why this happened?
   - What suggestions (guesses, theories) do you have about the cause of this?
   - Can you explain why it might have happened?
   - What do you think is the cause of . . . ?

Questions that focus on interpretation and explanation should be open-ended and divergent and should be pursued for a sufficient time to get responses from several students. This strategy helps to ensure that ideas and explanations at a variety of levels of abstractness are at hand for students of different abilities to consider.

Note the use of the personal pronoun *you* in the examples of explanation questions. Framing questions in this way helps to make them more open-ended, allowing children to respond at their own level of thought. An explanation question such as "What ideas do *you* have about why . . . ?" (rather than "Why did this happen?") focuses more on the act of thinking than on correct answers. This questioning approach frees children of the burden of knowing in advance why something took place. It encourages them to think about *possible* reasons for the cause of a puzzling event and to offer suggestions or theories to build on. Their initial responses need not be absolutely correct. The teacher, through sensitive listening, careful and caring questioning, and appropriate scaffolding, can help the class as a whole formulate a satisfying response that is age and grade level appropriate.

Questioning to Guide Discussions of Applications to New Situations

Children need opportunities to apply new knowledge and understanding in many problem-solving situations. Problems can be generated in various ways. For example, you may plan the problem situations, or they may arise from students' creative ideas and interests. As they work on fresh problems, students try out their recently learned ideas by transferring them to the new situations, thereby refining and elaborating their developing understanding. The application phase of a lesson thus allows students to make new connections and construct more useful schemas from the knowledge they gained in previous activities.

Application can often encompass science-technology-society (STS) approaches to studying human problems. As societies grow and change, particularly as they adapt to technological advances, problems are bound to arise. The process of problem solving typically includes analyzing problems of human adaptation, determining alternative choices, charting cost/benefit/risk factors, making decisions, and taking action (Pizzini, Bell, & Shepardson, 1988).

Here are some sample questions that focus on different aspects of application.

Extension of New Ideas to New Phenomena. To elicit thinking about how new knowledge and understanding might be extended to different phenomena, ask such questions as:

- How do you think . . . applies to . . . ?
- In what ways does this idea compare/contrast with . . . ?
- How can we use this principle to explain . . . ?
- What new problems does this suggest?
- What might happen if . . . ?

In the Annenberg Video Case Study featuring Erien (first year), Erien's fifth grade class studies STS issues related to wetlands areas. Which of these elaboration questions might be applied to focus and extend the lesson? A study guide for this video can be found in this chapter.

Investigating Science-Technology-Society Issues. To guide students to apply new learning in studying STS issues and problems, ask such questions as:

- How would you state the problem?
- What decisions need to be made?
- What are the alternative choices?
- How does what we have just learned apply here?

Making Decisions and Taking Action. To guide students to weigh risks and benefits of each choice and to consider different courses of action, ask:

- What are the consequences/benefits/risks of this choice?
- Who will be affected by this decision and in what way?
- What personal and societal values are related to this choice?
- In what ways are the choices related to these values?
- Which choice do you think is the best choice?
- What do you think should be done next?

Application opens up the opportunity for students to explore the natural and technological world more deeply and to realize how extensively science and technology affect people.

Next we look at ways you can respond to students' answers to facilitate and encourage inquiry.

Responding Strategically to Student Ideas

Instructional research indicates that student growth is influenced by teacher actions that involve students in the development and extension of ideas (King, 1994). There are three main ways you can respond strategically to nurture and extend children's ideas during inquiry (see Table 5-2). You can *accept* student responses without judging them; you can *extend* student responses by adding something new to what was said; and you can *probe* student responses by asking questions based on their responses.

Accepting Student Responses

Your inquiry teaching repertoire should incorporate an attitude of initial *acceptance* of student ideas, even when they contain errors, mistakes, and alternative conceptions. Students

TABLE 5-2 TEACHER RESPONSES THAT NURTURE AND EXTEND STUDENT INQUIRY	
Teaching Purpose	**Description of Response**
By responding strategically, teachers encourage critical discourse and communication of procedures, data, and explanations.	*Accepting.* Acknowledge and reinforce student responses; repeat or paraphrase student responses. *Extending.* Clarify, compare, or contrast student ideas; summarize and assess group progress; apply student ideas to explanations or problem solving. *Probing.* Building on ideas students have proposed, ask questions to get them to follow up on their own or other students' ideas, such as seeking clarification, justification, or verification of hypotheses.

VIDEO CASE STUDY: *ERIEN (YEAR ONE)*

Previewing the Video
As you watch this case study, use the Questions for Reflection for each of the three modules to guide your note taking, analysis, and discussion. For group discussions, choose a group facilitator to solicit various perspectives and keep the discussion on track.

Introducing the Case

Erien is a master's degree student doing her student teaching in a fifth grade classroom in a suburban school. Erien is an environmental science major and has chosen teaching as a career because she finds that helping students learn is exciting. The school in which Erien is student teaching is built near a wetlands environment: she has been asked to develop science activities about the wetlands that other teachers in the school can use. Erien begins this task by directing fifth graders to explore the soil in the wetlands area.

Questions for Reflection

1. What are some questions Erien poses to the students during the outside soil activity to help them focus on the *observations* they need to make?
2. What are some observations that students made of the soil in the school wetlands area?
3. Erien's science education mentor, Dr. Tom Dana of Pennsylvania State University, says that when teachers constrain students' inquiry a bit and get them focused, they are better able to get something out of an activity. Review the questions Erien asks students as they develop their soil profiles. What does Erien want students to understand about the soil they observe? What specific questions does Erien ask that "focus" her students on their task?
4. What tools does Erien have her students use to encourage their observations?
5. Why does Erien think that the students' outdoor experiences will result in an active classroom discussion?

Trying New Ideas
Erien asks her students to work within their groups and draw a large poster that illustrates their soil profiles. She then asks each group to describe their profile to the whole class. As you watch the presentations, reflect on the quality of the group posters, the descriptions students give, and the quality of the questions students ask one another.

When you review the students' group posters and class presentations, look and listen for the following:

- Description of soil properties
- Evidence of change based on depth
- Description of soil particles

Questions for Reflection

1. What surprised you about the various perspectives from which each group drew their soil profiles? How would you assess students' understanding of the lesson objectives based on their posters and presentations?
2. Dr. Dana indicated that although classroom discussions are generally loosely structured environments, they are valuable. Why? What added value to the classroom discussion you viewed for this case study module?

> "We really want children to be explorers and investigators and we want them to try to dictate for themselves what is the problem they should be exploring and what ways they are going to go about exploring that problem."
>
> *Dr. Thomas M. Dana, Pennsylvania State University*

Reflecting and Building on Change   *In the final module of this video case study, Erien engages students in a science-technology-society (STS) task. Although the task itself was a solid idea, classroom management became somewhat of an issue. What could Erien have done differently to ensure greater success with her culminating activity for this lesson?*

Questions for Reflection

1. How does Erien use the problem-solving activity and subsequent mock town meeting activity to lead students to generate and answer one another's questions?
2. Review what Erien's collaborating teacher, Judy Scannel, suggested to improve the town meeting activity. In what ways do you think such an activity might be modified to provide the student groups with more of the necessary information for asking and answering questions?
3. What ideas did Erien use in this STS activity that you might want to use in a similar activity? Review the table (below) of STS problem solving. What Procedures/Practices and Decision Making/Action Taking steps are present in Erien's lessons?
4. Look at the examples of application questions on pages 136–137. Which of these questions might be used to focus and extend the town meeting simulation?

Phases	Procedures/Practices	Decision Making/Action Taking
Seach (community events relevant to students' lives)		
Solve (students apply previously learned processes, procedures, and information to seek solutions)		
Create (students collect and analyze data)		
Share (students interact and communicate findings)		
Act (students act on their findings)		

should feel that they have the "right to be wrong." Because the very process of inquiry involves the challenge of trying the unknown, it necessarily must result in mistakes. The need to be always right, whether imposed by teachers, peers, or self, is a limiting and threatening position. Teachers have a major responsibility to help students explore new experiences and new meanings without penalizing the mistakes and wrong turns that are certain to accompany the process. By "accepting" children's ideas without initially judging or evaluating them, the teacher helps establish a climate in which students feel they can risk their ideas.

Teachers can show acceptance of student ideas by acknowledging, repeating, and reinforcing.

Acknowledging. When *acknowledging*, you should refrain from evaluating students' responses. This leaves the door open for further discussion. For example:

- OK.
- All right.
- Let's list your idea on the board.
- Let's keep your idea in mind.

You might also use nonverbal behaviors, such as a nod, to tell students that their responses have been heard and accepted.

Repeating. You can also show that you accept a student's idea by repeating it almost verbatim, or by paraphrasing the idea, without changing or adding to it significantly.
For example:

Student: Maybe it's the air leaking.
Teacher: OK. You think it may be the air leaking. (Repeating); or,
Teacher: OK. You think the bubbles may be caused by escaping air. (Paraphrasing)

Blosser (1991) cautioned against the overreliance on repeating student responses. If students know you are going to repeat responses, they may tend not to listen to one another but wait for your repetition. If you think the whole class has not heard a response, you might say something like:

Teacher: That's an interesting idea. I don't think the whole class heard it though. Would you say it again so everybody can hear?

Reinforcing. A third type of accepting behavior is *reinforcing* student ideas. It is an established principle of behavioral psychology that a person's tendency to display an action is dependent on events that follow the action. These special events are called reinforcements. In order to encourage student participation in discussion, a teacher may need to reinforce the act of responding. Teachers may also wish to reinforce good thinking and good ideas.
One way of reinforcing student responses is with praise. For example:

- Good!
- Fine!
- Excellent!

A stronger way of reinforcing children's responses is through praise followed by a word of explanation about the reason for the praise:

- Great! I like the way you are contributing.
- Good job! Your idea is particularly good because it relates your theory to your observations.
- Fine! I like the way you compared your idea to Celeste's idea.

Praise is important but should not be given in such a way that students think the idea praised is the only possible one. Other children might thus give up on their own lines of thought. Even when the idea you are seeking is voiced by a student, reinforce the child but let the class know there is more to be done. For example,

> *Teacher: Great thinking! Your idea is one we will have to consider. (Then, to the class) What other ideas do you have on why this happened?*

Reinforcement will be more effective if it follows an unpredictable schedule. If the student is able to predict that the teacher will say "very good" after every response, this form of praise will lose its effectiveness. For best results, the teacher should vary the type of reinforcements.

Reinforcement is, of course, more than a matter of what the teacher says. Both research and practice show that students are less inhibited about making responses and show more productivity and achievement when their teachers tend to be approving, to provide emotional support, to express sympathetic attitudes, and to accept their feelings.

Extending Student Responses

When students give vague, incomplete, unorganized, or partially incorrect responses, or when they are on the right track but need assistance, the teacher may act to nurture and extend their ideas. Perhaps the best reinforcement for students comes when they see their own ideas used by the teacher. Several techniques for extending student responses are described next.

Clarifying Student Ideas. To help clarify a student idea, a teacher may restate the idea in simpler terms, reorganize the idea, or perhaps summarize it. For example, suppose a student has given an unclear and unorganized response. The teacher may reply:

- In other words, the air takes up more space when heated. (Or)
- If I understand you correctly, you are saying that the air takes up more space when it is heated.

Compare or Contrast Student Ideas. When two or more students make suggestions that have significant similarities or differences, the teacher may wish to extend the ideas by comparing or contrasting them:

- Your idea is similar to Jamal's in that . . .
- Notice the difference in Kenesha's suggestion and Sean's suggestion. Kenesha said the wire would expand when it was heated; Sean said it would expand when it cooled. Both are good hypotheses. How could we test them?

Correcting Student Responses. There is uncertainty among teachers about how to handle incorrect ideas and misconceptions held by students. On the one hand, a student who is told that his idea is all wrong may be reluctant to participate in discussions again. On the other hand, misconceptions left unchallenged can cause confusion and interfere with correct explanations. Teachers need tactful ways of helping students confront and change wrong notions. One possibility is to determine if part of the student's answer is correct and to reinforce this part. For example:

> *Teacher: Yes, heat does play a part in the expansion of the copper rod, but melting does not take place. Remember, in melting, the solid rod would become a liquid. Can you make another suggestion?*

Applying Student Ideas in Constructing Explanations. Applying an idea suggested by a student in building an explanation is an excellent method of extending student ideas. However, teachers should be careful not to shift from extending student ideas to simply giving the desired information through lecture.

Summarizing Group Progress. To move the inquiry along, occasionally summarize the group's discussion and assess the various suggestions. This will not only extend students' ideas but also promote further inquiry. When the concepts involved are abstract or vague, when there are many responses, when student answers have been lengthy, or when some investigations have taken a great deal of time, you might say:

- Briefly, please summarize what you have just said.
- Tell us in your own words what we have learned.
- What were the main ideas discussed today?

Probing Student Responses

After a student has contributed an idea to a discussion, the teacher may attempt to produce greater critical awareness by probing (McDonald & Allen, 1967). Probing is a strategy in which the teacher reacts to student responses by asking penetrating questions that require students to go beyond superficial, first-answer responses.

Probing student ideas is different from *extending* student ideas in one main way: In extending, teachers add to student ideas; in probing, students are asked to add to their own ideas or those of others. A variety of probing techniques are given next.

Seeking Clarification of Ideas. A teacher may ask the child to clarify the response by giving more information, explaining a term used, or restating the response in other words. For example:

- What do you mean?
- Could you put that in other words to make clearer what you mean?
- Can you explain that further?
- What do you mean by the term . . . ?

The following interaction illustrates the clarification technique:

Teacher: What do you think is the relationship between the pressure of the air and its volume?
Student: The pressure got more and the gas condensed?
Teacher: Can you tell us what you mean by condensed? (Or) Can you restate that in terms of volume?

Seeking Justification of Ideas. Here you are asking the student to justify a response rationally. You might say:

- What are you assuming here?
- Why do you think that is so?
- I'm not sure I follow your reasoning. Tell us how you arrived at that answer.
- What evidence supports your idea?

Seeking Verification of Ideas. Here you are calling on the student to suggest means for testing or confirming a theory. For example, you may say:

- What would you do to test your idea?
- What would it take for that to be true?

- What evidence (additional information, data) would we need to test your explanation (suggestion)?
- What experiment could we do to test your idea?

Asking Questions Based on Student Ideas. Here the teacher takes a student response and builds a question based on it. For example:

- You have said that the bubbles are caused by escaping air. What do you think happens to the air pressure in the tube when some of the air escapes?

Develop Your Own Questioning and Responding Strategies

Developing personal competence in strategically guiding students in inquiry is a matter of

- fixing each questioning and responding skill and its purpose in mind,
- planning lessons carefully,
- using the inquiry discussion strategies in lessons with students, and
- analyzing the results.

This sequence should be followed by more practice in using the discussion strategy in teaching situations.

Analyze the teaching example in the next section to help you learn to use questioning and strategic responses in teaching science as inquiry.

Analyzing Inquiry Teaching Behaviors

Study the following dialogue in which teacher statements are numbered 1–22. Using the discussion in the previous sections and Tables 5-1 and 5-2 as guides, identify the specific type of question (observing or explaining) or responding skill (accepting, extending, or probing) that fits each of the teacher's questions or statements. Record your answers in the space provided. Note that some of the questions and statements may not fit any of the identified teaching skills.

In this dialogue, a discrepant event presented via video served as the engagement for the lesson segment. In the film, clear liquid was poured from two pitchers into two identical glasses. An ice cube was placed in each glass. Surprisingly, the ice cube floated in one glass but sank in the other (see Figure 5-2).

Dish 1   Dish 2

Figure 5-2 Why does one ice cube float and the other one sink?

Code each teacher question or response as one of the following:
a. Observation question
b. Explanation question
c. Accepting response
d. Extending response
e. Probing response
Answers are provided on pages 145–146.

_____ 1. Teacher: *What were some of the things you noticed in the film, Brad?*
Brad: *(Pause . . .) What did you say?*

_____ 2. Teacher: *Tell me some things you saw in the film.*
Brad: *There were two glasses of water. He put an ice cube in each glass.*

_____ 3. Teacher: *Good, Brad.*

_____ 4. Teacher: *Can you add anything, Sarah?*
Sarah: *The ice cube sank to the bottom in the glass on the right, but it floated in the other one. Maybe the ice cubes were different.*

_____ 5. Teacher: *OK, Sarah has an idea about why it happened—why one floated and the other one sank.*

_____ 6. Teacher: *But before we work on the "why," let's talk about what else you observed.*

_____ 7. Teacher: *What else did you notice in the film, Deion?*
Deion: *He poured the water out of different glasses.*

_____ 8. Teacher: *Good observing.*

_____ 9. Teacher: *But are you sure it is water?*
Deion: *Well it was clear; it was a clear . . . liquid. Maybe it was not water.*

_____ 10. Teacher: *OK.*

_____ 11. Teacher: *Let's go ahead and talk about why it happened.*

_____ 12. Teacher: *What needs explaining here? What do you wonder about, Chan?*
Chan: *I thought that ice always floats. Why did the ice cube sink?*
Linda: *Were the liquids the same?*
Erin: *Were the ice cubes the same? Maybe one was larger.*

_____ 13. Teacher: *Good. We have several questions to deal with.*

_____ 14. Teacher: *Actually, both cubes were plain ice cubes.*

_____ 15. Teacher: *What would happen if one cube were larger than the other one?*
Maria: *I don't think it would matter. Even icebergs float—like in* Titanic.

_____ 16. Teacher: *Good point, Maria.*

_____ 17. Teacher: *Big ice cubes and little ice cubes still float in water. Remember, we talked about density when we did the clay boats investigation. Big and little ice cubes have the same density and both float. Ice cubes get heavier as they get larger, but their volume—their size, the space they take up—also increases. That means they don't get too heavy for their size and sink.*

_____ 18. Teacher: *Why did one of the ice cubes float and the other one sink? Does anyone have an idea? Deion?*
Deion: *Maybe one of the liquids is not water.*

_____ 19. Teacher: *All right.*

_____ 20. Teacher: *Suppose one of the clear liquids is something other than water.*

_____ 21. Teacher: *What would that have to do with the ice cubes, Jennie?*
Jennie: *Maybe ice cubes don't float in all liquids. The egg floated in salty water but not in regular water.*

_____ 22. Teacher: *Perhaps. Would you like to investigate to find out?*

At this point in the lesson, the students wanted to experiment with different clear liquids to see if ice would float in each of them. The teacher had prepared for this particular investigation. With children helping her, she tried ice in tap water, salt water, bottled water, and Sprite, and it floated in each case. She also tried ice in rubbing alcohol, but the ice sank. The children excitedly said that the second liquid in the film was rubbing alcohol. The teacher confirmed this conclusion.

Using discrepant events can launch meaningful inquiry and questioning. In this mystery box, students speculate why moving the cardboard lever on one side of the closed box moves the lever on the other side.

If you have classified each of the teacher statements, let us talk about the lesson. After showing the brief videotape of the discrepant event, the teacher initiated the discussion with an *observation question* (question 1) intended to focus student thought at a level of observation. The student did not hear the question; the teacher resisted the impulse to admonish the student for not listening and simply phrased the *description question* (question 2) again. She *accepted* (3) Brad's answer, and *redirected* the *description question* (4) to another student. Note that the teacher was careful to ask the question first, then call on a particular student. This way, students could not relax because they did not know in advance who the question was for.

Sarah gave additional descriptive information but jumped to an explanation level with a suggestion about the two liquids. The teacher *accepted* (5) the student observations through acknowledging ("OK") and rephrasing them but brought the discussion back down to the description level (6). She was aware that the more descriptive information is on the table, the more likely the children would be able to sustain thought at the higher level.

The teacher redirected the original *description question* (7) to Deion. The teacher *accepted* (8) Deion's answer but chose to *probe* (9) it to get him to think a little deeper about what he had said. She then *accepted* (10) Deion's answer. Next the teacher made a comment showing that she had determined to raise the level of thought to interpretation (11). Rather than defining the problem herself, however, she asked the children to tell what needed explaining (12). She *accepted* (13) the students' problem statements, and then *extended* (14) one of the student's ideas by giving information about the ice cubes.

Next, the teacher constructed an explanation question (15) related to the size of the ice cubes. She *accepted* (16) a student's response, then chose to *extend* (17) the response with a little lecture, helping children to bring to mind some things they had already worked on. She then developed an explanation question (18) around another aspect of the problem. She *accepted* (19) a student response with the short "All right," then rephrased the response, which is also categorized as *accepting* (20). She then asked a *probing question* (21) to get the students to think a little more on the response. Finally, the teacher brought out the materials she had prepared so the children could go to nature to check their ideas. The final question (22) is simply rhetorical.

Let us look at a first grade classroom dialogue illustrating how teachers can use questioning to guide children's inquiry in constructing new knowledge in science.

Questioning Strategies in the Classroom: Properties of Air in First Grade

In this classroom dialogue, Ms. Newhall is teaching her first grade children that "air" is a real material substance that, like solids and liquids, takes up space. She is also trying to help them become better observers and use their observational evidence in drawing conclusions.

In the lesson, Ms. Newhall has a fish bowl about three-quarters full of water and a small, transparent glass. She plans to push the small glass, open-end down, all the way under the water, as in Figure 5-3, and to ask the children what they saw and why they think it happened. In preparation for studying the classroom dialogue, you should do the activity for yourself. Then, as you study the dialogue, think about the type and function of each of the questions the teacher asks and the responses that she gives to student statements and questions.

Before beginning the actual demonstration, Ms. Newhall questioned the children to ascertain their prior knowledge.

> *Teacher: I'm going to push this glass into the water until it is all the way under the water. What will happen? Terry, what do you think?*
> *Terry: It's going to stay at the bottom. . . . Sink.*

Ms. Newhall wanted the children to focus on the air and the water rather than the glass. So, with a nod acknowledging Terry's answer, she turned to another student who had her hand up.

> *Teacher: Samantha.*
> *Samantha: Me and my dad took a glass into the pool one time. We put the glass under the water. We kept it straight, and if you keep it straight, no water will come in. The air will stay in there, but if you tip it up the water will come in.*
> *Teacher: Interesting.*

Samantha's answer revealed that she had significant prior experience and knowledge about what would happen in the demonstration. Some of her knowledge came from personal discoveries. She had also acquired some knowledge from discussions with her father about the pool-glass activity. Samantha used the term *air* appropriately, but Ms. Newhall was not sure what she really *understood* about the concept of air.

Ms. Newhall acknowledged Samantha's answer and filed it away for later use. But she wanted to know what the other children knew

This dialogue is from a Merrill video called *Properties of Air in First Grade Science*. This video is included in the set of videos on science education available to instructors using this book. Excerpts from the video lesson described here can be seen in the *Virtual Classroom* link on the Companion Website for Chapter 5 at http://www.prenhall.com/carin.

A variety of lesson activities on properties of air can be found in *Activities for Teaching Science as Inquiry*, the companion volume to this text.

Figure 5-3 What happens when a glass is pushed open-end down into a container of water?

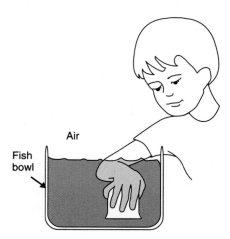

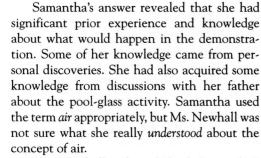

about air and what they thought would happen in the demonstration. So she turned to the class again.

> *Teacher: Is there anybody else who thinks if you put this whole glass under the water, nothing is going into the glass? What do you think, Michelle?*
> *Michelle: Water may go in the glass.*

After giving the rest of the class time to offer opinions, Ms. Newhall polled the students to see which of the two ideas they supported. There was about equal support for Samantha's idea that the air would keep the water out and Michelle's idea that the glass may fill up with water. Then the teacher continued with the demonstration.

> *Teacher: OK. We have two ideas. Let's test these ideas.*

Ms. Newhall called on a student to help her with the demonstration. First, she asked the student to check to make sure the glass was dry. To encourage careful observation, she told the students to "watch with your eyes." Then she pushed the glass open-end down all the way under the water. Most students noted that the water did not get into the glass, but one student was not sure.

Ms. Newhall then dried the glass carefully, took a paper towel, and crumpled it into the bottom of the dry glass. She pushed the glass with its open end down under the water again. When she removed the glass from the water, she asked a child to examine the paper towel, and the child observed that it was dry. The teacher then attempted to lift the children's thought from a level of description to a higher cognitive level through asking an explanation question.

> *Teacher: Why did it stay dry? What do you think, Jessica?*
> *Jessica: Because it was inside that glass and the rest is outside.*
> *Teacher: But what kept the water out? Anthony?*
> *Anthony: A water seal. It was pooled up. There was water on the bottom, but not on the inside.*
> *Teacher: But if there's all that water around the outside, why didn't it go in here (pointing to the inside of the glass)?*
> *Student: Because the air was in there.*
> *Teacher: The air. . . . Oh . . . Is that what kept the water out?*

The initial answers to Ms. Newhall's question about why the paper towel stayed dry indicated that the children did not yet have a good understanding of air. Although they knew the term *air* and had connected it to some physical situations such as wind and breathing, they had difficulty applying the concept in interpreting the demonstration. When one child said that the air kept the water out, Ms. Newhall decided to follow up on Samantha's earlier contribution.

> *Teacher: Samantha said something earlier. When she put the glass down straight the glass stayed dry, but when she pushed it down and tipped it, the glass got wet.*

Ms. Newhall then demonstrated that when she tilted the glass, bubbles came from the glass and rose in the water. She tried to get the children to describe the bubbles as bubbles of air. However, the children described the bubbles as "water bubbles" and in other ways, but no one used the term "air bubbles." So, the teacher attempted to extend the children's thinking by giving them a hint.

> *Teacher: In the bottom half of the glass is water; in the top half of the glass is . . .*
> *Student: Dry.*
> *Teacher: What is in there?*

No answers were forthcoming, so the teacher then gave an explanation.

> *Teacher: When I tip it (a small amount), the water keeps the air in. When I tilt it far enough, the air can come out.*

There is much for you to model from the teacher in this lesson. She strategically used some exceptional science questioning techniques.

- First, she asked prediction questions to ascertain the students' prior knowledge.
- Then, she asked observation questions to get the children to focus on *what* happened and to help them improve their observational skills.
- Only after sufficient evidence had been introduced into the discussion did she ask explanation questions, focusing on *why* the events happened.
- She did not immediately acknowledge that Samantha's initial answer was correct but kept the discussion open so that all children could enter in and possibly construct knowledge about air for themselves.
- Also, she asked her questions before calling on a student by name, thus helping to ensure that all students would have to listen to the questions.
- She kept the discussion orderly, asking students to raise their hands when they wished to volunteer an answer.
- She called on a diversity of students, making sure she included both boys and girls and children of all ability levels.

Despite the teacher's use of model teaching techniques, the children had difficulty constructing notions about air and its properties that would be useful in *understanding* why the paper in the glass remained dry. That is, the children still had problems in *applying* their knowledge to *explain* or make sense of the demonstrations involving air.

From the perspective of child development theory presented in Chapter 3, most of these young students have simply not yet developed the type of relational thinking that will support the construction of complex explanations. Nevertheless, through their discoveries and the teacher's discussion, the children are building knowledge to apply in future knowledge construction experiences when they are more developmentally ready.

Some Considerations in Questioning

Through your questioning, your body language, your treatment of students, and your general demeanor, you are establishing the climate of your classroom. Here are some general considerations to think about as you guide students through questioning, listening to them, and responding.

Increase Your Wait-Time

Elementary and middle school teachers often feel pressured to cover everything in the few hours that students are in the classroom each day. So it is no surprise that teachers try to rush through many of the things they do, even question-and-answer times. Rowe (1973, 1987) found that most teachers usually wait less than a second for a response after asking a question! These very brief intervals, or **wait-times**, encourage rote, verbatim recall, usually of textbook or teacher-made information. In contrast, inquiry requires time for students to reflect, make connections, and construct inferences and explanations.

What differences in student responses do you think were found with longer teacher wait-times? Rowe found that teachers who waited three seconds or longer got greater speculation, conversation, and argument than those teachers with shorter wait-times. She also found that when teachers are trained to wait an average of more than three seconds before responding, the following positive student behaviors happen:

1. The length of student response increases by 400 to 800%.
2. The number of unsolicited but appropriate responses increases.
3. Failure to respond decreases.
4. Confidence increases.
5. The number of questions asked by students increases.
6. Slow students contribute more.
7. The variety of types of responses increases. There is more reacting to each other, structuring of procedures, and soliciting.
8. Speculative thinking increases by as much as 700%.
9. Discipline problems decrease.
10. Achievement improves in cognitively complex items on written tests (Rowe, 1987).

Rowe also found that teachers trained to prolong wait-time changed their teaching behavior in the following ways:

1. The number of teacher questions decreased, because more students responded and the responses of students became longer.
2. The number of teacher questions that called for reflection and clarification increased.
3. Teacher expectations for student performance were modified. (Teachers were less likely to expect only the brighter students to reply and viewed their class as having fewer academically challenged students.)
4. Teachers changed the direction of discussion from teacher-dominated to teacher-student discussion.

There are two types of wait-time. **Wait-time 1** is the pause that follows a question by the teacher. The students may answer quickly, but if they do not, the teacher waits. **Wait-time 2** is the pause that follows a burst of responses by the students. The teacher waits before responding or asking another question to see if the students will continue to talk.

Of the two, Rowe (1987) indicated that wait-time 2 is more important for a teacher to develop. She found a 500 to 700% increase in student responses when teachers used it. The responses from the academically challenged students, furthermore, increased significantly when teachers increased their wait-time after student talk.

Instructors need to increase their wait-time tolerance so learners have more opportunities to think, create, and fully demonstrate their potential.

Gradually Fade Your Questioning Support

Teachers model, coach, and scaffold thinking behaviors through their questions. But gradually, students should come to ask self-regulatory questions themselves as teachers fade their support (Bransford, Brown, & Cocking, 1999). This approach highlights the importance of students' **metacognition** in planning, monitoring, and adjusting their own learning and inquiry behaviors. Thus, as teachers use questioning strategies, they are not just scaffolding student understanding, they are teaching students how to formulate productive inquiry questions for themselves.

Listen to One Another

Listening carefully and sensitively—not only to the answer but to the thinking behind the answer—provides you with much information about your students. The way teachers perceive their roles is undoubtedly related to their listening skills. If you see your function as mainly to develop or achieve some subject matter concept or principle, you naturally will focus on its achievement. However, if you perceive your role as helping students develop cognitively and construct their own concepts and understanding, you will tend to focus on the students, as well as on the content. To help students make discoveries and use their own developing thought processes, listen intently to what they have to say. Formulate questions and responses only when they have finished. There is no substitute for a teacher who is primarily interested in people and really listens to them.

Try not to analyze, evaluate, or judge what students are saying until after they have completed their thoughts about the questions. Unfortunately, some teachers start to dissect what students say before they have had a chance to finish. Many students' ideas are good, but they suffer from poor verbalization. If you wait until students finish their answers before reacting, you will grasp their ideas better and be more likely to convey in nonverbal ways that you are sincerely interested in their ideas. If you are not clear about what the children are saying, you can engage them in discussion to clarify their meanings, by asking a probing question.

Students often do not learn and achieve as well as they could because they have not developed their own listening skills. By modeling good listening yourself, you can help your students become better listeners.

Consider Cultural Implications of Your Questions

Because of students' diverse backgrounds, questions may take on different meanings for different students (Bransford et al., 1999). For example, research indicates that African American parents engage in different patterns of questioning with their children than do their white counterparts. African American parents are likely to emphasize metaphorical questions ("What is that like?") rather than fact-gathering questions ("What is that?"). Thus, African American students may not understand the purposes of white teachers' inquiry questions. According to Bransford et al. (1999), the answer to cultural mismatch between schools and communities "is not to concentrate exclusively on changing children or changing schools, but to encourage adaptive flexibility in both directions" (p. 99).

Some Native American students are averse to responding when called on in class. It may be that they perceive the traditional classroom, where teachers control all activities and interactions with one student as classmates look on, as very different from their community social events, where there are no clear leaders and no clear separation between performers and audience. These students usually perform better one-on-one with the teacher or in cooperative settings with small groups of classmates (Vasquez, 1990).

You must know your students well so that your manner of questioning and presentation does not conflict with their cultural backgrounds.

Remember, We All Need Strokes!

Research indicates that teachers should use praise judiciously when they guide discussions. Praise can provide a signal to students that their contributions to discussion are appropriate. But praise of one student's answer might also tend to stop discussion. Other students may think that the purpose of the inquiry discussion is to find the right answer, not to probe more deeply into nature. Students look to their teacher for guidance and approval.

However, it is important to recognize students during individual work and group work for specific things they have done well (Lepper & Hodell, 1989). Teachers who try to look for good in every student and who inform them specifically and privately about these things are effective. They also are more likely to enjoy teaching. It is possible to look for something good to say to each individual, for example, when they come into class or in private discussions. As Abraham Maslow indicated in his theory of human needs, we all need to be recognized as valuable persons so our self-concepts continue to grow positively (Maslow, 1987).

Use the self-assessment questions for Chapter 5 at http://www.prenhall.com/carin to assess how well you understand this chapter and how prepared you are for a test over its contents.

SUMMARY

- Questioning is at the heart of inquiry teaching. By questioning effectively you can ascertain what students already know, guide them in establishing questions for inquiry and in collecting relevant data, help them construct explanations, and lead them to apply their new knowledge in different situations.

- Open-ended questions are more likely to promote inquiry than closed questions. Questions can be used to assess the prior knowledge and conceptions of students. Questions can also be used to engage the interest and motivation of students, to guide them in exploring systems, and to lead them in building explanations. Questions are also important in leading students to apply what they are learning to new situations, including societal issues and concerns.

- How you respond to students' answers is very important in ongoing inquiry discussion. To keep students involved, be accepting of all their (relevant) answers; to keep them on target and supply needed information, extend their answers by adding to them; to lead them to think about their own ideas more deeply, probe their responses by building additional questions on them.

- After asking a question and calling on a student, teachers often wait only a second or two for students to compose and state their answer. When teachers wait just a little longer, three seconds or more, students tend to think more deeply, give longer answers, provide a wider variety of answers, and respond to one another more often.

- Learning to use questions effectively and productively in inquiry teaching takes practice, feedback, and reflection. Keep honing your questioning and responding tools to better guide children's inquiry.

REFERENCES

American Association for the Advancement of Science. (1993). *Benchmarks for science literacy*. New York: Oxford University Press.

Blosser, P. (1991). *How to ask the right questions*. Arlington, VA: National Science Teachers Association.

Bransford, J. D., Brown, A. L., & Cocking, R. R. (Eds.). (1999). *How people learn: Brain, mind, experience, and school*. Washington, DC: National Academy Press. (Also available at http://www.nap.edu)

Bronowski, J. (1974). *The ascent of man*. Boston: Little Brown.

Carin, A. A., & Sund, R. B. (1978). *Creative questioning and sensitive listening techniques: A self-guided approach*. Upper Saddle River, NJ: Merrill/Prentice Hall.

Cliatt, M. J. P., & Shaw, J. M. (1985). Open questions, open answers. *Science and Children, 23*(3), 14–16.

Gilbert, S. W. (1992). Systematic questioning. *The Science Teacher, 59*(90), 41–46.

King, A. (1994). Guiding knowledge construction in the classroom: Effects of teaching children how to question and how to explain. *American Educational Research Journal, 31*(2), 338–368.

Kober, N. (1993). *EDTALK: What we know about science teaching and learning*. Washington, DC: Council for Educational Development and Research.

Kuhn, D., Amsel, E., & O'Loughlin, M. (1988). *The development of scientific thinking skills*. New York: Academic Press.

Lepper, M. R., & Hodell, M. (1989). Intrinsic motivation in the classroom. In C. Ames & R. Ames (Eds.), *Research on motivation in education: Vol. 3. Goals and cognitions.* San Diego, CA: Academic Press.

Maslow, A. H. (1987). *Motivation and personality* (3rd ed.). New York: Harper and Row.

McDonald, F. J., & Allen, D. W. (1967). *Training effects of feedback and modeling procedures on teaching performance.* Palo Alto, CA: Stanford Center for Research and Development in Teaching, Stanford University.

Merrill Education. (1999). *Properties of air in first grade science.* Upper Saddle River, NJ: Merrill/Prentice Hall.

National Research Council. (1996). *National science education standards.* Washington, DC: National Academy Press.

Pizzini, E. L., Bell, S. A., & Shepardson, D. P. (1988). Rethinking thinking in the science classroom. *The Science Teacher, 55*(9), 22–25.

Rowe, M. B. (1973). *Teaching science as continuous inquiry.* New York: McGraw-Hill.

Rowe, M. B. (1987). Wait-time: Slowing down may be a way of speeding up. *American Educator, 11*(1), 38–47.

Vasquez, J. A. (1990). Teaching to the distinctive traits of minority students. *The Clearing House, 63,* 299–304.

Wigfield, A., Eccles, J. S., & Rodriguez, D. (1998). The development of motivation in school contexts. In P. D. Pearson & A. Iran-Nijad (Eds.), *Review of research in education* (Vol. 23). Washington, DC: American Educational Research Association.

6

T eaching and assessment are mirror images of one another. Assessment guides instruction, and instruction guides assessment. . . . Assessment should be a continuous process
involving listening, observing, and asking questions to promote intellectual growth.

(Foster & Heiting, 1994)

Assessing Science Learning

🦟 *Students observe as a classmate strokes a needle with a magnet, then lays the needle on a Styrofoam chip floating in a container of water. The floating needle moves around a bit, but when it settles down, it seems to point in a fixed direction. The students each draw a line down the middle of a page in their science logs. On one side, they write everything they know about what they just saw; on the other side, they list questions and things they would like to know about what happened in the investigation and why it happened. Small groups pool their knowledge and questions before sharing them with the class.*

🦟 *After watching the moon every night for 2 weeks, students respond to multiple-choice questions on moon phases and their causes and explain their answers through drawings, in writing, and, later, in discussion. A teacher studies the answers and explanations to determine student misconceptions that might interfere with learning about lunar phases.*

🦟 *A student ponders a written statement: "You have just found an unusual rock in the park. Draw a concept map and use it to show how you would determine whether the rock is sedimentary, igneous, or metamorphic."*

🦟 *A teacher displays rolls of three different brands of paper towels to the class. She says: "Your job is to test these paper towel brands for a consumer magazine. What factors will you test? How will you determine which brand is the best buy?" Students work together in small groups to formulate and carry out a plan for investigation, write a brief report, and present their results to the rest of the class. The teacher circulates among the groups, keeping notes and marking a check sheet.*

What do these four situations have in common? All of them involve assessments that are closely linked to instruction. Assessment takes place at the beginning of instruction (the first case), during instruction (the second and fourth situations), and at the end of instruction (the third case). In the first two situations, students' conceptions and misconceptions are being assessed prior to instruction; understanding of concepts learned in instruction is being assessed in the third situation; and inquiry skills are being assessed in the fourth situation. Assessment is an ongoing process, not one that occurs just at the end of a period of instruction.

Assessment methods and uses are changing to correspond to new understandings of learning and teaching. In the past, concern with assessment techniques took a back seat to

NSES You can review the Assessment Standards that are part of the *National Science Education Standards* online. Go to http://www.nap.edu/readingroom/books/nses/html.

Collect responses to these questions as you find them in the chapter. The focus questions also appear on the Companion Website at http://www.prenhall.com/carin.

learning theory and instructional reforms. Today, assessment is an integral part of the teaching-learning process. According to the *National Science Education Standards* (National Research Council, 1996), in the new view of science education,

> assessment and learning are two sides of the same coin. The methods used to collect educational data define in measurable terms what teachers should teach and what students should learn. And, when students engage in an assessment exercise, they should learn from it. (p. 76)

To participate in this assessment transformation, you will need to develop new assessment techniques, and you will need to use traditional techniques in more creative ways. In this chapter we will consider the following questions:

> *What is meant by "assessment" and what are the purposes of assessment in science classrooms?*
> *What is meant by "formative assessment" and "summative assessment"? How does formative assessment link to inquiry instruction?*
> *What is performance assessment and how does it differ from traditional assessment methods?*
> *What are the components of an effective performance assessment task?*
> *What specific assessment techniques can be used to assess science knowledge, understanding, and inquiry procedures as described in the* Science Standards?

What Is Assessment?

Assessment is a process. Teachers gather information on student learning through tests, performance tasks, worksheets, checklists, watching and listening to students, and so on. By emphasizing multiple means of collecting student data on a variety of variables, assessment goes beyond mere testing.

Uses and Users of Assessment Data

Assessment and evaluation are closely related concepts. Assessment involves collecting data, while evaluation involves using that data in judging student performance and making decisions. Teachers, students, parents, administrators, and legislators need different kinds of assessment information for different purposes (see Table 6-1).

Administrators must have accurate assessment data to make decisions about budgets, policies, personnel, space and time allotments, student promotion and graduation, student placement in special programs, and many other aspects of schooling. Legislators increasingly need assessment results to make judgments related to the accountability of schools, equitable opportunities for all students to learn, and legislative actions. The assessment data used by administrators and legislators usually comes from standardized, multiple-choice tests administered once each year. Because critical decisions about students, teachers, and schools are often made from such tests, they are sometimes referred to as "high-stakes" tests.

In order to work in tandem with the school, parents need information about their children's learning performance and progress. Assessment results can be communicated to parents through such means as report cards, progress reports, telephone calls, and informal notes. Informed parents can help improve their children's learning in myriad ways, such as by stressing the importance of school learning, providing learning incentives, providing a place and time for children to do homework, seeing that school assignments are completed, and working with their children in supplementary learning experiences.

Users of Assessment Data	Purposes	Frequency	Results	Assessment Types
TABLE 6-1 DIFFERENT AUDIENCES USE DIFFERENT TYPES OF ASSESSMENT RESULTS FOR DIFFERENT PURPOSES				
Teachers	planning, monitoring, evaluating, and adjusting instruction and learning procedures; assisting students in learning; assigning grades	daily	immediate; gained through classroom observation of student performance and products	variety of assessment types, formal and informal performance assessment tasks, traditional tests
Students	feedback about learning performance and progress	daily	communicated directly from teacher	traditional tests, performance tasks, teacher observation, self-assessment
Administrators, Legislators	accountability; budget, policy, and personnel decisions; student placement, promotion, and graduation	once each year	delayed, calculated outside of schools and made available at a later date	standardized tests; multiple-choice and short-answer items so many objectives can be assessed in a short period of time
Parents	feedback about their children's learning performance and progress	as needed, at least once each grading period	immediate or delayed, communicated directly from teachers or students	traditional tests, performance tasks, teacher observation

Assessment should help make students' work and progress understandable to students and parents. It should also guide further instruction.

Assessment results should be shared with students. By continually sharing assessment procedures and results with students, increased interest, direction, and motivation can be attained. Knowledge of formal and informal assessment results can

1. clarify the most important learning objectives for the students;
2. engage students more actively in their own learning;
3. inform students of what they understand and do not yet understand about a topic;
4. invite students to set realistic and attainable goals for themselves;
5. show students that progress has been made, no matter how small, to help them attain satisfaction and a desire to continue learning;
6. guide students to become increasingly self-directed as they put into perspective where they have been, where they are now, and where they should be in the future; and
7. show students that an adult really cares about their progress.

Our focus in this chapter is with the use of classroom assessment data by teachers. Think of classroom assessment as a tool used in the service of learning and instruction. The following three principles describe what should be done to connect assessment to learning and instruction in the classroom:

- Teachers should provide students opportunities to learn *Standards*-based science in active ways.
- Students should be required to show evidence of their learning through formal or informal assessments.
- Teachers should use the results of assessments to modify instruction and guide the improvement of student learning.

Effective assessment does not just happen by chance. It must be well thought out and executed daily from your first to your last day of school. In realistic terms, you use assessment procedures each time you engage in *any* teaching function with your students. Every question you ask and every observation you make in the learning process is an assessment probe to find out more about your students, what they do and do not know, and how they are reacting to your teaching. This is the type of information you need to make decisions about modifying teaching to improve learning.

 NSES   **Assessment Standard A**

Assessments must be consistent with the decision they are designed to inform.

- Assessments are deliberately designed.
- Assessments have explicitly stated purposes.
- The relationship between the decision and data is clear.

Assessment Standard B

Achievement and opportunity to learn science must be assessed.

- Achievement data should focus on the science content that is most important for students to learn.
- Equal attention must be given to the assessment of opportunity to learn and to the assessment of student achievement.

Diagnostic, Formative, and Summative Assessment

It is useful to think about and plan for student assessments in terms of diagnostic, formative, and summative purposes.

Diagnostic assessment, sometimes called preassessment, is used *before* you start teaching material to discover needed information about your students' knowledge, interests, abilities, and preferences. Diagnostic questions asked and observations made at the beginning of a lesson (in the engagement phase of the 5-E instructional model, for example) can help you identify what students already know about a topic, the misconceptions and alternative theories they carry, and what they are interested in learning. By using informal questioning, performance assessments, paper-and-pencil tests, and inventories diagnostically *before* you begin teaching, you can decide what specific experiences will best encourage students' science progress. Diagnostic data will help you adjust your instructional strategies to your students' individual differences.

Formative assessment is the crucial classroom-based element of a balanced assessment system. **Formative assessment** is used *during* your teaching to discover what your students are learning (or not learning) and to supply you with feedback to modify your lesson plans and teaching methods where needed.

The interactive approach in teaching science as inquiry provides teachers with unique opportunities to make reflective judgments based on concrete evidence of students' accomplishments. By asking key questions, using the performances and products of students, and administering assessment tasks of various designs, teachers can quickly spot science areas that students have been exposed to previously, ascertain the quality of their understanding and inquiry strategies, probe their misconceptions and alternative theories, and sense their attitudes and predispositions toward science. Knowledge of where the students are in learning provides teachers a basis on which to improve understanding, skills, and attitudes.

To act on formative assessment information, you must decide how you can scaffold learning. How can you provide just the level of assistance each student needs to move up the learning ladder to higher levels of achievement, understanding, and performance? Based on formative assessment data you might decide to

- simplify the learning task by breaking it into smaller components for the learner;
- ask meaningful questions that students can use to move to the next level;
- lead learners to clarify, elaborate, or justify their responses;
- define terms, invent concepts, and supply necessary information or direct learners to appropriate sources;
- carefully describe thinking processes students should model in inquiry; and
- provide graphic organizers, such as diagrams and concept maps, to aid students in making difficult connections (Grigorenko, 1998; Roehler & Cantlon, 1997).

In the daily adventure of assessing where students are, you should discover many more things to do to help them attain targeted goals.

Student participation is a key component of successful formative assessment. If students are to participate successfully in the process, they need to be clear about the objectives and criteria for good work, to assess their own efforts in light of the criteria, and to share responsibility in taking action (Atkin, Black, & Coffey, 2001).

Summative assessment is used *after* you have taught the material to assess what students have learned. Summative assessments may be used to assign grades, share data with students, provide progress reports to parents, and make judgments about what teaching and learning steps to take next. Traditional tests given at the end of a period of instruction, at the end of a 6-week or semester period, for example, are summative assessments.

A glossary containing definitions of important terms used in this chapter can be found on the Companion Website for Chapter 6 at http://www.prenhall.com/carin.

TABLE 6-2   DIAGNOSTIC, FORMATIVE, AND SUMMATIVE ASSESSMENT STRATEGIES

	Diagnostic	Formative	Summative
When?	*Before* teaching	*During* teaching	*After* teaching
Why?	Assess student needs and prior knowledge.	Continue diagnostic assessment.	Assess retention and understanding.
	Probe for naive theories and alternative conceptions.	Determine current levels of student learning.	Assess conceptual change.
	Match student needs with teaching methods.	Determine what students need to do to reach optimum learning levels.	Use for assigning grades, for promotion, and for graduation.
		Modify teaching of concepts.	Assess how much students have learned before moving on to the next topic.
		Provide scaffolding to bridge to higher level of learning.	Report to parents, administrators, and community.
		Provide immediate feedback to guide student learning.	
How?	For diagnostic, formative, and summative assessment use: a. student discourse b. paper-and-pencil tests c. student projects and written reports d. student performance tasks e. teacher observation and judgment		

State-mandated tests, such as those required by the federal *No Child Left Behind* statute, are also summative tests. Much of the public attention to assessment is based on these large-scale, standardized examinations that are developed, and usually scored, outside the classroom (Atkin et al., 2001). At the very least, district- and statewide assessments should be aligned with the inquiry goals of the *Science Standards* so the tests do not interfere with essential science learning in the classroom.

Table 6-2 provides a summary view of when, why, and how diagnostic, formative, and summative assessments can be used in your teaching.

Assessment and Inquiry Science

Assessment in inquiry science is based on two guiding questions (Atkin et al., 2001):

1. Where are students trying to go? (Identify and communicate learning goals and objectives.)

2. Where are students now? (Use assessment techniques, including student self-assessment, to determine current levels of learning.)

Teaching actions commensurate with the questions are given in parentheses.
Let us examine the first of those two questions.

What Shall Students Learn in Science?

In considering what students should learn in science, it is important to distinguish between goals and objectives. *Goals* are overarching and long-term statements. They serve to give general direction to science programs. Goals are stated broadly in terms such as *to know* or *to understand* something. Objectives are short-term outcomes that tell us specifically what we should teach and assess in order to reach goals. Objectives are generally stated in terms of performances that can be observed and assessed, such as to *identify, name, interpret,* or *predict.*

There is growing consensus that the *National Science Education Standards* define the goals that should be achieved in science at different grade levels. It is the responsibility of state education agencies, district curriculum personnel, and classroom teachers to determine the specific objectives that will lead to the attainment of the goals set forth in the *Science Standards.*

Assessment in the past centered too often on what was easy to measure with multiple-choice items: the *recall* of facts, concepts, principles, and theories. The *Science Standards* have not lost sight of the importance of a strong knowledge base, but they go beyond knowledge and place emphasis on students understanding and applying science concepts and principles, as well as being able to use a variety of investigative procedures.

Figure 6-1 presents a framework that can help you keep in mind the various emphases of the *Science Standards* as you prepare for instruction and assessment. The framework is adapted from Anderson and Krathwohl's (2001) revision of Bloom's (Bloom, Englehart, Furst, Hill, & Krathwohl, 1956) *Taxonomy of Educational Objectives.*

The framework consists of two dimensions: **science knowledge** and **cognitive processes.** Consistent with the *Science Standards,* the science knowledge dimension focuses on three kinds of knowledge: *factual knowledge*, related to the learning of facts, details, and attributes; *conceptual knowledge*, related to scientific concepts, principles, and theories; and *procedural knowledge*, including essential tasks of scientific inquiry and processes of science.

The cognitive processes dimension includes *knowing, understanding,* and *applying.* Action words that help delineate the various cognitive processes and serve as performance terms for objectives are included in the framework.

The three types of knowledge in the framework can be combined with the three kinds of cognitive processes to produce nine cells defining areas of learning, teaching, and assessing science. Sample science objectives for the various cells are given in the figure. Each objective would relate to a goal defined by the *Science Standards.* For example, consider these two objectives given in Figure 6-1:

- State the complete circuit rule for electrical current.
- Apply complete circuit rules to predict and explain what happens in series and parallel circuits.

Both objectives relate to this principle from the K–4 *Science Standards:*

> Students should understand that electrical currents require a complete loop through which an electric current can pass. (National Research Council, 1996, p. 127)

The cells in Figure 6-1 help define what we should teach and assess in science. That is, we should teach for memory of factual and conceptual knowledge, as well as understanding

David Krathwohl, who was instrumental in developing the revision of Bloom's **taxonomy**, also worked with Benjamin Bloom in the 1950s on the committee that developed the original taxonomy of educational objectives.

	Cognitive Processes Dimension		
Science Knowledge Dimension	**1. Remembering** • recall • identify • name • define • state • describe	**2. Understanding** • classify • interpret • explain • infer • analyze • connect • predict • apply • demonstrate • implement • evaluate • construct • synthesize	**3. Applying** • plan • generate • construct • create • use • solve
A. Factual Knowledge (Scientific facts, terms, details, attributes)	**Example Objectives** • Describe the parts of a seed. • State facts and define main terms related to evaporation and condensation.		
B. Conceptual Knowledge (Scientific concepts, principles, models, and theories)	**Example Objectives** • State the complete circuit rules for electric current. • Describe the main components and functions of the human circulatory system.	**Example Objectives** • Construct inferences about why the cotyledon of a seed shrivels up as the plant begins to grow. • Explain the water cycle, showing how the different parts of the cycle are related.	**Example Objectives** • Apply complete circuit rules to predict and explain what happens in series and parallel circuits.
C. Inquiry Procedures (Processes of science, procedures and strategies of inquiry)	**Example Objectives** • Name the essential tasks of inquiry. • List and define science process skills.	**Example Objectives** • Distinguish between inferences and observations. • Explain how processes of science are related to inquiry procedures.	**Example Objectives** • Construct hypotheses about factors affecting the rate of swing of a pendulum. • Construct a plan to investigate the behavior of mealworms. • Demonstrate skills of observing, measuring, and graphing in investigating plant growth.

Figure 6-1 A Framework for Assessing Science Learning

Source: From Lorin W. Anderson & David R. Krathwohl *A Taxonomy for Learning, Teaching, and Assessing.* Published by Allyn & Bacon, Boston, MA. Copyright © 2001 by Pearson Education. Adapted by permission of the publisher.

162

and application of knowledge. We should also teach for knowledge, understanding, and ability to apply inquiry procedures. The framework covers cognitive objectives only. We will look at affective objectives later.

Each cell in the framework is important, but need not be emphasized every day and in every science lesson. For example, simply recalling factual knowledge can be important for elementary and middle school students, and lessons and assessments emphasizing memory may be taught. However, much more time should be allotted to understanding concepts and planning and applying inquiry procedures. Applying the framework in assessment can remind us to teach for a broad range of cognitive objectives over the course of the school year.

Next we will examine assessment techniques teachers can use to determine where students are in their learning progress.

What Assessment Techniques Shall We Use to Determine Where Students Are in Science?

Two main types of assessment measures are available to teachers in science: traditional assessments and performance assessments.

Traditional Assessment. Traditional methods of assessment are typically the multiple-choice, true-false, short-answer, and essay items given on tests at the completion of lessons on a topic. Multiple-choice and true-false items are sometimes called forced-choice items, while short-answer and essay items are referred to as constructed-response items. These types of assessments offer teachers a number of advantages, but they also have some disadvantages.

Multiple-choice and short-answer items are easy to administer and score. They enable teachers to measure a wide range of knowledge over a short period of time. However, multiple-choice and short-answer items do not usually require students to show their reasoning. Further, traditional multiple-choice items measure more than just knowledge; the reading level, language ability, and vocabulary of students can also affect their choices of answers.

Carefully constructed essay items have the advantage that they require students to generate information in their own words, rather than to just recognize correct answers. Such items can also provide teachers with knowledge about how the student arrived at the answers. Essay items also give students an opportunity to practice and improve their writing skills. A disadvantage of essay items is that poor writing skills can mask the student's science understanding.

Traditional assessments can be used formatively if teachers are careful to follow through and give feedback to students on learning. However, more powerful methods of assessment are being developed to fit the expanded, formative purposes of classroom assessment. In recent years, there has been an increasing emphasis on a new type of assessment, called performance assessment.

Performance Assessment. When compared with traditional assessment measures, performance assessment offers students a wider range of options for communicating what they understand in science and what they are able to do with their understanding. In formative assessment, performance assessment tasks are embedded in daily instruction rather than administered at the end of the week or after a series of lessons. Students are generally more comfortable with performance assessments, because they often have the look and feel of regular hands-on learning situations.

The PALS (Performance Assessment Links in Science) Website has collected many excellent performance assessment examples from the World Wide Web. Peruse the site at http://pals.sri.com/index.html.

All performance assessment tasks have a performance that can be observed or a product that can be examined. Student performances in science assessment tasks might include measuring, observing, collecting and organizing data, constructing a graph, making a visual or audio presentation, presenting an oral defense of work, or presenting a how-to explanation of a procedure. Products presented for assessment could include such tangible things as data tables, graphs, models, reports, and written explanations and problem solutions.

Fitting Assessment Methods to Learning Objectives. Your choice of whether to use traditional or performance assessment methods in science will depend largely on the type of objectives you wish to assess. Look again at Figure 6-1. If you wish to assess recall of factual or conceptual knowledge, traditional multiple-choice or short-answer items are suitable. Traditional assessments might also be appropriate to assess student attainment of objectives related to understanding of science knowledge, particularly if you use essay items or combine multiple-choice responses with written explanations of why a particular response was chosen.

However, you might be able to probe deeper into student understanding when you use performance assessments that enable students to demonstrate their understanding during a learning or problem-solving task. Finally, performance methods are much more appropriate than traditional assessments when you wish to assess how well students can apply knowledge and plan and carry out inquiry procedures.

Here are some guidelines to assist you as you design and select assessment tools to fit your own science lessons.

1. A wide range of assessment data, instruments, and procedures are necessary to understand and display what each student has learned.
2. Both traditional and performance assessments can be used for diagnostic, formative, and summative purposes.
3. Traditional assessment items are useful for assessing memory and basic understanding of science knowledge.
4. Performance assessments are a valuable addition to the assessment picture in *Standards*-based science classrooms.
5. Performance assessments can be used at any time to assess student understanding or ability to apply conceptual knowledge. Such techniques are also important in assessing the inquiry abilities of students.
6. Materials and procedures of performance assessment are to be developed and used in ways such that they are integral to, not apart from, the other learning and instructional processes in a course.
7. Performance assessment procedures can be particularly effective when students and teachers work together in their development, implementation, and revision. Performance assessment should provide students opportunities to demonstrate, summarize, and interpret what they have accomplished. It should not be restricted to securing numerical data for marks and grading.
8. Quality of thinking, development of competencies in critically examining evidence and justifying explanations, and reflection on and integration of learning will take priority over moving on to new subject areas whenever these alternatives are in contention for class time (Raizen et al., 1989).

Next, we will examine how teachers can use performance assessment techniques to improve student learning.

In the Annenberg Video Case Study featured in this chapter, Tom explores a variety of nontraditional assessment methods to assess what students are thinking and understanding. For example, he has his students create cinquain poems to describe their understanding of electrical circuits.

Designing a Performance Task

Creating a good performance task involves determining the focus of the task, setting the context for the task, writing directions, and developing a scoring guide (Kentucky Department of Education, n.d.).

Focus

The first step in developing a performance assessment is to decide what students are expected to learn and how they can demonstrate that they have learned it. This becomes the *focus* of the performance task. Focus is closely related to learning objectives. In determining the focus, state very precisely what you expect your students to know, understand, and be able to do. Once you have determined a focus for the assessment task, a context should be created.

Context

The context of a performance assessment usually includes a background and a question related to the focus objective. The background may be presented in a variety of ways, including in written form and through hands-on activities. The focus question should center on a problem to which students will want to find an answer or solution. The background scenario and focus question represent the "hook" that draws students in and engages them in the task. The scenario should be made as authentic, or as close to the "real thing," as classroom conditions will allow (Jarolimek & Foster, 1997). Authentic contexts better portray the nature of science, relate classroom learning to the real world, are more intrinsically motivating to students, and serve not only as assessments but also as interesting learning situations. To make the task more authentic, you might describe it in terms of activities that are familiar to students. Also, specifying the audience for a presentation or product, such as younger children, classmates, or the city council, helps make the focus more authentic and engaging. Some general examples of performance assessments that can be made authentic by relating them to real-world contexts are provided in Table 6-3.

Directions

Directions for performance tasks should explain what students are expected to do and should describe the final performance or product to be assessed. It is very important to make sure that the directions are clear. You should ask other teachers and some students to review the directions for clarity.

Scoring Guides

The scoring guide provides a means for judging the quality of the assessment performance or product. Begin creating the scoring guide by describing what a high-quality performance

NSES   **Assessment Standard C**

- Assessment tasks are authentic.
- Students have adequate opportunity to demonstrate their achievement.

TABLE 6-3   GENERAL PERFORMANCE ASSESSMENT TECHNIQUES

In performance assessments, students may perform these activities involving complex behaviors not easily assessed by traditional paper-and-pencil tests.

plan and conduct an experiment	graph data
write a story, composition, or poem	construct a concept map
give an oral report	research information in the library
design and make a videotape	complete an art project
construct a scientific model	draw a chart or diagram
program a computer	give a photo or slide presentation
tutor a classmate	compose a song
keep a science journal	write science questions
interview a scientist	record long-term plant growth
guide classmates on a local trip	care for/keep records of an animal
correspond with a scientific author	organize a healthy luncheon

Students can collect samples of the above items over a long time for inclusion in a portfolio.

Source: Modified from *Educational Psychology: Principles and Applications,* 3rd ed. (p. 606), by Jeanne Ellis Ormrod, © 2000. Reprinted by permission of Pearson Education, Inc., Upper Saddle River, NJ.

or product will look like. The next step is to decide how many performance criteria or performance levels are needed. Descriptions of each criterion or level can then be written.

Three common types of scoring guides—checklists, rubrics, and holistic scoring guides—are described here. Other types of scoring guides may share features with these three.

Checklists.   A checklist is simply a list of the specific key elements that a teacher wishes to consider in judging a student performance or product. Scorers observe student perfomances and examine products and check *yes* or *no* for each element on the checklist. The check shows only whether the element was observed; no effort is made on a checklist to assess *how well* the skill was performed. Checklists are easy, quick, and handy to use. They help keep teacher observations focused. In making your own checklist, consider these items:

1. Do an analysis of what tasks are necessary for achieving a particular learning goal. To facilitate this process, you might refer to the scope and sequence chart in your science textbook teacher's manual, your school district or state science curriculum, or commercial science programs.
2. Once elements to be learned are identified, choose how often you will observe and record on the checklist.
3. Your checklist should have sufficient spaces to conform to the observation frequency you have determined and for your comments, if you wish.
4. Keep a separate record for each student. Review it with students periodically to assess their progress in specific skills.

Figure 6-2 is a sample checklist for observing students' skills in using a microscope. For another example, see the checklist on observing and investigating mealworm behavior

VIDEO CASE STUDY: Tom

Previewing the Video
As you watch this case study, use the *Questions for Reflection* to guide your note taking, thoughts, and discussion. For group discussion, choose a group facilitator to solicit various perspectives and keep the discussion on track.

Introducing the Case

Tom's philosophy of teaching and his beliefs about children's learning are reflected in the ways in which he chooses to assess learning. Tom thinks that all children can learn. Further, he believes that student learning is dependent upon the way a teacher sets up the learning experience. "It doesn't do any good if a teacher says, 'The child has never done this before…. I don't expect the child to be able to do this.' What worse words can you say about a child?" As you review the lesson in which students determine how enzymes help the body break up food, consider Tom's nontraditional methods for assessing student learning.

"Assessment isn't the final step in education— it's the first."

—*NSTA Pathways to the Science Standards*

Questions for Reflection

1. What expectations does Tom have for students' learning in the enzyme activity?
2. What different means does Tom discuss and use to assess students' science learning?
3. Why is it important to use multiple ways, in the most authentic contexts possible, to assess students' understanding?

Trying New Ideas *In exploring a variety of nontraditional assessments for science, Tom finds success with a number of different methods. Each method he uses certainly taps into individual learning styles. For example, in creating cinquain poems, students are asked not only to describe their understanding of electrical circuits but to follow a writing pattern that uses creative descriptors as they highlight conceptual understanding. In addition, pictorial representations and journal writing offer Tom ways to continuously assess what students are thinking and understanding.*

Want to Try Writing a Cinquain?

First line: One-word concept or idea
Second line: Two words describing the concept
Third line: Three action words that describe the concept
Fourth line: Tell how you feel about the concept
Last line: Write a one-word synonym

Cumulus
Evaporating, Saturating
Collecting Moist Air
Menacing, Scary
Thunderhead

Tiffany
Grade 4

Questions for Reflection

1. Using different modes of assessment is a practice that is supported by the National Science Education Standards (NSES). Review Table 7-A to see the change in emphases the NSES Assessment Standards require. How do Tom's methods of assessment align with the intent of the Assessment Standards? How do Tom's methods fall short?

2. According to the National Science Teachers' Association (NSTA), assessment is different from evaluation in that assessment uses a variety of formats to derive information about student understanding, whereas evaluation implies judgment and decision making based on assessment information. Assessment methods should determine what students are able to do and reveal how they can use their new information and knowledge. Review the five Assessment Standards of the National Science Education Standards (Table 7-B). How do Tom's assessment methods measure up to the Standards? Be sure to support your statements.

Table 7-A
Changing emphases envisioned in the National Science Education Standards.

Less Emphasis on	More Emphasis on
Assessing what is easily measured	Assessing what is most highly valued
Assessing discrete knowledge	Assessing rich, well-structured knowledge
Assessing scientific knowledge	Assessing scientific understanding and reasoning
Assessing to learn what students do not know	Assessing to learn what students do understand
Assessing only achievement	Assessing achievement and opportunity to learn
End-of-term assessments by teachers	Students engaged in ongoing assessment of their work and that of others
Development of external assessments by measurement experts alone	Teachers involved in the development of external assessments

Source: From *NSTA Pathways to the Science Standards* by Lawrence F. Lowry, Ed., 1997, Arlington, VA: National Science Teachers Association, pp. 21–22. Reprinted by permission.

Table 7-B

NSES	The Five Assessment Standards

1. Designing an assessment is a difficult task; the resulting data drives the curriculum and influences decision making about students. Every assessment tool should be crafted so that educators can measure clearly stated outcomes accurately.

2. As teachers measure student achievement, they must always compare their results to the standard of "opportunity to learn." Test scores reflect what students know, and also teachers' knowledge and skills, the degree of coordination in the program, the equipment and environment available for student experiences and the community support behind student growth.

3. Assessment data fuels decisions about students, teachers, programs, and systems. There must be confidence in the technical quality of that data. Assessment must be valid, authentic, and reliable. Decision makers must have data in which the confidence level is consistent with the consequences of the decision to be made.

4. In assessment, as in teaching, care must always be taken to avoid stereotypes and bias. Just as the styles of learners differ, their perspectives may vary based on their background, environment, or areas of ability. Assessment practices must accommodate diversity, and assessment data must always be examined for signs of bias.

5. Assessments influence the plans teachers make for students, courses, and programs. As teachers move toward the Standard, they will rely on data each step of the way. It is crucial that in each decision, teachers keep in mind the strengths, weaknesses, assumptions, and inaccuracies inherent in every assessment.

Source: From *NSTA Pathways to the Science Standards* by Lawrence F. Lowry, Ed., 1997, Arlington, VA: National Science Teachers Association, pp. 21–22. Reprinted by permission.

Venn Diagram Illustrating Interdependency of Two Kinds of Animals

Horsehoe Crabs

- spawn in May/June
- egg-laying females bury eggs in shallow nests in sand
- males release sperm over nests

Inter-dependency

- horseshoe crabs lay eggs in Delaware Bay
- birds stop in Delaware Bay to feed on eggs
- eggs supply rich energy source for birds
- birds' short beaks only reach exposed eggs

Migratory Shorebirds

- 3000-mile Spring migration from S. America depletes all body fat
- birds must replenish energy to continue journey to Arctic
- bird populations have inexplicably declined in recent years

Marcus
Grade 7

Reflecting and Building on Change *In the last module, Tom models for students how to create a concept map. Concept maps can show student understanding by visually representing the connections students make between major concepts and other, subsidiary concepts.*

Questions for Reflection

1. Think about activities or lesson models you have seen in this text. How would concept maps be useful as a pre-assessment? How would concept maps be used as an ongoing assessment tool while students are engaged in lesson activities?

2. Consider the Venn diagram Tom had students use to compare electric motors and electric generators. What types of science experiences might be useful for students to draw on in constructing this Venn diagram? What science experiences and knowledge do teachers need to set up this meaningful assessment tool?

3. After you have completed reading chapter 7, explain how performance tests and portfolios could be effective in assessing and/or evaluating science knowledge and understanding.

4. How do Tom's ideas on assessment fit with the 5-E model of instruction? How are each of the different phases of the 5-E model utilized in Tom's lesson activities?

Student's Name _____										
Behavior/Skills	Date	Yes	No	Date	Yes	No	Date	Yes	No
Is careful in handling microscope									
Cleans lenses properly									
Focuses instrument properly									
Prepares slides correctly									
Arranges mirror for correct amount of light									

Figure 6-2   Checklist for observing microscope skills.

given in Figure 6-21. Student results determined with checklists might be used both to provide feedback on learning and to adjust instruction.

Rubrics. A rubric is a type of scoring guide consisting of a number of evaluative criteria that are precisely described according to level of quality, usually with points assigned to each level. The number of levels should be based on the needs of your class and your observations of what your students are actually doing in science activities. Four-level rubrics are frequently used.

Names of proficiency levels in a four-level rubric are generally variations of the following:

- *Level 3: Advanced, Excellent.*   Outstanding quality of performance or product.
- *Level 2: Proficient, Satisfactory.*   Acceptable quality of performance or product.
- *Level 1: Basic, Below Expectations.*   Partial proficiency; demonstrated incomplete understanding or severe misconceptions.
- *Level 0: Unacceptable, Unsatisfactory.*   Student did not do the task, complete the assignment, or show comprehension of the activity.

Figure 6-3 provides examples of generic rubrics showing different levels of performance for four types of science tasks. You must provide enough information about each performance level for scorers to reliably observe differences in the quality of the students' performances or products.

Holistic Scoring Guides. In holistic scoring, teachers make judgments about learning by considering simultaneously all of the criteria that go into a high-quality product or performance (Stiggins, 1994, p. 196). Holistic scoring guides are sometimes referred to as holistic rubrics.

An example of a holistic rubric is shown in Figure 6-4. The performance task requires students to make predictions about what happens in an illustrated circuit when switches or either open or closed, to construct the circuit and use it to test predictions, and to write out an explanation of what happens to each of the bulbs in the test. This performance task gauges how well students solve a real-world scientific problem in a laboratory setting. It is

Figure 6-3 Criteria and scoring levels for rubric on major science categories. *Source:* From Elizabeth Meng and Rodney L. Doran, *Improving Instruction and Learning Through Evaluation: Elementary School Science* (Columbus, OH: ERIC Clearinghouse for Science, Mathematics, and Environmental Education, 1993), 162–163.

Knowing Science Information

1. Responds only in terms of specific examples experienced in class or presented in instructional materials.
2. Responds in terms of generalizations of these experiences but is unable to show relationships or to go beyond that which was experienced.
3. Demonstrates thorough understanding by applying information in a new context or by explaining relationships, implications, or consequences.

Using Science Concepts and Generalizations

1. Rarely connects previous learning with new situations in which it could be applied unless told what skill or idea is relevant.
2. Uses previous experiences in new situations once the relationship between the new and previous situation has been pointed out.
3. Works out what earlier learning could be applied in a new context by using relationships between one situation and another.

Doing Written Reports and Projects

1. What he writes or says is disorganized and difficult to follow; takes time to understand information in books or verbal directions.
2. Seems to have a clear idea of what he wants to express but does not always find the word to put it precisely or concisely; prefers to seek information orally than to use books.
3. Expresses himself clearly, using words appropriately and economically and at a level which can be understood by whomever receives the message; expands his knowledge through reading.

Experimenting/Investigating

1. Is unable to progress from one point to another in a practical investigation or inquiry without help, failing to grasp the overall plan.
2. Tries things out somewhat unsystematically unless the various steps in a practical inquiry are planned out for him, in which case he uses materials and collects results satisfactorily.
3. Has a clear idea of the reason for the various steps in an investigation; can work through them systematically, making reasonable decisions with only occasional guidance.

This performance task might accompany activities on electricity like the ones described in Chapter 4.

appropriate for students in about grade 4 or above. The scoring guide in Figure 6-4 is a holistic one because teachers made judgments about task performance by considering simultaneously all of the criteria that go into a high-quality product or performance. Teachers observe, assess, and evaluate each student's written responses to the questions. The teachers also assess and evaluate the student's performance in constructing and using the test circuit.

We devised this holistic scoring guide for a specific circuit task, but it can easily be adapted to simpler or more complex circuits. Variations of the scoring guide can also be used with other types of science problems.

Stiggins (1994) argues that holistic scoring should be minimized in favor of analytic procedures that consider each key dimension or criterion of a performance individually. Analytic rubrics provide a more precise method of judging performance.

Include your students in establishing scoring criteria and in the process of scoring task performance. When students are involved in the assessment process, they become more

Performance Task:

A. PREDICT: Study the diagram of the electric circuit. Make a prediction about what will happen to each light bulb if switch 1 is closed and switch 2 is open.

My Predictions:

Bulb 1: Lit   Not Lit   (Circle Lit or Not Lit)

Bulb 2: Lit   Not Lit   (Circle Lit or Not Lit)

Bulb 3: Lit   Not Lit   (Circle Lit or Not Lit)

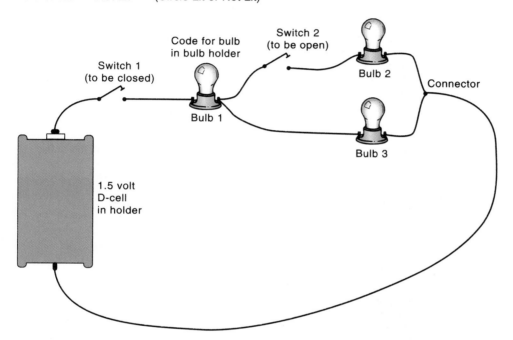

B. CONSTRUCT: Obtain a kit of materials from your teacher. Using the materials, build the circuit illustrated.

C. TEST: Use your circuit to test your predictions. Arrange the circuit so that switch 1 is open and switch 2 is closed. What happened to each bulb?

My Observations:

Bulb 1: Lit   Not Lit   (Circle Lit or Not Lit)

Bulb 2: Lit   Not Lit   (Circle Lit or Not Lit)

Bulb 3: Lit   Not Lit   (Circle Lit or Not Lit)

D. EXPLAIN: Use your knowledge of circuits to explain your observations of what happened to each bulb when you opened switch 1 and closed switch 2 of the test circuit.

My Explanation: (Write out your explanation here.)

_____

_____

_____

_____

Figure 6-4   Holistic scoring rubric for an electric circuits task.

Score: 0 Points

The student does not attempt to solve the problem. A 0-point score is characterized by most of the following:

- No predictions are given.
- There is no attempt to build the circuit.
- No observations are made.
- No explanations are given.

Score: 1 point

The overall responses are inconsistent with sound scientific thinking and investigation procedures. The responses indicate the student has little or no understanding of the problem and of circuit ideas. A 1-point response is characterized by most of the following:

- Predictions are inaccurate or missing.
- The student makes a limited attempt to build the test circuit; the circuit, if constructed, has many faults.
- The student's attempts to test the predictions are unsuccessful; the observations are missing.
- Explanations are missing or they are illogical and cannot be supported; understanding of circuit concepts is not demonstrated.

Score: 2 points

The responses represent a limited attempt at applying a sound scientific approach to the problem. Although the responses exhibit errors, incompleteness, and/or omissions, the student demonstrates some understanding of how to predict, how to construct a test circuit, and how to use the circuit to test predictions. Little understanding of the concept of circuits is demonstrated. A 2-point response is characterized by most of the following:

- The student makes two or more inaccurate predictions.
- The student attempts to build a test circuit but it is faulty.
- The students uses the constructed circuit to test the predictions.
- Observations of what happens to the bulbs in the test are inaccurate.
- Explanations are illogical and cannot be supported; clear understanding of the circuit concepts is not demonstrated.

Score: 3 points

The overall response is largely consistent with a sound scientific approach to design. The response indicates that the student has a general understanding of the problem, of how to make predictions, how to construct a circuit, and how to use it to test predictions. The quality of the explanation is good, although minor errors may be present. A 3-point response is characterized by most of the following:

- The student makes generally accurate predictions, with no more than one error.
- The student's test circuit is well constructed with only minor faults.
- The student uses the circuit to test predictions; one or two observations may be inaccurate.
- The explanation is logical and, for the most part, is consistent with observations and shows understanding of circuit ideas.

Score: 4 points

The responses are consistent with a sound scientific approach. The responses indicate that the student has a clear understanding of the problem and of how to predict, construct circuits, and use the circuits to test predictions. The explanation may, in some cases, define additional aspects of the problem or include extensions beyond the requirements of the task. Some inconsistencies may be present, but they are overwhelmed by the superior quality of the responses. A 4-point score is characterized by most of the following:

- The student makes accurate predictions.
- The circuit is well constructed, with no flaws.
- The circuit is successfully used to test the predictions; all observations in the test are accurate.
- The explanation is clear and detailed, and is convincingly supported with the data collected and an accurate presentation of circuit concepts.

Figure 6-4 *(continued)*

aware of learning expectations, and are enabled to take more responsibility for their own learning. Performance assessments have been criticized as being too subjective, but when good scoring guides are used, consistent scoring can be obtained.

In the following sections, we provide a large bank of assessment examples that you can draw on in developing your own science assessments.

Examples of Science Assessment Items and Tasks

The various examples presented in this section are organized according to the taxonomy given in Figure 6-1. Table 6-4 provides a guide to the assessment examples to help you sort through and keep up with the various assessment procedures illustrated in the chapter.

You should begin now to build up assessment items and sources for each subject you teach. You can find many good assessment examples on the Internet, in teachers' guides, in the education literature, and so on. In most cases, it is necessary to modify examples so that they fit your own classroom situation. And of course, you should begin to create, try out, and revise your own performance and traditional assessments.

> Table 6-4 follows the organizational format of Figure 6-1.

Assessing Knowledge of Science Facts, Concepts, Principles, and Procedures

Knowledge of science facts, concepts, principles, and procedures can be assessed with both performance and traditional items.

Assessing Science Knowledge with Performance Tasks. Sometimes performance tasks are part of the regular learning activity. The focus, context, and direction of the performance tasks are derived directly from the learning activities. For example, students often keep journals of their observations. These observation journals can reveal the students' developing knowledge about a topic. The journals can take many forms. We will examine student experience charts, record pages, and science logs. These types of journals are particularly useful at lower grades.

> A large bank of assessment procedures and examples are provided in this chapter. Use the chapter as a resource guide, referring to it often as you design and construct your own assessments.

Science Experience Charts. Science experience charts represent a type of performance task that can be used to assess science knowledge, including observations of details. Keeping records is a key aspect of doing science. It is through records that we compare and analyze science experiences. Students need to do this, too. Through their own record keeping, your students will build scientific knowledge and expand their scientific vocabulary.

The first records your students keep may contain a minimum of words but lots of pictures. For example, one record may be a small group or total class experience chart, in which students record things they observed after a field trip to the park. The experience chart may look like the one shown in Figure 6-5. Adding drawings to the chart can enhance it.

Experience charts are used primarily for feedback on learning, rather than for grading purposes. When assessing experience charts, consider the following questions (Shepardson & Britsch, 2001):

- Does the drawing or writing relate to and accurately correspond with what was observed or done?
- Does the child label or name the objects used?
- Does the drawing or writing elaborate on the details of what was observed or done?

TABLE 6-4   SCIENCE ASSESSMENT EXAMPLES

Assessment Purpose	Performance Assessment Examples	Traditional Assessment Examples
Assessing Recall of Science Knowledge	Student experience charts: Figure 6-5 Science record pages: Figure 6-6 Science logs: Figure 6-7	Multiple choice: Items 1–4 Short answer: Items 5–6 Essay: Item 7
Assessing Understanding and Application of Conceptual Knowledge in Science	Oral/written pictorial interpretations: Figure 6-8 Concept mapping: Figure 6-10 Anecdotal records: Figure 6-11 Discrepant events, student activities: Figures 6-15, 6-16	Standard multiple choice: Item 8 Justified multiple choice: Figure 6-12 Enhanced multiple choice: Figure 6-13 Essays: Items 9, 10 Essay with investigation data: Items 11, 12, 13
Assessing Science Processes, Inquiry Procedures, and Attitudes	Growing plants performance task: Figure 6-17 Observation checklists: Figure 6-18 Data capture—assessing observation, measurement, and communication skills: Figure 6-19 Scientific processes—mealworms task: Figures 6-20, 6-21 Graphing data: Figure 6-22 Checklist for science processes and inquiry procedures: Figure 6-23 Hands-on practical assessment—TIMSS tasks: Figures 6-24, Figure 6-25 Checklist for science attitudes: Figure 6-26 Performance and essay tasks: Items 19, 20, 21, 22, 23	Multiple choice, short answer: Items 14, 15 Cluster of multiple-choice and essay items with investigation data: Items 16, 17, 18
Assessing Multiple Objectives in Science	Model building: Page 202 Student demonstrations: Page 202 Student project—Aquarium design: Page 202 Student science fair project: Figure 6-27 Portfolio assessment: Figure 6-28	

Our Trip to the Park

Things We Saw	Things We Heard	Things We Smelled
Sally: Branches moving in wind	Birds singing	
Greg: Little bugs crawling		Fresh air
Tom: A bird's nest	An airplane	Flowers
Amy: Yellow flowers in grass	Dog barking	
Juan: Squirrel running	Twigs snapping	Dirt (soil)
Jill: Water drops on grass	Our class laughing	Wet grass

Figure 6-5 Class science sensory experience chart of field trip observations.

- Does the drawing or writing provide a context of people, materials, and processes from the science activity in which the child was engaged?
- Does the child relate the materials or activity to contexts in which they might be encountered outside the classroom?

Provide scaffolding to improve learning whenever it is warranted by your assessment data.

Science Record Pages. Record keeping for older students can include brief descriptions of what they did, observed, and thought, in addition to specific evidences of the number of objects they observed, counted, measured, and so forth. At first, you may want to use a group activity such as the experience chart illustrated in Figure 6-5.

As your students learn how to give brief descriptions of what they did in groups, they are ready to start their own individual record keeping. You can design a page such as the one shown in Figure 6-6, on which your students record their sink-or-float experimentation. The figure offers students three focused assignments:

- *Write* a description of what they did.
- *Draw* a picture of the activity.
- *Record observations* in the chart supplied.

Once students become familiar with this strategy, encourage them to devise their own observation format.

A rubric for assessing science record pages at the knowledge level might be constructed by adapting the rubric in Figure 6-17. Again, provide feedback to improve learning whenever it is appropriate.

Science Logs. Collecting, recording, sharing, and reading their science logs or science journals (or any other name given by you) give students much practice in observing and recording their observations. Science logs represent a student product you can use to assess what they have learned.

You and your students can make your own science logs or minibooks. They can be class collections of student reports, computer-generated materials, logs, or other written works illustrated with students' drawings or instant photos. Individuals or small groups of students could also make their own science logs.

To begin, select a size that appeals to you and your students. The size may be dictated by the materials available. Have the students put in their science logs things they have studied and found for a particular science topic, field trip, and so on. These might include

Table 6-4 shows how the sample assessments in this chapter are organized. Refer to this table as you study the various tasks, items, and scoring guides.

You have been working with things that sink or float. What did you do to find out which objects sink or float? Write a description and draw a picture.

We put objects in the bowl of water. If the object floated, we put it in box with the Float label. If it sank, we put it in box Sink. Then we tried all the objects in the Float box to check if they all floated. We did the same with the objects in the Sink box.

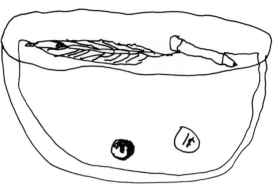

What did you find about which objects sink or float? Record your observations on the chart below.

OBJECT	MADE OF	SINK	FLOAT
PENNY	METAL	X	
PENCIL	MOSTLY WOOD		X

Figure 6-6   Hands-on/minds-on science record page.

experiments or other activities, observational records, drawings, magazine pictures, and handwritten or typed science content.

Have your students add front and back covers, illustrate them, laminate and bind them together, or put them in a binder. The students can share their science logs with each other. Some schools have even set up a special section in their libraries for student science logs. This is an excellent opportunity to integrate science with reading, writing, art, mathematics, and other subjects. Figure 6-7 shows how science log covers can be made attractive. Do not forget to avail yourself of the wonderful, copyright-free clip art available for computers.

Use holistic scoring, checklists, or rubrics to assess students' knowledge as shown in their products. Your main goal here is to improve learning rather than to obtain a summative grade.

Assessing Science Knowledge with Traditional Items. Traditional multiple-choice, short-answer, completion, and essay items are very useful for assessing science knowledge.

Using Multiple-Choice Items to Assess Science Knowledge. You will probably use multiple-choice items frequently in your assessment program to measure the attainment of science knowledge. Remember, to *know* is to be able to *recall*. Following are some sample multiple-choice items that assess recall.

Note that science goals related to each item are also given. The goals are derived from the *National Science Education Standards*. Several different items involving such tasks as

Figure 6-7   Student science log minibooks, grades K–12.

naming, identifying, stating, and describing would be needed to assess students' knowledge related to a goal.

Goal. Students should understand that
* water circulates through the atmosphere in what is known as the "water cycle" (NSES 5–8).

Item 1. Which of the following is *not* a form of precipitation?
    A. hail
    B. wind
    C. rain
    D. snow

Source: 2000 National Assessment of Educational Progress (NAEP), 4th grade level.

Goal. Students should understand that
* each plant or animal has different structures that serve different functions in growth survival and reproduction (NSES K–4).

Item 2. Which part stores food for a bean seed?
    A. cotyledon
    B. seed coat
    C. embryo plant
    D. roots

Goal. Students should understand that

• the earth is the third planet from the sun in a system that includes the moon, the sun, and eight other planets and their moons. The sun is the central and largest body in the solar system (NSES 5–8).

Item 3. The earth's moon is
    A. always much closer to the sun than it is to the earth.
    B. always much closer to the earth than it is to the sun.
    C. about the same distance from the sun as it is from the earth.
    D. sometimes closer to the sun than it is to the earth and sometimes closer to the earth than it is to the sun.

Source: 2000 National Assessment of Educational Progress (NAEP), 4th grade level.

Goal. Students should develop understandings about scientific inquiry (NSES K–4, 5–8).

Item 4. Which task would you undertake first in scientific inquiry?
    A. collect relevant data
    B. ask a question that can be investigated
    C. report your investigation and findings to others
    D. use data in forming explanations

In constructing your own multiple-choice items, keep these things in mind.

1. Multiple-choice questions have three parts:
    • *Stem:* presents the task to your students
    • *Distractors:* incorrect responses
    • *Correct response*
2. Be sure your stem
    • asks a direct question or poses a problem in a simple and clearly worded manner, and
    • avoids use of confusing negatives or highlights negative terms if they are used.
3. Check your answer choices to ensure that
    • there is only one correct response.
    • choices (including distractors and correct response) are kept to about four. More choices are unwieldy, and fewer make guessing too easy.
    • you avoid the phrases *all of the above* or *none of the above*, because these responses may confuse some students.
    • you avoid words like *never* and *all*, which can provide verbal clues.
    • the relative length of the choices does not provide a clue to the correct response.
    • all distractors are plausible.
    • the order of the choices is random, so there is not a discernible pattern (e.g., favoring the first or last answer) (Shick, 1990).

One quick way to provide feedback is to ask students to record their answers on two answer sheets, one for you and one for them. As students finish a short multiple-choice test (five or six items), collect one answer sheet from them. Then let students work together in small groups to develop an "answer key" for you. You can quickly score answer sheets and have plenty of time to walk around and listen, watch, and learn as students work together teaching science to one another. Students learn an immense amount as they dig into this task. You can keep a record of students' performance on the first answer sheet for formative and summative purposes.

Using Completion, Short-Answer, and Essay Items to Assess Science Knowledge. Short-answer, completion, and essay items require students to generate, not just recognize, correct answers, as is shown in the following examples of assessing memory of scientific facts, knowledge, and procedures. Note that item 5 is a modification of item 1.

Item 5. Name three forms of precipitation.

_____

_____

_____

Goal. Students should develop the ability to
* employ simple equipment and tools to gather data and extend the senses (NSES K–4).

Item 6. A(n) _____ is an instrument that would help you to look at the stars, the planets, and the moon more closely.

Goal. Students should develop
* abilities necessary to do scientific inquiry (NSES K–4, 5–8).

Item 7. A science fair judge asks you, "What is a controlled investigation?" Write out your answer.

_____

_____

_____

Scoring criteria for item 7: The student's answer must show clearly that

* a responding variable is selected;
* what is investigated is how the responding variable changes in response to changes in a manipulated variable; and
* all other variables are controlled or held constant.

From these four scoring criteria, the teacher might develop a rubric to use as a scoring guide. The rubric would show the quality of the responses relative to each criterion necessary for the student to receive full, partial, or no credit.

Score all assessments as quickly as possible, give feedback to students on their results, and use the assessment results to modify your own instruction to improve student learning.

Assessing Understanding of Conceptual Knowledge in Science

Understanding the natural world is a key goal of elementary and middle school science. When students understand, they are able to do something with their knowledge. They can interpret concepts and principles and use them along with observational evidence in inferring, predicting, analyzing, and explaining.

Using Performance Tasks to Assess Science Understanding. Understanding can be assessed by both performance and traditional assessments. Let us look first at performance tasks for assessing understanding.

Oral/Written Pictorial Interpretations. Teachers can gain insights into their students' understanding of concepts and principles by using assessments that ask them to respond to pictorial situations. Look for more than mere observations. Assess for hidden meanings, underlying patterns, and explanatory schemas that bring coherence to the students' observations. Such an assessment is intended to determine students' abilities to communicate the trends and sequences of the pictorial situation.

Decide on the learning objective (the *focus* of the performance task), show a science pictorial situation (the *context*), then give *directions* for how to respond to the questions. This can be done orally for younger students or those with limited reading skills, and in written form for others. Figure 6-8 illustrates such an activity.

An example of a *scoring guide* to assess students' responses to the snowman item of Figure 6-8 is given in Figure 6-9. The scoring guide relates to each of the three questions in the pictorial assessment. This scoring guide is similar to a checklist in that the teacher is to examine students' responses for specific criteria. However, points are to be assigned for

Figure 6-8 Pictorial interpretation assessment.
Source: From *Material Objects Student Manual,* Section 5, Chapter 18, SCIS3, 1992, Hudson, NH: Delta Education, Inc. Copyright 1992 by Delta Education, Inc. Reprinted with permission.

> Teacher shows pictures and says to children:
>
> What differences do you see in these three pictures?
> Which do you think will happen first? Second? Last?
> Why do you think the snowman is changing?

Figure 6-9 Scoring guide for pictorial interpretation assessment.

Element	0–8 Points
Differences among pictures	At least three key differences are clearly stated. Differences might relate to the snowman's height, size, position of arms, depiction of eyes. (0–3 points)
Ordering of pictures	Pictures arranged in correct order (picture 1, picture 2, picture 3). (0–1 point)
Reasons for changes	Judge how well the reasons for changes relate to the *evidence* in the pictures and to *knowledge* of heating and melting. Examples: The sun came out and melted the snowman; the longer the sun was out, the more the snowman melted. The snowman melted because he got hot. The snow changed to water because of the sun. (0–4 points)
Scoring	Outstanding: 7–8 points Satisfactory: 5–6 points Needs improvement: 3–4 points Unsatisfactory: 0–2 points

each relevant response. Teachers must use their own experience to judge the quality of the response and to assign points.

The assessment in Figure 6-8 could be used formatively to improve student understanding, or summatively in assigning student grades.

Using Concept Maps to Assess Science Understanding. We introduced the notion of concept maps in Chapter 3. A **concept map** (Novak, 1996) shows the relationships among facts, concepts, principles, and ideas of a science topic. Children can be taught to construct their own concept maps. Concept maps can be a powerful tool for formatively assessing quality of understanding, informing instruction, providing learning feedback to students, and showing progress (Edmondson, 1999).

By examining student concept maps during instruction, teachers can discover learners' conceptual understandings and their misconceptions (Novak & Musondra, 1991). Children's concept maps can then be used by the teacher as a guide to instruction.

For example, note on the concept map of Figure 6-10 that the learner recognizes that reptiles *are cold-blooded* and *have scales*. The learner also shows that, like reptiles, fish *are*

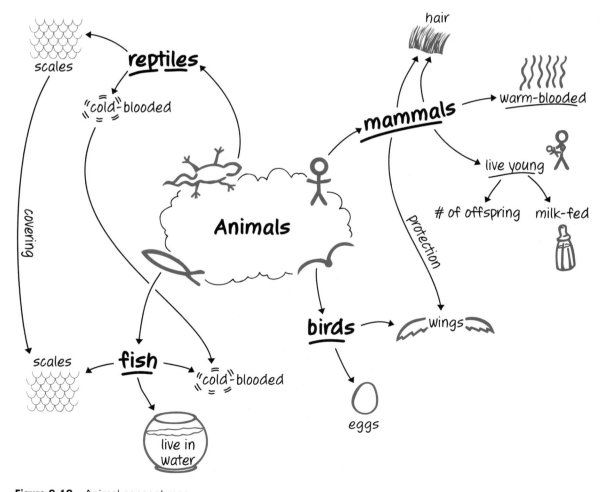

Figure 6-10 Animal concept map.
Source: Prime Time! Strategies for Lifelong Learning in Mathematics and Science in the Middle and High Schools (p. 56) by Hal Hemmerich, Wendy Lim, and Kanwal Neel, 1994, Markham, Ontario: Pembroke Publishers. By permission.

cold-blooded and *have scales*, but fish *live in water*. Similarly, both mammals and birds have defining characteristics. However, the concept map seems to show that the learner thinks that mammals have wings. Thus, the teacher should help the learner distinguish better between bird and mammal characteristics.

Using Anecdotal Records to Assess Understanding. Teachers have always observed their students and made mental notes about their learning progress. The **anecdotal record** procedure merely requires written notes so they can be analyzed over time; they are a simple way to informally assess your students' strengths and weaknesses, their accuracy in describing objects and events, how they use evidence and theories in arriving at explanations, their misconceptions, and so on. Anecdotal record keeping reflects the emphasis you teach in science: that people should write down their observations because they forget things and may not remember when they need the data. Your records can be brief notations of student observations, reactions to hands-on activities, and scientific questions raised by students. Figure 6-11 depicts a form that can be used for anecdotal records for each student.

Using Traditional Items to Assess Understanding. Multiple-choice assessments can be used to go beyond simple recall to assess student understanding of science concepts and principles. Standard multiple-choice items and justified multiple-choice items can be designed that require students to integrate information and to use knowledge in thinking and problem solving.

Using Standard Multiple-Choice Items to Assess Understanding. Here is an example of a multiple-choice item that measures understanding, rather than mere recall.

Goal. Students should understand that
- energy is a property of many substances and is associated with heat, light, electricity, mechanical motion, sound, nuclei, and the nature of a chemical (NSES 5–8).

Item 8. Beans and coal both have stored energy. Where did the energy come from that is stored in beans and coal?
    A. from the earth's gravity
    B. from the sun's light
    C. from the heat in the earth's core
    D. from the airs in carbon dioxide

Source: 2000 National Assessment of Educational Progress (NAEP), 4th grade level.

Date	Learning Activity	Observation/Student Reaction

Figure 6-11   Individual student anecdotal record form.

This item assesses understanding because it requires students to think about two different examples of stored energy and then to examine each possible source of energy to find one that fits both samples. The item was designed by the NAEP project to be used as a summative assessment, but it can be used formatively if teachers score it quickly, give immediate feedback, and provide opportunity for students to learn from their mistakes.

Assessing Understanding with Justified Multiple-Choice Items. In justified multiple-choice questions, students first mark the best answer and then explain in several sentences why they chose that answer. An example of justified multiple choice is shown in Figure 6-12.

Assessing Understanding with Enhanced Multiple-Choice Items. Enhanced multiple-choice questions occur in clusters that provide the context and setting for students. An enhanced multiple-choice example is shown in Figure 6-13.

Assessing Understanding with Essays. Essays represent an important way for students to demonstrate understanding. Through an essay, a student might interpret data, describe and explain an event, or show relationships among facts, generalizations, definitions, values, and skills. Like all assessment devices, the essay has disadvantages as well as advantages:

1. Essays show how well the student is able to organize and present ideas, but scoring may be subjective without firm answers unless you have a clear scoring guide.

Figure 6-12 Justified multiple-choice assessment.

Directions

Three candles, exactly the same size, were put in different boxes like those in the drawing below and lit at the same time. Then the boxes were closed.

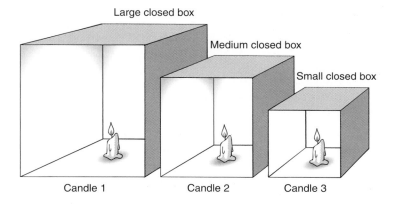

Large closed box

Medium closed box

Small closed box

Candle 1   Candle 2   Candle 3

Circle the letter that shows the order in which the candle flames most likely will go out.

A.   1, 2, 3   C.   3, 1, 2
B.   2, 3, 1   D.   3, 2, 1

Explain (in two or three sentences) why you think the answer you selected is correct.

Figure 6-13 Enhanced multiple-choice assessment.

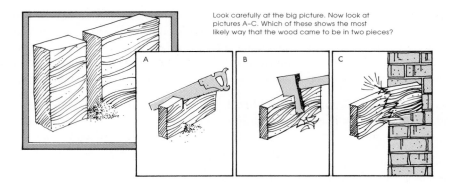

2. Essays show varying degrees of correctness, because there is often not just one right or wrong answer, but scoring requires excessive time.
3. Essays assess abilities to analyze problems using pertinent information and to arrive at generalizations or conclusions, but scoring is influenced by spelling, handwriting, sentence structure, and other extraneous items.
4. Essays assess deeper meanings, reasoning, and interrelationships rather than isolated bits of factual materials, but questions may be either ambiguous or obvious unless you carefully construct them.

To offset the disadvantages of essays, you must carefully construct each essay question. Word the question so students will be limited, as much as possible, to the concepts being tested.

Here are two related essay questions to assess your students' ability to interpret scientific concepts in their own words. Item 10 requires the student to generalize ideas from item 9 to a new setting.

Goal. Students should understand that
- unbalanced forces will cause changes in the speed or direction of an object's motion (NSES 5–8).

Item 9.   In the Cartesian diver you made, why did the medicine dropper go up and down as you squeezed the plastic bottle?

_____

_____

Item 10. Using your knowledge of the Cartesian diver, explain what might be done to a submarine to make it submerge (go down) and surface (come back up).

_____

_____

The following related items show essay questions used with an investigation. The essay items are adapted from a fourth grade National Assessment of Educational Progress (NAEP) test. Items 11 and 12 ask students to interpret data from an investigation. Item 13 requires students to apply the concepts and relationships from items 11 and 12 in a novel situation.

Goal.
1. Students should understand that energy is transferred in many ways (NSES 5–8).
2. Students should develop
   - abilities necessary to do scientific inquiry (NSES K–4, 5–8).

One hot, sunny day Sally left two buckets of water out in the sun. The two buckets were the same except that one was black and the other was white. She made certain that there was the same amount of water in each bucket. She carefully measured the temperature of the water in both buckets at the beginning and end of the day. The following pictures show what Sally found.

Before Sitting
in the Sun

After Sitting
in the Sun

Item 11. Look at the pictures of Sally's experiment. What can Sally conclude from her experiment?

_____

_____

Item 12. What is the evidence for Sally's conclusion?

_____

_____

Item 13. How does the experiment help explain why people often choose to wear white clothes in hot weather?

_____

_____

Source: Adapted from released items, including diagrams, from the 4th grade National Assessment of Educational Progress. http://nces.ed.gov/nationsreportcard/science/.

You will be able to overcome or minimize subjectivity in scoring essay questions by preparing a scoring guide beforehand and scoring each question separately. If a list of the important ideas you expect is made before scoring, there is less chance for ambiguity while scoring.

Figure 6-14 NAEP scoring guide for essay item 13.

Score and Description
Complete
Student explains that white clothes reflect more heat from the sun than black clothes, or that black clothes absorb more heat from the sun than white clothes.   a. Black clothes soak up the heat from the sun.   b. The sun's rays bounce off white clothes.
Partial
Student explains that black clothes attract more heat or that white clothes do not attract as much heat.
Unsatisfactory/Incorrect
Student provides little or no explanation that is related to the heat-absorbing properties of dark-colored clothes and light-colored clothes, or gives unrelated answers.   a. They stay cooler in white clothes.   b. The sun likes dark clothes better.

Figure 6-14 shows the scoring guide used by NAEP to evaluate responses to item 13. This item proved to be quite difficult for the national sample of fourth grade students who took the NAEP tests. Only 12% of the national sample wrote complete explanations and 15% supplied partial explanations, while 73% gave unsatisfactory, incorrect, or off task answers.

For more on this item and examples of other items, access the NAEP Website at http://nces.ed.gov/nationsreportcard/science/. Go to the PALS Website (mentioned earlier) and to the state assessment links on the PALS site for more good essay-based items that can be used in formative assessments in science.

Assessing the Application of Concepts and Principles

The normal cycle of engagement, exploration, explanation, elaboration (application), and evaluation used in the 5-E model of instruction provides teachers opportunity to assess students' abilities to apply concepts and principles.

During the engagement phase of instruction, a boy blows across the top of a piece of paper (see Figure 6-15). Before reading on, try this investigation for yourself to see what happens.

Unexpectedly, the paper moves up rather than down. In the *exploration* phase of instruction, students try out the demonstration. They are then guided to describe the demonstration through questions like these:

What objects are involved in the demonstration?
What is happening to the paper?
What else do you notice in the demonstration?

In the explanation phase of instruction, teachers first ask open-ended questions that require students to use prior knowledge to construct inferences, predictions, and explanations about why the discrepant event took place. Here are some divergent questions you might ask about the event in Figure 6-15:

What is puzzling here? What needs explaining?
What might cause the paper to move upward?

See Chapter 5 for an extended discussion on using different types of questions, including open-ended questions, observation questions, and explanation questions, to guide and assess student thinking.

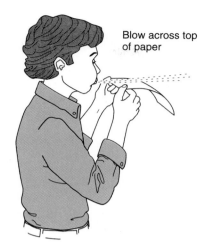

Blow across top of paper

Figure 6-15 What happens when the boy blows across the top of the paper?

Under what conditions could this be possible?
In what situations have you seen similar happenings?

Still in the explanation phase, the students are directly taught a principle that can be combined with observational evidence to explain the phenomenon. The relevant principle for this event is called Bernoulli's principle:

When air flows rapidly across a surface, the air pressure on the surface is reduced.

This is the basic principle of flight.

Students are then guided to apply this principle to explain the demonstration. When air is blown across the top of the paper, the air pressure *above* the paper is reduced. The greater air pressure *below* the paper pushes the paper upward.

In the elaboration or concept application phase of 5-E instruction, students try to apply their learning about the event in Figure 6-15 to a new event. Small groups can be guided with minimal instructions to perform the activity in Figure 6-16. Before they try the activity, each student is given an investigation report sheet and instructed to write a prediction about what might happen in the new activity. Using the principle learned in the investigation of Figure 6-15, what do you think will happen to the paper wad in Figure 6-16?

After making a prediction, students can do the experiment to see what happens. Students write their observations on the investigation reports. If they have done the activity appropriately, the paper wad moves out of the bottle. Students are then asked to individually write on their investigation reports an explanation about why the paper wad moved out of the bottle. What is your explanation for the new event?

A scoring guide for student investigation reports might be developed from the generic rubrics of Figure 6-3. Look especially at the rubrics for *Knowing Science Information* and *Experimenting/Investigating*. What you are looking for in assessment of application is the students' understanding of concepts, principles, and explanations from the first investigation, their abilities to apply their conceptual understanding to the second investigation, and their abilities to coordinate evidence and theory in explaining the two events.

Through this assessment technique, you can gain a better understanding of where each of your students might need assistance in learning. You can use this technique with many topics that lend themselves to teaching through the 5-E model of instruction.

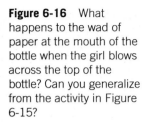

Figure 6-16   What happens to the wad of paper at the mouth of the bottle when the girl blows across the top of the bottle? Can you generalize from the activity in Figure 6-15?

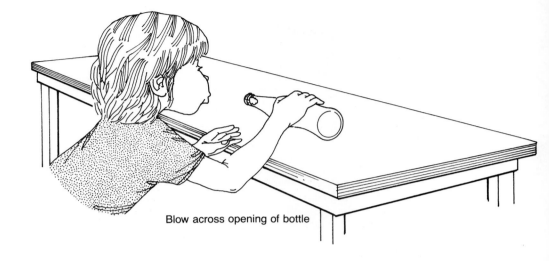

Blow across opening of bottle

Assessing the Application of Inquiry Procedures and Science Processes

A distinctive element of the *National Science Education Standards* is the dual focus on students attaining science understanding and at the same time improving their abilities to inquire. Assessing inquiry procedures and science processes, both formatively for improvement and summatively for accountability and grading, is an important part of elementary and middle school science programs.

Using Performance Tasks to Assess the Application of Inquiry Procedures and Science Processes. In an inquiry-oriented classroom, there are many opportunities to extend learning activities by making them the centerpiece of performance tasks for assessing science processes and procedures.

Using Data Gathering, Recording, and Analysis to Assess Application of Processes. Figure 6-17 shows an example of a performance task for assessing knowledge, understanding, and ability to apply processes of science. On this task, students measure, record data, and determine patterns and trends from the data. The performance task requires students to observe pairs of growing plants over time and answer questions about them. The product to be judged is the students' oral or written answers to the questions. The scorer judges the quality of the answers using a four-point rubric, shown in Figure 6-17, as a scoring guide. Because the rubric is detailed, teachers will need to adapt it to their particular situations.

Assessing Observation Skills. Observation requires the use of all appropriate senses. Figure 6-18 shows a performance task and rubric for assessing the use of the sense of touch. In the activity, students touch a number of objects, infer the properties of the objects, and decide which object is rubber. Prior to beginning, the teacher tells them there are five objects in the box. The scoring key assigns

- one point for correctly identifying rubber, and
- one point for each property identified (must be one that could distinguish rubber from the other materials to a maximum of two points).

Sample Scoring System

Question One. Students are asked to measure the height of two seedlings and to record their results.

Scoring Rubric for Question One

0 = The student either did not record results or reported measurements that were inaccurate by more than a certain percentage determined by the teacher.

1 = The student did not record results, but did report approximate measurements. The teacher needs to determine the meaning of "approximate." This will depend on such things as the markings on students' rulers and students' classroom experiences.

2 = The student recorded approximate measurements.

3 = The student recorded accurate measurements. The teacher needs to determine the meaning of "accurate."

Question Two. Students are asked to explain their recorded measurements to their teacher.

Scoring Rubric for Question Two

0 = The student provided either no explanation or one that makes no sense to the teacher or is unrelated to any unit activities.

1 = The student's explanation related to unit activities but did not explain the growth pattern.

2 = The student provided an explanation for the growth pattern.

3 = The student gave more than one reasonable explanation for the growth pattern.

Figure 6-17 Rubric for performance assessment in a unit on plants.
Source: From "Scoring Active Assessments: Setting Clear Criteria and Adapting Them to Your Students Are the Key to Scoring Classroom Performance," by Sabra Price and George E. Hein, Oct. 1994, *Science and Children 32,* no. 2, p. 29. Copyright 1994, National Science Teachers Association, 1840 Wilson Blvd., Arlington, VA 22201–3000.

This scoring key lends itself to many variations (e.g., identifying all five materials and properties or substituting liquids for solids). What additional tests can you invent and what rubric or scoring key would you use?

Data Capture—Assessing Observation, Measurement, and Communication Skills. Data capture refers to the process of students observing and recording data about objects, organisms, and events. Figure 6-19 shows a data capture assessment that provides teachers with knowledge of students' observing and communicating skills. It is suitable for use with students from K–8, depending on their prior experiences and levels of cognition. It may be adapted for a variety of science topics.

When assessing data capture, consider the following questions:

- How well does the written communication relate to and accurately correspond with what was observed with each sense?
- Does the child accurately label or name the objects observed?
- Does the communication provide details of what was observed?

Assessing the Application of Scientific Processes. The assessment of scientific processes in practical activities can be structured or formalized to guide teacher observations. In one activity,

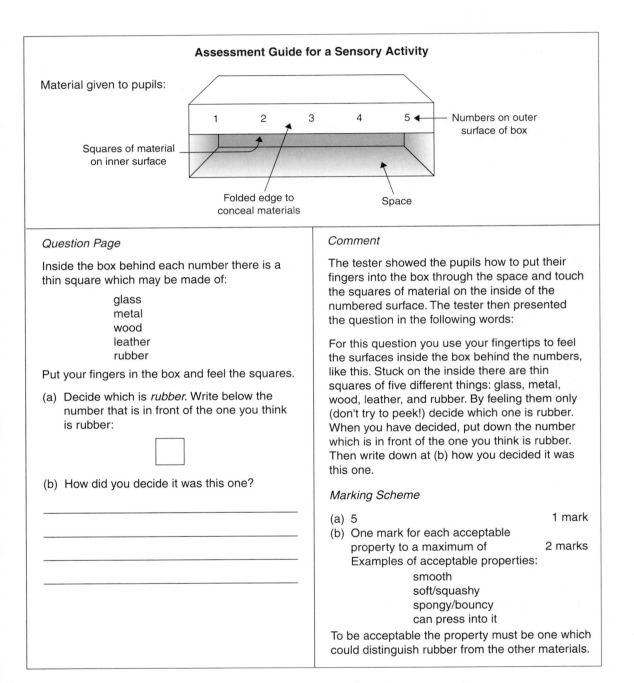

Assessment Guide for a Sensory Activity

Material given to pupils:

1   2   3   4   5 ← Numbers on outer surface of box

Squares of material on inner surface

Folded edge to conceal materials

Space

Question Page

Inside the box behind each number there is a thin square which may be made of:

    glass
    metal
    wood
    leather
    rubber

Put your fingers in the box and feel the squares.

(a) Decide which is *rubber.* Write below the number that is in front of the one you think is rubber:

☐

(b) How did you decide it was this one?

_____

_____

_____

_____

Comment

The tester showed the pupils how to put their fingers into the box through the space and touch the squares of material on the inside of the numbered surface. The tester then presented the question in the following words:

For this question you use your fingertips to feel the surfaces inside the box behind the numbers, like this. Stuck on the inside there are thin squares of five different things: glass, metal, wood, leather, and rubber. By feeling them only (don't try to peek!) decide which one is rubber. When you have decided, put down the number which is in front of the one you think is rubber. Then write down at (b) how you decided it was this one.

Marking Scheme

(a) 5   1 mark
(b) One mark for each acceptable
    property to a maximum of   2 marks
    Examples of acceptable properties:
        smooth
        soft/squashy
        spongy/bouncy
        can press into it
To be acceptable the property must be one which could distinguish rubber from the other materials.

Figure 6-18 Criteria and scoring key for hands-on/minds-on performance assessment.
Source: From Elizabeth Meng and Rodney L. Doran, *Improving Instruction Through Evaluation: Elementary School Science* (Columbus, OH: ERIC Clearinghouse for Science, Mathematics, and Environmental Education, 1993), p. 146.

Observing Leaves

NSES

Science Standards

All students should develop understanding of:

■ Characteristics of organisms (K–4).

Investigation

■ Collect different kinds of leaves. If possible, allow children to gather their own leaves around their homes and the school.

■ Give each group of students a small collection of leaves. Instruct the students to observe the different characteristics (properties, attributes) of the leaves. Ask: *What do you notice about the leaves in your collection? How are they alike? In what ways are they different?* Provide rulers and magnifying glasses for the children to use in observing the leaves. Encourage the children in each group to discuss with one another the similarities and differences among their leaves.

■ Let each child choose two leaves to observe and describe. Instruct the students work individually to compare the leaves according to each of these characteristics: size, color, number of points, and number of veins. Give them the "Leaves Data Sheet" to record their observations.

Figure 6-19   Data capture assessment.
Source: "Leaves: An Investigation" and "Leaves Data Capture Sheet" (pp. 67–68), in *TCM771 Science Assessment,* 1994, Westminster, CA: Teacher Created Materials, Inc. Copyright 1994 by Teacher Created Materials, Inc. Reprinted with permission.

---

students are introduced to mealworms, provided necessary materials, including mealworms and different foods, and directed to find out the food preferences of the mealworms.

A student record page, such as the one in Figure 6-20, can be set up as shown for observational notes and results. The teacher may provide a cue, prompt, or question if students are stuck and cannot continue, or if the teacher seeks students' thinking or reason for some action.

For example, the teacher might make this suggestion: "One way you can try to find the food preference is to make a mark in the middle of the paper. Take some of each food and place it at the same distance from the mark and then put some mealworms on the mark" (Meng & Doran, 1993).

The student laboratory behavior checklist in Figure 6-21 lists problem-solving skills for the observer to focus on. If cues or prompts are given, the observer should make a record of them. The checklist spotlights specific behaviors to look for as students progress toward

Figure 6-19   *(continued)*

Leaves Data Sheet

Name _____ Date _____

■ Draw a picture of Leaf #1   ■ Draw a picture of Leaf #2

[blank box]   [blank box]

Look at Leaf #1.   Look at Leaf #2.

■ What is its color or colors?   ■ What is its color or colors?

_____   _____

_____   _____

■ How many centimeters is   ■ How many centimeters long
  Leaf #1?   is Leaf #2?

_____   _____

_____   _____

■ How many points does Leaf #1   ■ How many points does
  have?   Leaf #2 have?

_____   _____

_____   _____

■ Describe the veins in Leaf #1.   ■ Describe the veins in Leaf #2.

_____   _____

_____   _____

---

finding answers to the question. Emphasis is placed on observable behaviors such as: "places approximately equal quantities of food on the sections of the paper."

When the checklist is used formatively, scaffolding instruction is provided as needed on specific checklist criteria to individuals, small groups, or the class as a whole. Consider the checklist as an example that shows how to construct an assessment checklist that uses content (the behavior of mealworms) as the vehicle to gather data on the skills and processes used by students in scientific investigation or problem solving.

Which of your science activities lend themselves to this type of assessment?

Mealworms

> Find out if the mealworms prefer some of these foods to others. If they do, which ones do they prefer?

a) Put down here any notes and results as you go along:

b) Write down here what you found about the foods the mealworms prefer:

Figure 6-20 Example of student record page for mealworms activity.
Source: From Elizabeth Meng and Rodney L. Doran, *Improving Instruction and Learning Through Evaluation: Elementary School Science* (Columbus, OH: ERIC Clearinghouse for Science, Mathematics, and Environmental Education, 1993), p. 93.

Assessing Graphing Skills. Many activities and assessment devices in science involve using graphs or pictorial and tabular display. The abilities of students to collect data and make and interpret graphs are important skills stressed in elementary and middle school science programs. Therefore, devices for assessing graphing skills must be carefully selected.

The difficulty level of graphing skills required in a task may vary depending on how much is already done for the student and how much the student must do. Here are levels of graphing difficulty:

- lowest—student only needs to record data on the graph
- middle—some assistance in constructing the graph (e.g., axes are already labeled with names of variables)
- upper—must construct accurate graph from raw data

Figure 6-22 is an example of an assessment device that requires upper-level graphing skills.

A checklist to assess the quality of student graphs might be built around the following questions:

1. Is the manipulated variable on the x axis and the responding variable on the y axis? (2 points)
2. Are the variables named along the appropriate axes? (2 points)
3. Is the unit, such as centimeters or weeks, given for each variable? (2 points)
4. Are the axes scaled appropriately to fit the data? (2 points)
5. Are the data points plotted precisely? (2 points)

We examine the uses of graphing in science and mathematics classes in more depth in Chapters 2 and 8.

For excellent descriptions and examples of graphing assessments, see Meng and Doran (1993, pp. 29–31, 138–144).

Figure 6-21 Laboratory student behavior checklist.
Source: From Elizabeth Meng and Rodney L. Doran, *Improving Instruction and Learning Through Evaluation: Elementary School Science* (Columbus, OH: ERIC Clearinghouse for Science, Mathematics, and Environmental Education, 1993), p. 124.

Uses hand lens correctly

Hint given for using hand lens

Deliberately provides mealworm with choice; i.e., at least 2 foods at once

Employs an effective strategy such as:
- (i)   uses 6 or more mealworms if all 4 foods compared at once
- (ii)   compares foods in all possible pairs with 1 mealworm
- (iii) tries at least 4 mealworms with one food at a time

Attempts to provide equal quantities of different foods

Places approximately equal quantities of food on the sections of the paper

Attempts to release mealworms at equal distance from all foods *or* arranges mealworms to be randomly distributed around food

Arranges to release mealworms from points equidistant from foods, *or* places mealworms randomly around foods

Arranges for all mealworms to have same time to choose (i.e., puts them all down together or uses a clock)

Uses clock to time definite events

Allows about 4–7 minutes for mealworms to make choice (not necessarily timed)

Examines behavior carefully (to see if food is being eaten)

Counts mealworms near each pile after a certain time (or notes which food the mealworm is on for strategy [ii] above)

Makes notes at (a) on record page (however brief)

Records details such as time of choice and numbers near each food

Can read stop clock correctly (to nearest second)

Makes a record of finding at (b) on record page without prompting

Results at (a) and (b) consistent with evidence (even if only rough)

Results based on and consistent with quantitative evidence

Since the primary purpose of assessment in the classroom is to improve learning, student results on the graphing activity might be used to guide reteaching of selected elements of graphing. The learning goal is for all students to succeed in graphing accurately.

Checklists for Assessing Scientific Processes and Procedures. Hands-on inquiry activities provide an authentic setting for assessing children's abilities to do scientific inquiry. Figure 6-23 displays a checklist that can be used to judge students' use of specific science process and inquiry procedures. Think about using the checklist over the course of a year. Thus, you might

- keep a checklist record on each child,
- consider each child's performance in a variety of science activities,
- note whether or when each child exhibits the indicated task or behavior,
- add comments to guide learning and instruction, and
- work with all students to help them improve in their abilities to use each process or skill.

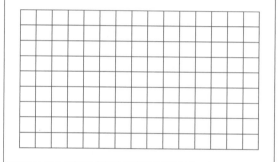

Our class planted bean seeds, watered them as needed, observed them, staked them on sticks, and measured their growth each Friday afternoon. Here are the average heights when we started measuring (when plant had grown above ground) and for six weeks after:

0 week ....10 cm

1 week ....15 cm

2 weeks.................25 cm

3 weeks.................50 cm

4 weeks.................60 cm

5 weeks.................70 cm

6 weeks.................75 cm

Draw any kind of graph (one of those we studied or any other kind you might want) to show how our beans grew over time.

Figure 6-22 Assessing graphing skills—upper level of difficulty.

Using Traditional Items to Assess the Application of Science Processes and Inquiry Procedures. Adding traditional items to your plan for assessing the application of science processes and inquiry procedures can help to achieve balance in assessment. Such items are often easy to construct, are quick to score, and can provide the basis for immediate feedback for the improvement of learning.

Assessing Science Processes with Justified Multiple-Choice Items. Ability to apply scientific procedures can be assessed with standard multiple-choice items, especially if they are combined with essays as is shown in this example.

Goal. Students should develop

- abilities necessary to do scientific inquiry (NSES K–4, 5–8).

Item 14. John cuts grass for several different neighbors. Each week he makes the rounds with his lawn mower. The grass is usually different in the lawns. It is tall in some lawns, but not in others. Which of the following is a suitable hypothesis he could investigate related to this situation?

A. Lawn mowing is more difficult when the weather is warm.

B. The amount of fertilizer a lawn receives is important.

Student Name: _____

Process or Skill	Task or Behavior	Task Observed?	
		Date	Comment
Questioning	Asks a variety of questions, including questions that can and cannot be investigated		
	Recognizes differences between questions that can be investigated and questions that cannot be investigated		
	Asks testable questions from predictions and explanations made in activities		
Placing Priority on Evidence	Has some idea of what evidence to look for to answer the question		
	Chooses a realistic way of measuring or comparing to obtain results		
	Takes steps to ensure that the results obtained are accurate		
Observing	Uses several senses in exploring objects		
	Uses magnifying glasses and other instruments to extend the senses		
	Identifies details in objects, organisms, and events		
	Notices patterns, relationships, or sequences in events		
Inferring	Uses evidence and scientific knowledge in making inferences		
	Explains basis for inferences		
	Makes inferences that are reasonable and fit the evidence and scientific knowledge		
	Suggests how to test inferences		
Predicting	Uses evidence in making a prediction		
	Explains basis for predictions		
	Makes predictions that are reasonable and fit the evidence, whether accurate or not.		
	Makes interpolations and extrapolations from patterns in information or observation		
	Suggests how to test predictions		
Explaining	Gives explanation consistent with evidence and scientific knowledge		
	Explains basis for explanations		
	Shows awareness that other explanations may fit the evidence		
	Suggests how explanation can be checked		
	Shows awareness that explanations are tentative and subject to change		
Communicating	Talks freely with others about activities and ideas		
	Listens to others' ideas and looks at their results		
	Reports observations coherently in drawings, writing, and charts		
	Uses tables, graphs, and charts to report investigation results		

Figure 6-23 Checklist for science processes and inquiry procedures.

Source: Adapted from Wynne Harlan and Sheila Jelly (1990). *Developing Science in the Primary Classroom.* Portsmouth, NH: Heinemann (pp. 46–48). Copyright © by Pearson Education Limited. Used with permission.

C. Lawns that receive more water have longer grass.
D. The more hills there are in a lawn, the harder it is to cut.

Item 15. Explain in a few sentences why you think your answer choice in item 14 is better than the other choices.

Complete answers to item 15 should note that

- the variable of interest in the item stem is *length of grass*;
- length of grass is a variable only in answer choice C; and
- answer choice C implies a hypothesis/question that can be investigated: *What effect does the amount of watering have on grass length?*

Assessing Application of Inquiry Abilities with Clusters of Items. Expanded multiple-choice items can also be used to assess understanding of scientific procedures. Such clusters can provide for constructed responses, as is shown in the following set of items.

Goal. Students should develop
- abilities necessary to do scientific inquiry (NSES K–4, 5–8).

Shannon decided to compare different kinds of popcorn to find out which was the best buy. She bought three kinds of popcorn: regular white popcorn, regular yellow popcorn, and gourmet yellow popcorn. She put 50 kernels of each kind in the popper. She kept the popper running for each batch until the popcorn stopped popping. Then she counted the number of kernels of each kind that popped. She repeated the procedure two more times and averaged the results for each kind of popcorn. Next, she put 5 popped kernels of each kind into a measuring cup to find out which kernels popped the biggest. Then she tasted some of each kind of popcorn. Her results are shown in the following chart.

Kind of popcorn	Average number of kernels that popped	Volume of 25 popped kernels	Price for a 16-ounce bag	Shannon's taste test
Regular white	38	60 ml	$1.19	OK
Regular yellow	46	60 ml	$1.19	BEST
Gourmet yellow	45	80 ml	$1.50	OK

Item 16. Shannon's brother looked at her results and decided that the gourmet popcorn was the best buy. What evidence from the chart supports his decision?
A. There is no evidence from the chart to support his decision.
B. More of the gourmet popcorn popped.
C. There is more popcorn in the bag of gourmet popcorn.
D. The gourmet popcorn kernels popped the biggest.

Item 17. If Shannon's brother repeated the popcorn test, which results would have the greatest probability of being different for the new test?
A. the average number of kernels that popped
B. the volume of 25 popped kernels
C. the price for a 16-ounce bag
D. the results of the taste test

Item 18. Shannon decided that the regular yellow popcorn was the best popcorn to buy. Identify two pieces of evidence from the chart that support her decision.

_____

_____

Scoring guide for item 18:

2 points for two acceptable reasons
1 point for one acceptable reason
0 points for no acceptable reasons

Acceptable reasons include:

Yellow popcorn had the largest number of kernels (46 out of 50 popped).
Yellow popcorn had the best taste.
Yellow popcorn is one of the cheaper kinds/is cheap.

Source: Adapted from released items from the Michigan Educational Assessment Program, 4th grade level.

Assessing the Planning and Implementing of Inquiry Procedures in Science

Performance assessments are especially useful for assessing the planning and implementing of inquiry procedures in science, as is shown by the following examples.

Hands-on Practical Assessment. Since the 1980s, assessment data have been collected in the United States and other countries from students in elementary and middle school grades on a series of practical hands-on science activities (Chan, Doran, & Lenhardt, 1999; Doran, 1990). The 1995–1996 Third International Mathematics and Science Study (TIMSS) collected data on a half million students from 41 nations. U.S. students were well above the average science performance of students worldwide at the fourth grade level, being surpassed only by students from Korea (U.S. Department of Education, 1997). U.S. eighth graders were slightly above the international average in science but trailed the average performance of students in 16 other countries (U.S. Department of Education, 1996).

Figure 6-24 describes seven performance tasks given at the eighth grade level in science on the TIMSS (Chan et al., 1999). These tests used science content and equipment from physics, chemistry, and biology. Students completed the tasks at tables where the necessary materials were provided. The shadows and plasticine tasks integrated science and mathematics. Students were asked to manipulate equipment and materials; observe, reason, and record data in test booklets; and interpret data.

Figure 6-25 provides the directions and questions for the TIMSS solutions task. In this task, students first planned procedures to determine what effect different water temperatures have on the speed with which effervescent antacid tablets dissolve. The students then carried out tests, measuring water temperatures and corresponding times for the tablets to dissolve. Students were asked to use the evidence from their tests to draw conclusions about the effect of different water temperatures on the speed with which a tablet dissolves. Finally, the students were instructed to explain why different temperatures have different effects. Student activities in this performance assessment closely parallel the tasks of inquiry (Figure 1-3) identified by the writers of the *National Science Education Standards*.

Although interpretations of data from the TIMSS and the earlier international comparisons vary, information from these studies is important for the development of educational policies at national and state levels.

Task	Description	Task	Integrated tasks (science and mathematics)
Pulse	Student investigates changes in pulse rate during exercise, records and analyzes data, and explains results.	Shadows	Student manipulates the position of light source and object to find three positions at which a shadow is twice the width of an object and expresses the relationship of distance of the light and object to the screen as a general rule.
Magnets	Student determines the stronger of two magnets and describes strategies to support the conclusion.	Plasticine	Given only two standard masses, student develops and describes strategies to determine the masses of lumps of various specified masses.
Batteries	Student determines which of four batteries is worn out, describes strategies, and uses concept knowledge to explain proper arrangement of batteries in a flashlight.		
Rubber Band	Student attaches increasing numbers of masses to a rubber band, investigates the effect on the length, and explains results.		
Solutions	Student investigates the effect of different temperatures on rate of tablet disintegration; collects, records, and analyzes data; and explains results.		

Figure 6-24 Description of eighth grade performance assessment tasks from the Third International Mathematics and Science Study (TIMSS).
Source: From "Learning from the TIMSS," by Alfred Chan, Rodney Doran, and Carol Lenhardt, 1999, *The Science Teacher, 66*(1), p. 20. Copyright 1999 by National Science Teachers Association. Reprinted with permission.

Table 6-5 shows the average percentage scores on each question for the solutions performance assessment. How do U.S. eighth graders' average percentage scores compare with the international average? On what tasks are U.S. eighth graders above average? below average? Why do you think these trends exist? For example, why do U.S. students lag behind in planning investigations but exceed international averages in drawing and explaining conclusions?

Survey your science program to see where you can use these suggestions to develop performance assessment measures suited to your immediate needs.

Essays Plus Performance Tasks for Assessing the Planning of Investigations. To assess ability to plan science investigations, we must ask students to move beyond "cookbook experiences" where everything is planned for them. They must be asked to devise other ways of investigating, as is shown by this cluster of items.

Figure 6-25 Directions and questions for the TIMSS solutions task.
Source: From "Learning from the TIMSS," by Alfred Chan, Rodney Doran, and Carol Lenhardt, 1999, *The Science Teacher, 66*(1), p. 20. Copyright 1999 by National Science Teachers Association. Reprinted with permission.

Materials:
Hot and cold water
Several beakers
Effervescent antacid tablets
Stirrer
Clock or watch with a second hand
Thermometer
30 centimeter ruler

Task: Plan an experiment to find out what effect different water temperatures have on the speed with which the tablets dissolve.

Part one. Write down a plan that includes what will be measured, how many measurements will be taken, and how the measurements will be presented in a table.

Part two. Carry out the test(s). Make a table and record all measurements.

Part three. According to the investigation, what effect do different water temperatures have on the speed with which a tablet dissolves?

Part four. Explain why different water temperatures have different effects.

Part five. If the plan must be changed, describe the changes and explain why they will be made. If there are no changes, write "no change." Empty all beakers into the waste container, dry them, and leave everything the way it was found.

TABLE 6-5   AVERAGE PERCENTAGE SCORES ON EACH PERFORMANCE CRITERIA FOR THE TIMSS SOLUTIONS TASK

Sample	Overall Task Average	Q1 Plan Investigation	Q2 Conduct Investigation		Q3 Draw Conclusions	Q4 Explain Conclusion	Q5 Evaluate Design
			Presentation	Data Quality			
International	49	44	62	59	77	22	30
United States	48	33	64	59	82	27	24

Source: From "Learning from the TIMSS," by Alfred Chan, Rodney Doran, and Carol Lenhardt, 1999, *The Science Teacher, 66*(1), p. 21. Copyright 1999 by National Science Teachers Association. Reprinted with permission.

Goal. Students should develop
• abilities necessary to design and conduct a scientific investigation (NSES 5–8).

We just finished investigating static electricity and ways of producing and controlling it.

Item 19. Use the information from your investigations to explain why you get a "shock" when you slide across the plastic seat covers in your parents' car.

Item 20. Suggest a way to prevent the shock; develop and carry out a plan to test your hypothesis.

Item 21. Write a report communicating to a classmate your hypothesis, investigation plan, results of your tests, and explanations. Be sure to use your investigative evidence and prior knowledge in forming your explanation.

Planning skills can also be assessed by asking students to set up problem-solving procedures; for example:

Item 22. We are on a class picnic and field day. As the bus stops at the park, three volunteers go to find us a good picnic spot. They all come back excited about their finds for the spot. What questions would you ask them to decide which spot to pick? Give the reasons you picked your particular questions.

Each of these examples delves into students' thinking and encourages communication.

Assessing the Use of Information in Planning. The ability to gather information and use it in problem solving can be assessed using a variety of techniques. You might structure this type of question:

Goal. Students should develop
- abilities of technological design (NSES 5–8).
- understanding that perfectly designed solutions do not exist; all technological solutions have trade-offs, such as safety, cost, efficiency, and appearance (NSES 5–8).

Item 23. We have just come back from a trip to our city's landfill. We were told that there was too much trash being discarded and placed in the landfill. How would you gather information on the amount of different types of trash placed in landfills? Gather the information and use it to set up a trash management and reduction plan for our school.

In developing a scoring guide for this assessment, analyze the problem situation, planning techniques, and communication skills to identify specific things you think should be evident in the students' answers. Use either a rubric or a checklist to guide you in scoring the answers.

What are some topics of interest to you, your students, and the community that might lend themselves to this type of assessment?

Assessment of Science Attitudes

As discussed in Chapter 1, developing positive attitudes toward science is an important goal of science education. Although there are many affective goals that should be attained in science, five main attitudes, values, and habits of mind discussed in that chapter are especially relevant to successful inquiry. They are

- being curious,
- insisting on evidence,
- being predisposed to apply science knowledge,
- being willing to critically evaluate ideas, and
- working cooperatively.

It is very difficult to measure attitudes reliably, but attitudes cannot be improved without an understanding of students' existing attitudes (Shepardson & Britsch, 2001, pp. 126–127). Figure 6-26 shows a checklist that can be used to gain some understanding of students' science attitudes. The checklist draws on the work of Harlan and Jelly (1990) and Shepardson and Britsch (2001). By analyzing attitudes into a number of different components, the checklist allows teachers to watch for specific indicators of these important science attitudes.

As with the science processes checklist (see Figure 6-27), you might keep an assessment checklist for each student, noting when you judge that the child has displayed the

Student Name: _____

Attitude	Component Behavior	Behavior Observed	
		Date	Comment
Curiosity	Notices and attends to new things and situations		
	Shows interest through careful observation of details		
	Asks questions		
	Uses resources to find out about new or unusual situations		
Respect for Evidence	Searches for evidence to answer questions posed		
	Checks evidence that does not fit the pattern of other findings		
	Challenges conclusions or interpretations where there does not seem to be sufficient evidence		
Predisposition to Apply Knowledge in Problem Solving	Searches for available scientific knowledge to apply in problem solving		
	Uses available knowledge to guide exploration of problem situation		
	Uses available knowledge and evidence in generating explanations and problem solutions		
Willingness to Critically Evaluate Ideas	Changes existing ideas when there is sufficient evidence		
	Considers alternative ideas to her own		
	Willing to examine positive and negative aspects of his own investigations		
	Seeks alternative ideas rather than just the first idea		
	Realizes that it may be necessary to change an existing idea		
Working Cooperatively	Talks freely with other students about topic-related ideas in small group and whole group settings		
	Shows respect for others in groups		
	Considers multiple viewpoints within groups		
	Readily assumes and fulfills assigned role in inquiry group		
	Assists others in investigation and learning tasks when appropriate		

Figure 6-26 Checklist for assessing science attitudes.

Source: From *Assessment in Science: A Guide to Professional Development and Classroom Practice* (pp. 119–147), by D. P. Shepardson and S. J. Britsch, 2001, Boston: Kluwer. Adapted with permission.

Judging Criteria	Indicators
Creativity	• Creativity is shown in the selection of a problem to investigate. • Ingenuity in the design and development of the project is shown.
Scientific Thought	• The problem selected is appropriate. • The question and hypothesis are clear, well formulated, and sufficiently narrow to be investigated empirically. • Experimental variables are clearly defined and appropriate controls are used. • Data are well organized and accurate graphs are shown. • Data collected serve as adequate evidence to support the conclusions formed.
Thoroughness	• The project shows thorough planning. • Review of background information is thorough. • All data are accurate. • All data collected were used in drawing conclusions. • A project notebook sufficiently documents the student's work from beginning to end.
Skill	• The project clearly represents the student's work. • The project is sturdy and well constructed. • The student clearly understands the equipment used. • The project shows continual attention to safety standards.
Clarity	• The student kept and displayed an original, bound logbook. • The project report was well done and easily understandable, with appropriate documentation. • The project display was eye-appealing, with appropriate materials, posters, charts, and graphs. • Lettering, signs, and diagrams are neat and accurate. • Visual aids assist the reader or judge in understanding the project.

Figure 6-27 Science fair judging criteria.
Source: Multiple science fair judging sheets found on the Internet.

attitude or failed to display the attitude when it matters. Information gained via the checklist should be used formatively to improve attitudes, learning, and instruction, rather than summatively for grading purposes.

Assessing Multiple Objectives in Science

Students use previously acquired science knowledge and understanding to solve problems in situations that are new or different from those to which they were exposed. In assessing multiple objectives in science, we might ask whether students understand a particular idea well enough to apply it in another context, for example in model building, student demonstrations, and student projects. We might ask students to show us both their understanding of science knowledge and their abilities to inquire, such as on a science fair project. Or we might ask students to select and draw together a variety of assignments, tasks, and items to show their understanding, such as with a portfolio.

Model Building. Physical models that illustrate students' understanding of natural objects, organisms, structures, and phenomena are excellent products for assessment. Students are required to research relevant information, discover what kind of models illustrate the scientific concept(s) to be shown, collect needed scientific supplies and equipment, plan and build the model, and explain it to the class and teacher. Students have successfully accomplished these things for models of the solar system, geological structures, physiological systems of the human body, and so forth.

Student Demonstrations. Students can divulge much of what they know about scientific concepts and their interrelationships through planning, manipulating, and demonstrating with scientific supplies and equipment. The audience may be their own classmates and teacher, other classes, their parents, or other persons. Individual students or groups may give the demonstrations, such as showing how electrical circuits work, exhibiting static electricity in everyday situations, or demonstrating what happens when colored lights are mixed.

Student Projects: Designing an Aquarium. Student projects may uncover much about students' understanding and thinking. Project assessments provide the teacher with insight into how well students have learned, recorded, and put their knowledge into practical use. The teacher and students should work out expectations of what the projects will encompass *before* students start their projects. Primary grade students often make something as part of their science learning.

In the example of project assessment that follows, groups of second grade students work together to design an aquarium. A description of this performance task and the detailed rubric for it can be found at http://ebbj.htmlplanet.com/. The project is built around a "WebQuest" in which students use the Internet or a library to gather needed information to design an aquarium. Here is the students' task.

> **You are a zoologist at a city zoo. Many people have suggested adding aquariums to the zoo. So, your task as a zoologist is to (a) choose a type of water habitat; (b) choose three animals that can coexist in the water habitat; and (c) design an aquarium so that it is an appropriate habitat for the three animals.**

The students would need to have explored the needs of organisms in previous activities. In this activity, they use reference books and the Internet to gather information on the habitat and animals selected. They will need to find information concerning the different components of the habitat, such as plants and rocks, the food that should be available for their animals, and what enables each of the animals to live in a water habitat.

Their aquarium design can be presented to the teacher and the class in the form of a *Kid Pix* or *PowerPoint* display or as an actual aquarium. As the teacher, you will be there to scaffold learning and provide input. But do not give too much assistance—this is a student project.

A rubric is used to assess the students' aquarium designs and their performance on an oral exam. The rubric might include these three main criteria:

1. The student identifies and distinguishes between freshwater and saltwater habitats.
2. The student lists three animals that live in the chosen water habitat and gives information about each, including the food, shelter, and part of the body that enables them to live in the environment.

NSES Students should understand that all organisms have basic needs; for example, animals need air, water, and food; organisms can survive only in environments in which their needs are met (K–4).

3. The aquarium design includes an appropriate habitat for each of the three animals, including shelter and a source of food for each.

Take some time to develop the aquarium task rubric by writing quality descriptions for three levels: high, medium, and low quality.

This performance task may be challenging for second graders. It can be a good one, however, because it relates to many cells of the assessment framework (see Figure 6-1) and combines assessment with learning opportunities. How does the project call for the development of factual knowledge, conceptual knowledge, and science processes and procedures? How are knowing, understanding, and applying used in the project by the second graders and assessed by the teacher?

Science Fair Projects. Students in many elementary and middle schools are required to develop science fair projects at one grade level or another. Projects are usually evaluated by external judges, using a common set of judging criteria. Figure 6-27 shows a composite view of judging criteria used in many science fairs.

The first step in creating a good science fair project is for the student to select an interesting, sufficiently narrow question to investigate. In Chapter 2 we identified and gave examples of three types of scientific investigations: descriptive, classificatory, and experimental. Judging criteria often favor experimental investigations, with hypotheses, responding and manipulated variables, and adequate controls designed into the investigation. Because true experiments are difficult for younger learners, we suggest that school and district-wide science fairs be for students from the fourth or fifth grade up. Younger students might be involved in descriptive and classificatory investigations displayed in their own classrooms.

In carrying out experimental investigations, students must perform a test to answer their research questions. If they were interested in earthworms, for example, they might perform a test to see if temperature had an effect on how earthworms move. Students would have to get some earthworms, find a way to vary the temperature of the soil in the earthworm container, and measure what happened at different temperatures.

The hypothesis, background information, experiment design, and results might be recorded in a bound notebook. The data collected would be used as evidence to answer the question posed. Students would need to carry out the project with only a little help from parents, teachers, or friends.

The project would need to be clearly and dramatically displayed, perhaps using show boards. Finally, the student would explain the project in detail through an interview with a judge.

For elementary and middle school students, downplay the competitive nature of projects. The goal is for students to improve in their abilities and understanding of science, not necessarily to "win." Thus, you should use the project assessment formatively to improve student learning, rather than summatively for grades.

Science fair projects are fun. Students will learn a great deal, and they will display to others what they know and have learned.

Portfolios. Teachers use a wide range of assessment procedures to evaluate students' progress in science and to communicate to students, parents, and others about their achievement and growth. A portfolio can be used to authentically assess knowledge, understanding, and ability to apply science concepts, principles, and procedures.

Portfolios are containers (folders, boxes, crates, etc.) into which students and teachers place student products or other evidences of their knowledge, skills, and attitudes in science, such as written assignments, logs, group work, tests, homework, projects, models, drawings, and other creative expressions. Besides being valuable for *teacher* data on student performance, portfolios can also be used by *students* to reflect on their science learning achievement. Samples of student work presented in portfolios should present *evidence* of growth in scientific content knowledge, concept construction, processes, skills, and attitudes (Barnes & Barnes, 1991).

Expressed in terms of Vygotsky's theory as discussed in Chapter 3, portfolios show the upper limits of a student's learning zone (zone of proximal development) as revealed over a long period of time. Portfolio item selections should be *positive* (e.g., what students did correctly, even with scaffolding assistance) rather than *negative* (student mistakes). Either the teacher (for younger students) or the student can catalog items with an index or table of contents listing each item, its date, descriptions of each assignment, and any other pertinent information.

The purpose of the portfolio usually determines items to be included. Items selected, in turn, determine the type of portfolio container to be used. Students can customize their own portfolios. By having students pick the items *they* want to include as evidence of their achievement, there is strong learner ego involvement, leading to greater learning and self-assessment. Selecting items for inclusion in their portfolio also prompts students to make a greater commitment and feel more ownership about their work. Students may be guided to choose among the following samples of work (or others of their own choice) to be included in their science portfolios:

science observations	book reviews
journals	data collection
projects	writing samples
research reports	tests
computer work	digital photographs
graphs	trip evaluations
drawings	dramatics
models	self-assessment checklists

Students and teachers must work together to establish selection and assessment criteria for portfolio items. With student input, you can develop rubrics or checklists to use as a scoring guide. Share the scoring guide with your students beforehand. Part of portfolio assessment should involve students' self-assessment through use of an agreed-on rubric or checklist. This makes students more active learners as they develop their own internal criteria for selecting and assessing each portfolio item. Figure 6-28 is an example of a portfolio checklist used for self-assessment.

Teacher Self-Reflection on Instruction

To improve student learning, it is generally necessary to improve instruction. Teachers need time and techniques to reflect on instruction. Self-reflection tools such as journals, audiotapes, videotapes, and portfolios allow teachers to capture their teaching, track their development over time, analyze their progress, and identify needs for further learning (National Research Council, 1996, p. 69).

As you examine your own teaching, consider the types of opportunities you give to students. Checklists like those in Figures 6-23 and 6-26 might form the basis for teacher self-reflection. Rather than examining student behavior, however, reflect on the opportunities you have provided for students to attain each indicator included in a checklist.

Name _____

Portfolio item _____

Date _____

Worked alone _____   **Worked with** _____

Answer only those questions that fit this portfolio item.

■ Why did you pick this item? _____

_____

■ What did you learn from working on this item? _____

_____

■ If you had more time with this item, what else would you do? _____

_____

■ What problems did you have while working on this item? _____

_____ How did you solve them? _____

_____

■ What area(s) of interest would you like to explore that resulted from

working on this item? _____

Figure 6-28   Portfolio item self-assessment.
Source: Modified from *The Great Northern Science Book* (p. 30), Nancy Murphy, K–8 Alaska Science Consortium, 1992, Fairbanks, AK: University of Alaska Fairbanks.

Examining questioning behavior from audiotape or videotape recordings can also be useful. Beginning with a short segment of one of your class discussions (about 15 minutes would be sufficient), you might ask these questions about your own questioning techniques (as discussed in Chapter 5):

- How much time was spent at the observational level and the explanation/problem-solving level in discussion?
- What cognitive processes (knowing, understanding, applying) did I try to develop?
- How did I respond to student discussion? Did I *listen to* and *use* student responses? Was I *accepting?* Did I *extend?* Did I *probe?* Did I use sufficient *wait-time* after my questions and after student responses?
- How much time was involved in teacher talk compared with student talk?
- What types of inferring and predicting questions did I use? Did I ask students to explain their reasoning? Did I ask them for their evidence to support reasoning?

You might also concentrate on how you open or structure the lesson or other aspects of the class discussion.

Other techniques you might use in reflecting on your teaching include peer observation, coaching, and mentoring. Make self-reflection an ongoing commitment. Remember, the integrated knowledge needed to teach science well develops over time.

Science Assessment: Putting It All Together

Teaching and assessing science learning requires thorough planning, skillful execution, and careful, constant review and modification. Here is a suggested format to assess student learning and your science teaching:

1. Identify the specific scientific skills, knowledge, and processes you will emphasize during your science teaching. Identify your objectives clearly. Good objectives are specific, capable of being observed (and therefore assessed), and varied.
2. Identify what will constitute evidence for students attaining the objectives.
3. Develop an assessment plan based on your goals and objectives for teaching science.
4. Choose appropriate assessment techniques. Table 6-6 shows how to match your group structure (individual, group, or class) to your assessment procedures.
5. Select and use a variety of assessment techniques. Avoid overdependence on any one type of evaluation device. Include a wide range of tests and performance assessment devices such as those discussed in this chapter.
6. If you assess your students continually, you can lessen their anxiety about assessment, especially if the results are used for instruction instead of just for grades.
7. Involve your students in your assessment. Invite your students' comments on your assessments and even have them try making up their own.

TABLE 6-6   MATCHING PERFORMANCE ASSESSMENT PROCEDURES TO SCIENCE TEACHING GROUP STRUCTURES

	Performance Assessment Procedures		
	Oral	Written	Performance
Group Structure:			
Individual	A student can be called on in class to give a brief summary of basic information discussed in class that day.	A student can be asked to write a review of a science program shown on television.	A student can take responsibility for studying an experiment and presenting a demonstration of it to the class.
	A student can be asked to critique an experiment conducted by a fellow classmate or critique a published study.	A student can be asked to write a brief report of research he conducted.	
Group	Students can collaborate on presenting a summary of the key concepts studied in a unit.	Students can collaborate on producing a bibliography of important books or articles.	Students can share the responsibility for preparing and presenting an experiment or discussion on an interesting topic to the class or school.
	Students can conduct a roundtable discussion of an important topic.		
Class	A class might conduct an assembly on a topic of interest or concern to the entire school.	A class might keep a log of their science experiments and provide written comments and critiques of each other's work.	A class might dramatize an important event in the history of science.

8. Scrutinize your assessment procedures often and revise them as a result of your students' responses to them.
9. Study the implications of your assessment data for future teaching. If you stress memorization or recall, students will memorize. If understanding, application, inquiry processes, and problem solving are important to you, make certain your assessment reflects these values.
10. Continue your self-reflection. Teachers today must be committed to improving the learning of all students. Use assessment results to look more closely at your students. At the same time, look more introspectively at your own teaching to examine the impact of your goals, teaching methods, and assessment techniques. Such self-assessment will also make you more effective with students who are physically or mentally challenged, or who have culturally diverse backgrounds. Assessment will help you see more clearly and sensitively the individual differences of your students.

 Use the self-assessment questions for Chapter 6 at http://www.prenhall.com/carin to assess how well you understand this chapter and how prepared you are for a test over its content.

Learning to use assessment effectively will help you become a better teacher and your students better learners. It is clearly worth the effort.

SUMMARY

- In constructivist models of teaching science, assessment is a continual process: for planning, guiding, and enriching students' learning; for communicating with students, school administrators, parents, and the public; for monitoring outcomes of your science program; and for influencing science curriculum and teaching.
- Various principles form the foundation for assessment; they critically affect the *what, how,* and *how well* of your science teaching/learning. Assessments can be *diagnostic* (before starting teaching), *summative* (after teaching), and *formative* (during teaching).
- Assessment is focused on three questions: *Where are learners going? Where are they now?* and *How can we help them reach their goals?* In answer to the first question, local, state, and national standards define the science facts, concepts, and principles, and the inquiry processes and procedures students should know, understand, and be able to apply. A wide variety of traditional assessment items and performance assessment tasks can be used to determine where learners are now. The results of assessments can then guide teachers as they work with individual students to help them reach learning goals.
- Authentic performance assessments are particularly relevant for inquiry science. Performance assessment tasks

are authentic whenever they simulate tasks that scientists, students, or other citizens might be called on to perform in real-world contexts. Developing performance assessment tasks involves determining the focus, context, directions, and scoring guides for the tasks. Types of scoring guides discussed included holistic scoring guides, checklists, and rubrics. Rubrics are particularly important in performance assessment. Keep these things in mind as you write your own rubrics:

- Set clear assessment standards to interpret the specifics of your students' work.
- Determine levels of rubric scoring—often on a four-point scale—that are applicable to the unique scientific processes, skills, content, and attitudes you are teaching.

- A large bank of traditional items, performance assessment tasks and techniques, checklists, and rubrics have been provided as resources for you to draw on in developing your own assessment program.
- Assessment is a critical component of inquiry learning and instruction. The assessment revolution is here to stay.

REFERENCES

Anderson, L. W., & Krathwohl, D. R. (2001). *A taxonomy for learning, teaching, and assessing: A revision of Bloom's taxonomy of educational objectives.* New York: Longman.

Atkin, J. M., Black, P., & Coffey, J. (Eds.). (2001). *Classroom assessment and the national science education standards.* Washington, DC: National Academy Press.

Barnes, L. W., & Barnes, M. B. (1991). Assessment, practically speaking. How can we measure hands-on science skills? *Science and Children, 28*(6), 14–15.

Bloom, B. S. (Ed.), Englehart, M. D., Furst, E. J., Hill, W. H., & Krathwohl, D. R. (1956). *Taxonomy of educational objectives: Handbook 1: Cognitive domain.* New York: David McKay.

Chan, A., Doran, R., & Lenhardt, C. (1999). Learning from the TIMSS. *The Science Teacher, 66*(1), 18–22.

Doran, R. (1990). What research says . . . about assessment. *Science and Children, 27*(8), 26–27.

Edmondson, K. M. (1999). Assessing science understanding through concept maps. In J. J. Mintzes, J. H. Wandersee, & J. D. Novak (Eds.), *Assessing science understanding: A human constructivist view* (pp. 223–248). New York: Academic Press.

Foster, G. W., & Heiting, W. A. (1994). Embedded assessment: This method not only helps teachers to evaluate students but also guides instruction. *Science and Children, 32*(2), 30.

Grigorenko, E. L. (1998). Mastering tools of the mind in school (Trying out Vygotsky's ideas in classrooms). In R. J. Sternberg & W. M. Williams (Eds.), *Intelligence, instruction, and assessment.* Mahwah, NJ: Erlbaum.

Harlan, W., & Jelly, S. (1990). *Developing science in the primary classroom.* Portsmouth, NH: Heinemann.

Hemmerich, H., Lim, W., & Neel, K. (1994). *Prime time! Strategies for lifelong learning in mathematics and science in the middle and high school.* Portsmouth, NH: Heinemann.

Jarolimek, J., & Foster, C. D., Sr. (1997). *Teaching and learning in the elementary school* (6th ed.). Upper Saddle River, NJ: Merrill/Prentice Hall.

Kentucky Department of Education. (n.d.). *Designing a performance assessment.* Frankfort, KY: Author.

Meng, E., & Doran, R. L. (1993). *Improving instruction and learning through evaluation: Elementary school science.* Columbus, OH: ERIC Clearinghouse for Science, Mathematics, and Environmental Education.

National Research Council. (1996). *National science education standards.* Washington, DC: National Academy Press.

Novak, J. (1996). Concept mapping: A tool for improving science teaching and learning. In D. F. Treagust, R. Duit, & B. J. Fraser (Eds.), *Improving teaching and learning in science and mathematics.* New York: Teachers College Press.

Novak, J., & Musondra, D. (1991). A twelve year longitudinal study of science concept learning. *American Educational Research Journal, 29,* 117–153.

Ormrod, J. E. (2000). *Educational psychology: Principles and applications* (3rd ed.). Upper Saddle River, NJ: Merrill/Prentice Hall.

Price, S., & Hein, G. A. (1994). Scoring active assessment: Setting clear criteria and adapting them to your students as the keys to scoring classroom performance. *Science and Children, 32*(2), 27.

Raizen, S., Baron, J. B., Champagne, A. B., Hartel, E., Mullis, I. V. S., & Oakes, J. (1989). *Assessment in elementary school science education.* Andover, MA: National Center for Improving Science Education.

Roehler, L. R., & Cantlon, D. J. (1997). Scaffolding: A powerful tool in social constructivist classrooms. In K. Hogan & M. Pressley (Eds.), *Scaffolding student learning: Instructional approaches and issues.* Cambridge, MA: Brookline Books.

Science Curriculum Improvement Study. (1992). *Material objects student manual* (Section 5, chap. 18). Hudson, NH: Delta Education, Inc.

Shepardson, D. P., & Britsch, S. J. (2001). Tools for assessing and teaching science in elementary and middle schools. In D. P. Shepardson (Ed.), *Assessment in science: A guide to professional development and classroom practice* (pp. 119–147). Boston: Kluwer.

Shick, J. (1990). Textbook tests: The right formula? *The Science Teacher, 57*(6), 33–39.

Stiggins, R. (1994). *Student-centered classroom assessment.* Upper Saddle River, NJ: Prentice Hall.

Teacher Created Materials. (1994). *TCM771 science assessment* (pp. 67–68). Westminster, CA: Author.

U.S. Department of Education. (1996). *Planning excellence: A study of U.S. eighth-grade mathematics and science teaching, learning, curriculum, and achievement in international context.* Washington, DC: U.S. Department of Education, Office of Educational Research and Improvement.

U.S. Department of Education. (1997). *Introduction to TIMSS: The third international mathematics and science study.* Washington, DC: U.S. Department of Education, Office of Educational Research and Improvement.

7

*T*eachers are designers. An essential act of our profession is the design of curriculum and learning experiences to meet specified purposes. . . . We are not free to teach any topic we choose. Rather, we are guided by national, state, district, or institutional standards that specify what students should know and be able to do. These standards provide a framework to help us identify teaching and learning priorities and guide our design of curriculum and assessments.

(Wiggins & McTighe, 1998, pp. 7–8)

Preparing for Inquiry Instruction

IN EARLIER CHAPTERS you were introduced to contemporary ideas about learning, teaching, and assessing science as inquiry. We emphasized that learning is an active process in which students construct their own knowledge, that instruction in science should focus on science understanding and provide opportunities for students to develop inquiry abilities, and that assessment should be based on a variety of techniques with primary concentration on performance assessment strategies. This chapter is about putting theory into practice.

Preparing to teach science can be thought of in terms of five tasks: planning lessons, designing learning environments, forming classroom management strategies, considering safety precautions, and planning implementation strategies. Negotiating these planning tasks will involve many decisions and require professional knowledge and skills.

Working within a context of local curriculum guidelines and state and national standards, you will select and organize science content, decide on learning activities, and choose and design assessments to foster student understanding and the development of inquiry abilities. You will also determine how to arrange your classroom, manage materials, group students for learning, establish a learning community, and maintain an orderly classroom in which optimum learning can take place safely.

As you study this chapter and continue to develop your background for teaching science as inquiry, think about the following questions:

- *What science content will you teach? How can you develop your own science background to support teaching? What resource materials are available for planning science lessons?*

- *How can you develop and write objectives and create and sequence activities that engage students in meaningful learning?*

- *How can you effectively design the learning environment, group students, and manage your classroom for learning?*

- *What safety precautions should you and your students take in doing science?*

- *How can you bring it all together to effectively implement inquiry teaching plans in your own classroom?*

First, let us look at designing effective inquiry science lessons.

Collect responses to these questions as you find them in the chapter. The focus questions also appear on the Companion Website at http://www.prenhall.com/carin.

Designing Inquiry Science Lessons

The first step in planning science lessons is to examine the science content knowledge that you wish to teach.

In the Annenberg Video Case Study featuring Erien (year two), Erien notes that although the science curriculum is often mandated by the local district or state, when and how to teach the content is left up to the teacher. A study guide for this video is included in this chapter.

NSES   You can review the *National Science Education Standards* online. Go to http://www.nap.edu/readingroom/books/nses/html. Review the *Benchmarks* document online at http://www.project2061.org

The activities in *Activities for Teaching Science as Inquiry*, the companion volume to this text, are referenced to specific NSES *Science Standards* and *Concepts and Principles* underlying the standards.

Selecting Appropriate Science Knowledge

The *National Science Education Standards*, *Benchmarks for Science Literacy*, and state and local curriculum frameworks present encompassing goals for science education. These are essential documents to study in determining what science to teach at each grade level. Although there is a movement to integrate the different science subjects, the *Science Standards* continue to divide science into three overlapping branches: physical science, life science, and earth and space science. *Content standards* describe the essential science knowledge that children should develop at different grade levels for each science branch.

As an example, Figure 7-1 provides expectations from the *National Science Education Standards* of what students should learn about the nature and properties of matter in grades K–4 and 5–8. Take a moment to examine this figure. Notice that both the *Science Standards* and the *Concepts and Principles* underlying the standards are specified. At grades K–4, children build on prior knowledge and interests by observing, measuring, and describing the properties of many different types of objects and grouping or classifying objects on the basis of their common properties. During these early grade levels, experiences with classifying lead to the notion that objects can differ in various ways but still be made up of the same material. Further investigations with matter lead to the idea that materials—water, for example—may exist in different states, as solids, liquids, and gases. The activities we presented on water in Chapter 1 and properties of white powders in Chapter 2 are good examples of early grade activities that support the content standards on matter.

Understanding the nature and structure of matter requires many experiences over a long time. Look again at Figure 7-1. Note that at grades 5–8, students expand their studies of properties of objects and materials by investigating **characteristic properties** of matter, such as density and boiling point. They also investigate changes in matter and the effects of these changes on characteristic properties. For example, when water freezes, its density changes. Knowledge of the different densities of water and ice can provide a basis for middle school students' understanding of why ice floats in water and why lakes freeze from the top down.

Students in grades 5–8 also investigate how different substances mix or combine. When some substances are mixed, they may be separated. When iron filings are mixed with sugar, for example, the iron can be recovered from the mixture with a magnet. Students discover that some substances react chemically with other substances to form new substances (**compounds**) with new properties, as when an effervescent antacid tablet reacts with water to form a bubbling gas (carbon dioxide).

For elementary and middle school children, notice that the *Science Standards* do *not* focus on atoms, electrons, protons, and neutrons—the building blocks of all matter. The theory of atomic structure and the evidence for it are quite complex and abstract, involving formal operational thinking. According to the *Science Standards*, an emphasis on explaining the nature of matter in terms of the structure of atoms and molecules and the electrical forces between protons and electrons should be reserved for grades 9–12.

Ron Jones, who has taught middle school science for many years, points out that science knowledge is increasing so fast that no one can teach it all. "After you've taught content for a while, you can see the heart of the subject matter," he says. "You can pick out the fundamentals and teach those clearly." Jones selects topics based on his wide background

NSES

Science Standards

As a result of their science activities, all students should develop an understanding of:

- Properties of objects and materials (K–4).
- Properties and changes of properties in matter (5–8).

Concepts and Principles

Fundamental concepts and principles underlying these standards include:

- Objects have many observable properties, including size, weight, shape, color, temperature, and the ability to react with other substances. Those properties can be measured using tools, such as rulers, balances, and thermometers (K–4).

- Objects are made of one or more materials, such as paper, wood, and metal. Objects can be described by the properties of the materials from which they are made, and those properties can be used to separate or sort a group of objects or materials (K–4).

- Materials can exist in different states—solids, liquids, and gases. Some common materials, such as water, can be changed from one state to another by heating or cooling (K–4).

- A substance has characteristic properties, such as density, a boiling point, and solubility, all of which are independent of the amount of the sample. A mixture of substances often can be separated into the original substance using one or more of the characteristic properties (5–8).

- Substances react chemically in characteristic ways with other substances to form new substances (compounds) with different characteristic properties. In chemical reactions, the total mass is conserved. Substances often are placed in categories or groups if they react in similar ways; metals are an example of such a group (5–8).

- Chemical elements do not break down during normal laboratory reactions involving such treatments as heating, exposure to electrical current, or reaction with acids. There are more than 100 known elements that combine in a multitude of ways to produce compounds, which account for the living and nonliving substances that we encounter (5–8).

Figure 7-1 What students are expected to learn about the properties of objects and materials in grades K–4 and 5–8, according to the *National Science Education Standards*.
Source: Reprinted with permission from *National Science Education Standards* by the National Academy of Sciences, courtesy of the National Academies Press, Washington DC.

in science, many years of experience teaching science, and continued study of science and science teaching resources.

What can you do to build your own science background for planning and teaching science lessons?

Developing Your Science Background

Science knowledge is often complex and abstract. As discussed in Chapter 3, science for children must be developmentally appropriate. To teach science, you must not only understand a science topic yourself but also know how to present it to children in ways that enable them to explore and explain the world at their own level. Fortunately, there is a wealth of resources available for elementary and middle school science teachers to build their own science background.

VIDEO CASE STUDY: *ERIEN, YEAR TWO*

Previewing the Video

As you watch the three modules for this case study, use the Questions for Reflection to guide your thoughts and notes for any group discussion or individual feedback. If you watch the video as a group and then participate in a group discussion, choose a group facilitator to solicit various perspectives and keep the discussion on track.

Introducing the Case

Erien, the student teacher you were introduced to in Chapter 5, has been hired to work in the school where she did her student teaching. She is now a seventh grade teacher who is responsible for teaching a science curriculum that includes a study of human body systems. Erien relates that although the science curriculum is often mandated by the local or state school districts, when and how to teach the content is left up to the teacher. Because Erien is also responsible for teaching her students language arts, she looks for ways to integrate the teaching of both.

Questions for Reflection

1. What are the many creative ways Erien's students explore concepts about the function and form of the excretory system?
2. How did Erien's students benefit from one another reviewing the respiratory system? Did you have any concerns about this type of reviewing activity? If so, how would you address those concerns?
3. What does Erien do well to motivate her students and engage them in their learning?

Erien asked students to be creative and find magazine pictures that represented human body systems.

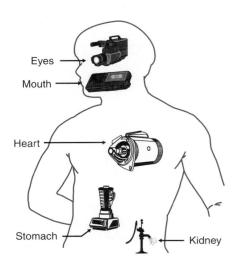

> "An important transition in doing science is taking a hands-on experience and making it into a minds on experience, and without that transition you run the risk of not allowing students to have the opportunity to make meaning of something."
>
> *Sue Mattson, Science Educator, Smithsonian Institute*

Trying New Ideas
Erien wants to foster critical thinking by her students. She engages them in an exciting and motivating activity to study bacteria and the spread of diseases. Science educator Sue Mattson from the Smithsonian Institute serves as a mentor to Erien and suggests using journal writing to advance students' science thinking.

Questions for Reflection

1. What does Erien have students do to engage them in their inquiry about diseases and the spread of bacteria? How does she have them explore this inquiry? What does Erien do to get students to elaborate on the lesson concepts and explain what they understand? How does she evaluate their understanding?

2. How might journal writing—before, during, and after students' inquiry—advance their thinking?

Building and Reflecting on Change
Near the end of the year, Erien wanted to have each student group come up with their own question for study. She decided to require students to use science journals to get them to think more critically about their science venture. She began by asking students to write in their journals changes they observed in the wetlands from their first visit to the site a few weeks earlier.

Questions for Reflection

1. Review the inquiry questions for which students were seeking answers. How does Erien account for the high caliber of these student questions?

   ◆ *What decomposes faster? (a leaf, a penny, an orange peel, or a piece of paper)*

   ◆ *In what depth of water do you find more frogs?*

   ◆ *Which material works best at keeping gypsy moths from getting to the top of the tree?*

   ◆ *What types of insects are attracted to what types of trees?*

   ◆ *Where do we find more insects—in the moist areas or in the dry areas?*

2. Sue Mattson explained to Erien that journal writing has become a natural part of science education. She noted that asking students to use writing to interpret what they understand provides students an opportunity to look at something they've done and to make meaning of it. How did Erien's students use their journals to make meaning of their wetlands inquiry?

3. In Erien's follow-up activity, she required students to use writing to further their investigations. Review the students' answers and explain why this follow-up activity was meaningful.

For example, teachers' guides in funded science programs usually provide background information intended to help teachers better understand what they are teaching. As they improve their own background knowledge, teachers "can better guide students to ever higher levels of understanding" (Full Option Science System, 2000). The background knowledge sections in FOSS (Full Option Science System) modules lay a foundation for the content that will be taught to children through a variety of activities. Before planning a lesson on sound, for example, you might want to study the science background section of the FOSS Physics of Sound module. It includes discussions of such topics as.

- characteristics of sound;
- sound vibrations;
- sources, mediums of transfer, and receivers of sound;
- how sound travels; and
- how we hear sounds.

In enhancing teachers' knowledge, the background discussion often goes well beyond what most elementary and middle school students are expected to learn. To develop your own background knowledge on a science topic that you will be teaching, you should

- read widely, especially science books written for children;
- examine lessons from funded and other available science programs;
- use an Internet search engine such as Google, Alta Vista, or Yahoo to locate appropriate science lessons;
- be sure to check the science education resource database at the Eisenhower National Clearinghouse at http://www.enc.org;
- talk to other teachers and science education specialists;
- attend college courses and institutes for teachers; and
- attend relevant sessions at national, regional, and state conferences for science teachers.

As you gain confidence in your understanding of the science content, you will be ready to develop and write science lesson plans.

Writing a Science Lesson Plan

National, state, and local curriculum documents provide a framework and describe the *types* of knowledge and skills that children at different levels should learn. Teachers are accountable for planning when and how to teach different science topics to help students attain local, state, and national expectations.

Science lessons that are consistent with the *National Science Education Standards* should focus on developing both science understanding and inquiry skills. This requires that lessons provide opportunities for children to ask questions that can be investigated empirically; to engage in hands-on explorations; to collect and organize data; to acquire background knowledge, concepts, and theories needed to make sense of their observations; and to use observational evidence and developing knowledge to explain phenomena and answer their questions. Lessons should, whenever possible, be set within authentic, real-world contexts and involve materials and problems that may already be familiar to students. Furthermore, students should have opportunities to participate actively in different group structures as members of a community of inquirers. Lesson plans help you prepare to attain these ideals in a practical way.

The federal government often funds programs at universities and colleges for science and mathematics teachers at every level. A typical program focuses on a narrow range of content and uses hands-on approaches. Funds for tuition, fees, books, abundant materials, and expenses to a state science conference are often provided for teacher-participants. These professional development opportunities are not only educational but also great fun.

As you develop your content outline and lesson objectives, review the National Science Education Standards *state and local curriculum documents, books, and Internet links. This can enrich what you plan.*

Well-designed science lesson plans generally have four components:

- Science content outline or concept map
- Instructional objectives
- Learning activities
- Assessment tasks and procedures

We discussed assessment tasks and procedures extensively in Chapter 6. In the following sections we will examine the other components of science lesson plans.

Describing and Organizing the Science Content. Content outlines and concept maps show details about concepts and relationships within a content area. Thus, they provide an organizational framework for lesson planning. You can develop a science content outline or concept map from your own growing knowledge of a science topic. You need not include everything about the topic, just what you plan to teach and intend for students to learn. The first column of Table 7–1 shows an outline of the content to be learned over

NSES

According to the program standards of the National Science Education Standards:

- All students, regardless of gender, cultural or ethnic background, physical or learning disabilities, or future aspirations, should have the opportunity to experience the richness and excitement of knowing about and understanding the natural world.
- Clear goals and expectations for students must be used to guide the design, implementation, and assessment of all elements of the science program.
- Science content should be embedded in curriculum patterns and activities that are developmentally appropriate, interesting, and relevant to students' lives.
- The science program must emphasize inquiring into and understanding natural phenomena and science-related social issues.
- The science program should connect to other subjects.

TABLE 7-1	CONTENT, OBJECTIVES, AND ACTIVITIES FOR THE FOSS (FULL OPTION SCIENCE SYSTEM) MODULE ON THE PHYSICS OF SOUND	
Science Content Description	**Science Objectives**	**Synopsis of Activities**
1. Characteristics and Causes of Sound • Objects can be identified by the sounds they make when dropped. • Sounds have identifiable characteristics. • Sounds can convey information. • Sound is caused by vibrations. • A sound source is an object that is vibrating. • A sound receiver detects sound vibrations.	Students should be able to: • *Describe* sounds made by objects when dropped. • *Communicate* with others using a code. • *Compare* sounds to develop discrimination.	**Dropping In** Students explore their ability to discriminate between sounds, by dropping objects into a drop chamber and identifying each object by the property of its sound. They develop a code by assigning letters to objects and send messages to one another by using their drop code.
2. Pitch and Vibrating Sources • Sound originates from vibrating sources. • Pitch is how high or low a sound is. • Differences in pitch are caused by differences in the rate at which objects vibrate. • Several variables affect pitch, including size (length) and tension of the source material.	Students should be able to: • *Demonstrate* that sound originates from a vibrating source. • *Compare* high-, low-, and medium-pitched sounds. • *Record* observations on sound. • *Relate* the pitch of a sound to the physical properties of the sound source.	**Good Vibrations** Students explore sound generators and musical instruments in mini-activities to find out what causes sound and what changes the pitch. They investigate variables that affect changes in pitch: the length of vibrating objects and the tension on vibrating strings.
3. How Sound Travels • Sound vibrations need a medium to travel. • Sound travels through solids, water, and air. • Sound that is directed travels better through air. • Our outer ears are designed to receive, focus, and amplify sounds.	Students should be able to: • *Describe* evidence that sound travels through solids, water, and air. • *Compare* how sound travels through different mediums. • *Record* observations on sound.	**How Sound Travels** Students work in collaborative groups on miniactivities that introduce a sound source and a medium of sound travel. They observe and compare how sound travels through solids, water, and air.
4. Sources, Mediums, and Receivers of Sound • Several variables affect pitch, including size (length), tension, and thickness of the source material. • Sound can be directed through air, water, or solids to the sound receivers. • The medium that sound passes through affects its volume and the distance at which it can be heard.	Students should be able to: • *Describe* the outer ear and *explain* that it is designed to receive sounds. • *Compare* different ways of amplifying sounds and making them travel longer distances. • *Record* observations of how sound travels. • *Report* findings in a class presentation.	**Sound Challenges** Students investigate the nature of our sound receivers, ears. They are challenged to put their knowledge of sound sources, sound travel, and sound receivers to work. They take one of the instruments they used earlier and change its pitch, make its sound travel farther, or make it louder.

Source: Adapted from FOSS® (Full Option Science System®) Physics of Sound, Overview. © The Regents of the University of California and published by Delta Education. Adapted with permission.

Science Standards

Students should develop an understanding of:

- The position and motion of objects (K–4).

Concepts and Principles

Fundamental concepts and principles underlying this standard include:

- Sound is produced by vibrating objects.
- Changing the rate of vibration changes the pitch of the sound.

several lessons in the FOSS Physics of Sound module. This is a good example to follow. The second and third columns of the table also provide instructional objectives and descriptions of science activities from the sound module, but we will get to those later.

Notice in the first column of Table 7-1 that the content description for the FOSS module on sound has four main sections:

- Characteristics and causes of sound
- Pitch and vibrating sources
- How sound travels
- Sources, mediums, and receivers of sound

If you are planning to teach a series of lessons on sound, you might wish to expand the outline by adding a section on "applications of sound," including such familiar topics as megaphones, microphones and speakers, stethoscopes, and ultrasound. Keep in mind that you do not have to teach every topic identified in the content outline; sometimes the outline just shows where instruction and learning might lead at a later time.

By placing concepts and principles of sound together in outline form, you can present a better picture of the coherence and connections of the topic. The content outline can also be used as a framework for developing instructional objectives.

Specifying Instructional Objectives. In planning for instruction, you must translate standards and content knowledge statements into instructional objectives—specific learning targets for your students to achieve during lessons. Specific objectives aid teachers in planning instruction, serve as a guide in the process of teaching, convey learning expectations to students, and facilitate the assessment of student learning.

Domains of Objectives. Instructional objectives have traditionally been divided into three domains: cognitive, affective, and psychomotor. Characteristics of each of these domains are given in Table 7-2. Cognitive objectives relate to factual knowledge, conceptual knowledge, and inquiry processes and procedures to be learned; affective objectives relate to attitudes, habits of mind, and values; and psychomotor objectives relate to physical skills. Inquiry-oriented lessons, by their very nature, generally include objectives from all three domains.

Take a moment to study and classify the objectives in the following list. What domain— cognitive, affective, or psychomotor—would each objective fit?

A glossary containing definitions of important terms used in this chapter can be found on the Companion Website at http://www.prenhall.com/carin.

TABLE 7-2 SCIENCE LESSONS SHOULD ENCOMPASS THESE DOMAINS OF OBJECTIVES	
Domain	**Description**
Cognitive domain	Objectives related to remembering, understanding, applying, and creating knowledge and inquiry procedures
Affective domain	Objectives related to attitudes, values, and habits of mind
Psychomotor domain	Objectives related to physical skills

At the conclusion of the activities on sound, students will be able to

1. *ask* questions about sound, *plan* investigations and *collect* data, *form* explanations to answer questions, and *report* investigations and findings to the class.
2. *describe* the outer ear and *explain* how it receives sounds.
3. *compare* different ways of amplifying sounds and making them travel longer distances.
4. *record* observations of how sound travels.
5. *construct* a simple stringed instrument.
6. *demonstrate* the production of different pitches of sound using the instrument.
7. *explain* the production of different pitches from a simple stringed instrument.
8. *demonstrate appreciation* of the importance of safety rules related to hearing and sound through consistently *practicing* them.
9. *show* respect for partners when working in cooperative groups by listening attentively and responding courteously to their ideas and suggestions.

How did you classify the objectives? Objective 1 is a cognitive objective, but with an inquiry skills focus. Objectives 2, 3, 4, and 7 are also cognitive objectives. Objective 5 is a psychomotor objective. Objective 6 combines cognitive and psychomotor aspects of objectives. Objectives 8 and 9 are affective objectives.

Writing Instructional Objectives. These objectives on sound contain three essential characteristics found in most objectives statements in science and other subjects. First, the phrase "students will be able to" designates students as the audience of the objective.

Second, the action verbs in italics—such as *describe, explain, compare, record, construct, report, demonstrate,* and *show*—designate different performances or behaviors that display student knowledge, understanding, appreciation, and skills related to sound.

Figure 7-2 defines several action words denoting different types of cognitive performances that are particularly useful for science instruction. The developers of the *Science—A Process Approach* (SAPA) program used only 10 action words, including most of those in Figure 7-2, in specifying all of the objectives—several hundred of them—to be learned in grades K–6.

Third, in instructional objectives, what is to be acted on by the students is usually specified. For example, in the objective "students describe the outer ear," the *outer ear* is what is described by the students.

Traditionally, instructional objectives have included a fourth component—statements about the degree of performance expected by students for mastery. For example, *students will be expected to define at least three of four designated terms.* The phrase "three of four designated terms" describes the expected level of performance. Note that in the various examples of objectives we have given, no degree of expected performance has been stated.

Cognitive Processes	Action Words
Remembering	**Identify.** To select (by pointing to, touching, or picking up) the correct object or designating the object property, in response to its name. **Name.** To supply the correct name for an object, property, or event. **Define.** To state the meaning of a term. **State.** To make a verbal statement that conveys a fact, concept, principle, or procedure.
Describing	**Distinguish.** To show how potentially confusable objects or events are different. **Describe.** To name the necessary objects, properties, events, or relationships in a situation. **Compare.** To note similarities and differences in two or more things.
Understanding	**Classify.** To place objects into groups based on common properties. **Interpret.** To express the meaning in one's own words of a concept, principle, or model, or to find and express patterns and relationships in data. **Explain.** To draw conclusions about relationships involved in an event, giving special attention to links between observational evidence and prior knowledge that serve to support the conclusions. **Apply.** To use a concept, principle, or procedure to derive an answer to a question or problem. **Demonstrate.** To perform the operations involved in a given procedure, such as using instruments, collecting and organizing data, or carrying out a controlled investigation.

Figure 7-2 Some action words that are especially useful in writing cognitive objectives for inquiry-oriented science lessons.
Source: Adapted from *Science—A Process Approach* (SAPA), American Association for the Advancement of Science, 1965. Adapted with permission.

Rather than specifying degree of expected performance within objectives, we recommend the use of rubrics. As described in Chapter 6, rubrics define several different levels of knowledge and understanding in specific terms. Thus, teachers can use rubrics to specify the ideal levels of student performance on lesson objectives and assess their actual level of attainment.

Figure 7-3 shows a sample rubric related to three of the objectives on sound (objectives 5, 6, and 7) that we examined previously. This rubric defines the level of expected performance on each of the objectives.

Designing Lesson Activities. In designing lesson activities, teachers determine what specific learning experiences and teaching approaches relate to the content outline, lead to the attainment of specified objectives, and promote understanding, interest, and excellence.

Organize Learning Activities Using an Inquiry Instructional Model. Instructional models, such as the 5-E model described in Chapter 4, can be used in organizing lesson activities. Inquiry instructional models build on the NSES *Science as Inquiry Standards* and on the essential features of inquiry described in previous chapters.

Objectives

5. Construct a simple stringed instrument.
6. Demonstrate the production of different pitches of sound using the instrument.
7. Explain the production of different pitches from a simple stringed instrument.

	3 Points	2 Points	1 Point	0 Points
Rubric for Objective 5	Instrument is well constructed.	Instrument is sturdy but with some flaws.	Instrument has major flaws.	No instrument constructed.
Rubric for Objective 6	Student clearly demonstrates production of different pitches, by varying the length and tension of the string.	Satisfactory demonstration of the production of different pitches, though the demonstration may be incomplete.	Unsatisfactory demonstration of the production of different pitches.	No attempt to demonstrate the production of different pitches of sound.
Rubric for Objective 7	Student clearly explains production of different pitches, using notions of length and tension of string.	Satisfactory explanation of the production of different pitches, though the explanation may be incomplete.	Unsatisfactory explanation of the production of different pitches.	No attempt to explain the production of different pitches of sound.

Figure 7-3   Rubrics can be used to define the level of expected performance of students.

All models of inquiry instruction build on questions. In planning for inquiry, focus on questions that students can answer through collecting and using their own observational data.

The three approaches to investigation emphasized in Chapter 2 are especially important for elementary and middle school students (National Research Council, 1996, p. 123):

- *Descriptive investigation*, involving collecting, observing, and describing objects
- *Classificatory investigation*, in which students sort and classify objects according to one or more properties to learn more about the objects and to answer initiating questions
- *Experimental investigation*, involving planning and carrying out experiments to determine causes of events

In each of these approaches, students collect data that can be used in forming explanations and arriving at conclusions to answer the initiating questions.

As students engage in investigations, be sure to provide opportunities for them to practice and develop simple skills, such as how to observe, measure, classify, infer, predict, hypothesize, and communicate. Students should routinely use rulers, thermometers, watches, spring scales, and balance beams to measure important variables. And they should learn to use magnifying lenses and microscopes to see finer details of objects and organisms.

Students need time to present their data to others and to think about what the data mean. Build into your inquiry lessons opportunities for students to go beyond the data given and to construct inferences, make predictions, and build explanations that make sense of the world. You, of course, are their guide in this all-important part of inquiry.

Light
ray

(a)   (b)   (c)

Figure 7-4 Anchor a coin to the bottom of an opaque container. (a) Ask students to stand directly above the coin so they can see it from above. (b) Then, tell students to step back gradually until the coin is just out of sight. (c) Slowly pour water into the container. The students will see the coin appear to float upward into view. As the light rays emerge from the water into air, they refract or bend enough to reach the students' eyes.

Incorporate Concept Instruction Activities. When engaging in inquiry, students always need scientific knowledge. What will you do to facilitate students' learning of needed concepts and principles?

In children's inquiry, teachers should refrain as much as possible from supplying answers and providing information. Nevertheless, in simplifying scientific inquiry for children, it is sometimes necessary to invent or provide direct instruction on needed terms, concepts, principles, and procedures. This may be the most appropriate place to read text materials related to the concepts involved in the investigation. Although inquiry teachers may use a direct instruction method or reading to teach concepts and principles, the instruction should always build on children's recent prior activities.

Consider Using Discrepant Events. A discrepant event is a novel or unusual phenomenon in which there is an inconsistency between what is expected to happen and what is observed to happen. Observing and trying to explain discrepant or puzzling events is highly motivational and exciting for students. Discrepant events might be particularly appropriate to raise questions during the engagement phase, or they might be introduced in the elaboration phase of instruction.

As an example, here are the instructions for a discrepant event involving light (see Figure 7-4).

* Obtain an opaque, cylindrical container (such as a margarine "tub") that is about 15 cm deep and 15 cm across.
* Use a small amount of clay or some transparent tape to anchor a coin to the bottom of the container, in the very center.
* Ask students to stand above the container so that they can see the coin. Then direct them to move back slowly, still looking at the coin, until the coin just disappears from view.
* With the students fixed in place and the coin just out of sight, gradually pour water into the container, taking care that the coin is not moved by the water.
* As the water level in the container rises, the coin appears to gradually float into view.

This illusion is so convincing that most people have to look twice to make sure that the coin has not actually floated upward. You should do this little investigation yourself before reading on.

Discrepant events provide excellent opportunities for students to form hypotheses and design ways to test them. Explaining the floating coin illusion requires knowledge of these two principles of light:

1. Light ordinarily travels in straight lines.
2. Light *refracts* or bends when it passes from air to water and vice versa. Light bends inward when it goes from air to water; light bends outward when it goes from water to air.

If the floating coin illusion is used as an engagement activity, these principles would be learned in the exploration and explanation phase of instruction. If the discrepant event is presented in the elaboration phase, students would apply knowledge of light learned through previous instructional phases.

Here is an explanation for the floating coin illusion, demonstrating how knowledge about light can be used as a tool for problem solving.

> Light rays coming from the coin refract or bend outward when they pass from the water into the air. Because they have been refracted or bent, the light rays from the coin can then reach our eyes, even though we are not in a direct line of sight with it. Since light ordinarily travels in straight lines, we think the light reaching our eyes comes from high in the water.

Figure 7-4 provides a graphic illustration of this explanation.

It will take a great deal of experience, instruction, and effort for students to attain deep understanding of puzzling phenomena like this. Yet, for many students and teachers, thinking about puzzling and discrepant events is the best part of science.

Consider Using Less Structured Activities. The teacher may provide the problem and materials for students but then, in the exploration phase of instruction, allow them time and freedom to simply "mess about." For example, you might give cooperative groups of students glass soft drink bottles and pitchers of water (and newspapers and plenty of paper towels to mop up spills). You might then ask the groups to discover what they can do to change the pitch of the sounds produced with the bottles. In producing sounds, some groups might think to strike the bottles with a wooden object. Others might blow across the open ends of the bottles. They may discover that putting water in the bottles changes the pitch produced by their actions on the bottles. After allowing students to investigate for some time, collect the equipment and discuss what was discovered. This activity may be followed by more structured assignments. Students might also write in their journals and read about wind instruments.

For less structured activities, the teacher's role is to present the materials to the learners and ask open-ended, divergent questions. For example, "How can you use these materials to produce different pitches?" Teachers should interject questions only when they see that students are losing interest or are off track. Teachers might then ask questions to redirect the students' investigations. For example, "What do you think would happen if you were to blow across the top of the bottle? What do you think would happen if you added water to the bottle?"

Less structured inquiry activities not only teach science concepts but also allow students a great deal of autonomy, so they become more self-directed and creative inquirers. Through their own physical and mental actions, children learn to generate questions and solve problems. If teachers always tell students what to do, students are less likely to become responsible for their own learning or to develop their own creativity and social competence.

PREPARING FOR INQUIRY INSTRUCTION 225

Science Lesson Plans on the Internet

There are literally hundreds of science lesson plans available on the Internet. Go to a search engine such as Google Search and type in *science lesson sound* or *science lesson insects*, for example, and you will find a wide variety of lesson plans. The Internet lesson plans will usually include objectives, a list of materials, activities, and suggestions for assessing understanding.

Almost all of the lesson plans will provide useful information, but a word of caution is in order: There is little quality control on the lessons included in most Internet sites. Many of the elementary and middle school science lesson plans on the Internet are not inquiry- and constructivist-oriented; they do not focus on helping children construct significant science knowledge through their own inquiry activities.

Here are some questions to ask in analyzing Internet science lessons:

1. **Questions.** What is the focus question for the lesson? Is the question one that might arise out of the activities of students with simple, everyday materials? Are the students involved in formulating the question?
2. **Investigations.** To what extent are the students involved in developing the procedures for investigating the question? Are the students required to make observations and measurements, and collect, organize, and record data?
3. **Evidence and Explanations.** To what extent are students led to construct generalizations, inferences, predictions, and explanations, and to use investigative evidence to support them?
4. **Communication.** How are students expected to report procedures, findings, evidence, and explanations to others?
5. **Assessment.** What are students asked to do to show evidence of their understanding? Do they have opportunities to defend conclusions and show how evidence links to explanations? Are students required to apply new science knowledge or inquiry skills to new situations?

You can modify almost any lesson plan to make it more inquiry- and constructivist-oriented.

Focus on Inquiry but Also Use Other Teaching Methods. Although hands-on activities are essential in science learning, this does not mean that every science lesson must have students handle science materials and generate new data. Your lessons should include a variety of teaching and learning approaches, including listening and speaking, reading and writing, and watching, as well as doing. Films and videos, books, research reports, computer activities, Internet searches, field trips, and so on, can also provide excellent learning opportunities for students.

In the next section, we will see how the different parts of a lesson plan fit together by examining how two preservice teachers developed a lesson plan for teaching a series of activities on floating and sinking to fourth grade students.

An Example Lesson Plan on Floating and Sinking

In preparing a series of lessons for fourth graders, one pair of preservice teachers in a science methods class chose to focus on the properties of matter related to whether objects float or sink in a liquid. They would be teaching the topic to small groups of fourth grade children in a local elementary school classroom for 5 days. Through observing, assisting, and conducting formal and informal assessments in the classroom, the preservice teachers had already formed some ideas about the children's prior knowledge and developmental levels.

Figure 7-5 Content knowledge outline for floating and sinking unit.

I. Floating and sinking
   A. Several variable factors contribute to whether an object floats or sinks:
      1. Volume (size)
      2. Weight
      3. Design
II. Some characteristics that affect floating and sinking can be measured and compared
   A. Volume (size)
   B. Weight
III. Theory/rules for floating and sinking in fresh water
   A. The weight and volume (size) of objects are compared in predicting whether they will float or sink.
   B. Objects float if they are light enough for their size.
   C. Objects sink if they are too heavy for their size.
IV. Investigating boat designs
   A. The buoyant force on a boat is increased when the amount of space of the boat underwater is increased.
   B. Boats can weigh the same but be designed so that they occupy different amounts of space underwater.
   C. Boats that occupy more space underwater can carry the largest cargo.

Content Outline. The preservice teachers developed the content knowledge outline shown in Figure 7-5 for the lessons on floating and sinking. Before creating this outline, they studied a variety of sources, including state-level frameworks and local curriculum guides, chapters within the science textbook adopted by the local district, the activities sections of science methods textbooks, and lessons developed by national curriculum groups. They also consulted with the classroom teacher and the science methods instructor.

The preservice teachers' science content outline focuses on grade-level-appropriate concepts of weight and volume and the relationship between weight and volume for floating and sinking objects. By considering the design of boats in the outline, the content knowledge is expanded, related to technology, and applied to the children's real-world experiences.

Objectives. Using the content outline as a guide, the preservice teachers could then decide on specific learning objectives, activities, and assessments. The lesson objectives on floating and sinking written by the pair are shown in Figure 7-6. Notice that the content outline is somewhat broader than the list of objectives. Other aspects of the outline may be covered in informal learning, in other lessons, and at later grades. Also, note that rather than listing the objectives separately and risking their isolation from one another, the preservice teachers have grouped related targets together, often within the same objective, to indicate that they wish to teach for connections and deeper understanding.

Learning Activities. Figure 7-7 shows learning activities developed by the preservice teachers for the lessons. They organized their learning activities using the 5-E model of instruction. Several of the activities are drawn from a unit called *Floating and Sinking* that is a part of the Science and Technology for Children (1995) program developed by the National Science Resources Center, and a unit called *Floaters and Sinkers*, developed by the AIMS (Activities Integrating Math, Science, and Technology) group.

You may wish to review the form of the 5-E lesson plans on position and motion (Chapter 2) and moon watching (Chapter 4).

At the conclusion of the floating and sinking unit, students should be able to:

1. *Define* the term "prediction," *distinguish* between predictions and guesses, and *describe* how predictions can be tested.
2. *Construct* predictions and *explain* their thinking about whether objects in a set will float or sink.
3. *Test* predictions about floating and sinking, *compare* and *discuss* their predictions and their tests, and *report* the results of their investigations.
4. *State* the following rules and *apply* them to floating and sinking objects:
   a. Objects sink in water if they are too heavy for their size.
   b. Objects float in water if they are light enough for their size.
5. *Design* and *construct* a clay boat that floats and holds as much cargo as possible.
6. *Explain* how the floating and sinking rules apply to clay boats of different designs.

Figure 7-6 Objectives for lessons on floating and sinking.

Implementing the Lesson Plan. The preservice teachers had the opportunity to grow professionally through planning, implementing, receiving feedback, and reflecting on the lessons on floating and sinking. Let us look at how they implemented their lesson plan with the fourth grade class.

Engagement. In implementing the series of lessons, each of the two preservice teachers taught half the class. The preservice teachers *engaged* their miniclasses in thinking about floating and sinking through a demonstration and inquiry discussion of a raisin elevator activity (see Chapter 5, Activity 5-1). Such activities stimulate curiosity and can be very motivating for students.

Next, the preservice teachers involved the children in a demonstration and inquiry discussion about whether a variety of objects would float or sink in water. All student answers were accepted, with students occasionally being asked to state, clarify, or justify their reasoning. No new information or concepts were taught to the students at this point.

Exploration. For the *exploration* phase of the lesson, the preservice teachers provided materials to students who worked in pairs at learning stations discussing, predicting, and testing which objects in a set floated and which sank. Students recorded all of their data and conclusions individually on specially prepared worksheets. The sets of materials for students included a golf ball that sank and one that, surprisingly, floated. The secret to this discrepant event was that one of the golf balls was manufactured to be a "floater." It differed from the other in its internal composition and was thus lighter. As the preservice teachers had hoped, some of the children suggested that the two golf balls were the same in every way, except that one was lighter. The preservice teachers noted that other children, failing to detect the role of weight and volume, thought that what was inside the golf balls was the determining factor in whether a ball floated or sank.

Explanation. When the students finished investigating with all of the materials, they returned to large group configurations for the *explanation* phase of the lesson. The preservice teachers began by leading a discussion on *what* the children observed and *why* they think things float or sink. Without relying on direct instruction, the teachers guided the students to *compare* the weight and volume (or size) of the objects in each case. Eventually, the

Engagement

1. *Why do some things float and other things sink?*
   - The teacher initiates the lesson with a raisin elevator activity. Raisins are placed in a glass of clear, carbonated soda water. The raisins are seen to continually ascend and descend in the liquidlike elevators. The children discuss their ideas about why the raisins move up and down.
   - Within a large group, students will name things that float or sink and brainstorm why some things float while others sink.
   - The teacher will lead the discussion and record student ideas on chart paper.
2. *What is a scientific prediction, and how is a prediction different from a guess?*
   - *Ask:* What is the difference between a scientific prediction and a guess? *Response:* A scientific prediction is a forecast of a future event based on observations and prior knowledge. Guesses are not based on prior knowledge. Weather forecasts are predictions, not guesses, when they are based on weather data.
   - The teacher has an assortment of objects that float and sink in fresh water. Children predict which objects float and which sink and explain the reasons for their predictions. By placing each object in water, the teacher tests the children's predictions.

Exploration

3. *Predict and test whether objects in a set float or sink.*
   - Students work in pairs to predict, discuss, and test whether objects in a set float or sink. Each individual writes his own predictions and reasons on a record sheet. Two pairs of students share a container of water. Within a set of four students, one pair is given a regular golf ball and the other a special "floater" golf ball. As students compare predictions and observations, they are surprised that some golf balls can float. Children are asked to discuss this discrepant event in pairs and quartets and write reasons why one golf ball sank and the other one floated.

Explanation

4. *Why do objects float or sink?*
   - The children discuss their predictions and tests. The children are led to suggest that one golf ball is lighter than the other one. Students then test this hypothesis by using a balance to compare the weights of golf balls that sink and float.
5. *Inventing a theory of floating and sinking.*
   - Building on the discoveries and constructed understanding of the children, a theory of floating and sinking is invented. The theory consists of two rules:
   a. Objects float if they are light enough for their size.
   b. Objects sink if they are too heavy for their size.

Elaboration

6. *What is the best design for clay boats?*
   - Pairs of children are given a small ball of clay. The size of the clay balls is the same for each group. Students use their invented theory of floating and sinking to design a clay boat that will hold the maximum amount of cargo (pennies) possible. Children test their clay boats in a classroom lake, loading pennies one by one onto their boats until they sink.

Evaluation

7. *How can you make a Coke float?*
   - As an assessment, a can of Coke and a can of Diet Coke are placed in a tank of water. Surprisingly, the Diet Coke can floats while the regular can of Coke sinks.
   - Individually, children are instructed to think about the demonstration in terms of the invented rules (which they may look at) and to write down reasons why they think one can floated and the other one sank. The teacher assesses the children's reasoning in terms of their usage of the terms "weight" and "volume."

Figure 7-7   Activities for the floating and sinking lesson plan.

teachers *invented* a simple theory, consisting of two rules that students could use in predicting whether objects will float or sink:

- Objects float if they are light enough for their volume or size.
- Objects sink if they are too heavy for their volume or size.

Thus, in determining whether objects will float or sink, children had to compare the weight and the volume of objects in some way. The teachers led the children in applying their new rules to each object at their learning stations and to some new objects. In discussion, the teachers emphasized that the children had to fit their observations and the rules together to make predictions and explanations.

Although *size* is an ambiguous term, the teachers allowed the children to substitute it for the term *volume*. Consistent with Piaget's developmental theory, fourth graders generally have difficulty with the notion of volume because they do not easily separate the volume of an object from its weight. The floating and sinking activities will give the children experiences to help them later distinguish between these two variables.

Elaboration. In the *elaboration* phase of the lesson, children worked in their cooperative groups designing and constructing clay boats that would, hopefully, float. This activity was an experimental investigation in which students kept the weight of a clay boat constant, changed the shape, and observed what happened to the boat in water. Children discovered that balls of clay sink in water because they are too heavy relative to their size. By reshaping the balls into boats, the clay was made to float. The *effective volume* of the clay—that is, the volume of the clay that was underwater—had been increased. The children brought their boats to classroom "lakes" to see if they would float.

If a boat floated, the children added pennies one at a time to determine how much cargo the boat would hold. This constitutes another experimental investigation with the effective volume of the boat kept constant while the weight was varied by adding pennies. The children recorded their data on data sheets replete with appropriate drawings of ships and a shipping manifest.

After the clay boat activity, children reassembled as miniclasses to discuss their boat designs and how the floating and sinking rules applied. The children concluded that they had increased the effective volume of the clay by changing its shape, thus enabling the clay boat to float. Then, by adding pennies, they had increased the effective weight of the clay boat. When a particular boat and its cargo became too heavy relative to its new size, the boat sank. Boats that were designed to displace more water were able to support the most cargo. After the discussion, children were required to write in journals about their clay boats, using the terms *weight* and *size* to explain why their boats floated and eventually sank.

Evaluation. In assessing attainment of the learning objectives (see Figure 7-6), the preservice teachers listened to the students, checked their worksheets, and observed their performances during hands-on activities, demonstrations, and discussions. The teachers kept student record sheets and a reflection journal in which they recorded notes and anecdotes indicating student understanding of new ideas. Figure 7-8 shows a rubric the teachers used to assess student performance on the clay boat activity.

To assess the children's understanding of floating and sinking, the teachers demonstrated another discrepant event. They placed a can of regular Coke and a can of Diet Coke in a large container of water (see the Evaluation section of the lesson activities in Figure 7-7). The regular Coke sank, but, surprisingly, the Diet Coke can floated. The Diet Coke floated because it was lighter, although the two cans had the same volume. Regular Coke contains sugar, making it heavier than an equal volume of Diet Coke.

Details of the Coke float activity are given in the Life Science section of *Activities for Teaching Science as Inquiry*. The emphasis of the activity in that section is on the sugar content of diet and regular soft drinks.

Objectives

Students should be able to:

5. Design and construct a clay boat that floats and holds as much cargo as possible.
6. Explain how floating and sinking rules apply to clay boats of different designs.

	3 Points	2 Points	1 Point	0 Points
Rubric for Objective 5	Boat is well designed and constructed and holds substantial cargo.	Boat is well designed but with some flaws which limit cargo.	Boat has major flaws.	No boat constructed.
Rubric for Objective 6	Student clearly explains that the boat floats until the weight of the cargo becomes too heavy in relation to the size of the boat.	Student uses notion of the size of the boat *and* the weight of the cargo in explaining floating and sinking, but explanation has some flaws.	Unsatisfactory explanation of the role of size and/or weight in whether the boat floats or sinks.	No attempt to explain floating and sinking of the clay boat.

Figure 7-8 Rubric for assessing student performance and understanding on clay boats objectives.

Before the Coke float demonstration was discussed, the children wrote about and explained the activity. The teachers used a rubric (similar to Figure 7-8) to evaluate the children's explanations in terms of how they used concepts of *weight* and *volume* to explain why one can floated and the other can sank. After the written explanations were collected, the group discussed the demonstration and how the floating and sinking rules applied. If children wished to, they were allowed to rewrite their explanations.

Throughout the lessons, the teachers took opportunities to read about and discuss boats, submarines, and life preservers, and other real-world experiences related to floating and sinking. The children also recorded and drew labeled diagrams of their experiences in a science journal, describing their observations and conclusions.

The activities in the Science and Technology for Children and AIMS lessons on floating and sinking proved to be quite helpful for the preservice teachers as they planned their lessons. Project-developed programs are generally well planned and well written, and have excellent grade-level-appropriate activities and materials for your science program. However, lesson plans are not scripts, and even the very best set of activities must be adjusted to your own objectives, the needs of individual students, and classroom facilities. Still, ideas can be gathered from such programs for use in your science activities. What else can you glean for your students from the project-developed programs available today?

Now let us turn to how you can best arrange your classroom for inquiry learning and teaching.

Arranging the Science Classroom for Learning

Well-designed lesson plans and thoughtful teaching approaches are essential if students are to learn. But it is just as important for your students to have a positive, supportive learning environment. How you manage your classroom, more than anything else, determines the learning environment for your students.

Classroom management requires organizing and maintaining classroom environments that support learning.

NSES   **National Science Education Standards Program Standard D**

The K–12 science program must give students access to appropriate and sufficient resources.

- Conducting scientific inquiry requires that students have easy, equitable, and sufficient opportunities to use a wide range of equipment, materials, supplies, and other resources for experimentation and direct investigation of phenomena.
- Collaborative inquiry requires adequate and safe space.
- Good science programs require access to the world beyond the classroom.

"As the number of students increases in a school, they all have less elbow room and less space of their own," science teacher Ron Jones (1990) observes. "In a well-designed classroom, students know where their space is, which equipment is theirs, and what they're responsible for. They have more space and more ownership of that space."

The physical arrangement of the classroom is an important part of the experience Jones has designed for his students. He has set up a centralized lecture area, although he does very little "lecturing." Lab tables line three walls of the room. Each lab area has two drawers of equipment, one with slides and other materials for working with microscopes and one with beakers and test tubes for chemistry activities. Each lab area also is assigned one of the microscopes that are kept in a nearby cabinet. In addition, Jones has trays of equipment that he gets out when a class needs them for what he calls "cut and paste": scissors, glue, markers, and so on.

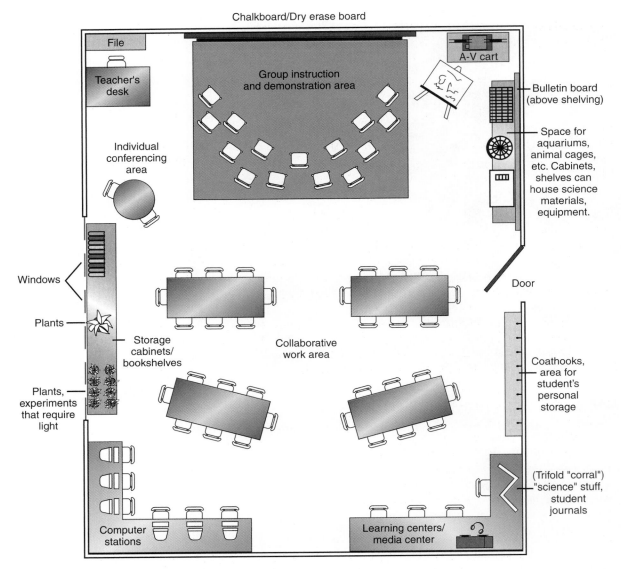

Figure 7-9   Self-contained classroom stressing active student involvement.

Jones's classroom organization is one key to his success, one reason why former students have written him notes that say "The only reason I came to school each day was because of science." Students like his science class, Jones says, because they want to "do science, not read about it."

What should you consider in planning the arrangement of your own classroom? Figure 7-9 shows how different areas might be arranged in a self-contained elementary classroom to facilitate learning in science and other subjects. You may want the following areas in your classroom:

- Group instruction and demonstration area
- Collaborative work areas

- Learning resource areas (e.g., writing and art supplies, library resources, and materials for following through on individual activities)
- Subject matter centers (science, social studies, math, etc.)
- Media and other technology areas (e.g., computer stations, audiovisual equipment, etc.)
- Flexible space that can change as needs change

Note especially that the classroom fosters collaboration and inquiry, but that each area serves learning needs.

With inquiry-oriented activities, you will constantly need to store many small items. Saving containers for collecting, organizing, and storing materials will help keep them available and ready for use in activities.

Science Classroom Learning Centers

In classrooms where students actively engage in inquiry, learning centers can be a good addition. Learning centers are created and directed by the teacher. They motivate, guide, and support the learning of individuals and small groups. Science learning centers will better enable you to meet individual needs and provide students with self-directed learning opportunities. They will encourage student responsibility, especially to keep accurate records to communicate their observations and understanding.

Set aside at least one area of your classroom as a discovery science learning center. This center should contain collections of natural objects (shells, rocks, and so on), other appropriate materials for inquiry activities, data sheets, and directions on what to do. Generally, science learning centers are set up to (O'Sullivan, 1984)

1. present new science ideas.
2. reinforce previously learned ideas.
3. develop a process skill.
4. drill on specific science information.
5. develop other science interests and creativity.
6. make efficient use of limited class time.
7. utilize educational technology resources.
8. encourage students to work independently.

Science learning centers allow teachers to design supplemental science curricula that closely match the developmental levels of their individual students. Tasks at the center can range from hands-on activities to written and research assignments (Orlich, Gebhart, Harma, & Ward, 1982). Learning centers are places where one or more students may work apart from your regular, ongoing science activities. Students are relatively free to explore, discover, experiment, or just tinker.

Figure 7-10 offers a view of a typical elementary or middle school classroom using learning centers. The different learning centers may be separated by dividers such as movable screens, workbenches, display or bulletin boards, planters, tables, or shelves. Classroom space and the availability of materials often dictate the arrangement of learning centers.

Types of Science Learning Centers. Two types of science learning centers are directed discovery learning centers and science process centers.

The **directed discovery learning center** focuses on specific science concepts. For this type of center, place materials in shoe boxes with a series of guiding discovery questions, such as, "Using the materials in this box, how would you show that light appears to travel in a straight line?" Directed learning centers may be set up with one theme or separate problems.

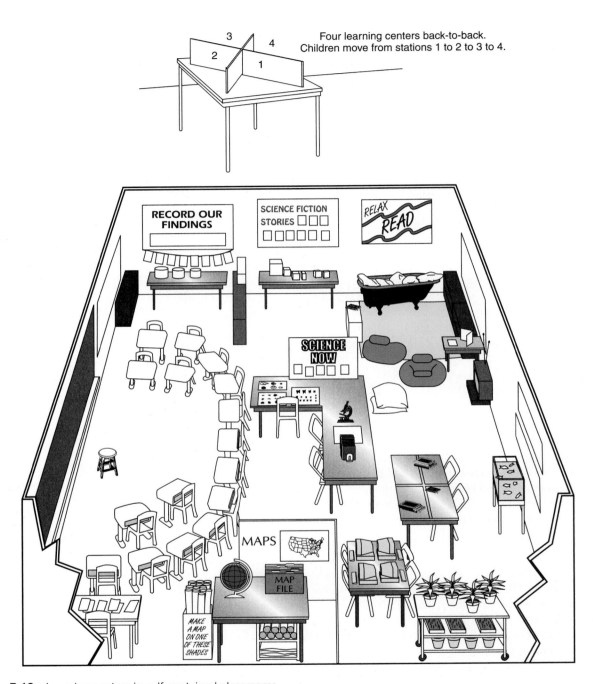

Four learning centers back-to-back. Children move from stations 1 to 2 to 3 to 4.

RECORD OUR FINDINGS

SCIENCE FICTION STORIES

RELAX READ

SCIENCE NOW

MAPS

MAP FILE

MAKE A MAP ON ONE OF THESE SHADES

Figure 7-10 Learning centers in self-contained classrooms.

A **science processes learning center** focuses on developing science processes, such as observing, predicting, and measuring. For example, using collections of materials and guiding questions, you could ask your students to measure the items in a box in both metric and standard measurements (Lehman, 1994).

Live Animals in the Classroom

According to the National Science Teachers Association (1991) *Guidelines for Responsible Use of Animals in the Classroom,*

> Studying animals in the classroom enables students to develop skills of observation and comparison, a sense of stewardship, and an appreciation for the unity, interrelationships, and complexity of life. This study, however, requires appropriate humane care of the organism. Teachers are expected to be knowledgeable about the proper care of the organism under study and the safety of their students.

Thus, you and your students must be aware of your responsibilities and use precaution when keeping live animals in the classroom. Here are some directions to help the students care for and adopt a humane attitude toward the living things they are observing.

Small animals, such as insects, frogs, and fish, may be kept for short periods of time, from 24 hours to several weeks, if the habitat in which they were found is simulated as closely as possible in captivity. Teachers should be aware that diseases such as salmonellosis can be transmitted to students who handle classroom animals. The small painted turtles that are frequently kept in elementary classrooms have been found to carry salmonella (Texas Safety Standards, 2002, p. 63). Keeping the cages clean of fecal remains will reduce the presence of bacteria that may cause an illness.

Always insist that students wash their hands before feeding the animals, as well as after they have handled the animals or touched materials from an animal's cage. They should research information about identification, characteristics, feeding habits, and values. The animals should eventually be released unharmed in an appropriate natural area or as prescribed in safety guidelines.

Each state publishes a safety manual that is made available to teachers. Safety guidelines for keeping a variety of animals such as earthworms, mealworms, crickets, guppies, and butterflies can be also found in the FOSS (Full Option Science System), STC (Science and Technology for Children), and AIMS (Activities that Integrate Math and Science) teachers' guides.

To be well prepared for living things brought into the classroom, have these kinds of containers always available:

- Insect cages
- Small animal cages
- Aquariums
- Terrariums

See Appendix D for information on constructing and using these houses for living things. Food and other requirements for a variety of water and land animals are presented in Appendix F.

Science Learning Just Outside Your Classroom

Every school—whether in an urban, suburban, or rural area—has areas just outside the classroom that are excellent laboratories for extending scientific inquiry into the local environment. The school yard, a vacant lot, a community park, or the school itself provide

Project Wild has developed excellent approaches to studying animals and the environment in elementary science. See the Project Wild Website at http://www.projectwild.org.

Also consult the NSTA Science Store Website (http://www.nsta.org/scistore) for various helpful how-to publications on living things in the classroom.

Good examples of the use of outdoor areas for scientific inquiry can be seen in Video Case Studies featuring Jennie's kindergarten lessons on snow and leaves and Erien's fifth grade lessons on wetlands. Video guides for these case studies are provided in Chapters 1 (Jennie) and 5 (Erien).

almost endless opportunities for students to examine soil composition; make measurements of everyday weather phenomena; hone observation skills looking for changes and patterns in their local environment; or investigate playground puddles, ice and snow, common local plants and animals, weeds, grasses, and trees throughout the various seasons.

Outdoor science extends the classroom walls. Students enlarge their science studies by taking nature walks and doing data collection and scientific analysis in the "real world." Outdoor science activities give students the feeling that science is not something just relegated to a schoolroom.

Even the most concrete-covered urban environment is rich in science possibilities. Here are a few just-outside-the-classroom science activities:

- Adopt a tree, bush, or plant on the school grounds or in the neighborhood, and observe and record observations bimonthly. Identify and share STS ideas with other classes or the community by way of a Neighborhood Environment Newspaper. Brainstorm or solicit ways to solve environmental problems in the community.
- Cultivate a native ecosystem or develop a plan to landscape your school grounds to protect and advance native species of plants. Enlist the assistance of your school administration, local gardeners, your school custodian, interested parents, or high school teachers and students.

For useful activities, great teaching suggestions, and essential information be sure to check out the GEMS (Great Explorations in Math and Science—Lawrence Hall of Science) guide, *Schoolyard Ecology* (http://lhsgems.org/GEMSschooleco.html).

The purpose of the outdoor learning centers is to provide science activities that will enable your students to construct greater knowledge and appreciation for their immediate environment. Here is an example of appropriate objectives and activities:

Objective: Students will observe and record data, and use the data as evidence to explain the interrelationships between plants, animals, and insects in their school site habitat.

Activities: Students will visit the site often to observe and record in journals what happens to plants, animals, and insects when people do not use insecticides, chemical plant killers, and fertilizers, or mow or tamper with nature in any other way.

Grouping Students for Learning

The way you group students in science is critical to the effectiveness of instruction and learning and in building communities of inquirers. Expert teachers use a variety of classroom arrangements for science and other subjects. These include (Lowery, 1998)

- *whole class structure* (e.g., the teacher lectures, demonstrates, or guides the whole class in discussion);
- *cooperative group structure* (e.g., students in small groups cooperatively collect, organize, and exchange data, and arrive at collaborative conclusions);
- *pair structure* (e.g., two students work together to construct an explanation of some action in a demonstration); and
- *individual structure* (e.g., each student works individually on an investigation, collecting data, recording data in a science journal, and answering relevant questions).

Used thoughtfully and strategically, these four types of classroom arrangements can be effective tools for improving learning and instruction.

Small groups of students working cooperatively are especially important in contemporary elementary and middle school science classrooms. Collaborating in small groups, students consider problems and assignments together, verbalize what they know, consider the multiple viewpoints of group members, take data together, and come up with group solutions to problems.

One collaborative group structure that works for elementary classrooms involves specific roles for group members. However groups are organized, students should share responsibilities within a small group. Each group could, for example, have a principal investigator (PI), a recorder/reporter, a materials manager, and a maintenance director:

- *Principal investigator.* In charge of all team operations, including checking assignments, communicating activity directions, asking teacher informational questions, assisting group members, conducting group discussions about activity results, and either carrying out each activity or assigning it to other team members.
- *Materials manager.* Gets and distributes materials to the team and inventories and returns materials after the activity. The materials manager is usually the only one moving about the room without special permission (Jones, 1990).
- *Recorder/reporter.* Collects, records, and certifies data on lab sheets; reports results to whole class orally or in writing on class summary chart posted on chalkboard.
- *Maintenance director.* Assigns team members to help clean up and return materials and equipment to their appropriate storage space or container. Directs the disposal of used materials and is responsible for team members' safety.

Throughout the year, each student should have an opportunity to take the responsibilities of each cooperative learning job.

The value of grouping comes from the collaboration that takes place among students. Small group structures build learning communities by providing students opportunities to interact and learn from one another. In addition, using cooperative teams can facilitate classroom management by providing for group sharing of limited science materials, giving students responsibility to manage materials, and involving students in helping team members with assignments and problems.

Some suggestions on building learning communities and promoting discourse within them are given in Chapter 3, p. 92, and Chapter 4, p. 102.

Safety in the Science Classroom

Safety in the science classroom is critical. Teachers are legally responsible for the safety of students in their classroom (Gerlovich, 1996). But the law does not require teachers to be superhuman in their efforts. It is only expected that teachers be reasonable and prudent in their judgment when performing their duties with students. Teachers must attempt to anticipate hazards, eliminate them, or be prepared to address them.

Safety is often closely tied to the room arrangement. As you arrange your room, think out patterns of student movements and avoid overcrowding any area. Here are some other safety considerations to follow as you work to protect your students:

- Examine each of your science activities carefully for possible safety hazards. Eliminate or be prepared to address all anticipated problems.
- Be alert to potential hazards related to children handling and caring for animals. Instruct children in the proper care and handling of classroom pets, fish, or other live organisms used as part of science activities.
- Consider eliminating all activities using open flames. Use hot plates as heat sources, but make sure that the hot plates are not in an area where children might touch them.
- Consider eliminating activities in which students are required to taste substances.
- Caution students to protect their eyes from small objects such as iron filings, sharp objects such as electrical wire, and flying objects such as rubber bands. Require

Additional safety precautions for elementary and middle school science classrooms are given in Appendix G.

students to wear American National Standards Institute approved safety goggles (with Z87 printed on the goggles) whenever activities are done in which there is a potential risk to eye safety.

At the onset of the school year, you should generate and post a list of safety rules that students should always follow. Review these rules as appropriate throughout the year. Here is a set of general classroom safety rules you might provide for your students (Full Option Science System, 2000):

- Always follow the safety procedures outlined by your teacher.
- Never put any materials in your mouth.
- Avoid touching your face, mouth, ears, or eyes while working with chemicals, plants, or animals.
- Always wash your hands immediately after using chemicals.
- Be careful when using sharp or pointed tools. Always make sure that you protect your eyes and those of your neighbors.
- Wear American National Standards Institute approved safety goggles (with Z87 printed on the goggles) whenever activities are done in which there is a potential risk to eye safety.
- Report all accidents, even small ones, to your teacher.
- Follow directions and ask questions if you are unsure of what to do.
- Behave responsibly during science investigations.

As you are developing your science background, you will usually encounter additional safety precautions relative to each topic you will teach.

Classroom Discipline

Maintaining an orderly learning environment is crucial in inquiry classrooms. Students are naturally active—getting materials, performing experiments, discussing procedures and results with one another and with you, and moving to different group structures. Still, you must establish rules for behavior, monitor students' activities, and enforce disciplinary consequences when necessary.

Keep in mind that all misbehavior is not equal. Classify misbehavior as *off task* (attention wandering, failing to attend to the task at hand), *inappropriate* (doing something that is against the agreed-on rules), or *disruptive* (inappropriate behavior that prevents learning or is potentially dangerous). Deal with each case in an appropriate way, such as regaining attention indirectly or stopping inappropriate behavior and cautioning the student.

Assess the behavior of individuals or groups during science lessons to see if you need to address any of these obstacles:

- Some students may be too immature for group work. You may have to work with them individually while the rest of the class works in groups. The goal is to help each student develop strategies for following class rules and participating in activities effectively. Do not just give up on a student and stop trying to help him.
- If there is a chronic offender in your class, you might
  1. talk with the student;
  2. try to determine her interests;
  3. ask for the student's perceptions of the problem and schedule a student-parent-teacher conference to see what can be done; and

4. if necessary, invite the principal, school psychologist, social worker, or other professional to attend the conference or observe the behavior of the student in the classroom.

Dealing strongly with disruptive students is essential if they and their neighbors are going to learn science effectively in inquiry settings. Here are some special precautions and actions you might consider:

1. Prepare contingency plans for problem situations, for example, deliberate damage to science supplies or explosive student behavior (fighting and pushing).
2. Consider beforehand the pros and cons of various methods of discipline, such as removing a student from the situation, so you can use the methods effectively if necessary. Consider developing routine procedures for handling improper actions so students understand the consequences of bad behavior. If it fits within your school or district policy, you might review the following policy with students and then display it in the classroom:
   - *First offense:*   warning addressed to student by name in clear, calm voice.
   - *Second offense:*   student given 10-minute time-out in an isolated part of the classroom, another teacher's classroom, or school office. Never use learning centers.
   - *Third offense:*   student given 15-minute time-out in isolation.
   - *Fourth offense:*   phone call to student's parents or guardian.
   - *Fifth offense:*   conference with student, parent or guardian, school principal, and/or school psychologist or counselor (Baron, 1992).
3. If you feel the lesson is getting away from you, do not hesitate to end it. Assess what went wrong and plan the next lesson to eliminate the problem.

Implementing Learning Activities

In preparing to implement learning activities, an ounce of prevention is worth a pound of cure. Thinking and planning can help you spot many potential trouble areas. Here are some things to keep in mind as you plan lessons, make teaching preparations, and move into that most important phase of teaching your students in the classroom.

Phase A: Teacher/Student Preparation

- Formulate your content outline, objectives, activities, and assessment design into a lesson plan.
- Collect supplies and equipment you and the students will need.
- Plan the room arrangement and other logistics for the activity.
- Organize the class into learning groups. Organize science materials before starting activities. If possible, place materials into separate kits in sacks, plastic bags, or boxes, or on trays for each group. The organization and distribution of materials and the transition from one activity to another can make or break your science lesson (Seefeldt & Barbour, 1994).
- Practice all activities in advance to eliminate or reduce potential problems.

Phase B: Pre-Activity Teacher/Student Discussions

- Establish with students a minimum set of rules and working directions that primarily cover classroom and cooperative group behavior that is fair and courteous. Wherever

Some additional discipline and classroom management strategies are provided in Chapter 9 on pages 294–295.

possible, give students a reason for the rule. Post the rules so all students can see them.
- Establish and consistently use a system for distributing and collecting science supplies and equipment, as well as cleanup procedures.
- Working within the framework of inquiry instruction, lead the students to pose questions that can be investigated and to suggest procedures for investigating them.
- Before students move into groups, give them time to ask questions, discuss what will be done, and exchange ideas. It is important for students to internalize what will be done and to form working relationships with other students.

Phase C: Distribution and Collection of Science Materials
- Once students are in their groups, review briefly what they will do, what they need, and how they will proceed before having them go for supplies. Make sure each group knows exactly what to get. Then ask the materials manager from each group to go to the supply stations, two or three at a time, and get the needed items (which you have prepackaged for each group).
- Work efficiently and quickly in all pre-activity tasks. Remember, time is of the essence. Students should be working in their cooperative groups within a very few minutes after the start of the science period.

Phase D: Beginning the Activity
- With all the groups in place with their supplies, move quickly from group to group, checking once more to see that each group knows what to do. Sometimes it helps to ask the students who have the most difficulty, so that you can be sure all team members understand the directions.

Phase E: During the Activity
- As your students engage in their group work, move about the room. Do not plant yourself in the front of the room, but move quietly to each group.
- Encourage communication among the students in each group.
- Be sure to spend only a brief time—less than a minute—with each group. When working with one group, keep an eye and ear on the other groups in the classroom. Remember, as a teacher *you must have eyes in the back of your head.*
- Assess the student behavior in each group and see if it is appropriate for the specific activity. If it is not, you might try these solutions:
    1. Establish beforehand a signal calling for quiet (e.g., putting lights out for a moment, ringing a bell, raising a hand in the air). When everyone becomes attentive, remind the class that it is too noisy. Ask the students to quiet down.
    2. Move to the offenders and quietly remind them to lower their voices.
    3. Temporarily remove individual students from their groups if they are displaying disruptive behavior and ask them to watch groups that are working well together. In a few minutes you might say, "Jason, I know you want to work with your group, so when you're ready, quietly go back to them and see if you can now work quietly and share your materials properly."
    4. Conclude the lesson if you are unable to quiet the class. Do this only as a last resort.
- Praise students who are working well instead of criticizing those who are not working well. Be specific so students know exactly the behavior you are praising, such as,

"Notice how quietly Ann's group is discussing what effect the length of the pendulum cord has on its swings."

- Be enthusiastic!
- Show respect for students by speaking politely and listening to each student in an unhurried manner.
- Do not add to class noise by shouting above students' voices. Calm and quiet the students with a firm but soft voice.

Phase F: After the Activity

- At the conclusion of the hands-on phase of the activity, ask materials managers to inventory equipment and materials and return them to the collection stations. Remind students to clean up their group work area. This helps teach them to share responsibility in caring for equipment, materials, and the classroom environment.
- The whole group may then be assembled to share data, examine different ways data have been organized, discuss conclusions, and review what they have learned.
- Throughout the class discussion, use the questioning, listening, and responding strategies of Chapter 5. Focus deliberately on observations before shifting the level of thought to interpretations; accept, extend, and probe student responses, building toward understandable explanations. As an alternative to questioning, promote higher-level thinking through group presentations of their investigations, findings, and conclusions. Students from other groups should be encouraged to ask questions and make suggestions to the presenting group.
- Use the conceptual change strategies of Chapter 4 to deal with misconceptions and encourage conceptual change: identify misconceptions and alternative theories; lead students to be dissatisfied with their alternative ideas; and use discrepant events that challenge alternative theories.
- "Invent" needed terms and concepts. Guide students in using prior and invented knowledge, along with observational data, in constructing explanations that help them make sense of the problems posed.
- Use science textbooks as resources *after* students have engaged in hands-on, minds-on activities that have helped them develop the knowledge base necessary for comprehending text materials.

 Use the self-assessment questions for Chapter 7 at http://www.prenhall.com/carin to assess how well you understand this chapter and how prepared you are for a test over its content.

School, district, or regional in-service sessions are often available to help beginning teachers handle classroom management; to guide them in choosing lessons, activities, and labs; and to show them how to modify activities to meet their students' needs. If your district does not offer this kind of support, you might suggest it, along with a "hands-on" learning day that involves teachers in making science discoveries, just like students.

SUMMARY

- Working within a framework of national, state, and local district expectations for science learning, teachers are responsible for planning effective science lessons and managing learning environments.
- Designing science lessons is a complex task requiring professional knowledge and skills. In lesson planning, you must make decisions related to four generic lesson components: science content, instructional objectives, learning activities, and assessment procedures. Science content outlines and concept maps specify and organize the science facts, concepts, principles, theories, and inquiry procedures to be taught. Objectives state what students will do to demonstrate the attainment of skills, knowledge, understandings, attitudes, and values related to the content. Learning activities

describe the opportunities you will provide for students to attain the objectives. Assessment procedures detail how you will use specific performances of students and the products they develop to determine what they are learning and to adjust your instruction to improve learning.

● Inquiry-oriented lessons can include a variety of types of teaching and learning methods, such as listening-speaking, reading-writing, and watching-doing. Examples are included in this chapter and other chapters to serve as guides as you design your own lessons.

● Building an effective learning environment is also an important task in preparing to teach. Various physical arrangements of the classroom, including storage for materials, small items, and living things, are suggested in the chapter. Science learning centers allow your students to explore, discover, and experiment on their own in structured or less structured situations.

● How you manage your science classroom, including managing materials and student behavior, can make or break your science teaching. The main purposes of classroom management are to ensure safety and to facilitate learning. Specific practical examples of classroom management and discipline guidelines are highlighted in the chapter.

REFERENCES

American Association for the Advancement of Science. (1965). *An evaluation model and its application, Science—a process approach*. Washington, DC: Author.

American Association for the Advancement of Science. (1993). *Benchmarks for science literacy*. New York: Oxford University Press.

Baron, E. B. (1992). Discipline strategies for teachers. *Fastback, 344*. Bloomington, IN: Phi Delta Kappa Educational Foundation.

Full Option Science System. (2000). *Overview: Physics of sound*. Nashua, NH: Delta Education.

Gerlovich, J. A. (1996). Developments in laboratory safety. In J. Rhoton & P. Bowers (Eds.), *Issues in science education*. Arlington, VA: National Science Teachers Association.

Jones, R. M. (1990). *Teaming up! The inquiry task group management system user's guide*. LaPorte, TX: ITGROUP.

Lehman, J. H. (1994). Measure up to science. *Science and Children, 31*(5), 30–31.

Lowery, L. F. (1998). Classroom arrangements and teaching. *FOSS Newsletter, 11*, 6–9.

National Research Council. (1996). *National science education standards*. Washington, DC: National Academy Press.

National Science Teachers Association. (1991). *Guidelines for responsible use of animals in the classroom: A position statement*. Arlington, VA: Author. (Also available at http://www.nsta.org/159&psid=2)

Orlich, D. C., Gebhardt, R. F., Harma, R., & Ward, G. L. (1982). Science learning centers: An aid to instruction. *Science and Children, 20*(1), 18–19.

O'Sullivan, K. A. (1984). Creating a learning center. *Science and Children, 24*(6), 15–17.

Science and Technology for Children. (1995). *Floating and sinking: Teacher's guide*. Burlington, NC: Carolina Biological.

Seefeldt, C., & Barbour, N. (1994). *Early childhood education* (3rd ed.). Upper Saddle River, NJ: Merrill/Prentice Hall.

Texas safety standards for kindergarten through grade 12 (2nd ed.). (2002). Austin, TX: Charles A. Dana Center, the University of Texas at Austin. (Also available at http://www.tenet.edu/teks/science/stacks/safety/safety_manual.html)

Wiggins, G., & McTighe, J. (1998). *Understanding by design*. Alexandria, VA: Association for Supervision and Curriculum Development.

8

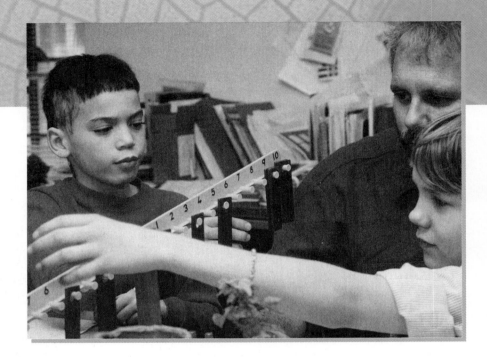

O ver the past few years, the need for and interest in curriculum integration has intensified
throughout the country. . . . It is not that schools should avoid dealing with specific
disciplines; rather, they also need to create learning experiences that periodically demonstrate
the relationship of the disciplines, thus heightening their relevancy. There is a need to actively
show students how different subject areas influence their lives, and it is critical that students
see the strength of each discipline perspective in a connected way.

(Jacobs, 1989, pp. 3, 5)

Connecting Science with Other Subjects

ALTHOUGH THE CURRICULUM and the school day are neatly divided into separate subjects, real-world approaches to problems and issues cut across disciplinary lines. Scientists, for example, use mathematics as a tool to explore, represent, and explain patterns in data from investigations. They draw on their language and literacy skills as they read scientific literature, formulate problems, write proposals, plan investigations, record data, and communicate findings and conclusions to others. Furthermore, scientists as well as other citizens enter into discussions and make decisions about societal problems and issues arising out of the applications of science and technology. In the real world, then, science, mathematics, reading, writing, social studies, and other disciplines are not isolated from one another, but connected.

Just as scientists use mathematics and language arts as tools, children should have opportunities to apply and enhance their mathematics, reading, and writing skills in investigating the natural world. This heightens the relevance of mathematics and language arts, enhances their usefulness, and promotes greater learning in science. Similarly, in their studies of both science and social studies, children should have the opportunity to examine the cause-and-effect relationships between science, technology, and societal change. Students might, for example, identify the impact of new technologies on communities around the world or study and offer solutions to environmental problems in the local community or other communities (Texas Education Agency, 1999).

In this chapter, we help you confront and begin to develop answers to questions about curriculum connections between science and other subjects. As you study the chapter, consider the following questions:

How can mathematics and science be connected in practical instructional activities so that knowledge, understanding, and skills in both subjects are enhanced?

How can reading and writing be used to enrich science learning? How can science be used to promote and improve children's abilities to read and write?

How do events and issues studied in social studies connect to science and technology?

How can science, social studies, mathematics, reading, writing, and other subjects be integrated to promote learning of the essential knowledge and skills of each of these subjects?

Let us start by examining connections between science and mathematics.

 Companion Website

Collect responses to these questions as you find them in the chapter. The focus questions also appear on the Companion Website at http://www. prenhall.com/carin.

NSES   You can review the *National Science Education Standards* online. Go to http://www.nap.edu/readingroom/books/nses/html. For an overview of the *Principles and Standards for School Mathematics*, go to http://nctm.org/standards/overview.htm.

Connecting Science and Mathematics

Mathematics has been called the language of science. It is the ultimate human method for exploring, representing, and expressing patterns. Thus, mathematics is an indispensable tool used to investigate, discover, model, and communicate the order and patterns found in the real world (Activities That Integrate Mathematics and Science, 1999).

The *National Science Education Standards* stress that science "requires the use of mathematics in the collection and treatment of data and in the reasoning used to develop concepts, laws, and theories" (National Research Council, 1996, p. 214). *The Curriculum and Evaluation Standards for School Mathematics* (National Council of Teachers of Mathematics, 1989) emphasize that students must learn to view mathematics as a practical subject that can be applied to real-world situations and to problems arising in other disciplines. Science is a natural place for students to develop this view of mathematics.

Table 8-1 shows the array of mathematical concepts, operations, and skills that can be emphasized in both mathematics and science classes in elementary and middle schools. Figure 8-1 depicts a connections model for science and mathematics, which graphically relates the mathematical ideas of Table 8-1 to scientific inquiry. In the following sections, we

TABLE 8-1   WAYS OF APPLYING MATHEMATICS IN SCIENTIFIC INQUIRY

I. Quantifying the Real World
- Identifying variables
- Counting objects and events
- Estimating number and size
- Measuring all sorts of things using standard and nonstandard units

II. Organizing and Interpreting Data
- Depicting data in pictures and diagrams
- Constructing data tables
- Constructing different kinds of graphs: bar graphs, histograms, line graphs
- Searching for and expressing patterns in graphs, including linear, proportional, geometric, and other relationships

III. Using Patterns and Relationships
- Using patterns and relationships from tables and graphs in explaining events and making predictions
- Using ratios, rates, proportionalities, and formulas in explaining events and making predictions

IV. Operating on Numbers
- Adding, subtracting, multiplying, dividing
- Using fractions, decimals, and percentages
- Calculating averages
- Estimating probabilities
- Calculating products, ratios, and rates
- Recognizing equalities and inequalities
- Constructing proportionalities

Sources: Adapted from *Curriculum and Evaluation Standards for School Mathematics*, National Council of Teachers of Mathematics, 1989, Weston, VA: NCTM; and an analysis of the Third International Mathematics and Science Study (TIMSS) in *Splintered Vision: An Investigation of U.S. Science and Mathematics Education*, by William H. Smith, Curtis C. McKnight, and Senta Raizen, 1997, Boston: Kluwer Academic Publishers.

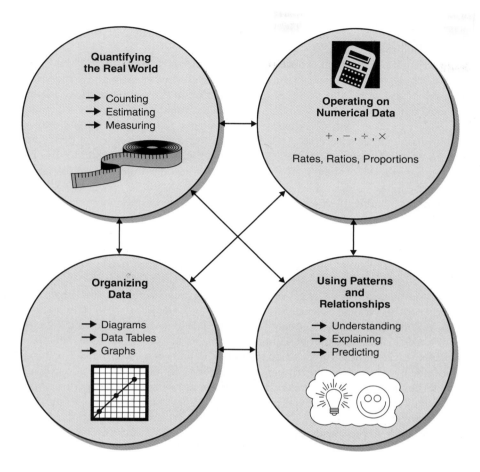

Figure 8-1 A connections model for science and mathematics.

will expand on the connections model and show you a variety of ways that mathematical ideas can be used and enhanced in scientific inquiry.

Quantifying the Real World

Expressing and thinking about the real world in terms of numbers is the first step in connecting science and mathematics (see Figure 8-1). By examining how infants respond to different stimulus situations, researchers have shown that number concepts are used to organize physical arrays and repetitive events as early as 5 to 7 months of age, if the arrays or events vary from two to four. From as early as 5 months, children can use concepts of

NSES

Program Standard C

The science program should be coordinated with the mathematics program to enhance student use and understanding of mathematics in the study of science and to improve student understanding of mathematics.

addition and subtraction to recognize when objects have been added to or subtracted from a small array (Bransford, Brown, & Cocking, 2000, p. 89).

The growth and development of mathematics concepts are often rooted in physical experiences. In school, children quantify the world through counting, estimating, and measuring all kinds of real-world variables that they encounter in the process of investigating. Children may *count* the number of seeds found in different fruits or the number of pennies added as cargo to a clay boat. They may *estimate* weights and volumes in determining whether objects might float or sink. And they might *measure* the weights of pendulum bobs, lengths of stems of growing plants, time for an antacid powder or tablet to dissolve in water, and so forth. All of these mathematical operations help children begin to quantify objects and events.

Let us look in more detail at measurement, one main task of students in quantifying their world.

Measuring. Measuring is emphasized in both science and mathematics standards. When children engage in problem-solving activities in either subject, they need skills for measuring length, volume, weight, time, temperature, and other variables.

Measuring is founded on processes of observing and comparing. "Children naturally make comparisons" (National Science Resources Center, 1996, p. 3). They stand back to back to see who is taller; line up their feet to see whose is longer; and match their bodies to different-sized clothing to see what will fit.

The need to make comparisons leads to the notion of units of measure, enabling things that are not side by side to be indirectly compared. At first, children may use nonstandard units to make comparisons. For example, they stretch their own arms, use their own bodies, or use handy objects like pencils or plastic spoons as nonstandard units to measure length. However, nonstandard units have a main disadvantage. Because spoons and pencils, as well as children's arm spans and bodies, vary in length, it is often difficult to use them to consistently compare objects that cannot be held side by side.

By second grade, children use standard units—centimeters, seconds, grams, and degrees Celsius or Fahrenheit—marked on different kinds of scales to measure in their investigations. Standard units enable consistent descriptions and comparisons of measured objects. As an example of measuring, we will examine length.

Mathematics Standards for Measurement

In grades K–4, the mathematics curriculum should include measurement so that students can

- understand the attributes of length, capacity, weight, mass, area, volume, time, temperature, and angle;
- develop the processes of measuring and concepts related to the units of measurement;
- make and use estimates of measurement; and
- make and use measurements in problems and everyday situations.

In grades 5–8, students should

- estimate, make, and use measurements to describe and compare phenomena; and
- select appropriate units and tools to measure to the degree of accuracy required in a particular situation. (National Council of Teachers of Mathematics, 1989)

Measuring Length. The logic of length measurement is deceptively complex. It encompasses such ideas as the conservation of length, the notion of standard units, unit iteration (counting the number of standard units in a length), and how to use standard measuring instruments, such as rulers. According to research by Clements (1999), however, children do not have to master all of these logical complexities to learn to measure the lengths of objects using a ruler, if the teacher provides appropriate scaffolding.

When length measurements are set within the contexts of real-world investigations and a *need to know* is established, even young children can learn to use rulers successfully. Learning to use a ruler, even by rote, provides a framework for children to begin to understand the logical complexities of length measurement.

Real-world measurements often present a challenge to children. For example, measuring the length of plant roots in germination bags (as discussed in Chapter 2) can be difficult because the roots are not straight, but curved and twisted. A simple ruler cannot be used to directly measure the roots. Children must invent ways to measure them with nonstandard measuring devices, perhaps by laying a curving string along the roots, then straightening out the string and measuring it with a ruler.

The process of measuring length in science contexts provides children an opportunity to rehearse, and consequently enlarge, their measurement knowledge. Rehearsal is an important concept in learning theory. *Practice* means to do something over and over again the same way to improve a performance (Ormrod, 1999). What is learned in practice is a specific skill applicable in a specific context. *Rehearsal*, in contrast, takes place "when people do something again in similar but not identical ways to reinforce what they have learned while adding something new" (Lowery, 1998, p. 28). In using measurement and other mathematics skills in science, children not only practice what they have already encountered in mathematics classes, but add something new to it. Mathematics schemas are expanded with the new additions from science activities. Children's mathematics skills are then less likely to be bound to specific tasks and are more likely to be transferable and useful in a variety of ways (Lowery, 1998).

A glossary containing definitions of important terms used in this chapter can be found on the Companion Website for Chapter 8 at http://www. prenhall.com/carin.

A number of innovative elementary science programs emphasize connections between mathematics and science, including AIMS (Activities That Integrate Mathematics and Science), GEMS (Great Explorations in Mathematics and Science), FOSS (Full Option Science System), and Science and Technology for Children (STC). STC has produced a series of very good lessons for first grade classes on comparing and measuring length. Through the 16 lessons of the STC unit *Comparing and Measuring* (National Science Resources Center, 1996), children begin to understand that

- comparing involves observing similarities and differences;
- one way to make comparisons is by matching;
- a common starting line is required to make fair comparisons;
- using beginning and ending points and placing units end to end are important factors when measuring;
- nonstandard units of measure can be used in comparing; and
- standard units of measure produce more consistent results than nonstandard units (p. 2).

Addresses for AIMS, FOSS, GEMS, STC, and other exemplary science programs are provided in Appendix K.

Science, Mathematics, and the Metric System. The metric system, termed the International System of Units (SI), is used exclusively in science. It is also used exclusively in daily life in all English-speaking countries except the United States. Although use of units such as feet and pounds is customary in the United States, the need for SI units has already affected machine tools, packaging, and temperature measurements. Competition with the rest of the world will continue to accelerate the use of SI in business, science, and government.

The metric system is convenient because it is based on the mathematics of place value and uses decimals rather than fractions. Thus, the metric system is often easier to use than U.S. customary units. It is easier for children to add 4.5 cm and 4.2 cm, for example, than to add 1 3/4 and 1 2/3 inches.

U.S. children must continue to learn and be familiar with both metric and customary units, but the NCTM standards (National Council of Teachers of Mathematics, 1989) deemphasize the memorization and use of conversion factors between the two systems. When a student measures something 6.5 cm long, for example, accept that as a description of its length. Do not ask how many inches it is. Students' concepts of a unit of length will be just as good without knowing the exact equivalent in the U.S. standard unit system.

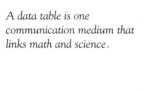

More on metric and customary units can be found in Appendix H.

Using Graphs to Organize and Interpret Data

In science activities, once data have been obtained through measurements, they must be organized and interpreted. Organizing data into diagrams, tables, and graphs is another key step in scientific inquiry (see Table 8-1 and Figure 8-1). Data tables display numerical data in column form. Graphs provide visual displays of data. Putting data obtained from scientific investigations into tables and graphs better enables students to

- relate their data to their investigative procedures;
- make comparisons among data;
- see relationships and patterns; and
- communicate their data to other people.

The FOSS K–6 science program developed at the Lawrence Hall of Science provides many opportunities for children to construct and interpret graphs. In the FOSS program, graphs are prepared at three levels of abstraction:

- *Concrete:*   organizes real objects to facilitate comparisons and reveal patterns
- *Representational:*   uses organization of pictorial representations to reveal relationship

A data table is one communication medium that links math and science.

• *Symbolic:*   uses numbers and data points to reveal relationships and facilitate interpretation

There are different types of graphs. The graphs most often used in scientific applications in elementary and middle schools are bar graphs, histograms, and line graphs.

Bar Graphs. Bar graphs vividly show *differences* in data collected. Bar graphs can be used, for example, to show the number of children with each different type of hair or eye color. Data about how many students in a class have blue eyes, brown eyes, green eyes, and so on, may be displayed visually in bar graphs.

In the Annenberg Video Case Study featuring Jennie described in Chapter 1, we saw kindergarten children constructing a large bar graph of the types of leaves they had collected. This graph is at the *concrete* level of abstraction, because it was constructed by placing the actual leaves above a designation of the leaf types.

A bar graph at the *representational* level is shown in Figure 8-2. This graph depicts the number of leaves of different colors collected by the children. In constructing the graph, children use colored dots that correspond to or stand for the color of each leaf collected. The left side, or *vertical axis* of the graph, shows the number of leaves. The bottom line, or *horizontal axis*, shows leaf color. Students stack gummed dots of the appropriate color at the appropriate number: Four orange, six red, three yellow, and two purple leaves have been collected.

Some other good examples of bar graph activities may be found in a *Science and Children* article by Susan Pearlman and Kathleen Pericak-Spector (1995) called "Graph That Data!"

Histograms. Histograms display the *number of times* a *number event* occurs in a large set. Histograms differ from bar graphs in that the *x* axis on a bar graph simply names a category, while the *x* axis on a histogram is a number line representing a variable. A familiar example of data that might be displayed in a histogram is how many students made each score on a test. Here, all possible scores are arranged in a number line on the *x* axis; the frequencies, or number of occurrences, of scores are arranged in a number line on the *y* axis. Another example, shown in Figure 8-3, is how many unshelled peanuts in a large bag are of each designated length (or small range of lengths).

Line Graphs. Line graphs are more advanced; students from about grade 4 can learn to construct and interpret them. With line graphs, your students can graphically show numerical data that are continuous. A line graph displays visually the changes in a *responding* or *dependent variable* in an investigation corresponding to changes in the values of a *manipulated*

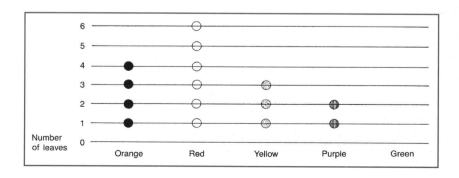

Figure 8-2   Bar graph of collected fall leaves with different colors.

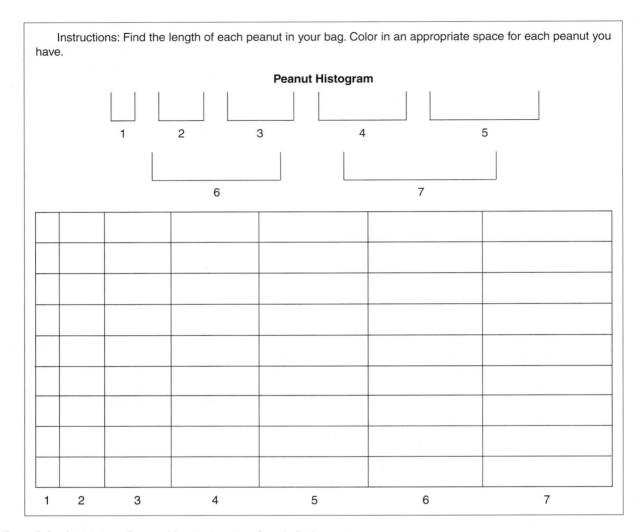

Instructions: Find the length of each peanut in your bag. Color in an appropriate space for each peanut you have.

Peanut Histogram

Figure 8-3   A histogram for graphing the lengths of unshelled peanuts.
Source: Used with permission from Larry Malone, Lawrence Hall of Science, University of California, Berkeley.

or *independent variable*. Figure 8-4 shows an example of a line graph depicting the bounce height versus the drop height of golf balls. In collecting data for the graph, children varied the drop height of a golf ball systematically and recorded the rebound height of the ball for each drop height.

Line graphs in science are usually constructed according to the graphing criteria given in Figure 8-5. Study the line graph in Figure 8-4 to see how these graphing conventions are applied. For example, if students are studying bouncing golf balls, the vertical axis shows bounce height (the responding variable in centimeters) and the horizontal axis shows drop height (the manipulated variable, also in centimeters). Using the chalkboard or overhead, show your students how to place a point on the graph to represent the data, as well as how to draw smooth, best-fit lines indicating the pattern or relationship of the data.

Students should understand that in using mathematics in scientific investigations, they will "encounter all the anomalies of authentic problems—inconsistencies, outliers,

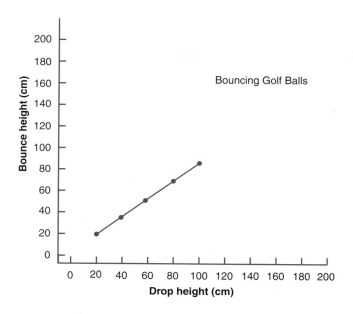

Figure 8-4 A line graph depicting the bounce height versus the drop height of a golf ball.
Source: Graph made with "Data Explorer" software. © 1998 Sunburst Technology Company. Information from "Data Explorer," used with permission of and copyright 1998 by Sunburst Technology Company. All rights reserved.

1. The manipulated variable is graphed on the horizontal axis, or *x* axis.
2. The responding variable is graphed on the vertical axis, or *y* axis.
3. The name of each variable is placed along the appropriate axis.
4. The unit of measurement of each variable is included along with its label.
5. The axes are uniformly scaled and numerals are placed at regular intervals along each axis.
6. The graph is given a descriptive title.
7. Data points are plotted on the graph.
8. A smooth line, either straight or curving, is drawn through or near each point on the graph to show the best-fit pattern of the data.

Figure 8-5 Criteria for constructing line graphs in science.

and errors—which they might not encounter with contrived textbook data" (National Research Council, 1996, pp. 214, 218). Thus, if certain data points do not fall on a projected trend line, students should consider whether the points might be anomalies or errors and retake that data.

In connecting mathematics and science, it is important that students not only construct tables and graphs but also interpret them.

Using Patterns and Relationships

Science and mathematics can also be connected through finding mathematical patterns and relationships and using them in interpreting physical situations (see Table 8-1 and Figure 8-1). Patterns and relationships found in tables and graphs enable students to

- make predictions from collected data;
- formulate and test possible relationships between variables in the science/mathematics activities performed;
- construct hypotheses about possible patterns of change in their obtained data; and
- draw conclusions and inferences from data (Curcio, 1989).

In Chapter 10 on educational technology, we discuss the use of electronic spreadsheets and graphing programs to facilitate the construction of charts and graphs from investigative data.

Recall from Chapter 2 that a prediction is a forecast of an outcome based on knowledge of patterns or trends. A line graph visually displays the pattern of the relationship between two variables.

Let us look at some examples of using charts and graphs to make interpretations in science.

Making Predictions from Graphs. Predicting is an excellent way for students to interpret their data and for you to assess student understanding. Predictions can be made, for example, from the bouncing ball graph in Figure 8-4.

After some time investigating the bouncing ball and constructing graphs (as described in the previous section), ask students to predict what they think the rebound height will be for, say, a 200 cm drop height. To do this, students should first extend the graph line, making sure that it follows the pattern of the graphed data. Next, they should locate the 200 cm point on the *x* axis and draw a vertical line straight up from it until it intersects the graph line. Students can then read across to the *y* axis to predict the rebound height for a ball dropped from 200 cm. With appropriate safety precautions, teams should check their predictions by dropping the ball from the new height and measuring the rebound height.

The solution to this problem relates to air resistance and the fact that the Ping-Pong ball reaches a terminal velocity.

For golf balls, children should find that their measured rebound height for a 200 cm or greater drop height is very close to their predicted rebound height. Interestingly, this is not the case for Ping-Pong balls. Why do you think this is so? You can find the solution to this problem in a fun article by Elizabeth Dudley Holmes (1997) on using spreadsheets in mathematics and science.

Another investigation that can promote data collection and graphical analysis concerns the swing time for pendulums.

Swingers. FOSS has provided an interesting activity on pendulums, in which collected data are displayed on a concrete line graph. In the activity, students are given long strings and directed to attach a small weight to one end of each string. Students then trim each string to a specific length, such as 13 cm, 15 cm, 17 cm, 18 cm, 20 cm, and so on. The students determine the number of swings in 15 seconds for their particular pendulum lengths. Next, they hang their pendulums from pushpins arranged along a number line to uniformly display the number of swings in 15 seconds for different length pendulums. The strings have been cut so that there are whole numbers of swings in 15 seconds, for example 13 swings in 15 seconds.

When all of the data have been collected and the pendulums hung from the number line, the pendulum strings are seen to form a gentle curve (see Figure 8-6). The curve shows a relationship that can be detected and expressed by students: The longest length pendulums have the fewest number of swings in 15 seconds, and the shortest pendulums have the most swings in 15 seconds. That is, the longer the pendulum length, the fewer the number of swings in 15 seconds.

A research study investigating how general education and special education students form generalizations from pendulum data is described in Chapter 9, pp. 289–291.

As part of the pendulum swingers activity, the students are given a swing rate for which swing data have not been collected, for example, 15 swings in 15 seconds or 6 swings in 15 seconds. They are asked to use their graph to predict the length of the pendulum that would produce that swing rate. In making predictions, the students simply hold a new string up to the graph and fix the new string length so that it will continue the gentle curve pattern established. Students then test their predictions by counting the number of swings in 15 seconds for their new pendulums to see if the length they chose produces the desired swing rate.

Operating on Numerical Data

Operating on numerical data is another way to connect mathematics and science (see Table 8-1 and Figure 8-1). Numbers obtained in scientific investigations through counting and measurement processes often need to be operated on mathematically. Lengths may

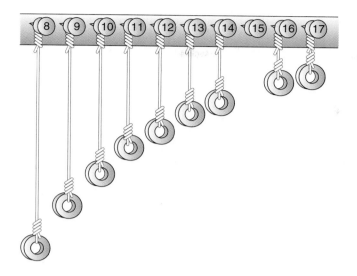

Figure 8-6 A concrete line graph depicting the number of swings pendulums of different length take in 15 seconds. *Source:* Adapted from FOSS® (Full Option Science System®) Variables, Investigation 1: Swingers. © The Regents of the University of California and published by Delta Education. Apapted with permission.

need to be *added*, and weights of containers may need to be *subtracted* from total weights to determine the weights of contents. Areas might be calculated through *multiplication;* ratios, such as densities, and rates, such as speeds, must be obtained through *division;* averages must be determined through *addition* and *division* operations; and so on. Understanding mathematical operations on numbers is essential for students in understanding concepts in prealgebra and algebra.

Children encounter mathematical relationships from a very early age, such as when pulling a wagon uphill. From experience, the child might predict that more force will be needed to pull a wagon up a steeper hill. An upper elementary or middle school student may take data on the required force to pull a cart up planes of different angles of inclination, put the data in a chart of ordered pairs, and graph the data.

At later grades (upper middle school or above), the student may search for an equation to model the mathematical relationship. Once an equation is developed, it may be manipulated through algebraic and arithmetic operations to predict the exact amount of force required to move an object of a given weight up inclined planes of different heights. The equation is connected back to the real world through the graphs, tables, measurements, verbal descriptions, and physical manipulations that serve to represent the mathematical relationship at different levels of thought. Historically, one of Galileo's great contributions to modern science was his pioneering use of mathematics to describe physical situations (Sobel, 2000).

Let us look at the mathematics of the equal-arm balance as an example of how mathematics can be used to better understand a real-world situation.

Mathematics in the Balance. Children experience balancing from very early ages. For example, young children physically balance themselves as they walk on narrow rails, play on seesaws, or learn to ride a bicycle. Children's actions reveal the ways they think about balancing. When they start to fall to one side when walking on balance boards, they shift their weight to the other side by extending an arm or leg. A lighter child might balance a heavier child on a seesaw by sitting farther out toward the end of the seesaw board. These actions show that young children are implicitly using mathematical ideas in understanding and adapting to physical reality. The seeds of mathematical thinking are present in the children's mental and physical actions.

The math balance, illustrated in the chapter opening photo and sold by Delta Education and other equipment companies, is an excellent tool for studying balancing from kindergarten through middle school. Addresses for equipment companies are given in Appendix C.

In one FOSS (Lowery, 1998) investigation, students attempt to balance a cardboard cutout figure on the end of a finger. Children quickly discover several ways to balance the figure. They are then challenged to place clothespins at different points on the figure (to shift its center of gravity) and to discover new ways to balance it. Children solve the problem by finding a balance point that enables the weights to be distributed around it.

Qualitative Thinking about the Balance. Consistent with Piaget's theoretical research (Inhelder & Piaget, 1958; Siegler, 1986) and the practical experiences of teachers in the classroom, the NCTM standards have emphasized the importance of the qualitative dimensions of children's mathematical learning. When children think qualitatively, they compare and make judgments about whether variables are equal, or one is greater or less than another, without regard to exact numbers or measurements. According to the mathematics standards,

> The mathematical ideas that children acquire in grades K–4 form the basis for all further study of mathematics. Although quantitative considerations have frequently dominated discussions in recent years, *qualitative* considerations have greater significance. (National Council of Teachers of Mathematics, 1989, p. 16, emphasis added)

You can study fourth graders' responses to the balance beam problem at the *Inquiry in Virtual Classrooms* link on the Companion Website for Chapter 8 at http://www.prenhall.com/carin.

Children's success with quantitative thinking and problem-solving activities in mathematics and science programs at later grade levels depends largely on the qualitative foundations established in the earlier years of school.

Inhelder and Piaget (1958) carried out a detailed study of children's mathematical thinking about an equal-arm balance. Around ages 8 or 9, at the concrete operational level, balance is seen to be a function of four variable factors working together:

- Weight on one side of the balance
- Distance of that weight from the pivot point
- Weight on the other side
- Distance of the other weight from the pivot point

Through discovery activities and teacher invention, these four variables can be coordinated into rules, though the rules are qualitative or nonnumerical at this stage. Two main rules are learned initially:

- Equal weights at equal distances will balance [see Figure 8-7(a)].
- Heavier weights that are close in can balance lighter weights farther out [see Figure 8-7(b)].

The first rule is a symmetry rule. Children predict that, for an equal-arm balance, if weights are equal and distances are equal, the crossbar will balance. Younger children may implicitly know the symmetry rule, but they tend to focus on either the weights *or* the positions, not *both* at the same time. Thus, younger children may take incomplete data and fail to apply the symmetry rule appropriately. Children in third or fourth grade who are at the concrete operational level can consider the weights and distances simultaneously and use the symmetry rule to predict balance.

The second balance rule, placing heavier weights closer to the center, is also a qualitative rule. It involves a nonnumerical combination of weights and distances. In making qualitative comparisons using the rule, children may note, for example, that one weight is considerably heavier than the other. If the two weights are to balance, the first one must be much closer to the central pivot point than the second one.

These two rules (which are not likely to be stated explicitly by children) open up the possibility of a whole range of compensating actions that can potentially be applied to establish balance. For example, if there is too much weight on one side, the child can

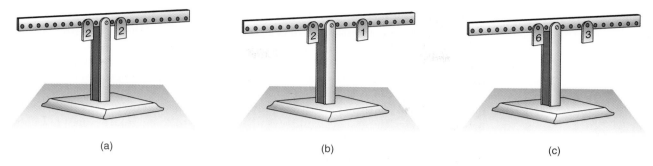

(a)   (b)   (c)

Figure 8-7   (a) Qualitative Rule #1: Equal weights at equal distances will balance. (b) Qualitative Rule #2: Heavier weights close in can balance lighter weights farther out. (c) Quantitative Rule: When the product of the weight and distance on one side of the pivot is equal to the product of weight and distance on the other side, the balance bar will be horizontal.

- take off weights from the first side,
- add weights to the other side,
- decrease the distance of the weights on the first side, or
- increase the distance on the other side.

The children's qualitative rules govern their trial-and-error learning as they add and take off weights and move them to different positions. This reversible and flexible way of thinking about qualitative relationships makes complex thought about numerical operations truly possible.

Quantitative Thinking about the Balance. Around fifth or sixth grade, many children can extend their qualitative rules through using exact numbers to represent weights and distances. When one side of a balance beam has more weight, the young mathematical scientist goes beyond qualitative questions about more and less and asks such questions as:

- How much heavier is it? How much farther out is it?
- What is the proportion? Is it twice as much or three times as much?

If the weight on one side is twice as much, for example, then to compensate, either the weight or the distance on the other side has to be twice as much for balance. If this type of thinking is to be very useful, it must build on the qualitative thinking at an earlier level.

At some point in the formal operational stage, the student begins to understand the use of formal mathematics to coordinate the four numerical variables. The quantitative rule of the balance can then be understood and applied [see Figure 8-7(c)]. Stated in the form of an equation, the quantitative rule of the balance is

$$(WL) \times (DL) = (WR) \times (DR)$$

where W = weight, D = distance, L = left side, and R = right side of the balance. Thus, the product of the weight and distance on one side is equal to the product of weight and distance on the other side. Try the equation for yourself using Figures 8-7(a), (b), and (c). The products of the weights and distances on the left side will equal the products on the right side for each of these three cases.

This equation summarizes experiences at the qualitative level; for example, heavy weights must be placed closer to the pivot for balance. The quantitative rule, however, tells the child exactly how much closer to the pivot the heavier weight would need to be for balance.

The principle governing equal-arm balances also governs the operation of levers. Using a small force far out from a fulcrum, a person can lift a heavy load. Using the equation, students can predict how much force is needed to lift a load of a given weight when the distances involved are known. It is through using mathematics to summarize (or model) past experiences and to analyze real-world situations that true mathematical understanding is demonstrated.

Balances and other manipulatives provide students opportunities to bridge from the concrete world to the abstract world of mathematics. In so doing, students must talk about concrete objects and their actions on them, find qualitative ways to represent their thinking, and eventually construct ways of coordinating numerical variables that describe the real world. When they learn to think about mathematics and its applications in this way, students are better prepared to negotiate the complex ideas of advanced mathematics and science in later grades.

There are many more opportunities for you to integrate mathematics into your science program. To augment your own creativity, examine the abundance of excellent lessons in contemporary funded science programs and on the Internet that connect science and mathematics.

Next, we will discuss connections between science and language arts.

Connecting Science and Literacy

Teachers of all subjects should be engaged in language instruction. As stated in the *Standards for the English Language Arts* (International Reading Association, 1996),

> Language is the most powerful, most readily available tool we have for representing the world. . . . Language is not only a means of communication, it is a primary instrument of thought. . . . Encouraging and enabling students to use language effectively is certainly one of society's most important tasks. (p. 12)

Literacy instruction in schools generally includes four areas: reading, writing, speaking, and listening. These critical elements of language learning occur in all curricular areas and should not be separated from substantive content in science, mathematics, social studies, and other subjects. An emphasis on literacy across the curriculum is a natural way for students to learn and use language skills to communicate and reason in specific domains, as well as in their everyday lives (Robbins, 1990).

Evidence suggests that language experiences across the curriculum help students with language and logical development. Several studies have found, for example, that young chil-

---

These reading standards from the *Standards for the English Language Arts* can be addressed in science (International Reading Association, 1996, p. 25):

1. Students read a wide range of print . . . texts to build an understanding of texts, of themselves, and of . . . cultures . . . ; to acquire new information; to respond to the needs and demands of society and the workplace; and for personal fulfillment.
2. Students apply a wide range of strategies to comprehend, interpret, evaluate, and appreciate texts. They draw on their prior experiences, their interactions with other readers and writers, their knowledge of word meanings . . . , their word identification strategies, and their knowledge of textual features.

---

dren's experiences with observing, describing, and interpreting natural phenomena in active science programs improved their reading readiness and reading skills (Welman, 1978).

A teacher of science can do many things to help students enhance their language abilities and, at the same time, enrich their science learning. The elements of literacy are valuable for students in doing science and should be promoted through science instruction as well as in language arts classes. For example, in helping students develop language and thinking processes, teachers of both science and language arts are called on to

- develop, extend, and refine the knowledge base of students;
- assist students to organize knowledge into useful schemas;
- invent vocabulary that is related to topics being studied;
- provide students with opportunities to use reading, listening, and viewing behaviors; and
- supply many opportunities for practice and rehearsal in communicating through writing, speaking, and representing things visually (Ormrod, 1999; Scott, 1993).

Let us focus first on reading. How can science and reading be connected for students?

Science and Reading

Santa and Alvermann (1991) noted, "Science and reading teachers have very similar goals for their students. Foremost is the pursuit of meaning" (p. vi). In science, students construct meaning from the natural world; in reading, they construct meaning from text. Although investigative processes in science and comprehension processes in reading are quite different, processing strategies remain at the heart of both disciplines. As we noted in Chapter 2, both science and reading teachers want their students to be able to describe events, make inferences, interpret information, draw conclusions, and make and test predictions (Padilla, Muth, & Padilla, 1991; Tompkins & Hoskisson, 1994).

Contemporary learning theories in both science and reading follow a constructivist view. In the traditional view of reading, meaning resided in the text; the reader's task was to ferret it out. In the constructivist view, "the reader creates meaning based on the text, and her or his existing knowledge about its content, language and structure" (Orasanu & Penney, 1986, p. 2). Thus, prior knowledge, reading strategies, and knowledge about language are essential in the reading process.

Reading specialists have identified a large number of strategies that are useful in helping students construct meaning from information presented in writing. For example, in learning from textbooks students must learn to

- actively distinguish between major ideas and minor details in presented information;
- regularly summarize the most important information;
- organize information into coherent structures;
- draw inferences by filling in information omitted in the text;
- use text statements to predict what is coming next; and
- continually monitor comprehension, such as through self-questioning (King, 1994; Mayer, 1998).

The application of such strategies may be mediated by the teacher; however, they are most powerful when students learn to apply them on their own.

Prior Knowledge and Comprehending Science Text. Science text materials, whether in activity guides, laboratory manuals, or textbooks, are notoriously difficult for students at

A very useful collection of articles on the "why," "how," and "precautions" about using science texts in instruction can be found in *Science Learning: Processes and Implications* (Santa & Alvermann, 1991). This volume, with contributions from reading and science specialists, is sponsored by the International Reading Association.

every level to read. In successfully comprehending a topic presented in science texts, a student's prior knowledge must be extensive, accurate, and consistent with the information presented in the text (Finley, 1990). Finley (1991) has suggested that teachers must make sure that readers have sufficient prior knowledge of terms, facts, concepts, and relationships to understand an assigned text selection. Thus, it makes sense to follow the dictum suggested in Chapter 3: *investigation first; reading later* (Lowery, 1998).

Students need extensive and repetitive experiences with hands-on, minds-on activities to develop connected, accurate, and useful knowledge. It is this type of prior knowledge that students must be able to draw on in reading science books.

Access to Prior Knowledge. To be able to comprehend written information, students must not only have prior existing knowledge but also access what they know and apply it appropriately. Students differ in the degree to which they use potentially available knowledge in order to learn and understand (Brown, Bransford, Ferrara, & Campione, 1983). Science teachers should scaffold learning to assist students in accessing and using what they know in comprehending text material.

Finley (1991) and others have suggested various ways that science teachers can help students draw on and use their existing knowledge. Teachers can help students assess prior knowledge by having them

- write initial descriptions and explanations of phenomena;
- construct concept maps of what they know;
- draw pictures and diagrams of events, accompanied by written explanations; and
- present their ideas to the class so that alternative descriptions and explanations might be considered.

All of these examples portray the student as an active learner, both in acquiring new knowledge and in accessing it in reading.

In addition to helping students acquire and use prior knowledge, teachers can help students approach reading more strategically.

An instructional tool often used to teach reading, a K–W–L chart can help you assess students' prior knowledge before beginning a new topic of study. (K–What Do You Know? W–What Do You Want to Learn? L–What Did You Learn?)

Strategies for Comprehending Science Textbooks. Teachers should assist students in pre-reading, reading, and postreading strategies to help them make sense of text.

Prereading Strategies. In beginning a reading assignment in science, students should be clear about what they are expected to learn. The teacher might begin by having students speculate about the text content before reading (Padak & Davidson, 1991). This helps students think about the relationships between the text information and their prior knowledge. In a case study reported by Padak and Davidson, students who learned to speculate about text content before reading were able to read for a wider variety of purposes than before. Rather than reading simply to answer the teacher's questions or questions in the passage, they read to learn more about science concepts, to verify predictions that they or others had made, and to connect text presentations to their prior knowledge.

Using Strategies During Reading. Students should be taught to use comprehension-monitoring strategies during reading. These strategies include such tasks as raising questions about the text, clarifying terms, identifying main ideas and supporting statements, paraphrasing and summarizing text meanings, making and verifying inferences and predictions about text meaning, and so on. Such strategies are not easily learned from direct instruction or from teacher modeling, because the learner tends to be a passive observer in both cases (Brown et al., 1983).

King (1994) has adapted reciprocal reading procedures developed by Palincsar and Brown (1986) to science teaching and learning. In King's adaptation, two children work cooperatively in reading a science text, with the children alternating the roles of dialogue leader and student. King has used prompt cards to successfully teach fourth and fifth grade children to deliberately ask themselves and one another questions to access prior science knowledge, comprehend what they have read, and make connections in constructing science explanations. A sample prompt card, which students may keep in front of them as they read for understanding, is shown in Figure 8-8.

Postreading Strategies. Discussion of the text is an important way to help students check on their comprehension. In discussion, go beyond asking factual questions about what was read. Focus on helping students

- link text ideas with their prior knowledge and experience;
- make connections between main ideas and supporting details;

These writing and research standards from the *Standards for the English Language Arts* can be addressed in science (International Reading Association, 1996, p. 25):

1. Students apply a wide range of strategies as they write and use different writing process elements appropriately to communicate with different audiences for a variety of purposes.
2. Students apply knowledge of language structure, language conventions . . . , media techniques, figurative language, and genre to create, critique, and discuss print and nonprint texts.
3. Students conduct research on issues and interests by generating ideas and questions, and by posing problems. They gather, evaluate, and synthesize data from a variety of sources . . . to communicate with different audiences for a variety of purposes.

Figure 8-8 A sample prompt card for interactive reading procedures.
Source: From "Guiding Knowledge Construction in the Classroom: Effects of Teaching Children How to Question and How to Explain," by Allison King, 1994, *American Educational Research Journal, 31*(2), pp. 338–368. Copyright 1994 by American Educational Research Association. Reprinted with permission.

DIRECTIONS:

Discuss the lesson with each other.

Ask each other questions.
Answer each other's questions by giving explanations.

Prompt card given to students to facilitate understanding of science texts

Comprehension questions
    Describe . . . in your own words.
    What does . . . mean?
    Why is . . . important?

Connection questions
    Explain why . . .
    Explain how . . .
    How are . . . and . . . similar?
    What is the difference between . . . and . . . ?
    How could . . . be used to . . . ?
    What would happen if . . . ?
    How does . . . tie in with . . . that we learned before?

- recognize and think about text statements that conflict with their own ideas;
- work to resolve conceptual confusion; and
- use concepts presented in text to explain other real-world phenomena (Roth, 1991).

These prereading, reading, and postreading strategies help readers pay attention to how they create meaning based on the text, their own existing content knowledge, and their knowledge about language (Orasanu & Penney, 1986).

Next, we will examine ways science and writing can be connected.

Writing in Science

The writers of the *Standards for the English Language Arts* (International Reading Association, 1996) asserted that

> Reading and writing are intertwined. . . . Just as students need an array of strategies to comprehend . . . text written by others, so too do they need to apply an array of strategies as they write. (p. 34)

To build these strategies, students need frequent opportunities to write on different topics and for different purposes. Science provides students with many opportunities to write. Writing in science improves science learning; it also enhances students' writing skills and strategies.

VIDEO CASE STUDY: *Donna*

Introducing the Case

Donna, a twenty-two-year veteran of the classroom, has learned that building on ideas that have relevance for her students allows her to capture their interest, advance their knowledge, and value their heritage. Donna focuses on the heritage of her students to illustrate for them how all people—regardless of race, gender, or culture— contribute to the body of knowledge we call science. Look at the first module in the video case to see how she accomplishes this task.

> "Science is just another word for nature."
>
> Dr. Thom Alcoze, Northern Arizona University

Questions for Reflection

1. What evidence is there that Donna effectively uses cultural traditions of Native Americans to teach science?
2. Donna began with stories and myths to engage her students and lead to questions about the peoples who had lived in the area. How does Donna employ the rest of the 5-E model in her archeological study?

Trying New Ideas *Donna's focus on reviewing the traditions of Native Americans led her to arrange for her students to take a field trip to ancient ruins and to participate in an archeological dig. Donna's students learned a variety of skills in their opportunity to be archeologists.*

Questions for Reflection

1. What kinds of evidence in an archeological dig illustrate for students the need to understand soil, weather, the physical properties of different kinds of matter, sources of energy, the differences among living things, and so on?
2. Consider the skills students developed at the archeological dig. How did the site map (see last page) they used to plot what they found contribute to their study, understanding, and respect for past culture?

Field Record

Date _____ Location Coordinates _____ Recorder _____

Length _____ Width _____

Full Description _____

_____

_____

_____

How was it used? _____

What does it tell you about these people? _____

_____

Source: From *Digging into Archeology* by Julie Coan, 1999, Pacific Grove, CA: Critical Thinking Books & Software, www.criticalthinking.com. Reprinted by permission.

Reflecting and Building on Change *By asking her students to create middens, Donna requires students to use what they have learned to evaluate their own understanding of how human artifacts contribute to the knowledge of a culture and how those artifacts might change over time. Because this is an assessment activity, Donna expects students to use their new knowledge to role-play how science, technology, and society result in decision making that can affect future generations.*

Questions for Reflection

1. How do students determine what artifacts to use in their middens? Why is it important for students to use artifacts that represent several generations?
2. How can students use a field square plan (see last page) to identify where they locate artifacts in a dig or to know how to place artifacts in middens?
3. What connections did Donna want to make between valuing people in the past and preparing her students for the future?
4. What are your perspectives about the nature of science and its relationship to ethics?

Looking for artifacts requires that students work carefully, noting how deep the stratum is where they are digging.

After students gently sift soil from their dig, they will analyze what they find, based partly on where they found it.

Two Archeological Principles

1. Objects found in the same stratum—horizontal layer—at the same location probably are from the same time period.

2. Superposition implies that, given any undisturbed layer, the bottom layer is the oldest and the layers above it are successively younger. Thus, objects uncovered nearest the surface are generally the most recent.

Field Square Plan

Completed by: _____

	A	**B**	**C**	**D**	**E**
7					
6					
5					
4					
3					
2					
1					

Source: From *Digging into Archeology* by Julie Coan, 1999, Pacific Grove, CA: Critical Thinking Books & Software, www.criticalthinking.com. Reprinted by permission.

Writing Investigative Reports. One important writing task for students in science is writing reports of investigations. Writing reports forces students to consider their audience, clarify their questions, organize and present their data more clearly, and form more secure links among data, prior knowledge, and conclusions. Organizing and presenting their findings and conclusions to others helps students make new information their own and connect it to their prior understandings. Furthermore, according to the *National Science Education Standards*,

> oral and written communication skills are developed in science when students record, summarize and communicate the results of inquiry. . . . Coordination suggests that these skills receive attention in the language arts program as well as the science program. (National Research Council, 1996, p. 214)

See Hand and Keys (1999) for a well-designed science writing heuristic for developing reports on inquiry investigations in science. A discussion of inquiry reports is also included in our Chapter 2 discussion of a seed germination project and our Chapter 6 discussion of assessment.

Journal Writing in Science. Journals provide another opportunity for students from primary grades through middle school to enhance their science learning and writing approaches (Santa, Alvermann, & Havens, 1991). Journals may contain observations of a demonstration, personal explanations of a discrepant event, reactions to a film or oral presentation, personal notes from a reading assignment, and so on. Journals allow students to write informally and personally explore content.

Next we will examine connections between science and social studies.

Connecting Science and Social Studies

Making connections between science and social studies helps students create a more complete picture of the world. While science emphasizes how the natural world works, social studies addresses the multiple roles of humans as they adapt to their surroundings and reorganize ways they relate to each other.

Social studies cuts across and combines several disciplines. According to the National Council for the Social Studies (NCSS; 1994),

> Social studies is the integrated study of the social sciences and humanities to promote civic competence. Within the school program, social studies provides coordinated, systematic study drawing upon such disciplines as anthropology, archaeology, economics, geography, history, law, philosophy, political science, psychology, religion, and sociology, as well as appropriate content from the humanities, mathematics, and natural sciences. The primary purpose of social studies is to help young people develop the ability to make informed and reasoned decisions for the public good as citizens of a culturally diverse, democratic society in an interdependent world. (p. 3)

As with science, mathematics, and language arts, national standards have been written for social studies, as well as for civics, history, geography, and economics. The social studies standards can be found in the document *Expectations of Excellence: Curriculum Standards for the Social Studies*, developed by the NCSS (1994).

The social studies standards can be found on the NCSS Website at http://www.socialstudies.org.

Plan Lessons Around Science/Technology/Society Themes

Science and technology play a vital part in helping students understand their relationship to the world around them. One of the 10 themes of the NCSS standards is "Science, Technology, and Society." This theme is also found in various state-level frameworks for

The Texas Essential Knowledge and Skills for Social Studies, an example of state social studies standards, can be found on the Internet at http://socialstudies. tea.state.tx.us/teks_and_taas/ teks.htm.

social studies, which draw on the standards. For example, the Texas Essential Knowledge and Skills (TEKS, pronounced *Tex*) for Social Studies includes a strand for each grade level called "Science, Technology, and Society." Throughout the elementary and middle school grades, the TEKS challenge students to understand how science and technology have affected human life—past and present. As appropriate to their levels of development, students are expected to

- describe how science and technology have changed transportation, communication, medicine, agriculture, industry, and recreation;
- explain how science and technology have changed the ways people meet their basic needs;
- analyze environmental changes brought about by scientific discoveries and technological innovations;
- give examples of the contributions of scientists and inventors that have shaped society;
- explain how resources, belief systems, economic factors, and political decisions have affected the use of technology from place to place, culture to culture, and society to society; and
- make predictions about future social, economic, and environmental consequences that may result from future scientific discoveries and technological innovations.

In state-level frameworks for both science and social studies, student expectations are often closely related. Both types of frameworks call for students at different grade levels to study common topics such as the use of natural resources, the history of science and scientists, the effects of physical processes on the environment, and the societal impact of energy usage. Social studies processes shared with science include representation, problem solving, decision making, data collection, data interpretation, and critical thinking.

Weather Watchers: A Science and Social Studies Lesson for Grades K–2. An excellent example of merging social studies and science expectations can be found in a K–2 Internet lesson called "Weather Watchers." It was written by Noelle Kreider, a teacher in the San Bernardino County Schools of California. This 3-week lesson is written in a WebQuest format.

Kreider's "Weather Watchers" lesson can be found on the Internet at http://www.itdc.sbcss.k12.ca.us /curriculum/weather.html# sequence. You can find out more about WebQuest at http://edweb.sdsu.edu/ webquest/webquest.html.

WebQuest, the creation of Dr. Bernie Dodge of San Diego State University, is a bank of inquiry-based lessons posted on the Web in which all or part of the information comes from the Internet. WebQuest lessons are written by contributors from all facets of education. Each WebQuest follows a prescribed format and is evaluated by a rubric developed by Dodge.

The overall goal of the weather watchers lesson is for students to explore concepts of weather and determine how weather affects human life in various regions. Students work in groups to record the weather in different geographic regions, such as Argentina, Cambodia, Australia, Mexico, Canada, Portugal, South Africa, and Russia.

For direct links to Websites given in Chapter 8, go to the Web Destinations section at http://www. prenhall.com/ carin.

In order to apply weather information in decision making, each student makes a doll that "travels" to a certain location in the world. In adapting to the weather in each area, the dolls change clothes that have been created by the students. The students write daily journal entries about the weather, the people, and unique features of the region.

Web information available to students includes physical and weather maps of each region and pictures that give identity to each area. Web resources used in the lesson include:

Lonely Planet Destinations	http://www.lonelyplanet.com/
CNN Weather Page	http://cnn.com/WEATHER/
The Cloud Catalog	http://ww2010.atmos.uiuc.edu/(Gh)/guides/ mtr/cld/home.rxml
Environmental Canada	http://www.pnr-rpn.ec.gc.ca/index.en.html

As the lesson progresses each day, students develop both science and social studies concepts by exploring how humans adapt to physical processes related to weather and climate. Students also use current events to determine how weather affects the way people live. Further, students develop essential computer skills as they become weather watchers.

In concluding the lesson, students answer questions such as: How does the weather change? How is weather different in various regions? Why is weather important to us? Why is it helpful to predict the weather? These questions get to the heart of social studies and science because they lead students to understand the characteristics of weather, the instruments and processes real scientists use to describe and explain weather, the effects weather has on humans, and how humans adapt to constantly changing weather phenomena.

The following Websites that pertain to weather might also be used in a weather unit:

KGAN WeatherEye Homepage	http://weathereye.kgan.com
The Weather Unit	http://faldo.atmos.uiuc.edu/ WEATHER/ weather.html
Weather Here and There	http://www.ncsa.uiuc.edu/edu/ RSE/RSEred/ WeatherHome.html
Weather Channel: Weather Education	http://www.weather.com/education/

There are a multitude of other Web sources on weather. Use an Internet search engine such as Google to identify them.

A River Ran Wild: A Science and Social Studies Lesson for Grades 3–5. An example of connecting science and social studies at grades 3–5 centers around a study of the book *A River Ran Wild* by Lynne Cherry (1992). The goal of this learning experience is to guide students in understanding that the history of a given environment can reveal how humans have affected an ecosystem in both responsible and irresponsible ways. In this study, students expand their understanding of the environment and its relationship to humans by merging the theme of "Science, Technology, and Society" with other social studies themes, including "People, Places, and Environment," "Time, Continuity, and Change," "Civic Ideals and Practices," and "Culture."

The class is divided into five groups, with each group assigned to answer one of these five guiding questions:

1. In what ways have humans historically affected particular ecosystems?
2. How do cultural beliefs and practices affect the quality of the environment?
3. What physical and human factors cause an environment to change over time?
4. How can humans help change a polluted environment?
5. How can industry exist and progress within an ecologically sound environment?

Each group researches their question and illustrates their answer by making posters or by creating a multimedia presentation. The presentations include the portion of *A River Ran Wild* that deals with their question as well as answers from two other sources such as the Internet, resource books, newspaper articles, or interviews.

After students have presented their answers to the first five questions, a sixth question is posed for all of the students:

6. What do people in my community do to preserve our environment?

A community expert is enlisted to guide the students in answering this question. Before the expert comes to class, students write a letter summarizing what they have learned from the class presentations. This informs the expert about the students' background knowledge and also gives the students an opportunity to demonstrate understanding of all the issues raised in the guiding questions. The expert not only talks to students and answers their questions but also may arrange field trips or other appropriate means for students to attain information. As a culminating activity, once students have answered the sixth question, they develop a rubric for an ecologically balanced community and rank their community on the basis of the rubric. Where there are problems, students may write a request to state, county, or city officials asking them to address the situations. Where there are environmentally sound practices, students write letters thanking the people who are responsible for creating a safe environment for all living things.

Through their encounter with *A River Ran Wild* and by being engaged in the lesson's procedures, students meet the expectations outlined in the national standards and grow as informed, environmentally aware, and responsible citizens.

The Lewis and Clark Expedition: A Science and Social Studies Lesson for Grades 5–8. "Sent by President Thomas Jefferson to find the fabled Northwest Passage, Meriwether Lewis and William Clark led the most important expedition in American history—a voyage of danger and discovery from St. Louis to the headwaters of the Missouri River, over the Continental Divide to the Pacific" (Burns, 1997). An analysis of the 1804–1806 expedition of the Corps of Discovery, the group of explorers led by Lewis and Clark, brings together many of the themes of social studies. However, students cannot reach a full understanding of this feat without appreciating scientific goals and contributions of the fantastic voyage of the Corps of Discovery.

Joint social studies and science lessons on Lewis and Clark's expedition can lead students to appreciate the accomplishments of the journey and to understand that humans adapt to, overcome, and alter challenges presented by the physical environment.

Overall guiding questions for the joint lessons might include the following:

1. What was the mission of the Lewis and Clark expedition?
2. What is the historical background for the expedition?
3. Through what current states and near which current cities did the Corps of Discovery travel?
4. What new plants and animals did the explorers discover?
5. What human and geographic features shaped the events and outcome of the expedition?
6. What technologies did Lewis and Clark use to accomplish their mission?
7. What technological exchanges did the Native Americans and members of the Corps have?
8. What was the scientific and social significance of the Lewis and Clark expedition for the people of the United States at the time of the exploration? What is the significance of the expedition for people today?

Students launch their analysis of the Lewis and Clark expedition by reading a selection from the letter that President Jefferson wrote to Lewis (see Figure 8-9). As the students read

---

For some creative ideas about using community resources to extend this study, see Lois R. Stanley (1995), "A River Runs Through Science Learning: Tap Community Resources to Create an Integrated Science and Social Studies Unit," *Science and Children*, 52(4), 12–15, 58.

Connecting social studies and science in studying the Lewis and Clark expedition is particularly appropriate at this time as the nation celebrates the 200th anniversary of the expedition.

To Meriwether Lewis, Esquire, captain of the first regiment of infantry of the United States of America

Your situation as secretary of the president of the United States, has made you acquainted with the objects of my confidential message of January 18, 1803, to the legislature; you have seen the act they passed, which, though expressed in general terms, was meant to sanction those objects, and you are appointed to carry them into execution.

Instruments for ascertaining, by celestial observations, the geography of the country through which you will pass, have been already provided. . . .

The object of your mission is to explore the Missouri River, & such principal stream of it, as, by its course and communication with the waters of the Pacific ocean, whether the Columbia, Oregon, Colorado or any other river may offer the most direct & practicable water communication across this continent for the purposes of commerce.

Beginning at the mouth of the Missouri, you will take observations of latitude & longitude, at all remarkable points on the river, & especially at the mouths of rivers, rapids, at islands & other places & objects distinguished by such natural marks & characters of a durable kind, as that they may with certainty be recognized hereinafter, the courses of the river between these points of observation may be supplied by the compass, the long-line & by time, corrected by the observations themselves, the variations of the compass too, in different places, should be noted. . . .

Your observations are to be taken with great pains & accuracy, to be entered distinctly, & intelligibly for others as well as yourself to comprehend all the elements necessary, with the aid of the usual tables, to fix the latitude and longitude of the places at which they were taken. . . .

The commerce which may be carried on with the people inhabiting the line you will pursue renders a knowledge of these people important, you will therefore endeavor to make yourself acquainted, as far as a diligent pursuit of your journey shall admit, with

the names of the nations & their numbers;
their relations with other tribes or nations;
their language, traditions, monuments;
their ordinary occupations in agriculture, fishing, hunting, war, arts, & the implements for these;
their food, clothing & domestic accommodations;
the diseases prevalent among them, & the remedies they use. . . .

And considering the interest which every nation has in extending & strengthening the authority of reason & justice among the people around them, it will be useful to acquire what knowledge you can of the state of morality, religion & information among them, as it may better enable those who endeavor to civilize & instruct them, to adapt their measures to the existing notices & practices of those on whom they are to operate.

Other objects worth of notice will be
the soil & face of the country, its growth & vegetable productions . . . ;
the animals of the country, generally . . . ;
the remains and accounts of any which may be deemed rare or extinct;

Figure 8-9 President Thomas Jefferson's letter to Meriwether Lewis, commissioning a search for the Northwest Passage, related equally to science and social studies.

Figure 8-9 Continued.

> *the mineral productions of every kind; but more particularly metals, limestone,*
> *coal & salpetre; salines & mineral waters, noting the temperature of the last*
> *& such circumstances as may indicate their character;*
> *Volcanic appearances;*
> *climate as characterized by the thermometer, by the proportion of rainy,*
> *cloudy & clear days, by lightning, hail, snow, ice, by the access & recess of*
> *frost, by the winds, prevailing at different seasons, the dates at which partic-*
> *ular plants put forth or lose their flowers, or leaf, times of appearance of par-*
> *ticular birds, reptiles or insects. . . .*
>
> *In all your intercourse with the natives treat them in the most friendly & con-*
> *ciliatory manner which their own conduct will admit; allay all jealousies as to the*
> *object of your journey, satisfy them of its innocence, make them acquainted with*
> *the position, extent, character, peaceable, & commercial dispositions of the U.S. of*
> *our wish to be neighborly, friendly & useful to them, & of our dispositions to a*
> *commercial intercourse with them. . . .*
>
> *Should you reach the Pacific ocean inform yourself to the circumstances which*
> *may decide whether the furs of those parts may not be collected as advantageously*
> *at the head of the Missouri (convenient as is supposed to the waters of the Colorado*
> *& Oregon or Columbia) as at Nootka sound, or any other point of that coast; and*
> *that trade be consequently conducted through the Missouri & U.S. more benefi-*
> *cially than by the circumnavigation now practiced. . . .*
>
> *Given under my hand at the city of Washington, this 20th day of June 1803*
> *Th. Jefferson*
>
> *Thomas Jefferson*
>
> *Pr. U.S. of America*

the letter, they highlight the instructions from the president using two colors: one to indi-cate Jefferson's instructions relating to social studies and the other to indicate instructions relating to science. Observing the color-coded letter, students conclude that there is a bal-ance of science and social studies in the responsibilities described by President Jefferson. You should read Jefferson's letter yourself to gain an understanding of how social studies and sci-ence were intertwined in the expedition.

The students are divided into groups with each group analyzing one particular charge outlined in the letter. For example, one group might want to investigate all of the instruc-tions from the president regarding the Native Americans. Within that group, a pair of stu-dents might concentrate on "the diseases prevalent among them and remedies they use."

In the analysis, students define their charge, identify science and social studies rela-tionships, and investigate how the charge was carried out by the Corps of Discovery. Us-ing journals written by Lewis, Clark, and other members of the Corps, students cite evidence of details relating to the accomplishments of the expedition, including de-scriptions of hardships, mishaps, discoveries, delights, and deeds of the party. Other re-sources students can use include the Ken Burns (1997) PBS video, *Lewis and Clark,* resource books, and scores of Internet sites. Figure 8-10 lists some useful Websites for stu-dent investigations.

Students display their findings in multimedia slide shows and present them to a local historical society or civic group. Each student also writes a letter to President Jefferson

PBS Lewis and Clark Website
http://www.pbs.org/lewisandclark/

This site includes biographies of the members of the Corps of Discovery, descriptions of each Native American tribe Lewis and Clark encountered, an archive section including a time line, maps, and journal entries of the corps, a simulation of the expedition, and 17 lesson plans.

Lewis and Clark on the Information Superhighway
http://www.lcarchive.org/

Go West Across America with Lewis and Clark
http://www.nationalgeographic.com/west/

This site includes a simulation that involves students in decision making. Excerpts from the explorers' journal reveal the decision the leaders actually made.

Lewis and Clark Bicentennial
http://www.lewisandclark200.org/

Lewis and Clark Trail Heritage Foundation
http://www.lewisandclark.org

Discovering Lewis and Clark
http://www.lewis-clark.org/

The EOS Education Lewis and Clark Project
http://www.lewisandclarkeducationcenter.com/

Sponsored by NASA at the University of Montana, this site has photographs of the trail from space, ecological regions, and other scientific information.

LewisAndClarkTrail.Com
http://www.lewisandclarktrail.com

This is an interactive site that takes the visitor through each state the expedition covered. The site invites visitors to relive the adventure.

National Museum of the American Indian (Smithsonian Institution)
http://www.nmai.si.edu/

Dakota Information
http://puffin.creighton.edu/lakota/index.html

This site gives historical and contemporary information about the Dakota Sioux.

Native American Nations
http://www.nativeculture.com/lisamitten/nations.html

Native Americans
http://www.americanwest.com/pages/Indians.htm

Grizzly Bears
http://www.bearden.org/brnbear.html

Figure 8-10 Lewis and Clark resources on the Internet.

summarizing how each of the charges was successfully met and requesting recognition before Congress for each member of the Corps of Discovery. This activity gives students an opportunity to demonstrate understanding of the whole expedition as well as the part they investigated in depth.

To determine how geographic factors of the territory the Lewis and Clark expedition passed through have altered since 1806, students e-mail students in schools situated along the trail. In the e-mail, students might inquire about the human and physical characteristics of the region and how the Lewis and Clark expedition is commemorated there. They might also ask about human alterations such as the rerouting of rivers, construction of dams, building of cities and towns, dispersal of Native American people, and changes to animal habitats. After the e-mails have been answered and shared with all class members, students write an essay about the scientific and social significance of the Lewis and Clark expedition to people of the United States both in the days of the journey and today.

The lessons about weather, *A River Ran Wild*, and the Lewis and Clark expedition illustrate how science and social studies fit together well for effective student understanding

(a) *Sacagawea guides the Lewis and Clark expedition into Oregon.*

(b) *The landscape of Portland, Oregon, today.*

(c) *Land now occupied by Gavins Point Dam in South Dakota.*

How would tracing environmental changes that have occurred since Lewis and Clark's expedition further integrate science and social studies?

of the earth. Students benefit when teachers merge science and social studies concepts, processes, and approaches to learning on appropriate occasions and in a manner that fosters learning the essential elements of both science and social studies.

Integrating the curriculum can be an important goal in elementary and middle school classrooms.

Curriculum Integration

Curriculum integration usually means organizing the whole curriculum, including science, mathematics, social studies, language arts, music, and art, around a particular theme such as energy, the environment, space and space travel, or oceans.

Researchers assert that

- integrated learning activities are more appealing because they require fewer scheduling changes and can be done by one teacher (Kober, 1993);
- both science and the other subjects are learned more effectively (Koballa & Bethel, 1985); and
- the integration of science with other disciplines has potential for improving both the quantity and quality of science instruction and learning (Pappas, Kiefer, & Levstik, 1990).

Educators have explored a variety of ways to effectively integrate subjects in elementary and middle schools.

Insects as the Theme of an Integrated Curriculum Unit

Figure 8-11 shows how a middle grade teacher integrated science and other subjects in a study of insects (Tompkins & Hoskisson, 1994). All of the activities extend students' learning about insects, while giving direct experiences with a wide variety of subject matter and skills. Such an integrated lesson speaks to the broad range of learning levels and styles of students. You can easily adapt and use this model in your own classroom.

The Environment and Native American Culture as the Theme of an Integrated Unit

Donna, a fifth grade teacher featured in an Annenberg Case Study in Science Education, has integrated the curriculum for her students around the themes of the environment and Native American cultural heritage. In Donna's classroom, 25% of the students are Native American, while another 25% are Hispanic. One of Donna's main goals for her students is that they all "feel they have a very important heritage . . . all people have contributed to the body of knowledge we call science."

As part of a study of native plants and animals, Donna asks students to study and retell Native American myths and folktales. She emphasizes that these myths and folktales are not true stories, but they incorporate various accurate observations about nature. Donna wants her students to understand that the observations expressed in the myths often have scientific understandings at their foundation. The students share the stories with their class members using various means, including narratives, plays, and puppet shows.

The study guide of the Annenberg Video Case Study featuring Donna and her students is provided in this chapter.

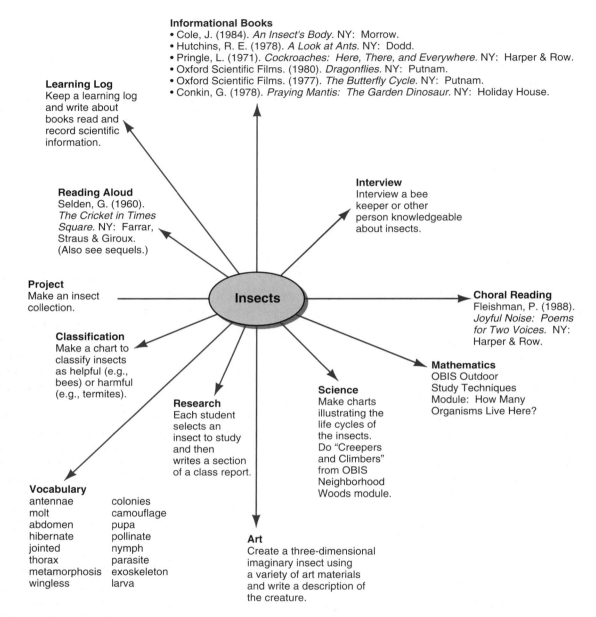

Figure 8-11   Thematic cluster of curricular subject matter on insects.
Source: Modified from *Language Arts: Content and Teaching Strategies* (p. 545), 3d ed., by Tompkins, © 1995. Adapted by permission of Pearson Education, Inc., Upper Saddle River, NJ.

The students take field trips to two ancient Native American sites and participate in an ongoing archaeological dig, using their mathematics skills to document the precise location of artifacts they discover. They also write stories that reveal their ideas on why people living in the area centuries ago might have abandoned their settlements.

In a culminating activity, students complete a chart identifying elements that are common to different cultures, such as food, shelter, medicine, and transportation. Then they construct shoe-box middens in which they have buried household items that represent their own "clan." Middens are exchanged between groups, who "excavate" the shoe-box middens to study the past as evidenced by the artifacts.

A main problem in curriculum integration is how to combine different disciplines in such a way that the unique standards, goals, and objectives of every subject are recognizably present in the lesson plans, instruction, and assessments provided for students (see McShane, 1994). As shown by these two examples, when integration is truly achieved, the curriculum is enriched for all children.

 Use the self-assessment questions for Chapter 8 at http://www.prenhall.com/carin to assess how well you understand this chapter and how prepared you are for a test over its content.

SUMMARY

- National standards in every discipline support connections between subjects in the school curriculum. There are important connections to be made between science and mathematics, language arts, social studies, and other school subjects.

- Connections between science and mathematics can center around four main themes: quantifying the world, organizing and interpreting data, using patterns and relationships, and operating on numbers.

- Children begin to quantify the world through counting, estimating, and measuring all kinds of real-world variables that they encounter in the process of investigating. Measuring should be emphasized in both science and mathematics. When children encounter measurement in problem-solving activities in science, they go beyond practice to engage in rehearsal. Through rehearsal, they not only develop skills, they add something to them.

- Organizing data into diagrams, tables, and graphs is a key step in scientific inquiry. The types of graphs most often used in elementary and middle schools are bar graphs, histograms, and line graphs. Putting data obtained from scientific investigations into tables and graphs better enables students to relate data to their investigative procedures, make comparisons among data, see relationships and patterns, and communicate their data to other people.

- Science and mathematics can also be connected through using mathematical patterns and relationships in interpreting physical situations. Patterns and relationships found in tables and graphs enable students to make predictions, formulate and test hypotheses, and draw conclusions and inferences from data.

- Operating on numerical data is another way to connect mathematics and science. Understanding mathematical operations on numbers obtained from investigations is an essential prerequisite for understanding the use of functions in prealgebra and algebra, and in high school science courses. In science and mathematics, quantitative treatments of data should be preceded by qualitative, nonnumerical investigations. The development of children's mathematical thinking about an equal-arm balance is a good example of how qualitative considerations should lay a foundation for more precise mathematical thinking.

- Connecting science to reading and writing is critically important in the elementary and middle school classroom. Science teachers can help students succeed in reading through helping them acquire necessary prior knowledge, guiding them in using comprehensive strategies, and following up after science reading assignments. There are also many opportunities in science for learners to use and improve their writing skills as they communicate their inquiries to others.

- Science, technology, and society themes are common to science and social studies standards. Lessons built around such topics as weather and the environment show how science and social studies can be linked. For example, the Lewis and Clark expedition of 1804–1806 relates equally to social studies and science. There are many opportunities for students to connect these two disciplines as they embark on re-creations of this fantastic voyage of discovery.

- Curriculum integration involves bringing all subjects together in the study of a special theme. A variety of themes, ranging from insects to moon watching to Native American cultures, are useful for this purpose.

REFERENCES

Activities That Integrate Mathematics and Science. (1999). *AIMS programs and product catalog*. Fresno, CA: AIMS Education Foundation.

Bransford, J. D., Brown, A. L., & Cocking, R. R. (Eds.). (2000). *How people learn: Brain, mind, experience, and school*. Washington, DC: National Academy Press. (Also available at http://www.nap.edu)

Brown, A. L., Bransford, J., Ferrara, R., & Campione, J. (1983). Learning, remembering, and understanding. In J. N. Flavell & E. M. Markman (Eds.), *Handbook of child psychology* (Vol. 3, 4th ed., pp. 79–166). New York: Wiley.

Burns, K. (1997). *Lewis and Clark: A Public Broadcasting Services film by Ken Burns*. Burbank, CA: Warner Home Video.

Cherry, L. (1992). *A river ran wild*. New York: Harcourt Brace Jovanovich.

Clements, D. (1999). Teaching length measurement: Research challenges. *School Science and Mathematics, 99*(1), 5–11.

Curcio, F. R. (1989). *Developing graph comprehension: Elementary and middle school activities*. Reston, VA: National Council of Teachers of Mathematics.

Finley, F. N. (1990). Variations in students' prior knowledge. *Science Education, 69*, 697–705.

Finley, F. N. (1991). Why children have trouble learning from science texts. In C. M. Santa & D. E. Alvermann (Eds.), *Science learning: Processes and applications* (pp. 22–27). Newark, DE: International Reading Association.

Full Option Science System. (1990). *Swingers*. Berkeley, CA: Lawrence Hall of Science.

Full Option Science System. (1991). *Graphs in the elementary science program*. Berkeley, CA: Lawrence Hall of Science.

Hand, B., & Keys, C. W. (1999). Inquiry investigation: A new approach to laboratory reports. *The Science Teacher, 66*(4), 27–29.

Holmes, E. D. (1997). The spreadsheet: Absolutely elementary. *Learning and Leading with Technology, 24*(8), 6–11.

Inhelder, B., & Piaget, J. (1958). *The growth of logical thinking: From childhood to adolescence*. New York: Basic Books.

International Reading Association. (1996). *Standards for the English language arts* (a project of the International Reading Association and the National Council of Teachers of English). Newark, DE: Author.

Jacobs, H. H. (1989). The growing need for interdisciplinary curriculum content. In H. H. Jacobs (Ed.), *Interdisciplinary curriculum: Design and implementation*. Alexandria, VA: Association for Supervision and Curriculum Development.

King, A. (1994). Guiding knowledge construction in the classroom: Effects of teaching children how to question and how to explain. *American Educational Research Journal, 31*(2), 338–368.

Koballa, T. R., Jr., & Bethel, L. J. (1985). Integration of science and other subjects. In D. Holdzkom & P. B. Lutz (Eds.), *Research within reach: Science education. A research-guided response to the concerns of educators*. Charleston, WV: Appalachia Educational Laboratory, Inc.

Kober, N. (1993). *EDTALK: What we know about science teaching and learning* (p. 46). Washington, DC: Council for Educational Development and Research.

Lowery, L. (1998, November). How new science curriculums reflect brain research. *Educational Leadership, 56*(3), 26–30.

Mayer, R. E. (1998). Cognitive theory. In N. L. Lambert & B. L. McCombs (Eds.), *How students learn: Reforming schools through learner-centered education*. Washington DC: American Psychological Association.

McShane, J. B. (1994). Editor's note: Integrate with integrity. *Science and Children, 31*(7), 4.

National Council for the Social Studies. (1994). *Expectations of excellence: Curriculum standards for the social studies*. Washington, DC: Author.

National Council of Teachers of Mathematics. (1989). *Curriculum and evaluation standards for school mathematics*. Weston, VA: Author.

National Research Council. (1996). *National science education standards*. Washington, DC: National Academy Press.

National Science Resources Center. (1996). *Science and technology for children: Comparing and measuring*. Burlington, NC: Carolina Biological Supply.

Orasanu, J., & Penney, M. (1986). Introduction: Comprehension theory and how it grew. In J. Orasanu (Ed.), *Reading comprehension: From research and practice* (pp. 1–9). Hillsdale, NJ: Erlbaum.

Ormrod, J. (1999). *Human learning*. Upper Saddle River, NJ: Merrill/Prentice Hall.

Padak, N. D., & Davidson, J. L. (1991). Instructional activities for comprehending science text. In C. M. Santa & D. E. Alvermann (Eds.), *Science learning: Processes and applications* (pp. 76–85). Newark, DE: International Reading Association.

Padilla, M. J., Muth, K. D., & Padilla, R. K. (1991). Science and reading: Many process skills in common? In C. M. Santa & D. E. Alvermann (Eds.), *Science learning: Processes and applications* (pp. 14–19). Newark, DE: International Reading Association.

Palincsar, A., & Brown, A. (1986). Interactive teaching to promote independent reading from text. *The Reading Teacher, 39*, 771–777.

Pappas, C. C., Kiefer, B. Z., & Levstik, L. S. (1990). *An integrated language perspective in the elementary school: Theory into action*. New York: Longman.

Pearlman, S., & Pericak-Spector, K. (1995). Graph that data! *Science and Children, 32*(4), 35–37.

Robbins, P. A. (1990). Implementing whole language: Bridging children and books. *Educational Leadership, 47*(7), 50–54.

Roth, K. (1991). Reading science texts for conceptual change. In C. M. Santa & D. E. Alvermann (Eds.), *Science learning: Processes and applications*. Newark, DE: International Reading Association.

Santa, C. M., & Alvermann, D. E. (Eds.). (1991). *Science learning: Processes and applications*. Newark, DE: International Reading Association.

Santa, C. M., Alvermann, D. E., & Havens, L. T. (1991). Learning through writing. In C. M. Santa & D.E. Alvermann (Eds.), *Science learning: Processes and applications* (pp. 122–133). Newark, DE: International Reading Association.

Scott, J. (Ed.). (1993). *Science and language links: Classroom implications*. Portsmouth, NH: Heinemann.

Siegler, R. S. (1986). *Children's thinking*. Upper Saddle River, NJ: Prentice Hall.

Smith, W. H., McKnight, C. C., & Raizen, S. (1997). *A splintered vision: An investigation of U.S. science and mathematics education*. Boston: Kluwer.

Sobel, D. (2000). *Galileo's daughter*. New York: Penguin Books.

Texas Education Agency. (1999). *Texas social studies framework, kindergarten–grade 12*. Austin, TX: Author.

Tompkins, G. E., & Hoskisson, K. (1995). *Language arts: Content and teaching strategies* (3rd ed., p. 521). Upper Saddle River, NJ: Merrill/Prentice Hall.

Welman, R. T. (1978). Science: A basic for language and reading development. In M. B. Rose (Ed.), *What research says to the science teacher* (Vol. 1, pp. 1–12). Washington, DC: National Science Teachers Association.

9

The increasing diversity of the school age population, coupled with differential science performance among student demographic groups, makes the goal of "science for all" a national challenge.

(Lee, 2002, p. 23)

Science for All Learners

YOUR ELEMENTARY OR MIDDLE school science classroom will include a diversity of students. In addition to general education students, you will be responsible for teaching students with disabilities, students from different cultural and linguistic backgrounds, and students with special gifts and talents. The *National Science Education Standards* emphasize that science must be for all students: All students—regardless of race, gender, cultural or ethnic background, disabilities, aspirations, or interest and motivation in science—should have the opportunity to attain high levels of scientific literacy (National Research Council, 1996, p. 20). This principle is one of equity and excellence. It challenges science teachers to meet the needs of all students, requiring them to recognize the diversity of students and to prepare science experiences to address these differences.

All children are unique. They will achieve understanding in different ways and at different depths as they explore answers to questions about the natural world (National Research Council, 1996, p. 20). Some children will have special learning needs. You may need to adapt science activities for students who have disabilities, or you may need to work much more closely with them to scaffold learning. Students with language barriers may need science materials written in their primary language, or they may need to work with other students who can help them access material more readily. Gifted and talented students may challenge you to find ways to lead them to ever-deeper understanding.

Whatever adaptations you need to make, you will want to consider the following questions to help you plan for the diverse backgrounds and abilities of your students:

- *Who are the students with special learning needs? What are the learning challenges and special needs of individual students in your classroom?*

- *How can you be a personal resource for all children in your classroom?*

- *What shall be the goals of science for students with special learning needs?*

- *What special modifications in materials, equipment, instruction, and assessment strategies should be made for students with special learning needs?*

The following sections will help you begin to build a bank of resources that you can draw from as you teach science in an inclusive classroom.

NSES You can review the *National Science Education Standards* online. Go to http://www.nap.edu/readingroom/books/nses/html.

Watch the Annenberg Video Case Study featuring Jean to get a glimpse of the diversity of students in today's elementary and middle school classrooms. A video guide to this case study can be found in this chapter.

Collect responses to these questions as you find them in the chapter. The focus questions also appear on the Companion Website at http://www.prenhall.com/carin.

VIDEO CASE STUDY: JEAN

As you watch the three modules for this case study, use the Questions for Reflection to guide your thoughts and notes for any group discussion or individual feedback. If you watch the video as a group and then participate in a group discussion, choose a group facilitator to solicit various perspectives and keep the discussion on track.

Introducing the Case

Jean, like most elementary teachers, is a generalist. She often prepares for teaching science to her students by first going to the library to research the topic she needs to teach. To reach her very diverse group of third grade students, including several students with special needs, she then develops multisensory learning experiences so that all her students will benefit from them.

Questions for Reflection

1. Do you think the diversity of students in Jean's classroom is representative of most elementary classrooms? Why or why not?
2. Why is teaching through different learning modalities an important way to address the diversity of children?

Trying New Ideas   *Jean engages her students in a Grand Adventure, challenging students to "act" like scientists and test five different mystery powders to figure out what each unknown powder is.*

Questions for Reflection

1. How does Jean accommodate for the cognitive level of her students? What does she do ahead of time to structure the activity and organize the classroom to help ensure that students have an ideal environment to engage in their inquiries?
2. What do Jean's students do to figure out what each numbered powder is? What process skills and critical thinking skills do they use?
3. What prior knowledge did Jean's students have to recall that would allow them to be successful with this culminating activity?
4. What accommodations did the special education teacher use to help Eric be successful with the activity?
5. How would you describe the interactions among the children? What evidence is there to indicate that the teacher and the children are respectful and caring of one another and that they consider themselves part of a learning community?

Reflecting and Building on Change   *The last science study of the year is a study of amphibians. To assess students' understanding of the life cycle of amphibians, where they "fit" on the food chain, and other science concepts, Jean had students engage in a number of multisensory activities.*

PROPERTIES OF MYSTERY POWDERS

	Sugar	Salt	Baking Soda	Cornstarch	Plaster of Paris
Distinguishing Properties	• grainy • fine crystals	• grainy • cube-shaped crystals	• light powder	• very light powder	• powder
Indicators	• dissolves in water • melts, bubbles, and turns black when heated	• dissolves in water	• turns orange with iodine • fizzes with vinegar	• turns black with iodine	• makes water cloudy • forms paste with water • hardens in about 15 minutes when water is added • generates heat with water • turns yellow with iodine

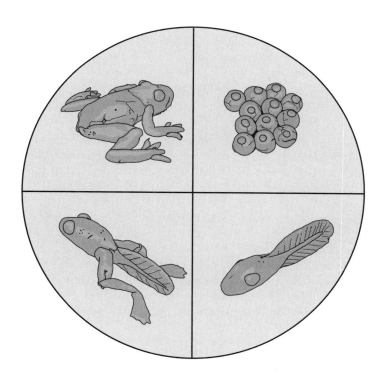

Questions for Reflection

1. What different opportunities did Jean give students to describe their understanding about frogs?
2. How did Jean's learning activities provide different children opportunities to be more successful in sharing what they know?
3. Why are field trips valuable learning experiences for children? What did Jean have students carry with them on the field trip to document their learning experience?

Students with Special Learning Needs

Who are the learners with special needs who will likely be included in your classroom? Although we run the risk of losing sight of individual values and differences when we categorize students, it is useful with the enormous numbers of students in public education to group diverse learners into these categories (Mastropieri & Scruggs, 2004, pp. 8–10):

- *Students with Disabilities:*   According to the federal **Individuals with Disabilities Education Act (IDEA),** formerly Public Law (PL) 94-142, students in this category must be provided with a free appropriate education, including receiving instruction in the "least restrictive environment." This is interpreted as students with disabilities being taught in general education classrooms to the greatest extent possible, an educational practice known as *inclusion.*
- *Gifted and Talented Students:*   These students exhibit abilities above those of their age in academic achievement, visual or performing arts, or athletics. Today, rather than being taught in special classes, gifted and talented students are more often included in regular classrooms. Special adaptations or accommodations may be appropriate for them.
- *Students with Linguistically and Culturally Diverse Backgrounds:*   These students are linguistically and culturally different from the majority U.S. culture. Some of these students will be in bilingual or English as a second language (ESL) programs for part of the day, but many of them will be a regular part of your inclusive classrooms. Teachers should plan and implement instruction that is sensitive to students' language and cultural differences.

Although students in each of these groups may exhibit special learning needs, federal legislation addresses educational modification for only the first category, students with disabilities. Various states have passed laws relating to the identification and education of students in other categories. However, in many cases funding for accommodations is inadequate or not provided.

Grouping students according to their special learning needs can mask an essential truth: All of us are unique. Even within the same culture, community, or family, we are all different. Your students will have different intellectual abilities and learning styles, diverse language and cultural backgrounds, and physical, social, and emotional differences. All will enter your classroom having experienced life differently. Thus, their understanding of the world will be different. The varied experiences, background knowledge, and abilities of your students will influence how you plan for and teach science.

A glossary containing definitions of important terms used in this chapter can be found on the Companion Website for Chapter 9 at http://www. prenhall.com/carin.

IDEA provides funds to state and local education agencies to assist in the education of students with disabilities.

Teachers as Bridge Builders

As a teacher, you are the key resource to help students bridge the gap from their varied experiences, language and knowledge backgrounds, and abilities to a scientific way of investigating and understanding the natural world.

What does it mean to be a resource for your students?

Examining Your Attitude

As you plan how to mediate effective science experiences for all of your students, consider your own preconceptions. What do you think when you visit a classroom with students who have disabilities or come from diverse cultures or speak English only haltingly? What expectations do you have for their learning? What is your attitude toward students who have special learning needs?

Your attitude will model for all your students how they should react to the diversity in your classroom—and the diversity in the world. If you are sensitive, supportive, and respectful of each student, you will create a classroom environment where students are willing to collaborate and cooperate with one another to ensure that everyone's ideas are heard and valued.

People-First Language

When working with students who have special learning needs, it is important to avoid using labels when talking with other teachers, other professionals, parents, or the students themselves. Using a categorical label when discussing a child with a special need devalues the child. Rather, using the child's name first and then identifying the need, if appropriate, indicates your recognition of the child as a person first (Caroline, my student who has mental retardation . . .). Practicing this use of "people-first" language and avoiding the use of labels will contribute to the acceptance of any child with special learning needs into your classroom community.

Recognizing Students' Abilities

You will find that students with special learning needs, like their general education peers, have capabilities and strengths that you as a teacher can identify, highlight, and build upon. It is important not to equate individual special needs with reduced abilities overall. A physician once said, "My colleagues sometimes lose sight that our duty is to treat people and not symptoms!" Teaching to students' "symptoms" or individual needs instead of treating students as people who just happen to have certain needs is often a trap teachers find themselves in when they label and categorize students.

Please visit the Companion Website at www.prenhall.com/carin for a set of inquiry science activities ideal for students with special needs.

The Role and Importance of Friendship

Neither cooperative grouping nor peer tutoring guarantees friendship. Elementary and middle school students, including students with diverse needs, rely on friendships for companionship and emotional support. But friendship is about choice and cannot be readily defined, much less forced. This is precisely its magic. However, teachers and others do have some influence over the nature of proximity. Thus, to create and foster an environment in which it is possible for friendship to emerge might be a reasonable goal (Van der Klift & Kunc, 1994).

As you provide opportunities for students to interact in cooperative groups or ask students to tutor one another, you can also encourage collaboration, social interaction, and friendship.

Combating Learned Helplessness

Sometimes one student helps another student so much that the student who is "helped" learns to rely on others and does little or nothing on his own. This *learned helplessness* compromises the process and goals of learning. Constructive learning is effortful. If a student becomes used to having someone do things for him, he does not learn to accept the challenge of learning tasks. The student learns to be helpless and ends up with little knowledge, undeveloped skills, and low self-esteem because he does not have the opportunity to achieve learning on his own (Turnbull, Turnbull, Shank, & Smith, 2004, p. 109). Your goal as a bridge builder is to help your students learn to accept assistance but maintain responsibility in ways that boost their learning and self-esteem.

Involving Parents

It is certainly true that the effort parents make at home can make a difference in their children's achievement. Coordinate home and school learning with parents of all of your students. Explain to parents the desirability of motivating and supporting their child's learning. Stress the importance of the parents making available supplemental science books such as the *How and Why Wonder Book* series. In addition, encourage parents to seek out television programs that stimulate and enrich children's science interests (e.g., *Nova*, *Bill Nye—The Science Guy*, and *Discovery Channel* and *National Geographic* specials). Also, note that science videos can be borrowed from many public libraries or rented to be viewed and discussed at home and at school with teachers and peers.

Common Standards, Common Assessments, Diverse Pathways

Although different learning pathways and modifications in teaching approaches may be necessary for individuals and special groups, the goals of science instruction are the same for all learners. The *National Science Education Standards* (National Research Council, 1996) state that

> The understandings and abilities described in the content standards are for all students; they do not represent different expectations for different groups of students. (pp. 221–222)

The *Science Standards*, then, assert that all students should be expected to achieve the same science knowledge and inquiry standards—though learning approaches and levels of achievement may vary.

According to the *No Child Left Behind Act* of 2002 (see Chapter 1, p. 14), all children, including children with disabilities and children with diverse language backgrounds, must be tested yearly in reading and math in grades 3–8. Beginning in 2007, all students must be tested in science at least once in each of these grade spans: 3–5, 6–9, and 9–12. Schools must demonstrate adequate yearly progress (AYP) toward the goal of 100% proficiency in reading, math, and science for all students within 12 years. Although state standards in science, which must be set by all states by the 2005–2006 school year, may vary from national standards, the goal is for all students within each state to pass statewide, standards-based assessments. If the students within local schools do not exhibit annual progress toward this goal, the whole school faces a host of sanctions (Mastropieri & Scruggs, 2004, pp. 14–15; Turnbull et al., 2004, pp. 46–47). Assisting all learners to achieve proficiency in science, as well as in mathematics and reading, is a national challenge.

Assisting All Students to Attain Proficiency in Science

The results of a research study by Rowe (1973, pp. 367–373) highlighted the difficulties teachers face in helping all students attain proficiency on a learning task requiring concept understanding, not just recall, as well as insight and reasoning. In the study, first grade boys were shown a bar magnet, an iron bar, and a heavy plastic bar. All three objects were the same size and shape. The children were also shown three closed, cloth bags and told that

NSES

"Teachers of science guide and facilitate learning; recognizing and responding to student diversity and encouraging all students to participate fully in science learning."

(National Science Education Standards, Teaching Standard B)

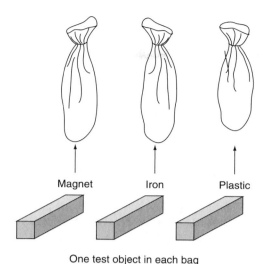

Magnet   Iron   Plastic

One test object in each bag

the bags contained objects like those in front of them. One bag contained a magnet, one held an iron bar, and the other had a plastic bar (see Figure 9-1). The children's task was to determine what was in each bag without looking.

The key to solving the problem was for children to use their knowledge of magnet rules as tools for problem solving, rather than simply to recall the rules as memorized information. Successful children found that they could use magnet rules learned in previous activities to gather evidence to solve the problem.

Using the magnet outside the bag as a probe, and using the magnet rules to guide investigation, the successful children found out that

- the probe magnet can be made to either attract or repel the object in the first bag;
- the probe magnet attracts but does not repel the object in the second bag; and
- the probe magnet neither attracts nor repels the object in the third bag.

Applying this information and their knowledge about magnets, successful students reasoned that a magnet was in the first bag because it was both attracted to and repelled by the probe magnet; an iron bar was in the second bag because it was only attracted to the probe magnet; and a plastic bar was in the third bag because it was neither attracted to nor repelled by the probe magnet.

Rowe (1973) found that only 4 of 60 of the first graders were able to solve the magnets problem spontaneously. Hints were supplied as scaffolds to 15 other children in Rowe's study. The most productive hints prompted the children to think about what they could find out using the magnet rules. For example, Rowe provided one cue by holding up an object and saying,

Suppose I met you around school one day, and I told you that I found this piece of metal. I thought it was a magnet, but I was not sure. Could you help me find out whether it was a magnet or not? (p. 369)

No matter how the student replied, the investigator called attention to the three bags and asked how the student could find out which one had the magnet, which one had the iron bar, and which one had the plastic bar. This hint enabled 10 of the 15 students receiving hints to be successful on the task.

Results of this small-scale study highlighted the learning difficulties of the 5 children, one-third of the 15 student sample, who were not successful on the task. These students did not spontaneously solve the problem nor were they successful with a moderate amount of scaffolding. What modification in the learning task or instructional approaches might have helped these children to be successful? When we encounter students who are unsuccessful in science activities, what can we do to assist them in learning?

Let us look at some characteristics of learners within various diverse groups and consider how we might modify materials, instruction, and assessment strategies to help them learn science with understanding at optimal levels.

Students with Disabilities

Planning for individual student needs in science requires knowing the general characteristics of students with different disabilities. IDEA recognizes about a dozen disabilities (see Table 9-1). Students with disabilities represent more than 10% of the public school student population. Over 6 million students with identified disabilities require special education services.

An analysis of Table 9-1 shows that more than half of students with disabilities were categorized as having specific learning disabilities. The first four categories—specific learning disabilities, speech or language impairments, mental retardation, or emotional disturbance—account for 88% of all students with disabilities.

Six principles of IDEA govern the education of students with disabilities (see Figure 9-2). IDEA directs that all students have a right to a full, free public education in the *least restrictive environment*. This means that schools are required to educate students with disabilities with nondisabled students to the maximum extent appropriate for the students with disabilities. Statistics from the National Center for Education Statistics (http://www.nces.ed.gov) indicate that in 1998–1999, 47% of students with disabilities spent at least 80% of the school day in regular education classrooms, a figure that was up noticeably from the 31% of 1988–1989.

TABLE 9-1   CHILDREN 6–21 YEARS OLD SERVED IN FEDERALLY SUPPORTED PROGRAMS FOR THE DISABLED, BY TYPE OF DISABILITY: 1999–2000 SCHOOL YEAR

Disability	Number	Percent
Specific learning disabilities	2,872,000	50.5
Speech or language impairments	1,090,000	19.0
Mental retardation	614,000	10.8
Emotional disturbance	470,000	8.2
Hearing impairments	72,000	1.3
Orthopedic impairments	71,000	1.3
Other health impairments	254,000	4.5
Visual impairments	27,000	0.46
Multiple disabilities	113,000	2.0
Deaf-blindness	2,000	0.03
Autism	65,000	1.3
Traumatic brain injury	14,000	0.24
Developmental delay	19,000	0.38

Source: U.S. Department of Education. (1999). *To Assess the Free Appropriate Education of All Children with Disabilities: Twenty-First Annual Report to Congress on the Implementation of the Individuals with Disabilities Education Act.* Washington, DC.

- **Zero reject:** No student with disabilities can be excluded from a free, appropriate education.
- **Nondiscriminatory evaluation:** Schools must evaluate students fairly (without bias) to determine if they have a disability, identify what kind of disability the student has, and identify how extensive it is.
- **Appropriate education:** Schools must tailor education for individual students (Individual Education Plan, IEP) based on nondiscriminatory evaluation. Schools are also required to augment that education with related support services and supplementary aids.
- **Least restrictive environment:** Schools must educate students with disabilities alongside students without disabilities to the maximum extent appropriate for the students with disabilities. The school may not remove a student from general education unless the student cannot be educated there successfully.
- **Procedural due process:** IDEA provides safeguards for students against schools' actions including a right to sue in court.
- **Parental and student participation:** Schools must collaborate with parents and adolescent students in designing and carrying out special education programs.

Figure 9-2 Six principles of IDEA that govern the education of students with disabilities.
Source: Adapted from Individuals with Disabilities Education Act 20, U.S.C. & 1400 et seq. (1997).

In general, not all students with exceptionalities are educated in inclusion classrooms. Students in the first two categories of Table 9-1, specific learning disabilities and speech or language impairments, will be more typical of the students with special needs you will have in your classroom. Chances are good that you will have one or more students with these special needs in your inclusion classroom.

Making Modifications for Students with Special Learning Needs

There are a variety of considerations to remember as you plan learning experiences, make modifications, and implement instruction for students with disabilities.

Individualized Education Plans. Many of your students with disabilities will have already been identified as needing special education services through nondiscriminatory evaluation. Thus, some students will enter your classroom with an IEP (individualized education plan) in place. You should view the IEP as a dynamic, working document intended to improve student learning, rather than a set of legalities to be fulfilled. Recorded on each IEP are learning goals and objectives designed for individual students. Once a student with special needs has been assigned to your class, you will want to review her IEP goals and objectives to see what science activities or experiences will help to meet these goals. For example, one goal in an IEP might read: *Develop communication skills and interactions with peers.*

Science instructors can help to meet this individual learning goal by including the student in a cooperative learning group. Within this group students may be asked to engage in an inquiry activity that requires meaningful student interaction to discover and communicate findings revealed by the data. The student with a disability could be required to communicate her understanding of the phenomena she observes to her peers, and together they could determine how to report these findings.

Even though the IEP lists general goals to advance the education and socialization of the student with special needs, you should develop specific science objectives that will move the student from what she knows to learning new information, concepts, and inquiry strategies called for in state and district standards and curriculum frameworks. Just as you would strive to do this for nondisabled students, based on their abilities, so you would do this for your students with disabilities. Ascertain their areas of interest and the conceptions they have of science knowledge. It will make sense to engage some students in learning science that will assist them in developing greater independence in their adult life. For example, a student with mental retardation may benefit from practical knowledge about the properties of common household chemicals and how to safely use and store them.

Barrier-free Education. A challenge you will face as a science teacher is to ensure that the curricular materials you prepare or access for students with special learning needs are free from barriers that would prevent participation. An obvious example is a video for science instruction, which is not closed-captioned for a student who is deaf. Many barrier-free materials are available for teacher use. IEP objectives can often help you determine what modifications and supports are needed to remove barriers. A few minutes of research on the Internet will give you names of products and manufacturers of furniture, innovative devices, or software that are designed to make learning more accessible for a variety of disabilities. In some cases you will need assistance from special educators and administrators to see that students with disabilities are provided specialized equipment such as barrier-free furniture to accommodate wheelchairs, talking calculators, or computer software that utilizes keyboard shortcuts or voice input/speech recognition.

In addition to the general accommodations you make for students with disabilities, there are specific suggestions that you can use to meet individual needs. The following sections provide concrete ideas for working with students who have varied cognitive differences, students with emotional or behavioral disorders, students with orthopedic disabilities, students who are blind or have low vision, and students who are deaf or hard of hearing.

Go to the Website at http://www.prenticehall.com/carin to find links to the National Information Clearing House for Handicapped Children and Youth or ERIC Clearinghouse on Disabilities and Gifted Education set up by the Council for Exceptional Children. These sites provide ideas for adapting science instruction.

Science for Students with Learning Disabilities

The students in your classroom will come to you with a variety of cognitive abilities and disabilities. Some will have been identified as having learning disabilities. Defined by IDEA, the term *specific learning disability* means a disorder in one or more of the basic psychological processes involved in understanding or in using language, spoken or written. A disorder may manifest itself in imperfect ability to listen, think, speak, read, write, spell, or do mathematical calculations (Individuals with Disabilities Education Act, 1997).

Students with learning disabilities are commonly in the normal range of intelligence. Sometimes, in fact, they are gifted intellectually. However, students with learning disabilities are generally achieving below their current grade level, or are several grade levels below where they should be, in one or more basic academic skill areas such as reading, written language, or math.

Most states use a discrepancy between intelligence and achievement to support the identification of learning disabilities. However, this practice has been challenged on theoretical and practical grounds. The President's Commission on Excellence in Special Education (2002) has recommended a move toward a "response to instruction" model of identification. According to this model, a student's learning problem must first be addressed by numerous, differing instructional attempts in general education before special education placement is considered. It is likely that an alternative to discrepancy criteria will be implemented in the future (see Mastropieri & Scruggs, 2004, pp. 69–70).

What Teaching Approaches in Science Are Most Appropriate? Students with learning disabilities are a very heterogeneous group and can have overlapping problems. This makes it difficult to classify their learning discrepancies and prescribe learning activities and approaches for them. However, research and practical experience support some general strategies to enhance science instruction. These include the use of

- activities-based science;
- intensive scaffolding;
- learning strategies;
- visual presentations and multimedia in general; and
- mnemonics and graphic organizers.

Select an Inquiry Approach. Two main methods of science teaching are a traditional text-book approach and an inquiry approach, such as is emphasized in the *Science Standards* and described throughout this book. The textbook approach typically consists of textbooks and worksheets as the major instructional materials, supplemented with teacher lecture, class discussions, demonstrations, videotape presentations, or other short activities (Mastropieri, Scruggs, & Magnusen, 1999). Most textbooks place high demands on students' reading, language, and memory skills and present large amounts of vocabulary.

Tom Scruggs and Margo Mastropieri, a husband-wife team at George Mason University, have conducted a variety of research studies to investigate the most appropriate methods of teaching science to special education students. With two colleagues (Scruggs, Mastropieri, Bakken, & Brigham, 1993), they carried out a controlled investigation comparing textbook and activities-based, inquiry approaches to teaching science to students with learning disabilities (LD). In the study, 26 seventh and eighth grade students with LD received instruction on two science topics—rocks and minerals, and electricity and magnetism. All students received instruction through an activities approach on one of the topics and a textbook approach on the other. Lessons for the activities-based approach were from FOSS (Full Option Science System) modules. For example, in exploring electricity and magnetism, students constructed and investigated circuits, switches, an electromagnet, and a telegraph.

In the activities approach, teachers first presented problems to be investigated by students (*engagement* according to the 5-E model). Students then performed activities in small groups of three to five students (*exploration*). The lesson was concluded with a whole class session, in which the activities were summarized and discussed (*explanation*). FOSS materials were available for students to use in describing and recording their observations.

Lessons for the textbook approached paralleled the activities approach in content. In the textbook approach, teachers presented information, and students read text materials and examined pictures (such as pictures of circuits, switches, electromagnets, or telegraphs). The children engaged in independent and guided practice activities using worksheets.

Both approaches were well structured and involved daily review, active engagement by students, formative evaluation of student products, and questioning. Teachers in the activity approach raised questions and guided students to raise questions about what happened and why, but generally refrained from directly answering them. Instead, they encouraged and challenged students to answer questions for themselves. Questions in the textbook approach were most often directed toward promoting student attention and prompting direct recall of information provided.

Tests were given individually to students in both conditions for the lessons covering the two science topics. The tests emphasized recall of what students did in the science lesson, recall of facts and vocabulary, and application of concepts, principles, and procedures. Students were also asked four questions related to their enjoyment of the two approaches.

Results strongly favored the activities-based approach to science. Students in the activities approach scored significantly higher on the tests. Additionally, almost all of the students enjoyed the activities approach more. Scruggs et al. (1993) concluded:

> Results of the present investigation suggest that activity-based, inquiry-oriented approaches, when appropriately structured, may facilitate the acquisition of content knowledge of students with LD. . . . In the present context, when students were taught by experiential, more indirect methods, they learned more, remembered more, and enjoyed learning more than when they were taught by more direct instructional methods. (pp. 10–11)

Fradd and Lee (1999) have suggested that, rather than debate about whether a textbook or inquiry approach is best, it may be more fruitful to consider how to use the two approaches in a complementary way to meet students' needs. In the study by Scruggs et al. (1993), what seemed to be most important was that the lessons be well structured, reflect designated instructional objectives, enable students to process information and modify it to meet their personal needs, and lead them to draw their own inferences and make logical connections.

Use Questioning to Guide Active Thinking. An advantage of inquiry science for diverse learners, according to Mastropieri (Brownell & Thomas, 1998) is that it facilitates the efforts of classroom teachers to make appropriate modifications to accommodate different learning needs. (See the accompanying box for Margo Mastropieri's comments on the benefits of inquiry science for students with special needs.)

One modification teachers often make is to provide more scaffolding assistance to certain learners. Consider this example in which a teacher uses questioning to provide sup-

---

Margo Mastropieri on Science Education and Students with Disabilities

"Science focuses on everyday life and daily experiences that we have interacting with our environment. As a result, science contains important life experiences and critical content for students with disabilities. For many students, science is high interest and motivating; they see science all around them and have opportunities to experience and understand this content in ways that may not be as readily available in other content areas. Studying science helps students with disabilities develop better general observation and problem-solving skills. They learn to observe in a systematic manner, classify, think critically about what they see, make logical predictions, and then test those predictions. . . .

Activities-based approaches facilitate the efforts of classroom teachers and specialists to make appropriate modifications to accommodate different learning needs. . . . Lower literary requirements (of activities-based science) facilitate participation that helps students with disabilities to feel better about themselves and view school more positively. . . . Interestingly, when activities-based science instruction is well structured, teachers report that many student behavior problems were reduced significantly. The students are so focused on interesting learning experiences that they do not have time to misbehave."

Source: From "An Interview with Margo Mastropieri: Quality Science Instruction for Students with Disabilities" by M. T. Brownell and C. W. Thomas, 1998, *Intervention in School and Clinic, 34,* pp. 118–122. Copyright 1998 by PRO-ED, Inc. Reprinted with permisson.

port for a group of seventh grade students with learning disabilities and mild mental retardation to help them draw conclusions from their observations. The students have participated in an activity in which white flowers were placed in water containing food dye and were observed over a period of time:

> Teacher: . . . What do you think happened? I have a flower in blue water and a flower in green water, a white flower, right? Ken, what is the color of this flower?
> Ken: Blue.
> Sam: White.
> Teacher: White and blue. Julie, what color is this flower? (designating the second flower)
> Julie: Green.
> Teacher: White and green. How did I get the colors there? How did I get the colors there, Shawn?
> Shawn: That's from a stain in there like . . .
> Teacher: A stain? What do you think? Ken, how did this blue get here?
> Ken: . . . Oh, you watered it with food coloring.
> Teacher: But I didn't put any up here, did I?
> Ken: You put it in the dirt.
> Teacher: But there's no dirt.
> Ken: Oh.
> Teacher: OK, Jimmy, what do you think?
> Jimmy: It went all the way up to here.
> Teacher: Went all the way through water? The what, Mary?
> Mary: A stem.
> Teacher: The stem. It went all the way through the stem, you're right. (Mastropieri et al., 1999, p. 243)

This example shows us how difficult it can be for some students to generalize from real-world experiences and form new science concepts. The students in the example did not initially generalize from their observations that water was transferred through the plants along stems. The children answered the teacher's questions only through a highly structured questioning approach.

Use Intensive Coaching to Guide Thinking. How well, compared to their general education peers, can special education students form generalizations from their science experiences? How much coaching will general education students and special education students need to make generalizations? These were questions addressed in an informative study by Mastropieri, Scruggs, and Butcher (1997).

A total of 54 junior high students participated in the study, including 20 general education students, 18 students with LD, and 16 students with mental retardation (MR). Students were seen individually by a teacher-examiner. Each student was shown a pendulum and taught how to count the number of complete back-and-forth swings the pendulum made in 10 seconds. Then, the pendulum was set in motion and the student counted the number of swings while the teacher-examiner kept the time.

The first pendulum made 10 swings in 10 seconds. The examiner recorded the number of swings on a sticker below the pendulum. The student and examiner then took data on three more pendulums. The number of swings each pendulum made in 10 seconds was recorded on a sticker below the appropriate pendulum. When the four pendulums were displayed together, the labeled number of swings read, from left to right, 10, 6, 12, and 8. The corresponding lengths of the pendulums, from left to right, were second longest, fourth longest (shortest), longest, and third longest.

Inductive reasoning is the process of generalizing, or drawing general rules based on a number of specific observations. In the 5-E approach to science teaching, students are often required to generalize during the explanation phase from data taken during the exploration phase of instruction. The task of students in the pendulum study was to generalize from observations of four instances that the longer a pendulum, the fewer number of complete back-and-forth swings it makes in 10 seconds.

Participants in the study were provided a graded series of five prompts as needed to assist them to make the correct generalization about pendulum length and rate of swing. Here are the prompts:

1. The examiner asked, "Thinking about these pendulums, can you think of a general rule about pendulums?" If the student was not successful, the examiner went to the next prompt.
2. Students were asked to compare the number of swings in 10 seconds for the shortest and longest pendulums and then make a generalization.
3. Students were asked to sequence all of the pendulums from the shortest to the longest, compare the number of swings in 10 seconds for the pendulums, and then form a generalization.
4. The teacher pointed out that when the pendulums were sequenced, the strings got longer and the rates got smaller; based on this direct information, students were then asked to form a generalization.
5. Finally, if needed, the examiner gave the generalization, saying, "Isn't it that, as the string gets longer, the number of swings they make get smaller?" The examiner then demonstrated the rule until the students expressed understanding.

The number of prompts needed for a student to be successful on the task was taken as a measure of inductive reasoning. As shown in Table 9-2, the results indicated that 75% of the nondisabled students were successful after the first prompt and 100% were successful by the fourth prompt. For students with LD, 50% were successful with the first prompt, while 72% were successful after the fourth prompt. For students with mild mental retardation, no students were successful with one prompt, while only 19% were successful after four prompts.

Additionally, students were asked to apply the rule to a new pendulum problem. The students were shown a new pendulum intermediate in length between the 8-swing pendulum and the 10-swing pendulum and asked how many swings it would make in 10 seconds.

TABLE 9-2   CUMULATIVE PERCENTAGE OF STUDENTS MAKING CORRECT INDUCTION OF THE PENDULUM PROBLEM IN RESPONSE TO NUMBER OF PROMPTS

Number of Prompts	Nondisabled	Learning Disabled	Mild Mental Retardation
1	75%	50%	0%
2	95%	61%	6%
3	95%	67%	12%
4	100%	72%	19%
5	100%	100%	100%

Source: From "How Effective Is Inquiry Learning for Students with Mild Disabilities?" by M. A. Mastropieri, T. E. Scruggs, and K. Butcher, 1993, *The Journal of Special Education, 31*(2), pp. 199–211. Copyright 1993 by PRO-ED, Inc. Reprinted with permission.

On this application problem, 90% of the nondisabled students, 50% of students with LD, and none of the students with MR provided the correct answer.

According to Mastropieri et al. (1997), general education junior high school students may readily make generalizations from data, with only a moderate amount of scaffolding assistance. Students with LD may also succeed on an induction task, but may need more assistance. "On the other hand," the investigators concluded, "the very low performance of students with MR on this task suggests (but does not prove) that inquiry-based teaching methods and tasks that are appropriate for normally achieving students may not be developmentally appropriate for similarly aged students with MR" (Mastropieri et al., 1997, p. 208).

Teach Learning Strategies. Successful students develop many skills and strategies that they use when integrating, remembering, and using information. However, students with special needs may require explicit instruction in the use of these strategies (Ellis, n.d.; Mastropieri & Scruggs, 2004).

One important strategy in learning is elaboration. Elaboration of an idea occurs when one transforms an idea without losing the essence of its meaning. Ellis (n.d.) notes that students with LD often lack the language-based cognitive skills necessary to engage in effective elaboration, but can be taught to use elaboration strategies. In teaching students with or without LD to elaborate, teach them how to create a visual image of an idea, how to paraphrase and summarize information about an idea, how to raise a series of questions about the idea, and how to use the idea in drawing inferences and forming predictions.

Students with LD may have particular difficulties in collecting, organizing, and using data (Gersten & Baker, 1998), skills that are critical in science inquiry. Thus, they may benefit from explicit instruction on how to record data and how to construct and interpret charts and graphs.

Cawley and Foley (2002) have emphasized the importance of teaching students with exceptionalities the inherent relationships involved in data tables. Help your students learn to recognize relationships by involving them in connecting data to measurement procedures, describing data, filling in blank spaces in data tables, and using data to make predictions of new measurements.

In the pendulum investigation described previously, students with LD benefited from prompts related to examining the data (prompt 2), arranging it in order to form a concrete graph (prompt 3), and interpreting the graph to form a generalization about pendulum length and time for 10 swings (prompt 4). Nondisabled students in general did not need these prompts, presumably because they had learned to analyze data on their own. Students with LD need to be provided explicit instruction in constructing and working with tables, charts, and graphs.

To teach students with disabilities to use charting and graphing strategies (Mastropieri & Scruggs, 2004, pp. 470–471), prefamiliarize them with graph paper and various types of charts and graphs, such as bar graphs, histograms, and line graphs. Use very concrete examples in your instruction. For example, create a class bar graph based upon students' favorite foods, colors, or television shows. Talk with the class about what might be learned from the graph. Is each person's favorite displayed? Is there a "class favorite"? Use pictures of the objects being graphed to help reinforce what the graph represents.

Consider grouping students with and without disabilities together and allow them to record and graph data cooperatively. Peers may be able to assist with some of the more difficult components of the task. As students work together, take time to teach specific cooperative skills, such as turn taking and listening. In teaching cooperative skills, use explicit instruction procedures, such as modeling, pointing out examples and

Edwin Ellis, a professor at the University of Alabama, advocates that we "water up" rather than "water down" the curriculum for students with LD by integrating the teaching of learning strategies with instruction on content. Read Dr. Ellis's informative comments in LD Online (http://www.ldonline.org/teaching/ellis/biography.html).

See Chapter 8 for a discussion of the construction of different types of graphs, including concrete graphs.

nonexamples, role-playing, and providing feedback. In this way, students with and without exceptionalities can learn to actively and successfully be part of cooperative learning groups.

Gersten and Baker (1998) have recommended the use of *procedural facilitators*, such as "think sheets" and semantic maps, to assist in the use of learning strategies. Procedural facilitators assist performance by reminding students of options, strategies, and questions to ask themselves as they attempt to learn and solve problems. Students with and without disabilities may also benefit from metacognitive training to better monitor and regulate their own learning efforts (Mastropieri & Scruggs, 2004).

Teach Mnemonics. Students with LD often have difficulty with short-term memory. One of the strategies identified for assisting students with LD is mnemonics. In their research, Mastropieri and Scruggs (1993) found the use of mnemonics very effective with students who have LD. Figure 9-3 is an example of a mnemonic strategy. In this example, a pegword strategy (rhyming words) helps students remember the three classes of levers. The figure of an oar is an example of a first-class lever because it has the fulcrum at the middle and the force and load or resistance at opposite ends. To remember that an oar is an example of a first-class lever, students were given a picture of an oar with a package of buns (pegword for one) at the fulcrum. To remember that a wheelbarrow is an example of a second-class lever (with the fulcrum at one end and the force at the other), a picture of a wheelbarrow on a shoe (pegword for two) was depicted. Finally, a rake was used as an example of a third-class lever (with the fulcrum at one end and the force at the middle), to provide a picture of a rake leaning against a tree (pegword for three).

Use Graphic Organizers. A variety of graphic organizers are available to aid students with LD in visualizing how to order or sequence conceptual ideas. Figure 9-4 is one example. In

Figure 9-3 Pegword mnemonic strategy for classes of levers.
Source: From *A Practical Guide for Teaching Science to Students with Special Needs in Inclusive Settings* (p. 154), by M. A. Mastropieri and T. E. Scruggs, 1993, Austin, TX: PRO-ED. Copyright © 1993 by Purdue Research Foundation. Reprinted with permission of author.

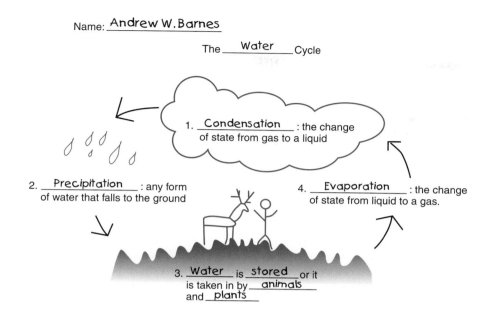

Name: Andrew W. Barnes

The _____Water_____ Cycle

1. _Condensation_ : the change of state from gas to a liquid

2. _Precipitation_ : any form of water that falls to the ground

4. _Evaporation_ : the change of state from liquid to a gas.

3. _Water_ is _stored_ or it is taken in by _animals_ and _plants_

Figure 9-4 Graphic organizer modified for a student with a disability. *Source:* From *The Inclusive Classroom: Strategies for Effective Instruction* (p. 514), by M. A. Mastropieri and T. E Scruggs, 2000, Upper Saddle River, NJ: Merrill/Prentice Hall. Copyright © 2000 by Merrill, an imprint of Prentice-Hall, Inc. Reprinted by permission of Pearson Education, Inc. Upper Saddle River, NJ.

using this graphic organizer, students fill in the blank spaces about the phases of the water cycle as the information is presented or as they engage in relevant activities.

Activities-based approaches involving inductive reasoning are quite appropriate for students with LD, but may not be the most beneficial method for teaching science to students with mental retardation. Let us examine the characteristics of students with MR and approaches to science that may be more beneficial for them.

Science for Students with Mental Retardation

Students with mental retardation show greater cognitive discrepancies than students with learning disabilities. The American Association on Mental Retardation provides this definition of mental retardation:

> Mental retardation is a disability characterized by significant limitations both in intellectual functioning and in adaptive behaviors as expressed in conceptual, social, and practical adaptive skills. (Turnbull et al., 2004, p. 226)

Current understanding of this disability "represents a shift away from conceptualizations of mental retardation as an inherent trait or permanent state of being to a description of the individual's present functioning and the environmental supports needed to improve it" (Heward, 2000, p. 211). It is assumed that with appropriate personalized supports over a sustained period of time, the functioning of the person with MR generally will improve (Turnbull et al., 2004, p. 226).

To improve functioning of persons with MR, science teachers might provide learning experiences that promote self-care, home living, community use, communication, self-direction (problem-solving and decision-making skills), and functional academics as appropriate.

An example of a science program that meets the needs of students with MR is *You, Me, and Others* developed by BSCS (Biological Sciences Curriculum Study). This K–6 program introduces basic genetic concepts and is made up of three units: Variety (grades K–2),

Change (grades 3–4), and the Chain of Life (grades 5–6). Each booklet includes four or five lessons and comes with teaching materials. *You, Me, and Others* is distributed by the March of Dimes Birth Defects Foundation (1-800-367-6630).

Research indicates that students with mild MR can learn some basic science concepts, but they often have difficulty generalizing learned information to novel situations (Mastropieri & Scruggs, 2004, pp. 77–80). In one study (Scruggs & Mastropieri, 1994), students with mild retardation learned concepts better when they were guided to construct them through questioning than when the information was presented directly to them. Additionally, a study of the thinking of fourth grade students with mild disabilities during an ecology unit indicated that they can actively engage in such processes as observing, describing, comparing, recording, and predicting—with appropriate assistance (Scruggs & Mastropieri, 1994).

It is very likely that you will have at some time students with mild MR in your general education classroom. Consider that students with mild retardation often have difficulty focusing on one aspect of an activity at a time. Therefore, it is best to limit your goals for each science lesson. If you want to discuss the students' findings at the conclusion of a lesson, collect all materials before starting the discussion, because students may be easily distracted by the materials before them.

Students with mild retardation can be effectively educated in a self-contained, general education classroom with individualized instruction, the help of peers, and specialists such as a resource teacher. Students who are moderately or severely retarded, however, generally need a highly specialized program and may be pulled out to work in a resource room or attend a class with students who have the same learning impairments.

Science for Students with Emotional/Behavioral Disorders

Despite your best efforts, some students may exhibit disruptive or asocial behaviors in your classroom. Recall that Chapter 7 covered typical classroom disciplinary problems. However, you may have students who are identified as having serious emotional or behavioral disorders (EBD).

Working cooperatively with their general education peers assists students with exceptionalities to learn science effectively.

According to IDEA, students with emotional disorders exhibit one or more of these characteristics:

- An inability to learn not due to intellectual, sensory, or health factors
- An inability to exhibit appropriate behavior under ordinary circumstances
- An inability to maintain relationships with peers or teachers
- An inappropriate affect such as depression or anxiety
- An inappropriate manifestation of physical symptoms or fears in response to school or personal difficulties (Turnbull et al., 2004, p. 80)

These criteria for assessing emotional disorders have been challenged on theoretical and practical grounds (Cullinan, Evans, Epstein, & Ryser, 2003). The President's Commission on Excellence in Special Education (2002) has recommended that criteria for EBD and other high-incidence disabilities be reexamined.

Because students with EBD may be included in your classroom, a few words of wisdom may be helpful. Consider that labels often get in the way of seeing these students as children. Even as they are aggressive, antisocial, or disruptive, you could also identify them as smart, good soccer player, lively, helpful, creative, tenacious, and daring. Picture the student(s) in your class exhibiting these positive characteristics and choose carefully the words you use to describe them. Finally, as you review the strategies in this section that will help you work with students who have EBD, note that your utmost concern is to provide a safe and supportive environment for all of your students.

Behavior Modification. To work successfully with students whose conduct is often disorderly, try viewing their deficit of appropriate social behaviors just as you would academic deficits—skills that need to be taught. Do not condone inappropriate behaviors; teach alternative, appropriate ways to interact. With patience and guidance, some students can learn to "correct" social behaviors just as they can learn to be more successful academically. One way to teach correct behavior is to use behaviorist principles.

Behavior modification is one approach that systematically applies behaviorist principles to classroom practices and therapeutic settings. Hundreds of research studies reveal that behavior modification improves not only classroom behaviors but academic performances as well (Ormrod, 1999). Behavior modification is often effective when other techniques are not, because (1) students know exactly what is expected of them, (2) through the gradual process of shaping, students attempt to learn new behaviors only when they are truly ready to acquire them, and (3) students find that learning new behaviors usually leads to success.

These four steps are routinely used in behavioral modification:

1. Identify problem behavior to be modified.
2. Log behavior with regard to how often and under what conditions it occurs.
3. Reinforce desired behavior(s) by initiating a system that reinforces or rewards appropriate, positive behavior.
4. Determine the type of positive reward or reinforcer to use: manipulatives (computer games, interactive videos, games); visuals (videos, CD-ROMs); physical (extra gym or recess privileges, dance); social (praise, attention, status); tactile (art time); edibles (food and drink); auditory (music as choices of audiotapes or CDs); and others selected by students. Positive (or negative) reinforcers can vary.

Science for Students with Orthopedic Impairments

Students with orthopedic impairments can have a variety of physical differences, such as large muscle dysfunctions (causing mobility or balance problems) or small muscle malfunctions (causing loss of coordination, dexterity, hand strength, or erratic muscular spasms). Students with physical disabilities may need crutches, braces, wheelchairs, walkers, or other assistive devices.

For many students with physical impairments, the greatest obstacles are attitudinal and architectural barriers. Generally, students with physical disabilities have normal intellectual abilities. If you are to be effective in helping students overcome some limitations of their physical disabilities, you must strive to understand the nature of their individual physical conditions and the parameters of their physical capabilities. Often, with a little ingenuity, you will enable students with orthopedic impairments to be active learners in your science class. Here are some ways to begin.

Meeting Physical Needs. Be aware of the various ways you can modify your classroom environment for students with orthopedic disabilities:

- Provide adequate space for movement by wheelchair, walker, crutches, and other devices.
- Ensure barrier-free movement by clearing aisles and keeping traffic lanes uncluttered.
- Ensure safety by placing seats or wheelchairs near exits wherever possible.
- Be sure desk and table heights are appropriate for wheelchairs. Use trays to hold materials for science activities.
- Provide plastic bags or buckets that can be carried over the shoulder by students who use canes or walkers, so they can carry simple science materials.
- Make outdoor areas accessible to wheelchairs or canes. Alternatively, transport students with physical disabilities in a wagon or carry them.
- Provide book holders or book scanners if students cannot hold books or turn pages. Students who have impaired hand coordination may need pencil holders, tape recorders, adapted computer keyboards, or other assistive technology.

Meeting Learning Needs. You can modify your teaching and learning activities to accommodate students with physical impairments. Some suggestions include the following:

- Pair students with no physical impairments with those who have physical impairments.
- In pairing students, expect students with physical disabilities to do as much for themselves as they can.
- Capitalize on the well-developed sensory channels students with physical disabilities are likely to have when you present science lessons.
- Look for adaptations, modifications, and opportunities for manipulations in hands-on science activities or multisensory activities, such as the following:
  a. In a lesson on interaction of materials with a magnet, tape a magnet to the arm or hand of a student with no or limited limb control. This will enable the student to feel and see which objects interact.
  b. Have students wheeled around in a circle by their nonimpaired classmates to represent the orbit of the earth in a lesson on the revolution of the earth around the sun.
- Position yourself so your demonstrations and other teaching methods are visible, especially for students unable to move their heads. Avoid pacing or moving around the room while teaching if it could hinder students' ability to learn.

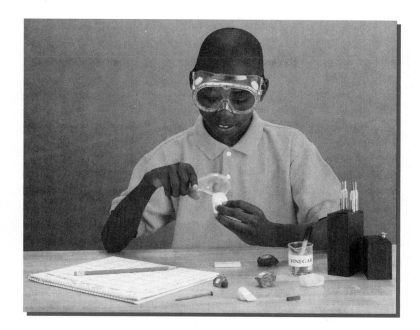

Inquiry science programs help schools to meet the needs, interests, and expectations of students.

- Encourage students with physical impairments to participate as fully as they can. Think of ways you can modify your teaching so they will be able to engage in inquiry activities.

Science for Students with Visual Impairments

You may have students with visual impairments in your classroom from time to time. These students include anyone who needs special aids or instruction to read ordinary print (low vision), students with low vision who typically use Braille for efficient reading and writing (functionally blind), and those who do not receive meaningful input through the visual sense (totally blind). These individuals use tactile and auditory means to learn about their environment.

Planning for Mobility Orientation. One of the first accommodations a teacher must make for students with visual impairments is a classroom arrangement that ensures students are oriented to the placement of furniture, activity materials, and any science equipment. Let students with visual impairments practice finding their way around the room when other students are out of the classroom. You will need to tell students who are sighted how important it is not to move objects from their usual location and to replace materials where they find them. You will also need to caution them to be careful not to leave bookbags or other cluttering materials on the floor where any student, including students who are blind or have low vision, may trip and fall over them.

Refer to the following Website sponsored by the Center for Rehabilitation Technology at Georgia Tech for information on technological equipment that facilitates the movements of students with disabilities: http://barrier-free.arch.gatech. edu/Research/concepts.html.

Adapting Learning Materials. One of your main tasks if you have a student with visual impairments is to figure out how to adapt classroom materials to make them accessible. Textbooks, blackboards, handouts, and science instruments are not generally accessible for students with visual impairments. Thus, you may need to create alternative formats for printed materials (handouts and textbooks) and computer-based materials, and you may even have to adapt science instruments or tools. Currently, using alternative formats remains an imperfect process, but audiotapes, enlarged print, Braille, and some computer text are somewhat viable.

You may want to find out how to access printed science materials in Braille or prepare grades in Braille that you can affix to lab reports, papers, or quizzes. When appropriate, students themselves could prepare Braille labels and affix them to scientific equipment. In addition, some software can produce synthetic speech from ASCII text, which offers students who are blind greater levels of independence.

Providing Opportunities for Incidental Learning.   One of the greater challenges for students who are blind is the lack of opportunities for incidental learning. Individuals with visual impairments do not have the same opportunities for learning about the world as their nondisabled peers. They cannot see the earth's features that are big or distant (mountains, oceans, the sun, the horizon), animals that are small (ants, grasshoppers), matter that changes (snowflakes, ice), or events that are dangerous (fire, earthquakes) (Turnbull, Turnbull, Shank, & Leal, 1999). Some of their limitations—in the range and variety of experiences, in the ability to get around, and in interactions with the environment—can be satisfied with inquiry activities.

Activities like those developed by the Center for Multisensory Learning, Lawrence Hall of Science, Berkeley, California, are especially appropriate. The materials published by the Lawrence Hall of Science for students with visual or physical disabilities are called SAVI/SELPH. SAVI represents Science Activities for the Visually Impaired, and SELPH represents Science Enrichment for Learners with Physical Handicaps. These programs have been combined and reworked into a single program, mostly for upper elementary school and beyond, but nine modules are adapted for primary grade students.

SAVI/SELPH consists of sets of activity folios, with a section overview, background, purpose, materials, anticipating (what to do before starting), doing the activity, and follow-up. For an example of a running summary of how the program developers provided metric measurement activities for visually impaired students, see Figure 9-5.

In addition to SAVI/SELPH, several other curriculum developers have created science materials for students who are blind or have low vision. These include Adapting Science Materials for the Blind (ASMB) and Full Options Science System (FOSS) developed at the Lawrence Hall of Science and published by Delta Education.

Science for Students with Hearing Impairments

Students who have impaired hearing range in their hearing ability from hard of hearing (use of amplification) to total deafness. Because there are substantial differences between aided and unaided hearing (Turnbull et al., 1999), there is no consensus about how to refer to people with hearing impairments. A people-first approach—persons who are deaf—will be used in this section.

Language and Concept Development.   One of the major problems of persons who are deaf is language development. Just as incidental learning accounts for the lack of certain kinds of prior knowledge for persons who are blind, persons who are deaf generally struggle with language development. Thus, psychosocial development—an interaction with the world through language—is a key need for students who are deaf or hard of hearing. Sign language, lip reading, and the reading of body and facial movements help these students with

Science Education in the Balance

During the past spring and fall, SAVI answered the cry for metric measurement activities for visually impaired students with the SAVI **Measurement Module.** The six hands-on activities contained in this module introduce youngsters to standard units of metric measurement.

To develop the concept of *mass,* we needed a measuring tool that would be suitable for use by the visually impaired. We finally decided to use a balance instead of a spring scale or other device and this decision resulted in some unexpected dividends for the project.

We looked at a lot of balances before we made the decision and even built a few of our own. Finally, we chose a simple, vacuum-formed model that is commercially available at a reasonable price. Then, we went to work on it!

First, we cut the bottoms of the two balance pans so that a paper or plastic cup could be dropped securely into the hole and then removed easily. Then, we added a tactile balance indicator. These slight modifications made it possible for blind students to determine weight to an accuracy of one gram!

The removable cup was the breakthrough we need to make accurate weighing easy for visually impaired students. Both the weights (20 g, 10 g, 5 g, 1 g plastic pieces) and the objects or substances to be weighed automatically centered in the cups, thus eliminating discrepancies due to the position of objects in the cups. An object, substance, or liquid can be removed from the balance—cup and *all;* a new cup can then be inserted and a new material weighed. There's no more trouble "getting all the powder out," or "transferring the beans"; the objects stay in the cups.

The students use the balances to verify that 50 ml of water (measured with a modified SAVI syringe) weigh 50 g, thereby establishing the relationship between volume and mass.

Since its introduction, the SAVI balance has crept into other modules. The forthcoming **Kitchen Interactions Module** will feature an activity that focuses on the concept of *density.* Density is defined operationally using the SAVI balance: equal volumes of two different liquids are compared on the balance and the heavier one is identified as the denser liquid.

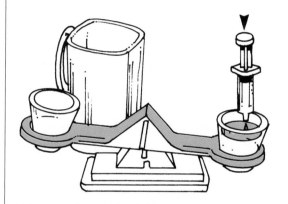

Figure 9-5   Science activity for students with visual impairments.
Source: Reprinted by permission of The Center for Multisensory Learning, Lawrence Hall of Science, University of California, Berkeley, CA 94720.

communication. However, without intervention, there are increasing gaps in vocabulary, concept formation, and the ability to understand and produce complex sentences for people who are deaf; without intervention, both language and intellectual development may be affected.

Inquiry science activities can provide a variety of learning experiences that enhance both language and cognitive growth. Here are some suggestions for implementing these types of science activities in your classroom.

Use Hands-on Science Activities to Develop Vocabulary.   Hands-on activities can help show students differences in the meanings of words. Begin with familiar objects from the students' everyday environment. Stress handling the objects during language/concept development. Introduce other words related to the properties of objects, such as color, size, and texture. Engage older students in activities to observe chemical changes. This process follows the constructivist Learning Cycle where the learner manipulates materials and then the teacher introduces or "invents" words for the scientific concepts.

Use Multimedia Materials for Concept Invention and Development. Introduce or explain concepts using pictures, drawings, models, and closed-captioned TV programming or videotapes. Screen all materials first to see if they are appropriate for your students who are deaf and to decide what modifications you must make. Older students who can read can be given written materials before they view visual materials for orientation to new concepts. Note that the written language appropriate for your students who are deaf may need to be a grade or more below that of your average class level, because the reading skills of people who are deaf often develop more slowly.

Adaptations for Inquiry Activities. Encourage students who are deaf to participate in the same activities as their peers. Whenever practical, you might pair students who are deaf with students who can hear.

Use modifications such as the following ones to change auditory observations to visual ones:

- Use a light in a circuit instead of a buzzer.
- Substitute a "probe box" for a "mystery box."
- Have students feel vibrations rather than listen to pitch.
- Show vibrations of strings and tuning forks in water waves and sand movements.

In addition, you might make language cards to be used as students who are deaf engage in the activities. These help students identify with and relate to the activity, instructions, vocabulary, and concepts. Use diagrams and pictures to enrich the cards. Further, encourage students who are deaf to verbalize as much as possible to practice relating their experiences, observations, discoveries, and interpretations.

Science for Gifted and Talented Students

Ten-year-old Alan developed an unlikely interest in Einstein's theory of relativity. Alan's teacher invited a college professor to the classroom to talk about the theory with the boy. The child said to the professor, "I understand that Einstein described the universe in terms of four variables, but I can only think of three of them." As they discussed the problem, the professor told Alan that at age 16, Einstein set this puzzle for himself: *What would happen if I traveled along at the speed of light and held up a mirror to my face? What would I see?* The professor explained that Einstein needed the three variables of space and an additional variable of time to eventually answer this question at age 26. Somehow, this information helped Alan to bring together a variety of things he had read and thought about. He then took up the explanation, laying out Einstein's problem and solution in such an insightful way that the astounded professor began to understand them more deeply himself.

Students such as Alan provide a different kind of challenge for teachers. These students have above average intelligence and possess unusual skills, interests, talents, and attitudes about learning. Words such as *creativity, vitality, potential, motivation,* and *joy* tend to describe their approach to learning (Armstrong, 1998). Such students are identified as having special gifts or talents.

As a teacher, you will quickly learn that there is no typicality associated with students who are gifted, but most have general intellect, specific academic ability, creative and productive thinking, leadership ability, or abilities in visual and performing arts that stand out from their classmates. Students who are gifted or talented love to participate in many activities and usually enjoy being challenged with meaningful enrichment activities. The following suggestions may prove useful.

Make Real Inclusion a Goal

Make gifted and talented students in your classroom feel welcome and accepted. Previously, these students were accelerated to higher or special pullout classes. Currently, greater emphasis is placed on inclusion, incorporating changes in science content and activities to introduce higher levels of abstract and independent thinking and problem-solving skills. Your challenge is to help your gifted and talented students modify, adapt, and learn how to discover new skills and concepts for themselves.

Most highly motivated, bright students need little encouragement. For those who do, try these suggestions:

A. Provide recognition for their efforts, but be wary of gifted students with know-it-all tendencies. Encourage cooperative efforts.
B. Challenge students to come up with questions they think are difficult and then work in small groups to find answers to the questions.
C. Encourage student-initiated projects and alternative activities sometimes in lieu of standard kinds of class activities.
D. Introduce elementary and middle grade students to research methods.
E. Encourage students to use a variety of media to express themselves in creative ways such as drawing, creative writing, drama, and role-playing.
F. Help students organize and publish a classroom or school science magazine.

However, a caution is in order: Students who are gifted must also acquire basic knowledge, understandings, and procedures, even as they are given more freedom to move in their own directions.

Stimulate Gifted Students by the Way You Teach

Your teaching methods can encourage students who are gifted and talented. In our society, students' thinking is often trained to focus on the right answer, which sometimes discourages them from taking risks in academic situations. Students may be confused or feel threatened with failure when they are faced with tasks in which there are either no clear answers or a variety of correct answers. Be sure to use some of these inquiry techniques to encourage them:

1. Use a series of questions rather than giving information.
2. Use hypothetical questions beginning with "What if . . . ?"
3. Ask students to develop open-ended situations where no one answer is correct.
4. In science tasks involving mathematics, where specific answers are usually required, encourage students to estimate their answers.
5. Instead of information, emphasize concepts, principles, relationships, and generalizations.
6. Provide opportunities and assignments that rely on independent reading and research as appropriate. Ask students to report on their research and experimentation; this helps them acquire a sense of sharing knowledge.
7. Provide students multiple opportunities to learn how to use technology to research information and gather data from a variety of global resources.
8. Challenge students to engage in, and perhaps design or originate, more open-ended, hands-on inquiry activities.
   - Start by working with the entire class or a group. Later, when routines are established, invite individuals to explore on their own.
   - Keep the experimentation within the limits of time, talents, and available apparatus. Explore these limitations before suggesting problems.

- Be alert to the open-endedness of this type of exploration. Expect questions to arise such as, "Suppose we vary the experiment in this way, what will happen?"
- Do not assume that the gifted student will have a sustained interest in the problem. You must continually check on progress.

Connecting science and mathematics is important for all students, particularly gifted students. Challenge them to go beyond describing what happens and why and to explore *how much* or what *quantitative relationships exist between variables*. Ask students to quantify their findings, and encourage them to use graphing when communicating their findings.

Provide Opportunities for Leadership

Ask gifted and talented students to be science assistants to help with preparing materials, dispense and collect equipment and supplies, collect information about experiments, and assist classmates. Often, peer teaching and learning is more effective than learning from teacher-pupil exchanges. Students who are gifted and talented in science may also create physical models related to the science units being studied, such as models of the solar system or scale models of local environmental or ecological systems.

As you promote the leadership skills of your students, be careful that gifted students are not singled out as the "smart ones." Nor should they be cast in a role in which they are continually taking over cooperative learning situations and group projects.

Learn with and from Your Gifted and Talented Students

Most elementary school teachers have not majored in science and, therefore, find that some of their students know more about certain areas of science than they do. Feeling somewhat incompetent with science should not stop you from encouraging gifted and talented students to do more advanced work than the rest of the class. Students enjoy seeing their teachers get excited about the results of their work. Facilitate the academic environment of students who are gifted by posing challenging questions and offering constructive feedback. Also, identify community people who are available to work with gifted and talented students in a mentor program. Be sure to provide some guidance to those who are knowledgeable in their fields but do not know how to motivate and teach students.

Remember that for all their knowledge and abilities, gifted students are still elementary or middle school students whose social, emotional, and physical development mirrors the development of their peers. They need your mature adult guidance, professional training, and practical experience. They will seek caring and emotionally stable adults. That's you!

Science for Students from Linguistically and Culturally Diverse Backgrounds

Our nation's motto is **e pluribus unum,** "out of many, one." Nowhere in our society is the rich mosaic of people that embody the United States better represented than in our schools. Meeting the needs of the diversity of children in our classrooms has become an important issue in education.

Many students from diverse ethnic backgrounds are in the process of acquiring the U.S. mainstream language, culture, and discourse patterns in schools. For many of these students a language other than English is spoken at home.

TABLE 9-3   PERCENTAGE OF PUBLIC ELEMENTARY AND SECONDARY STUDENTS BY RACE/ETHNICITY FOR THE 2001–2002 SCHOOL YEAR

Race/Ethnicity	Percent
White, non-Hispanic	61.2%
Black, non-Hispanic	17.2%
Hispanic	16.3%
Asian/Pacific Islander	4.1%
American Indian/Alaska Native	1.2%

Source: National Center for Education Statistics (http://nces.ed.gov/pubs2002).

Hispanic students make up the large majority of the English language learners (ELL) or limited-English-proficient (LEP) students in American schools. According to the National Center for Educational Statistics, in the 2001–2002 school year, Hispanic students made up 16.3% of the approximately 47 million students enrolled in public elementary and secondary schools (see Table 9-3). Statistics indicate that 57% of Hispanic students in grades K–12 spoke mostly English at home, 25% spoke mostly Spanish, and 17% spoke English and Spanish equally. This translates to more than 3 million Hispanic students who are encountering English as a second language in U.S. public schools. Providing equal educational opportunities to students who are not proficient in English is a special challenge.

Inquiry science programs, with their emphasis on exploring, investigating, and manipulating concrete materials, are especially valuable for students who wrestle with the development of a new language, customs, friendships, and less advantageous community environments. Providing inquiry activities equalizes the opportunity for success because success is not generally dependent on the students' ability to read a textbook, answer questions from the textbook, or complete worksheets that depend on students' understanding of what they have read. Hands-on, inquiry activities will help all students span the gap between their past experiences and the development of language within their immediate environment.

Limited-English-Proficient Students and Inquiry Science

Learning language is much more than learning vocabulary. Language learning is a complex process of developing relationships among ideas, terms, and meanings (Lee & Fradd, 1998). A great deal of language can be learned in the context of science and other subjects. Context enables children to build on what they already know to infer the meaning of new words and verbal constructs. According to Lapp (2001, p. 2), "For children who are learning science by means of an inquiry-centered approach, classroom investigations and the activities surrounding them can provide context. These experiences can be springboards for growth in verbal fluency and literacy."

In learning science through inquiry approaches, students have opportunities to develop verbal fluency as they talk about what they are doing, record their observations, summarize their findings, and create written explanations that draw on their understanding of science concepts. They also read science articles and books, write essays and stories, and do library and Internet research to complement their classroom work (Lapp, 2001).

Language is only one of the internal learning systems students need to learn science and other subjects. Students also need knowledge of facts, concepts, and principles and knowledge of how to apply them in making sense of problem situations (Bransford, Brown,

Simplifying the output	Check frequently for understanding
• Slower speech rate • Clear enunciation • Controlled vocabulary • Controlled sentence length • Use of cognates • Limited use of idioms	• Confirmation checks • Comprehension checks • Clarification requests • Repetitions • Expansions • Vocabulary emphasis • Variety of question types
Use contextual clues	**Design appropriate lessons**
• Gestures • Facial expressions • Act out meaning • Props • Graphs • Realia • Overheads • Maps • Manipulatives • Visuals	• Appropriate to English fluency • Listening and speaking activities precede reading and writing activities • Reading assignments include prereading, during reading, postreading activities • Writing activities preceded by prewriting • Cooperative activities and grouping • Topical rather than grammatical emphasis • Hands-on activities • Use of various modalities

Figure 9-6   Teaching suggestions for implementing hands-on, minds-on science for LEP students.
Source: Jennifer W. Harris, "Sheltered Instruction: Bridging the Language Gap in the Science Classroom," *The Science Teacher 62,* no.2 (February 1995), 26. Reprinted with permission from NSTA Publications, copyright © 1995 from *The Science Teacher,* National Science Teachers Association, 1840 Willson Boulevard, Arlington, VA 22201–3000.

& Cocking, 1999, pp. 183–184). Inquiry science can help students learn how to construct understanding through teaching them the scientists' approach to solving problems—an approach that has proved successful in every culture.

Figure 9-6 provides tips for implementing inquiry science with LEP students. This method of teaching science and English to LEP students—with minimum dependency on language, concentration on concept development, and nonlanguage cues and prompts—is called **sheltered instruction.**

Here are some general strategies you can use to help improve the English of students who are LEP, even when all your teaching is conducted in English (Buck, 2000):

1. LEP students may learn to read English before they learn to speak it. So you may try using writing more than you otherwise might. For example, prepare for a lesson by writing the list of vocabulary you will introduce during the lesson on a large sheet of paper. Tape these sheets to the wall in full view of all students to create a word wall. Point to each word when you say it, explore concepts in hands-on activities as students experience it, and then talk about it.

2. Always print (upper- and lowercase) legibly. Most writing that LEP students encounter out of school is in print.

3. Plan regulations or procedures with students as a class. Act out procedures to model them. Write regulations on the chalkboard as they are "performed." Review regulations frequently. Each time you remind students of one of these regulations, point to the chart and read the words aloud.

4. When you give directions, give them one at a time, step by step.

5. When students do not understand what you have said, rephrase using different words and simpler sentences. Use body language or concrete objects while you explain what you are saying.

6. Summarize what has been taught at frequent intervals. Print the key points on the board, or refer to a wall chart.

7. As appropriate for the age level of your students, require all class members to keep journals written in English.

Perhaps the best way to include LEP students in your classroom is to view these students as an asset to the learning of all students. LEP students can contribute language enrichment for native English-speaking students and abundant occasions for cross-cultural teaching and learning.

Students from Culturally Diverse Backgrounds and Inquiry Science

Meeting the needs of students from diverse cultural backgrounds has become an important issue in education (Lee, 2002). The National Science Teachers Association recognizes and appreciates the strength and beauty of cultural pluralism. In its 2000 Position Statement on Multicultural Science Education, NSTA asserted that

- children from all cultures are to have equitable access to quality science education experiences that enhance success and provide the knowledge and opportunities required for them to become successful participants in our democratic society;
- curricular content must incorporate the contributions of many cultures to our knowledge of science; and
- science teachers are knowledgeable about and use culturally related ways of learning and instructional practices.

Additionally, science teachers have the responsibility to expose culturally diverse children to career opportunities in science, technology, and engineering.

The NSTA statement on multicultural science education calls for you to become knowledgeable about the learning styles of your students from diverse cultures and how their cultures aid or hinder their science learning. The prior cultural experiences of some students may actually interfere with inquiry science. For example, newly arrived students may experience difficulties with scientific inquiry in school because they have not been previously encouraged to ask questions or devise plans for investigation. Students from cultures that respect authority may be more receptive to teachers directing and telling them than to inquiry, exploration, and seeking alternative ways (Lee & Fradd, 1998).

Students unfamiliar with more exploratory approaches to learning may need explicit instruction to acquire the skills for effective participation. Fradd and Lee (1999, p. 15) suggested, "With teachers' encouragement, students learning English can also learn to pose questions, devise plans, test hypotheses, collect and analyze data, engage in science discourse, and construct theories and explanations."

In teaching science, you should employ a wide range of content and teaching strategies to meet the learning needs and interests of students with different cultural backgrounds. You should also build on and broaden the prior knowledge of multicultural students by deepening their learning experiences.

View the NSTA position statements on multicultural science education and other issues at http://nsta.org/position/.

Please visit the Companion Website at www.prenhall.com/carin for a set of inquiry science activities ideal for students with special needs.

Fostering the Learning and Acceptance of All Students

In a sense, all students are culturally diverse because each family is unique and has its own cultural identity. Although the following recommendations are some you have seen within

Use the self-assessment questions for Chapter 9 at http://www.prenhall.com/carin to assess how well you understand this chapter and how prepared you are for a test over its content.

the discussion on students with special needs, they bear repeating because they foster acceptance for all students:

1. Foster collaboration in cooperative learning groups.
2. Capitalize on the broad cultural diversity within your classroom. Recognize the variety of cultural backgrounds and heritages of different students by asking them to share unique native foods, dances, or songs with the class.
3. Provide a reasonable, caring, and supportive interpersonal environment for all students.
4. Work to improve home and school relations through frequent communication with parents.
5. Strive to foster a classroom atmosphere that has success as the expected norm for every student.

SUMMARY

- The *National Science Education Standards* emphasize that science is for all students. Students come to your classroom with a wide range of learning abilities and styles, diverse cultural backgrounds, and physical, social, and emotional differences. Some will have a limited proficiency using the English language, and all will have had different sensory experiences and prior knowledge. It is your challenge to provide worthwhile science learning activities for every student.

- The Individuals with Disabilities Education Act (IDEA) mandates that individuals with disabilities from birth to age 21 have the right to a full, free public education in the least restrictive environment. This has led to the current trend of inclusion, which means that all students, including those with a wide range of disabilities (physical, social, and cognitive), are in regular classrooms for the entire school day.

- Practical teaching and learning techniques provide for the needs of students who have learning disabilities, are mentally retarded, have emotional disturbances, have orthopedic disabilities, or have sensory impairments. More

important than the individual means by which you can adapt instruction is your attitude and expectations for working with each of these students to provide a sensitive and supportive learning community.

- Gifted and talented students present different kinds of challenges for teachers. Students who have unusual talents or are intellectually gifted can benefit from doing relatively unstructured explorations, engaging in enrichment activities such as studying abstract topics to integrate connections, and observing how math and science are connected.

- A National Science Teachers Association position paper recognizes and advocates a quality science education for students from diverse cultural and linguistic backgrounds. This challenges all science teachers to employ a wide range of science content and teaching methods to meet the learning needs and interests of students with different cultural backgrounds. Hands-on science teaching and learning activities have many benefits for students from diverse backgrounds, especially limited-English-proficient students.

REFERENCES

Armstrong, T. (1998). *Awakening genius in the classroom.* Alexandria, VA: Association for Supervision and Curriculum Development.

Bransford, J. D., Brown, A. L., & Cocking, R. R. (Eds.). (1999). *How people learn: Brain, mind, experience, and school.* Washington, DC: National Academy Press. (Also available at http://www.nap.edu)

Brownell, M. T., & Thomas, C. W. (1998). An interview with Margo Mastropieri: Quality science instruction for students with disabilities. *Intervention in School and Clinic, 34*(2), 118–122.

Buck, G. A. (2000, November/December). Teaching science to English-as-second-language learners. *Science and Children,* 38–41.

Cawley, J. F., & Foley, T. E. (2002). Connecting math and science for all students. *Teaching Exceptional Children, 34*(4), 14–19.

Center for Rehabilitation Technology. (2000, January). Concepts: Disabilities and curriculum plans. In *Barrier free education.* Atlanta, GA: The IMAGINE Group at the College of Architecture at Georgia Tech. (Also available at http://barrier-free.arch.gatech.edu/Research/concepts.html)

Cullinan, D., Evans, C., Epstein, M. H., & Ryser, G. (2003). Characteristics of emotional disturbance of elementary school students. *Behavioral Disorders, 28*(3), 94–111.

Ellis, E. S. (n.d.). Making real-world connections when teaching major concepts in inclusive classrooms. *LD Online.* Retrieved August 2003, from http://ldonline.org/ld_indepth/teacher/ellis_relate.html

Fradd, S. H., & Lee, O. (1999). Teachers' roles in promoting science inquiry with students from diverse language backgrounds. *Educational Researcher, 28*(6), 14–20.

Harris, J. W. (1995). Sheltered instruction: Bridging the language gap in the science classroom. *The Science Teacher, 62*(2), 26–27.

Heward, W. L. (2000). *Exceptional children: An introduction to special education* (6th ed., p. 211). Upper Saddle River, NJ: Merrill/Prentice Hall.

Individuals with Disabilities Education Act 20, U.S.C. § 1400 et seq. (1997).

Lapp, D. (2001). Bridging the gap. *Science Link (Newsletter of the National Science Resources Center), 12*(1), 2.

Lee, O. (2002). Promoting scientific inquiry with elementary students from diverse cultures and languages. In W. C. Secada (Ed.), *Review of research in education* (Vol. 26, pp. 23–69). Washington, DC: American Educational Research Association.

Lee, O., & Fradd, S. H. (1998). Science for all, including students from non-English-language backgrounds. *Educational Researcher, 27*(4), 12–19.

Mastropieri, M. A., & Scruggs, T. E. (1993). *A practical guide for teaching science to students with special needs in inclusive settings* (p. 154). Austin, TX: PRO-ED.

Mastropieri, M. A., & Scruggs, T. E. (2004). *The inclusive classroom: Strategies for effective instruction* (2nd ed.). Upper Saddle River, NJ: Merrill/Prentice Hall.

Mastropieri, M. A., Scruggs, T. E., & Butcher, K. (1993). How effective is inquiry learning for students with mild disabilities? *Journal of Special Education, 31*(2), 199–211.

Mastropieri, M. A., Scruggs, T. E., & Magnusen, M. (1999, Fall). Activities-oriented science instruction for students with disabilities. *Learning Disability Quarterly, 22,* 240–249.

National Research Council. (1996). *National science education standards.* Washington, DC: National Academy Press.

Ormrod, J. E. (1999). *Human learning: Theories, principles, and educational applications* (3rd ed., pp. 402–403). Upper Saddle River, NJ: Merrill/Prentice Hall.

President's Commission on Excellence in Special Education. (2002). *A new era: Revitalizing special education for children and their families (final report).* Washington, DC: U.S. Department of Education. (Also available at http://www.ed.gov/inits/commissionsboards/whspecialeducation/index.html)

Rowe, M. B. (1973). Teaching science as continuous inquiry. New York: McGraw-Hill.

Scruggs, T. E., & Mastropieri, M. A. (1994). The construction of scientific knowledge by students with mild disabilities. *Journal of Special Education, 28*(3), 307–321.

Scruggs, T. E., Mastropieri, M. A., Bakken, J. P., & Brigham, F. J. (1993). Reading versus doing: The relative effects of textbook-based and inquiry-oriented approaches to science learning in special education classrooms. *Journal of Special Education, 27*(1), 1–15.

Turnbull, A., Turnbull, R., Shank, M., & Leal, D. (1999). *Exceptional lives: Special education in today's schools* (2nd ed.). Upper Saddle River, NJ: Merrill/Prentice Hall.

Turnbull, A., Turnbull, R., Shank, M., & Smith, S. J. (2004). *Exceptional lives: Special education in today's schools* (4th ed.). Upper Saddle River, NJ: Merrill/Prentice Hall.

Van der Klift, E., & Kunc, N. (1994). Epilogue: Beyond benevolence—friendship and the politics of help. In J. Thousand, R. Villa, & A. Nevin (Eds.), *Creativity and collaborative learning: A practical guide to empowering students and teachers* (pp. 391–402). Baltimore: Brookes.

10

Our educational system must produce technology capable kids. They will live, learn, and work within an increasingly complex and information-rich society. For them, literacy will demand effective communication, critical thinking, creative problem solving, and lifelong learning. They are our children. Who is to prepare them to function effectively in this future world? If not us—teachers, parents, community members, all of America's educational stakeholders—then who?

(International Society for Technology in Education, 1999)

Educational Technology and the Science Curriculum

MI AND HER THREE TEAMMATES watch the monitor closely as the lost space probe sends back images of the planet where it has crashed. They can see craters, so they know the planet is terrestrial rather than gaseous. But which one is it?

"Temperatures here range from very mild to $-135°$ Celsius," the probe informs them.

Mi, the meteorology expert on the team, quickly searches her data to learn more about the weather on the terrestrial planets. "Only Earth and Mars have mild weather," she tells her teammates, "and only Mars has temperatures as low as $-135°C$. The probe must be on Mars!"

After listening to information from the probe in their areas and consulting their own expert data, they concur: The lost probe crashed on Mars.

"I'm going to check it out," Cassie says. She clicks the mouse on the Mars symbol on the screen to test her team's hypothesis. The screen confirms their inference: The probe is on Mars!

"But," Gerald says, "where on Mars?" Gerald and Cassie decide from their collective historical data that there are only four possible locations where the probe could have landed. Angelo, the team's geology expert, clicks the mouse on the probe's elevation detector. The probe informs the team that its location is 4 km deep. Angelo quickly searches through his geological database. "The probe must be either in Valles Marineris or Argyre Basin," he tells his teammates. "The other two locations aren't that deep." Then Angelo tries a rock analysis. He clicks on the rock analysis label on the probe. The probe tells the team that it senses violent activity within Mars's crust.

"It has to be Valles Marineris!" Angelo tells them. "That's where there's folding and faulting of the surface due to Marsquakes!"

What student—or teacher—could resist an activity like this? *The Great Solar System Rescue* by Tom Snyder Productions is one of a number of computer-based programs that includes not only absorbing simulations but lesson plans and worksheets that encourage students to make predictions, experiment, and test their ideas. This particular package combines computer graphics with footage from real space probes; it also offers a section on ancient sky watchers, adding a multicultural perspective.

Advances in educational technology certainly have much to offer science teachers. There is a mass of advanced computer hardware and peripherals on the market. Software, ranging from simple instructional programs to sophisticated interactive learning environments, presents endless possibilities for learning. Application programs from desktop publishing to multimedia presentation packages enhance the art of communication. Data loggers and probes enable real-time collection of data that is simultaneously displayed as a graph. Spreadsheets, databases, and data analysis programs facilitate organization of information and attempts to extract meaning from it. Digital imaging and image processing software expands opportunities for observations and measurements of scientific phenomena. The Internet offers a gold mine of opportunities for classroom use, such as online data sources, Web-based lessons, and worldwide connectivity. These imaginative products of the information technology age virtually expand the classroom walls to encompass the globe.

This chapter provides a framework and some suggestions for connecting science curriculum and educational technology. Because technology changes rapidly, however, you will need to continue to take advantage of professional development opportunities to keep up with the latest innovations. As you study the chapter, consider these questions:

Collect responses to these questions as you find them in the chapter. The focus questions also appear on the Companion Website at http://www.prenhall.com/carin.

What technology standards should we enable all students to meet?

What software, simulations, productivity tools, data collection and analysis tools, multimedia tools, and telecommunication resources can enhance the teaching and learning of science?

What hardware is needed in your classroom to take advantage of these educational technology resources? How should the hardware be arranged and managed?

How does educational technology fit within the broader context of inquiry and constructivist learning of science? How can educational technologies be connected to your own science curriculum without dominating it?

How can you stay on the cutting edge of learning technology throughout your teaching career?

Are you prepared to learn to use educational technology in the most effective way in your science instruction? This chapter will help you see possibilities of incorporating educational technology into a hands-on, inquiry science program in your classroom.

Educational Technology

Computer technology is a prime example of technology in general. As discussed in Chapter 1, technology refers to any process or product that has been invented to assist humans in adapting to their natural, constructed, and social environments. Computers have certainly changed the way people do science, handle personal affairs, and run businesses, and they have the potential to change the way schooling takes place. Technology promises a variety of potential benefits for education (Kay, 1995):

- Through computers and related technologies, students can gain instant access to a wide array of available media. Texts, images, sounds, and movies can be readily accessed, manipulated, and placed in appropriate form to support learning.
- Educational technology provides for great interactivity. Students can mold presentations to fit their own tastes, and explore ideas from many different perspectives.
- Educational technology allows teachers and students to go beyond static presentations to dynamic simulations and models of attributes, processes, and relationships that can be used to understand and test theories.
- Pervasively networked computers provide a universal library, offering global information resources to individuals.

NSES   **Content Standards**

Children in grade K–4 should develop skills in the use of computers and calculators for conducting investigations. (National Research Council, 1996, p. 122)

Students in grade 5–8 should be able to use computers to access, gather, store, retrieve, and organize data using hardware and software designed for these purposes (National Research Council, 1996, p. 145).

In science classes, the use of educational technology can demonstrate the course of technological progress, enrich instructional presentations, encourage students to become more active explorers of their environment, and significantly enhance curiosity and motivation. Using educational technology enables students to practice science and technology in ways similar to professionals in the field, leading to a deeper understanding of concepts and improved thinking and problem-solving capabilities.

Technology Standards

The International Society for Technology in Education (ISTE) has collaborated with other educational organizations, business, government, and private foundations to develop technology foundation standards for students. These standards are presented in Figure 10-1. They are developed and related to curriculum in *National Educational Technology Standards for Students: Connecting Curriculum and Technology* (International Society for Technology in Education, 1999).

For more information on technology standards, contact International Society for Technology in Education, 480 Charnelton Street, Eugene, OR 97401-2626. Telephone: 541-302-3777. Internet: http://www.iste.org.

Technology Standards and Science Education

Science classes represent an ideal context in which to develop the technology standards, and educational technology provides a variety of excellent tools to help students master science content. In considering how to connect educational technology and science, it is useful to place the ISTE technology standards into three categories (see Figure 10-2):

- Learning *about* technology—understanding computers as a major example of technology, learning how to use them in classroom settings, and considering societal implications of technology use
- Learning *from* technology—using computer-assisted instruction, tutorials, simulations, and multimedia presentations to enhance science learning
- Learning *with* technology—using technology resources in science classes as tools to enhance productivity, communications, research, problem solving, and decision making

In the following sections, we will examine how educational technology and the science curriculum connect as students learn *about*, *from*, and *with* technology.

Learning about Technology in Science Classes

Educational technology literacy starts with knowledge of technology systems and how to use them for particular purposes, such as multimedia presentations and communication through the Internet. It also entails understanding social, ethical, and human issues related

For an interesting expansion on computer literacy for teachers, refer to the article by Dyrli and Kinnaman (1995).

Technology Foundation Standards for All Students

The Technology Foundation Standards for students are divided into six broad categories. Standards within each category are to be introduced, reinforced, and mastered by students. Teachers can use these standards as guidelines for planning technology-based activities in which students achieve success in learning, communication, and life skills.

1. Basic operations and concepts
   * Students demonstrate a sound understanding of the nature and operation of technology systems.
   * Students are proficient in the use of technology.
2. Social, ethical, and human issues
   * Students understand the ethical, cultural, and societal issues related to technology.
   * Students practice responsible use of technology systems, information, and software.
   * Students develop positive attitudes toward technology uses that support lifelong learning, collaboration, personal pursuits, and productivity.
3. Technology productivity tools
   * Students use technology tools to enhance learning, increase productivity, and promote creativity.
   * Students use productivity tools to collaborate in constructing technology-enhanced models, preparing publications, and producing other creative works.
4. Technology communications tools
   * Students use telecommunications to collaborate, publish, and interact with peers, experts, and other audiences.
   * Students use a variety of media and formats to communicate information and ideas effectively to multiple audiences.
5. Technology research tools
   * Students use technology to locate, evaluate, and collect information from a variety of sources.
   * Students use technology tools to process data and report results.
   * Students evaluate and select new information resources and technological innovations based on the appropriateness to specific tasks.
6. Technology problem-solving and decision-making tools
   * Students use technology resources for solving problems and making informed decisions.
   * Students employ technology in the development of strategies for solving problems in the real world.

to technology usage. You should resolve to continue to develop your own technological literacy and your understanding of how to use technology effectively in teaching and learning.

This section draws on a 1998 publication, *Education on the Internet: A Student's Guide*, written by Andrew T. Stull and adapted for Merrill Education by Randall Ryder.

Internet Basics

The Internet is an important technology tool for teaching and learning in all subject areas. It is a vast connection of computers that was initially developed for communication among scientists and now is used in businesses, governments, homes, and schools around

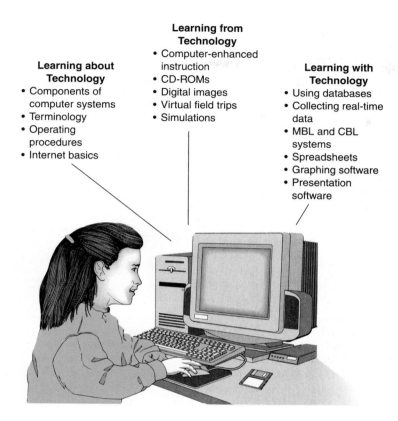

Learning about Technology
- Components of computer systems
- Terminology
- Operating procedures
- Internet basics

Learning from Technology
- Computer-enhanced instruction
- CD-ROMs
- Digital images
- Virtual field trips
- Simulations

Learning with Technology
- Using databases
- Collecting real-time data
- MBL and CBL systems
- Spreadsheets
- Graphing software
- Presentation software

Figure 10-2 Learning about, from, and with technology in the science classroom.

the globe (Stull, 1998). If your computer is connected to the Internet, you can access and exchange information with millions of computers worldwide. The World Wide Web, which was developed in 1989, allows users to access text, visual images, video, and audio presentations. Web browsers, such as Netscape Navigator and Internet Explorer, are software packages that enable users to navigate along the electronic superhighways that crisscross the Internet.

Suppose you wish to find out what is available on the Internet about a specific topic. You can use search engines such as Yahoo! at http://www.yahoo.com or Google Search at http://www.google.com/ to find hundreds of sites related to the topic. To use a search engine, type in a descriptor of the topic in the appropriate space and begin.

Develop Technology Literacy Through Science Classes

In addition to the efforts of specialists in technology classes for students, it is important that classroom teachers also work to build technology literacy among students. In your science classes, you should tie computers to science, technology, and society (STS) issues by showing

- how computers were made possible through advances in science;
- how computer technology affects people's lives now and in the future;
- how scientists use technology systems in their work;
- how to use the Internet responsibly;
- what cutting-edge technologies are being used by research scientists; and
- what career opportunities are available for people with computer technology skills.

Innovative technology can facilitate science teaching and learning. The technology shown here allows the teacher to place a slide on a microscope so the whole class can view it at once by video.

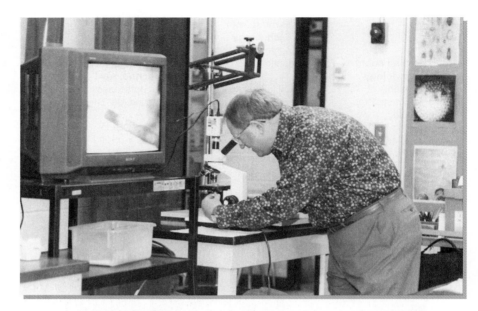

Learning from Educational Technology in Science Classes

Previous chapters have emphasized the learning of science through inquiry, as well as through other approaches. Think of a technology system as a tool to enrich your science teaching and your students' learning. In teaching and learning from educational technology, the computer takes over at least a portion of the role of instruction. Students may learn *from* computers through

- instructional presentations, including concept invention and direct instruction with drill and practice;

* interactive dialogues and tutorials;
* virtual field trips; and
* simulations and models of phenomena, concepts, and theories.

A variety of software programs are available on disks, CD-ROMs, or the Internet to enhance instructional presentations. Commercial and teacher-made programs might be used to guide and augment inquiry. Some multimedia commercial programs even involve hands-on activities. Computer-assisted instruction might also be used to present information directly and to provide for practice and review. Additionally, teachers and students can use multimedia application programs such as *PowerPoint*, *HyperStudio*, *Kid Pix*, and *Inspiration* to develop their own instructional presentations.

Let us examine more closely some ways educational technology can enhance the teaching and learning of science.

Embed Electronically Stored Images into Your Instruction

Picture yourself teaching elementary or middle school students about volcanic action. You would love to have them experience the sights, sounds, and other sensory aspects of these dramatic forces of nature. But how? Take them to a volcano? That is not practical for most of us, and it is potentially dangerous.

But CD-ROMs can give some of these sensory impacts. A single CD-ROM can store whole encyclopedias (e.g., *Grolier's Electronic Encyclopedia*) or the data from 380 floppy disks. A CD-ROM can hold more than 600 MB of data, the equivalent of about 250,000 pages of text or 20,000 images.

CD-ROMs embellish science teaching and learning by dispensing instant individual illustrations and sound for hard-to-grasp material. They invite creativity for teachers and students. And best of all, they are easy to use. It is little wonder they are among the most popular teaching and learning technologies. For example, to use CD-ROMs to explain the concept of phototropism, select time-lapse shots and slides of plants growing toward the light to make the learning more dramatic and meaningful. These technological tools allow you to pause at critical points, show entire sequences in slow motion, and review important concepts quickly and easily.

CD-ROMs provide a library of images and text for students as they research, study, and present reports. Your students can use the materials stored on CD-ROMs just as they would an encyclopedia. When they are ready to present their reports, they can display pertinent images to dramatically illustrate their understanding.

Many new computers also have DVD (digital video disk) drives allowing direct access to digital information stored on this even more powerful medium. DVD players can be connected to a television to enable viewing of a DVD without a computer. DVDs enable students and teachers to use menus to quickly select certain topics or segments of the presentation to view. DVDs are, therefore, more flexible than the older videotape technology. However, because of the continued availability of video cassette player/recorders and televisions in classrooms, much quality educational programming is still available on videotapes.

High-speed Internet access also makes downloading of still and video images from the World Wide Web a practical approach to supplementing teaching with visual material.

Digital cameras and video cameras are now affordable tools for schools. Their availability makes it possible for teachers and students to electronically record images of objects and events in their environment. This capability adds a real-world connection to science learning. Visual as well as written and drawn observational records can be stored for future analysis. A photographic record of the seasonal changes in the school yard, the growth of plants in a classroom investigation, or the position of shadows at different times during the day can provide familiar visual data for students to observe, sequence, and analyze.

Use Computer-Assisted Instruction Packages

Computer-assisted instruction (CAI) packages may range from text-based drill and practice or tutorial software to open-ended multimedia environments that support student's exploration of information (Reynolds & Barba, 1996). Tutorials present information to the student, often like an electronic textbook. Drill and practice, or review and reinforcement, programs provide opportunities for students to rehearse their knowledge and get immediate feedback about the accuracy of their answers. Though both of these approaches have developed negative connotations over the years, they can be effective learning tools when used in conjunction with other learning approaches.

In their book *Technology for the Teaching and Learning of Science*, Reynolds and Barba (1996) present a concise review of the research into the effectiveness of CAI, then summarize the research-based implications for computer-assisted instruction as follows:

> From the research of the past two decades, we have learned that computer-assisted instruction is a powerful learning tool for improving students' knowledge of science concepts at the knowledge and comprehension levels. Drill-and-practice packages help students decrease learning time, while increasing their achievement levels. Students enjoy working in electronic environments and enjoy learning in electronic microworlds. Computer-assisted instruction provides science teachers with supplementary resources to enrich basic science instruction. (p. 41)

A variety of innovative instructional packages, often incorporating interactive multimedia activities and presentations, are currently available to schools. Computer presentations can enhance the learning of science topics such as the circulatory system, the organs in the respiratory system of a fish, the parts of a microscope, constellations and star names, and so on.

Visit Sammy's Science House. *Sammy's Science House* by Edmark is designed to introduce science skills and concepts to preschool and primary students in a fun, risk-free learning environment. Guided and supported in their exploration by Sammy, a gender-neutral snake, children can engage in five different learning games. They can

- build a machine or toy from available parts in the workshop;
- sequence still pictures and then view them as a movie;
- categorize various plant, animal, and mineral objects at the sorting station;
- use the weather machine to see the effects of varying temperature, rainfall, and wind on the resultant weather; and
- visit the acorn pond to watch plants and animals change through the seasons.

Take Your Case to Science Court. Science Court (for grades 4–6) and Science Court Explorations (for grades 2–4) are innovative series of programs developed by Tom Snyder Productions (http://tomsnyder.com) on such topics as friction, sound, work and machines, flight, electrical current, and the water cycle. Each episode engages students in a scientific question presented in a funny, animated video. The case ends up in Science Court, where lawyers and expert witnesses seek the answer to the question. Before the case is decided, students form hypotheses and test them through hands-on activities. They then use their findings to predict the verdict in the Science Court trial.

An example of a program that explores human anatomy (basic organization and terminology, bones and body organs, and body systems and how they relate to each other) is *A.D.A.M. The Inside Story* from A.D.A.M. Software http://www.adam.com.

For example, in the case of the electric circuit, I. M. Richman refuses to relinquish his ping-pong trophy to the new champion, Mary Murphy. But he does agree to let her look at it. On the way into Richman's mansion, Mary trips and breaks the wire for Richman's alarm system. He repairs the break by inserting his dog's leash in the circuit, but later discovers that his alarm system is not working. Did Mary attempt to steal the trophy, or does the broken alarm system have to do with the way the wiring was repaired? The case is argued before the Science Court. Before the answer is revealed on the CD-ROM, students discuss the case, form hypotheses, and test them through hands-on activities with electric circuits.

Cool Science for Curious Kids. *Cool Science for Curious Kids* (http://www.hhmi.org/coolscience/index.html) is a website supported by Howard Hughes Medical Institute's Precollege and Public Science Education Program. It is designed to involve children in grades K–3 in science learning. Two activities on this site exemplify computer-assisted instruction. In "Classifying Critters," children are challenged to match pictures of animals and select summary statements as they develop the concept of classification of vertebrates. In "Plant Parts Salad," children select a picture of a plant part and the name of the plant part. If they match, the plant part goes into a salad bowl. These simple reinforcement games give students a chance to check their knowledge of concepts.

To see a collection of space–science related games that include tutorials and drill and practice approaches, visit the "Spacey Things to Do" section of *The Space Place* (http://spaceplace.jpl.nasa.gov/do.htm). There you will find a variety of memory and matching games, puzzles of images, crosswords, word finds, and so on, that exemplify CAI approaches.

Keep Up with Science Software. To keep up with software for science instruction, read the reviews in such education journals as *Science and Children*, *Science Scope*, *The Science Teacher*, and *Learning and Leading With Technology*. *NSTA Reports*, an NSTA publication, often provides addresses of software producers (as well as sources of free science software). Also, when you attend state, regional, and national science teacher conferences, frequent the commercial exhibits to find out more about available software.

There are currently many quality instructional websites available on the Internet. The Eisenhower National Clearinghouse (ENC) maintains a database of instructional materials for mathematics and science teaching that is available at http://www.enc.org. Each month ENC identifies its "Digital Dozen," twelve exemplary Websites related to science and math instruction. Besides viewing the current handpicked selections, teachers can browse hundreds of carefully chosen sites and identify the perfect application of instructional technology for their class.

Use Computer Simulations

The best way for elementary or middle school students to learn something is through first-hand experiences (with appropriate reflection, of course). However, this is not always practical, cost-effective, or safe. Simulating the experience by computer can be an effective substitute. Simulation follows the constructivist idea that learners construct their own unique concepts through active participation.

Simulations have great potential as a teaching tool. The computer can simulate activities that are difficult or impossible to do in your classroom, such as ocean wave properties, organism population growth, introduction of new organisms into a food chain, dissections, and inheritance of traits. Students enjoy engaging with the colorful, animated displays. They are placed in a situation where they control an environment by interacting with the computer. They collect data, correlate results, and learn skills, attitudes, and concepts. Your job is to help your students understand the relationship of the simulation to reality.

In simulations, struggling students may type in as many requests for assistance as necessary without embarrassment. A computer never gets angry or impatient; its pace adapts to the student using it. Conversely, advanced students may skip parts of a program that they already understand and proceed at their own pace. Simulations move students to higher or lower levels as needed.

Students must constantly be creating ideas to keep the simulation going. They must construct sentences, solve problems, and make decisions. By being active participants in the simulation, students get practice in solving problems in situations with which they can easily identify.

Explore the Universe Through Simulations. We have already seen how students respond to *The Great Solar System Rescue*. Many other good simulation programs are available that let your students explore an unknown universe. *Voyager Stargazer: A Guide to the Heavens* by Carina Software (2003) is a planetarium simulation that displays the sun, moon, planets, and stars in their correct spatial positions for any day of the year, from the distant past, through the present, to the future. As a dynamic simulation, *Voyager Stargazer* allows students to do compressed time studies of motions of objects in the sky. In a few seconds, students can watch the circumpolar constellations as they revolve about the North Star throughout a 24-hour period, follow the moon on its cycle around the earth, or keep track of a planet as it moves through the night sky.

Computer simulations can be used to understand sky relationships. For example, the positions of sunrise along the horizon for different days throughout the year might be measured using *Voyager Stargazer*. Students would note that the sun rises along the northeastern horizon around June 21, due east around September 21, along the southeastern horizon on December 21, and due east again around March 21. Through studying the sun's movements, students can construct a better understanding of the causes of the seasons. Additionally, students can better understand and appreciate the annual movements of the sun along the horizon, a means people thousands of years ago used to establish a solar calendar. *Voyager Stargazer* even allows students to map the changing areas of day and night on the earth's surface at different times and dates to help them explore the reasons for seasons.

Some simulation programs allow learners to conduct experiments in a virtual setting. *Virtual Labs: Light* by Edmark allows students to use virtual lasers and optical tools to safely investigate the nature of light, reflection, refraction, and color, rather than setting up light beams, mirrors, and lenses in a laboratory. *Virtual Labs: Electricity* by Edmark enables students to construct virtual circuits by clicking and dragging labeled icons that specify electrical components—batteries, bulbs, resistors, wires, and so on. Students can discover the basic properties of a circuit and the purpose of devices such as switches and fuses without the expense or potential safety issues of exploring with electrical components in the laboratory. The school version of this program includes structured learning activities, opportunities for open exploration, thinking questions and challenges, and embedded assessment activities. For example, "Broken? Fix It!" requires students to alter two circuits that do not work to make them functional.

Some simulations involve learners in a scenario that maintains their interest in the learning tasks. An example of this approach is *Bill Nye—The Science Guy: Stop the Rock* by Pacific Interactive. To stop a giant meteoroid from destroying earth, the learner must use various machines and devices within the virtual world at Nye Labs to uncover the answers

Another quality computer planetarium simulation appropriate for the classroom is *Starry Night EDU* by Space Holding Corp. This program has many of the same features as *Voyager Stargazer* and is packaged with a printed teacher's manual with reproducibles. Visit http://www.starrynight.com to learn more about this program's features.

to seven science riddles. The needed information can be uncovered by exploration, observation, and experimentation guided by humorous clues provided by the story's characters. By requiring active discovery rather than passive interaction, this program not only teaches science principles and facts but also teaches how to observe, hypothesize, test, and conclude.

Virtual field trips also represent excellent examples of simulations.

Take a Class on a Virtual Field Trip. Consider what you do when you organize a traditional field trip. You pick a location, plan the day's schedule, and guide the group from one spot to the next (Dockterman, 1997). You are creating an educational experience that supports your curriculum objectives and classroom activities. On a real field trip—whether to a local pond, aquarium, wetlands area, museum, zoo, planetarium, or any one of dozens of other exciting places—students experience new things and relate the experiences to concepts previously encountered in the classroom. Taking an electronic field trip can offer many of the same advantages as real field trips. Additionally, virtual field trips can enhance students' skills in using word processors, spreadsheets, databases, presentation programs, and the Internet (Bitner, Wadlington, Austin, Partridge, & Bitner, 1999).

Successful electronic field trips that support your curriculum need to be well planned (Dockterman, 1997). You can choose what your students will visit and what you expect them to learn, or you can let your students plan their own pathways through the software. Alternatively, you can let the software serve as a guide through the virtual landscape.

Explore the Rainforest: A Field Trip to the Rainforest Deluxe by Sunburst transports your students to the enchanted and fragile environment of three of the world's major rainforests: South America, Africa, and Southeast Asia. In the Discovery Screen, students can click on plants and animals to take a closer look at the organisms' adaptations and behaviors in relation to their environment. Other features that support learning include an interactive on-screen field guide to research climate, people, products, and the future of the rainforest; hyperlinks to a glossary; a data table that contains information about 150 rainforest organisms and provides a good introduction to the use of databases for sorting, classifying, and organizing data; and a journal where students can record notes, text, and pictures to create reports.

Visit Tourist Attractions. The Internet also provides opportunities for children to take virtual field trips to museums, zoos, or science centers without ever leaving the classroom (Ebenezer & Lau, 1999). For example, visit the *Exploratorium*, a San Francisco–based interactive science museum, at http://www.exploratorium.edu. An "exhibit cam" captures live views of Exploratorium visitors interacting with featured exhibits in the hall. The "roof cam" provides real-time images of the surrounding area, and you can select the direction it points. It is almost like being there. Additionally, there are "on-line exhibits" featuring optical illusions that let your students try out some of the museum's exhibits through interactions with their computer.

> To find current links to virtual field trips on the Internet, just search for "virtual field trips." You will discover many sites that provide links to virtual places to visit.

Visit Factories. How Everyday Things Are Made, published online by Alliance for Innovative Manufacturing (AIM) in cooperation with Stanford University, provides links to narrative video clips and collections of still images of manufacturing processes ranging from the production of airplanes and golf clubs to jellybeans and denim (http://manufacturing. Stanford.edu/). The links on this page can take you to 40 different virtual factory tours. Students interested in engineering and how familiar products are made will be impressed with the diversity of products included. Those with a sweet tooth will be satisfied, too, since eight of the links are to candy factories.

Join the Great Ocean Rescue. You read in the introduction to this chapter about the virtual field trips students take during *The Great Solar System Rescue.* Tom Snyder Productions also has a similar program, *The Great Ocean Rescue,* which is very educational and motivational for students. The program contains four ocean rescue missions—the Fishin' Mission, the Case of the Pollution Pirates, Grief on the Reef, and the Leaky Bottom Mission. In undertaking a mission, students work in teams of four, with each team member playing the role of a different scientist (geologist, environmental scientist, marine biologist, and oceanographer).

To begin an ocean rescue, teams view a transmission presenting a mission through written descriptions, still pictures, and video, accompanied by audio narratives. Information necessary for teams to accomplish the mission is embedded within the transmission. Expert scientists also have booklets providing background knowledge and information that is useful in achieving the mission. Teams work cooperatively to locate the trouble spot described in the transmission. Once the trouble spot has been identified, the team selects tests to help provide more information. Pooling their data, the team then decides which of four options to take to accomplish the mission. Mixing multiple media, cooperative learning, and accurate information on oceans, *The Great Ocean Rescue* provides an exciting and worthwhile learning opportunity for students.

Board the Magic School Bus. Kindergarten to sixth grade students are introduced to a meaningful multimedia science adventure with Scholastic's *The Magic School Bus Explores* series. These computer programs are based on the best-selling series, *The Magic School Bus* books, and the popular PBS television series of the same name.

In the programs, Ms. Frizzle, a high-spirited teacher, takes her class on extraordinary field trips by means of a magical school bus. The bus changes size and shape so students can grasp science topics through original and interesting viewpoints.

The Magic School Bus Explores the Solar System has Ms. Frizzle's class on a trip to the planetarium, when the bus "morphs" into a rocket ship and blasts off into outer space. Then Ms. Frizzle disappears and the class has to find her in the solar system. Students gather information from interactive experiments and reports as part of their search for Ms. Frizzle.

You can incorporate computer-based presentations, tutorials, simulations, and virtual field trips into your own lessons. Computer programs allow students to enjoy lessons while absorbing valuable science concepts. Make sure computer activities fit your objectives and are age appropriate for your students. Your responsibilities include providing closure and analysis and encouraging expressions of the concepts learned through such activities as writing, drawing posters, and role-playing. Use computer activities to enrich your science lessons and discussions; do not use them as substitutes for real experiences.

Learning with Educational Technology in Science Classes

Learning *with* educational technology means to use technology tools to enhance the construction of new knowledge and understanding. In constructivist learning approaches, students actively construct meaning from their own activities. They connect, learn to use, and test personal ideas through collaborative research and data taking with real-world events, problems, and issues. Through communicating their findings and conclusions to others, they clarify and extend their own ideas and learn from other people's comments. Educational technology can be especially useful to students in undertaking such constructivist tasks as

For additional information about *The Magic School Bus Explores* interactive science series, contact Scholastic, Inc., 555 Broadway, New York, NY 10003. Telephone: 212–343–6100.

To join in a discussion on "What are some ways you have seen the Internet and other educational technologies used in the classroom? What educational technology experiences might help elementary and middle school students learn science, mathematics, and other subjects better?" go to the Message Board module for Chapter 10 at http://www.prenhall.com/carin.

- accessing databases and other information through CD-ROMs and the Internet;
- data gathering through electronic sensors;
- using charts and graphs to display, analyze, and interpret data;
- communicating with other students, other classes, and scientists about research problems and ideas;
- presenting investigations and conclusions through multimedia communication, including word processors, graphics, and presentation software; and
- recording observations with digital imaging techniques and analyzing the visual data with image processing software.

Let us examine some of the ways that students can learn *with* technology.

Contribute to and Use Computer Databases

Useful data collected over long periods of time are available to students and scientists today on the Internet and CD-ROMs. Your science classroom computer can be used to search through database materials from throughout the United States and other parts of the world. **Databases** (electronically stored information) exist in all curricular areas, including science. For instance, if your students are studying the interrelationships between wind direction, speed, and weather conditions, they can instantly gather information from a variety of geographic locations without leaving your classroom. This not only motivates students and encourages them to use higher-thinking processes but also helps students learn how to effectively select and secure information.

Through using the computer, students can

- access commercial databases and information services;
- do collaborative research with other teachers and students locally or around the world;
- get up-to-the-minute weather and other science-related data;
- communicate using electronic mail;
- join discussions on bulletin boards, news groups, and computer conferences about science topics; and
- correlate various data sets using geographic information system (GIS) programs to see relationships among variables.

Global Learning and Observations to Benefit the Environment (GLOBE) is a model for international cooperation in monitoring the environment. GLOBE is an Internet-based research program involving scientists, students, and teachers worldwide (Ebenezer & Lau, 1999; Rock, Blackwell, Miller, & Hardison, 1997). GLOBE students learn to observe the environment by taking scientific data, such as the maximum and minimum temperature of the atmosphere, precipitation, cloud cover, and cloud type; and the temperature, pH, dissolved oxygen, and alkalinity of bodies of water. Students then send their data via the Internet to the GLOBE student data archive. Environmental and earth scientists use the data to accurately map such features as rivers, lakes, reservoirs, forest types, wetlands, and urban areas. The data are then available for students to use in their own research projects.

You can access the GLOBE Website at http://www. globe.gov.

NASA's S'COOL (Students' Cloud Observations On-Line) project provides another opportunity for students to contribute to real scientific research by making and sharing their observations. Classes provide *ground truth* measurements to assist in the validation of the CERES (Clouds and the Earth's Radiant Energy System) instrument. Students make visual cloud observations at the same time as the satellite does and share their findings electronically with NASA. Then the two observations are compared to validate the analysis of the

For more information about this collaborative NASA project, visit the S'COOL Website at http:// asd.www.larc.nasa.gov/SCOOL/.

satellite data. Students can also compare the surface- and space-based observations to learn more about clouds and climate.

In 2003, almost 1,500 schools in all 50 states and in over 60 countries were involved in S'COOL. The project is suggested for students in fourth grade or above, but classes of younger students have also participated successfully. Instructional materials and all materials necessary for participating in S'COOL are free. If you are teaching about clouds and weather, consider letting your students help NASA scientists do their work.

Scientific databases are also available on CD-ROMs. Michael Passow (1996) and his eighth grade science students have used a CD-ROM called the *Global Tropical/Extratropical Cyclone Climatic Atlas* to study historic storms. The *Climatic Atlas* CD-ROM was produced by the National Climatic Data Center of the National Oceanic and Atmospheric Administration (NOAA).

In one activity, Passow's class (1996) studied storms along the East Coast of the United States. Selecting a North Atlantic option on the CD-ROM allowed them to view a list of storms that occurred between 1871 and 1992. From the list, they found that most of the storms (21) in the North Atlantic occurred in 1933. They chose a particular 1933 storm and used the CD-ROM data to map its path from its beginning to its ending dates. The storm formed in the Atlantic Ocean, moved along the East Coast, and struck land in North Carolina on August 23, 1933.

Another CD-ROM in the NOAA series allowed students to study historical climatic data from more than 2,000 stations worldwide. Thus, they could select a station near their city and determine such things as annual temperature and wind patterns.

Passow (1996) concluded that CD-ROM and other new technologies

> Lie at the heart of the Standards' vision of "Science as Inquiry," where students sharpen observing, inferring, and experimenting skills while increasing their knowledge and using scientific reasoning and critical thinking. (p. 23)

GIS programs use computers and software to display geographically related data on maps. This allows students to view, understand, question, interpret, and visualize data in ways simply not possible in rows and columns, aiding them in finding patterns and solving problems.

ArcView is one GIS software package that is being used in middle and secondary schools. The book *Mapping Our World: GIS Lessons for Educators* by Malone, Palmer, and Voigt (2002) provides a 1-year license for ArcView, a teacher resource CD, and lesson plans for a variety of science and geography investigations. For example, in "The Earth Moves: A Global Perspective" students will observe patterns of earthquake and volcanic activity on the earth's surface and the relationship of those patterns to the location of diverse landforms, plate boundaries, and the distribution of population. Based on their exploration of these relationships, students will form a hypothesis about the earth's distribution of earthquake and volcanic activity and identify world cities that face the greatest risk from those phenomena (p. 49).

Use MBLs and CBLs to Collect and Process Data

Nothing adds to student excitement and links to real-world science like **microcomputer-based laboratory (MBL)** or **calculator-based laboratory (CBL)** systems. MBLs and CBLs are electronic systems used to collect, organize, and process real-world data automatically. MBL and CBL technologies need not replace direct measurements of temperature, time, force, air pressure, and so on. The direct measurement of variables in your classroom sci-

To learn more about ArcView and GIS applications to education, visit http://www.esri.com.

Graphing calculators can be thought of as handheld computing devices. They are able to perform many of the functions of microcomputers.

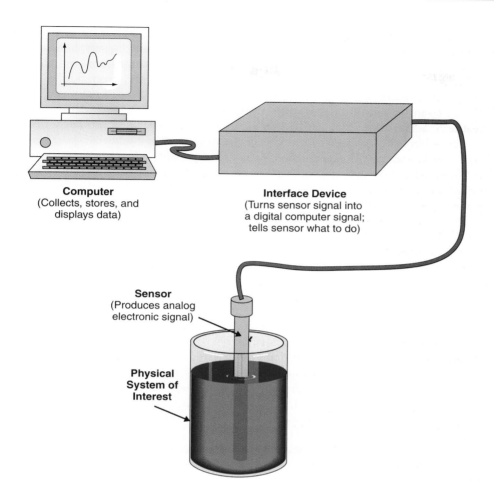

Computer
(Collects, stores, and displays data)

Interface Device
(Turns sensor signal into a digital computer signal; tells sensor what to do)

Sensor
(Produces analog electronic signal)

Physical System of Interest

Figure 10-3 There are three main components in microcomputer-based laboratory (MBL) and calculator-based laboratory (CBL) systems.
Source: Adapted from "Student Data Acquisition," by Alice B. Kreuger, Patrick D. French, and Thomas G. Carter (p. 160), 1997, in Karen C. Cohen, Ed., *Internet Links for Science Education.* New York: Plenum Press, 157–176. Copyright 1997 by Plenum Press. Adapted with permission.

ence program is still very important. However, the use of electronic data taking can help shift the focus from mechanical procedures to higher-level and more creative scientific processes, such as analyzing and hypothesizing. MBLs and CBLs allow students to focus on thinking about data, not merely gathering it (Nachmias & Linn, 1987; Price, 1989).

There are three main components in MBL and CBL systems (see Figure 10-3):

- A **sensor** or **probe**, which measures real-time physical data such as temperature, light intensity, loudness of sound, air pressure, pH, and heart rate. A sensor converts the physical quantity being measured into an electronic signal.
- An **interface** device, which tells the sensor what to do and stores the data that the sensor collects.
- A **computer** (for MBLs) or **graphing calculator** (for CBLs) into which the data are downloaded for display, organization, and processing.

In its *Hands-On Elementary Science Project Leader's Manual*, TERC (1993) states that "MBL provides more opportunity for learners to pay attention to the data—to interpret it, redisplay it, and analyze it to inform their understanding of the phenomenon. Since the time span between changing a variable in their investigation and seeing the results is shortened, learners can ask more 'what if' questions and are more likely to revise their test

TERC originally stood for Technical Education Research Center. Now the organization is known simply as TERC. Check out their website at http://www.terc.edu/.

design and try it again" (p. A-21). They suggest that MBL introduces learners to some standard representations of science data, including bar graphs and line graphs and assists them in acquiring the "language of graphing" (p. A-22). This instructional technology is especially applicable when trying to measure events that happen very slowly or very quickly, that change over a very small range, or that must be measured indirectly.

Data sensors and interfaces working together have been called "data grabbers" (Albrecht & Firedrake, 1998, 1999). A data grabber is a self-contained instrument that operates without being connected to another device. It captures and stores data over long periods of time without the experimenter having to be present. When you want the stored data, you connect the data grabber to a computer or graphing calculator and download the data. Data grabbers are used extensively by scientists and technicians working on real-world problems. Their use in the classroom helps to make school science activities more authentic.

According to Caniglia (1997), "collecting data, questioning results, consulting resources, exchanging ideas, and reaching conclusions are core activities in both science and mathematics" (p. 22). By enabling students to gather and graphically display data more quickly and frequently than through traditional procedures, MBL and CBL activities can be instrumental in helping learners forge stronger links between abstract graphical representations and real-world events.

Caniglia (1997) has pointed out that the exchange of ideas and results is just as important in science as collecting and analyzing data. When engaging in MBL and CBL activities, students do more than just look for patterns in graphs. They also argue about experimental procedures, discuss inconsistencies, draw conclusions, and make connections to the physical processes underlying the data. These are core activities in both science and mathematics. MBL and CBL investigations offer exciting opportunities for students to model real-world events and make needed connections between science and mathematics.

A variety of MBL and CBL packages are available commercially (see Table 10-1).

Use Spreadsheets to Organize and Analyze Data

Spreadsheets can facilitate and extend the organization and analysis of real data taken by students. This software tool is especially important in processing directly measured data or data collected from Internet databases. A **spreadsheet** is a computer program for organiz-

> Teachers are continually searching for ways to help students make connections among subject areas. Using MBL and CBL activities can be a critical way to help students tie mathematics and science together.

TABLE 10-1 SOME MBL AND CBL SUPPLIERS	
Company	**Website**
Acculab Products	http://www.sensornet.com
Data Harvest Company	http://www.dataharvest.com
iScience Project	http://iscienceproject.com
Pasco	http://www.pasco.com/hs
Team Labs Corporation	http://www.teamlabs.com
Texas Instruments	http://education.ti.com/success
Vernier Software	http://www.vernier.com

ing data in columns and manipulating it in various ways through the use of mathematics. **Graphing software** contained within spreadsheet programs enables students to display data in different types of graphs. Although students routinely study the use of spreadsheets in computer literacy classes, they should understand that they are recent innovations, becoming widely used in business and industry only since the 1980s.

In her article *The Spreadsheet—Absolutely Elementary*, Holmes (1997) has provided clear instructions and ideas on how to use spreadsheets in elementary science and mathematics. You will find her spreadsheet solution of the age-old problem posed by Mother Goose, How Many Were Going to St. Ives?, entertaining and instructive.

One of the most common spreadsheet programs available today is Microsoft® Excel. Its inclusion in Microsoft® Office packages has made it available on many home and school computers. It is a very powerful program that can be used successfully by teachers and students alike with proper training.

Communicate Through Multimedia Presentations

Multimedia software programs such as *PowerPoint*, *HyperStudio*, and *Kid Pix* enliven presentations, reports, and projects for both teachers and students. With these multimedia programs, users can build colorful and creative slides and combine them into the desired presentation product (Lee & Patterson, 1997). Program users have access to prebuilt graphic templates, word processing and drawing tools, built-in graphics, and high-quality clip art. *Kid Pix* includes movie clips as well. All three programs enable the user to insert items from other sources, including the Internet.

Kid Pix is an especially friendly tool for both students and teachers. The very young child can maneuver through the program via its system of symbols, while older children can perform more sophisticated tasks. For example, in word processing, the user can choose to stamp letters one at a time on a slide or use the keyboard for more conventional writing. Developing a slide show with *Kid Pix* is fun. Although the product's name implies that *Kid Pix* is only for the young, people of all ages delight in the vivid colors, funny movies, and vast selection of pictures and sounds within the program.

Teachers can create motivating slide shows that capture students' attention for instruction and model how students can present their own ideas through technology. In science instruction that follows the 5-E model, teachers might use a graphics presentation program to

- add catchy, animated graphics to the *engagement* phase;
- print directions for the *exploration* phase and project them onto a screen for students to view and follow;
- build concept maps and augment invention of new concepts and ideas in the *explanation* phase;
- assist students in the *elaboration* phase to develop understanding by linking invented concepts to previous activities and to new investigations; and
- present tests, rubrics, and other assessment items to students in the *evaluation* phase of instruction.

Using teacher-developed slide shows as models, students might construct reports of their investigations and prepare interesting presentations for the class. The very act of creating products with a multimedia program forces students to clarify, extend, and refine their ideas, and thus helps them in constructing understanding.

Additionally, teachers and students might use a multimedia program to create single slides to illustrate a point, to create theme files, to construct and print displays for bulletin

Step-by-step instructions for creating the St. Ives spreadsheet in *ClarisWorks* are available in the L&L (Learning and Leading with Technology) section of the ISTE Website at http://www.iste.org/L&L/archives/vol24/no8/index.html. Click on "Online Article Supplements" to access the file.

PowerPoint is one of a suite of programs available in *Microsoft Office*. HyperStudio is produced by Roger Wagner Publishing: http://www.hyperstudio.com. *Kid Pix* is produced by Broderbund: http://www.broderbund.com.

boards and projects, to design and produce safety and lab procedure posters, or to create announcement flyers to post in the classroom or send home to parents.

In this chapter, we have looked mostly at isolated uses of educational technology in teaching. Refer to the science and social studies lessons given in Chapter 8 on weather, river ecology, and the Lewis and Clark expedition for sample lessons that can meet standards from science and other disciplines, as well as the *National Educational Technology Standards*.

Successfully integrating technology with the rest of the curriculum requires that classroom technology resources be managed effectively.

Managing Educational Technology in the Science Classroom

Educational technology resources in schools are usually arranged in one or more of these ways: Technology resources may be housed in a centralized computer center or lab with computers for every student, classrooms may have only a single computer, or classrooms may be equipped with several computers in a multimedia arrangement.

Schoolwide Computer/Multimedia Center or Lab

Some elementary and middle schools set up computer or technology centers or labs for class-sized groups. Classes are scheduled into the technology center, and either an educational technology specialist conducts computer lessons, or individual teachers work with their own classes there. It is often quite difficult to connect educational technology to the ongoing curriculum with centralized technology centers.

The One-Computer Classroom

If you have one computer in your classroom, like Dotty in the Video Case Study for this chapter, you may have a problem (Brown, 1998). How are you going to use the computer? Will it be used primarily for presentation by the teacher, or as a tool for students in creating projects? How often will students use the computer? Will you encourage cooperative learning with the computer?

Fortunately, there is a variety of help available for the teacher in a one-computer classroom. Dockterman (1997) has compiled some good ideas in his *Great Teaching in the One Computer Classroom*. Kahn (1998) has also written a versatile and practical guide, *Ideas and Strategies for the One-Computer Classroom*, which provides many helps for teachers. Additionally, *Learning and Leading with Technology (L&L)*, a journal of the International Society for Technology in Education, includes a periodic section on teaching in the one-computer classroom.

In the October 1998 issue of *L&L*, Cindy Brown suggested that an important use of a single computer in a classroom is for teacher and student presentations. If you use the computer for instructional presentations, your computer will need to be connected to a large-screen monitor or liquid crystal display (LCD) projection system. You, or your students, work at the computer, and images are displayed on-screen for the entire class to view. Interaction can take place as students view the screen and discuss what they see.

In an Annenberg Video Case Study in Science Education, Dotty's middle school students use the one computer in their classroom primarily for telecommunication. In the video, we see the students collecting and testing water samples for pH and dissolved oxygen. They use telecommunications to exchange data with students from other schools in

 A video guide for the Annenberg Video Case Study featuring Dotty appears in this chapter.

their area; they also send e-mail messages to students in all 50 states asking for water samples. Telecommunications, set within an STS context, allows these students from rural Tennessee to feel connected to students in other parts of the state, the nation, and the world.

According to Brown (1998), another important way to use a single computer in a classroom is as a learning center. Mary Ellen Swadley, an innovative sixth grade teacher of science, mathematics, and social studies, uses the computer as one of several ongoing learning stations for her two classes of about 20 students. Each class meets for a 3-hour block of time. Students work in the learning stations—on either science, math, or social studies content—in small cooperative groups. All computer activities are related to the topic being taught in the class. For example, students may engage in *The Great Ocean Rescue* as part of a study of oceans, or they might use a multimedia package to develop a report or prepare a presentation on a topic being learned.

Every child in Ms. Swadley's classes uses the computer at least 20 minutes each day as a member of a cooperative group. Additionally, students might work on the computer on their own at different times during the day, including before and after school. Although Ms. Swadley started her adventure into educational technology with only one computer in her classroom, she has found creative ways to add five more.

More Than One Computer—A Multimedia Arrangement

It is possible that you will have more than one computer in a multimedia arrangement in your self-contained classroom. Here are some guidelines for setting up and managing computers and other electronic technology equipment for a class of 20 to 25 students:

1. A variety of educational technologies should be used to accommodate the range of learning styles and backgrounds of your students (e.g., texts, videos, hands-on materials, computers, MBLs or CBLs, software, and Internet).
2. Tables should be arranged so students can work in cooperative learning groups.
3. The following learning stations might be set up for groups of four students: a listening station, a video station, a hands-on materials station, a word processing station, an MBL/CBL station, and a writing station. Figure 10-4 gives a suggested floor plan for a science/technology-oriented classroom incorporating these stations.
4. The teacher's workstation should have a computer (the central server for students' computers and the Internet), an LCD projection system or large-screen monitor, an electronic writing board, a printer, and a modem connected to a telephone outlet.
5. Your classroom can contain these types of computer stations:
   - Student computer workstation with multimedia presentation software and Internet capability for data collection and sending science e-mail and bulletin board/news group correspondence
   - MBL or CBL systems for student-conducted science activities
   - A videocassette, interactive videodisc, and CD-ROM station for viewing and engaging in the videos and software
6. Arrange to lock the computers when they are not used. Many schools engrave the name of the school on all components and bolt them to tables or portable carts.
7. Arrange your classroom schedule so that students who are responsible can use the computers on a sign-up basis when they have completed their other classroom responsibilities. You will find that computers are very popular and can positively motivate students to complete assignments. Encourage this.
8. Periodically review technology literacy content and skills with simple tests, and introduce your students to new software as it becomes available.

VIDEO CASE STUDY: *DOTTY*

Previewing the Video
As you watch the three
modules for this case study,
use the Questions for
Reflection to guide your
thoughts and notes for any
group discussion or individual feedback. If you watch
the video as a group and
then participate in a group
discussion, choose a group
facilitator to solicit various
perspectives and keep the
discussion on track.

Introducing the Case

Dotty is a participating teacher in the Tennessee Valley Project, which was designed and funded to improve science education in eight rural school districts in eastern Tennessee. During the summer, participating teachers determined they would each develop two STS (science, technology, society) projects for their classes to do. As part of their required participation, teachers needed to integrate the use of telecommunications, establish partnerships with environmental groups in their area to assist with their projects, and address the National Science Education Standards for environmental science. At their initial meeting, teachers engaged in the Tennessee Valley Project discussed how they would need to use new teaching and learning approaches to accomplish their appointed tasks.

Questions for Reflection

1. What did teachers decide to try to accomplish in the teaching and learning goals of the Tennessee Valley Project?
2. What reservations did Dotty and other teachers have about changing the teaching method-ologies they had traditionally used?

Trying New Ideas   *Back in the classroom, Dotty and her class began a water quality study. After two or three students brought in local water samples, the whole class then determined that they would use e-mail to contact people from all 50 states and ask them to send water samples to their class for testing.*

Questions for Reflection

1. How did STS provide a context in which to use telecommunications? How did Dotty and her class interpret what STS meant to them?
2. In what ways did Dotty and her students utilize telecommunications to complete their project?
3. What do you think "inquiry-based" teaching means? How did the use of technology facili-tate Dotty in letting go of "control" of her classroom teaching?
4. Describe how Link-Up Day provided a unique way to culminate the water quality project.

Reflecting and Building on Change

Continuing in their study of the environment and water quality, Dotty's class engaged in a study of hydroelectricity. A number of area resources supported Dotty and her class in these efforts. Students' accomplishments and enthusiasm in this new approach to learning left Dotty with a number of questions about traditional assessment measures.

Questions for Reflection

1. What technological "glitches" did Dotty and her students run into? What recommendations would you make to a local school district about technology needs for your classroom?
2. How did Dotty's class prepare for their field trip to the Tennessee Valley Authority to learn about hydroelectricity?
3. What nontraditional ways did Dotty use to assess students' understanding about water quality and hydroelectricity? How would you prepare students to do effective peer evaluations and self-evaluations?
4. Do you agree with Dotty that traditional methods of assessment would now be contradictory to the way students in her class learned about water quality and hydroelectricity? Why or why not?
5. How do you see future technology further developing students' ability to take a more active role in their own learning? How do think your role as a teacher will change based on the use of that technology?

For an interesting quest to determine the varying amounts of nitrate in natural bodies of water and drinking water, go to http://www.aqua.org/education/teachers/activities/ act18.html and try Activity 18 with students. An online form will allow students to share the nitrate results of your part of the country with other schools. Online results can also allow students to create a map that shows nitrate levels in bodies of water across the country.

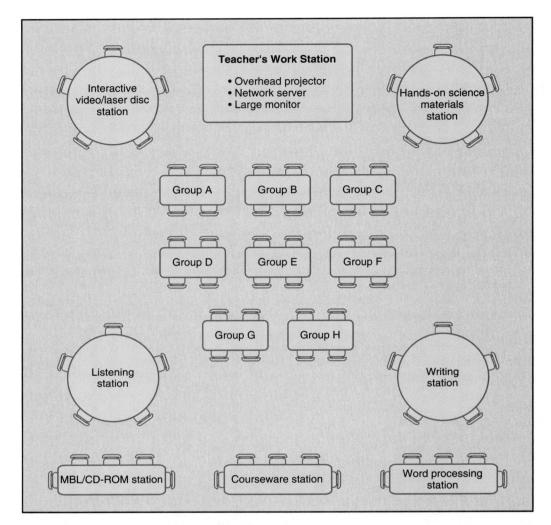

Figure 10-4   Technology-oriented self-contained science classroom.
Source: Designs for Elementary School Science and Health (p. 50), A cooperative project of Biological Science Curriculum Study (BSCS) and International Business Machines (IBM), © 1989, Colorado Springs, CO. Reprinted by permission.

Student Personal Computer Learning Stations. You should set up computer learning stations where students can work on learning software, word processing, and multimedia presentations. These would be similar to the learning centers described in Chapter 6, where collections of materials are arranged for students to work on individually or in small groups. Follow these guidelines:

1. Locate your computer learning stations so you can see them from anyplace in your classroom.
2. Provide written instructions on the basics of turning on and loading (booting) a computer, and any other necessary simple directions for beginning technology literacy. Post them near the computer.
3. Select two or three students who have used computers, and train them to be peer computer experts. They will have to know the hardware and software in your

room, how to operate the computer, and how to positively help their classmates. Post the names of these students and assign them specific times when each one will be available for help.

4. Set up a schedule so students can sign up for computer time at the computer station. Include some open or free times. Your schedule should record time spent on the computer by each student, so you can ensure that everyone gets computer time.

Selecting Science Software and Internet Sites

Computer programs and Internet sites vary greatly in suitability for use with elementary and middle school students. Many programs are designed to supplement or be an integral part of science programs and textbooks. You may be called on to suggest which software your school should buy in the coming years or to screen and select Websites for student use. In the selection process, start with your instructional objectives, not the mass of available software and Websites. First decide what you want to do with educational technology; then it is relatively easy to determine what hardware and software you will need.

Here are some questions to guide you in selecting and evaluating software for your elementary and middle school science program:

1. Is the program easy to use?
2. Is the program design flexible?
3. Is the menu complete?
4. Is the program content accurate and well designed?
5. Does the program offer a complete learning package, including a teacher's guide that can be correlated with your science curriculum?
6. Is the reading level what you need?
7. Are the graphics direct, attractive, and appropriate?
8. Is there a program purchase warranty?
9. Has the software been reviewed or recommended?
10. Are follow-up or enrichment science activities or demonstrations offered?

There are a multitude of appropriate and inappropriate sites available on the Internet. Here are some questions to ask when selecting Internet sites for student use (Gray, 1997):

1. Do the instructional objectives and content of the site provide a high degree of correlation to your science curriculum and to national, state, and local standards?
2. Does the site's use of unique Web features, such as communication and information access, promote a significantly broader and deeper understanding of ideas, concepts, and theories than more traditional instructional materials?
3. Does the online resource facilitate person-to-person interactivity and increased understanding through the use of telecommunications?
4. Are learners able to link to additional online resources that provide related information?
5. Is the site rich in content and aesthetically pleasing? Is text easy to read, and do graphics enhance the basic instructional design of the site?
6. Is the online resource well structured and easy for students to work with?
7. Is the site without cultural, gender, or racial bias in content and format?

Another important issue related to Internet use is the determination of the information's credibility. Everyone can learn to detect dubious assertions, strategies which are particularly applicable to assessing scientific claims and information students may encounter on the Internet. Students can detect less credible information by looking for the following signs:

- Premises of arguments are not explicit.
- Evidence does not lead logically to conclusions.
- Fact and opinion are not clearly distinguished.
- Celebrity is quoted as authority.
- Specific references are vague or missing.
- Graphs are misleading.
- Measures taken to guard against distortion in self-reports are not described.
- Percentages are given without stating total sample size (Kreuger & Sutton, 2001).

According to Kreuger and Sutton (2001, p. 76), scientifically literate students will respond appropriately to the barrage of information that technology provides. Separating sense from nonsense is a critical response skill that must be developed in all students.

In some cases, you will be able to download free software or programs from Internet sites. You can also join online discussion groups to find out what other teachers think of the programs, Websites, or materials you are considering for your classroom. Some descriptions list schools where computer-based materials and learning models have been field-tested or reviewed. In addition, some software companies offer previews of their products and encourage teachers to return products that do not meet their needs. Be sure to explore the programs, packages, and approaches that can help you and your students take advantage of information technology.

Acceptable Use Policies for the Internet

Soholt (1999) has cautioned that "the Internet is wide open. There are sites which no child should see" (p. 43). You need to protect your students and yourself. Thus, every school should have acceptable use policies in place for children and the Internet. These policies should relate to such things as e-mail use, giving out information requested by different sites, what students should do when they confront an inappropriate image or site, and when students can use the Internet. Figure 10-5 shows an acceptable use policy for one school.

Take the Plunge—Join the Information Age

Change is taking place so rapidly in the educational technology field that it is easy to feel overwhelmed by all the new products and resources. Fortunately, help is available. A number of professional magazines review computer-based materials and provide articles that guide you through the technology maze. The journals *Science and Children* and *The Science Teacher* regularly feature articles related to educational technology. *Learning and Leading with Technology* and *Multimedia Schools* are devoted specifically to the *what, how, where,* and *how well* of incorporating technology into teaching and learning. In addition, the Eisenhower National Clearinghouse for Mathematics and Science Education (http://www.enc.org/) offers an online catalog that includes extensive information about available curriculum resources, plus prices.

Computers and other electronic multimedia technology open many vistas for teaching science in the elementary and middle schools. Consider them another tool in your teaching arsenal. Be curious, but critical. Attend computer workshops, conferences, and exhibitions. Keep up with the latest advances in educational technology by reading widely. Most importantly, take the plunge and find out why students are so enthusiastic about computers and other electronic technologies. Learn to share their enthusiasm.

Internet Standards at Sandia Elementary

The following standards must be adhered to by all students and staff at Sandia Elementary. Violation of **any** of these standards will result in immediate suspension of Internet privileges. Continued and habitual violations will result in permanent suspension of Internet privileges.

1. Students and staff must have on file a signed Acceptable Use Policy in order to use any network services at Sandia Elementary, including e-mail and Internet access.
2. Students may not have individual e-mail accounts. All accounts will be in the teacher's name.
3. Students must have specific permission from their teacher to conduct a search on the Internet.
4. Students may not add "Bookmarks" without specific permission from a teacher.
5. Students may not give the following information out on the Internet without prior permission of their teacher.
   - your last name
   - a picture of yourself or any other students
   - your home address
   - your telephone number
   - any personal information asked for by someone you do not know
6. If you ever find an inappropriate site or image, immediately hit the back key and contact an adult.
7. If you ever feel uncomfortable about a certain site or message, contact an adult immediately.
8. No chat rooms!
9. There will be no Internet or e-mail access when a substitute teacher is in the room.

Figure 10-5 A school policy for acceptable Internet use.
Source: Using Technology Effectively in Your Classroom (p. 44), by Gordon Soholt, 1999, Bellevue, WA: Bureau of Education and Research, P.O. Box 96068, Bellevue, WA 98009.

SUMMARY

- A variety of multimedia technologies are available to elementary and middle school classrooms and can be as valuable as your other teaching aids in teaching science. Additionally, science classes are a natural place for students to achieve technological literacy and technology education standards.

- There are many ways to use computing technology in your science teaching. You and your students must learn *about*, *with*, and *from* computers. Your science teaching can be enhanced through computer-assisted instruction, simulation, virtual field trips, and data gathering, analysis, and processing. There are many software programs available for each of these uses.

- An inquiry-based science program can be enriched with microcomputer-based laboratory (MBL) or calculator-based laboratory (CBL) systems. Other electronic resources available for teaching and learning science are videodiscs, CD-ROMs, liquid crystal display (LCD) projection systems, interactive TV, and the Internet. Using the Internet can be beneficial, but you must also use caution and should establish an Internet use policy.

- Follow the suggested guidelines for evaluating software and Internet sites for your elementary science program. There are also many sources for learning what other teachers think of specific resources.

- This chapter is only introductory, opening up for you the many possibilities of using technology to enhance learning and motivation in your science classroom. Take advantage of the multiple professional development opportunities available to foster your technological literacy.

REFERENCES

Albrecht, B., & Firedrake, G. (1998). Grabbing data: What you need to log and use real world data. *Learning and Leading with Technology, 26*(1), 36–40.

Albrecht, B., & Firedrake, G. (1999). Blowin' hot and cold about my data. *Learning and Leading with Technology, 26*(5), 32–36.

Bitner, N., Wadlington, E., Austin, S., Partridge, E., & Bitner, J. (1999). The virtual trip. *Learning and Leading with Technology, 26*(6), 6–9, 25.

Boraiko, A. A. (1982). The chip. *National Geographic, 162*(4), 420–457.

Brown, C. A. (1998). Presentation software and the single computer. *Learning and Leading with Technology, 26*(2), 18–21.

Caniglia, J. (1997). The heat is on! Using the calculator-based laboratory to integrate math, science, and technology. *Learning and Leading with Technology, 25*(1), 22–27.

Carina Software. (2003). *Voyager stargazer: A guide to the heavens.* San Ramon, CA: Carina Software.

Designs for elementary school science and health. (1989). A cooperative project of Biological Science Curriculum Study (BSCS) and International Business Machines (IBM). Dubuque, IA: Kendall/Hunt.

Dockterman, D. (1997). *Great teaching in the one computer classroom.* Watertown, MA: Tom Snyder Productions.

Dyrli, O. E., & Kinnaman, D. E. (1995). What every teacher needs to know about technology. Part 2: Developing a technology-powered curriculum. *Technology and Learning, 14*(5), 46–51.

Ebenezer, J., & Lau, E. (1999). *Science on the Internet: A resource for K–12 teachers.* Upper Saddle River, NJ: Merrill/Prentice Hall.

Explore the Rainforest: A Fieldtrip to the Rainforest Deluxe [computer software]. (1998). Elgin, IL: Sunburst Communications.

Gray, T. (1997). ED's Oasis (Guidelines for evaluating educational web sites). *Learning and Leading with Technology, 25*(1), 44–45.

The Great Ocean Rescue [computer software]. (1997). Watertown, MA: Tom Snyder Productions.

The Great Solar System Rescue [computer software]. (1997). Watertown, MA: Tom Snyder Productions.

Holmes, E. D. (1997). The spreadsheet—Absolutely elementary. *Learning and Leading with Technology, 24*(8), 6–12.

International Society for Technology in Education. (1999). *National educational technology standards for students: Con-* necting curriculum and technology (a poster presentation of the standards). Eugene, OR: Author.

Kahn, J. (1998). *Ideas and strategies for the one-computer classroom.* Eugene, OR: International Society for Technology in Education.

Kay, A. (1995). Computers, networks, and education. In *The Computer in the 21st Century, Scientific American, Special Issue, 6*(1), 148–155.

Kreuger, A., & Sutton, J. (Eds.). (2001). Instructional technology in science. In *EDThoughts: What we know about science teaching and learning* (pp. 69–79). Aurora, CO: Mid-continent Research for Education and Learning.

Kreuger, A. B., French, P. D., & Carter, T. G. (1997). Student data acquisition. In K. C. Cohen (Ed.), *Internet links for science education* (pp. 157–176). New York: Plenum Press.

Lee, J. R., & Patterson, W. R. (1997). It's show time! Six hints for PowerPoint presentations. *Learning and Leading with Technology, 24*(5), 6–11.

Malone, L., Palmer, A., & Voigt, C. (2002). *Mapping our world: GIS lessons for educators.* Redlands, CA: ESRI Press.

Nachmias, R., & Linn, M. C. (1987). Evaluations of science laboratory data: The role of computer presented information. *Journal of Research in Science Teaching, 24*(5), 491–506.

National Research Council. (1996). *National science education standards.* Washington, DC: National Academy Press.

Passow, M. (1996). Storm studies. *The Science Teacher, 63*(3), 21–23.

Price, C. L. (1989). Microcomputer applications in science. *Journal of Science Education, 1*(2), 30–33.

Reynolds, K., & Barba, R. (1996). *Technology for the teaching and learning of science.* Needham Heights, MA: Allyn & Bacon.

Rock, B. N., Blackwell, T. R., Miller, D., & Hardison, A. (1997). The GLOBE program: A model for international environmental education. In K. C. Cohen (Ed.), *Internet links for science education: Student-scientist partnerships.* New York: Plenum Press.

Soholt, G. (1999). *Using technology effectively in your classroom* (p. 44). Bellevue, WA: Bureau of Education & Research.

Stull, A. T. (1998). *Education on the Internet: A student's guide* (adapted for Merrill Education by R. J. Ryder). Upper Saddle River, NJ: Merrill/Prentice Hall.

TERC. (1993). *Hands-on elementary science project leader's manual.* Cambridge, MA: TERC Communications.

Activities for Teaching
Science as Inquiry

I

Teaching Inquiry Science Activities

NSES *Inquiry is a set of interrelated processes by which scientists and students pose questions about the natural world and investigate phenomena; in doing so, students acquire knowledge and develop a rich understanding of concepts, principles, models, and theories. Inquiry is a critical component of a science program at all grade levels and in every domain of science. (National Research Council, 1996, p. 214)*

Terrariums offer a wonderful opportunity for children to investigate the world by questioning and hypothesizing, describing and classifying, manipulating and experimenting, inferring and predicting. Sharon Olson began a series of terrarium lessons with her second graders by asking: "What might you find on a forest floor?" As the class discussed this question, Ms. Olson held up the different materials the students suggested (soil, sand, leaves, seeds, fruit, plants, water, twigs, grass, and so on). She then told the students these were some of the things they would put in a container to make a home for living things. For the next few days, small groups of students built and investigated their own terrariums (Hosoume & Barber, 1994). Using readily available containers, such as large, plastic soda-water bottles (Ingram, 1993), the children arranged soil in the bottom of the containers, planted plants, sprinkled seeds, added moisture, and introduced earthworms and pill bugs to their new homes.

This scenario draws on activities described in this book. Here, you will find directions for more than 150 inquiry activities in physical science, life science, and earth and space science designed for elementary and middle school students. The activities presented here do not comprise a comprehensive science curriculum, but they do represent a large number of examples that will

1. provide you with concrete suggestions for teaching science as inquiry;
2. provide a bank of activities that you can draw on in teaching science as inquiry to children; and
3. help you connect science in the classroom to the *National Science Education Standards* in a very practical way.

You do not have to be a science specialist to engage your students in these activities, merely curious and willing to learn along with them.

Let us look more closely at what it means to teach science as inquiry.

When Scientists and Students Inquire

Science is an attempt to understand the natural world. Doing science can be as simple as one individual conducting field studies or as complex as hundreds of people across the world working together on a major scientific problem. Whatever the circumstances or level of complexity, scientists are likely to work from some common assumptions, have some common goals, and use some common procedures. When scientists inquire, they

- ask questions about objects, events, and systems;
- employ simple equipment and tools to make observations and measurements to obtain data and seek evidence;
- use accepted scientific concepts and principles to develop tentative explanations that make sense of collected evidence;
- make predictions to test explanations;
- blend logic and imagination;
- identify and avoid bias; and
- reach conclusions or *not* (American Association for the Advancement of Science (1993); Rutherford & Ahlgren, 1990, pp. 5–9; National Research Council, 1996, pp. 122–123).

Although what scientists do is a model for science instruction, because of developmental differences children may not be able to engage in inquiry as scientists do in professional communities. Thus, elementary and middle school science instruction occurs in a simplified form that enables children to participate with understanding (Lee, 2002).

The key ingredient in accommodating scientific inquiry to the level of children is the teacher, who plans, prepares, poses, presents, hints, prompts, questions, informs, guides, directs, scaffolds, tells, and explains—all in the context of children's hands-on engagement with the objects, organisms, and activities of the real world.

Phases of Inquiry Instruction

Inquiry instruction can be thought of in terms of five main components or tasks: *engage, explore, explain, elaborate,* and *evaluate.* You may recognize these five instructional phases as the components of the 5-E model of instruction. The roles of the teacher and the students are quite different in the 5-E model and the traditional textbook-oriented approach to science. See Tables I-1 and I-2 to identify these roles.

Engagement

Inquiry is initiated at the engagement phase. In this phase, teachers probe prior knowledge and conceptions (and misconceptions) of learners and generate a question to be investigated. Ideally, inquiry in the classroom should begin with authentic questions developed by students from their own experiences with objects, organisms, and events in the environment (American Association for the Advancement of Science, 1993, pp. 9–12). In classroom practice, teachers have to be prepared to provide guidance in forming initiating questions. Students learn from teachers how to ask good questions. Teachers can maintain the spirit of inquiry by focusing on questions that can be answered by collecting observational data, using available knowledge of science, and applying processes of reasoning (National Research Council, 1996, p. 189).

TABLE I-1   APPLYING THE 5-E INSTRUCTIONAL MODEL

Stage of the Instructional Model	What the TEACHER does	
	that is consistent with this model	that is inconsistent with this model
Engage	• Creates interest • Generates curiosity • Raises questions • Elicits responses that uncover what the students know or think about the concept/topic	• Explains concepts • Provides definitions and answers • States conclusions • Provides closure • Lectures
Explore	• Encourages students to work together without direct instruction from the teacher • Observes and listens to students as they interact • Asks probing questions to redirect students' investigations when necessary • Provides time for students to puzzle through problems • Acts as a consultant for students	• Provides answers • Tells or explains how to work through the problem • Provides closure • Tells students that they are wrong • Gives information or facts that solve the problem • Leads students step by step to a solution
Explain	• Encourages students to explain concepts and definitions in their own words • Asks for justification (evidence) and clarification from students • Formally provides definitions, explanations, and new labels • Uses students' previous experiences as the basis for explaining concepts	• Accepts explanations that have no justification • Neglects to solicit students' explanations • Introduces unrelated concepts or skills
Elaborate	• Expects students to use formal labels, definitions, and explanations provided previously • Encourages students to apply or extend the concepts and skills in new situations • Reminds students of alternative explanations • Refers students to existing data and evidence and asks: "What do you already know?" "Why do you think . . .?" (Strategies from Explore apply here also.)	• Provides definitive answers • Tells students that they are wrong • Lectures • Leads students step by step to a solution • Explains how to work through the problem
Evaluate	• Observes students as they apply new concepts and skills • Assesses students' knowledge and/or skills • Looks for evidence that students have changed their thinking or behaviors • Allows students to assess their own learning and group-process skills • Asks open-ended question, such as: "Why do you think . . .?", "What evidence do you have?", "What do you know about x?", "How would you explain x?"	• Tests vocabulary words, terms, and isolated facts • Introduces new ideas or concepts • Creates ambiguity • Promotes open-ended discussion unrelated to the concept or skill

Source: Teaching Secondary School Science, 7th ed., (p. 249), by Leslie Trowbridge and Rodger Bybee, © 2000, Merrill/Prentice Hall, Inc. Reprinted by permission of Pearson Education, Inc. Upper Saddle River, NJ.

TABLE I-2   APPLYING THE 5-E INSTRUCTIONAL MODEL

Stage of the Instructional Model	What the STUDENT does	
	that is consistent with this model	that is inconsistent with this model
Engage	• Asks questions, such as: "Why did this happen?", "What do I already know about this?", "What can I find out about this?" • Shows interest in the topic	• Asks for the "right" answer • Offers the "right" answer • Insists on answers or explanations • Seeks one solution
Explore	• Thinks freely, but within the limits of the activity • Tests predictions and hypotheses • Forms new predictions and hypotheses • Tries alternatives and discusses them with others • Records observations and ideas • Suspends judgment	• Lets others do the thinking and exploring (passive involvement) • Works quietly with little or no interaction with others (only appropriate when exploring ideas or feelings) • Plays around indiscriminately with no goal in mind • Stops with one solution
Explain	• Explains possible solutions or answers to others • Listens critically to one another's explanations • Questions one another's explanations • Listens to and tries to comprehend explanations offered by the teacher • Refers to previous activities • Uses recorded observations in explanations	• Proposes explanations from thin air with no relationship to previous experiences • Brings up irrelevant experiences and examples • Accepts explanations without justification • Does not attend to other plausible explanations
Elaborate	• Applies new labels, definitions, explanations, and skills in new, but similar, situations • Uses previous information to ask questions, propose solutions, make decisions, design experiments • Draws reasonable conclusions from evidence • Records observations and explanations • Checks for understanding among peers	• Plays around with no goal in mind • Ignores previous information or evidence • Draws conclusions from thin air • Uses in discussions only those labels that the teacher provided
Evaluate	• Answers open-ended questions by using observations, evidence, and previously accepted explanations • Demonstrates an understanding or knowledge of the concept or skill • Evaluates his or her own progress and knowledge • Asks related questions that would encourage future investigations	• Draws conclusions, not using evidence or previously accepted explanations • Offers only yes-or-no answers, memorized definitions, or explanations as answers • Fails to express satisfactory explanations in his or her own words • Introduces new, irrelevant topics

Source: *Teaching Secondary School Science*, 7th ed., (p. 248), by Leslie Trowbridge and Rodger Bybee, © 2000, Merrill/Prentice Hall, Inc. Reprinted by permission of Pearson Education, Inc. Upper Saddle River, NJ.

Exploration

The essence of science is to use whatever methods fit to gather evidence that can be used in making sense of the natural world. There are various types of investigations for scientists and children to use in doing science. Different types of questions call for different forms of investigation.

In the early grades, investigations are largely based on systematic description and classification of material objects and organisms (Lowery, 1997), such as we have seen in the terrarium lessons. Young children's natural curiosity motivates them to explore the world by manipulating and observing, comparing and contrasting, and sorting simple objects in their environment.

By grade 4 or 5, children begin to engage in experimental inquiry—posing questions, collecting information through experiments, and arriving at logical conclusions. Controlled experiments or fair tests can be very important parts of experimental investigations, especially in the upper elementary and middle grades. In controlled investigations, students manipulate one variable at a time, determine its effect on a responding variable, and control all other relevant variables. Carefully guided variations of experiments might also be introduced at earlier grades.

As students engage in these inquiry activities, they develop simple skills such as how to observe, measure, cut, connect, switch, pour, tie, hold, and hook. Beginning with simple instruments, they learn to use rulers, thermometers, watches, spring scales, and balance beams to measure important variables. Students learn to use magnifying lenses and microscopes to see finer details of objects and organisms. They may also begin to use computers and calculators in investigations (National Research Council, 2000).

Explanation

This phase of inquiry involves the interpretation of collected data. To interpret is to go beyond the data given and to construct inferences, make predictions, and build explanations that make sense of the world. Interpretations use reasoning processes to coordinate scientific knowledge and observational evidence to answer initiating questions.

In children's inquiry, teachers should refrain as much as possible from supplying information and providing explanations that children could attain on their own. Nevertheless, it is often necessary for teachers to directly teach terms and concepts, experimental procedures, and scientific principles. Although inquiry teachers may use expository methods to teach principles, the instruction always builds on children's recent activities, and what is learned is applied to new situations to assist the students in comprehending it.

Elaboration

If understanding is to be a result of inquiry, students must have opportunities to apply their new knowledge to new issues and problems (Bransford, Brown, & Cocking, 1999). In the elaboration phase, students identify additional questions to investigate, collect pertinent evidence, and connect their newly constructed knowledge to the evidence through such processes as classifying, relating, inferring, predicting, and explaining. Students communicate their investigations to one another and critique and analyze their work and the work of others. By applying their new knowledge in investigating new situations, students continually build understanding.

Evaluation

Evaluation in inquiry teaching involves use of assessment data to discover what students are learning (or not learning) and to provide feedback to modify lesson plans and teaching methods where needed. Continuous assessment through asking key questions, observing and judging the performances and products of students, and administering assessment tasks of various designs will help you probe your students' understanding, consider how misconceptions and alternative theories are affecting their learning, and determine how they are able to apply what they know in new situations.

Student participation is a key component of successful assessment and evaluation systems. If students are to participate successfully, they need to be clear about the objectives and criteria for good work, assess their own efforts in light of the criteria, and share responsibility in making judgments and taking action (Atkin, Black, & Coffey, 2001).

Teaching science as inquiry is especially compatible with a new type of assessment, called *performance assessment*. Performance assessment techniques make it possible to gather data on the processes of learning rather than just the outcomes, and to assess *how* students know rather than merely what they know. Performance assessments are often embedded in daily instruction, rather than administered at the end of the week or after a series of lessons.

All performance assessment tasks have a performance that can be observed or a work product that can be examined. Student performances might include measuring, observing, collecting and organizing data, constructing a graph, making a visual or audio presentation, participating in group discussion, presenting an oral defense of work, or presenting a how-to explanation of a procedure. Products presented for assessment could include data tables, graphs, models, reports, and oral or written explanations and problem solutions. Detailed scoring guides, such as checklists and rubrics, are developed and used with performance tasks to judge performance.

Characteristics of Inquiry Classrooms

At every step of inquiry instruction, learning takes place within classrooms characterized by student discourse, cooperative group activities, and teacher scaffolding.

Discourse

Children love to talk about their experiences. Inquiry science provides a rich context in which to develop language and thought (Rowe, 1973). Confronted with puzzling phenomena, and given some freedom to investigate, children work hard at expressing their experiences in language.

Just as communication among scientists is central in the construction of scientific knowledge, students learn by talking among themselves and writing about and formally presenting their ideas. Oral and written discourse focuses the attention of students on *what* they know, *how* they know it, and *how* their knowledge connects to the knowledge of other people, to other subjects, and to the world beyond the classroom (National Research Council, 1996, p. 36).

Teachers make students' ideas more meaningful by commenting and elaborating on them and asking students to clarify, expand, and justify their own emerging conceptions and those of others. Conversational partnerships with the teacher allow students to build on and use the teacher's thinking processes to support their own efforts to think in more flexible and mature ways.

Cooperative learning groups play a vital role in the learning community.

Cooperative Groups

Glenn T. Seaborg, 1951 Nobel Prize winner in chemistry and the principal investigator for GEMS (Great Explorations in Math and Science) at the Lawrence Hall of Science, reminds us that cooperation is the norm in science:

The PALS (Performance Assessment Links in Science) Website has collected many excellent performance assessment examples from the World Wide Web. Peruse the site at http://pals.sri.com/index.html.

In the case of all great "discoveries" it must be remembered that science is a group process. When we devise experiments and research today, we do so on the basis of an enormous body of knowledge contributed by people from all over the world over thousands of years. . . . Research effort is above all a team effort. (Seaborg, 1991)

In the context of inquiry instruction, cooperative learning is an important process that asks students to work together and support one another's learning. It entails students working collaboratively in small groups to

- consider a problem or assignment together;
- share limited supplies and science equipment;
- verbalize what they know and what they want to find out;
- plan investigations;
- collect and compare the data;
- consider the multiple viewpoints of group members; and
- propose group solutions to the problem.

Setting Up Cooperative Learning Groups (CLGs). Initially, you should assign students to teams because they tend to gravitate to friends only. For primary grade students, or older students who have not worked previously in CLGs, it is best to start with two students. As students acquire basic cooperative group skills, combine two groups of two as a working team. Generally, CLG teams of three or four are recommended once your classroom is comfortable and knowledgeable about the process.

When you form groups you will want to integrate students with various abilities, disabilities, and cultural backgrounds. Once you have established a cooperative group routine, keep teams together for at least 3 to 6 weeks so teammates have time to learn to work with each other. As a team builder, let each team choose its own name. After 3 to 6 weeks, change team membership, so students get to work with other students and learn the differences in team dynamics.

CLG Job Functions and Assignments. A specific job is assigned to each CLG team member. The names and functions are quite similar in all CLGs. The following are from Robert Jones's (1990) *Inquiry Task Group Management System:*

- *Principal investigator.* In charge of team operations including checking assignments, seeing that all team members can participate in activities, and leading group discussions. The principal investigator is also the one group member who communicates with the teacher when questions arise. This enables a more orderly atmosphere and limits the number of questions the teacher must respond to. Often groups can solve their own problems without consulting the teacher.
- *Materials manager.* Gets, inventories, and distributes materials to the team.
- *Recorder/reporter.* Collects and records data on lab sheets and reports results to whole class orally or in writing on class summary chart posted on chalkboard.
- *Maintenance director.* With the assistance of other team members, cleans up and returns materials and equipment to their appropriate storage space or container. Directs the disposal of used materials and is responsible for team members' safety.

An alternative set of cooperative group roles used in FOSS (Full Option Science System) activities is shown in Figure I-1.

CLG Job Badges. To enable easy identification of team members' jobs and responsibilities, students should wear job badges (see examples in Figures I-2 and I-3). Job badges will make it easier for students to remember their responsibilities and for you to spot students

Figure I-1 Cooperative group roles for FOSS (Full Option Science System) science activities.

- **Getters.** There are two Getters for each group. One (Getter 1) gets equipment from the materials station and the other (Getter 2) returns it.

- **Starter.** One person is the Starter for each task. This person makes sure that everyone gets a turn and that everyone has a chance to contribute ideas to the investigation.

- **Reporter.** The Reporter is the person who makes sure that everyone has recorded information on student sheets or in science journals. This is also the person who reports group data to the class or records it on the board or class chart.

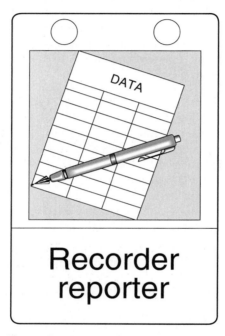

Figure I-2 Cooperative learning group (CLG) job badge.
Source: Reprinted by permission from Robert M. Jones, *Teaming Up! The Inquiry Task Group Management System User's Guide.* LaPorte, TX: ITGROUP, December 1990, 55.

Figure I-3 Cooperative learning group (CLG) job badge.
Source: Reprinted by permission from Robert M. Jones, *Teaming Up! The Inquiry Task Group Management System User's Guide.* LaPorte, TX: ITGROUP, December 1990, 43.

who should not be straying away from their group's space. Younger students will especially enjoy displaying an ID badge. As students get older, they may be reticent about wearing badges unless there is a level of sophistication to their design. You may liken the students' badges to the security badges that adults often wear in the workplace.

Scaffolding

In *scaffolding* student learning, the teacher supplies enough external support for students to be successful with the various inquiry tasks. The teacher might help learners at various steps in the inquiry process as they formulate the focus question for an investigation, plan and carry out procedures for data collection, and make sense of the data and answer the question posed. The younger the children and the less experience they have with scientific inquiry, the more scaffolding assistance they will probably need and the more structured the inquiry lessons will need to be.

To scaffold the learning process for students, teachers can (Grigorenko, 1998; Roehler & Cantlon, 1997) consider these types of assistance:

- start by making the learning task one that is challenging and interesting with an appropriate degree of novelty;
- if necessary, simplify the task so that the learner can manage it;
- facilitate student talk in small group and large group settings;
- ask meaningful questions at just the right time;
- lead students to clarify, elaborate, or justify their responses;
- supply necessary information or direct learners to appropriate sources;
- provide cues, prompts, and even direct instruction on needed concepts and principles;
- provide models of thinking processes; and
- provide external support, such as diagrams and concept maps, to aid students in making difficult connections.

An important task in the art of teaching is to know when to scaffold a student's learning and when to allow it to take its own course. Just as scaffolds in a building project are designed to be taken down when the building walls are strong, scaffolding support in teaching should be gradually removed or "faded" (Ormrod, 1999) as students develop science knowledge and inquiry processes. In the long run, students should develop their own self-regulated strategies to guide learning.

Planning for Inquiry Instruction

Thoughtful planning and organization is needed to prepare meaningful inquiry lessons. The science content you focus on will probably be dictated by your local or state curriculum guidelines. These guidelines will likely reflect the *National Science Education Standards*. That means that science content includes not only science knowledge but also essential inquiry skills and an understanding of the nature of science itself.

Once you have determined concepts and principles to be learned, find a series of activities, such as those in this book, that support investigations involving the science principles and concepts you want your students to understand. Be sure students have opportunities to experience, investigate, and think about phenomena so that they can begin to understand how science principles work in the world in which they live. Your lessons should enable students to learn how to form questions, design and conduct investigations, and use collected data and developing knowledge to answer the questions posed.

Getting Started with Inquiry Science

Now that you have selected lesson activities for students, how do you get started using inquiry in your science classroom? Here are some suggestions:

Step 1: Preparation. Prepare the inquiry activity for whole class or small group work.

- Arrange classroom furniture to facilitate inquiry and avoid excessive noise, movement, or confusion. Consider the furniture configuration illustrated in Figure I-4.
- Organize students into cooperative groups.
- Organize materials needed by teams in small boxes or bags, or on trays.

Figure I-4 Furniture arrangement for inquiry science.

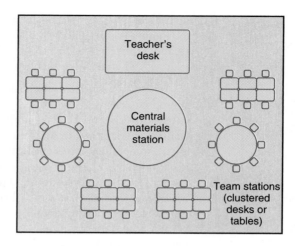

- Try out activities before they are introduced to students. By trying out activities beforehand, you can anticipate questions and ensure that the activity will work. Finding out in the middle of a lesson that you do not have enough materials or you cannot get the equipment to work properly can discourage you or your students.

Step 2: Engagement. Present an initiating activity designed to engage the students in pursuing the learning objectives.

- Keep the activity brief and open-ended.
- Ask or help the students ask specific key questions about the initiating activity.
- Ask questions to find out students' prior knowledge and conceptions or misconceptions.
- Tell students they will be exploring this and other related questions.
- Review general and specific safety procedures with students (see Figure I-5).
- Introduce or review pertinent activity information and cooperative group procedures such as, "When we begin, move quickly and quietly into your team. Stay with your team at all times. Speak softly, listen and respond to one another, and take turns. Concentrate on your assigned job."

Step 3: Distribution of Science Materials. Do not begin distributing materials until all of step 2 is completed. Then, have all the materials managers collect science materials from the central materials station and deliver them to each team station. This step can make or break the best-planned activity. Make certain that materials managers are reliable and know the specifics of their jobs before they begin!

Step 4: Exploration.

- As each team begins its work, move from team to team to ensure the proper distribution of materials has occurred and that teams have necessary materials and are proceeding safely.
- Be careful that you do not give away the "answer" during the exploration phase. Tell students very little about what can be expected to happen. You want students to make observations, discuss what they observe, and have a chance to make predictions or inferences from their observations. Otherwise, they are likely to discover exactly what you have told them they will discover. Part of the joy of exploring is not knowing what to expect!

1. Make certain you have the necessary science equipment and supplies in sufficient amounts to allow your students to participate in the lab activity. Have materials at a central workstation already set up with an adequate number of science materials and equipment for individual or group use.
2. Perform initial steps like boiling water, heating or cooling materials, and double-checking supplies before an activity begins.
3. If any chemicals are used, even diluted vinegar, make sure students wash up immediately following the activity.
4. Whenever possible, substitute plastics for all glassware. However, be certain when using heat that the plastics are able to withstand high temperatures. Whenever students use plastic bags, make sure the bags are too small to fit over their heads.
5. Avoid open flames in the classroom except under absolute necessity. Check your local school policies because the use of open flames in classrooms may be forbidden. Open flames should not be used in primary grade classrooms. Students should NEVER be allowed to use an open flame in any classroom activity. Candles and matches or a Bunsen burner should be used in teacher demonstrations only. If you must use an open flame, be sure a fire extinguisher is available and give instructions for its use.
6. Avoid the use of materials in your classroom that could cause serious damage to classroom facilities such as plaster of paris. Flushing excess plaster of paris powder down a sink drain can cause it to harden in the pipes. Check local guidelines before using any science materials to ensure you are aware of school policies regarding their use.
7. Avoid completely the use of electrical house current (110 volts) for student activities. Use dry cell batteries with students who are handling electrical equipment directly.
8. Assemble glass tubing and stoppers yourself and preferably before class. If possible and convenient, store glass tubing and connecting stoppers rather than disassembling and reassembling each time you need them.

Figure I-5 Guidelines for activity preparation and safety (additional safety suggestions are listed in Appendix G).

- Hold off on presenting science vocabulary. Do not give students the vocabulary words that will describe what they observe *before* they do the activity. Let students engage in the inquiry and experience the phenomena they observe. It is after exploration that science vocabulary will have more meaning for students.

Step 5: Explanation and Discussion of Results.

- Instruct reporter/recorders to post team results on a class summary chart visible to all. Conduct a discussion of the posted results. Then ask for students' conceptions of ideas and skills learned and discuss the similarities and discrepancies of team data.
- As students exchange their ideas, listen to how they have conceptualized what they think. Often, they will have developed erroneous beliefs about how something "works." Misconceptions are difficult to change. Simply pointing out alternative and naive conceptions will not generally change what students believe. There are several strategies you can employ to help students confront and reconsider their alternative conceptions:
  a. Ask questions that challenge students' current beliefs.
  b. Present phenomena that students cannot adequately explain within their existing perspectives.
  c. Engage students in discussions of the pros and cons of various explanations.
  d. Point out, explicitly, the differences between students' beliefs and "reality."
  e. Show how the correct explanation of an event or phenomenon is more plausible or makes more sense than anything students themselves can offer (Ormrod, 1999; Roth & Anderson, 1988).

- Although the child must do the interpretation work, teachers must be ready to assist in the process. During the explanation phase of inquiry, it is appropriate for teachers to supply vocabulary terms, invent relevant concepts and principles, and give hints and even complete explanations to children. But always follow this principle: Tell only after student inquiry.

Step 6: Elaboration. Suggest questions and activities that allow students to apply what they have learned to new and novel situations. Principal investigators then lead their teams in inquiring into the new questions. Follow up with appropriate class discussion. Also, have students extend their learning with readings, worksheets, Internet research, or other individualized reinforcement of concepts and principles being learned.

Step 7: Evaluation. Vary your methods for assessing understanding of individual team members and the group as a whole. Performance tasks and traditional assessment items could be used. Assess student understanding in every phase of your inquiry teaching. For example, determine:

- What information do students know about an activity before they begin exploration? What facts, concepts, and principles are mentioned?
- How well are students able to use the materials provided for the exploration activities? Do they discuss their observations? Are students able to provide reasons for their observations? Do they relate their observations to the initiating questions?
- Do students use their data to make predictions? How well were students able to provide reasons for their predictions? Are the reasons plausible?
- Are students providing plausible explanations for their observations? Are the students' reasons becoming more detailed? Do students provide more than one reason for their explanations?

Step 8: Team Cleanup. Maintenance directors, with the assistance of team members, arrange materials so they can be easily reused, return all supplies to designated areas, and ensure that work areas are cleaned. Note that cleanup is a team effort.

Using the Science Activities in This Book

The activities in this book are set within the context of specific **National Science Education Standards. Objectives** are given to provide specific focus for instruction, learning, and assessment, and to help tie the inquiry activities to the standards. **NSES Concepts and Processes** related to the *Science Standards* are also given. **Materials** needed for the lesson are specified, and a series of **activities** with an implied sequence is provided. The activities are keyed to specific phases of the **5-E Model.**

The science activities in the book focus on children raising questions about and exploring the natural world, learning concepts and principles and using them with observational evidence to make sense of natural phenomena, and developing inquiry procedures and abilities. The activities represent a bank of resources to use in developing your own inquiry lessons.

The activities are intended to be used flexibly as you design inquiry lessons. Feel free to add or subtract from them. Some activities are conducive for cooperative groups and some for teacher demonstrations. Activities that might be better done as teacher demonstrations are so marked.

The most important element in these inquiry activities is that students can discover the joy and wonder of science. And so can you. Have fun!

Many exciting science programs for children have been developed across the years (see Appendix K). Type acronyms such as FOSS, GLOBE, GEMS, AIMS, STC, and BSCS into a search engine such as Google to identify sources from groups that have long been recognized for their outstanding contributions to science education. You will find a variety of relevant and motivating activities for your classroom use.

REFERENCES

American Association for the Advancement of Science. (1993). *Benchmarks for science literacy.* New York: Oxford University Press.

Atkin, J. M., Black, P., & Coffey, J. (Eds.). (2001). *Classroom assessment and the national science education standards.* Washington, DC: National Academy Press.

Bransford, J. D., Brown, A. L., & Cocking, R. R. (Eds.). (1999). *How people learn: Brain, mind, experience, and school.* Washington, DC: National Academy Press.

Grigorenko, E. L. (1998). Mastering tools of the mind in school (Trying out Vygotsky's ideas in classrooms). In R. J. Sternberg & W. M. Williams (Eds.), *Intelligence, instruction, and assessment.* Mahwah, NJ: Erlbaum.

Hosoume, K., & Barber, J. (1994). *Terrarium habitats.* Berkeley: Great Explorations in Math and Science (GEMS), Lawrence Hall of Science, University of California.

Ingram, M. (1993). *Bottle biology.* Madison: Bottle Biology Project, Department of Plant Pathology, College of Agricultural and Life Sciences, University of Wisconsin.

Jones, R. M. (1990, December). *Teaming up! The inquiry task group management system user's guide.* LaPorte, TX: ITGROUP.

Lee, O. (2002). Promoting scientific inquiry with elementary students from diverse cultures and languages. In W. C. Secada (Ed.), *Review of research in education* (Vol. 26, pp. 23–69). Washington, DC: American Education Research Association.

Lowery, L. F. (Ed.). (1997). *Pathways to the science standards: Elementary school edition.* Arlington, VA: National Science Teachers Association.

National Research Council. (1996). *National science education standards.* Washington, DC: National Academy Press.

National Research Council. (2000). *Inquiry and the national science education standards: A guide for teaching and learning.* Washington DC: National Academies Press.

Ormrod, J. (1999). *Human learning.* Upper Saddle River, NJ: Merrill/Prentice Hall.

Roehler, L. R., & Cantlon, D. J. (1997). Scaffolding: A powerful tool in social constructivist classrooms. In K. Hogan & M. Pressley (Eds.), *Scaffolding student learning: Instructional approaches and issues.* Cambridge, MA: Brookline Books.

Roth, K., & Anderson, C. (1988). Promoting conceptual change learning from science textbooks. In P. Ramsden (Ed.), *Improving learning: New perspectives.* London: Kogan Page.

Rowe, M. B. (1973). *Teaching science as continuous inquiry.* New York: McGraw-Hill.

Rutherford, F. J., & Ahlgren, A. (1990). *Science for all Americans.* New York: Oxford University Press.

Seaborg, G. T. (1991, Fall/Winter). Some thoughts on discovery. *GEMS Network News.* Berkeley: Lawrence Hall of Science, University of California, p. 5.

Trowbridge, L., & Bybee, R. (2000). *Teaching secondary school science* (7th ed.). Upper Saddle River, NJ: Merrill/Prentice Hall.

SECTION II
Physical Science Activities

Based on the *National Science Education Standards*, this section presents physical science activities that involve the investigation of matter, forces, sound, heat, light, magnetism, and electricity. Through engaging in these activities, children develop a better understanding of how the physical world works. At the same time, they develop their abilities to inquire—to ask questions about the world around them, to investigate and gather data, and to use their observations as evidence to construct reasonable explanations for the questions posed.

Each activity in the section is organized according to the 5-E model of instruction, which draws on the *Science as Inquiry Standards* (see box). In following the 5-E approach to instruction, teachers guide students to:

Engage. Ask a question to initiate inquiry about objects, organisms, and events in the natural world.

Explore. Plan and conduct simple investigations to collect relevant data.

Explain. Use data to construct knowledge and generate interpretations, including descriptions, classifications, predictions, and explanations, that make sense of the world and answer their questions.

Elaborate. Investigate new problems and questions to extend concepts and principles.

Evaluate. Demonstrate knowledge, understanding, and ability to use inquiry strategies through formal and informal assessments.

Although the activities in this section may be used individually, most of them are arranged sequentially to provide a comprehensive view of the phenomena, concepts, and principles of each topic.

I. PROPERTIES OF MATTER

The simple activities on properties of matter included here enable children to exercise their natural curiosity as they manipulate, observe, and classify common objects and materials in their environment and continue to form explanations of the world. Consistent with the *National Science Education Standards*, topics studied include properties of material objects, and the nature of solids, liquids, and gases (air).

A. PROPERTIES OF MATERIAL OBJECTS

▶ *Science Background*

All material objects may be described by their unique properties. By dynamically investigating properties of different objects, children can function much as research scientists do. They will learn to question, observe, classify, design and perform experiments, collect and analyze data, explain, and test explanations. In the process, they will begin to acquire a level of understanding of the world compatible with their own levels of development.

NSES **Science Standards**

All students should develop an understanding of

- properties of objects and materials (K–4).
- changes of properties in matter (5–8).

Objectives for Students

1. Define *property* as a characteristic of an object—something you can see, touch, hear, smell, or taste.
2. Use simple equipment and tools that extend the senses to gather data about properties of objects and materials.
3. Develop descriptions and classifications of objects according to their properties.
4. Use description and classification to identify the most significant properties of buttons and how different properties of buttons might be related.

NSES **Concepts and Principles**

Activities I and 2 address these fundamental concepts and principles related to the *Science Standards*:

- Objects have many observable properties (K–4).
- Objects are made of one or more materials (K–4).
- Properties can be used to separate or sort a group of objects or materials (K–4).

---

1. HOW ARE BUTTONS ALIKE AND DIFFERENT? (K–2)

Materials

For each group:

- Collection of 20 to 30 buttons differing in many ways, including color, shape, number of holes, and material from which they are made
- One small tray to hold buttons or other objects to be observed and grouped

Safety Precautions

Caution the students not to put the buttons or other small objects in their mouths, ears, nostrils, or eyes.

ENGAGE: ASK A QUESTION ABOUT OBJECTS, ORGANISMS, OR EVENTS IN THE ENVIRONMENT.

a. With the children in a large group, hold up an object, such as a ball. Ask: *What can you tell me about this object? Yes, it is a ball, but what else can you tell me about it? What is its shape, its color, its texture?*

Discuss with children the various words that can be used to describe the object. Tell the children that, in science, the term *property* means the characteristics of objects—things you can observe with your senses or with instruments like magnifying lenses and stethoscopes that extend your senses. Discuss other uses of the word *property* with the children.

EXPLORE: PLAN AND CONDUCT SIMPLE INVESTIGATIONS TO COLLECT RELEVANT DATA.

b. Organize children into cooperative groups. Give each small group of children about 20 different buttons on a tray.

Ask: *How many properties of these buttons can you name? What do we have to do to discover the properties of an object?*

Tell children to observe the buttons and describe them to one another. Using a gamelike format similar to "I Spy," allow each child to describe a button in sufficient detail (without touching it or otherwise designating it) for the other children in the small group to pick it out. Characteristics to be described might include the button's color, its shape, its texture, the material it is made from, the number of holes it has, and other properties.

EXPLAIN: USE DATA TO GENERATE INTERPRETATIONS, INCLUDING DESCRIPTIONS, CLASSIFICATIONS, AND EXPLANATIONS.

c. Gather children as a whole class and ask: *What are the properties of the buttons you have observed?*

On the board, make a list of each of the properties identified by the children.[1]

2. WHAT ARE SOME DIFFERENT WAYS YOU CAN GROUP BUTTONS? (K–2)

Materials

Button collections
Button bingo cards
Collection of fabric swatches, samples of wood panels or tiles, or pieces of metal

ENGAGE: ASK A QUESTION ABOUT OBJECTS, ORGANISMS, OR EVENTS IN THE ENVIRONMENT.

a. Ask: *How can you group your buttons? How many different ways can you find to group them?*

EXPLORE: PLAN AND CONDUCT SIMPLE INVESTIGATIONS TO COLLECT RELEVANT DATA.

b. Tell the children to sort their buttons into groups based on the properties of the buttons. For example, children might have collections of red buttons, blue buttons, green buttons, and multicolored buttons.

---

[1]For a delightful introduction to properties of buttons, see *The Button Box* by Margarette S. Reid (illustrated by Sarah Chamberlain), New York: Dutton Children's Books, 1990.

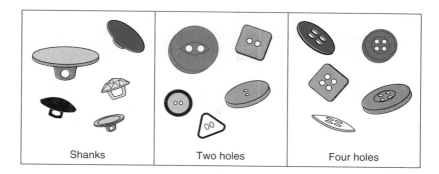

| Shanks | Two holes | Four holes |

As children sort their buttons, circulate among them and ask such questions as: *How are the buttons in this group alike? How are they different from one another?*

c. Show the children how to classify their buttons according to two stages. For example, in the first stage of classification they may get a class of all red buttons. In the second stage of classification, they may group the red buttons into two groups, such as round and not round. Thus, they end up with a group of red buttons that are round and a group of red buttons that are not round.

d. Let two cooperative groups come together. Members of one group should study the button classification system of the other group and guess the basis of the classification.

   Ask: *How did you sort the buttons? How are the buttons in one group alike? How are they different from one another?*

EXPLAIN: USE DATA TO GENERATE INTERPRETATIONS, INCLUDING DESCRIPTIONS, CLASSIFICATIONS, AND EXPLANATIONS.

e. Ask: *What are buttons for? How are buttons used?* Answers might relate to the function of buttons to fasten garments or the ornamental nature of buttons. *What properties of buttons relate to how they work? What properties of buttons relate to their ornamental use?*

   Building on children's observations and descriptions, guide them to suggest and explain that buttons are fasteners. They attach to garments in different ways, and they hold garments together in different ways. Investigating how different buttons are designed to be attached to garments and to hold garments together is a good way to extend the concepts studied.

How could you help children understand what scientists do?

f. Ask: *Why do scientists classify things? What is the purpose of classification?* Through discussion, bring out the advantage that through classification, we can simplify our thinking by dealing with a few groups rather than many individual elements. Also, explain that it is through classification of properties of buttons that we begin to identify their most significant properties. These include how buttons are attached to garments, how they function as fasteners, how they are ornamental, and so on.

ELABORATE: EXTEND CONCEPTS, PRINCIPLES, AND STRATEGIES TO NEW PROBLEMS AND QUESTIONS.

g. Give each group a pile of objects containing fabric swatches, samples of wood paneling or tile (obtained from a decorating store), pieces of metal, and so on. Give each group an envelope with several index cards, each stating a different basis for grouping. A pair of children take a card and group the objects on the basis of the property or properties stated. The other children must guess the basis of the grouping. Use singular properties such as "red" objects, "rough" objects, "metal" objects, or "cloth" objects. Also, place multiple properties on some cards, such as "rough and red." Challenge children to do a multistage classification of the materials based on the two properties.

Additionally, challenge children to create their own cards with their own desired multiple properties and to group materials according to the properties.

h. Prepare several different 9-square (3 by 3) button bingo cards, with button properties named in each square. As in the diagram, include single properties such as red, round, two-holed, wooden, and cloth. Also include some multiple-property squares, such as red and round, or two-holed and plastic.

RED	RED AND ROUND	NOT RED
CLOTH	ROUND	WOODEN
NOT ROUND	TWO HOLES AND PLASTIC	TWO HOLES

SAMPLE BUTTON BINGO CARD

i. Pass a button bingo card facedown to each pair of children. Give each pair several bingo tokens. Draw buttons from a bag of buttons. Call on children to name different properties of each button you draw. Instruct the children that they are to place a token in each square on their cards that contains a property named. Circulate among the children and interact with them about their understanding of the meaning of properties and classification. If you use a competitive group structure, winners might be the children who are able to correctly place three tokens in a row, column, or diagonally, or the children who are able to place the most tokens on their button bingo card. (You may think of other ways to play button bingo to give students additional practice at observing and classifying properties, and recognizing classification systems.)

B. PROPERTIES OF LIQUIDS

▶ *Science Background*

Students can conduct simple investigations with water that can be explained through use of an abstract model. In the model of water developed through the activities in this section, water consists of tiny particles or droplets. These particles of water are attracted to each other. Scientists refer to this force of attraction as *bonding*. For children, water drops are *sticky* or *grabby*.

Because water drops are sticky, water can heap up in a cup much more than first expected. Water at the surface of a filled cup attracts new water drops as they are added to the cup. Eventually, as the water being added heaps up too much, its weight causes it to overcome the stickiness of water and it flows over the edge of the cup.

As they develop new understandings of liquids, students also continue to develop their abilities to inquire.

Science Standards

All students should develop an understanding of

• properties of objects and materials (K–4).
• changes in properties in matter (5–8).

Objectives for Students

1. Use simple apparatus and tools to gather data and extend the senses.
2. Describe the behavior of water and other liquids under various conditions.
3. Use observational evidence and a model of the bonding of liquid particles to explain the behavior of water and other liquids under different conditions.

Concepts and Principles

Activities 1–8 address these fundamental concepts and principles related to the *Science Standards*:

• Materials can exist in different states—solid, liquid, and gas (K–4).
• Objects (such as liquids) have many different properties (K–4).

1. HOW MUCH WATER CAN HEAP UP IN A CUP? (2–4)

Materials

For activities 1–8, supply a kit of the following materials for each group:

- Two 30 ml medicine cups
- Beaker for water
- Magnifying lens
- Two medicine droppers (use identical droppers for the whole class)
- 6-inch squares of aluminum foil, wax paper, and plastic wrap
- 30–45 regular size paper clips

For the teacher:

- Small container of liquid dishwashing soap
- Toothpicks

Safety Precautions

Caution the students not to taste any liquid substances. When children work with water, provide table coverings, such as newspapers, and plenty of paper towels to absorb spills. Clean up spills promptly.

ENGAGE: ASK A QUESTION ABOUT OBJECTS, ORGANISMS, OR EVENTS IN THE ENVIRONMENT.

a. Pouring water from the beaker, students should fill the cup completely full of water until some overflows. When the children's cups seem completely filled, ask: *How many drops of water from a medicine dropper do you think you can add to your filled cup before it overflows?* Tell the children to make a prediction and record it before they carry out the activity.

EXPLORE: PLAN AND CONDUCT SIMPLE INVESTIGATIONS TO COLLECT RELEVANT DATA.

b. Tell your students to hold the medicine dropper about 2 cm above the cup as in the diagram. Slowly drop water into the cup, counting the number of drops needed for the water to overflow. As they count drops, students should observe the shape of the surface of water in the cup and what happens to water drops as they are added to the cup. Instruct them to bend down so that they are eye level with the 30 ml cup when they observe it. Show students how to use a magnifying lens (magnifying glass) to enhance their observations.

Allow reporters for cooperative groups to chart predictions and actual counts on the chalkboard or a transparency. Note and discuss variations in the data. If you think there is too much variation among groups, you might ask the groups to repeat their investigation under more common procedures.

EXPLAIN: USE DATA TO GENERATE INTERPRETATIONS, INCLUDING DESCRIPTIONS, CLASSIFICATIONS, AND EXPLANATIONS.

c. Ask: *How many drops did you add before the water spilled over the edge of the cup? How does your tested result compare with your prediction? How would you describe the shape of the water above the rim of the cup? What happens to each drop of water as it hits the surface of water in the cup? What happens to the last drop added to the cup, the one that makes the water overflow?*

d. Ask: *What is the property of water that makes it tend to heap up in a cup? That is, what keeps the water from overflowing as water drops are added?*

As children discuss possible answers to these questions, begin to develop a mental model of water, with water consisting of particles or drops that are all attracted to one another. Lead children to understand that water heaps up in medicine cups and does not overflow because water particles bond to, stick to, or grab on to one another. This simple model of liquids anticipates and lays a foundation for the introduction of atomic and molecular forces in later grades. If the children mention atoms and molecules of water (H_2O), listen but do not pursue the idea at this time. Rather, continue to focus on the notion that water is made up of tiny droplets that attract one another.

ELABORATE:
INVESTIGATE NEW
PROBLEMS AND QUESTIONS
TO EXTEND CONCEPTS AND
PRINCIPLES.

e. As an extension, ask: *How many drops of water do you think you can place on the surface of a clean penny? Can you add more drops to the head or tail of a penny?*
  Lead children to make and record predictions, and then to design and conduct investigations to answer their questions. Chart the results on the board and discuss the results.

2. HOW MANY PAPER CLIPS CAN YOU ADD TO A CUP OF WATER? (2–4)

ENGAGE: ASK A
QUESTION ABOUT OBJECTS,
ORGANISMS, OR EVENTS IN
THE ENVIRONMENT.

a. Using the beaker, students should fill the 30 ml cup completely full of water again. Ask: *How many paper clips do you think you can add to the water in the cup before it flows over the rim?* Tell the children to make and test a prediction.

EXPLORE: PLAN
AND CONDUCT SIMPLE
INVESTIGATIONS TO
COLLECT RELEVANT DATA.

b. Tell students to gently slide regular-size paper clips one at a time into the water in the cup and count the number of paper clips needed to make the water flow over the rim. Chart results on the board and discuss similarities and differences.

EXPLAIN: USE DATA
TO GENERATE
INTERPRETATIONS,
INCLUDING DESCRIPTIONS,
CLASSIFICATIONS, AND
EXPLANATIONS.

c. Ask: *How do your predictions compare with actual results? Why do you think so many paper clips could be added to the cup before the water overflowed?* Students should explain that the water did not overflow at first because of the attractive forces between water droplets.

How could you help
children understand
what scientists do?

d. As children carry out these investigations of water, occasionally emphasize to them that they are *doing* science and *being* scientists. They are asking questions, gathering evidence, building a model of water drops, and using their model to construct explanations of what they see.

3. CAN YOU GET A PAPER CLIP TO "FLOAT" ON TOP OF WATER? WHY DOES THE PAPER CLIP NOT SINK? (2–4)

ENGAGE: ASK A
QUESTION ABOUT OBJECTS,
ORGANISMS, OR EVENTS IN
THE ENVIRONMENT.

a. Ask: *What can you do to make a paper clip "float" on the surface of water? If you push the paper clip down, will it bob back up?*

EXPLORE: PLAN
AND CONDUCT SIMPLE
INVESTIGATIONS TO
COLLECT RELEVANT DATA.

b. Allow students to try to make a paper clip stay on the top of water in a medicine cup or glass. To accomplish this task, bend a second paper clip so that a cradle is formed (see diagram). Place the other paper clip on the cradle and lower it into the water as in the diagram. The paper clip should stay suspended on top of the water.

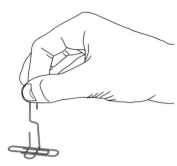

Use wire cradle to place another
paper clip on water.

EXPLAIN: USE DATA
AND SCIENCE KNOWLEDGE
TO GENERATE
INTERPRETATIONS,
INCLUDING DESCRIPTIONS,
CLASSIFICATIONS, AND
EXPLANATIONS.

Ask: *Why does the paper clip stay suspended on the top of the water? Is the paper clip floating?* Tell students that to explain why the paper clip "floated," we must connect observations to our model of water. Lead students to understand that because of the attractive forces among water drops, the surface of the water acts like a skin. The paper clip does not float in the water, like boats do, but is supported by water's skinlike effect. The paper clip rides on the top of the water's skin. If you push the paper clip down in the water, it breaks the skin and goes to the bottom of the container and will not bob back up. Scientists refer to the skinlike effect of water as *surface tension*.

ELABORATE:
INVESTIGATE NEW
PROBLEMS AND QUESTIONS
TO EXTEND CONCEPTS AND
PRINCIPLES.

c. Ask: *How do some bugs walk on water?* Explain that similar to the paper clip, a water strider is able to walk on the "skin" at the surface of the water.

4. WHAT DOES SOAP DO TO THE SKINLIKE EFFECT OF WATER? (2–4)

ENGAGE: ASK A
QUESTION ABOUT OBJECTS,
ORGANISMS, OR EVENTS IN
THE ENVIRONMENT.

a. Ask: *How can we break or overcome the skinlike effect of water?*

EXPLORE: PLAN
AND CONDUCT SIMPLE
INVESTIGATIONS TO
COLLECT RELEVANT DATA.

b. Tell students to use a beaker to fill the 30 ml cup completely full of water again. Tell them to add drops of water to the cup until it is about ready to flow over the rim. Take two toothpicks. Dip one of the toothpicks in a container of liquid dishwashing soap. Go from group to group, touching the end of the clean toothpick and then the soapy end of the other toothpick to the surface of the water in the cups.

EXPLAIN: USE DATA
TO GENERATE
INTERPRETATIONS,
INCLUDING DESCRIPTIONS,
CLASSIFICATIONS,
PREDICTIONS, AND
EXPLANATIONS.

c. Ask: *What did you see happen?* (The water flowed over the rim of the cup.) *What do you think was on the second toothpick? Why do you think the water flowed over the rim of the cup when it was touched with the soapy toothpick? Why did we use two toothpicks, a clean one and a soapy one?* (This is a controlled experiment. Using two toothpicks, a clean one and a soapy one, shows that it was not the toothpick, but what was on it that caused the water to overflow.)

d. Through discussion, lead the students to apply the model of water drops, adding the idea that soap tends to break the bonds that water drops have for one another. When the bonds are broken, the weight of the water allows it to flow over the rim of the cup.

5. WHAT HAPPENS TO WATER DROPS ON DIFFERENT SURFACES? (2–4)

ENGAGE: ASK A QUESTION ABOUT OBJECTS, ORGANISMS, OR EVENTS IN THE ENVIRONMENT.

a. Ask: *Do water drops look and act the same on different kinds of surfaces? How could we investigate to find out?*

EXPLORE: PLAN AND CONDUCT SIMPLE INVESTIGATIONS TO COLLECT RELEVANT DATA.

b. Provide each group small squares (about 15 cm by 15 cm) of wax paper, aluminum foil, and plastic wrap. Tell students to use a medicine dropper to place three or four drops of water on the wax paper. Ask: *How would you describe the shape of the water drops?*

c. Tell students to push the drops of water around with a pencil point. Ask: *What happens to the drop when you push on it with a pencil point? What happens when you push several drops near each other?*

d. Tell them to investigate and compare what water drops look like and what they do on each of the three surfaces—wax paper, aluminum foil, and plastic wrap (see diagram). Provide magnifying lenses to enhance student observations.

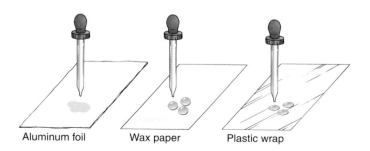

Aluminum foil　　Wax paper　　Plastic wrap

Ask: *What is the smallest size drop you can make? What is the largest size drop you can make? On which of the three surfaces does water heap up the most? spread out the most? What is the shape of water drops on wax paper? on aluminum foil? on plastic wrap?*

EXPLAIN: USE DATA AND SCIENTIFIC KNOWLEDGE TO GENERATE INTERPRETATIONS, INCLUDING DESCRIPTIONS, CLASSIFICATIONS, AND EXPLANATIONS.

e. Ask: *Why do you think the drops were heaped up on wax paper and spread out on aluminum foil?*

Using *evidence* from the children's investigations, invent (directly teach) the terms *cohesion* and *adhesion*. The bonding of a material to the same kind of material is known as **cohesion.** Water drops cohere to one another. The attraction of one material for another material is called **adhesion.** Adhesive tape bonds to different kinds of material, such as skin. Add the notions of cohesion and adhesion to the model of water drops bonding to one another.

Help children understand that the adhesive attraction between water and aluminum foil is greater than the adhesive attraction between water and wax paper. Thus, water drops can bead up more on wax paper because they do not have to overcome a great adhesive force for the surface.

ELABORATE: EXTEND CONCEPTS, PRINCIPLES, AND STRATEGIES TO NEW PROBLEMS AND QUESTIONS.

f. Ask: *Do you think it would be easier to use a toothpick to lead a drop of paper around on wax paper or on aluminum foil? Why do you think so? Try it and see. What differences do you observe for the two surfaces? Why do you think these differences happen?*

Guide children to plan and conduct an investigation and to use their data to answer these questions. With your assistance, children should reason that because there is greater adhesion (greater stickiness) between aluminum foil and water than between wax paper and water, it is harder to lead a drop of water around on aluminum foil than on wax paper. The aluminum foil grabs on to the drop more than the wax paper does.

NSES **Concepts and Principles**

Activity 6 also addresses these fundamental concepts and principles related to the *Science Standards:*

- Forces will cause changes in the speed or direction of an object's motion (5–8).

6. WHEN THE SURFACES ARE SLANTED, WILL WATER DROPS RUN DOWN FASTER ON WAX PAPER, PLASTIC WRAP, OR ALUMINUM FOIL? (3–5)

ENGAGE: ASK A QUESTION ABOUT OBJECTS, ORGANISMS, OR EVENTS IN THE ENVIRONMENT.

a. Ask: *When the surfaces are slanted, on which surface will water drops slide or roll down fastest? What could you do to find out?*

EXPLORE: PLAN AND CONDUCT SIMPLE INVESTIGATIONS TO COLLECT RELEVANT DATA.

b. Help students plan a *controlled experiment (fair test)* to determine on which surface the water drops run down more quickly (see the diagram). They might, for example, control the slant of the surface and vary the type of surface (aluminum foil, plastic wrap, or wax paper).

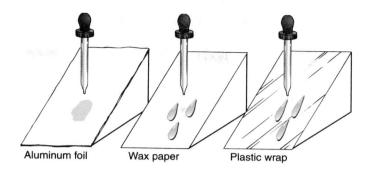

Aluminum foil   Wax paper   Plastic wrap

EXPLAIN: USE DATA TO GENERATE INTERPRETATIONS, INCLUDING DESCRIPTIONS, CLASSIFICATIONS, AND EXPLANATIONS.

c. Ask: *Why do you think the water drops ran more quickly down the wax paper ramp?* With your assistance, children should explain that water drops do not adhere or stick to wax paper as much as they do to aluminum foil and plastic wrap. Thus, the water drops ran down the wax paper ramp more quickly.

7. HOW DO THE COHESIVE AND ADHESIVE BONDS OF DIFFERENT LIQUIDS COMPARE? (2–4)

ENGAGE: ASK A QUESTION ABOUT OBJECTS, ORGANISMS, OR EVENTS IN THE ENVIRONMENT.

a. Ask: *Do water drops and drops of other liquids look and act the same on different surfaces?*

EXPLORE: PLAN AND CONDUCT SIMPLE INVESTIGATIONS TO COLLECT RELEVANT DATA.

b. Using a clean medicine dropper, the teacher should place a few drops of alcohol on the aluminum foil, wax paper, and plastic wrap of each group. Students should then place water drops near the alcohol drops on the surfaces and compare the properties of the two liquids on each surface. For example, tell students to compare the sizes of water drops and alcohol drops on the different surfaces, compare how small drops of each kind cohere to form larger drops, or try to lead water drops and alcohol drops around with a toothpick. Provide magnifying lenses to enhance students' observations.

Safety Precautions

Only the teacher should have access to the container of alcohol.

EXPLAIN: USE DATA TO GENERATE INTERPRETATIONS, INCLUDING DESCRIPTIONS, CLASSIFICATIONS, AND EXPLANATIONS.

c. Ask: *Does alcohol or water have stronger internal bonding forces? What is your evidence?* Lead the students to notice that water drops bead up more on each surface than alcohol drops. Help them infer that because water drops bead up more, they must have stronger internal bonds than alcohol drops, that is, water drops are more cohesive.

How could you help
children understand
what scientists do?

d. Ask: *What does it mean to explain something? How do scientists make up explanations? How do they know their explanations are correct?*

   Through discussion, lead children to understand that to explain an event means to use observations and science knowledge to show that the event is reasonable and could be expected to occur. Explain that scientific explanations are guesses about the way things are. They can be altered with new observations and new scientific knowledge.

---

8. WHY DO SEVERAL STREAMS OF WATER COHERE INTO ONE STREAM? (2–4)

ENGAGE: ASK A
QUESTION ABOUT OBJECTS,
ORGANISMS, OR EVENTS IN
THE ENVIRONMENT.

a. About 2 cm apart as shown in the diagram, puncture four very small holes in a horizontal line about 2 cm from the bottom of a 1 gallon plastic jug. Put masking tape over the holes.

Note: Do not make the holes too large. Also, be sure the holes are very close together.

Ask: *What do you think will happen when water is poured into this container and the masking tape is removed?*

   How many jets of water will you get coming out of the holes in the bottom of the plastic jug?

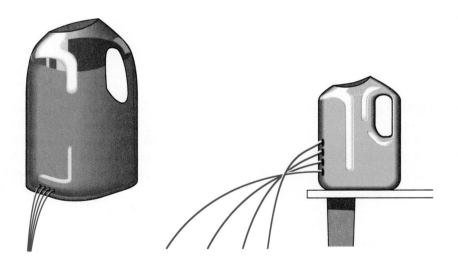

EXPLORE: PLAN
AND CONDUCT SIMPLE
INVESTIGATIONS TO
COLLECT RELEVANT DATA.

b. This activity might be conducted as a teacher demonstration with students assisting. Hold the jug over a sink or large tub, pour water into the jug, and remove the tape.
   Ask: *What do you observe?*
   Tell students to pinch the four jets of water together just as if they were going to pinch someone.

EXPLAIN: USE DATA
TO GENERATE
INTERPRETATIONS,
INCLUDING DESCRIPTIONS,
CLASSIFICATIONS, AND
EXPLANATIONS.

c. Ask: *What do you observe? Why do you think this happened?*
   Lead students to use the water drop model and the concept of cohesion (the bonding of water drops) to explain why the four streams of water cohered into one stream.

C. PROPERTIES OF SOLIDS: OOBLECK

▶ *Science Background*

Investigating and describing the properties of oobleck can be a fascinating task for students grades 1–8. Oobleck is the name given to a special mixture of cornstarch, water, and food coloring that has some unique properties. The substance flows like liquid when you pour it, but keeps its shape like a solid when you hit it hard and fast. Many substances, like syrup and cooking oil, become more viscous and flow more easily when they are heated and less viscous when they are cooled. Oobleck is one of a number of puzzling *non-Newtonian* fluids that get more viscous when they are stirred or pressed.

You may have recognized the name oobleck from the Dr. Seuss children's book, *Bartholomew and the Oobleck*. In this little tale, a strange green rain falls from the sky. The properties of this green rain—Oobleck—cause quite a mess in the kingdom. Other books that treat this substance or its variations include *Horrible Harry and the Green Slime* by Suzy Kline and *The Slimy Book* by Babette Cole. You may want to read one or more of these books with your class in language arts as you investigate oobleck in science, focusing as you read about the properties of materials.

Information, recipes, and activities related to oobleck are excerpted from the GEMS teacher's guide, *Oobleck: What Do Scientists Do?* by Cary L. Sneider (Lawrence Hall of Science, University of California at Berkeley).

NSES   **Science Standards**

All students should develop an understanding of

- properties of objects and materials (K–4).
- changes in properties in matter (5–8).

Objectives for Students

1. Conduct simple investigations to determine the properties of oobleck.
2. Describe properties of oobleck and compare them with various properties of solids and liquids.
3. Explain how their investigations of oobleck are like what scientists do when they investigate.

NSES   **Concepts and Principles**

Activity I addresses these fundamental concepts and principles related to the *Science Standards:*

- Objects have many observable properties (K–4).
- Materials can exist in different states—solid, liquid, and gas (K–4).

···

1. WHAT ARE THE PROPERTIES OF OOBLECK? (1–6)

Materials	Four boxes cornstarch Food coloring Plastic bowls
Preparation	About 2 hours before class add 15 drops of food coloring to 4 1/4 cups of water. Pour the light green water into a large bowl and add four boxes of cornstarch and another 2 1/2 cups of water. Swirl and tip the bowl to level the mixture, then set the bowl aside.

Safety Precautions

- Oobleck is strange but is safe to handle.
- However, oobleck can be quite messy. Have plenty of newspaper around for children to use as a surface to work on. Impress on the children that part of doing science is to maintain a clean, orderly laboratory for investigating. Thus, they must be actively responsible for the cleanliness of their own work area.
- To protect their clothing, let the children wear large shirts over their regular clothes, as in art. Or give the children "lab coats" made of plastic grocery sacks with armholes and a neck hole cut in the bottom.
- Do not put oobleck down the sink as it will clog the drain. If oobleck falls on the floor, scoop most of it up and mop up the remainder with a damp sponge. If it falls on a carpet area, scoop up what you can, then vacuum after it dries.

ENGAGE: ASK A QUESTION ABOUT OBJECTS, ORGANISMS, OR EVENTS IN THE ENVIRONMENT.

a. Remind the children that a *property* is a characteristic of something that can be seen, heard, smelled, or felt by the senses or detected by instruments, such as magnifying lenses, that extend the senses.

Tell the children that you have a very strange substance that you will call oobleck, after the Dr. Seuss story, *Bartholomew and the Oobleck*. Ask: *What are the properties of oobleck? What can you do to find out?*

EXPLORE: PLAN AND CONDUCT SIMPLE INVESTIGATIONS TO COLLECT RELEVANT DATA.

b. Tell children they are to play the role of scientists in investigating the properties of this strange substance. Instruct them to write down as many properties of oobleck as they can discover, but to put a star by the two or three properties they think are most important.

c. Pour about a cup of oobleck into plastic bowls, give a bowl to each cooperative group, and let the fun begin. Some properties children might observe include:

It is gooey, sticky, and green; you can throw it like a ball; it is soft when you move your hand through it slowly, and hard when you move your hand fast; it dries out when left on paper for more than 10 seconds.

EXPLAIN: USE DATA TO GENERATE INTERPRETATIONS, INCLUDING DESCRIPTIONS, CLASSIFICATIONS, AND EXPLANATIONS.

d. Ask cooperative group reporters to write on the chalkboard one property their group has found. Continue until all properties have been exhausted. Place a star beside the two or three properties the children think are most distinctive for oobleck.

e. Show the children a solid object and a liquid in a container.

Ask: *What are the main properties of these two things?* Discuss whether oobleck is best classified as a liquid (flowing easily and taking the shape of its container) or a solid (maintaining its shape). Discuss whether oobleck should be called a solid or a liquid—or do we need a third category?

How could you help children understand what scientists do?

f. Ask the students to identify and list the ways they acted like scientists during their investigation of oobleck. In their lists they might include asked questions, talked, searched, planned, used magnifying lenses, experimented, recorded, explained, discussed, argued, defined, criticized, changed ideas, decided, asked more questions.

Discuss with students how what they did fits within these more formal statements in the *National Science Education Standards* of what scientists do when they inquire:

- Ask a question about objects, organisms, and events in the environment.
- Plan and conduct an investigation, using simple equipment and tools to gather data and extend the senses.
- Use data to construct descriptions, classifications, and explanations.
- Communicate investigations and explanations.

Ask students to give specific examples of what they did that is like one or more of these processes of scientists.

D. PROPERTIES OF SOLIDS: MYSTERY POWDERS

▶ *Science Background*

Investigating the physical and chemical properties of materials forms the basis for an exciting inquiry for children. This set of activities involves the study of four common white powders: granulated sugar, table salt, baking soda, and cornstarch. At first, it seems hard to distinguish among the powders; they appear to have closely similar properties. But when observed through a magnifying lens, an instrument that extends the sense of sight, the powders are found to be quite distinctive. Further, chemical tests reveal that the white powders react differently from one another when drops of water, iodine, and vinegar are added to them.

When given a mystery mixture of two powders, children use magnifying lenses and chemical indicator tests to identify the powders in the mixture. In the process of investigating the powders, children function as research scientists as they observe, design and perform chemical tests, and collect, record, analyze, and explain data. They also add to their own understanding of our fantastically diverse world.

NSES   Science Standards

All students should develop an understanding of

- properties of objects and materials (K–4).
- changes in properties in matter (5–8).

Objectives for Students

1. Use simple tools and instruments that extend the senses to gather data.
2. Carry out chemical indicator tests to determine how different powders react with water, iodine, and vinegar.
3. Accurately record and analyze data.
4. Use data to draw conclusions.

1. WHAT ARE THE DISTINGUISHING PROPERTIES OF COMMON WHITE POWDERS? (3–6)

Materials

For each pair of students:

- Small quantities of salt, granulated sugar, baking soda, and cornstarch
- Medicine droppers
- Plastic spoons
- Plastic wrap
- Magnifying lenses
- Safety goggles
- Small containers of water, vinegar, and iodine

Safety Precautions

- Students should wear safety goggles for these investigations with powders.
- Caution children not to taste any of the powders or liquids and to wash their hands after they test each powder.
- Do not put powders in the sink as they may clog drains.

ENGAGE: ASK A QUESTION ABOUT OBJECTS, ORGANISMS, OR EVENTS IN THE ENVIRONMENT.

a. Ask: *How are sugar and salt different? How are they alike? If you have several white powders, how can you tell them apart?*

Tell the students they will be doing chemical tests, acting like scientists (e.g., forensic chemists) to see what happens when different indicators (water, vinegar, and iodine) are added.

Show students the prepared data table and conclusion sheet and how to enter data in it. Explain that the data table provides a record of observations and experiments that we can refer to later. If necessary, remind students how to use a magnifying lens to extend the sense of sight.

> **Using a Magnifying Lens**
>
> To observe an object through a magnifier or magnifying lens, hold the magnifier close to the object, look through the magnifier at the object, then lift the magnifier toward your eye, stopping when the object begins to blur.
>
> Many science classrooms have magnifiers with three lenses. The large lens usually provides a twofold magnification, the medium-sized lens provides a sixfold magnification, and the small lens an eightfold magnification. To provide increased magnification, two or even three magnifiers can be fitted together and used as a single magnifier.

DATA TABLE AND CONCLUSIONS FOR INVESTIGATING WHITE POWDERS

Observations	Powder 1 Granulated Sugar	Powder 2 Table Salt	Powder 3 Baking Soda	Powder 4 Cornstarch
Visual (Magnifying Glass)				
Water Test				
Iodine Test				
Vinegar Test				
Conclusions:				

EXPLORE: PLAN AND CONDUCT SIMPLE INVESTIGATIONS TO COLLECT RELEVANT DATA.

b. *Visual Observation*. Instruct students to use a magnifying lens to visually observe each powder, and to write down their observations on the data table.

c. *Preparation*. Give each group of students a sheet of plastic wrap. The plastic wrap will serve as a tray for their investigations. Show them how to place white powders in a row on the plastic wrap. Data will be recorded on the data table.

d. *Water Tests*. Students should place a small spoonful of each powder in a row on top of the plastic wrap. They should then add several drops of water and mix with a tooth-pick to see what happens. Observations should be recorded in the data tables.

e. *Iodine Tests*. Instruct students to place a small spoonful of each powder in a row on top of the plastic wrap. Then, they should add a drop or two of iodine to each powder and write down the results in their data tables. Caution the students to be careful! Iodine can stain hands and clothing.

f. *Vinegar Tests*. Students should place a small spoonful of each powder in a row on top of the plastic wrap. They should then add a drop or two of vinegar to each powder and write down the results in their data tables.

EXPLAIN: USE DATA TO GENERATE INTERPRETATIONS, INCLUDING DESCRIPTIONS, CLASSIFICATIONS, AND EXPLANATIONS.

g. *Compare*. Discuss the properties of the five powders that have been revealed through the different chemical tests. Help students to compare the results of their tests with the class master chart of properties of white powders. If necessary, ask students to repeat tests to see what happens.

PROPERTIES OF WHITE POWDERS

Observations	Powder 1 Granulated Sugar	Powder 2 Table Salt	Powder 3 Baking Soda	Powder 4 Cornstarch
Visual (Magnifying Glass)	White crystals	White box-shaped crystals	Fine white powder	Fine yellowish white powder
Water Test	Dissolves in water	Dissolves in water	Turns milky water	Makes water cloudy
Iodine Test	Turns yellow with iodine	No reaction with iodine	Turns yellow orange with iodine	Turns red, ends black with iodine
Vinegar Test	Dissolves in vinegar	No reaction with vinegar	Fizzes with vinegar	Gets thick, then hard with vinegar

2. HOW CAN YOU DETERMINE THE IDENTITY OF A MYSTERY POWDER? (3–6)

Materials

Flour
Materials from Activity 1
Mixtures of flour and one of the original white powders for each pair of students

ENGAGE: ASK A QUESTION ABOUT OBJECTS, ORGANISMS, OR EVENTS IN THE ENVIRONMENT.

a. Ask: *If you had a mixture of powders, how could you find out what is in the mixture?*

EXPLORE: PLAN
AND CONDUCT SIMPLE
INVESTIGATIONS TO
COLLECT RELEVANT DATA.

EXPLAIN: USE DATA TO
GENERATE INTERPRETATIONS,
INCLUDING DESCRIPTIONS,
CLASSIFICATIONS, AND
EXPLANATIONS.

How could you help
children understand
what scientists do?

b. Give each pair of students small samples of a mixture of two white powders, flour, and one of the original white powders.
   Ask: *What powders are these?* Challenge children to determine if each powder is one they have encountered previously, and if so, which one. (Children would not have studied the properties of flour.) Ask: *What is the evidence for your conclusions?*

c. Let students present and discuss their procedures and their conclusions. Ask students to explain the basis for their conclusions.

d. Lead a discussion about how the children's activities in these investigations are like those of scientists. Ask: *What are some of the ways you have acted as scientists in this investigation of powders?* Common activities of children and scientists might include asking questions, talking, searching, planning, using magnifying lenses, experimenting, recording, explaining, discussing, arguing, defining, criticizing, exchanging ideas, deciding, asking more questions.

e. Students should throw away plastic wrap and toothpicks, return powders and test supplies to teacher-designated spot, clean and dry anything dirty—including their hands. Caution students not to put any of the powders in the sink since they can clog drains.[2]

E. PROPERTIES OF AIR

▶ *Science Background*

Although we cannot see, taste, smell, hear, or feel air (if we reach out our hand to grab it), we know that air is a real substance because of the way it interacts with objects that we can see.
   Through the following activities, discussion, and expository teaching you will help the students begin to develop an understanding of these principles about air:

▶ *Principles about Air*

1. Air, like solids and liquids, is a real material substance (made up of particles too small to see).
2. Bubbles in water indicate the presence of air.
3. Air exerts pressure; it can press or push on things.
4. We live at the bottom of an ocean of air that exerts a great pressure on all things on the surface of the earth.
5. Objects tend to be moved from regions of high air pressure toward regions of low air pressure.
6. Air tends to exert more pressure when it is heated; it exerts less pressure when it is cooled.

Together, these principles can be used to *explain evidence* gathered about a wide variety of phenomena. The principles are appropriate for students from about grades 3 or 4 (ages 9–10 or older), provided the children have had plenty of opportunities to lay a foundation for the principles by raising questions, investigating, and trying out their explanations.

---

[2]More information on these activities on white powders can be found at these Internet sites: http://www.csulb.edu/~lhenriqu/mysterypowder.htm, http://etc.sccoe.k12.ca.us/i98/ii98units/cross/mystery/text/powders.html, http://eduref.org/cgi~bin/printlessons.cgi/virtual/lessons/science/chemistry/chm0200.html.

Science Standards

All students should develop an understanding of

*   properties of objects and materials (K–4).
*   changes in properties in matter (5–8).

Objectives for Students

1. Investigate and describe natural events related to air and air pressure.
2. Demonstrate and describe evidence for each of the principles about air and air pressure.
3. Use observational evidence and the principles about air to explain what happens in various investigations and phenomena.

 Concepts and Principles

Activity 1 addresses these fundamental concepts and principles related to the *Science Standards*:

*   Materials can exist in different states—solid, liquid, and gas (K–4).
*   Objects (such as gases) have many different properties (K–4).

1. WHAT DO KITES NEED TO FLY? (2–4)

Materials

Plastic, such as that used by dry cleaners, to cover the kite
Small pieces of wood to form the kite supports
String, transparent tape or glue, and cloth for the tail

Safety Precautions

*   Caution children about flying kites near power lines. Point out that they should never use wire instead of string to fly a kite because of the danger involved if the wire hits a power line.
*   Also warn children of the danger of putting plastic wrapping over their heads or on their faces.

ENGAGE: IDENTIFY A TECHNOLOGICAL PROBLEM.

a. *Note:* This activity is about technology—about human designs and constructions—rather than about the natural environment.
    Ask: *What is a kite? How are kites designed? How can we make kites? What will we need?*

EXPLORE: DESIGN AN APPROACH TO SOLVE THE PROBLEM AND IMPLEMENT THE APPROACH.

Encourage students to plan in small groups how they are going to make their kites before they construct them. Guide them in discussing what they know about air and how it might affect how kites fly and how they should be built. After they have done this, you might bring in some books on kites. Discuss the role of the tail and how it helps to stabilize the kite.

b. Assist groups as they plan and build their kites. Perhaps have a kite available to serve as a model.

EXPLAIN: TEST THE PROBLEM SOLUTION.

c. Arrange for students to fly their kites.
    Ask: *How do kites provide evidence that air is a real material substance?*

Concepts and Principles

Activities 2–9 address these fundamental concepts and principles related to the *Science Standards:*

- Objects have many observable properties (K–4).
- Materials can exist in different states—solid, liquid, and gas (K–4).

2. IS AIR A REAL MATERIAL SUBSTANCE LIKE SOLIDS AND LIQUIDS? (1–4)

Materials

For Activities 2–9:

Large syringes
Several medicine droppers
Containers for water

Soda straws
Potato

▶ *Teaching Suggestions*

We suggest that you use Activities 2–9 as teacher demonstrations in inventing and developing principles about air. Emphasize that these principles are based on evidence and are useful in explaining phenomena and predicting outcomes. The demonstrations might then be made available later to your students, perhaps at learning stations.

ENGAGE: ASK A QUESTION ABOUT OBJECTS, ORGANISMS, OR EVENTS IN THE ENVIRONMENT.

a. Show the children three plastic food storage bags, one filled with a solid (such as sand), a second with water, and a third with air. Ask: *What is in each bag?*

After children discuss the contents of each bag, ask: *How do you know what is in each bag? What is your evidence?*

Some children may say that air is in the third bag. Ask: *Since you cannot see, hear, feel (if you place your hand in the bag), smell (if you open the bag), or taste what's in the bag, how do you know that air is really in the bag?*

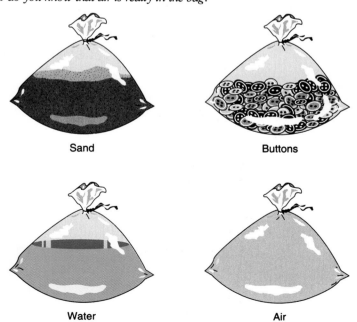

Sand

Buttons

Water

Air

b. Discuss the meaning of the term *evidence* (observations that we can use to support conclusions). Use the term in story form, such as:

> Two boys came out of the house and noticed that the driveway was wet. One boy said, "It has rained." The other boy said, "No, my Dad washes his car every Saturday."

What *evidence* might have supported the first boy's conclusion? What was the implied conclusion of the second boy? What evidence might have supported the second boy's conclusion?

EXPLORE: PLAN AND CONDUCT SIMPLE INVESTIGATIONS TO COLLECT RELEVANT DATA.

c. Lead students to note that although we cannot see air, evidence for the existence of air comes from many activities, such as activities with medicine droppers and syringes.

Place a medicine dropper or a syringe underwater. Squeeze the bulb of the medicine dropper or push in on the plunger of the syringe. Ask: *What do you observe? How can you explain what you see?*

EXPLAIN: USE DATA TO GENERATE INTERPRETATIONS, INCLUDING DESCRIPTIONS, CLASSIFICATIONS, AND EXPLANATIONS.

d. Use this activity to introduce and develop these two principles about air:

Principle 1. Air is a real material substance. Although we cannot observe air directly, we can observe its effects as it interacts with other materials.

Principle 2. Bubbles in water indicate that air is present. The bubbles are filled with air.

ELABORATE: EXTEND CONCEPTS, PRINCIPLES, AND STRATEGIES TO NEW SITUATIONS AND QUESTIONS.

e. Ask: *What other evidence can you think of to show that air is a real material substance?* Through discussion, help your students come up with many examples involving interactions with air, such as wind, rustling of leaves in a tree, paper airplanes, kites, balloons, your breath on a cold morning, or a dropped sheet of paper floating down to the floor.

3. HOW DOES AIR INTERACT WITH WATER? (1–4)

ENGAGE: ASK A QUESTION ABOUT OBJECTS, ORGANISMS, OR EVENTS IN THE ENVIRONMENT.

a. Ask: *Can air and water be in the same space?*

EXPLORE: PLAN AND CONDUCT SIMPLE INVESTIGATIONS TO COLLECT RELEVANT DATA.

b. Push an "empty" glass straight down into a container of water. Ask: *What do you observe? How can you explain what you see?*

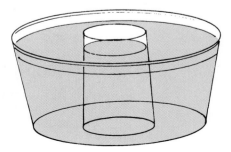

Excerpts from a video of a teacher demonstrating the "crumpled paper in the glass" activity at grade 1 is available on the Virtual Classroom in Chapter 2 of the Companion Website for this book: http://www.prenhall.com/carin.

c. Tilt the glass while it is underwater. Ask: *What do you observe? Why do you think this happens?*

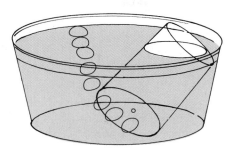

EXPLAIN: USE DATA TO GENERATE INTERPRETATIONS, INCLUDING DESCRIPTIONS, CLASSIFICATIONS, AND EXPLANATIONS.

d. Through discussion, lead students to apply the principle that air is a real material substance. Air keeps the water from coming into the glass. Although the glass looks empty, we infer that it contains air.

e. Ask: *Why were bubbles seen in the water when the glass was tilted?*

   Through discussion and direct instruction, help students use Principle 2 to explain that bubbles show that air is escaping into the water from the glass.

4. HOW CAN AIR KEEP WATER OUT OF A CONTAINER? (1–4)

ENGAGE: ASK A QUESTION ABOUT OBJECTS, ORGANISMS, OR EVENTS IN THE ENVIRONMENT.

a. Crumple up a paper towel in the bottom of a dry, empty glass. Push the glass mouth down into a large container of water so that it is completely submerged. Ask: *What do you observe? Why do you think that the paper towel remains dry?*

EXPLAIN: USE DATA TO GENERATE INTERPRETATIONS, INCLUDING DESCRIPTIONS, CLASSIFICATIONS, AND EXPLANATIONS.

b. Help students use Principle 1 to explain what they see in this demonstration. Air is a real material substance that keeps water from coming up into the glass and wetting the paper towel. Tell the students that large, air-filled, inverted containers, called **diving bells,** have been used in underwater work for centuries. Ask: *Why does water not come into a diving bell when it is submerged?*

ELABORATE: EXTEND CONCEPTS, PRINCIPLES, AND STRATEGIES TO NEW PROBLEMS AND QUESTIONS.

c. Push an empty glass mouth down into a large container of water until it is completely submerged. Tilt the glass so that it fills with water. Ask: *How can you use a straw to replace the water in the glass with air? When you have emptied the glass of its water using the straw, how can you use the straw to replace the air in the glass with water again?*

EXPLAIN: USE DATA TO GENERATE INTERPRETATIONS, INCLUDING DESCRIPTIONS, CLASSIFICATIONS, AND EXPLANATIONS.

Your students will need Principle 1 to explain their observations. When air is blown into the glass through the straw, it replaces the water in the glass. When the air is removed through the straw, the water comes back in.

5. HOW CAN YOU USE A SYRINGE TO FEEL AIR PRESSURE? (3–5)

ENGAGE: ASK A
QUESTION ABOUT OBJECTS,
ORGANISMS, OR EVENTS IN
THE ENVIRONMENT.

a. With the plunger pulled part of the way out of a small- to medium-sized syringe, plug the opening of the syringe with your finger. Try to push the plunger in. Ask: *What do you observe? Why do you think the plunger of the syringe is so hard to push in?*

EXPLAIN: USE DATA
TO GENERATE
INTERPRETATIONS,
INCLUDING DESCRIPTIONS,
CLASSIFICATIONS, AND
EXPLANATIONS.

Use Principle 1 to help students understand that when you push in on the plunger, the air presses back. This demonstration is another type of evidence that air is a real material substance. The demonstration also shows that air can exert pressure. Building on this experience and the children's discussion of it, teach (invent) Principle 3.

Principle 3. Air exerts pressure; it can press or push on things.

NSES **Concepts and Principles**

Activities 6–8 also address these fundamental concepts and principles related to the *Science Standards:*

- The position and motion of objects can be changed by pushing or pulling. The size of the change is related to the strength of the push or pull (K–4).
- Unbalanced forces will cause changes in the speed or direction of an object's motion (5–8).

6. HOW DOES A MEDICINE DROPPER WORK? (3–5)

ENGAGE: ASK A
QUESTION ABOUT OBJECTS,
ORGANISMS, OR EVENTS IN
THE ENVIRONMENT.

a. Ask: *What do you have to do to get water up into a medicine dropper?*

EXPLORE: PLAN
AND CONDUCT SIMPLE
INVESTIGATIONS TO
COLLECT RELEVANT DATA.

b. Dip a medicine dropper into a container of water and fill the medicine dropper with water. Ask: *What did you see happen? What did I do to get water into the medicine dropper? Why do you think the water rose into the medicine dropper?*

EXPLAIN: USE DATA
TO GENERATE
INTERPRETATIONS,
INCLUDING DESCRIPTIONS,
CLASSIFICATIONS, AND
EXPLANATIONS.

c. Your students will likely say that the water was "sucked" into the medicine dropper. Help the students understand that, even though the term is commonly used, *suction* is a misconception; liquid is not pulled into the dropper by suction.

Ask: *What do you do to get water to come into the medicine dropper?* (You dip the tube of the medicine dropper in water, squeeze the bulb, release it, and water comes into the medicine dropper tube.) *What happens to the air in the medicine dropper tube when you squeeze it?* (Some air comes out of the tube.) Ask: *What happens when you pull up on the plunger?*

Lead the children to understand that when you squeeze air out of the tube, there is less air in the tube. When you release the tube underwater, the reduced number of air particles left exert less air pressure. Through discussion, lead the students to understand Principles 4 and 5.

Principle 4. We live at the bottom of an ocean of air that exerts a great pressure on all things on the surface of the earth.

Principle 5. Objects tend to be moved from regions of high air pressure toward regions of low air pressure.

Use Principles 4 and 5 to help children understand that the greater air pressure of the atmosphere pushes water up into the medicine dropper when we have removed air from it.

An understanding that water is pushed (rather than pulled) into the medicine dropper comes only gradually for students. The younger the students, the more partial and fragmented the explanation is likely to be and the more scaffolding support they will need to achieve optimal understanding.

ELABORATE: EXTEND CONCEPTS, PRINCIPLES, AND STRATEGIES TO NEW PROBLEMS AND QUESTIONS.

d. Ask: *In what ways might a syringe be like a medicine dropper? How do you think a syringe works to get air up into the dropper?* Help students to see that the two systems are similar. When you pull up on the syringe plunger, the air in the plunger tube has more space and less pressure. Since there is less air pressure in the syringe than before, the pressure of the atmosphere surrounding us then pushes down on the surface of the water, forcing some liquid up into the syringe.

7. HOW DOES A SODA STRAW WORK? (3–5)

ENGAGE: ASK A QUESTION ABOUT OBJECTS, ORGANISMS, OR EVENTS IN THE ENVIRONMENT.

a. Ask: *How does a soda straw work?*

EXPLORE: PLAN AND CONDUCT SIMPLE INVESTIGATIONS TO COLLECT RELEVANT DATA.

b. Use a clean soda straw to draw liquid up out of a container.
Ask: *In what ways is a soda straw like a medicine dropper? Using what you know about how water comes up into medicine droppers and syringes, how do you think water comes up through soda straws and into your mouth when you drink through a straw? How do you think the air pressure in the soda straw is reduced enough for atmospheric pressure to push liquid up into the straw?*

EXPLAIN: USE DATA TO GENERATE INTERPRETATIONS, INCLUDING DESCRIPTIONS, CLASSIFICATIONS, AND EXPLANATIONS.

c. Lead students to arrive at the explanation that when you drink through a straw, you expand your lungs and some air comes out of the straw into your lungs. Because some air went out of the straw, there is now less air and lower air pressure in the straw. The atmospheric pressure—remember, we live at the bottom of an ocean of air—pushes on the liquid surface, forcing some liquid up through the straw and into your mouth.

ELABORATE: EXTEND CONCEPTS, PRINCIPLES, AND STRATEGIES TO NEW PROBLEMS AND QUESTIONS.

d. Using a straight pin, put a tiny hole in a soda straw above the liquid line. Try drinking liquid through the straw. Ask: *What do you observe? Why do you think this happens?*

How could you help
children understand
what scientists do?

e. Ask: *What do scientists do when they explain something?* Through discussion, lead students to understand that when scientists explain an event, they connect observations and scientific concepts and principles in a reasonable way to make sense of the observations. When scientists propose an explanation, they appeal to scientific knowledge and observational evidence to support their explanation. Children should check their explanations against scientific knowledge, experiences, and observations of others.

8. HOW CAN YOU PUSH A SODA STRAW THROUGH A POTATO? (3–5)

ENGAGE: ASK A
QUESTION ABOUT OBJECTS,
ORGANISMS, OR EVENTS IN
THE ENVIRONMENT.

a. Ask: *Can you push a soda straw through a potato?*

EXPLORE: PLAN
AND CONDUCT SIMPLE
INVESTIGATIONS TO
COLLECT RELEVANT DATA.

b. Place a potato on a table and ask a student to hold it. Raise the straw about 5 inches above the potato and then quickly and forcibly stick the potato, as shown in (a) in the diagram.
    Ask: *What happened?*

c. Repeat step *b* but this time hold your thumb over the end of the straw as you stick the potato, as shown in diagram (b).
    Ask: *Why is this different from before?*

EXPLAIN: USE DATA
TO GENERATE
INTERPRETATIONS,
INCLUDING DESCRIPTIONS,
CLASSIFICATIONS, AND
EXPLANATIONS.

d. Explanation: The first straw usually bends and only partially penetrates the potato. The second straw does not bend and goes through the potato. Blocking the straw end traps and compresses the air inside the straw, creating greater air pressure. Some of the potato is forced into the straw, further increasing the air pressure.

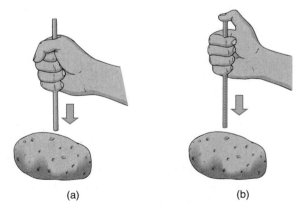

(a)   (b)

9. HOW CAN YOU DEMONSTRATE THAT AIR EXPANDS WHEN IT IS HEATED? (1–4)

ENGAGE: ASK A
QUESTION ABOUT OBJECTS,
ORGANISMS, OR EVENTS IN
THE ENVIRONMENT.

a. Ask: *What can we do to change the shape of a soap bubble on the mouth of a container?*

EXPLORE: PLAN AND CONDUCT SIMPLE INVESTIGATIONS TO COLLECT RELEVANT DATA.

b. Squirt some liquid soap into a large container of water with a wide opening at the top. Stir the water. Dip the open end of a test tube, medicine vial, or small juice can into the soapy water so that a soap film forms across the end of the container. Challenge students to get the soap film to expand. One way to get the soap film to expand is for students to wrap their hands around the container (without squeezing) so that their hands cover as much of the container as possible.

Ask: *What do you observe?*

c. Get a soap bubble on a small container, such as a test tube or medicine vial. Put the container in a bucket of ice. Ask: *What happens to the soap bubble?*

EXPLAIN: USE DATA TO GENERATE INTERPRETATIONS, INCLUDING DESCRIPTIONS, CLASSIFICATIONS, AND EXPLANATIONS.

d. Ask: *Why did the soap bubble expand when you held the container in your hands? Why did the soap bubble go down into the container when you placed the container in ice?*

Through their explorations, the students should note that when they hold the container in their hands, the soap film expands, becomes dome-shaped, and eventually pops. Lead students to understand Principle 6:

Principle 6. Air tends to exert more pressure when it is heated; it exerts less pressure when it is cooled.

The students' hands warmed the air in the small container, the air pressure in the container was increased, and the air expanded. When the container is in ice, the air in the container cools and its pressure is reduced. The outside air pressure then forces the soap bubble into the container.

ELABORATE: EXTEND CONCEPTS, PRINCIPLES, AND STRATEGIES TO NEW PROBLEMS AND QUESTIONS.

e. Obtain a very large can, such as a vegetable can from the school cafeteria. Get a soap film on a large can. Let several students wrap their hands around it to see if they can get the soap film to expand. Ask children to describe what they see and to explain why it happens.

II. MOTION AND FORCES

An object's motion can be described by noting how its position changes over time. To change the motion of an object—to start it moving or stop it, to speed it up or slow it down—a force is needed. An object continues in motion, in a straight line, unless interfered with by some outside force—some push or pull on the object. In most cases of moving objects on the earth, frictional forces act to slow objects down and eventually stop them.

There are many different kinds of forces in addition to frictional forces, such as the mechanical forces exerted by simple machines, gravitational forces, magnetic forces, static electric forces, and the bonding forces between water molecules. A force may be direct, as when we push on a lever arm, or it may be indirect, as when a magnet pulls on a piece of iron from a distance.

The study of simple forces at grades K–4 provides concrete experiences on which a more comprehensive study of forces and motion may be based in grades 5–8 and 9–12.

A. FRICTIONAL FORCES

▶ *Science Background*

Friction is the result of an interaction between a moving object and the surface on which it moves. Students' everyday experience is that friction causes all moving objects to slow down and stop. Through experiences in which friction is reduced (by a lubricant or through the use of wheels), students can begin to see that a moving object with no friction would continue to move indefinitely.

Science Standards

All students should develop an understanding of

- motions and forces (5–8).

Objectives for Students

1. Design and conduct an investigation to demonstrate the friction present as an object moves across a level surface.
2. Ask questions about friction and describe frictional effects as an interaction between an object and a surface.
3. Explain how wheels and lubricants can reduce friction.

Concepts and Principles

Activity I addresses these fundamental concepts and principles related to the *Science Standards*:

- The position and motion of objects can be changed by pushing or pulling (K–4).
- The size of the change is related to the strength of the push or pull (K–4).

1. WHAT IS FRICTION? HOW CAN FRICTION BE REDUCED? (3–6)

Materials

Screw hook
Block of wood
Rubber bands
Ruler
Sheets of coarse sandpaper
Five or six round pencils

ENGAGE: ASK A QUESTION ABOUT OBJECTS, ORGANISMS, OR EVENTS IN THE ENVIRONMENT.

a. Ask: *How can you measure the effects of friction?*

EXPLORE: PLAN AND CONDUCT SIMPLE INVESTIGATIONS TO COLLECT RELEVANT DATA.

b. Students should carry out these investigation procedures in cooperative groups.
   1. Turn the screw hook into the end of a block of wood. Attach a rubber band (or a spring scale) to the hook.
   2. With the rubber band on your finger, lift the block into the air and measure the stretch with a ruler, as in diagram (a). Design a data table and record your measurement in it.

3. Position the block on a table with the rubber band extended, as in diagram (b). Now drag the block on the table and measure the rubber band's stretch once the block begins to move. Record your measurements.

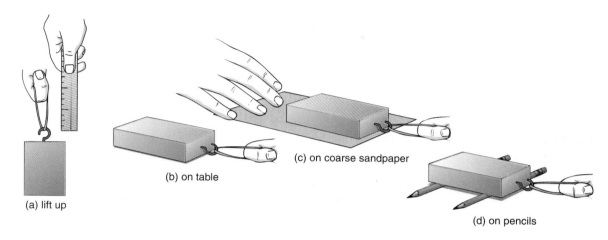

(a) lift up

(b) on table

(c) on coarse sandpaper

(d) on pencils

4. Repeat the procedure in step 3, this time with sandpaper beneath the block, as in diagram (c). Ask: *What change do you observe in the stretch of the rubber band when the block is dragged on the table and on sandpaper? What is the cause of the increase in force needed to move the object on sandpaper?* Introduce the concept of friction. Friction is a force opposing motion that results when two surfaces slide across one another.

5. Now place two round pencils underneath the block and drag it across the table, as in diagram (d). Measure the stretch of the rubber band just after the block begins to move. Ask: *What happens to the stretch of the rubber band this time? Why? In what way do wheels help objects to move?* Explain that wheels reduce friction.

6. Older students might repeat the activity using a spring scale.

EXPLAIN: USE DATA TO GENERATE INTERPRETATIONS, INCLUDING DESCRIPTIONS, CLASSIFICATIONS, AND EXPLANATIONS.

c. Invite students to present their procedures and findings. Ask: *How does the surface on which the block slides affect the force to move it? What is friction? How do wheels reduce the force needed to move a block across a table?*

B. EQUAL-ARM BALANCES

▶ *Science Background*

An equal-arm balance is a system consisting of a crossbar pivoted in the center and weights that can be placed at different positions on each side of the bar, as is shown in the diagram. The amount of each weight and its distance from the central pivot point are the relevant factors in determining balance.

Homemade balances can be constructed for the following activities, but if at all possible, students should use commercial plastic balances, often referred to as "math balances." The Invicta Math-Balance, sold by Delta Education and other equipment companies, is an excellent tool for studying balancing from kindergarten through middle school. Addresses for equipment companies are given in Appendix C.

Science Standards

All students should develop an understanding of

• motions and forces (5–8).

Objectives for Students

1. Use these qualitative rules to predict and explain balance on an equal-arm balance:
   - *Symmetry rule.* Equal weights at equal distances will balance [see diagram(a)].
   - *Relational rule.* Heavier weights close in can balance lighter weights farther out [see diagram (b) and diagram (c)].
2. Demonstrate and explain that balance occurs when the products of weights and distances on one side of the pivot equal the product of weights and distances on the other side of the pivot.

 Concepts and Principles

Activity 1 prepares students to learn these fundamental concepts and principles related to the *Science Standards:*

• Unbalanced forces will cause changes in the speed or direction of an object's motion (5–8).

1. WHAT FACTORS AFFECT THE EQUILIBRIUM OF AN EQUAL-ARM BALANCE? (3–6)

Materials

Equal-arm balance for each pair of students

ENGAGE: ASK A QUESTION ABOUT OBJECTS, ORGANISMS, OR EVENTS IN THE ENVIRONMENT.

a. Ask: *What affects the balance of an equal-arm balance scale? How can you predict accurately whether a balance will be level?*

EXPLORE: PLAN AND CONDUCT SIMPLE INVESTIGATIONS TO COLLECT RELEVANT DATA.

b. Distribute balances to your students. Try to obtain enough balances so that two, or no more than three, children work together on their own balance. If balances are limited, you may wish to set up stations that children can work at during the day.

   Give the children the following balance problems, one at a time. Allow ample time for students to work on each problem and discuss their findings, before giving the next one. Be noncommittal about patterns they may discover.

   1. Place two weights at the second peg from the center on the left side. Leaving the left side always the same, find at least three different ways to balance the crossbar by adding weights to a peg on the other side. (You can use as many weights as necessary, but be sure to add weights to only one peg at a time on the right side, not to two or three pegs.) Use drawings, words, or data columns to show what you did. Tell your teacher what you did to balance the crossbar.

2. Start with two weights on the left side at the third peg from the center. Find at least four ways to balance the crossbar. (Remember, you can use as many weights as necessary, but be sure to add weights to only one peg on the right side, not to two or three pegs.) Write down what you did and show your work to your teacher.
3. Start with four weights at the third peg on the left side. How many ways can you find to balance the crossbar? (Remember to add weights from only one peg at a time on the other side.)
4. Set up your own combinations of weights and distances on one side of the balance and use your developing knowledge to predict what might be done to the other side to produce balance.

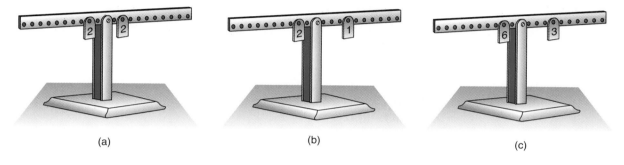

(a)   (b)   (c)

EXPLAIN: USE DATA TO GENERATE INTERPRETATIONS, INCLUDING DESCRIPTIONS, CLASSIFICATIONS, AND EXPLANATIONS.

c. Ask: *What did you do to balance the crossbar? Can you find patterns in the different ways you found to balance the crossbar? How can you test to determine if the pattern you found is a general one, applying in all cases?*

Through discussion, lead your students to understand the following balance patterns or rules:

- *Symmetry rule.* Equal weights at equal distances will balance [see diagram (a)].
- *Relational rule.* Heavier weights close in can balance lighter weights farther out [see diagram (b) and diagram (c)].

Both of these rules are qualitative, nonnumerical rules. They are understood by children from ages 8 or 9, but they may not be stated explicitly.

d. At some point, older students (from ages 10 or 11) may understand the use of formal mathematics to coordinate weights and distances. Challenge students to work with their data from step *b* to find a mathematical rule for the balance, a rule involving doing something with the actual numbers.

The mathematical rule for the balance is:

$$(W_L) \times (D_L) = (W_R) \times (D_R)$$

where W = weights, D = distances, L = left side, and R = right side of the balance. Thus, the product of the weight and distance on one side is equal to the product of weight and distance on the other side.

Lead older children to try this rule for themselves, using the data from different trials. If the crossbar is balanced, the products of the weights and distances on the left side will always equal the products on the right side for each of these three cases.

Interestingly, this rule applies even if weights are placed on more than one peg on each side. Then, the sum of the weights times distances on one side must equal the sum on the other side.

C. LEVERS

▶ *Science Background*

The rules governing equal-arm balances are important in science because they also apply to the operation of levers. A lever system has a crossbar, pivoted at a fulcrum. Using a small effort force far out from a fulcrum, a person can lift a heavy load (or move a resistance) that is nearer the fulcrum. At the lower grades, students can use the symmetry and relational rules of the equal-arm balance to explain and predict actions of a lever. Middle school students might use the balance equation to predict how much force is needed to lift a load of a given weight when the distances involved are known.

Levers have been classified as first-, second-, and third-class levers, depending on the relative placement of the fulcrum, effort force, and resistance or load. But the goal in teaching children about levers is not that they be able to identify the type of lever. Rather, the focus should be on descriptive and relational thinking. Students should learn to identify the fulcrum, load, load arm, effort, and effort arm for a variety of levers and explain how their physical arrangement in a particular lever affects the effort force needed to lift a given load. Students should be able to consistently demonstrate and explain that through the use of a lever, a small effort force far from the fulcrum can lift a heavy load that is near the fulcrum.

NSES **Science Standards**

All students should develop an understanding of

- motions and forces (5–8).

Objectives for Students

1. Identify the fulcrum, effort force, and load/resistance of different kinds of levers.
2. Explain how a lever is like an equal-arm balance.
3. Demonstrate and explain that a small effort force far from the fulcrum can lift or move a large load near the fulcrum.

NSES **Concepts and Principles**

Activities 1 and 2 prepare students to understand these fundamental concepts and principles related to the *Science Standards*:

- Unbalanced forces will cause changes in the speed or direction of an object's motion (5–8).

1. WHAT IS A LEVER? HOW COULD YOU USE ONE? (2–6)

Materials   Large stone or other heavy object
                                    Half-meter stick or 50 cm board

ENGAGE: ASK A QUESTION ABOUT OBJECTS, ORGANISMS, OR EVENTS IN THE ENVIRONMENT.

a. Tell students a story about two girls that were climbing a mountain. A rock slide deposited a large boulder on the leg of one of the girls. The boulder was too heavy to lift directly. What might her companion do to lift the boulder enough so that the girl could get her leg free?

Ask: *What do you think the second girl could do to help free her friend?*

EXPLORE: PLAN AND CONDUCT SIMPLE INVESTIGATIONS TO COLLECT RELEVANT DATA.

b. Lead students to consider getting a tree limb, finding something to use as a fulcrum (pivot), and then using the tree limb to lift the boulder enough for the girl to get her leg free. Model the situation in the classroom using a heavy box to represent the boulder, a half-meter stick for the lever arm, and a book as the pivot.

EXPLAIN: USE DATA TO GENERATE INTERPRETATIONS, INCLUDING DESCRIPTIONS, CLASSIFICATIONS, PREDICTIONS, AND EXPLANATIONS.

c. Ask: *Where was the load (or resistance) for this lever? Where was the fulcrum? Where was the force applied?*

Lead students to understand that a lever can be used to lift a heavy load, if the force on the lever is much farther from the fulcrum than the load is.

2. HOW IS A LEVER LIKE A BALANCE? (3–6)

ENGAGE: ASK A QUESTION ABOUT OBJECTS, ORGANISMS, OR EVENTS IN THE ENVIRONMENT.

a. Make sure that students have studied the equal-arm balance, following procedures similar to those in the previous section of these activities. Ask: *How is a lever like an equal-arm balance?* Ask the students to identify the fulcrum, effort, and resistance on a balance and on a lever.

EXPLORE: PLAN
AND CONDUCT SIMPLE
INVESTIGATIONS TO
COLLECT RELEVANT DATA.

b. Instruct the students to design an investigation to determine how much effort they must exert at different distances on one side of the balance/lever to lift weights at specific positions on the other side. For example, using the balance as a lever, they might place a load of 8 weights at a distance of 10 units from the fulcrum and note that the farther from the pivot/fulcrum they apply the effort force, the easier it is to lift the load. Through this activity, students can experience directly the great amount of effort force needed to move a heavy load when the effort force is much nearer to the fulcrum than is the load.

EXPLAIN: USE DATA
TO GENERATE
INTERPRETATIONS,
INCLUDING DESCRIPTIONS,
CLASSIFICATIONS, AND
EXPLANATIONS.

c. Ask: *How does the balance and lever principle apply to a seesaw?*

If possible, take your students to a playground seesaw. Or make a classroom seesaw by placing a solid 2 inch by 6 inch board about 6 to 8 feet long on another board under it to act as a pivot. Let the children investigate how a smaller child far out from the pivot of the seesaw can balance a larger child nearer to the fulcrum.

D. INCLINED PLANES

▶ *Science Background*

An inclined plane or ramp can be used as a simple type of machine to reduce the force needed to move an object up to a given height.

NSES **Science Standards**

All students should develop an understanding of

• motions and forces (5–8).

Objectives for Students

1. Describe and demonstrate how an inclined plane can be used to reduce the force needed to move an object up to a given height.
2. Name and describe examples of inclined planes in everyday life.

NSES **Concepts and Principles**

Activity I provides a foundation for students to understand these fundamental concepts and principles related to the *Science Standards*:

• Unbalanced forces will cause changes in the speed or direction of an object's motion (5–8).

1. WHAT IS AN INCLINED PLANE? HOW CAN YOU USE IT? (3–6)

Materials

Smooth board, 4 feet long
Block with screw eye in one end or a rubber band wrapped around it
Spring scale

ENGAGE: ASK A
QUESTION ABOUT OBJECTS,
ORGANISMS, OR EVENTS IN
THE ENVIRONMENT.

a. Ask: *What happens to the force needed to move an object up an inclined plane when the angle of the plane is increased?*

EXPLORE: PLAN
AND CONDUCT SIMPLE
INVESTIGATIONS TO
COLLECT RELEVANT DATA.

b. Lead students to plan and conduct an investigation similar to this one.
   1. Use the spring scale to find the weight of the block by lifting it straight up as shown in the diagram. Repeat this several times and find the average reading on the scale. Record the average weight.
   2. Take the 4-foot board and place two or three books under one end so that end of the board is raised about 10 cm. Place the block with the screw eye in it on the inclined board as shown in the diagram. Slip the hook of the spring scale through the eye of the block.
   3. Slowly and evenly pull the scale and block up the board.
   4. Record the amount of force needed to pull the block up the board and the height of the plane. Do this several times and record your observations. Using the data obtained, determine the average force required to pull the weight.

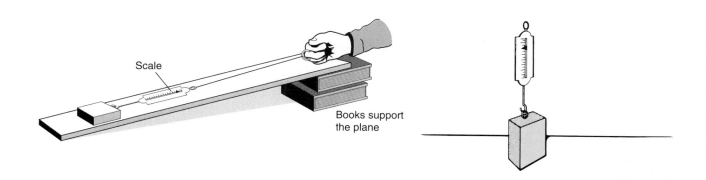

Scale

Books support
the plane

Ask: *How much force is required to pull the block up each plane? Is the force to move the block up the plane greater than, equal to, or less than the weight of the block? Why?*
   5. Repeat the activity but this time make the inclined plane steeper by changing the number of support books so that the end of the board is about 20 cm high.
   6. Again, find the average force needed to pull the weight up the board.

EXPLAIN: USE DATA TO GENERATE INTERPRETATIONS, INCLUDING DESCRIPTIONS, CLASSIFICATIONS, AND EXPLANATIONS.

c. Ask: *How do the forces to move the block up the two inclined planes compare? How is the force needed different when lifting the block straight up than when pulling the block up the board? Why?*

Guide students to understand that inclined planes are used for moving objects that are too heavy to lift directly. An inclined plane is a simple type of machine. Because of the slant of the plane, a smaller force is needed to move an object up an inclined plane than to lift it straight up the same height.

Ask: *What generalization can you make about the amount of force required to move a block as an inclined plane becomes steeper? What is the advantage of having a long inclined plane rather than a short inclined plane if both planes are the same height?*

ELABORATE: EXTEND CONCEPTS, PRINCIPLES, AND STRATEGIES TO NEW PROBLEMS AND QUESTIONS.

d. Ask: *Why do roads not go straight up and down mountains?*

Which of the following examples is an inclined plane?
  a. wheelchair ramp   d. stairway
  b. hill   e. vertical cliff
  c. gangplank   f. head of an ax

Where are there examples of inclined planes in the school or on the school campus?

E. PULLEYS

▶ *Science Background*

A pulley also can be used as a simple type of machine to reduce the force needed to lift an object to a given height.

NSES Science Standards

All students should develop an understanding of

• motions and forces (5–8).

Objectives for Students

1. Describe and demonstrate how pulleys can be used to reduce the force needed to lift an object to a given height.
2. Name and describe examples of pulleys in everyday life.

NSES Concepts and Principles

Activities 1 and 2 prepare students to understand these fundamental concepts and principles related to the *Science Standards:*

• Unbalanced forces will cause changes in the speed or direction of an object's motion (5–8).

---

1. WHAT IS A MOVABLE PULLEY, AND HOW CAN YOU USE IT? (3–6)

Materials

Ring stand and clamp for attaching pulleys
Two single pulleys
String for the pulley
Spring scale
100 g weight
50 g weight
Meterstick

ENGAGE: ASK A
QUESTION ABOUT OBJECTS,
ORGANISMS, OR EVENTS IN
THE ENVIRONMENT.

a. Ask: *What is a pulley? How do pulleys work? How can pulleys help us lift heavy objects?*

EXPLORE: PLAN
AND CONDUCT SIMPLE
INVESTIGATIONS TO
COLLECT RELEVANT DATA.

b. Lead students to conduct this investigation.
   1. Obtain a ring stand and a clamp for attaching a pulley, a single pulley, some string, a spring scale, and a 100 g weight. Assemble your equipment as shown in the diagram.
      Ask: *How much do you think you will have to pull on the scale to raise the 100 g weight?*

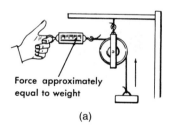

Force approximately
equal to weight

(a)

   2. Pull on the scale and raise the 100 g weight. Record the force needed to raise the weight.
   3. Repeat this activity several times and record each measurement.
      Ask: *What do you think will happen when you use two pulleys to raise the 100 g weight?*
   4. In addition to the equipment you have, obtain a second pulley and a 50 g weight. Assemble your equipment as shown in the diagram.
   5. Pull the 50 g weight and record your observations.
   6. Remove the 50 g weight and attach the spring scale to the free end of the string, as shown in the following diagram.
      Ask: *How much force do you think the scale will show when you raise the 100 g weight?*

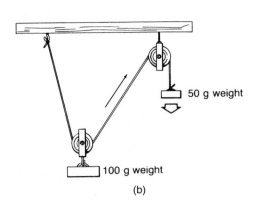

(b)

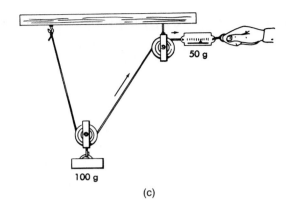

(c)

7. Raise the weight by pulling on the scale. Ask: *How much is the reading on the scale when you raise the weight?* Repeat the activity several times and record each measurement. Ask: *Why is there an advantage in using this type of pulley system?*

EXPLAIN: USE DATA TO GENERATE INTERPRETATIONS, INCLUDING DESCRIPTIONS, CLASSIFICATIONS, AND EXPLANATIONS.

c. Ask: *From your investigation, what can you generalize about pulley systems?* Design a pulley system to lift a piano weighing 300 pounds. Draw a sketch of that pulley system.

▶ *Teaching Background*

As you can see from the activities, more pulleys reduce the amount of force needed to lift a heavy weight. Actually, it is not the number of pulleys, but the number of ropes or strings pulling against the resisting weight that makes a difference. In diagram (a), one string pulls upward and the force needed to lift the block is the same as the weight of the block. In diagram (b), two strings pull upward against the load/block and the force needed to lift the load is one-half its weight. If four strings in a pulley arrangement pulled upward, how much force you would need to exert to lift the block (one-fourth the weight of the block).

2. HOW CAN A PULLEY ARRANGEMENT HELP YOU USE A SMALL FORCE TO OVERPOWER A LARGE FORCE? (4–6)

Materials

Two 1 3/4 inch dowel rods, about 36 inches long
20 feet of 1/2 inch nylon rope

Safety Precautions

Since a large force will be involved, make sure the dowel rods are short and very strong. Safe dowel rods can be cut from a shovel handle purchased from a hardware or building supply store.

ENGAGE: ASK A QUESTION ABOUT OBJECTS, ORGANISMS, OR EVENTS IN THE ENVIRONMENT.

a. Ask: *How can we design a pulley system out of dowel rods and a rope so that a small force can overcome a very large force?*

EXPLORE: PLAN AND CONDUCT SIMPLE INVESTIGATIONS TO COLLECT RELEVANT DATA.

b. Tie a strong loop in one end of the rope and loop it over one of the dowel rods. With one person holding one dowel rod in both hands and a second person holding the other dowel rod in both hands, pass the rope back and forth over the dowel rods about 4 times as in the illustration.

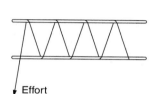

Effort

With a pulley arrangement, a small effort force can overcome a large resistance force.

c. Select four large volunteers and let them hold on to the ends of the dowel rods, with two against two in a tug-of-war. Let a smaller person pull on the free end of the rope.

EXPLAIN: USE DATA TO GENERATE INTERPRETATIONS, INCLUDING DESCRIPTIONS, CLASSIFICATIONS, AND EXPLANATIONS.

d. Ask: *What happens? Why?* (The force of the smaller person draws the two larger persons together. The rods and rope make up a pulley system with several pulleys. If the rope is looped four times over the rods, there are eight ropes pulling on a dowel. The smaller person will have to pull with one-eighth of the force of the four students trying to hold the rods apart. The effect of this pulley system is very dramatic.)

F. BERNOULLI'S PRINCIPLE

▶ *Science Background*

When air rushes over a surface, it has the effect of reducing the air pressure on that surface. This cause-and-effect relationship is called Bernoulli's principle, for Daniel Bernoulli (1700–1782), an important Swiss mathematical scientist who first described the relationship.

As an example of the application of this principle, take a strip of paper and hold it between your lips, with the long edge of the paper trailing down. Blow across the top of the paper. Because of the air rushing over the top surface of the paper, the air pressure on the top of the paper is reduced. The air pressure on the bottom of the paper, which has not changed, is now larger and pushes the paper strip upward.

Bernoulli's principle is the principle of flight. Wings of planes are designed so that as the plane is propelled through the air, air moves faster over the top of the wing than the bottom of the wing. This results in a lower air pressure on the top wing surface, and the air pressure on the bottom of the wing surface can then support the weight of the plane and hold it aloft.

Several activities that illustrate Bernoulli's principle are presented in this section. The activities may take a lot of practice from you and your students to get them to work appropriately.

 Science Standards

All students should develop an understanding of

- motions and forces (5–8).

Objectives for Students

1. State Bernoulli's principle and use it to analyze a rushing air situation.
2. Use Bernoulli's principle to explain what happens in various rushing air demonstrations.

 Concepts and Principles

Activities 1–4 address this fundamental principle related to the *Science Standards*:

- Unbalanced forces will cause changes in the speed or direction of an object (5–8).

1. WHAT IS BERNOULLI'S PRINCIPLE? HOW CAN YOU USE A PIECE OF PAPER TO INVESTIGATE IT? (4–6)

Materials

Notebook paper
Drinking straw

ENGAGE: ASK A QUESTION ABOUT OBJECTS, ORGANISMS, OR EVENTS IN THE ENVIRONMENT.

a. Conduct this demonstration for students.
   1. Obtain a piece of paper about 8 inches by 8 inches.
   2. Make a fold 1 inch wide along one side of the paper. Make another 1 inch fold on the opposite side as indicated in the diagram.
   3. Place the paper on a flat surface, with the folds acting as legs to hold the paper up.
      Ask: *What do you think will happen if I blow through a straw under this folded paper?*

4. Using a drinking straw, blow a stream of air under the paper.

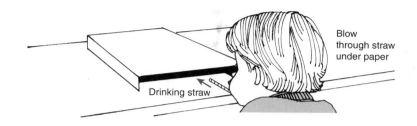

Blow through straw under paper

Drinking straw

EXPLORE: PLAN AND CONDUCT SIMPLE INVESTIGATIONS TO COLLECT RELEVANT DATA.

b. Provide paper and straws to students and allow them to repeat the demonstration.

EXPLAIN: USE DATA TO GENERATE INTERPRETATIONS, INCLUDING DESCRIPTIONS, CLASSIFICATIONS, AND EXPLANATIONS.

c. Ask: *What do you notice about the way the paper moves?* (The center of the paper moves down.)

How did the air move under the paper when you blew under it? (The air was moving in a stream under the paper.)

What can you infer about why the paper went down in the center? Guide students to understand that air pressure pushed the paper down.

Would the air pressure be greater on the top of the paper or on the bottom of the paper? Help students understand that the air pressure would be greater on the top if the paper was pushed down by the air pressure.

Why is the air pressure lower on the bottom of the paper? Invent Bernoulli's principle: When air rushes over a surface, the air pressure on that surface is reduced. Make sure that the students can use Bernoulli's principle, along with their observational evidence, to explain the example.

2. HOW CAN YOU USE A PIECE OF PAPER IN ANOTHER WAY TO INVESTIGATE BERNOULLI'S PRINCIPLE? (3–6)

ENGAGE: ASK A QUESTION ABOUT OBJECTS, ORGANISMS, OR EVENTS IN THE ENVIRONMENT.

a. Ask: *If you were to hold a strip of paper by each corner and blow across the top of the paper, what would happen to the paper? Why do you think so?*

EXPLORE: PLAN AND CONDUCT SIMPLE INVESTIGATIONS TO COLLECT RELEVANT DATA.

b. Assist students to conduct this investigation.
   1. Obtain a strip of paper about 3 inches by 11 inches.
   2. Along the 3 inch side, hold the upper left corner of the strip with your left hand and the upper right corner with your right hand.

3. Blow hard across the top of the paper (see diagram).

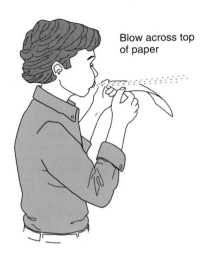

Blow across top of paper

EXPLAIN: USE DATA TO GENERATE INTERPRETATIONS, INCLUDING DESCRIPTIONS, CLASSIFICATIONS, AND EXPLANATIONS.

c. Ask: *What happens to the paper while you are blowing across it?*
Why does the paper move in this direction? Where does the air move faster, over the top of the paper or the bottom of the paper? Why do you think so?
Lead students to apply Bernoulli's principle to explain why the paper strip moves upward. The air pressure was reduced as air rushed over the top of the paper. The greater air pressure under the paper pushed the paper upward, overcoming the gravitational forces that tend to bend the paper downward.

ELABORATE: EXTEND CONCEPTS, PRINCIPLES, AND STRATEGIES TO NEW SITUATIONS AND QUESTIONS.

d. Discuss these questions with the class:
1. *Why is it unwise to stand close to the edge of a platform as a moving train is coming?*
2. *How does Bernoulli's principle apply to flying planes?*
   If a plane is moving fast enough, the upward pressure on the wings is enough to support the weight of the plane. The plane must keep moving to stay aloft. If the plane's engines cut out in midair, it would glide down immediately.
3. Look at the following diagram of an airplane wing. *Is the air moving faster at A or B? Why?*
4. *How do wing slopes vary and why?*

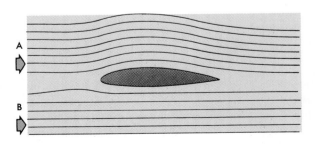

3. HOW CAN YOU USE A BOTTLE AND A PIECE OF PAPER TO INVESTIGATE BERNOULLI'S PRINCIPLE? (3–6)

Materials

Pop bottle

ENGAGE: ASK A QUESTION ABOUT OBJECTS, ORGANISMS, OR EVENTS IN THE ENVIRONMENT.

a. Ask: *Using what you know about the effects of rushing air on air pressure, what do you think will happen to a wad of paper placed in the opening of a pop bottle if you blow across the bottle opening? Will the paper go into the bottle or come out of the bottle? Make a prediction. Explain your reasoning.*

EXPLORE: PLAN AND CONDUCT SIMPLE INVESTIGATIONS TO COLLECT RELEVANT DATA.

b. Guide students to conduct this investigation.
   1. Wad a small piece of paper so it is about the size of a pea (about 0.5 cm diameter).
   2. Lay the pop bottle on its side.
   3. Place the small wad of paper in the opening of the bottle, next to the edge of the opening. (See diagram.)
   4. Blow across the opening in front of the bottle. Make sure you bend down so that you are level with the bottle.

Blow across opening of bottle

EXPLAIN: USE DATA TO GENERATE INTERPRETATIONS, INCLUDING DESCRIPTIONS, CLASSIFICATIONS, AND EXPLANATIONS.

c. Ask: *What happens to the wad of paper?* (It moves out of bottle.)
   Why is the wad of paper forced to do that?
   What do you infer about the air pressure in the bottle and the air pressure at the opening of the bottle when you blow across it? (Air pressure in the bottle is greater.)

ELABORATE: EXTEND CONCEPTS, PRINCIPLES, AND STRATEGIES TO NEW PROBLEMS AND QUESTIONS.

d. Ask: *What do you think will happen if you place a wad of paper in the opening of a pop bottle (as before) and blow directly into the bottle?*
   1. Blow hard directly into the bottle as shown.
   2. Record your observations.
      What do you conclude from your observations?

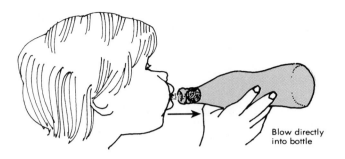

Blow directly
into bottle

4. HOW CAN YOU USE A FUNNEL AND PING-PONG BALL TO INVESTIGATE BERNOULLI'S PRINCIPLE? (3–6)

Materials

Ping-Pong ball
Thistle tube or funnel

ENGAGE: ASK A QUESTION ABOUT OBJECTS, ORGANISMS, OR EVENTS IN THE ENVIRONMENT.

a. Ask: *What will happen to a Ping-Pong ball if it is placed in the large end of a thistle tube or funnel and you blow through the small end of the thistle tube or funnel?*

EXPLORE: PLAN AND CONDUCT SIMPLE INVESTIGATIONS TO COLLECT RELEVANT DATA.

b. Let children observe as you perform this investigation.
   1. Hold the Ping-Pong ball in the wide, larger opening of the thistle tube or funnel, put your mouth on the other end, and blow with a long, steady breath. (See diagram.) *Hint:* Get a deep breath before you put your mouth on the tube end to blow.
   2. While blowing hard and steady through the tube end of the funnel, let go of the Ping-Pong ball.
   3. Tell students to record their observations.

Safety Precautions

Wash the funnel or thistle tube with soap and hot water before this activity. Do the activity only as a teacher demonstration.

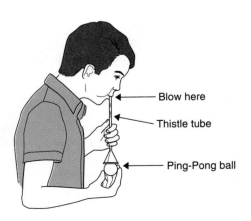

Blow here

Thistle tube

Ping-Pong ball

EXPLAIN: USE DATA TO GENERATE INTERPRETATIONS, INCLUDING DESCRIPTIONS, CLASSIFICATIONS, AND EXPLANATIONS.

c. Ask: *What happens to the ball? Why does the ball spin around in the thistle tube or funnel?*

G. PENDULUMS

▶ *Science Background*

Students typically identify three variable factors that might affect the rate of swing of a pendulum: the weight of the pendulum bob, the angle at which it is released, and the length of the pendulum string. Determining which factors are indeed relevant requires that students conduct controlled investigations in which one factor at a time is varied and its effect on the rate of swing of the pendulum is determined, while the other two variables are controlled or left unchanged.

Surprisingly, only the length affects the rate of swing. Varying the weight of the pendulum bob or the angle at which the pendulum is released has no effect on its rate of swing.

NSES Science Standards

All students should develop an understanding of

• the position and motion of objects (K–4).
• motion and forces (5–8).

Objectives for Students

1. Demonstrate procedures for measuring the rate of a pendulum's swing.
2. Design controlled experiments to test hypotheses about factors that might affect the speed of a pendulum.
3. Record, analyze, and draw accurate conclusions from data.
4. Construct and make predictions from graphs of data from pendulum investigations.

NSES Concepts and Processes

These pendulum activities address these fundamental concepts and principles that underlie the stated standards:

• Changes in systems can be quantified through measurement (5–8).
• Mathematics is essential for accurately measuring change (5–8).
• Rate involves comparing one measured quantity with another measured quantity (5–8).

(National Research Council, 1996, p. 118)

1. WHAT IS A PENDULUM? (5–8)

Materials

Watch with a second hand for each group, or clock with a second hand for the whole class
Paper clips
Pennies
Ball of string
Tongue depressors or pencils (to support the pendulums)
Masking tape (to tape the pendulum support to a desk)

Preparation

- Tie a paper clip to one end of several pieces of long string and insert one or more pennies into each paper clip to make the pendulum bobs (as in the drawing). Wedge the string into the slit of a tongue depressor as in the drawing. Students can adjust the length of string as needed by sliding it along the notch of the tongue depressor.

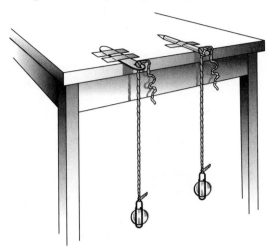

- Determine where teams of students can set up pendulums that can swing freely. To support the pendulums, students should tape or hold the tongue depressor or the pencil securely on the edge of a table.

ENGAGE: ASK A QUESTION OR PRESENT A PROBLEM TO INITIATE INQUIRY.

a. Show students a pendulum using the paper clip and pennies as a pendulum bob and a tongue depressor as a support. Start the pendulum swinging. Ask: *How does a pendulum move? How many ways can you think of to change the motion of the pendulum?* Write these two questions on the board or on chart paper.

Allow students time to talk with partners or classmates about answers to the questions.

EXPLORE: GUIDE STUDENTS TO PLAN AND CONDUCT SIMPLE INVESTIGATIONS.

b. Help each team of students construct and find a place to support their pendulum. Invite students to explore with their pendulums. Ask: *What can you find out about the motion of a pendulum?*

EXPLAIN: ASSIST STUDENTS TO DEVELOP CONCEPTS, PRINCIPLES, MODELS, AND EXPLANATIONS.

c. After about 10 minutes of open exploration, stop students and ask them what they have discovered. After students share some ideas, invite them to suggest questions they might investigate.

2. WHAT FACTORS MIGHT AFFECT THE RATE OF SWING OF A PENDULUM? (5–8)

ENGAGE: ASK A QUESTION OR PRESENT A PROBLEM TO INITIATE INQUIRY.

a. Ask: *Do all pendulums swing at the same rate, or do some swing slower or faster? How can you measure how fast a pendulum swings?* (Lead the students to count the number of swings in 15 seconds. Explain that this is called the rate of swing of the pendulum. Define a swing as one complete back-and-forth cycle.)

Ask: *How can you get a pendulum to swing faster or slower (more or fewer swings in 15 seconds)?*

b. After some discussion, ask students to focus on these three separate, measurable *variables* that might make a pendulum swing faster or slower:
   1. Length of the pendulum
   2. Weight or number of pennies that make up the pendulum bob
   3. Angle at which the pendulum is released

EXPLORE: GUIDE STUDENTS TO PLAN AND CONDUCT SIMPLE INVESTIGATIONS.

c. Instruct students to write down a separate question about each variable (e.g., How does the rate change when the weight of the pendulum bob is changed?). Then tell them to design and conduct controlled experiments to answer the questions they have asked.

d. Monitor students' experiments and provide assistance with the procedures, logic, and data interpretation for controlled experiments. Ask the students to record what they do and what they find out.

e. When students have had ample time to explore, help the class to standardize the way they measure weight, length, angle, and rate (number of back-and-forth swings in 15 seconds). At this time you should be ready to introduce the use of a data table like the one illustrated to help students organize their investigations, keep track of their data, and interpret their data to form conclusions.

PENDULUM DATA TABLE

Does length affect the rate of swing of a pendulum?		Does weight affect the rate of swing of a pendulum?		Does the release angle affect the rate of swing of a pendulum?	
What variable did you manipulate?		What variable did you manipulate?		What variable did you manipulate?	
What variables did you control?		What variables did you control?		What variables did you control?	
What responding variable did you measure?		What responding variable did you measure?		What responding variable did you measure?	
Length of Pendulum	Rate (number of swings in 15 seconds)	Weight of Pendulum (number of pennies)	Rate (number of swings in 15 seconds)	Angle of Pendulum Release	Rate (number of swings in 15 seconds)
20 cm		1		small	
40 cm		2		medium	
60 cm		3		large	
What can you conclude about length and rate of swing?		What can you conclude about weight and rate of swing?		What can you conclude about the angle of release and rate of swing?	

This data table is not only a place for students to record measurements so they can remember them but also a "think sheet" that facilitates the planning and conducting of investigations, guides the students in recognizing relationships, and assists them in drawing conclusions.

EXPLAIN: ASSIST
STUDENTS TO DEVELOP
CONCEPTS, PRINCIPLES,
MODELS, AND
EXPLANATIONS.

f. Instruct students to use their data to answer their questions about the factors that affect the rate of a pendulum.

    If students have changed more than one variable at a time (for example, changing length and weight together), discuss with them the importance of experimental design. Ask: *Why must you change only one variable at a time when investigating? Why must other variables be kept constant?* (So you can be sure which of the variables really made a difference.)

    Guide students to use their data to arrive at these conclusions:
1. The rate of swing decreases as the length of the pendulum increases.
2. The rate of swing is not affected by changes in the weight of the pendulum bob.
3. The rate of swing is not affected by changes in the angle of release.

ELABORATE: PRESENT
PROBLEMS AND ASK
QUESTIONS TO EXTEND
CONCEPTS AND PRINCIPLES.

Students often have great difficulty in controlling variables while experimenting. For a dramatic example, see the video clip and essay about designing pendulum investigations for seventh grade students in Chapter 3 of the Companion Website: http://www.prenhall.com/carin.

g. Using data from the whole class and an overhead transparency of a grid (or a computer graphing program or spreadsheet and LCD projector), show students how to construct a graph of *rate* versus *length* for pendulums. Rate (the number of swings in 15 seconds) should be graphed on the y axis (vertical axis). Length should be graphed on the x axis. Explain that scientists conventionally graph the *independent* variable (the variable deliberately *manipulated*) on the x axis and the *dependent* variable (the variable responding to the deliberate manipulation) on the y axis.

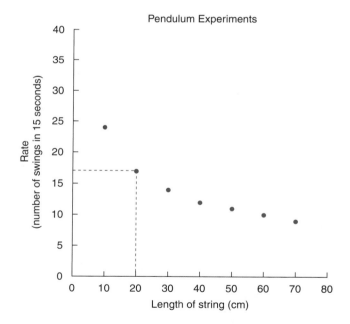

1. Explain to students that the graph visually depicts the *pattern of changes* in rate that occur when the length of the pendulum is changed.
2. Ask students how they can use the data tables and graph to predict future events as well as indicate their observations and arrive at conclusions.
3. Once they have recorded the number of swings per 15 seconds for string lengths of 20 cm, 40 cm, and 60 cm, for example, lead students to use the pattern of change represented by the graph to predict the rate for a pendulum length that is between two measured lengths (30 cm or 35 cm, for example) and the rate for a pendulum length that is greater than any length shown on the graph (an 80 cm pendulum, for example).

4. Ask students to test their predictions by making pendulums of the designated lengths and measuring the rate of swing for each one (the number of swings in 15 seconds).

Encourage students to notice pendulums in the world around them. Grandfather clocks, swings, and trapezes are all forms of pendulums.

EVALUATE: USE FORMAL AND INFORMAL MEANS TO ASSESS STUDENTS' KNOWLEDGE, UNDERSTANDING, AND INQUIRY SKILLS.

1. Performance assessment task for cooperative learning groups:
   - Instruct students to create a pendulum that swings from one extreme to the other in one second (7.5 complete back-and-forth swings in 15 seconds).
   - Encourage students to try to predict the appropriate length. (*Note:* A 100 cm pendulum is needed.) Students can use data from their previous investigations and gather additional data as needed. Remind students of the data tables and graph created previously.
   - Develop and use a rubric to assess levels of group performance in solving the task.
2. Assessment task for individuals:
   - Ask students to explain in writing: *How would you adjust a grandfather clock that was running too fast? too slow?* (Students should realize that the pendulum must be lengthened for the clock to slow down and shortened for the clock to run faster.)
   - You might develop and use a rubric to assess levels of individual performance in solving the task.

III. SOUND

Sound is an important part of our lives, enabling us to communicate with one another, be alert to different situations, and enjoy music and the sounds of the world around us. The simple activities included here enable children to begin to understand the basic physics of sound. Consistent with the *National Science Education Standards*, topics studied include sources of sounds, how sounds travel, and detectors of sound.

A. SOURCES OF SOUND

▶ *Science Background*

Sounds are produced when objects vibrate or move back and forth rapidly. An object that produces sound is called a sound source. Many different objects can generate sounds. For example, musical instruments produce sound when some part of them is made to vibrate.

Characteristics such as pitch and loudness allow us to distinguish one sound from another. Pitch is determined by the frequency, or rate of a vibration of sound. Humans can ordinarily hear pitches between about 15 Hz (15 vibrations per second) and 20,000 Hz. Dogs and cats can hear frequencies as high as 30,000 Hz. Ultrasound refers to high-pitched sounds beyond the range of human hearing. Physicians rely on the penetrating power of ultrasound to see inside the human body and examine internal organs or check the development of babies.

NSES   **Science Standards**

All students should develop an understanding of

- position and motion of objects (sound) (K–4).

Objectives for Students

1. Define *vibration* as the back-and-forth movement of an object.
2. Demonstrate, describe, and explain the generation of sound by various vibrating sources.
3. Define *pitch* as how high or low a sound is. Demonstrate, describe, and explain how the pitch of a sound may be varied.
4. Define *loudness* as the amount, amplitude, or intensity of sound. Demonstrate, describe, and explain how the loudness of a sound may be increased.

NSES Concepts and Principles

Activities 1–8 address these fundamental concepts and principles related to the *Science Standards:*

- Sound is produced by vibrating objects (K–4).
- The pitch of a sound can be varied by changing the rate of vibration (K–4).

1. HOW ARE SOUNDS PRODUCED? (2–4)

Materials   Craft sticks

ENGAGE: ASK A QUESTION ABOUT OBJECTS, ORGANISMS, OR EVENTS IN THE ENVIRONMENT.

a. Ask: *How can you use a craft stick to create sounds?*

EXPLORE: PLAN AND CONDUCT SIMPLE INVESTIGATIONS TO COLLECT RELEVANT DATA.

b. Instruct students to hold a 15 cm craft stick firmly against a desk with one hand. With the other hand, they should pluck the overhanging part of the stick, causing it to vibrate.

EXPLAIN: USE DATA TO GENERATE INTERPRETATIONS, INCLUDING DESCRIPTIONS, CLASSIFICATIONS, AND EXPLANATIONS.

c. Ask: *What is meant by vibration? Which part of the craft stick vibrates and produces sound?*

2. WHAT AFFECTS THE PITCH AND LOUDNESS OF A SOUND? (2–4)

Materials   Craft sticks

ENGAGE: ASK A QUESTION ABOUT OBJECTS, ORGANISMS, OR EVENTS IN THE ENVIRONMENT.

a. Ask: *How can you create sounds of different pitches with a craft stick?*

EXPLORE: PLAN AND CONDUCT SIMPLE INVESTIGATIONS TO COLLECT RELEVANT DATA.

b. Challenge students to produce a high-pitched sound by vibrating the stick and to produce a low-pitched sound by vibrating the stick.

EXPLAIN: USE DATA TO GENERATE INTERPRETATIONS, INCLUDING DESCRIPTIONS, CLASSIFICATIONS, AND EXPLANATIONS.

c. Ask: *What is meant by the pitch of a sound? How can you change the pitch of a vibrating craft stick? Does the craft stick vibrate faster or slower when more of it hangs over the edge of a desk?*

3. HOW IS SOUND PRODUCED BY A TUNING FORK? (2–4)

Materials   Tuning forks
                         Wood blocks
                         Container of water

Safety Precautions   To protect tuning forks from damage, strike them only against a wood surface or the sole of your shoe or with a rubber mallet to produce vibrations and sounds.

ENGAGE: ASK A QUESTION ABOUT OBJECTS, ORGANISMS, OR EVENTS IN THE ENVIRONMENT.

a. Ask: *What is a tuning fork? How does a tuning fork produce sounds?*

EXPLORE: PLAN AND CONDUCT SIMPLE INVESTIGATIONS TO COLLECT RELEVANT DATA.

b. Instruct students to observe while you conduct this demonstration:
   1. Hold the tuning fork by its stem.
   2. Strike a wood block or sole of your shoe crisply with the tip of one of the fork tines.
   3. Bring the fork near your ear and listen. Strike the fork again and lightly touch the tip of one of the fork tines to the surface of the water in a container.

EXPLAIN: USE DATA TO GENERATE INTERPRETATIONS, INCLUDING DESCRIPTIONS, CLASSIFICATIONS, AND EXPLANATIONS.

c. Ask: *What vibrates in producing sound from a tuning fork? What is your evidence that the fork tines are vibrating?*

4. HOW IS SOUND PRODUCED WHEN YOU TALK OR SING? (2–4)

ENGAGE: ASK A QUESTION ABOUT OBJECTS, ORGANISMS, OR EVENTS IN THE ENVIRONMENT.

a. Ask: *When you talk or sing, what part in your body vibrates to produce the sound?*

EXPLORE: PLAN AND CONDUCT SIMPLE INVESTIGATIONS TO COLLECT RELEVANT DATA.

b. Have students place their fingers on their voice box or larynx near the bottom of their throats. Tell them to buzz like a bee.

EXPLAIN: USE DATA TO GENERATE INTERPRETATIONS, INCLUDING DESCRIPTIONS, CLASSIFICATIONS, AND EXPLANATIONS.

c. Ask: *What did you feel in your voice box when you buzzed like a bee? What vibrates in your throat to produce sounds?*
   Help students understand that inside your throat is a voice box or larynx. When you buzz, speak, or sing, air passes across the voice box, causing it to vibrate and produce sounds.

5. HOW IS SOUND PRODUCED BY A DRUM? (2–4)

Materials

Cylindrical container
Puffed rice or wheat cereal
Large balloon or sheet rubber
Strong rubber band
Drumstick or pencil with eraser

ENGAGE: ASK A QUESTION ABOUT OBJECTS, ORGANISMS, OR EVENTS IN THE ENVIRONMENT.

a. Ask: *What vibrates in a drum to produce sound?*

EXPLORE: PLAN AND CONDUCT SIMPLE INVESTIGATIONS TO COLLECT RELEVANT DATA.

b. Stretch a large balloon or piece of sheet rubber over the open end of a cylindrical container, such as an oatmeal container. Place a rubber band around that end to hold the rubber sheet securely in place. This makes a simple drum. Sprinkle puffed rice or wheat cereal on the drumhead. Tell students to tap the drumhead softly with a drumstick or eraser end of a pencil and observe what happens. Then tell them to hit the drumhead harder and watch the cereal and observe the sound produced.

EXPLAIN: USE DATA TO GENERATE INTERPRETATIONS, INCLUDING DESCRIPTIONS, CLASSIFICATIONS, AND EXPLANATIONS.

c. Ask: *What part of a drum vibrates to produce sound? What is your evidence? What is meant by loudness? How do you vary the loudness of a drum?*

6. HOW IS SOUND PRODUCED BY A BANJO? (2–4)

Materials

Rubber bands of varying lengths and thicknesses
Small, open box or plastic cup

ENGAGE: ASK A QUESTION ABOUT OBJECTS, ORGANISMS, OR EVENTS IN THE ENVIRONMENT.

a. Ask: *What vibrates to produce sound in a stringed musical instrument, such as a banjo?*

EXPLORE: PLAN AND CONDUCT SIMPLE INVESTIGATIONS TO COLLECT RELEVANT DATA.

b. Tell students to make banjos by stretching rubber bands of varying lengths and thicknesses over a small box or plastic cup. Pluck the rubber bands to produce sounds.

EXPLAIN: USE DATA TO GENERATE INTERPRETATIONS, INCLUDING DESCRIPTIONS, CLASSIFICATIONS, AND EXPLANATIONS.

c. Ask: *What part of a rubber band banjo vibrates to produce sound? What is your evidence?* Many good activities on sound concern musical instruments. Rather than focusing on music or on band instruments, keep the focus on what is vibrating to produce the sound in each instrument. Studies in the physics of sound will lay a good foundation for musical training on the fundamentals of music, how specific band instruments are played, and how they work.

d. Ask: *What do you think might affect the pitch of the sound from a banjo?* Instruct students to investigate how the pitch of a sound is varied on a rubber band banjo by varying the tension and thickness of the rubber bands. Ask: *What two variables can you change to vary the pitch of a rubber band banjo? How do you vary the loudness of the banjo?*

ELABORATE: USE DATA TO GENERATE INTERPRETATIONS, INCLUDING DESCRIPTIONS, CLASSIFICATIONS, AND EXPLANATIONS.

e. Ask: *How can you vary the pitch of the sound produced by a stringed musical instrument, such as a guitar or ukulele?* Allow students to investigate how strings of differing thickness produce different pitches in guitars, ukuleles, or other stringed instruments. Demonstrate how the tension of a string can be varied to produce high- and low-pitched sounds with a guitar or other stringed instrument.

▶ *Teaching Background*

Each time a guitar player plucks a guitar string, it starts to vibrate. The rate of vibration determines the pitch of the string. Guitars have strings of differing thickness. Thinner strings vibrate more quickly and produce higher-pitched sounds than thicker ones. Strings under greater tension also vibrate more quickly and produce higher pitches than strings under less tension. The musician uses the tuning knobs on the guitar to adjust the tension of the strings. As she increases the tension of a string, that string vibrates more rapidly and the pitch gets higher. As she decreases the tension of a string, the string vibrates more slowly and the pitch gets lower.

Source: Full Option Science System, *Physics of Sound.* Lawrence Hall of Science, University of California, Berkeley.

7. HOW CAN YOU MAKE A DRINKING STRAW FLUTE? (2–4)

Materials

Drinking straws
Scissors

ENGAGE: ASK A QUESTION ABOUT OBJECTS, ORGANISMS, OR EVENTS IN THE ENVIRONMENT.

a. Ask: *What is a flute? How is sound produced in a flute? How can you vary the pitch of a sound produced by a flute?*

EXPLORE: PLAN AND CONDUCT SIMPLE INVESTIGATIONS TO COLLECT RELEVANT DATA.

b. Give each student a drinking straw. Have students use scissors to cut a V-shape at the end of the straw and pinch it closed to produce a reed.

Pinch here   Cut a V

Side view   Top view

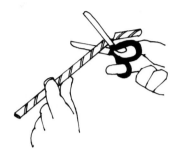

Have students blow on the "V" cut into the straw flute to produce a sound. (*Note:* They will need to experiment to get the proper lip vibration.) Now, have students cut the straw into different lengths and blow on the straw flute to get different pitches.

EXPLAIN: USE DATA TO GENERATE INTERPRETATIONS, INCLUDING DESCRIPTIONS, CLASSIFICATIONS, AND EXPLANATIONS.

c. As you circulate among students, or when you return to a whole class structure, ask: *What part of a straw flute vibrates to produce a sound? What can you vary to change the pitch of a straw flute? How do you think clarinets, oboes, and saxophones produce sounds?*

....

8. HOW CAN YOU MAKE A POP-BOTTLE PIPE ORGAN? WHAT AFFECTS THE PITCH OF THE SOUND PRODUCED BY A POP BOTTLE? (2–4)

Materials

At least eight identical glass pop bottles

ENGAGE: ASK A QUESTION ABOUT OBJECTS, ORGANISMS, OR EVENTS IN THE ENVIRONMENT.

a. Blow across a pop bottle that is about three-fourths full of water so that a sound is produced from the bottle. Ask: *How could you vary the pitch of the sound coming from the bottle?*

EXPLORE: PLAN AND CONDUCT SIMPLE INVESTIGATIONS TO COLLECT RELEVANT DATA.

b. Fill eight identical pop bottles with varying amounts of water. Blow across the open ends of the bottles. Arrange the bottles to play a simple tune.

EXPLAIN: USE DATA
TO GENERATE
INTERPRETATIONS,
INCLUDING DESCRIPTIONS,
CLASSIFICATIONS, AND
EXPLANATIONS.

c. *Ask: What part of a pop bottle vibrates to produce sound? How is the air in the pop bottle made to vibrate? What can you vary to change the pitch of a pop bottle? How do you think pipe organs and horns produce sounds?*

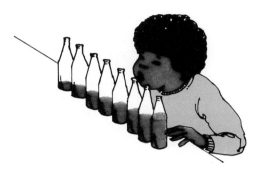

▶ *Teaching Background*

In a pipe organ, air is blown across the bottom opening of a metal pipe. The air in the pipe then vibrates to produce a sound. The pitch of the sound depends on the length and thickness of the pipe. Shorter pipes produce higher-pitch sounds.

When a musician blows air into the mouthpiece of a horn, the air in the open column of the horn vibrates and produces sounds. The pitch of the sound produced in a horn depends on the length and volume of the air column.

B. TRANSFER OF SOUND

▶ *Science Background*

Sound moves away from a source through a material medium. Air, water, and solids are all good media for carrying sound. Sounds travel through media in waves that are analogous to waves at the seashore. Sound cannot travel through a vacuum because there are no particles to vibrate and carry the sound waves. When sound waves bounce off some solid object in the distance, they return to the source as echoes.

Sound travels through air at about 760 miles per hour (1 mile in 5 seconds). In contrast, light travels at 186,000 miles per second. Traveling much slower than light, the sound of the thunder which was produced simultaneously with lightning reaches your ears a few seconds after you see a flash of lightning.

NSES   **Science Standards**

All students should develop understanding of

- position and motion of objects (sound) (K–4).
- transfer of energy (5–8).

Objectives for Students

1. Define *medium* as the material substance through which sound travels from a vibrating source to a receiver. Demonstrate and describe how sound travels through solid, liquid, and gas media.
2. Demonstrate properties of water waves. Describe how sound travels through different media in waves that are analogous to water waves.

3. Demonstrate and describe ways that sound can be directed and amplified.
4. Describe and explain echoes as the reflection of sound waves.

 Concepts and Principles

Activities I and 2 prepare students to understand these fundamental concepts and principles related to the *Science Standards*:

- Energy is transferred in many ways (5–8).
- Vibrations in materials set up wavelike disturbances that spread away from the source. Sound waves and earthquake waves are examples. These and other waves move at different speeds in different materials (*Benchmarks for Science Literacy*, 6–8).

....

1. DOES SOUND TRAVEL THROUGH AIR, SOLIDS, AND LIQUIDS? (2–4)

Materials

Lengths of garden hose
Metersticks
Pieces of metal or rocks
Bucket

ENGAGE: ASK A QUESTION ABOUT OBJECTS, ORGANISMS, OR EVENTS IN THE ENVIRONMENT.

a. Ask: *How does sound travel? Does sound travel through all kinds of materials? Can sound travel through the air in a garden hose? Does sound travel through solids? Does sound travel through water?*

EXPLORE: PLAN AND CONDUCT SIMPLE INVESTIGATIONS TO COLLECT RELEVANT DATA.

b. Have students listen to sounds through straight and curving lengths of garden hose. Make sure all of the water is drained out of the hose.
c. Have students work in pairs. One student should hold a meterstick to her ear. The partner should scratch the other end of the stick with a pencil. Repeat the activity with the meterstick held away from the ear a few centimeters.

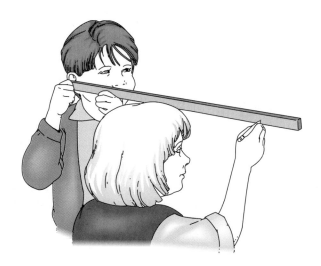

d. Obtain a large bucket of water. Ask students to take two pieces of metal or two rocks and hit them together under the water. Then, tell them to hit the objects together out of water.

EXPLAIN: USE DATA TO GENERATE INTERPRETATIONS, INCLUDING DESCRIPTIONS, CLASSIFICATIONS, AND EXPLANATIONS.

e. Ask: *How does the garden hose demonstration show that sound travels through air?*
What do you hear through the meterstick? How do you think the sound of the pencil travels through the meterstick?
What did you hear when you hit the objects together underwater? Was the sound louder or softer when you hit the objects together out of the water?
Which seemed to be a better conductor of sound: the solid meterstick, air, or water?

2. HOW IS THE MOVEMENT OF SOUND LIKE WAVES ON WATER? (2–4)

Materials

Dominoes
Large dishpan or other container

ENGAGE: ASK A QUESTION ABOUT OBJECTS, ORGANISMS, OR EVENTS IN THE ENVIRONMENT.

a. Ask: *How does sound travel through a material? Does sound travel like a water wave, or like a pulse along a line of dominoes?*

EXPLORE: PLAN AND CONDUCT SIMPLE INVESTIGATIONS TO COLLECT RELEVANT DATA.

b. Instruct students to drop a pebble or other small object into a large dishpan of water and observe what happens. Tell students to place a cork in the water and observe how it interacts with the water wave. Also tell them to notice how the pulses from the disturbance interact with the walls of the container.

c. Ask: *What happens to a curving line of dominoes when you push the first one down?*
Tell students to take 10 dominoes and stand them up on end in a straight row. Push the first domino over so that a chain reaction causes all the dominoes to fall.

EXPLAIN: USE DATA TO GENERATE INTERPRETATIONS, INCLUDING DESCRIPTIONS, CLASSIFICATIONS, AND EXPLANATIONS.

d. Ask: *What do you observe about water waves? What happens to the cork?* (Rather than moving along with the wave, it bobs up and down.) *How does the water wave interact with the walls of the container?* (The water wave reflects off the walls.)

e. Ask: *What travels along the row of dominoes? Is it a domino or a pulse caused by the first domino?*
How might the action of the dominoes be like waves traveling through water? (In both cases, pulses travel.)
How is the pulse traveling along the line of dominoes different from the water wave? (The domino chain reaction is a single pulse; the disturbance at the source of a water wave sends out many pulses coming one after the other.)

f. Ask: *How might the action of dominoes be like sound traveling through a solid, liquid, or air?* (Both sound and the domino pulse are created by an initial disturbance and travel along or through a material.)
Does sound travel more like a pulse along a line of dominoes or more like a wave from a disturbance in water? Why do you think so? How is the reflection of a water wave like a sound echo?

C. RECEIVERS OF SOUND

▶ *Science Background*

Receivers are instruments that detect sound. Sound is one of the many forms of energy. Our ears are marvelously designed receivers of sound that are tuned to keep us in touch with much of our environment.

NSES   **Science Standards**

All students should develop an understanding of

• position and motion of objects (sound) (K–4).

Objectives for Students

1. Explain how the outer ear and megaphone are similar in gathering incoming sound signals.
2. Explain that in receiving sound, a detector in the receiver is set in vibration by the incoming sound signals.
3. Identify and describe the operation of the sound detectors in the human ear and a stethoscope.
4. Compare the ear as a receiver of sound with the eye as a receiver of light.

NSES   **Concepts and Principles**

Activity I addresses these fundamental concepts and principles related to the *Science Standards*:

• Energy is transferred in many ways (5–8).
• Sound is a form of energy (5–8).

1. HOW CAN SOUNDS BE HEARD BETTER? (2–4)

Materials

Stethoscope
Megaphone
Listening tube

ENGAGE: ASK A QUESTION ABOUT OBJECTS, ORGANISMS, OR EVENTS IN THE ENVIRONMENT.

a. Ask: *What part of your body detects sounds? How is your ear specially designed to receive and detect sounds?*

EXPLORE: PLAN AND CONDUCT SIMPLE INVESTIGATIONS TO COLLECT RELEVANT DATA.

b. Roll a piece of poster board into a cylinder and fasten it on both ends with paper fasteners. Have students use the listening tube to listen to faint sounds.

c. To make a megaphone, curl a fan-shaped piece of cardboard into a cone. Fasten the cone with three brass fasteners. Ask students to place the small end of the megaphone to their ears and listen to the faint whispers of partners some distance away from them.

d. Ask students to tap their fingers together and listen to the sound. Have them tap their fingers together again and listen to the sound through a stethoscope. Then, have them tap their fingers underwater and listen to the sound without and with a stethoscope.

Safety Precautions

- Help students to clean earpieces of stethoscopes with alcohol and cotton swabs before using them.
- Caution students not to damage the diaphragm of a stethoscope by striking it against hard objects.

EXPLAIN: USE DATA TO GENERATE INTERPRETATIONS, INCLUDING DESCRIPTIONS, CLASSIFICATIONS, AND EXPLANATIONS.

Ask: *How do listening tubes enable sounds to be heard better?*

Ask: *How does the megaphone enhance hearing? How is a megaphone similar to the outer ear?*

Ask: *How does the stethoscope work? How does a stethoscope enable you to hear soft sounds better?*

Ask: *In what ways do the rolled cylinder, the megaphone, and the stethoscope extend the sense of hearing?*

▶ *Teaching Background*

A sound receiver must be able to detect sound pulses that reach it. The ear is a sound receiver. The outer part of the ear collects sound much like the large end of a megaphone when it is used as a listening tube. When sound energy strikes the eardrum, vibrations are set up which initiate the hearing process.

A stethoscope has a diaphragm that vibrates when sound strikes it. Faint sounds can be detected by the diaphragm. The sounds are then conducted from the diaphragm down the air-filled tubes to the ear. In a similar way, a telephone mouthpiece has a diaphragm that vibrates when sound energy strikes it. In a telephone, the vibrations in the diaphragm are converted electromagnetically to electrical energy. Electrical energy is then conducted from one telephone along telephone wires or from a series of towers to another telephone.

D. SOUND CHALLENGES: HOMEMADE TELEPHONES

 NSES   ### Science Standards

All students should develop an understanding of

- position and motion of objects (sound) (K–4).

Science and Technology Standards

Students should also develop

- abilities of technological design, including the ability to
  a. identify a simple problem of human adaptation in the environment;
  b. propose a solution;
  c. implement proposed solutions;
  d. evaluate a product or design; and
  e. communicate a problem, design, and solution (K–4).

Objectives for Students

1. Construct homemade telephones.
2. Explain the operation of a homemade telephone, using the concepts of vibrating source, conducting material, and receiver.
3. Design and carry out investigations to determine the best type of materials for a homemade telephone.
4. Demonstrate abilities of technological design.

 NSES   ### Concepts and Principles

Activities 1 and 2 address these fundamental concepts and principles related to the *Science Standards*:

- Sound is produced by vibrating objects (K–4).
- Energy is transferred in many ways (5–8).
- Sound is a form of energy (5–8).

1. CAN SOUND TRAVEL THROUGH A STRING? (2–4)

Materials   Spoon
String

ENGAGE: ASK A
QUESTION ABOUT OBJECTS,
ORGANISMS, OR EVENTS IN
THE ENVIRONMENT.

a. Ask: *Can sound travel through a long string?*

EXPLORE: PLAN
AND CONDUCT SIMPLE
INVESTIGATIONS TO
COLLECT RELEVANT DATA.

b. Loop a length of string around a spoon. Try to tie the spoon at about the middle of the string. Hold the two ends of the string in your ears. Bend over so the spoon hangs freely. Have your partner gently strike the spoon with another spoon.

EXPLAIN: USE DATA
TO GENERATE
INTERPRETATIONS,
INCLUDING DESCRIPTIONS,
CLASSIFICATIONS, AND
EXPLANATIONS.

Ask: *What do you observe? What is your evidence that the string is a good conductor of sound?*

ENGAGE: IDENTIFY A
SIMPLE PROBLEM OF
HUMAN ADAPTATION IN
THE ENVIRONMENT.

2. HOW CAN YOU MAKE A DEMONSTRATION TELEPHONE? (2–4)

Materials   String, wire, nylon fishing line
Cups of various kinds (Styrofoam, waxed cardboard, plastic, large, small)
Nail, paper clips, toothpicks

ENGAGE: ASK A
QUESTION ABOUT OBJECTS,
ORGANISMS, OR EVENTS IN
THE ENVIRONMENT.

a. Ask: *How can you design a "telephone" that will enable you to communicate across some distance using a string as a medium?*

EXPLORE: DESIGN AND
IMPLEMENT AN APPROACH
TO THE PROBLEM.

b. Show students how to construct a homemade telephone using plastic cups. In advance, use a small nail to punch a hole in the bottom of each cup. Tell pairs of students to cut a 20 foot (6 or 7 meter) length of string and thread the ends into cups. Tell them to tie a paper clip around each end to hold the string firmly in place inside the cup. Instruct them to try out their homemade telephones with their partners.

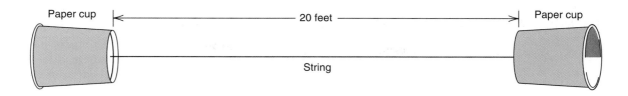

Paper cup |← ——————— 20 feet ——————— →| Paper cup

String

EVALUATE: EVALUATE THE PROBLEM SOLUTION.

c. Challenge students to improve the quality of their homemade telephones by investigating the effects of different string or wire media, different types of cups, and different ways to hold the string or wire against the bottom of the cups. Tell students to come up with standard ways to test their telephones so they can decide which parts are most effective.

EXPLAIN: USE DATA TO GENERATE INTERPRETATIONS, INCLUDING DESCRIPTIONS, CLASSIFICATIONS, AND EXPLANATIONS.

Ask: *What is the original source of sound for your telephones? What is set in vibration in the mouthpiece of the telephone? What is the conductor of sound? How is the sound detected at the other end of the telephone?*

▶ *Teaching Background*

A homemade telephone is a human-constructed product that connects well to scientific principles. Many concepts introduced in the activities on sound are used in this activity. The voice of one partner sets particles of air in vibration. The cup/mouthpiece of the string telephone is then set in vibration. The sound energy produced by the vibrating cup is conducted along the string to the other cup. Thus, the second cup is set in vibration. This vibrating cup sets the air in vibration, producing sound. The sound is then carried to the ear. Designing, constructing, and evaluating homemade telephones provides a good introduction to the technological design cycle.

IV. TEMPERATURE AND HEAT

▶ *Science Background*

Heat, like light, sound, and electricity, is a form of energy. Energy is one of the few concepts in science that children talk about accurately before they can define it. Children's ideas about energy—getting "quick energy" from a candy bar or turning off lights so as not to "waste energy"—may be imprecise but are reasonably close to the concept of energy that we want children to learn (*Benchmarks for Science Literacy*, American Association for the Advancement of Science, 1993, p. 81).

Technically, energy is the ability to do work. More intuitively, something has energy if it can bring about a change in another object or in itself. Heat can bring about many changes. For example, it can change the state of a substance from liquid to gas (evaporation) or from solid to liquid (melting); it can change the temperature of a substance; it can cause most things to expand; and it can change the rate of a reaction, such as how fast a substance dissolves. Changes in temperature give us an indication of how much heat energy has been transferred into or out of a system, but heat and temperature are not the same thing. This is a distinction that is complex and hard for children to understand. Children do not need to know precise definitions of energy, heat, and temperature to investigate them. These can come later in secondary school.

There are many sources of heat in our everyday lives—lights, radios, television sets, motors, computers, friction, and even people. Heat can be transferred or spread from an energy source to an energy receiver by conduction when things are in contact, by radiation across space, or in air and liquids through convection currents. Heat is transferred from the sun to the earth by radiation. Heat energy carried by ocean currents has a strong influence on climate around the world. Weather is also a product of the transfer of heat energy from solar radiation into and out of the earth's atmosphere.

 Science Standards

All students should develop an understanding of

- light, heat, electricity, and magnetism (K–4).
- transfer of energy (5–8).

Objectives for Students

1. Name and describe sources of heat and activities that produce heat.
2. Design, conduct, and interpret experiments to determine the effects of heat on the dissolving time of substances.
3. Describe what happens in the transfer of heat by radiation, conduction, and convection. Give examples of each.
4. Design, conduct, and interpret experiments to determine the effects of the color of a material on the amount of radiated heat absorbed by the material.
5. Design and conduct experiments to determine the final temperature of water mixtures.
6. Explain that heat flows from warmer substances to cooler substances until an equilibrium temperature is reached.

 Concepts and Principles

Activities 1 and 2 address these fundamental concepts and principles related to the *Science Standards:*

- Heat can be produced in many ways, such as burning, rubbing, or mixing one substance with another (K–4).

1. WHAT MAKES THINGS GET HOTTER? (K–5)

Materials

6 inch piece of wire coat hanger
Mineral oil
Brass button
Wool cloth
Piece of metal
Pencil eraser
Notebook paper
Ice cubes
Newspapers or paper towels
Miscellaneous magazines

ENGAGE: ASK A QUESTION ABOUT OBJECTS, ORGANISMS, OR EVENTS IN THE ENVIRONMENT.

a. Ask: *What happens when you bend a wire rapidly or rub your hands together rapidly?*

EXPLORE: PLAN AND CONDUCT SIMPLE INVESTIGATIONS TO COLLECT RELEVANT DATA.

b. Bend a 6 inch piece of wire hanger back and forth 10 times as shown. Quickly touch the wire at the point where you bent it.
    Ask: *What do you feel?* (The wire got hotter.) *What do you think will happen if you bend the wire more times, for example, 20, 25, 30, 35 times?* (Each time the wire gets hotter.)

Safety Precautions

Try out this activity first to find out how many bends will make the wire too hot for students to touch.

c. Rub your hands together very fast and hard. Ask: *What do you feel?* (Heat.) Now rub different things together and quickly touch them to your upper lip or the tip of your nose (sensitive parts of your body): brass button on a piece of wool, metal on paper, pencil eraser on paper, and so on.

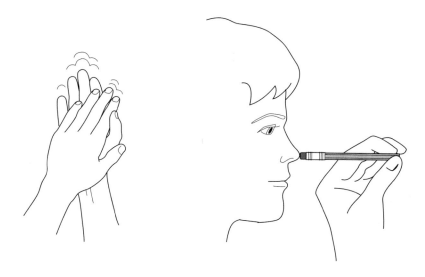

EXPLAIN: USE DATA TO GENERATE INTERPRETATIONS, INCLUDING DESCRIPTIONS, CLASSIFICATIONS, AND EXPLANATIONS.

d. Ask: *What did you observe in each case? How was heat produced in these two investigations?*
    Guide students to understand that bending things and rubbing things produces heat.

ELABORATE: EXTEND
CONCEPTS, PRINCIPLES,
AND STRATEGIES TO NEW
PROBLEMS AND QUESTIONS.

e. Try rubbing your hands together again, but put a few drops of oil or water on your hands first. Ask: *How do you think the second rubbing will feel different from the first rubbing?* Ask: *What did you observe? Why do you think it happened?*

2. HOW CAN YOU HEAT UP THE SAND IN A JAR? (3–6)

Materials

Baby food jar with screw top
Sand
Thick towel
Thermometer

ENGAGE: ASK A
QUESTION ABOUT OBJECTS,
ORGANISMS, OR EVENTS IN
THE ENVIRONMENT.

a. Ask: *What do you think will happen to the sand in a baby food jar if you shake it many times?*

EXPLORE: PLAN
AND CONDUCT SIMPLE
INVESTIGATIONS TO
COLLECT RELEVANT DATA.

b. Fill a baby food jar three-fourths full of sand, screw on the jar top, and then wrap it with a thick towel. Each person should take a turn doing the following things:

1. Measure the initial temperature of the sand, then shake the sand vigorously for 5 minutes.
2. Measure the temperature of the sand.
3. Write your findings on a record sheet like the one shown.

Person	Minutes of Shaking	Temperature in °C
1	5	
2	10	
3	15	
4	20	
5	25	

4. Pass the jar to the next person.
5. When everyone has had a turn, compare the temperature of the sand from the first to the last reading.
6. How were they different? (The temperature was higher after each shaking.)
7. Set up a graph like the one shown, then graph the data from the record sheets.

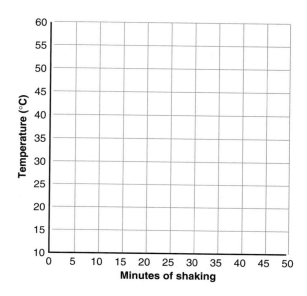

EXPLAIN: USE DATA TO GENERATE INTERPRETATIONS, INCLUDING DESCRIPTIONS, CLASSIFICATIONS, AND EXPLANATIONS.

c. Ask: *What did you observe? What do your data indicate? What was the source of the heat energy in the sand?* Explain that shaking something is a form of energy (mechanical energy; kinetic energy). Heat is also a form of energy. When you shook the sand, the energy of the sand's motion was transferred to heat energy when the sand grains struck one another and the glass. The heat energy in the sand caused its temperature to go up.

ELABORATE: EXTEND CONCEPTS, PRINCIPLES, AND STRATEGIES TO NEW PROBLEMS AND QUESTIONS.

d. Discuss these questions with the class:
1. Why do you rub a match against the side of a matchbox?
2. Why do matches not catch fire while sitting in a matchbox?
3. When you bend a wire back and forth several times, why does it get warm?
4. When you put two pencils together and rub them back and forth several times, what happens to your hands?
5. A person tried to strike a match against a piece of glass to light it. The match would not light. Why?
6. If you feel the tires of your car before you take a trip and then just after you get out of the car, they will not feel the same. How do you think they will differ? How would you explain the difference?
7. A person was chopping wood with an ax. After chopping very hard for about 10 minutes, she felt the ax. How do you think the ax felt and why?

Concepts and Principles

Activity 3 serves as preparation for learning these fundamental concepts and principles related to the *Science Standards:*

- Energy is a property of many substances and is associated with heat (5–8).

3. WHAT ARE SOME SOURCES OF HEAT? (K–5)

ENGAGE: ASK A QUESTION ABOUT OBJECTS, ORGANISMS, OR EVENTS IN THE ENVIRONMENT.

a. Ask: *What do we mean by a source of heat? Are sweaters or mittens sources of heat?* (No.) *Why are we "warm" under the covers on a cold night?* Conduct a brainstorming session on sources of heat. To initiate the following activity, ask: *What happens to an ice cube held in your hand?*

EXPLORE: PLAN AND CONDUCT SIMPLE INVESTIGATIONS TO COLLECT RELEVANT DATA.

b. Hold an ice cube in your hand over newspapers or paper towels. (*Note:* From experience, it is recommended that young students go to the bathroom before and after this activity!)

   Ask: *How does your hand feel with the ice cube in it?* (Cold.) *What is happening to the ice cube?*

c. Leave an ice cube in a nearby dish and notice the difference between this ice cube and the one in your hand.

EXPLAIN: USE DATA TO GENERATE INTERPRETATIONS, INCLUDING DESCRIPTIONS, CLASSIFICATIONS, AND EXPLANATIONS.

d. Ask: *What differences did you observe between the ice cube in your hand and the one in the dish? Why do you think the ice cube in your hand melted more?* (Your hand is a source of heat. Heat from your hand melts the ice cube faster than heat from the room melts the ice cube in the dish.)

Ask: *Which received heat—your hand or the ice cube you held?* (Ice cube; heat moved from hand to ice.)

Ask: *How is this the same as when you pour a warm soft drink over ice cubes?* (The warm drink gets cooler as heat moves from the drink to the ice.)

ELABORATE: EXTEND CONCEPTS, PRINCIPLES, AND STRATEGIES TO NEW PROBLEMS AND QUESTIONS.

e. Students in grades 3–5 could go on a "heat source hunt" in school and at home. Look for sources of heat, places where heat is produced (school or home heater or furnace, oven and stove, toaster, microwave oven, sunshine through windows, electric motors, car engines). List these places in a booklet or chart and illustrate them with magazine or computer pictures. Then, use these three questions to organize your list of heat producers:
   - Where did you see it?
   - What was the source of heat?
   - What was the receiver of heat, that is, what was heated?

Safety Precautions

Caution students not to touch heat-producing appliances or other hot objects.

> **NSES**   **Concepts and Principles**
>
> Activity 4 addresses these fundamental concepts and principles related to the *Science Standards:*
>
> - Most change involves energy transfer (5–8).

4. HOW DOES HEAT AFFECT THE DISSOLVING TIME OF SUBSTANCES? (3–6)

Materials

Six baby food jars or clear plastic tumblers
Sugar cubes
Colored cinnamon candies or jelly beans
Tea bags
Pencils
Two Pyrex or tin pans

ENGAGE: ASK A QUESTION ABOUT OBJECTS, ORGANISMS, OR EVENTS IN THE ENVIRONMENT.

a. Ask: *How does heat affect the dissolving time of substances? What could you do to find out?*

EXPLORE: PLAN AND CONDUCT SIMPLE INVESTIGATIONS TO COLLECT RELEVANT DATA.

b. Lead students to plan and conduct a controlled experiment to determine the effect of heat on dissolving time. Students could set up two sets of three containers of water as follows:
   1. Fill six baby food jars or plastic drinking glasses with water to within 2 cm of the top and let them stand until the water is room temperature.
   2. Slowly lower a sugar cube into each of two containers, a few cinnamon candies or jelly beans into two more, and a tea bag into the other two. (See diagram.) Set up two sets of three containers with sugar, cinnamon candies, and tea bags.

3. Place one set of containers in ice-cold water in a pan and the other set in a pan of very hot water.
4. Observe the two sets of containers and make records of what is seen every 10 minutes.

EXPERIMENT: Substances dissolving with stirring

EXPLAIN: USE DATA TO GENERATE INTERPRETATIONS, INCLUDING DESCRIPTIONS, CLASSIFICATIONS, AND EXPLANATIONS.

c. Ask: *In which containers do you think the materials will dissolve first? Why?*

From the experiment, you can conclude that heat affects dissolving time. The hotter the liquid, the faster a substance dissolves. This investigation uses the strategy of controlled experimenting. If you think your students are ready, you might introduce the concept of variables. The temperature of the water is the manipulated variable (independent variable) and dissolving time is the responding variable (dependent variable). All other conditions are controlled, such as the type of container, the amount of water, and whether or not you stir the water.

NSES   **Concepts and Principles**

Activities 5–7 address these fundamental concepts and principles related to the *Science Standards:*

• Energy is transferred in many ways (5–8).

5. WHAT AFFECTS THE TEMPERATURE CHANGE OF WATER HEATED BY RADIATION? (3–6)

Materials

Three tin cans of same size
Small can of shiny white paint
Small can of dull black paint
Two small paintbrushes
Styrofoam covers for cans
Three thermometers
Lamp with 150 to 300 watt bulb

ENGAGE: ASK A QUESTION ABOUT OBJECTS, ORGANISMS, OR EVENTS IN THE ENVIRONMENT.

a. Ask: *If something is left in sunlight, does its color affect how hot it gets? How could you investigate to find out?*

EXPLORE: PLAN AND
CONDUCT SIMPLE
INVESTIGATIONS TO
COLLECT RELEVANT DATA.

b. Guide students to plan and conduct a controlled experiment to determine the effect of color on heating in sunlight. These activities may be done in cooperative groups. For immature or unruly children, the teacher should demonstrate these activities.
   1. Obtain three identical-sized cans and remove all labels. Paint one can dull black and another can shiny white; leave the third can unpainted, shiny metal.
   2. Fill each can with the same amount of regular tap water.
   3. Put a Styrofoam cover on each can and insert a thermometer through each cover.
   4. Set the cans in direct sunlight or at equal distances from a 150 to 300 watt light bulb. (See diagram.)
   5. Prepare a table for data collection and record the temperature of the water in each can at 1-minute intervals. (Do not move the thermometers when you record the temperature each time.)

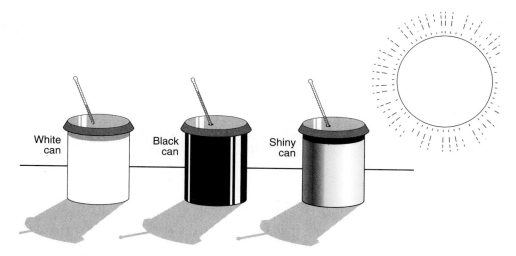

EXPLAIN: USE DATA
TO GENERATE
INTERPRETATIONS,
INCLUDING DESCRIPTIONS,
CLASSIFICATIONS, AND
EXPLANATIONS.

c. Ask: *What happens to the water temperature in the three different cans after being in the sun or near light bulbs for a while? If there are different temperatures, how would you explain that?* Explain that radiation is the transfer of heat across space, such as the transfer of heat energy from the sun to earth. Lead students to understand that the shiny surface of the unpainted can and the shiny white paint reflect radiant energy, whereas the dull black paint absorbs most of the radiant energy.

ELABORATE: EXTEND
CONCEPTS, PRINCIPLES,
AND STRATEGIES TO NEW
PROBLEMS AND
QUESTIONS.

d. Ask: *How would you relate the unequal heating in the tin cans to different land and water surfaces of the earth?* Guide students to understand that dark patches of ground absorb more radiant energy than do shiny water surfaces or lighter-colored land surfaces. The unequal heating of the earth contributes to climate and weather changes.

e. Ask: *What color space suits do astronauts wear? Why?*

6. HOW IS HEAT TRANSFERRED THROUGH CONVECTION? (3–6)

ENGAGE: ASK A
QUESTION ABOUT OBJECTS,
ORGANISMS, OR EVENTS IN
THE ENVIRONMENT.

a. Ask: *Where do you think the warmest and coolest spots are in your classroom?* Try this activity to see if you can find the answer.

EXPLORE: PLAN AND CONDUCT SIMPLE INVESTIGATIONS TO COLLECT RELEVANT DATA.

b. Guide students to plan and conduct this investigation.
1. As far away as possible from the room's source of heat, tape three thermometers to a wall at these places: near the ceiling, halfway up the wall, and near the floor.
2. Make a chart of the thermometer readings once an hour for 1 day.
3. Using the data collected, graph the temperature on the *y* axis (vertical axis) and time on the *x* axis (horizontal axis).
4. From your data and graph, answer these questions:
    Which thermometer consistently had the highest temperatures? the middle temperatures? the lowest temperatures? Why do you think the temperatures were different?

EXPLAIN: USE DATA TO GENERATE INTERPRETATIONS, INCLUDING DESCRIPTIONS, CLASSIFICATIONS, AND EXPLANATIONS.

c. Explain to students that **convection** is the transfer of heat by the movement of either a gas (air) or a liquid (water). When the air in the room is heated, it expands and becomes lighter per given volume. The lighter air then rises as heavier air settles under it. This rising and falling is called a **convection current.**

ELABORATE: EXTEND CONCEPTS, PRINCIPLES, AND STRATEGIES TO NEW PROBLEMS AND QUESTIONS.

d. Ask: *When you see "wiggly lines" rising from a blacktop parking lot on a sunny day, how is this the same as the convection current in our classroom? Why does a "cloud" fall down from a freezer that is above a refrigerator when you open the freezer door? Why does smoke usually rise up a chimney? Under what conditions would smoke come into the house through the fireplace opening? Why would a pinwheel start to spin if put over a lit light bulb?*

  Concepts and Principles

Activity 7 also addresses these fundamental concepts and principles related to the *Science Standards:*

- Heat can move from one object to another by conduction (5–8).

7. HOW IS HEAT TRANSFERRED THROUGH CONDUCTION? (4–6)

Safety Precautions

Because of the use of an open flame from a candle, you should demonstrate all or part of this activity yourself.

Materials

Candle
Matches
Nine thumbtacks
Tripod stand
One 4 3/4 inch square of aluminum foil
Silver or steel knife
4 inch length of copper tubing

ENGAGE: ASK A QUESTION ABOUT OBJECTS, ORGANISMS, OR EVENTS IN THE ENVIRONMENT.

a. Ask: *What do you think will happen to tacks that have been attached with wax to a strip of aluminum foil, to a silver or steel knife, and to a copper tube when the tips of these metals are heated?*

EXPLORE: PLAN AND CONDUCT SIMPLE INVESTIGATIONS TO COLLECT RELEVANT DATA.

b. Demonstrate the following activity for your students:
    1. Obtain a 4 3/4 inch square of aluminum foil, a candle, a match, and nine tacks.
    2. Roll the aluminum foil tightly.
    3. Light the candle. Drip some wax onto three tacks and the aluminum foil rod so the tacks stick to the foil.
    4. Obtain a tripod stand, a silver knife, and a 4 inch length of copper tubing.
    5. Stick three tacks each to the knife and to the copper tubing as you did with the foil.
    6. Place the foil, knife, and copper tubing on a tripod stand as shown in the diagram. Heat the tips of each of these with a candle flame. Have students observe and record what happens.

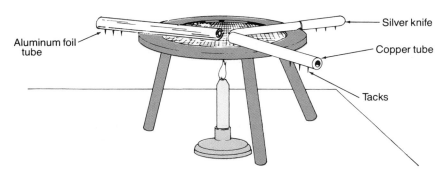

EXPLAIN: USE DATA TO GENERATE INTERPRETATIONS, INCLUDING DESCRIPTIONS, CLASSIFICATIONS, AND EXPLANATIONS.

c. Ask: *Why did the tacks not all fall at the same time? How do you think the heat affected the three metals?*
    Guide students to understand that heat is conducted from a heat source through materials. Heat is conducted through different materials at different rates. Heat is always conducted from hotter to cooler areas.

ELABORATE: EXTEND CONCEPTS, PRINCIPLES, AND STRATEGIES TO NEW PROBLEMS AND QUESTIONS.

d. The following questions relate to radiation, convection, or conduction of heat energy. Tell students to answer each question and to explain or give the evidence for their answers.
    1. When you stand in front of a fireplace and only the front of you is warmed by the fire, how is the heat transferred?
    2. How does heat energy come from the sun to the earth?
    3. What colors are more likely to absorb heat?
    4. Why do people generally wear lighter-colored clothes in the summer?
    5. In the can experiment, what kind of energy did the black surface absorb?
    6. How was the heat transferred from the black surface to the thermometer?
    7. Why is it desirable to have a copper-bottomed tea kettle?
    8. Why would you not want a copper handle on a frying pan?
    9. What metals conduct heat well?

10. What advantage would there be in having a white car rather than a black car?
11. What advantage might there be to having a lighter-colored roof on a house rather than a darker-colored roof?
12. Why would you prefer to put a hot dog on a stick rather than on a wire to cook the hot dog over a campfire?

NSES **Concepts and Principles**

Activity 8 addresses these fundamental concepts and principles related to the *Science Standards*:

- Heat moves in predictable ways, flowing from warmer objects to cooler ones, until both reach the same temperature (5–8).

8. WHAT AFFECTS THE FINAL TEMPERATURE OF A WATER MIXTURE? (3–6)

Materials

Styrofoam cups (at least 250 ml)
Graduated cylinder or measuring cup
Thermometers
Stirring spoon

ENGAGE: ASK A QUESTION ABOUT OBJECTS, ORGANISMS, OR EVENTS IN THE ENVIRONMENT.

a. Ask: *What happens to the temperature of bath water when you add hot water to cold water? Does the amount of hot water and cold water matter? How could you predict the new temperature when hot and cold water are mixed?*

EXPLORE: PLAN AND CONDUCT SIMPLE INVESTIGATIONS TO COLLECT RELEVANT DATA.

b. Tell students to plan an investigation to determine the final temperature when hot and cold water are mixed. Students could plan and conduct the following activity in cooperative groups:
  1. Pour the following volumes of water at the indicated temperatures into separate Styrofoam cups:
     - 100 ml of hot water
     - 100 ml of cold water
     - 50 ml of hot water
     - 50 ml of cold water
     - 150 ml of hot water
     - 150 ml of cold water
  2. Measure and record the temperature of the 100 ml samples of water in a copy of the prepared data table (see illustration). If possible, make all temperature measurements in degrees Celsius.
  3. In a third cup, carefully mix and stir the two 100 ml samples of water.
  4. When the temperature of the mixture stops changing, measure and record the final temperature.
  5. Repeat steps 2, 3, and 4 for the following mixtures:
     - 150 ml of hot water and 50 ml of cold water
     - 150 ml of cold water and 50 ml of warm water

TEMPERATURE OF WATER MIXTURES

	Amount of Water in Each Container	Initial Temperature of Water	Final Temperature of Mixture
Mixture 1	100 ml		
	100 ml		
Mixture 2	150 ml		
	50 ml		
Mixture 3	50 ml		
	150 ml		
Mystery Mixture			Predicted _____ Measured _____

c. Instruct cooperative group recorders to record their data on the class master data table.

EXPLAIN: USE DATA TO GENERATE INTERPRETATIONS, INCLUDING DESCRIPTIONS, CLASSIFICATIONS, AND EXPLANATIONS.

d. Ask: *Do you see a pattern to your final temperature for different mixtures?* Lead students to notice that if the volumes of two samples of water are the same, the final temperature will be halfway between the two initial temperatures. If the volumes of the two samples are different, the final temperature will be nearer the initial temperature of the larger sample.

ELABORATE: EXTEND CONCEPTS, PRINCIPLES, AND STRATEGIES TO NEW SITUATIONS AND QUESTIONS.

e. Tell students you are going to give them a new water mixing problem, but they will need to predict the final temperature before they mix the water samples and take data.

f. Prepare a large container of cold water at near freezing temperature (but with no ice). Prepare another large container of water at room temperature. Give materials managers a cup of cold water and a cup of room temperature water.

g. Instruct groups they are going to mix 175 ml of cold water with 50 ml of warm water. Ask groups to make a prediction of the final temperature and then to conduct the investigation. Predictions do not need to be exact. For example, a group may just predict that the final temperature will be halfway between the temperatures of the two samples or very near the temperature of the larger sample.

h. Instruct recorders to record the predicted and final temperatures of their mixtures on a class chart. Invite students to present and discuss their predictions, the basis of the predictions, and the final temperatures obtained.

Explain that the final temperature of a mixture depends on both the initial temperatures and amounts of the samples. When a large volume of water is mixed with a smaller volume of water, the final temperature will be nearer the initial temperature of the large volume. There are actually mathematical ratios here that can be dealt with at upper grades.

How could you help children understand what scientists do?

i. Ask: *What have you done in this investigation that is like what scientists do?*

Lead students to understand that they have formulated a problem, planned and conducted an investigation, used a thermometer and graduated cylinder to collect data, recorded data in a table, interpreted the data and formed an explanation for experimental results, and tested the explanations through a prediction. These are some of the things scientists do.

V. LIGHT

▶ *Science Background*

Visible light is a form of energy. Along with gamma rays, X-rays, microwaves, and radio waves, light is one of the many forms of electromagnetic radiation. Light is produced by the actions of electrons. Light can be modeled as a wave motion, something like water waves on a still surface. In empty space, light travels at a speed of 186,000 miles per second.

Because our eyes are light detectors, light is an especially important part of our lives, enabling us to see the world around us. We see objects when light that is either emitted or reflected from an object reaches our eyes. Further, light is the energy source for photosynthesis and the growth of plants which sustain both human and animal life. Thus, light is essential for life.

A. SOURCES AND RECEIVERS OF LIGHT

NSES   **Science Standards**

All students should develop an understanding of

• light, heat, electricity, and magnetism (K–4).

Objectives for Students

1. Distinguish between sources and reflectors of light.
2. Identify and describe human-constructed sources of light (e.g., light bulbs) and natural sources of light (e.g., the sun).
3. Explain that our eyes are detectors of light and that we can "see" an object only if light is emitted or reflected from the object.
4. Identify materials that are transparent, translucent, and opaque, and explain what we "see" when each of these materials is placed over an object.

NSES   **Concepts and Principles**

Activities 1 and 2 address these fundamental concepts and principles related to the *Science Standards*:

• Light interacts with matter by transmission (including refraction), absorption, or scattering (including reflection) (5–8).
• To see an object, light from that object—emitted by or scattered from it—must enter the eye (5–8).

1. HOW DO WE SEE THINGS? (1–5)

Materials   Flashlights
                                 Shoe box

Safety Precautions   As they study light, impress on students the importance of protecting their eyes at all times. Students should never look directly into the sun or any other bright light source. Also, they should never look into a laser light source nor shine a laser toward someone else.

ENGAGE: ASK A QUESTION ABOUT OBJECTS, ORGANISMS, OR EVENTS IN THE ENVIRONMENT.

a. Darken the room and write this statement on the chalkboard: "We cannot see without light." Tell students to read what you have written. Illuminate the sentence with a flashlight and tell students to read it. Ask: *How does light enable us to see things?*

EXPLORE: PLAN AND CONDUCT SIMPLE INVESTIGATIONS TO COLLECT RELEVANT DATA.

b. Cut two small holes in a shoe box, one for students to look into the box and the other to illuminate the inside of the box with a flashlight. Place an object in the box, cover the flashlight hole, and put the top on the box. Tell students to look into the box and describe the object. Illuminate the object with the flashlight and tell students to describe the object again.

c. Build a small electric circuit consisting of a bulb in a bulb holder, a battery in a battery holder, a switch, and wires. Place the circuit inside another shoe box with only one hole cut in the end of it. Arrange the circuit so the switch is outside the box and place the top on the box. Tell students to look into the box and describe the objects in it. Tell them to activate the switch and describe the objects again.

EXPLAIN: USE DATA TO GENERATE INTERPRETATIONS, INCLUDING DESCRIPTIONS, CLASSIFICATIONS, PREDICTIONS, AND EXPLANATIONS.

d. Ask: *How did light enable you to see the statement on the chalkboard? How did the flashlight enable you to see the object in the shoe box?* (Lead students to understand that we see things only when light from them reaches our eyes. Light from the flashlight reflected from the object to our eyes, enabling us to see it.) *Why were you able to see the bulb in the box?* (Lead students to apply the idea that we see things only when light from them reaches our eyes. Light coming from the bulb reached our eyes and enabled us to see it. Explain that there are natural sources of light, such as a flame, and artificial, human-constructed sources of light, such as the light bulb.) *Why are you able to see the sun? Why are you able to see the moon? What objects/things can you see in the classroom or outside now? What enables you to see these objects? Which sources of light are natural and which are artificial?* Fill in a chart like the one illustrated for the different rooms in your house.

▶ *Teaching Background*

Emphasize that we can see things only if light emitted or reflected from them reaches our eyes. The eye is a receiver of light, like the ear is a receiver of sound.

Room	Light source	Artificial or natural light

2. WHY CAN WE SEE CLEARLY THROUGH SOME MATERIALS AND NOT OTHERS? (K–2)

Materials

Transparent materials (clear plastic wrap, clear glass)
Translucent materials (wax paper, cloudy plastic)
Opaque materials (paper, cardboard)

ENGAGE: ASK A QUESTION ABOUT OBJECTS, ORGANISMS, OR EVENTS IN THE ENVIRONMENT.

a. Allow students to examine a small object placed underneath a sheet of wax paper or a piece of cloudy plastic. Ask: *What do you see? Why is the object not easily seen?*

EXPLORE: PLAN AND CONDUCT SIMPLE INVESTIGATIONS TO COLLECT RELEVANT DATA.

b. Give each group of students some samples of transparent, translucent, and opaque materials. Ask the students to place one kind of material at a time over a printed page. For each material, have students fill in a chart with one of these choices: (1) can see through it easily; (2) can see through it but not very clearly; (3) cannot see through it.

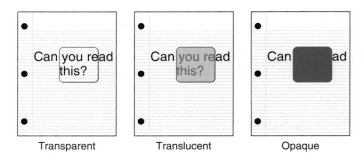

Transparent   Translucent   Opaque

EXPLAIN: USE DATA TO GENERATE INTERPRETATIONS, INCLUDING DESCRIPTIONS, CLASSIFICATIONS, PREDICTIONS, AND EXPLANATIONS.

c. Ask: *How does light interact with each of the different materials you used in the investigation?* Guide students to understand that light is transmitted through transparent media, such as air, water, and glass. Translucent objects transmit some light, but absorb some of the light energy. Opaque objects absorb all of the light energy striking them. We see things only if light reflected from them or passing through them strikes our eyes. A transparent object transmits light to our eyes; translucent objects transmit only a portion of the light from an object to our eyes; opaque objects absorb light so that none of the light is transmitted to our eyes.

B. HOW LIGHT TRAVELS

▶ *Science Background*

Light travels in straight lines until it is absorbed, reflected, or refracted by an object. Unlike sound, light cannot ordinarily bend around corners.

NSES Science Standards

All students should develop an understanding of

- light, heat, electricity, and magnetism (K–4).

Objectives for Students

1. Demonstrate that light travels in straight lines unless it is absorbed, refracted, or reflected by an object.
2. Compare the speed of light to the speed of sound.

NSES Concepts and Principles

Activities 1 and 2 address these fundamental concepts and principles related to the *Science Standards:*

- Light travels in straight lines until it strikes an object (K–4).

1. WHAT TYPE OF PATH DOES LIGHT TAKE AS IT TRAVELS? (1–4)

Materials

Flashlight or projector
Index cards
Hole puncher or pointed object (pencil)
Modeling clay
Wax paper

ENGAGE: ASK A QUESTION ABOUT OBJECTS, ORGANISMS, OR EVENTS IN THE ENVIRONMENT.

a. Tell a child to stand behind a barrier or just outside the classroom so that she can be heard but not seen. Instruct the child to speak softly. Ask: *Can you hear her talking? Can you see her? Why can you hear someone talking when the person is out of sight?*

EXPLORE: PLAN AND CONDUCT SIMPLE INVESTIGATIONS TO COLLECT RELEVANT DATA.

b. Holding three or four index cards together, punch a 1/4 inch (7 mm) hole in the center of each card. Stand each card up in a lump of modeling clay. Instruct students to space the cards about 30 cm apart and to arrange them in such a way that light from a flashlight passes through the center hole in each of the cards.

EXPLAIN: USE DATA
TO GENERATE
INTERPRETATIONS,
INCLUDING DESCRIPTIONS,
CLASSIFICATIONS,
PREDICTIONS, AND
EXPLANATIONS.

c. Ask: *What must you do to the holes in the index cards if light is to pass through them? Do you think that light travels along a straight or curved pathway? What is your evidence, or why do you think so? Can light travel around an opaque object? Can sound travel around an opaque object? How can you test your inference about how sound travels?*

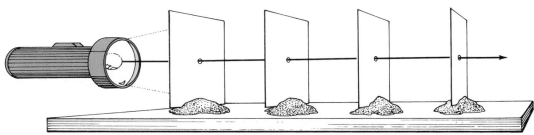

2. HOW ARE SHADOWS FORMED? (1–4)

ENGAGE: ASK A
QUESTION ABOUT OBJECTS,
ORGANISMS, OR EVENTS IN
THE ENVIRONMENT.

a. Have students observe their own shadows. Tell students to make some change so that their shadows are smaller or larger, lighter or darker. Point out shadows in the room, in the school building, and outside. Ask: *How are shadows formed?*

EXPLORE: PLAN
AND CONDUCT SIMPLE
INVESTIGATIONS TO
COLLECT RELEVANT DATA.

b. Place an object between a light source (flashlight or projector) and a screen (such as a white wall). Let students form shadows on the screen.

c. Have students make puppets from cardboard. Make a screen out of a heavy cardboard frame and wax paper. Place the puppet between the flashlight and the screen. Shine a flashlight on the puppet so that a shadow is formed on the screen as shown in the diagram.

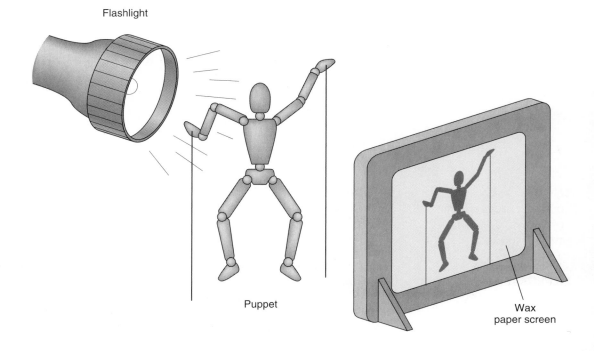

Flashlight

Puppet

Wax
paper screen

EXPLAIN: USE DATA TO GENERATE INTERPRETATIONS, INCLUDING DESCRIPTIONS, CLASSIFICATIONS, PREDICTIONS, AND EXPLANATIONS.

d. Ask: *How are shadows formed? What is the relationship (physical alignment) between the light source, opaque object, and screen when a shadow is formed? What can you do to make a shadow smaller or larger? How do shadows illustrate that light travels in straight lines until it is absorbed by an object?*

ELABORATE: EXTEND CONCEPTS, PRINCIPLES, AND STRATEGIES TO NEW SITUATIONS AND QUESTIONS.

e. Ask: *How is a lunar eclipse related to shadows? What is the light source for a lunar eclipse? What object forms a shadow on the moon?*

▶ *Teaching Background*

Shadows are formed when light from a source strikes the edge of an opaque object, with some light being absorbed and some light moving past the object in a straight line. The object casting the shadow is between the light source and the screen. Shadows can be enlarged by moving the object nearer the light source. Shadows are made smaller when the object is moved farther from the light source.

When teaching about light and shadows, you may wish to discuss lunar phases and eclipses. Lunar phases are not related to the earth's shadow. Lunar eclipses occur when the sun, earth, and moon are aligned. For a lunar eclipse, the earth blocks some sunlight, and a shadow of the earth falls on all or part of the moon. A solar eclipse also occurs when the sun, earth, and moon are perfectly aligned, but shadows are not involved. During a solar eclipse, all or a portion of the sun appears dark because the moon blocks the light.

C. LIGHT REFRACTION

▶ *Science Background*

Light ordinarily travels in straight lines, but it bends or refracts when it passes at an angle into a clear material, such as glass, plastic, or water. Lenses use the property of refraction to form images of objects. A magnifying lens bends the light coming from an object so that we see the object larger than it actually is. A lens can also be used to form an image of an object on a screen.

NSES   **Science Standards**

All students should develop an understanding of

• light, heat, electricity, and magnetism (K–4).

Objectives for Students

1. Describe the refraction or bending of light rays passing through water, clear plastic, or glass.
2. Use knowledge of refraction to explain different light phenomena.
3. Define *magnifying power* and relate it to the curvature of a lens.
4. Define *image* and describe the image of an object formed on a screen.

Activities 1–3 address these fundamental concepts and principles related to the *Science Standards*:

- Light travels in straight lines until it strikes an object (K–4).
- Light can be reflected by a mirror, refracted by a lens, or absorbed by the object (K–4).

1. WHAT IS REFRACTION? (3–6)

Materials

For the teacher:

- Glass
- Pencil
- Opaque cylindrical container such as a large butter tub
- Coin
- Modeling clay

For each group:

- Flashlight
- Black rubber or plastic comb
- Two cylindrical jars of different diameters

ENGAGE: ASK A QUESTION ABOUT OBJECTS, ORGANISMS, OR EVENTS IN THE ENVIRONMENT.

a. Place a pencil in a glass of water so that half of it is in water and half of it out of water. Ask: *What do you see? Why does the pencil seem distorted?*

EXPLORE: PLAN AND CONDUCT SIMPLE INVESTIGATIONS TO COLLECT RELEVANT DATA.

b. Provide each group with a flashlight, a comb, and two cylindrical jars of very different diameters. Show them how to form rays of light by laying the flashlight on a white poster board and shining the flashlight through the comb. Instruct students to follow these directions:
  1. Fill a jar almost full of water, place it in the path of the rays, and observe what happens.
  2. Repeat the procedure with the other jar.
  3. Record your observations. Include any differences you observed.

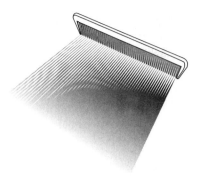

EXPLAIN: USE DATA TO GENERATE INTERPRETATIONS, INCLUDING DESCRIPTIONS, CLASSIFICATIONS, PREDICTIONS, AND EXPLANATIONS.

c. In a large group, invite students to discuss their procedures and observations.

Ask: *What did you observe? What differences did you observe in the effects of the two jars? Which jar, the larger or smaller diameter one, bent the light rays more and caused them to converge nearer to the jar?* Lead students to recognize that the smaller jar, which had the greater curvature of its surface, caused the most bending of the light rays.

Explain that light rays are bent when they pass into and out of a clear material, such as water, plastic, or glass. The bending of light rays is called *refraction*.

Ask: *Why do you think the pencil appeared distorted in the glass of water?* Lead the students to understand that the water bent or refracted the light rays coming from the pencil, causing it to appear distorted.

ELABORATE: EXTEND CONCEPTS, PRINCIPLES, AND STRATEGIES TO NEW SITUATIONS AND QUESTIONS.

d. Invite students to observe the following demonstration and use their knowledge of light to explain what happens.

1. Obtain an opaque, cylindrical container (such as a margarine "tub") that is about 15 cm deep and 15 cm across.
2. Use a small amount of clay or some transparent tape to anchor a coin to the bottom of the container, in the very center.
3. Ask students to stand above the container so that they can see the coin. Then direct them to move back slowly, still looking at the coin, until the coin just disappears from view.
4. With the students fixed in place and the coin just out of sight, gradually pour water into the container, taking care that the coin is not moved by the water.
5. As the water level in the container rises, the coin appears to gradually float into view.

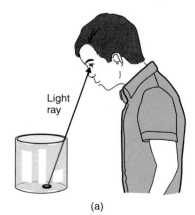

Light ray

(a)

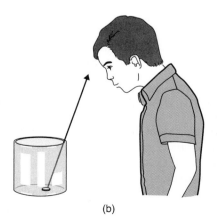

(b)

(c)

e. Ask: *What did you see?* (The coin floated into view.) *Why do you think it happened?* Through discussion, lead students to apply their knowledge of light rays to form this explanation.

> Light rays coming from the coin refract or bend when they pass from the water into the air. Because they have been refracted or bent, the light rays from the coin can then reach our eyes, even though we are not in a direct line of sight with it. Since light ordinarily travels in straight lines, we think the light reaching our eyes comes from high in the water, making the coin seem like it floated upward.

2. WHAT IS A MAGNIFIER? HOW DOES IT WORK? (3–6)

Materials

For each group:

- Two or more cylindrical, glass jars or jugs of different diameters
- Magnifying lenses, including at least two lenses of different magnifying power
- Clear plastic sheets, such as transparency sheets (sandwich bags might be substituted)
- Dropper

ENGAGE: ASK A QUESTION ABOUT OBJECTS, ORGANISMS, OR EVENTS IN THE ENVIRONMENT.

a. Obtain two cylindrical, glass jars of different diameters. Fill them with water within a few centimeters of the top. Allow students to look through each jar of water at some small writing. You can place the jars on a tray and carry them around the room for all students to see. Ask: *What do you see? Do you see the same thing through each jar? Which jar makes things appear larger? Why do you think the jars of water magnify? What other things will magnify?*

EXPLORE: PLAN AND CONDUCT SIMPLE INVESTIGATIONS TO COLLECT RELEVANT DATA.

b. Arrange students in small groups of three or four. Provide each group a clear plastic sheet, a dropper, and a small container of water. Tell students to place different-sized drops of water on the plastic sheet and to look through the drops at some very small writing. Ask: *What do you see through drops of different sizes? Do different-sized drops magnify differently?* (*Note:* Very small drops provide greater magnification.) Tell students to record their observations on a record sheet or in their science journals.

c. Provide at least two magnifiers of different magnifying power to each group. If necessary, show students how to use the magnifiers. Lead students to examine writing and different objects through each of the magnifying lenses. Lead students to compare the magnifying lenses. Ask: *How are your magnifying lenses different? What makes lenses have different magnifying power?*

EXPLAIN: USE DATA TO GENERATE INTERPRETATIONS, INCLUDING DESCRIPTIONS, CLASSIFICATIONS, PREDICTIONS, AND EXPLANATIONS.

d. Invite students to share their observations.

   Explain that what your students see through a lens is called an *image*. Lenses fool our eyes; we think the light comes from the image, when it really comes from the object and only appears to come from the image. The lens bends or *refracts* the light, making it appear to come from the image.

   Define the *magnifying power* of a lens as the number of times bigger it can make an object appear or how many times bigger the image is than the object. Ask: *Which jar had a greater magnifying power?* (The smaller one.) *Which water drop had a greater magnifying power?* (The smaller one.) *Why do you think this is so?* Guide students to understand that the smaller jar and smaller water drops have a greater curvature. Light is refracted or bent more when the surface at which refraction is occurring is curved more. The magnifying power of a magnifier depends on how much the surface of the magnifier is curved. The greater the curvature, the greater the magnifying power.

e. Ask: *Which magnifying lens had a greater magnifying power? Did that lens have a greater curvature?* If lenses are of the same diameter, the lens with greater curvature will be the one that is thicker in the middle.

ELABORATE: EXTEND CONCEPTS, PRINCIPLES, AND STRATEGIES TO NEW SITUATIONS AND QUESTIONS.

f. Challenge students to measure the magnifying power of each of their magnifying lenses. This might be done by examining a millimeter scale through a lens to determine the number of times bigger an image appears than the object.[3]

3. WHAT DO LENSES DO IN CAMERAS? (3–6)

Materials

For the class:

*   Lamp with 40 to 75 watt bulb

For each group:

*   At least two lenses of different magnifying power

ENGAGE: ASK A QUESTION ABOUT OBJECTS, ORGANISMS, OR EVENTS IN THE ENVIRONMENT.

a. Ask: *Where have you seen lenses? What things have lenses in them?* List students' answers on the board. Students might suggest eyeglasses, contact lens, the eye, microscopes, telescopes, projectors, binoculars, cameras, and other instruments.

   Ask: *What do lenses do in cameras? How do they work?*

EXPLORE: PLAN AND CONDUCT SIMPLE INVESTIGATIONS TO COLLECT RELEVANT DATA.

b. Arrange students in groups. Provide two lenses of different magnifying power to each group. Show students how to support a lens vertically by taping it to the bottom of a Styrofoam cup. Remove the shade from the lamp and place the lamp in the room so that all groups have an unobstructed view of it.

[3]Adapted and modified from *More than Magnifiers,* one of more than 75 teacher's guides in the Great Explorations in Math and Science (GEMS) series, available from the Lawrence Hall of Science, University of California at Berkeley. For more information, visit their website at www.lhsgems.org.

Provide these instructions to students:
1. Tape each of the two lenses to the bottom of cups. Label the cups and lenses A and B.
2. Place lens A, supported by a cup, on the table so that it faces the lamp.
3. Fold a white sheet of paper along two opposite edges so it will stand up.
4. Place the sheet of paper behind the lens and move it back and forth until you see an image of the lamp on the paper.

5. Measure and record the distance from the lens to the image on the paper.
6. Ask: *Is the image inverted or right side up?* (Inverted.) *Is the image of the lamp larger or smaller than the lamp itself?* (Smaller.) Record your answers on a record sheet or in your science journal.
7. Repeat the procedures for lens B. Is the image formed on the paper inverted or right side up? Is the image larger or smaller than the lamp?
8. Which lens, A or B, formed a larger image? For which lens, A or B, was the lens closer to the paper screen?

EXPLAIN: USE DATA
TO GENERATE
INTERPRETATIONS,
INCLUDING DESCRIPTIONS,
CLASSIFICATIONS,
PREDICTIONS, AND
EXPLANATIONS.

c. In a large group, invite students to discuss their procedures and observations.
Ask: *Why do you think the images formed of the lamp were inverted?* Draw the following diagram to show how light rays from the top of the lamp are bent or refracted by the lens and converge so that the lamp is upside down.

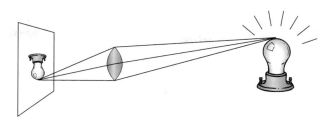

ELABORATE: EXTEND
CONCEPTS, PRINCIPLES,
AND STRATEGIES TO NEW
SITUATIONS AND
QUESTIONS.

d. Ask: *How are lenses used in cameras? What do the lenses do? Do you think the images formed in cameras are right side up or upside down? Are they larger or smaller than the object forming the image?*
Draw on the board the illustration of a camera and lens showing an image formed on a film. Explain that some of the light coming from the bulb strikes the lens. The light is bent and converges on the film so that the image is small and upside down. The film is coated with a light-sensitive chemical. When the film is developed, the image of the bulb is clearly seen.[4]

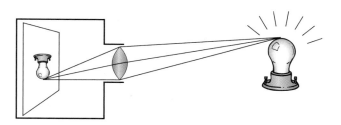

D. LIGHT REFLECTION

▶ *Science Background*

Reflection, the bouncing of light rays, follows a pattern that can be discovered through investigations. Light reflects from a smooth, plane surface in such a way that the angle at which it strikes the surface is equal to the angle at which it reflects from the surface. Mirrors are excellent examples of reflecting surfaces. As a consequence of reflection, images can be seen in mirrors. In a flat, plane mirror, an image is symmetric with the object forming the image, but the image is reversed.

---

[4]Adapted and modified from *More than Magnifiers*, one of more than 75 teacher's guides in the Great Explorations in Math and Science (GEMS) series, available from the Lawrence Hall of Science, University of California at Berkeley. For more information, visit their website at www.lhsgems.org.

NSES   Science Standards

All students should develop an understanding of

• light, heat, electricity, and magnetism (K–4).

Objectives for Students

1. Describe the reflection of light off reflecting surfaces.
2. Describe images in mirrors as symmetric with objects, but reversed.
3. State and apply the rule that an image is formed deep within mirrors at a distance equal to the distance of the object in front of a mirror.

NSES   Concepts and Principles

Activities 1–3 address these fundamental concepts and principles related to the *Science Standards:*

• Light travels in straight lines until it strikes an object (K–4).
• Light can be reflected by a mirror, refracted by a lens, or absorbed by the object (K–4).

1. WHAT ARE IMAGES IN MIRRORS LIKE? WHAT IS MEANT BY MIRROR SYMMETRY? (1–4)

Materials

Mirrors
Pictures of butterflies, flowers, and other things that might show symmetry

ENGAGE: ASK A QUESTION ABOUT OBJECTS, ORGANISMS, OR EVENTS IN THE ENVIRONMENT.

a. Ask: *What does the image in a mirror look like? Is your face reversed in a mirror? Is your face symmetric? Is the left side of your face identical to the right side? Is a butterfly symmetric? Is the left side of a butterfly like the right side? What letters of the alphabet are symmetric?*

EXPLORE: PLAN AND CONDUCT SIMPLE INVESTIGATIONS TO COLLECT RELEVANT DATA.

b. Allow children to examine their own images in mirrors. Show children how to use a mirror to explore the symmetry of different objects and patterns:
   1. Find an axis you think divides the object symmetrically.
   2. Place a plane mirror along that axis.
   3. Look at the image of one-half of the object in the mirror and compare it with the other half of the object.

c. Provide students an activity sheet with all of the letters of the alphabet displayed in block lettering. Tell students to use a mirror to identify all of the axes of symmetry for each letter. For example, ask: *Does the letter* **A** *have an axis of symmetry? How many axes of symmetry can you find for an* **H**?

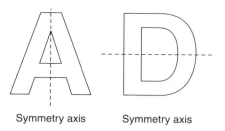

Symmetry axis   Symmetry axis

EXPLAIN: USE DATA TO GENERATE INTERPRETATIONS, INCLUDING DESCRIPTIONS, CLASSIFICATIONS, PREDICTIONS, AND EXPLANATIONS.

d. Ask: *What does the mirror image of your face look like?* Lead students to realize that the image of an object is reversed in a mirror. Ask: *What is meant by symmetry? Where is the axis of symmetry for a butterfly? Does the left side of the butterfly differ from the right side? What letters of the alphabet show symmetry?* Discuss with the students the axis or axes of symmetry of each letter of the alphabet.

2. HOW DOES LIGHT REFLECT FROM A MIRROR? (3–6)

Materials

Flashlight
Cardboard
Transparent tape
Mirrors

Preparation

Make a light-ray source by obtaining a stiff cardboard shield about the diameter of a flashlight, cutting a slit in the shield, and attaching the shield over the lens of a strong flashlight with transparent tape. A light ray is formed when light from the flashlight passes through the slit.

ENGAGE: ASK A QUESTION ABOUT OBJECTS, ORGANISMS, OR EVENTS IN THE ENVIRONMENT.

a. Ask: *Is there a pattern in the way light reflects from a mirror?*
b. Lay the flashlight source on a white poster board so you can see the light ray on the board. Attach a small, plane mirror to a block of wood with a rubber band. Put the mirror in the path of light. Tell children to mark a spot on the poster board and to orient the mirror so that the reflected ray hits the spot. Instruct the students to initially

use trial and error to align the mirror so that the reflected light ray hits the desired spot. Gradually, the students should make and test predictions of how the mirror should be aligned to direct the reflected light ray to the spot.

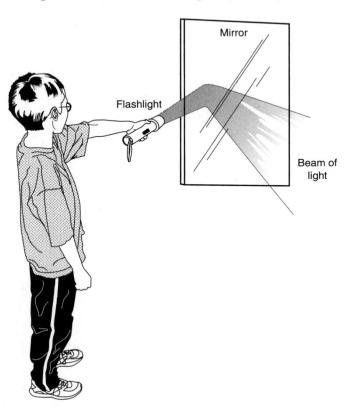

Mirror

Flashlight

Beam of light

EXPLAIN: USE DATA TO GENERATE INTERPRETATIONS, INCLUDING DESCRIPTIONS, CLASSIFICATIONS, PREDICTIONS, AND EXPLANATIONS.

c. Ask: *How does light reflect from a mirror? What pattern did you detect about how light reflects? How did you know how to align a mirror to make a reflected light ray hit a desired spot?* Lead students to understand that the angle formed between a reflected light ray and a mirror is the same as the angle between the incident light ray and the mirror.

3. WHERE ARE THE IMAGES FORMED IN REFLECTING SURFACES? (4–6)

Materials

Light sources
Empty glass aquarium

ENGAGE: ASK A QUESTION ABOUT OBJECTS, ORGANISMS, OR EVENTS IN THE ENVIRONMENT.

a. Place a candle upright in an aluminum pie pan in front of an empty aquarium. Place a second candle inside the aquarium. Light the first candle. Allow students to stand behind the lit candle and to look into the aquarium. Ask: *What do you see? Do you see an image of the candle and candle flame inside the aquarium? Where is the image?*

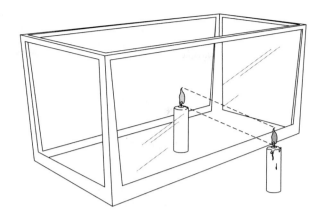

EXPLORE: PLAN
AND CONDUCT SIMPLE
INVESTIGATIONS TO
COLLECT RELEVANT DATA.

b. Locate a plate glass door within the school. Allow students to explore their own images formed within the door. If students do not come up with this idea, suggest that one person (the image partner) stand on the other side of the door right on top of the image of another person (the object partner). Provide metersticks and ask students to measure, record, and compare the object distance and image distance.

EXPLAIN: USE DATA
TO GENERATE
INTERPRETATIONS,
INCLUDING DESCRIPTIONS,
CLASSIFICATIONS,
PREDICTIONS, AND
EXPLANATIONS.

c. Ask: *What did you observe about the image of the candle flame?* (If the candle inside the aquarium is positioned correctly, the image of the flame can be seen right on top of the second candle, so that the second candle appears to be lit.) *What did you observe about your image in the door?* (The image was the same size as the object, but was reversed.) *How did the object distance compare to the image distance?*

E. LIGHT AND COLOR

Color is a response of the human eye to different frequencies of visible light. The color spectrum includes red, orange, yellow, green, blue, indigo, and violet. White is a combination of all colors. An object appears black when all colors are absorbed by it. The color of an object depends on the colors absorbed and reflected. A red object, for instance, will appear red because it reflects mostly red and absorbs other colors of light.

1. WHAT IS WHITE LIGHT? (K–4)

Materials

Prism
Sheet of heavy, white cardboard
Scissors
Felt markers or crayons
String

ENGAGE: ASK A QUESTION ABOUT OBJECTS, ORGANISMS, OR EVENTS IN THE ENVIRONMENT.

a. Obtain a prism. Place the prism in the path of a strong beam of light as indicated in the diagram.
    Ask: *What do you see? What happened to the white light when it passed through the glass prism? What colors do you see?*

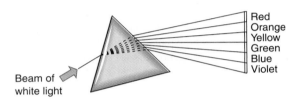

EXPLORE: PLAN AND CONDUCT SIMPLE INVESTIGATIONS TO COLLECT RELEVANT DATA.

b. Challenge students to construct color wheels by following these directions:
    1. Cut out a circle about 10 cm in diameter from stiff cardboard.
    2. Divide the circle into three pie-shaped sections.
    3. Use felt markers or crayons to color each section a different color.
    4. Punch two small holes about a centimeter apart in the center of the cardboard circle.
    5. Pass a string about 60 cm long through the two holes; tie the free ends of the string forming a loop.
    6. Hold the loop by the ends and turn the cardboard color wheel many times, twisting the string as you go.
    7. Pull the two ends of the string suddenly and watch the color wheel spin. What do you see? What colors do you observe as the color wheel is spinning?
c. Let different groups color their color wheel sections differently. Have groups compare what they see with different color wheels.

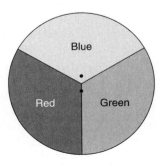

EXPLAIN: USE DATA TO GENERATE INTERPRETATIONS, INCLUDING DESCRIPTIONS, CLASSIFICATIONS, PREDICTIONS, AND EXPLANATIONS.

d. Invite students to report on their procedures and findings related to their color wheels.

Ask: *What did the prism do to the light?* (It separated white light into different colors.) *What did the color wheel do to the light?* (It combined different colors to form a white color.)

Lead students to understand that white light is produced by the combination of several different colors. A prism breaks white light into its constituent parts. A color wheel combines different colors, forming white.

F. A LIGHT CHALLENGE: PINHOLE CAMERA

▶ *Science Background*

A pinhole camera can be used to illustrate what happens in a regular camera. In a pinhole camera, light passes through a small hole in the end of a box and forms an inverted image on a wax paper screen. In a real camera, light is focused by a lens and forms an inverted image on a strip of film.

NSES   **Science Standards**

All students should develop understanding of

• light, heat, electricity, and magnetism (K–4).

Objectives for Students

1. Construct a pinhole camera and demonstrate how it works to form an image.
2. Describe the pathway of light as it passes through a hole in the end of a pinhole camera and forms an inverted image on a wax paper screen in the camera.

NSES   **Concepts and Principles**

Activity I addresses these fundamental concepts and principles related to the *Science Standards*:

• Light travels in straight lines until it strikes an object (K–4).

1. HOW CAN YOU MAKE A PINHOLE CAMERA? (3–6)

ENGAGE: ASK A QUESTION ABOUT OBJECTS, ORGANISMS, OR EVENTS IN THE ENVIRONMENT.

a. Ask: *How does a camera work? How can you make a type of camera that illustrates how a camera works? How does a camera use light?*

EXPLORE: PLAN AND CONDUCT SIMPLE INVESTIGATIONS TO COLLECT RELEVANT DATA.

b. Follow these directions to construct a pinhole camera. Students might construct and demonstrate their own pinhole cameras, or the teacher might make one and allow students to use it.
   1. Obtain a shoe box.

2. Cut a hole about 4 cm square in the end of the box. Cover the hole with a larger square of aluminum foil using transparent tape. Using a sharpened pencil, punch a small, clean hole in the center of the aluminum foil.

3. Cut a flap about 3 cm by 5 cm in the other end of the box to use as a window to see into the box.

4. Cut a heavy piece of corrugated cardboard the same size as the end of the box to use as a screen. Cut a rectangular hole in the cardboard, leaving about 2 cm on each side. Tape wax paper over the hole to form a screen.

5. Attach the screen to a small block of wood so that it can stand upright inside the box.

6. Stand the screen upright in the box. Place the lid securely on the box.

7. Point the pinhole in the aluminum foil at a bright object such as a lamp bulb. Look at the screen through the window in the box. Describe and record what you see on the screen. What is the size of the image? Is the image upright or inverted?

8. Point the pinhole camera at other things and report what you see. Record your observations on a record sheet or in your science journal.

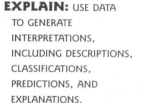

EXPLAIN: USE DATA TO GENERATE INTERPRETATIONS, INCLUDING DESCRIPTIONS, CLASSIFICATIONS, PREDICTIONS, AND EXPLANATIONS.

Ask: *What did you see on the pinhole camera screen when you looked at the lamp? Did you see an image of the bulb? How large was the image compared to the bulb? Was the image upright or inverted? How was the image formed in the pinhole camera? How is a pinhole camera like a real camera?*

Use the following diagram to help students understand how the image is formed on the screen in a pinhole camera. Light from the top of the bulb travels in a straight line, passes through the pinhole, and strikes the screen, forming an inverted image.

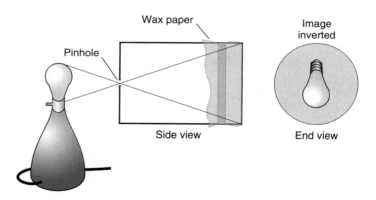

Pinhole   Wax paper   Image inverted

Side view   End view

VI. MAGNETISM

▶ *Science Background*

The *National Science Education Standards* emphasize that, through the study of its history and nature, students should begin to understand science as a human endeavor. The study of magnetism is a very good place for students to examine the long history of science and technology. As you guide students in learning about magnetism, provide them with interesting information about the history of the topic and make appropriate biographies and other books and resources available to them.

William Gilbert's book on magnetism is readily available as part of Volume 28 of the Great Books Series published by the Encyclopedia Britannica and found in many libraries.

More than 2,000 years ago, people knew that bits of a certain kind of rock, today called magnetite, would stick to iron objects. It was later discovered that when a piece of magnetite was placed on a cork floating in water, the cork would turn until the magnetite lined up in a north-south direction (as determined from observations of the North Star). Around a thousand years ago, this phenomenon was applied in the development of the magnetic compass. Because the magnetite could *lead* a person by indicating directions, it came to be known as a *lodestone (loadstone)* or *leading stone*.

Four hundred years ago, William Gilbert, an English physician, wrote a book titled *On the Loadstone and Magnetic Bodies*. It was the first important work in physical science published in England. Gilbert's book provides the first written account of numerous experiments on magnetism, experiments which can be readily carried out in elementary and middle school science today. Gilbert argued for a new method of knowing, dedicating his book to those "ingenuous minds, who not only in books, but in things themselves look for knowledge."

In the activities in this section, we will explore the following concepts, most of which were also set out by William Gilbert:

- Objects containing iron stick to a magnet.
- Magnets come in many sizes and shapes.
- Magnetism can occur naturally, or it can be induced in objects containing iron.
- All magnets, regardless of their size or shape, have two places, called poles, where magnetic forces are greatest.
- When two magnets are brought together, like poles repel (push one another apart), while unlike poles attract (pull one another together).
- The magnetic field around a magnet can be mapped by a compass or iron filings. The greater the distance from the pole of a magnet, the less the magnetic force.
- Magnetic forces act through most materials, although the magnetic interaction decreases with the thickness of the materials.
- The earth acts like a large bar magnet is buried within it, with an S-pole near the north geographic pole and an N-pole near the south geographic pole.
- The earth's magnetic poles are today almost a thousand miles from the geographic poles. (Gilbert assumed, erroneously, that the magnetic poles and geographic poles coincided.)

Some of the concepts and activities in this section are adapted from a FOSS (Full Option Science System) grade 3–4 unit on *Magnetism and Electricity*.

A. MAGNETS AND MAGNETIC MATERIALS

NSES Science Standards

All students should develop an understanding of

- light, heat, electricity, and magnetism (K–4).

Objectives for Students

1. Identify materials that interact with magnets.
2. State that magnets come in many sizes and shapes.
3. Demonstrate that only objects containing iron stick to magnets.
4. Demonstrate that magnetism will act through most materials.

1. HOW DOES A MAGNET INTERACT WITH DIFFERENT OBJECTS? (1–4)

Materials

For each group:

- Assortment of magnets, including bar magnets, U-shaped magnets, ring magnets, disc magnets, and other magnets
- Bag of assorted magnetic materials (objects containing iron, such as paper clips and most screws and nails) and nonmagnetic materials (such as wood, plastic, and paper objects, and non-iron metallic objects, such as aluminum nails, most soda cans, and brass fasteners)

Safety Precautions

- Keep computer disks, audio- and videocassettes, and credit cards away from magnets, as magnets can destroy information on them. Also, keep magnets away from computer and television screens and antique watches, as magnetism can damage them.
- Magnets must be treated with care so as not to destroy their magnetic effects. Magnets can be destroyed by dropping them, extreme heat, or storing two magnets of the same type together.

ENGAGE: ASK A QUESTION ABOUT OBJECTS, ORGANISMS, OR EVENTS IN THE ENVIRONMENT.

a. Give each student a magnet. Without pointing out what it is or calling it a magnet, tell students to find out how the object interacts with the things within reach of their seats. Explain that when things interact, they do something to one another. Many possible interactions may be observed, but the key one is that some objects stick to a magnet. Provide the term *magnet* as the name of the object the students have investigated.

Ask: *What other magnets have you seen or used? What were their shapes? What were they used for?*

Bar   V-shaped   U-shaped   Horseshoe   Cylindrical   Lodestone   Doughnut-shaped

EXPLORE: PLAN AND CONDUCT SIMPLE INVESTIGATIONS TO COLLECT RELEVANT DATA.

b. Ask: *What kinds of things will stick to magnets?*

Give each small group of students a bag of assorted magnetic and nonmagnetic materials. Instruct students to sort the objects into two piles, according to which objects they predict will stick to a magnet and which will not. When groups have made their predictions, give them magnets and ask them to test each object.

EXPLAIN: USE DATA TO GENERATE INTERPRETATIONS, INCLUDING DESCRIPTIONS, CLASSIFICATIONS, AND EXPLANATIONS.

c. Ask: *How accurate were your predictions? Were you surprised by any objects you tested?* (Students might mention the aluminum nail or the brass fastener.) *Are there any metal objects in the things-that-don't-stick pile? What do you think is the difference between the metal objects in the will stick and won't stick piles?*

▶ *Teaching Background*

Iron is the only common kind of metal that magnets stick to. Magnets will not stick to such metals as aluminum, copper, and brass. Magnets stick to steel because steel is mostly iron.

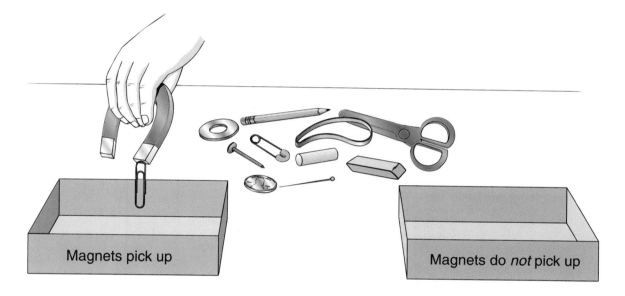

Magnets pick up

Magnets do *not* pick up

ELABORATE: EXTEND CONCEPTS, PRINCIPLES, AND STRATEGIES TO NEW PROBLEMS AND QUESTIONS.

d. Ask students to explore the room to determine which objects interact with magnets. Place "NO MAGNETS HERE!!" signs on computers, computer and television screens, computer disks, and audio- and videocassettes. Caution students not to bring magnets near these objects, because magnets can damage them.

e. Ask: *Which objects interacted with the magnet? Which objects in the room contain iron? What is your evidence? Did some objects, such as painted objects, turn out to contain iron when you thought they would not?*

2. CAN MAGNETS INTERACT WITH OBJECTS THROUGH DIFFERENT MATERIALS? (1–4)

Materials

Magnets
Paper clips

ENGAGE: ASK A QUESTION ABOUT OBJECTS, ORGANISMS, OR EVENTS IN THE ENVIRONMENT.

a. Ask: *Will magnets work through books and other materials?*

EXPLORE: PLAN AND CONDUCT SIMPLE INVESTIGATIONS TO COLLECT RELEVANT DATA.

b. Ask students to investigate if a magnet will attract a paper clip through different materials. Students should try a sheet of paper, cardboard, plastic tumblers, glass jars, aluminum foil, a tin can, and a sheet of steel, such as the walls of a filing cabinet.

EXPLAIN: USE DATA TO GENERATE INTERPRETATIONS, INCLUDING DESCRIPTIONS, CLASSIFICATIONS, AND EXPLANATIONS.

c. Ask: *What kinds of things did you find that magnetic forces act through?*

ELABORATE: EXTEND CONCEPTS, PRINCIPLES, AND STRATEGIES TO NEW PROBLEMS AND QUESTIONS.

d. Challenge students to investigate how many pages of a book magnets can act through.

▶ *Teaching Background*

Magnetic forces act through most materials, although the magnetic interaction decreases with the thickness of the materials.

B. MAGNETIC INTERACTIONS

NSES   Science Standards

All students should develop an understanding of

• light, heat, electricity, and magnetism (K–4).

Objectives for Students

1. Define the terms *force*, *attract*, and *repel* and apply them to the interactions between two magnets.
2. Demonstrate procedures for mapping magnetic fields.
3. State in their own words the meanings of the terms *pole*, *north-seeking* or *north pole*, and *south-seeking* or *south pole*.
4. Demonstrate a procedure for identifying the north and south poles of magnets.
5. State and demonstrate that like poles of magnets repel and unlike poles attract.

NSES   Concepts and Principles

Activities 1–5 address these fundamental concepts and principles related to the *Science Standards* and *Benchmarks for Science Literacy*:

• Magnets attract each other and certain kinds of other materials (K–4).
• Magnets can be used to make things move without touching them (*Benchmarks*, K–2).

1. WHAT HAPPENS WHEN TWO MAGNETS INTERACT? (2–4)

Materials

For each group:

- Three or four ring magnets

ENGAGE: ASK A QUESTION ABOUT OBJECTS, ORGANISMS, OR EVENTS IN THE ENVIRONMENT.

a. Ask: *How do two magnets interact with each other?*

EXPLORE: PLAN AND CONDUCT SIMPLE INVESTIGATIONS TO COLLECT RELEVANT DATA.

b. Give each pair or small group of students three or four ring-shaped magnets. Ask the students to find out what happens when magnets interact. Allow time for exploration. If necessary, challenge students to try
   - using one magnet to move another magnet without the two magnets touching; and
   - placing several ring magnets over a pencil in different ways to see what happens.

EXPLAIN: USE DATA TO GENERATE INTERPRETATIONS, INCLUDING DESCRIPTIONS, CLASSIFICATIONS, PREDICTIONS, AND EXPLANATIONS.

c. Ask: *What did you do to test how the magnets interact? What did you find out about how the two magnets interact?* Building on the children's activities, use discussion and expository teaching to help them understand the terms *attract*, *repel*, and *force* to describe magnetic interactions.
   - When two magnets or a magnet and an object come together, we say they attract.
   - When two magnets push apart, we say they repel.
   - A force is a push or a pull. We can see some forces, such as when you push someone in a swing. Some forces, such as magnetic forces, are invisible and act without direct contact between objects.
   - Magnets can attract or repel each other. When two magnets come together, there is a force of attraction. When two magnets push apart, there is a force of repulsion.

2. HOW DO THE ENDS (POLES) OF TWO MAGNETS INTERACT WITH EACH OTHER? (2–6)

Materials   Bar magnets
Masking tape

ENGAGE: ASK A QUESTION ABOUT OBJECTS, ORGANISMS, OR EVENTS IN THE ENVIRONMENT.

a. Place masking tape over the ends of bar magnets so the N-pole and S-pole designations are obscured. Provide each group with three identical bar magnets with taped ends. Ask: *Can you find a way to determine which ends of the magnets are the same?*

EXPLORE: PLAN AND CONDUCT SIMPLE INVESTIGATIONS TO COLLECT RELEVANT DATA.

b. The students should arrive at the idea that if the ends of two magnets are the same, then they interact in the same way with the end of the third magnet. For example, if the ends of two magnets both attract one end of a third magnet, the ends of the first two magnets are the same. Tell children to use red and blue crayons to designate the like ends of the three magnets. (*Note:* Do not introduce the terms *magnetic pole* and *north* and *south magnetic poles* yet. They will be introduced through later investigations.)

EXPLAIN: USE DATA TO GENERATE INTERPRETATIONS, INCLUDING DESCRIPTIONS, CLASSIFICATIONS, AND EXPLANATIONS.

c. Ask: *Now that you know which ends of the magnets are like and which are unlike, can you find a pattern or rule in how like and unlike ends of magnets interact?*

     Through exploration, discussion, and expository teaching of new concepts, make sure that students understand this rule:

* When two magnets are brought together, like poles repel (push one another apart), while unlike poles attract (pull one another together).

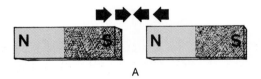

A

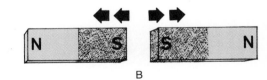

B

Ask the students to try out their rule with other types of magnets, such as ring-shaped magnets.

3. WHAT ARE MAGNETIC FORCE LINES? (2–6)

Materials   Magnets
Iron filings
Food storage bags

Preparation   Sprinkle iron filings into a large, transparent, food storage bag so that a thin layer covers about three-fourths of the area of one side of each bag. Prepare a bag for each cooperative group of students.

ENGAGE: ASK A QUESTION ABOUT OBJECTS, ORGANISMS, OR EVENTS IN THE ENVIRONMENT.

a. Ask: *How will a magnet interact with the material in this storage bag?*

EXPLORE: PLAN AND CONDUCT SIMPLE INVESTIGATIONS TO COLLECT RELEVANT DATA.

b. Ask students to explore what happens when a magnet touches or is brought near a storage bag. Explain that a magnetic field is the region around a magnet that interacts with other magnets or with magnetic materials. Iron filings can be used to map the magnetic force lines in the field of a magnet. Give students these instructions:
  - Spread an iron filings bag out flat on your desk. Tap the bag lightly so that the iron filings are evenly distributed. Slide a bar magnet under the bag. Tap the bag again so that the iron filings move about. (See the diagram.)
  - Draw a diagram of the magnet's field as shown by the iron filings.

  - Experiment with the field around two magnets placed end to end a few centimeters apart so that the magnets attract. Experiment with the field around two magnets placed end to end a few centimeters apart so that the magnets repel.

EXPLAIN: USE DATA TO GENERATE INTERPRETATIONS, INCLUDING DESCRIPTIONS, CLASSIFICATIONS, AND EXPLANATIONS.

c. Ask: *What did you observe about the magnetic field around a single bar magnet? What did you observe about the magnetic field for attracting bar magnets? What did you observe about the magnetic field for repelling bar magnets?*

d. Explain that all magnets have two regions where the magnetic interaction with other magnets or magnetic materials is strongest. These regions are called *poles*. Point out that the concentration of iron filings is greatest at the poles of the magnets.

4. HOW DOES A MAGNET INTERACT WITH THE EARTH, AND WHAT ARE NORTH-SEEKING AND SOUTH-SEEKING POLES OF A MAGNET? (2–6)

Materials

Ring magnets
String
Compasses

ENGAGE: ASK A QUESTION ABOUT OBJECTS, ORGANISMS, OR EVENTS IN THE ENVIRONMENT.

a. Ask: *How can you use a magnet to tell directions?*

EXPLORE: PLAN AND CONDUCT SIMPLE INVESTIGATIONS TO COLLECT RELEVANT DATA.

b. Suspend a bar magnet by a string from a nonmagnetic support as in the diagram. Note the directions the ends of the bar magnet point. Compare the directions pointed to by the bar magnet and the directions indicated by a compass. How does the bar magnet interact with a second bar magnet? (See the following diagram.)

EXPLAIN: USE DATA TO GENERATE INTERPRETATIONS, INCLUDING DESCRIPTIONS, CLASSIFICATIONS, AND EXPLANATIONS.

c. Ask: *What happens to the suspended bar magnet?* Lead students to compare the directions pointed to by the magnet and the directions indicated by the compass.

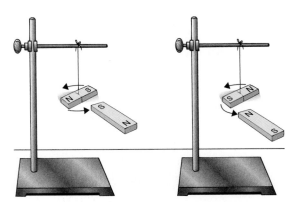

- One end of the magnet points toward the north (as indicated by the compass) and is called a north-seeking pole, or simply a north pole. The other pole of the magnet is a south-seeking pole or south pole.
- Our suspended magnet acts like a compass. The main part of a compass is a small permanent magnet attached to a pivot at the bottom of the compass.
- North and south are defined geographically by the rotational axis of the earth and astronomically by observations of the fixed North Star. The projection onto earth of a line drawn between us and our North Star, Polaris, will be within a degree of true, geographic north.
- The interaction between the earth and magnets can be explained in terms of a model in which the earth acts like it has a large bar magnet buried within it. Contrary to expectations, the earth's S-pole is near the north geographic pole and attracts the N-poles of magnets. The earth's N-pole is near the south geographic pole and attracts the S-poles of magnets.
- The earth's magnetic poles are nearly a thousand miles from the geographic poles. Thus, a compass may point several degrees away from true north.

5. HOW CAN YOU MAKE A MAGNET? (2–6)

Materials

For each group:

- Steel needle
- Bar magnet
- Cork
- Plastic bowl of water

ENGAGE: ASK A
QUESTION ABOUT OBJECTS,
ORGANISMS, OR EVENTS IN
THE ENVIRONMENT.

a. Ask: *How can you make a compass?*

EXPLORE: PLAN
AND CONDUCT SIMPLE
INVESTIGATIONS TO
COLLECT RELEVANT DATA.

b. Obtain a steel needle, a magnet, a cork (substitute a flat piece of Styrofoam), and a plastic bowl with a few centimeters of water in it. Holding the magnet in one hand and the needle in the other, stroke the needle about 25 times in one direction with the magnet.

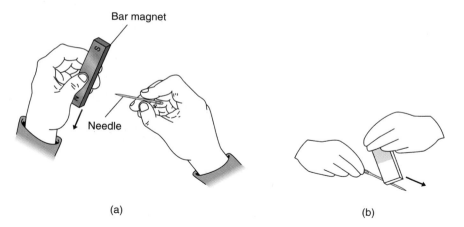

(a)   (b)

c. Float the cork in the water, and lay the needle on it.
   Ask: *What happens to the needle and the cork?* Rotate the needle and cork 90 degrees and then release it. *What happens to the needle-cork system when you release it?*

d. Bring the magnet near the needle on the cork. Ask: *What happens to the needle and cork now?*

EXPLAIN: USE DATA TO GENERATE INTERPRETATIONS, INCLUDING DESCRIPTIONS, CLASSIFICATIONS, PREDICTIONS, AND EXPLANATIONS.

e. Ask: *What is your evidence that stroking the needle magnetized it? What made the needle move when it was first placed on the cork? How is this like a compass? How can you make a compass? Which pole of the needle is the N-pole? What is your evidence?*

VII. ELECTRICITY

A. STATIC ELECTRICITY

▶ *Science Background*

More than 2,000 years ago, the Greeks were aware that when amber, a resinous substance, was rubbed with a cloth, the amber was able to attract small bits of straw. The Greek word for amber is electron, so the phenomenon came to be called electricity. In his book on magnetism, published in 1600, William Gilbert carefully distinguished between magnetism, which occurred naturally, and electricity, which had to be induced by friction. Gilbert also reported investigations showing that not only amber, but many other substances—including diamond, sapphire, opal, glass, sealing wax, and sulphur—demonstrated electric qualities when rubbed.

Benjamin Franklin, the American statesman and scientist, investigated electric phenomena in the 1700s. Franklin found that things could be not only attracted by electric forces but also repelled. Franklin proposed that the attracting and repelling forces of static electricity resulted from two kinds of electrical "fluids," which he called positive and negative fluids.

NSES   **Science Standards**

All students should develop an understanding of

• light, heat, electricity, and magnetism (K–4).

Objectives for Students

1. Describe electrostatic investigations and identify materials that can interact electrostatically.
2. Describe ways electrostatic interactions are different from magnetic interactions.
3. Explain in their own words what is meant by electrical charge and how objects become electrically charged.
4. State and demonstrate evidence for the electrostatic force rule: Like charged bodies repel; unlike charged bodies attract.
5. Demonstrate and explain what is meant by electrostatic induction.
6. Apply the model of electrostatic interaction to explain evidence from electrostatic investigations.

NSES **Concepts and Principles**

Activities 1 and 2 address these fundamental concepts and principles related to the *Science Standards* and *Benchmarks*:

- The position or motion of an object can be changed by pushing or pulling (K–4).
- The size of the change is related to the strength of the push or pull (K–4).
- Without touching them, a material that has been electrically charged pulls on all other materials and may either push or pull other charged materials (*Benchmarks*, 3–5).

1. HOW CAN YOU DEMONSTRATE STATIC ELECTRIC FORCES? (3–6)

Materials

Plastic or acetate sheet
Plastic rulers
Hard rubber comb or resin rod
Wool cloth
Balloons
Paper towels
Paper clips
Flour
Salt
Thread
Bits of paper

ENGAGE: ASK A QUESTION ABOUT OBJECTS, ORGANISMS, OR EVENTS IN THE ENVIRONMENT.

Moisture in the air can interfere with electrostatic effects. Thus, electrostatic investigations are best done on a cool, dry day.

EXPLORE: PLAN AND CONDUCT SIMPLE INVESTIGATIONS TO COLLECT RELEVANT DATA.

a. Have students rub a clear acetate sheet with a rough paper towel. (Coarse paper towels from restrooms work well.) Instruct them to bring the rubbed acetate near a pile of tiny bits of torn paper and observe what happens. Experiment to see what other materials interact with the acetate sheet. Try such materials as paper clips, bits of aluminum foil, flour, salt, cotton and nylon thread, and wood shavings from a pencil sharpener.
   Ask: *What did you observe in the investigation? Why do you think it happened?*

b. Rub a hard rubber comb or resin rod with a wool cloth. Try to pick up flour with the rubbed comb or rod. Ask: *What do you observe?*

Resin rod or hard rubber comb

Flour

c. Tie a 1 meter string around the mouth of an inflated balloon. Vigorously rub the inflated balloon with a piece of wool. Investigate to determine what materials interact with the balloon.

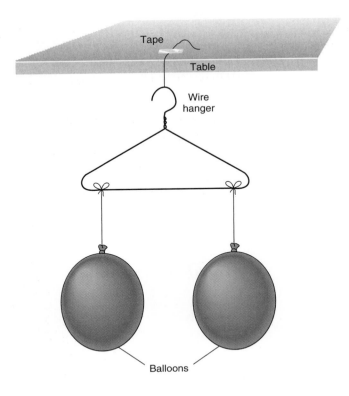

Tape

Table

Wire
hanger

Balloons

d. Inflate a second balloon. Tie a 1 meter string around the mouth of the balloon. Vigorously rub the two balloons with wool. Suspend the two balloons by their strings from a support as in the diagram and investigate how they interact with each other.

EXPLAIN: USE DATA
TO GENERATE
INTERPRETATIONS,
INCLUDING DESCRIPTIONS,
CLASSIFICATIONS, AND
EXPLANATIONS.

e. Ask: *What did your rubbed balloon attract? Why do you think it happened? In what ways is this investigation similar to your previous investigation? Which materials did the ruler pick up? What materials did the balloon attract?*

f. Ask: *What happened when the two rubbed balloons were brought near one another? What kind of force did you observe, attraction or repulsion?*

g. Introduce the notions of positive and negative electric charges and electrical forces. Help the students relate each part of the explanation to some part of their investigation.

1. There are two kinds of electric charges in all materials: positive charges and negative charges.

2. In ordinary substances, positive charges and negative charges are balanced. These substances are electrically neutral.

3. When some materials are rubbed together, the friction causes the materials to acquire electrical charges.

4. Two electrically charged substances can interact.

5. An electrically charged substance can interact with a neutral substance by a process called *induction*.

2. HOW CAN I DEMONSTRATE POSITIVE AND NEGATIVE ELECTRICAL CHARGES? (2–6)

Materials   Transparent tape (one roll for each cooperative group)

ENGAGE: ASK A QUESTION ABOUT OBJECTS, ORGANISMS, OR EVENTS IN THE ENVIRONMENT.

a. Stick a 20 cm strip of transparent tape (A) to a wooden tabletop. Press the tape down well with your fingers, leaving 2 or 3 cm loose as a handle. Very carefully, peel the tape away from the table. Attach one end of the tape to the end of a pencil. Test to see if the tape will pick up bits of paper. (Try to bring only the nonsticky side of the tape near the paper.)

Ask: *How does the strip of tape affect bits of paper? Why do you think this interaction took place? What is your evidence that the tape was charged? Were the bits of paper charged?* (No. The paper had not been rubbed.)

EXPLORE: PLAN AND CONDUCT SIMPLE INVESTIGATIONS TO COLLECT RELEVANT DATA.

b. Charge a second 20 cm strip of tape (B) by sticking it to the tabletop and peeling it away as before. Hang the strip of tape (B) to a wooden pencil or dowel. Bring it near the first strip of tape (A) to see how they interact.

EXPLAIN: USE DATA TO GENERATE INTERPRETATIONS, INCLUDING DESCRIPTIONS, CLASSIFICATIONS, AND EXPLANATIONS.

c. Ask: *How do the two strips of tape interact?* (They repel one another.) *Do you think the two strips of paper carry like or unlike charges?* (Like.) *What is your evidence?* (We did the same thing to each strip of tape.) *What can you conclude: Do like charged substances attract or repel?* (Repel.)

d. Stick a third 20 cm strip of tape (C) to the table, leaving a 2 to 3 cm handle. Stick a fourth strip of tape (D) on top of tape strip C, again leaving a handle. Press them down well. Remove the two tape strips, still stuck together, from the table. Run the tape strips over your lips or over a water pipe. Now carefully peel the two strips of tape apart. Investigate to see how they interact with one another. Also investigate to see how each of these two tape strips (C and D) interact with tape strip A.

Ask: *What did you observe?* (The tape strips attracted one another.) *Did tape strips C and D have like charges?* (They must not have had like charges because they did not repel one another.)

Explain that when tape strips C and D were peeled apart, they acquired opposite charges. Add these principles to the explanation in the previous activity:

- Unlike charged materials attract one another.
- Like charged materials repel one another.

B. CURRENT ELECTRICITY

▶ *Science Background*

In the section on static electricity, you learned that objects can be charged positively (more protons than electrons) or negatively (more electrons than protons). You also learned that like charged materials repel one another, while unlike charged materials attract.

Current electricity refers to a movement of electrical charge along a conducting path. Electrical energy is produced in a battery and converted to heat, light, or motion in an electrical component such as a light bulb or a motor. For energy to be transferred to an electrical component, there must be a complete conducting path—a complete circuit—from the battery along conducting wires through the electrical component and back to the battery along conducting wires.

If two or more electrical components are aligned so that current flows from one to the next, the circuit is a series circuit. If the components are arranged so that each is in an independent circuit, then the circuit is a parallel circuit. A switch is a device that breaks or opens a circuit so that it is not a continuous path and current cannot flow through it.

NSES **Science Standards**

All students should develop an understanding of

- light, heat, electricity, and magnetism (K–4).

Objectives for Students

1. Demonstrate and explain through words and drawings how to make a bulb light in various ways, given one or two batteries, one or two bulbs, and one or two wires.
2. State, explain, and demonstrate the complete circuit rule:
   For a bulb to light,
   - the bulb must be touched on the side and the bottom;
   - the battery must be touched on both ends; and
   - there must be a complete circuit or continuous path along the wires and through the battery and bulb.
3. Explain in their own words what a conductor is and how to test a material to determine if it is an electrical conductor.
4. Identify and construct series circuits and use the complete circuit rule to explain why the other bulbs in a series circuit go out when one bulb is removed from its holder.

5. Identify and construct parallel circuits and use the complete circuit rule to explain why the other bulbs in a parallel circuit stay lit when one bulb is removed from its holder.

6. Demonstrate a switch and use the complete circuit rule to explain how it works.

 Concepts and Principles

Activities 1–6 address these fundamental concepts and principles related to the *Science Standards*:

- Electricity in circuits can produce light, heat, sound, and mechanical motion (K–4).
- Electrical circuits require a complete conducting loop through which an electric current can pass (K–4).
- Electrical circuits provide a means of transferring electrical energy to produce heat, light, sound, mechanical motion, and chemical changes (5–8).

1. HOW CAN YOU CONSTRUCT A CIRCUIT IN WHICH A BULB LIGHTS? (2–6)

Materials

For each student, at least:

- One flashlight bulb
- One battery (1.5 volt D-cell)
- One 15–25 cm wire

(Students initially need their own materials but will later combine materials with one or more other students.)

Safety Precautions

Discussing safe habits to use with electricity is a must.

- Caution children not to experiment with anything but 1.5 volt flashlight batteries (D-cells) and flashlight bulbs. There is no danger of electrical shock from these batteries.
- Children should wear safety goggles to protect their eyes from the sharp ends of the copper wires used in the activities.
- Children should never experiment with the electricity from wall sockets or from car batteries.
- Do not use electrical appliances near water; for example, do not use a hair dryer near a water-filled sink.
- When you pull an electrical cord out of a wall socket, grasp it by the plug and pull firmly.

ENGAGE: ASK A QUESTION ABOUT OBJECTS, ORGANISMS, OR EVENTS IN THE ENVIRONMENT.

a. Give each child a small flashlight bulb, a length of wire, and a 1.5 volt D-cell. (*Note:* A 1.5 volt D-cell is commonly referred to as a battery, although batteries actually have multiple cells.) Ask: *Can you make the bulb light?* The question might be posed as part of a story about some hikers who lost their flashlight in a dark cave. One hiker had an extra battery, another had an extra bulb, and a third had a wire. *Can you help them light the bulb so they can get out of the cave?*

EXPLORE: PLAN
AND CONDUCT SIMPLE
INVESTIGATIONS TO
COLLECT RELEVANT DATA.

b. The story provides a focus for the activities of the children. Let the children work to light the bulb. Some children may take 20 minutes or longer to light the bulb. Resist the temptation to step in and "teach" them how to light the bulb. Encourage them to keep trying on their own. As they succeed, the children develop confidence in their own abilities to learn about electrical circuits.

As each child lights the bulb, ask: *Can you find another way to light the bulb?* Students may experiment by placing the bulb on its side or on the other end of the battery. If two or more children want to cooperate at this point, let them. More hands may be helpful. Be accepting and reinforcing of the children's efforts.

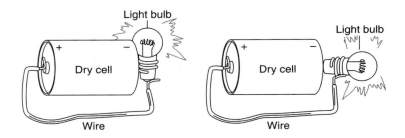

c. Give each pair of children a second wire. Ask: *Can you make the bulb light using two wires?* Children may simply twist the two wires together and make one wire of them. If so, ask: *Can you use two wires to light the bulb without the bulb touching the battery?*

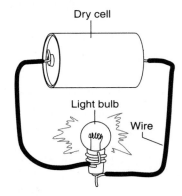

Lighting a bulb without it touching the battery.

d. Ask children, individually, to draw pictures of what they did to light the bulb with one battery and one wire. Look at the children's drawings carefully to see if they have observed that the electrical path (circuit) is a continuous or complete one.

Also ask them to draw a picture of what they did to light the bulb using two wires, with the bulb not touching the battery.

EXPLAIN: USE DATA TO
GENERATE INTERPRETATIONS,
INCLUDING DESCRIPTIONS,
CLASSIFICATIONS, AND
EXPLANATIONS.

e. Ask the children to explain their drawings to you and to one another. Look at the drawings carefully to see if the wires touch the bulb on the bottom and the side.

Ask: *What two places must you touch a bulb for it to light? Where must the battery be touched?*

Referring to actual circuits and drawings, children should state, explain, and write the complete circuit rule:

For a bulb to light,

- the bulb must be touched on the side and the bottom;
- the battery must be touched on both ends; and
- there must be a continuous path through the battery, bulb, and wires.

ELABORATE: EXTEND CONCEPTS, PRINCIPLES, AND STRATEGIES TO NEW PROBLEMS AND QUESTIONS.

f. Instruct children to do Prediction Sheet 1. It is a good idea to cut this activity sheet into two parts and hand out the second part after the first part is completed. The children should make a prediction for each frame (*Will the bulb light?*) and then experiment to test their prediction (*Try it and see.*). When the children have completed the prediction sheet, go back over it with them. (*Will this one light? Why won't it light? What could you do to get it to light?*)

As children predict, test, and explain, they have the opportunity to use and develop better understanding of the complete circuit rules.

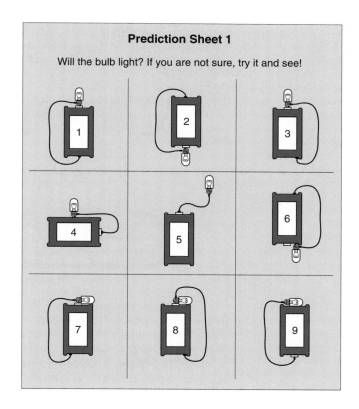

Prediction Sheet 1

Will the bulb light? If you are not sure, try it and see!

2. WHAT HAPPENS WHEN THERE IS MORE THAN ONE BULB OR BATTERY, OR A MOTOR IN A CIRCUIT? (2–6)

Materials

Batteries, bulbs, wires
Bulb holders
Small 1.5 volt electric motors

ENGAGE: ASK A QUESTION ABOUT OBJECTS, ORGANISMS, OR EVENTS IN THE ENVIRONMENT.

a. Instruct the children to explore different arrangements of batteries and bulbs. Ask: *What happens when you try two bulbs? Try two batteries. Can you use three batteries and two bulbs? Does the orientation of the batteries matter?*

EXPLORE: PLAN AND CONDUCT SIMPLE INVESTIGATIONS TO COLLECT RELEVANT DATA.

Let children explore and discover. Children may discover that when batteries are placed end-to-end (in series), a positive terminal of one battery must be connected to the negative terminal of an adjacent battery.

Safety Precautions

Do not allow children to experiment with more than three batteries. More batteries can result in burned-out bulbs.

Ask: *What happens to the bulbs when you use more than one battery?* (The bulbs get brighter.)

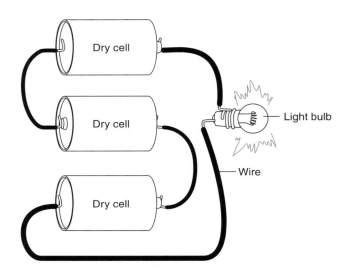

b. As the children try different arrangements, the need for a "bulb holder" arises. Give the children bulb holders and demonstrate how to use them in building one, two, and three bulb circuits.

c. Provide each group with a small electric motor (available from Radio Shack). The motors have two wires coming from them. Challenge the groups to connect the motor to a battery and observe what happens. Place a plastic or wooden propeller on the motor shaft and observe what happens.

Ask: *How could a motor be used to do useful work? Where around your home or school can you find electric motors being used?* (Fans, washing machines, hair dryers, blenders, vacuum cleaners, air conditioners, etc.)

Wire a motor in a circuit with a bulb in a bulb holder. You may need to give the motor shaft a little spin to start the motor whirring. Ask: *What happens to the bulb when the motor starts turning? What happens to the bulb when the motor stops turning?*

EXPLAIN: USE DATA TO GENERATE INTERPRETATIONS, INCLUDING DESCRIPTIONS, CLASSIFICATIONS, AND EXPLANATIONS.

d. Ask: *Can you trace the complete circuit path for each circuit you have built?* Help the children see that the bulb holder is constructed so that one part of it is connected to the metal side of a bulb and another part is connected to the bottom base of the bulb. The terminals of the bulb holder are then connected to the battery. So the bulb holder is doing the same thing the children were doing with their hands when they made the bulb light. The bulb holders provide a complete circuit path for the electricity.

3. WHAT IS A SERIES CIRCUIT? (3–6)

ENGAGE: ASK A QUESTION ABOUT OBJECTS, ORGANISMS, OR EVENTS IN THE ENVIRONMENT.

a. Show the children the accompanying circuit illustration. Ask them to build the circuit using their materials.

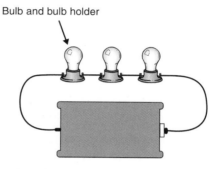

Bulb and bulb holder

   Tell the children that electricians, scientists, and engineers call this circuit a *series circuit* because the bulbs are lined up in a series and electricity flows from bulb to bulb.

EXPLORE: PLAN AND CONDUCT SIMPLE INVESTIGATIONS TO COLLECT RELEVANT DATA.

b. Ask: *What will happen to the other bulb in a series circuit if one of the bulbs is removed from its holder? Try it and see.* (The other bulb will go out.)

EXPLAIN: USE DATA TO GENERATE INTERPRETATIONS, INCLUDING DESCRIPTIONS, CLASSIFICATIONS, AND EXPLANATIONS.

c. Ask: *Why did the other bulb not light?* The children should tell you that the continuous path was broken when the bulb was removed.

4. WHAT IS A PARALLEL CIRCUIT? (3–6)

ENGAGE: ASK A QUESTION ABOUT OBJECTS, ORGANISMS, OR EVENTS IN THE ENVIRONMENT.

a. Show the children the accompanying circuit illustration and ask them to build it.

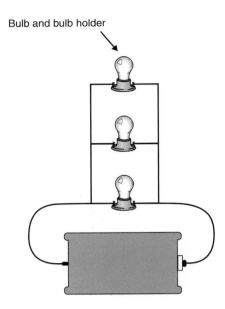

Bulb and bulb holder

This circuit is called a parallel circuit because there are parallel paths through the bulbs for the electricity. Each bulb is part of an independent circuit with the battery.

EXPLORE: PLAN AND CONDUCT SIMPLE INVESTIGATIONS TO COLLECT RELEVANT DATA.

b. Ask: *What will happen to the other bulb if one of the bulbs is removed from its bulb holder? Try it and see*.

EXPLAIN: USE DATA TO GENERATE INTERPRETATIONS, INCLUDING DESCRIPTIONS, CLASSIFICATIONS, AND EXPLANATIONS.

c. Ask: *What happened to the other bulbs when you removed one? Why did it happen?* The students should observe and explain that the other bulb stays lit because it is still part of a continuous path with the battery.

ELABORATE: EXTEND CONCEPTS, PRINCIPLES, AND STRATEGIES TO NEW PROBLEMS AND QUESTIONS.

d. Ask: *How are the electrical circuits in the classroom wired, series or parallel? If one light burns out, will the others light?* Through discussion, lead children to understand that electrical circuits in the classroom are wired in parallel. If the lights in the room are off, the TV or computers will still work. If one light bulb (or bank of lights) is out, the others still work.

   You might discuss strings of Christmas tree or holiday lights at this point. Most strings of lights sold today are wired in parallel. If one bulb burns out, the others still light. If the bulbs were in series, if one bulb burned out, none of the others would light. You would have to test each one of them to determine which one needed to be replaced.

5. WHAT ARE CONDUCTORS AND NONCONDUCTORS? (3–6)

Materials

Batteries
Bulbs
Wires
Bulb holders
Diverse array of conducting and nonconducting materials made from paper, cloth, wood, plastic, and metals of different kinds

ENGAGE: ASK A QUESTION ABOUT OBJECTS, ORGANISMS, OR EVENTS IN THE ENVIRONMENT.

a. Ask: *Do all things conduct electricity? Are some materials better conductors of electricity than others?*

EXPLORE: PLAN AND CONDUCT SIMPLE INVESTIGATIONS TO COLLECT RELEVANT DATA.

b. Make available to each cooperative group a diverse array of conducting and nonconducting materials. Instruct students to use the test circuit illustrated to find out which materials will and which will not conduct electricity. Place the test object (made of metal, cloth, wood, plastic, etc.) between the bare ends of the two pieces of wire. If the bulb lights, the material is a conductor. Ask: *What types of materials did you find are the best conductors?* (Metals.)

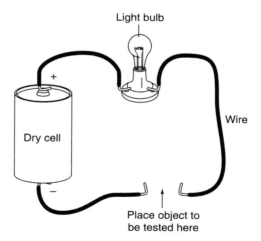

Light bulb

Dry cell

Wire

Place object to be tested here

EXPLAIN: USE DATA TO GENERATE INTERPRETATIONS, INCLUDING DESCRIPTIONS, CLASSIFICATIONS, AND EXPLANATIONS.

c. Through discussion lead children to understand that some materials will conduct electricity. Others will not. Materials that conduct electricity well are called *conductors*. Materials that do not conduct electricity well are called *insulators* or *nonconductors*.

6. WHAT IS A SWITCH AND HOW DOES IT WORK? (2–6)

Materials

Heavy cardboard
Brass paper fasteners
Paper clips

ENGAGE: ASK A
QUESTION ABOUT OBJECTS,
ORGANISMS, OR EVENTS IN
THE ENVIRONMENT.

a. Ask: *What does a switch do? How does a switch work? How can you make a switch?*

EXPLORE: PLAN
AND CONDUCT SIMPLE
INVESTIGATIONS TO
COLLECT RELEVANT DATA.

b. Ask your students to make an electrical "switch" using a 10 cm by 10 cm piece of corrugated cardboard, two brass paper fasteners, and a paper clip, as in the illustration. Tell them to connect the switch into an electric circuit as shown.

EXPLAIN: USE DATA
TO GENERATE
INTERPRETATIONS,
INCLUDING DESCRIPTIONS,
CLASSIFICATIONS, AND
EXPLANATIONS.

c. Ask: *What happens when the switch is open (with the paper clip not touching the second fastener)? What happens when the switch is closed (with the paper clip touching the second fastener)?*

The children should note that when the switch is closed, a complete circuit is formed and the bulb lights. When the switch is open, the circuit is broken and the bulb does not light. Take time for children to identify and talk about the electrical switches in the classroom.

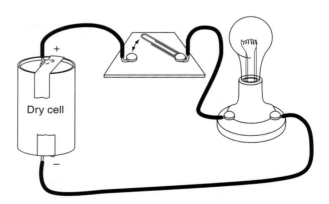

Dry cell

C. ELECTROMAGNETS

▶ *Science Background*

All magnetism is the result of moving electrical charges. When current flows in a wire, a magnetic field is set up. If the wire is placed over a compass, the magnetic field of the wire interacts with the magnetic field of the compass needle, causing it to deflect. Since the earth's magnetic field affects the compass needle strongly, the needle may deflect only a small amount. More coils of wire increase the magnetic effects of the current. When the current is less, which occurs when a bulb is wired into the circuit, the resulting magnetic field produced will also be less.

Even permanent magnets are the result of electrical currents. In the case of permanent magnets, the current is the result of the movement of electrons within the atoms of the iron from which the magnets are made.

NSES **Science Standards**

All students should develop an understanding of

• light, heat, electricity, and magnetism (K–4).

Objectives for Students

1. Describe interactions between compass needles and current-carrying wires.
2. Construct an electromagnet.
3. Design and conduct an experiment to determine the effects of variables such as the type of core, number of loops of wire, and amount of current on the strength of an electromagnet.
4. Explain the cause of electromagnetic effects.

NSES **Concepts and Principles**

Activities 1–3 address these fundamental concepts and principles related to the *Science Standards* and *Benchmarks*:

• Electricity in circuits can produce heat, light, sound, and magnetic effects (K–4).
• Electric currents and magnets can exert a force on each other (*Benchmarks*, 6–8).

1. HOW DO COMPASS NEEDLES INTERACT WITH CURRENT-CARRYING WIRES? (4–6)

Materials

Batteries
Bulbs
Wires
Iron nails or rivets
Switches
Paper clips

ENGAGE: ASK A QUESTION ABOUT OBJECTS, ORGANISMS, OR EVENTS IN THE ENVIRONMENT.

a. Instruct students to take a 50 cm length of wire and stretch it out on a table. Lay a compass over the wire as in the diagram. Orient the wire so the compass needle is perpendicular to the wire. Connect one end of the wire to one of the terminals of a D-cell. Quickly touch the other end of the wire to the other terminal of the D-cell and then disconnect it. Observe what happens to the compass needle. Move the wire so it points in different directions. Quickly connect and disconnect the wire to the D-cell.

Safety Precautions

Since there is no light bulb or other resisting component in the circuit in this investigation, it is a "short" circuit. You must connect and disconnect the short circuit quickly so that the wire does not get too hot and the D-cell is not drained of electrical energy.

EXPLAIN: USE DATA TO GENERATE INTERPRETATIONS, INCLUDING DESCRIPTIONS, CLASSIFICATIONS, AND EXPLANATIONS.

b. Ask: *What did you observe in this investigation?* (The compass needle moved.) *Why do you think this happened? What is your evidence that the electric current in the wire produced some magnetism?*

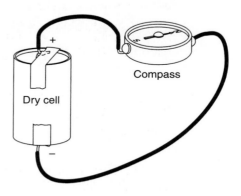

ELABORATE: EXTEND CONCEPTS, PRINCIPLES, AND STRATEGIES TO NEW PROBLEMS AND QUESTIONS.

c. Tell students to obtain a wire about 50 cm long and to wrap five loops of the wire around a compass as in the diagram. Leave the ends of the wire long enough to connect to a D-cell. Quickly connect and disconnect the wire to a single D-cell. Ask: *What did you observe?* (The compass needle deflected more than before.)

   Why do you think this happened? What evidence can you state that a magnetic interaction took place? Was the effect stronger or weaker than in the first investigation? What is your evidence that the electric current in the loops of wire produced some magnetism?

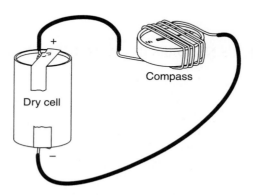

2. WHAT IS AN ELECTROMAGNET, AND HOW CAN YOU MAKE ONE? (3–6)

ENGAGE: ASK A QUESTION ABOUT OBJECTS, ORGANISMS, OR EVENTS IN THE ENVIRONMENT.

a. Show children an electromagnet. Demonstrate how it can attract small objects like paper clips. Ask: *How can we make an electromagnet?*

EXPLORE: PLAN
AND CONDUCT SIMPLE
INVESTIGATIONS TO
COLLECT RELEVANT DATA.

b. Give students these directions:
  1. Obtain a D-cell, a large iron nail or rivet, a 50 cm length of insulated (enameled) copper wire, some iron filings in a plastic bag, and some paper clips.
  2. Wrap the nail around the wire about 50 times as shown in the diagram.
  3. Place the nail on the bag of iron filings.
  4. Scrape the insulation off the two ends of the wire. Connect one end of the wire to one of the terminals of the D-cell.
  5. Holding the other end of the wire along the insulated portion, touch the bare end of the wire to the other terminal of the D-cell for only a few seconds. Move the nail around on the plastic bag and observe how it interacts with the iron filings.
  6. Repeat the activities using paper clips rather than iron filings to observe electro-magnetic effects.

Safety Precautions

Do not let the wire and terminal remain in contact for more than a few seconds because

  · intense heat builds up, and you could get a burn through the insulation; and
  · the electrical energy in the battery will be used up quickly.

EXPLAIN: USE DATA
TO GENERATE
INTERPRETATIONS,
INCLUDING DESCRIPTIONS,
CLASSIFICATIONS, AND
EXPLANATIONS.

c. Ask: *What happens to the iron filings and the paper clip when the circuit is completed (or when the wire is touched to the battery)? What happens to the iron filings and the paper clip when the circuit is broken (or when the wire is removed from the battery)? What is the evidence that the nail became a magnet temporarily?*

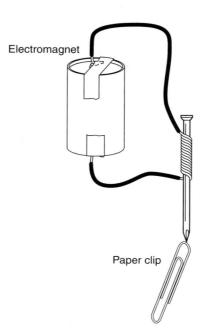

Electromagnet

Paper clip

d. Explain that when a loop of wire is placed around an iron object and current runs through the wire, the object becomes an electromagnet. The electromagnetic effect is suddenly reduced when current no longer runs through the wire.

3. HOW CAN YOU INCREASE THE STRENGTH OF AN ELECTROMAGNET? (3–6)

ENGAGE: ASK A QUESTION ABOUT OBJECTS, ORGANISMS, OR EVENTS IN THE ENVIRONMENT.

a. Ask: *What determines the strength of an electromagnet?* Through discussion, generate the hypothesis that the strength of an electromagnet might be increased by
  * increasing the number of wire loops around the iron object; or
  * increasing the current (or increasing the number of D-cells).

EXPLORE: PLAN AND CONDUCT SIMPLE INVESTIGATIONS TO COLLECT RELEVANT DATA.

b. Tell students to design and conduct a controlled experiment to determine how the number of coils of wire around the nail or rivet affects the strength of the electromagnet. Measure the strength of the electromagnet by how long a chain of paper clips it can pick up. Use 20 coils, 40 coils, and 60 coils of wire.

c. Ask: *What is the responding variable in this experiment?* (Number of paper clips lifted.) *What is the manipulated variable in the experiment?* (Number of loops of wire around the nail.) *What variables have you controlled in this experiment?* (Type of wire; number of batteries; length of wire.)

EXPLAIN: USE DATA TO GENERATE INTERPRETATIONS, INCLUDING DESCRIPTIONS, CLASSIFICATIONS, AND EXPLANATIONS.

d. Instruct students to display their data in a graph like the one shown here. Tell them to use the graph to predict how many paper clips the electromagnet can hold with 50 coils of wire and 80 coils of wire. Instruct students to test their predictions.

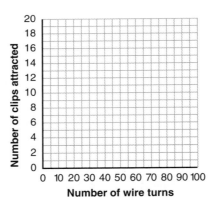

e. Ask: *What were your predicted and tested amounts of paper clips attracted to the electromagnet?*

SECTION III
Life Science Activities

Life is a complex, exciting, and mysterious subject for inquiry. Children should have the opportunity to develop a deep and personal appreciation for the variety and wonder of life. Children are naturally curious about the diversity of life around them. Studying characteristics of plants and animals and of their habitats also provides a very good context for students to develop inquiry skills. Investigations in life science might involve

1. asking different kinds of questions that suggest different kinds of scientific investigations;
2. observing and describing plants and animals;
3. classifying plants and animals (insects, fish, birds, mammals) according to their properties;
4. investigating plant and animal life cycles;
5. planning and carrying out investigations that show the function of different parts/structures of plants and animals;
6. investigating how different habitats or environments enable the needs of plants and animals to be met; and
7. investigating how the activities of people bring about changes in the environment.

As students learn more and more about plants, animals, and the environment, they become better prepared to assume responsibility for the well-being of living things on our planet.

Investigation Journals. Life science activities provide an excellent context for students to learn how to keep good records of investigations. Records may be kept in student observation journals, or you may want for students to keep their records on pages you prepare. Decorate prepared record pages with clip art designating the function of each part of the journal.

Here is a suggested format for student investigation journals and examples of a child's journal entries from a seed germination experiment.

	My Investigation Journal	
1. Key Question	• *Is moisture needed for seeds to sprout?*	
2. My Investigation	• *We put a sponge in a bowl of water and sprinkled grass seeds on it. We put grass seeds on a dry sponge. We watched the seeds for several days.*	
3. My Prediction	• *I think the dry seeds won't grow but the moist ones will.*	
4. What Happened		

Day	What I Observed on the Wet Sponge	What I Observed on the Dry Sponge
1	• *Nothing is happening.*	• *Nothing is happening.*
2	• *Nothing.*	• *Nothing.*
3	• *Some sprouts are coming up on the moist sponge.*	• *Nothing.*
6	• *There was lots of grass on the moist sponge but nothing growing on the dry one.*	• *Nothing.*

5. What I Concluded	• *Seeds need moisture to sprout.*

I. CHARACTERISTICS OF ORGANISMS

Children can begin to sense the astounding variety of living things on our planet as they investigate seeds, plants, insects, and birds.

A. SEEDS

▶ *Science Background*

Amazingly, seeds contain the ingredients of life. A living seed may lie dormant for years until it is awakened by just the right conditions. To begin the **germination** or sprouting process, seeds need moisture, air, and moderate temperatures.

Seeds typically have very hard **seed coats** that keep water from penetrating them. Thus, they will germinate more quickly after being soaked or scarified to allow water inside the seeds. Within every viable seed lives a tiny **embryo plant,** complete with leaf, stem, and root parts. When the seed begins to germinate, a temporary food supply, stored within the **cotyledons** of the seeds, nourishes the growing embryo. Eventually, as the leaves develop, the plant will obtain its energy for growth and survival from sunlight through the process of **photosynthesis.**

NSES **Science Standards**

All students should develop an understanding of

- characteristics of organisms (K–4).
- structure and function in living systems (5–8).
- life cycles of organisms (K–4).
- organisms and their environments (K–4).

Objectives for Students

1. Recognize the wide variation in seeds and where seeds are found.
2. Identify and describe different parts/structures of seeds (seed coats, cotyledons, embryo plants) and describe the functions of each.
3. Define *germination* and describe the sequence of events in the germination of a seed.
4. Ask questions about seeds that can be answered through investigations.
5. Design and carry out descriptive, classificatory, and experimental investigations to gather information for answering questions about seeds.
6. Use simple equipment and tools to gather data and extend the senses.
7. Through investigations, identify basic conditions for seed germination: air, water, and moderate temperature.
8. Use evidence from investigations and science knowledge to answer questions about seeds, construct explanations, and make predictions.

 Concepts and Principles

Activities 1–4 address or provide preparation for learning these fundamental concepts and principles related to the *Science Standards* or *Benchmarks for Science Literacy:*

- Some animals and plants are alike in the way they look and the things they do, and others are very different from one another (K–2).
- A great variety of living things can be sorted into groups in many ways using various features to decide which things belong to which group (3–5).
- Features used for grouping depend on the purpose of the grouping (3–5).
- Each plant or animal has different structures that serve different functions in growth, survival, and reproduction (K–4).

1. WHAT IS INSIDE A BEAN POD? (K–4)

Materials

Bean pods
Plastic knives
Assortment of fruits

Large bag of pea pods
Paper plates

ENGAGE: ASK A QUESTION ABOUT OBJECTS, ORGANISMS, OR EVENTS IN THE ENVIRONMENT.

a. Distribute two bean pods to each small group. Ask: *What are the properties of the bean pod? What do you observe inside the bean pod?* Introduce or review the term *property* as a characteristic of an object or something you can observe about an object using your senses.

EXPLORE: PLAN AND CONDUCT SIMPLE INVESTIGATIONS TO COLLECT RELEVANT DATA.

b. Distribute a plastic knife to each group. Provide instructions on safe use of the plastic knife. Challenge students to use the knives to open their bean pods. Encourage students to use all of their senses, except taste, to observe the inside of the bean pod. They should observe color, texture, size, shape, and other features.

EXPLAIN: USE DATA TO GENERATE INTERPRETATIONS, INCLUDING DESCRIPTIONS, CLASSIFICATIONS, PREDICTIONS, AND EXPLANATIONS.

c. Ask: *What observations did you make? What are the properties of what is inside the bean pods?* List the students' observations on the board. Discuss the various observations with them. Tell students that the pod is the part of the plant that holds the seeds, and the scientific term for that part of the plant is the fruit. Explain that although in everyday language we call bean pods *vegetables*, in scientific terms they are *fruits*.

....

2. WHERE ARE SEEDS FOUND? HOW ARE SEEDS ALIKE AND DIFFERENT? (K–2)

Materials   Paper plates
Plastic knives
Variety of fresh fruits (Children might be encouraged to bring a fruit from home. Tomatoes, apples, corn on the cob, apples, cherries, cantaloupes, and bell peppers make interesting fruits for children to observe.)

ENGAGE: ASK A QUESTION ABOUT OBJECTS, ORGANISMS, OR EVENTS IN THE ENVIRONMENT.

a. Ask: *Are there seeds in each of these fruits? How many seeds are in each of the fruits? How can we find out?*

EXPLORE: PLAN AND CONDUCT SIMPLE INVESTIGATIONS TO COLLECT RELEVANT DATA.

b. Distribute paper plates and several fruits to each group. Tell children to use their plastic knives to cut their fruits open. They should find and observe the seeds in each one.

EXPLAIN: USE DATA TO GENERATE INTERPRETATIONS, INCLUDING DESCRIPTIONS, CLASSIFICATIONS, AND EXPLANATIONS.

c. Ask: *Did you find seeds in your fruit? How many seeds did you find? What are the properties of the seeds? How are they similar? How do they differ?*

ELABORATE: EXTEND CONCEPTS, PRINCIPLES, AND STRATEGIES TO NEW SITUATIONS AND QUESTIONS.

d. Tell the students to take turns sorting the seeds on the paper plates. Ask: *How have you sorted the seeds?* Allow groups to describe and explain how they sorted the seeds. Lead students to compare and contrast the different ways they have sorted the seeds and to discuss the best ways to sort them.

....

3. HOW DO SEEDPODS VARY? (K–4)

Materials   Large number of pea pods
Paper plates

ENGAGE: ASK A QUESTION ABOUT OBJECTS, ORGANISMS, OR EVENTS IN THE ENVIRONMENT.

a. Ask: *Do all pea pods have the same number of peas?*

EXPLORE: PLAN AND CONDUCT SIMPLE INVESTIGATIONS TO COLLECT RELEVANT DATA.

b. Give two pea pods to each pair of students. Tell students to open the pods, count the number of peas in each pod, and put the peas and pods on their paper plates.

EXPLAIN: USE
DATA TO GENERATE
INTERPRETATIONS,
INCLUDING DESCRIPTIONS,
CLASSIFICATIONS,
PREDICTIONS, AND
EXPLANATIONS.

c. Ask: *Who found the most peas in their pods?* Record this number on the chalkboard. Also ask: *Who found the least number of peas in their pods?* Record this number on the board. Let each group report the number of peas they found in their pods.

d. Construct a histogram showing the numbers of peas in the different pods. Have one student from each pair come to the chalkboard and place an X above the numbers that correspond to the number of peas in each of their two pods. Ask: *What does the graph (histogram) show? What does it tell about peas and pods? If you open another pea pod, what might be the most likely number of peas in the pod? Why do you think so?* Discuss the notion of predictions and how predictions are based on collected evidence.

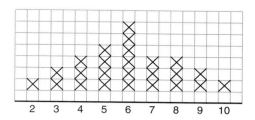

Give each pair another pea pod, and tell them to make predictions about the number of peas in each pod. Tell them to open the pea pods to test their predictions. Ask: *How accurate were your predictions? Why were your predictions so accurate (or so inaccurate)?*

ELABORATE: EXTEND
CONCEPTS, PRINCIPLES,
AND STRATEGIES TO NEW
PROBLEMS AND
QUESTIONS.

e. Ask: *Do you think there is a relationship between the number of peas in a pod and the length of the pod? How would you investigate to find out?* Carry out an investigation to see if the number of peas in a pod is related to the length (centimeters) of the pod. Display class data in a line graph (number of peas in a pod on the y axis; length of the pod in centimeters on the x axis). Use the graph to make predictions about the number of peas in pods of different lengths. Discuss the use of graphs to display data from investigations and to make predictions. Discuss how science can enable students to put mathematical skills, such as graphing, to work.

f. Ask: *How do other things in nature vary? How do dogs vary? What are some ways that children vary?*

4. WHAT ARE THE PROPERTIES OF SEEDS? (K–4)

Materials

Assortment of seeds, perhaps from old seed packets
Magnifying lens

ENGAGE: ASK A
QUESTION ABOUT OBJECTS,
ORGANISMS, OR EVENTS IN
THE ENVIRONMENT.

a. Give each group an assortment of 10 to 15 seeds. Ask: *How are the seeds alike? How are they different? How many different kinds of seeds do you have? What are the properties of each seed?*

EXPLORE: PLAN AND
CONDUCT SIMPLE
INVESTIGATIONS TO
COLLECT RELEVANT DATA.

b. Students should be encouraged to notice and talk about the color, shape, size, and texture of each kind of seed. Provide magnifying lenses to each group to better observe details.

For very young children, include other small objects with the seed assortments, such as marbles, small pebbles (gravel), jelly beans, and other small pieces of candy. As children observe and talk about their collection, discuss what is living and what is not living. Caution children not to place small objects in their mouths, noses, or ears.

c. Invite students within small groups to play "I'm thinking of . . ." with their assortment of seeds. One child describes a particular seed or a type of seed and the other children try to figure out which one is being described.

EXPLAIN: USE
DATA TO GENERATE
INTERPRETATIONS,
INCLUDING DESCRIPTIONS,
CLASSIFICATIONS,
PREDICTIONS, AND
EXPLANATIONS.

d. Ask: *What characteristics do seeds seem to have in common? What makes a seed a seed? How can you tell a seed from a nonseed?*

Concepts and Principles

Activities 5–7 address these fundamental concepts and principles related to the *Science Standards:*

- Each plant or animal has different structures that serve different functions in growth, survival, and reproduction (K–4).
- Plants and animals have life cycles that include being born, developing into adults, reproducing, and eventually dying. The details of this life cycle are different for different organisms (K–4).

5. WHAT DOES THE INSIDE OF A SEED LOOK LIKE? (K–4)

Materials

Lima bean seeds
Magnifying lenses

ENGAGE: ASK A
QUESTION ABOUT OBJECTS,
ORGANISMS, OR EVENTS IN
THE ENVIRONMENT.

a. Ask: *What do you think the inside of a seed looks like?* Discuss possibilities.

EXPLORE: PLAN
AND CONDUCT SIMPLE
INVESTIGATIONS TO
COLLECT RELEVANT DATA.

b. Give each pair or group of students four lima bean seeds, one-half cup of water, and a magnifying lens. Have them place two seeds in the water for 24 hours and observe them regularly. After 24 hours, ask: *How have the seeds in the water changed? How are the soaked seeds different from the unsoaked seeds?* (They are larger.) *Why are the soaked seeds larger?* (They have soaked up water.)

c. Ask: *What do you think was happening inside the seed?* Have students carefully peel the outer coat from one of the seeds and examine it with the magnifying lens. Show students how to pull the coatless seed in half with a fingernail. Ask: *What does the inside of the seed look like? What are the distinctive parts of a seed?* Tell students to draw a picture of the inside of the seed. Ask students to compare their drawings with the illustration.

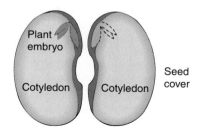

EXPLAIN: USE DATA TO GENERATE INTERPRETATIONS, INCLUDING DESCRIPTIONS, CLASSIFICATIONS, PREDICTIONS, AND EXPLANATIONS.

d. Provide names for the main parts of the bean seed: *seed coat* or cover; *cotyledon* or the meaty, pulpy part of the seed; and the *embryo*, the "beanie baby" with its embryo leaves, stem, and root.

6. HOW MUCH WATER CAN A BEAN SEED SOAK UP? (K–4)

Materials

Unsoaked lima bean seeds
Lima bean seeds that have been soaked overnight
Balances
1 g weights
Plastic containers

ENGAGE: ASK A QUESTION ABOUT OBJECTS, ORGANISMS, OR EVENTS IN THE ENVIRONMENT.

a. Ask: *If the seeds are soaking up water, how can we find out how much water they are holding?* Through discussion, arrive at the possibility of weighing the seeds before and after they have been soaked to gather data on how much water seeds can soak up.

EXPLORE: PLAN AND CONDUCT SIMPLE INVESTIGATIONS TO COLLECT RELEVANT DATA.

b. Provide each group 10 unsoaked bean seeds and a plastic container. Tell students to use a balance to find the mass of their 10 bean seeds and to record their measurements in the data table:

DATA TABLE

Mass of 10 soaked bean seeds	_____
Mass of 10 unsoaked bean seeds	_____
How much water did the bean seeds soak up?	_____

    c. Instruct students to add water to the container to a level of about 1 cm above the bean seeds. Set the bean seeds aside for 24–48 hours to soak up water. Allow students to add water to their containers if necessary during this time. After the bean seeds have soaked, tell students to use a balance to determine the mass of the soaked seeds and to record this measurement in the data table.

EXPLAIN: USE DATA TO GENERATE INTERPRETATIONS, INCLUDING DESCRIPTIONS, CLASSIFICATIONS, PREDICTIONS, AND EXPLANATIONS.

    d. Ask: *How much water did the bean seeds absorb?* Lead students to subtract the before-soaking measurement from the after-soaking measurement to determine how much water the seeds soaked up. Enter the difference in the data table.

    e. Ask: *How does the amount of water soaked up compare to the initial mass of the bean seeds? Is it larger, much larger, smaller, much smaller, or about the same? Why do you think water is important in the sprouting of the dry seeds?*

How could you help children understand what scientists do?

    f. Explain that scientists use mathematics in all aspects of scientific inquiry. Ask: *How did we use mathematics in this activity?* (Measuring, putting data in a table, subtracting, comparing.) Discuss that a practical value of mathematics is using it to answer questions in science. *Mathematics is the language of science.*

. . . .

7. WHAT HAPPENS TO SEEDS WHEN THEY GERMINATE? (K–4)

Materials

A 7 inch by 8 inch (quart size) plastic storage bag for each child
Paper towels
Stapler
Lima bean seeds
Ruler or centimeter-gram cubes

ENGAGE: ASK A QUESTION ABOUT OBJECTS, ORGANISMS, OR EVENTS IN THE ENVIRONMENT.

    a. Ask: *What are some things we do with seeds?* When students suggest that we plant them, ask: *What happens to seeds when they are planted?* Explain that if we plant the seeds in the soil, we cannot see what happens to them underground. Tell them we will place the seeds in a plastic bag and observe what happens for a few days.

EXPLORE: PLAN AND CONDUCT SIMPLE INVESTIGATIONS TO COLLECT RELEVANT DATA.

    b. Give each child a 7 inch by 8 inch (quart size) plastic storage bag. Show students how to line the inside of the bag with a paper towel. Place four or five staples along the bottom portion of the bag about 4 to 5 cm (2 inches) from the bottom. Place a lima bean seed above each staple inside the bag, as in the illustration. Gently pour water into the bag, being careful not to dislodge the seeds (the water should bulge slightly at the bottom of the bag to about a finger's thickness). There should be enough water to keep the seeds moist, but the seeds should not rest in water. Some of the seeds will germinate within 24–48 hours. Others may take longer.

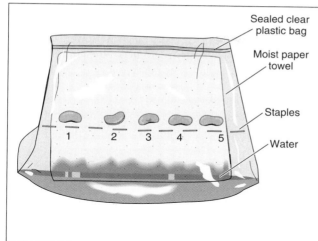

Sealed clear plastic bag

Moist paper towel

Staples

Water

- Line a 7 inch by 8 inch (quart size) sealable, transparent storage bag with a moist paper towel.
- Place six staples across the bag about 4 to 5 cm from the bottom, as shown in the diagram.
- Position each seed to be germinated above one of the staples.
- The seeds may be presoaked for about 24 hours.
- Gently pour water from a small container into the bag, being careful not to dislodge the seeds (the water should bulge slightly at the bottom of the bag to about a finger's thickness).

The water will soak the paper towel and keep the seeds moist. The staples keep the seeds from lying in the water at the bottom of the bag. The transparent bag allows the seeds and roots to be observed.

c. Children should observe their germinating seeds and developing plants regularly for 2 weeks or more, recording daily in their investigation journals or on a prepared chart any changes in color, length, shape, texture, special features, and so on.

d. This investigation is a good one to promote careful measurement. Tell students to use a ruler or centimeter-gram cubes (plastic cubes which are 1 cm on a side and interlock) to measure the length of the stem and root each day and to record the measurements in a chart. The chart should show length in centimeters for each day observed. The measurement data can then be displayed in a graph, which provides a picture of growth.

At lower grade levels, rather than measuring with a ruler, students can cut a green strip of paper to the length of the stem and a brown strip of paper to the length of the root. If the strips of paper are attached to a time line, such as a calendar, with the green strip above the line and the brown strip below, a visual display of growth over 2 or 3 weeks can be seen.

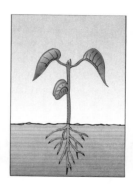

EXPLAIN: USE DATA TO GENERATE INTERPRETATIONS, INCLUDING DESCRIPTIONS, CLASSIFICATIONS, PREDICTIONS, AND EXPLANATIONS.

e. From their observational data, you want children to discover the sequence of growth changes for the beans from day to day—to learn that the root appears first and grows downward, that the stem is connected to the root and grows upward carrying the bean seed with it, and that leaves grow on the stems. To make the growth sequence clear, ask students to make drawings of changes they observe for one of their germinating bean seeds.

f. In addition to observing the sequence of growth, students should also learn to recognize the seed coat, cotyledons, and embryo plant of seeds, and the root, stems, and leaves of the developing plants. Provide the names of these seed and plant parts.

NSES Concepts and Principles

Activity 8 addresses these fundamental concepts and principles related to the *Science Standards:*

- Each plant or animal has different structures that serve different functions in growth, survival, and reproduction (K–4).

8. WHAT IS THE FUNCTION OF EACH SEED PART IN THE GROWTH OF THE PLANT? (3–6)

Materials

Transparent storage bags
Paper towels
Soaked bean seeds

ENGAGE: ASK A QUESTION ABOUT OBJECTS, ORGANISMS, OR EVENTS IN THE ENVIRONMENT.

a. Ask: *What are the parts of a seed? How do different parts of a seed change during germination? Which part of the seed do you think grows into a plant? How could we investigate to find out?* Lead children to observe that a lima bean seed has two cotyledons (it is a dicot), with the embryo embedded in one of them. Lead them to consider trying to germinate a cotyledon by itself, an embryo plant and cotyledon, an embryo plant by itself, and a whole lima bean, and to observe what happens.

EXPLORE: PLAN AND CONDUCT SIMPLE INVESTIGATIONS TO COLLECT RELEVANT DATA.

b. Assist children to set up a germination bag (as in Activity 7) containing
   1. one cotyledon by itself;
   2. one cotyledon with an embedded embryo plant;
   3. an embryo plant by itself; and
   4. a whole lima bean.
   Allow the students to observe their germination bags for several days, keeping records on their observations. *Note:* Open the bags daily for 15 minutes to prevent mold formation. Add just enough water to keep the paper towel slightly moist.

EXPLAIN: USE DATA TO GENERATE INTERPRETATIONS, INCLUDING DESCRIPTIONS, CLASSIFICATIONS, PREDICTIONS, AND EXPLANATIONS.

c. Ask: *Which of the seed parts, if any, started to grow? Why do you think that is so? Which parts did not grow at all? What do you conclude from your investigation about what seed parts are necessary for seed germination and growth into a plant?* (Only the whole seed and the one cotyledon and embryo produced growth.) *What do you think the role of the embryo was in sprouting? What do you think the role of the cotyledon was? Why do seeds not germinate (sprout) if the embryo is removed? Why do seeds not germinate if the cotyle-don is removed?*

NSES **Concepts and Principles**

Activity 9 expands on these fundamental concepts and principles related to the *Science Standards:*

- Organisms have basic needs. Plants require air, water, nutrients, and light (K–4).
- Organisms can survive only in environments in which their basic needs are met (K–4).

9. WHAT CONDITIONS ARE NEEDED FOR SEEDS TO GERMINATE OR SPROUT? (3–6)

Materials

Lima bean seeds
Radish seeds
Transparent storage bags
Paper towels
Stapler

ENGAGE: ASK A
QUESTION ABOUT OBJECTS,
ORGANISMS, OR EVENTS IN
THE ENVIRONMENT.

a. Ask: *What do seeds need to germinate?*

EXPLORE: PLAN
AND CONDUCT SIMPLE
INVESTIGATIONS TO
COLLECT RELEVANT DATA.

b. Ask: *How could we find out?* Lead children to suggest an investigation to determine if light is needed for seed germination. In the investigation, the same kinds of seeds are placed in two germination bags. One bag is placed in a well-lit place; the other in a very dark place. Ask: *What is the manipulated variable?* (The amount of light.) *What is the responding variable?* (The germination of the seeds.) *What variables should be controlled?* Emphasize that to be a controlled investigation, the moisture in each bag and its temperature have to be the same.

c. Let groups of children set up the investigation and observe the seeds for about 2 weeks, being careful not to expose the dark seeds to the light. Tell students to keep their observational records in a chart like the one illustrated.

Seed name and amount	Date planted	Germination date Predicted	Actual	Germination conditions	Number of seeds germinated

EXPLAIN: USE DATA TO GENERATE INTERPRETATIONS, INCLUDING DESCRIPTIONS, CLASSIFICATIONS, PREDICTIONS, AND EXPLANATIONS.

ELABORATE: EXTEND CONCEPTS, PRINCIPLES, AND STRATEGIES TO NEW SITUATIONS AND QUESTIONS.

d. Ask: *What did you observe? What do you conclude?* (That light is not necessary for seed germination. After all, seeds germinate underground in the dark.)

e. Ask: *Are there other factors that affect the germination of seeds? How could we determine the range of temperatures that seeds can tolerate and still sprout?* Lead the students to plan a controlled investigation using two germination bags, with one bag placed in the refrigerator and one in a warm, dark place. Discuss the responding variable (growth), the manipulated variable (temperature), and the variables to be controlled (amount of light, kinds of seeds, amount of water, etc.). Ask: *If one bag is placed in a refrigerator, why would the other one need to be in a "dark" place?*

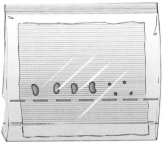
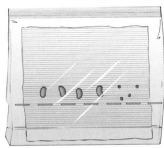

Refrigerator   Dark cabinet

f. Tell students to place three lima bean seeds and three radish seeds in two separate plastic germination bags. Have students carry out the controlled investigation they planned. Put one bag in a cool, dark place (e.g., inside a refrigerator) and one bag in a warm, dark place (e.g., inside a cabinet). Make sure the two bags have the same amount of moisture and light.

g. Instruct students to observe the two bags regularly for about 2 weeks and to record their observations in their chart (like the one in the previous illustration). *Note:* Open the bags daily for about 15 minutes to prevent the formation of mold. Also, keep the paper towels just slightly moist.

h. After 2 weeks of observations, ask: *How do the seeds in the two bags compare? How were the conditions for the two bags different? What do you think is the effect of temperature on germination (sprouting)? Why do you think so? What is your evidence?*

NSES **Concepts and Principles**

Activity 10 addresses these fundamental concepts and principles related to the *Science Standards:*

- All animals depend on plants (K–4).
- Some animals eat plants for food (K–4).

10. WHAT SEEDS DO WE EAT? (K–4)

ENGAGE: ASK A
QUESTION ABOUT OBJECTS,
ORGANISMS, OR EVENTS IN
THE ENVIRONMENT.

a. Ask: *What seeds or seed products do we eat?*

EXPLORE: PLAN
AND CONDUCT SIMPLE
INVESTIGATIONS TO
COLLECT RELEVANT DATA.

b. Hold a classroom "seed feast." Provide a variety of seeds for children to eat. Consider some of the seeds and seed products in the accompanying chart for the seed feast.

Safety Precautions

Make sure children are not allergic to any food you provide for them to eat, such as peanuts.

EXPLAIN: USE
DATA TO GENERATE
INTERPRETATIONS,
INCLUDING DESCRIPTIONS,
CLASSIFICATIONS,
PREDICTIONS, AND
EXPLANATIONS.

c. Using the chart, conduct a discussion of the various seeds and seed products we eat. Emphasize that rather than the cotyledons providing food for the seeds to germinate and begin growth, they are providing food energy for our survival and growth.

SEEDS AND SEED PRODUCTS WE EAT

Food	Seed or Seed Product
Peas	seeds (and fruit)
Beans	seeds (and fruit)
Corn	seeds
Rice	seeds
Peanuts	seeds
Sunflower seeds	seeds
Chocolate	made from seeds of cacao plant
Coffee	made from seeds of coffee plant
Vanilla	made from seeds of orchid
Cumin (spice)	made from cumin seeds
Flour	made from wheat, barley, or other grass seeds
Pretzels	made from flour
Bread	made from flour
Tortillas	made from flour or corn
Breakfast cereals	made from the seeds of grasses including wheat, rye, oats, and barley

Source: Adapted from National Gardening Association, 1990. *GrowLab.* National Gardening Association, Burlington, VT.

B. PLANTS

▶ *Science Background*

Biologists classify organisms on the basis of their structures and behaviors. Most organisms can be classified as plants or animals. Each plant or animal has different structures that serve different functions in growth, survival, and reproduction. All organisms have basic needs. Plants need light, air, water, and nutrients. Animals need air, water, and nutrients. Plants and animals can survive only in environments in which their needs are met. Roots absorb water and nutrients through small root hairs. Water and nutrients are carried from the roots to the leaves through small tubes, called capillaries, that are inside the stem. Plants get their energy for survival and growth directly from sunlight through a process called photosynthesis. Animals live by consuming the energy-rich foods initially synthesized by plants.[1]

NSES Science Standards

All students should develop an understanding of

- characteristics of organisms (K–4).
- structure and function in living systems (5–8).
- life cycles of organisms (K–4).
- organisms and their environments (K–4).

Objectives for Students

1. Recognize and appreciate the wide variation in plant life.
2. Identify and describe different parts/structures of plants (roots, stems, leaves) and describe the functions of each.
3. Observe and describe the life cycles of plants.
4. Ask questions about plants that can be answered through investigations.
5. Design and carry out descriptive, classificatory, and explanatory investigations to gather information for answering questions about plants.
6. Use simple equipment and tools to gather data and extend the senses.
7. Through investigations, identify basic needs of plants: air, water, nutrients, and light.
8. Use evidence from investigations and science knowledge to answer questions about plant life, construct explanations, and make predictions.

NSES Concepts and Principles

Activities 1–4 address or provide preparation for learning these fundamental concepts and principles related to the *Science Standards* or *Benchmarks for Science Literacy*:

- Some animals and plants are alike in the way they look and the things they do, and others are very different from one another (K–2).
- A great variety of living things can be sorted into groups in many ways using various features to decide which things belong to which group (3–5).
- Features used for grouping depend on the purpose of the grouping (3–5).
- Each plant or animal has different structures that serve different functions in growth, survival, and reproduction (K–4).

---

[1]Adapted from National Research Council (1996). *National Science Education Standards.*

1. WHAT IS A TREE LIKE? (K–2)

ENGAGE: ASK A QUESTION ABOUT OBJECTS, ORGANISMS, OR EVENTS IN THE ENVIRONMENT.

a. Ask: *What are the properties of trees? How do trees differ? How are they similar?*

EXPLORE: PLAN AND CONDUCT SIMPLE INVESTIGATIONS TO COLLECT RELEVANT DATA.

b. Have students hug a tree trunk, feel its surface, and describe how it feels. Encourage students to smell the bark. Have them draw and give a name to their favorite tree or cut pictures of trees out of magazines.

EXPLAIN: USE DATA TO GENERATE INTERPRETATIONS, INCLUDING DESCRIPTIONS, CLASSIFICATIONS, PREDICTIONS, AND EXPLANATIONS.

c. Ask: *What was your favorite tree like? What did it look like? How did it smell? How did it differ from other trees?* Discuss children's findings with them.

2. HOW DO THE CHARACTERISTICS OF LEAVES VARY? (K–2)

Materials

Assortment of leaves
Magazines
Newspapers
Colored paper
Paintbrushes
Poster paint

ENGAGE: ASK A QUESTION ABOUT OBJECTS, ORGANISMS, OR EVENTS IN THE ENVIRONMENT.

a. Ask: *What are leaves like? What are the similarities in leaves from different trees? What are the differences in the leaves from different trees?*

EXPLORE: PLAN AND CONDUCT SIMPLE INVESTIGATIONS TO COLLECT RELEVANT DATA.

b. Invite students to take a walk through a nature area at home or school, collect a variety of fallen leaves, and bring them to class.

Safety Precautions

Stress collecting fallen leaves only. Do not allow students to pick from living trees and plants.

EXPLAIN: USE DATA TO GENERATE INTERPRETATIONS, INCLUDING DESCRIPTIONS, CLASSIFICATIONS, PREDICTIONS, AND EXPLANATIONS.

c. Instruct students to spread the leaves out and compare them. Ask: *How are the leaves alike? How are they different? How do the leaves differ in shape? size? color? number of points? arrangement of veins? How do they differ in other ways? Why do you think the leaves vary so much from one another?*

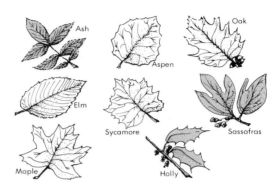

d. Tell the students to place the leaves in groups according to color, shape, size, or some other characteristic. Ask: *How many groups did you get?* Then tell them to rearrange the leaves according to other characteristics. Ask: *How many groups did you get?*

ELABORATE: EXTEND CONCEPTS, PRINCIPLES, AND STRATEGIES TO NEW SITUATIONS AND QUESTIONS.

e. Have students press some leaves between newspapers. Place books or something heavy on the newspapers. After several days, remove the weights and newspapers. Discuss how drying helps to preserve the leaves.

f. Tell students to place leaves on colored paper. Then show students how to dip brushes in poster paint and splatter it over the leaves to make a picture outline.

NSES   **Concepts and Principles**

Activity 3 addresses these fundamental concepts and principles related to the *Science Standards*:

- Organisms have basic needs. Plants require air, water, nutrients, and light (K–4).
- Organisms can survive only in environments in which their basic needs are met (K–4).
- Each plant or animal has different structures that serve different functions in growth, survival, and reproduction (K–4).

3. HOW CAN SOME PLANTS GROW WITHOUT SEEDS? (K–2)

Materials

Small tumblers (preferably clear plastic)
Small sweet potatoes, white potatoes, and carrot tops (with some root)
Toothpicks
Cuttings from coleus, philodendron, ivy, and other houseplants

ENGAGE: ASK A
QUESTION ABOUT OBJECTS,
ORGANISMS, OR EVENTS IN
THE ENVIRONMENT.

a. Ask: *What is needed for new plants to grow? How can we get new plants to grow without planting them in soil? How can we take good care of our new plants?*

EXPLORE: PLAN
AND CONDUCT SIMPLE
INVESTIGATIONS TO
COLLECT RELEVANT DATA.

b. Put three toothpicks each in a sweet potato, white potato, and carrot, as shown in the diagram. Place them in small tumblers of water. Take cuttings of houseplants and place them in small tumblers of water. Put all the tumblers in a well-lit place and make sure the water levels are maintained so that the water always touches the plants. Have students observe, measure, and record the changes in the plants, such as root development, height, number of leaves, and so on.

Coleus and philodendron   Sweet potato   White potato   Carrot

EXPLAIN: USE
DATA TO GENERATE
INTERPRETATIONS,
INCLUDING DESCRIPTIONS,
CLASSIFICATIONS,
PREDICTIONS, AND
EXPLANATIONS.

c. Ask: *Do new plants come only from seeds? What is your evidence?*
d. Ask: *What do plants need to grow?* Explain to students that plants require air, water, nutrients, and light. Plants can survive only in environments in which these basic needs are met. Ask: *How do you think these basic needs of plants are met when they are growing in water? How are the basic needs of plants met when they are growing in soil?*

NSES   **Concepts and Principles**

Activities 4–7 address these fundamental concepts and principles related to the *Science Standards:*

- Organisms have basic needs. Plants require air, water, nutrients, and light (K–4).
- Each plant or animal has different structures that serve different functions in growth, survival, and reproduction (K–4).

4. WHAT ARE ROOTS LIKE? (K–5)

Materials

Lima bean plants and radish plants growing in a germination bag
Magnifying lenses
Small, healthy coleus, geranium, or petunia plants
Potting soil
Planting containers (such as clean, empty milk cartons)

ENGAGE: ASK A QUESTION ABOUT OBJECTS, ORGANISMS, OR EVENTS IN THE ENVIRONMENT.

a. Ask: *What do the roots of a young plant look like? What could you do to find out?*

EXPLORE: PLAN AND CONDUCT SIMPLE INVESTIGATIONS TO COLLECT RELEVANT DATA.

b. Lead students to answer this question through their observations of the roots of bean plants and radish plants growing in a germination bag. Instruct students to use a magnifying lens and to record their observations, including drawings, of the structure of roots.
c. Continue the observation of the roots of plants for several days. Require students to make daily records of their observations in their journals.

EXPLAIN: USE DATA TO GENERATE INTERPRETATIONS, INCLUDING DESCRIPTIONS, CLASSIFICATIONS, PREDICTIONS, AND EXPLANATIONS.

d. After several days of observation, ask: *What do you notice about the roots? How are the roots of the bean plant and radish plant similar? How are they different? What are the small, fuzzlike projections coming from the roots?* (Root hairs.)

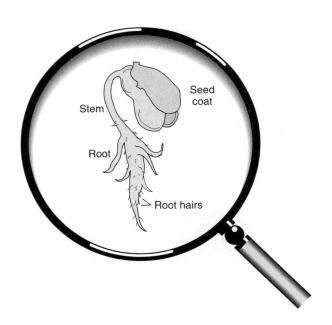

5. WHAT IS THE FUNCTION OF ROOTS? (K–5)

ENGAGE: ASK A QUESTION ABOUT OBJECTS, ORGANISMS, OR EVENTS IN THE ENVIRONMENT.

a. Ask: *What do you think is the function of the roots and the root hairs? What could you do to investigate to find out?* Lead students to suggest that functions of roots may be to absorb water and nutrients for plant growth and to provide support for plants. Ask: *How might you investigate these hypotheses?*

EXPLORE: PLAN AND CONDUCT SIMPLE INVESTIGATIONS TO COLLECT RELEVANT DATA.

b. Obtain two similar coleus, petunia, or geranium plants and remove all the roots from one plant. Fill the bottom half of two milk cartons or other planting containers with soil. Place the plant without roots down on top of the soil. Release the plant and observe what happens. Ask: *How might roots have helped this plant?* Explain that one function of the roots is to provide support for plants.

c. Push the bottom part of the stem of the plant without roots to a depth of about 5 cm into the soil. Water the plant daily. Observe the plant for 4 or 5 days. As a control, plant the other plant with roots in a container of soil.

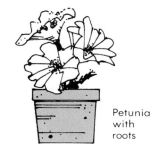 Petunia with roots

 Petunia without roots

EXPLAIN: USE DATA TO GENERATE INTERPRETATIONS, INCLUDING DESCRIPTIONS, CLASSIFICATIONS, PREDICTIONS, AND EXPLANATIONS.

d. Ask: *What did you observe about the two plants? Why do you think this happens?* Explain that one function of the root hairs is to absorb water and nutrients for the plant. Because the root hairs are critical to the life of the plant, it is important that they not be damaged when a plant is pulled up or transplanted.

Gently pull the plant without roots from the soil. If this plant has developed new roots, discuss the function of the newly developed roots.

e. Ask: *Why do you think some roots grow comparatively shallow and others grow deep? What are some ways people use the roots of plants?*

6. DO PLANTS GET WATER THROUGH ROOTS OR LEAVES? (K–5)

ENGAGE: ASK A QUESTION ABOUT OBJECTS, ORGANISMS, OR EVENTS IN THE ENVIRONMENT.

a. Ask: *Do plants get water through their roots or leaves? What could we do to find out?*

EXPLORE: PLAN AND CONDUCT SIMPLE INVESTIGATIONS TO COLLECT RELEVANT DATA.

b. To gather evidence to answer this key question, lead children to set up a controlled investigation like the one illustrated. This investigation involves two plants. Water is added to the soil of one plant so that it can reach the roots. Water is sprinkled on the leaves of the second plant, with a plastic bib keeping the water from reaching the soil and roots. All other conditions are controlled.

Pot A
Water soil

Pot B
Water leaves

plastic "bib"

dish

c. Tell the children to keep daily records of their observations.

EXPLAIN: USE DATA TO GENERATE INTERPRETATIONS, INCLUDING DESCRIPTIONS, CLASSIFICATIONS, PREDICTIONS, AND EXPLANATIONS.

d. After about 2 weeks, lead a discussion of the children's findings. Ask: *What did you do in the investigation? What did you observe? How did your findings compare with your predictions? What can you infer about the role of leaves in taking in water? Did you actually see roots taking in water? What makes you confident in your inference that water is taken in by roots? What factors might have affected the results of your investigation? (For example, watering might have damaged the leaves.)*[2]

7. WHAT IS THE FUNCTION OF A STEM? (K–5)

Materials

Carnations
Geranium or celery stem
Red and blue food coloring
Drinking glass or clear plastic cup
Paper towel

Preparation

Place the stem of a white carnation in a cup containing water with blue food coloring. Leave the carnation in the water until it has turned blue.

ENGAGE: ASK A QUESTION ABOUT OBJECTS, ORGANISMS, OR EVENTS IN THE ENVIRONMENT.

a. Ask: *Why is this carnation blue? Aren't carnations usually white? Do you think I planted a blue carnation seed? How does water get from the roots of a plant to the leaves? How do you think a florist produces blue carnations? If you wanted to change a white carnation into a blue carnation, what would you do? How could you find out if your idea was correct?*

---

[2]Adapted from National Gardening Association, 1990. *GrowLab: Activities for Growing Minds.* National Gardening Association, 180 Flynn Avenue, Burlington, Vermont 05401.

EXPLORE: PLAN AND
CONDUCT SIMPLE
INVESTIGATIONS TO
COLLECT RELEVANT DATA.

b. Fill a cup with water, tint with food coloring, and add a rolled paper towel, as in diagram (a).

  Ask: *What do you see happening to the paper towel? Why do you think this happens? How could this work in plants?*

c. Tell children to put some water in the drinking glass and add the food coloring. Cut a small slice off the bottom of the celery stem. Set the stem into the glass of colored water as in diagram (b). Allow it to sit in a sunny area for 2 hours. At the end of this period, cut open the stem. See diagram (c).

EXPLAIN: USE
DATA TO GENERATE
INTERPRETATIONS,
INCLUDING DESCRIPTIONS,
CLASSIFICATIONS,
PREDICTIONS, AND
EXPLANATIONS.

d. Ask: *What has happened to the celery stem? What parts of the stem appear to contain the colored water? How do you know? What can you conclude about the function of a stem?*

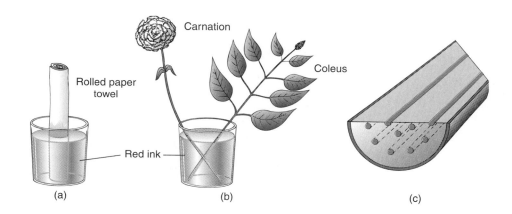

ELABORATE: EXTEND
CONCEPTS, PRINCIPLES,
AND STRATEGIES TO NEW
SITUATIONS AND
QUESTIONS.

e. Ask: *What do you think might happen if you put half of a split stem in one color of water and the other half in another color of water?* Try it and see.

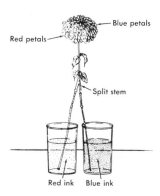

f. Ask: *What do you think might happen to the upward movement of water in a stem when the plant is in the dark or out of sunlight? How could you find out?*

NSES	Concepts and Principles

Activities 8–10 address these fundamental concepts and principles related to the *Science Standards*:

- Organisms have basic needs. Plants require air, water, nutrients, and light (K–4).

8. HOW MUCH WATER IS ENOUGH FOR HEALTHY PLANT GROWTH? (K–5)

Materials

Young bean or radish plants
Milk cartons or plastic cups
Graduated cylinder or measuring cup

ENGAGE: ASK A QUESTION ABOUT OBJECTS, ORGANISMS, OR EVENTS IN THE ENVIRONMENT.

a. Ask: *How much water do you need each day? How much water do you think a plant needs to grow in a healthy way? How could you find out?*

EXPLORE: PLAN AND CONDUCT SIMPLE INVESTIGATIONS TO COLLECT RELEVANT DATA.

b. Guide students to design an investigation to determine how much water a plant needs to grow.
   1. Set up three young bean plants in small pots, labeled A, B, and C.
   2. Give the plant in pot A one tablespoon of water each week.
   3. Place pot B in a bowl of water as in the diagram.
   4. Water the plant in pot C as needed.

EXPLAIN: USE DATA TO GENERATE INTERPRETATIONS, INCLUDING DESCRIPTIONS, CLASSIFICATIONS, PREDICTIONS, AND EXPLANATIONS.

c. Ask: *How do the conditions of the plants differ? Which one seems healthiest? What are the indications of health?*

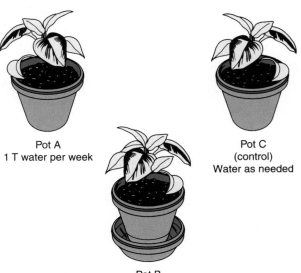

Pot A
1 T water per week

Pot C
(control)
Water as needed

Pot B
Leave pot in bowl of water

Children tend to overwater plants. Too much water can be as harmful as too little water. Lead students to observe plants to determine when they might need water.

9. HOW MUCH FERTILIZER IS ENOUGH FOR HEALTHY PLANT GROWTH? (K–5)

Materials

Young bean or radish plants
Milk cartons or plastic cups
Fertilizer
Graduated cylinder or measuring cup

ENGAGE: ASK A QUESTION ABOUT OBJECTS, ORGANISMS, OR EVENTS IN THE ENVIRONMENT.

a. Ask: *How much fertilizer do plants need?*

EXPLORE: PLAN AND CONDUCT SIMPLE INVESTIGATIONS TO COLLECT RELEVANT DATA.

b. Guide children to plan and set up an investigation similar to that in the illustration to determine how much fertilizer is enough for plants.

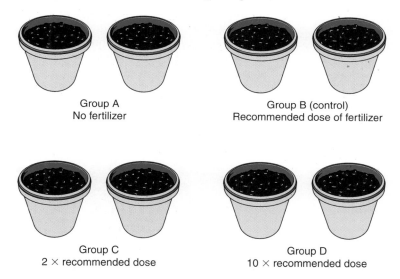

Group A
No fertilizer

Group B (control)
Recommended dose of fertilizer

Group C
2 × recommended dose

Group D
10 × recommended dose

c. Lead students to observe the plants and make records in their observation journals. They might observe, measure, and compare the height of each plant, leaf color, number of leaves, and leaf size.

EXPLAIN: USE DATA TO GENERATE INTERPRETATIONS, INCLUDING DESCRIPTIONS, CLASSIFICATIONS, PREDICTIONS, AND EXPLANATIONS.

d. Ask: *How do the conditions of the plants differ? Which one seems healthiest? What do you conclude about the amount of fertilizer a plant needs? What does fertilizer supply for plants?*

▶ *Teaching Background*

Plants require **mineral nutrients** for growth, repair, and proper functioning. Mineral nutrients are formed by the breakdown of rocks and other materials in the earth. Mineral nutrients can also be supplied by fertilizers applied by humans. Humans ordinarily obtain minerals from eating plants or animals. Nutrients can also be obtained from supplements.[3]

10. WHAT IS THE EFFECT OF LIGHT ON PLANT GROWTH? (3–5)

Materials

Germinated bean seeds
Sunny window or light source
Ruler
Potting soil
Clean milk carton
Shoe box with cover

ENGAGE: ASK A QUESTION ABOUT OBJECTS, ORGANISMS, OR EVENTS IN THE ENVIRONMENT.

a. Ask: *What effect does light have on the way a plant grows? What do you think might happen to a plant if the amount of light from a light source is very limited? What do you think might happen if a plant is placed near a window? What could you do to find out?*

EXPLORE: PLAN AND CONDUCT SIMPLE INVESTIGATIONS TO COLLECT RELEVANT DATA.

b. Plant four germinated bean seeds 3/4 inch to 1 inch (2 cm) deep in moist soil in a clean milk carton.
c. Place the milk carton in a shoe box that has only a single, 1 inch hole cut in the middle of one end. Cover the box and turn the opening toward bright sunlight or a strong lamp, as shown in the diagram.

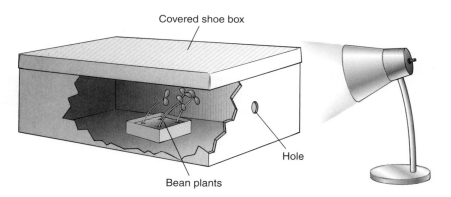

Covered shoe box

Hole

Bean plants

d. Lift the cover every 2 days and see how the bean plants are growing. Record observations. Add water as needed.

EXPLAIN: USE DATA TO GENERATE INTERPRETATIONS, INCLUDING DESCRIPTIONS, CLASSIFICATIONS, PREDICTIONS, AND EXPLANATIONS.

e. Ask: *What is happening to the stems and leaves? Why do you think they are growing as they are? What do you think might happen if you turned the milk carton with the plants completely around in the shoe box?*
f. Try it and observe what happens in 2 days.

---

[3]Adapted from National Gardening Association, 1990. *GrowLab: Activities for Growing Minds.* National Gardening Association, 180 Flynn Avenue, Burlington, Vermont 05401.

▶ *Teaching Background*

Students should see that the beans grow toward the opening in the shoe box. When turned around, they reverse their direction of growth toward the opening again. Green plants need sunlight and are forced toward the light by **phototropism,** which causes the cells on one side of leaves to grow faster than the other. This causes the turning effect of the leaves toward the sunlight.

    g. Ask: *Knowing what you do about* **phototropism,** *the effect of light on plants, why is it necessary to turn your plants at the windowsill every few days? What might happen if you did not turn them?*

Concepts and Principles

Activities 11–15 address these fundamental concepts and principles related to the *Science Standards:*

- Organisms have basic needs. Plants require air, water, nutrients, and light (K–4).
- Each plant or animal has different structures that serve different functions in growth, survival, and reproduction (K–4).

11. WHAT MAKES LEAVES GREEN? (3–5)

Materials

Double boiler pot
Hot plate
Assorted green leaves
Rubbing alcohol

ENGAGE: ASK A QUESTION ABOUT OBJECTS, ORGANISMS, OR EVENTS IN THE ENVIRONMENT.

    a. Ask: *What color are most leaves? Why do you think this is so?*

Safety Precautions:

Caution children to stay away from boiling water.

EXPLORE: PLAN AND CONDUCT SIMPLE INVESTIGATIONS TO COLLECT RELEVANT DATA.

    b. Teacher should demonstrate this activity for the students.
       1. With water in the bottom and green leaves and rubbing alcohol in the top, set up the double boiler pot on the hot plate.
          Ask: *What color are the leaves as we put them in the rubbing alcohol?*
       2. Heat the double boiler so that water boils for 10 minutes. Review parts of plants and discuss leaves while the water boils.
       3. Remove leaves from the pot and observe.

EXPLAIN: USE DATA TO GENERATE INTERPRETATIONS, INCLUDING DESCRIPTIONS, CLASSIFICATIONS, PREDICTIONS, AND EXPLANATIONS.

c. Ask: *What color are the leaves now?*
What color is the rubbing alcohol now? Why?
What do we call the "green stuff" in leaves? (This is called **chlorophyll.**)

12. WHAT MAKES LEAVES GREEN? (METHOD TWO) (3–6)

Materials

Rock
1 inch by 4 inch strip of filter paper or white coffee filter
Clear plastic cup

ENGAGE: ASK A QUESTION ABOUT OBJECTS, ORGANISMS, OR EVENTS IN THE ENVIRONMENT.

a. Ask: *What color are most leaves? Why do you think this is so?*

EXPLORE: PLAN AND CONDUCT SIMPLE INVESTIGATIONS TO COLLECT RELEVANT DATA.

b. Another method to find "hidden" colors in plant leaves uses the following technique, which students can perform under your supervision:
1. Use a rock to rub a leaf impression about 1 inch up on a 1 inch by 4 inch strip of filter paper or white coffee filter, as in diagram (a).
2. Place enough water to cover the bottom of a clear plastic cup and fold the paper so it hangs from the edge of the jar, just touching the bottom. See diagram (b). What do you think will happen?
3. Observe the changes.

EXPLAIN: USE DATA TO GENERATE INTERPRETATIONS, INCLUDING DESCRIPTIONS, CLASSIFICATIONS, PREDICTIONS, AND EXPLANATIONS.

c. Ask: *What happened? Why? What colors were revealed?*

ELABORATE: EXTEND CONCEPTS, PRINCIPLES, AND STRATEGIES TO NEW SITUATIONS AND QUESTIONS.

d. Try this activity with different leaves.

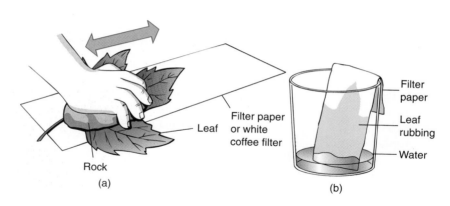

Leaf

Rock

(a)

Filter paper or white coffee filter

Filter paper

Leaf rubbing

Water

(b)

▶ *Teaching Background*

As the water slowly rises, it hits the plant leaf "stain" in the filter and separates out some of the pigments. This reveals the "hidden" colors of the leaf.

Note: Using acetone (nail polish remover) in place of the water will produce better results by separating pigments more effectively. If you use acetone, place it in a closed glass jar instead of an open plastic cup.

Safety Precautions

Acetone fumes can be harmful. Keep acetone in a closed container. Do not allow children to breathe the acetone fumes.

13. HOW DOES LIGHT AFFECT PLANTS? (K–2)

Materials

Two plants of the same type—one that has been growing in the dark for a week and the other in light
Healthy plant growing in pot
3M Post-it foil stars

ENGAGE: ASK A QUESTION ABOUT OBJECTS, ORGANISMS, OR EVENTS IN THE ENVIRONMENT.

a. Show students two plants of the same type—one that has been in the dark for a week and the other that has been in light. Ask: *How do you think they got this way?*

EXPLORE: PLAN AND CONDUCT SIMPLE INVESTIGATIONS TO COLLECT RELEVANT DATA.

b. Guide students to conduct this investigation:
   1. Select a healthy outdoor or indoor plant. Peel and stick a few foil stars on one or two leaves, while the plant is in the pot or ground and in growing conditions (has water, sun, etc.).
   2. Leave stars on for 1 week.
   3. Remove stars from leaves.

EXPLAIN: USE DATA TO GENERATE INTERPRETATIONS, INCLUDING DESCRIPTIONS, CLASSIFICATIONS, PREDICTIONS, AND EXPLANATIONS.

c. Ask: *What do you see? Why do you think this happened?*

d. Ask: *What do you think will happen to the spots that were under the stars if the plant is put back in the sun for 1 week?* Ask the children to try it, to observe what happens, and to record their data.

e. Ask: *What did you observe? Why did this happen?*

▶ *Teaching Background*

Plants are green because of **chlorophyll.** Chlorophyll absorbs light energy from the sun and helps plants make food. Without sunlight, plants use up the chlorophyll, the leaf starts to turn white, and the plant eventually dies.

14. WHAT COMES OUT OF LEAVES IN SUNLIGHT? (3–5)

Materials

Elodea water plants (obtained from classroom aquarium or pet store)
1 gallon widemouthed jar
Glass or plastic funnel
Test tube
Lamp or sunlight
Wooden splint
Matches
Magnifying lens

ENGAGE: ASK A QUESTION ABOUT OBJECTS, ORGANISMS, OR EVENTS IN THE ENVIRONMENT.

a. Ask: *What happens when your head is underwater and you let some air out of your mouth? What do you see?* (Remember from activities with air that bubbles indicate the presence of air.) *What do you think might happen to a plant if it is placed underwater in sunlight?*

EXPLORE: PLAN AND CONDUCT SIMPLE INVESTIGATIONS TO COLLECT RELEVANT DATA.

b. Do this activity:
   1. Put a water plant such as elodea in a 1 gallon widemouthed jar.
   2. Invert a glass or plastic funnel over the elodea and place a test tube completely full of water over the stem of the funnel, as shown in the diagram.
   3. Place the jar in direct sunlight for 3 days.

EXPLAIN: USE DATA TO GENERATE INTERPRETATIONS, INCLUDING DESCRIPTIONS, CLASSIFICATIONS, PREDICTIONS, AND EXPLANATIONS.

c. Ask: *What do you see coming up from the elodea plant?*
   What happened to the level of water in the test tube? Why do you think the water level changed?
   What do you think might be in the test tube?

ELABORATE: EXTEND CONCEPTS, PRINCIPLES, AND STRATEGIES TO NEW SITUATIONS AND QUESTIONS.

d. Ask: *How might you set up an experiment to find out what is in the test tube?*

e. *Note:* The teacher should perform this step as a demonstration: When most of the water in the test tube has been displaced, quickly remove the test tube and insert a glowing splint or lit match into the test tube, as shown in the diagram.

Ask: *What do you see happening to the wooden splint or lit match? Why do you think this happened?*

Guide students to understand that the splint burned brightly because of **oxygen** given off from the elodea plant in sunlight. Oxygen is given off by plants during photosynthesis.

Leaves have small pores called **stomata** through which air enters and gases escape (see drawings). Students can use magnifying lenses to view stomata as the oxygen is released from the green plant.

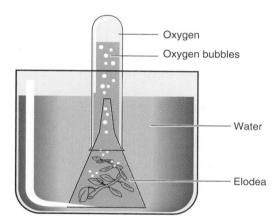

- Oxygen
- Oxygen bubbles
- Water
- Elodea

15. WHAT ELSE COMES OUT OF LEAVES IN SUNLIGHT? (3–5)

Materials

Two clear plastic bags
Two small, identical geranium plants
Plastic ties
Magnifying lenses

ENGAGE: ASK A QUESTION ABOUT OBJECTS, ORGANISMS, OR EVENTS IN THE ENVIRONMENT.

a. Ask: *What else might come out of leaves in sunlight?*

EXPLORE: PLAN AND CONDUCT SIMPLE INVESTIGATIONS TO COLLECT RELEVANT DATA.

b. Instruct students to do this activity:
   1. Place a clear plastic bag over one geranium and tie the bag around the stem, just above the soil level.
   2. Wave a second plastic bag through the air and tie it as well, as illustrated in the diagram.
   3. Put both plastic bags in direct sunlight for at least 3 hours.

EXPLAIN: USE DATA TO GENERATE INTERPRETATIONS, INCLUDING DESCRIPTIONS, CLASSIFICATIONS, PREDICTIONS, AND EXPLANATIONS.

c. After 3 hours, ask:

- *What do you see forming on the top of the plant in the plastic bag? Where do you think the moisture came from?* (From the leaves of the plant.)
- *What is your evidence that the moisture came from the leaves and not the soil?* (The plastic bag was tied off above the soil line.)
- *How is the plastic bag without the plant different after 3 hours? Why do you think this happened? Why do you think the empty plastic bag was used in this activity?*
- *What makes this investigation a controlled experiment?* (Two identical bags containing air are used, one with a plant and one without a plant. The condition varied—the manipulated variable—is whether or not a bag has a plant. The outcome or responding variable is the production of moisture.)

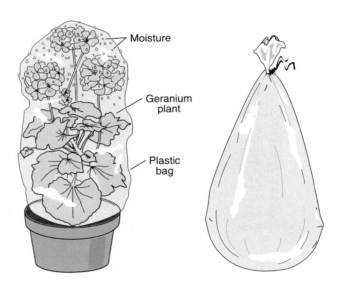

Moisture

Geranium plant

Plastic bag

▶ *Teaching Background*

Moisture is formed in the plastic bag with the plant as a by-product of **photosynthesis** in the leaves. The purpose of tying off the bag at the stem was to prevent moisture evaporating from the soil from entering the bag. The "empty" clear plastic bag is the control.

NSES   **Concepts and Principles**

Activity 16 addresses these fundamental concepts and principles related to the *Science Standards*:

- Organisms can survive only in environments in which their basic needs are met (K–4).
- Each plant or animal has different structures that serve different functions in growth, survival, and reproduction (K–4).

16. WHAT IS THE EFFECT OF GRAVITY ON THE GROWTH OF ROOTS AND STEMS? (K–5)

Materials

Young, growing bean plants
Paper towels
Two pieces of glass or thick plastic to place growing plants between
Tongue depressors or applicator sticks
Small pebbles
Tape

ENGAGE: ASK A QUESTION ABOUT OBJECTS, ORGANISMS, OR EVENTS IN THE ENVIRONMENT.

a. Ask: *What do you think might happen to roots of a plant if they were planted facing up or sideways rather than facing down? What do you think might happen to roots if something were in their way? What could we do to find out? What do you think would happen to the stems of plants that are planted upside down or sideways?* Lead students to design an investigation in which the plant is planted upside down so that the progress of roots and stems can be observed.

EXPLORE: PLAN AND CONDUCT SIMPLE INVESTIGATIONS TO COLLECT RELEVANT DATA.

b. This investigation might be done as a class demonstration. Place four young bean plants between two moist paper towels. Put the paper towels with the seedlings between two pieces of glass or rigid, clear plastic. Put small pebbles under each root. Place the applicator sticks or tongue depressors between the pieces of glass or clear plastic, and tape as shown in the diagram.

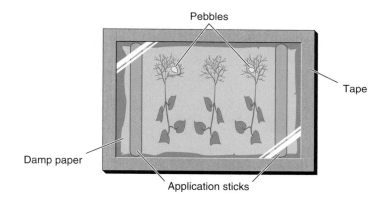

Pebbles

Tape

Damp paper

Application sticks

c. Stand the glass so the roots point up and the stems point down. Instruct the students to observe the plant growth for several days and record their observations.

EXPLAIN: USE DATA TO GENERATE INTERPRETATIONS, INCLUDING DESCRIPTIONS, CLASSIFICATIONS, PREDICTIONS, AND EXPLANATIONS.

d. Ask: *What did you observe about the roots? What did you observe about the stems? Why do you think this happened?* Through discussion, lead students to conclude that roots grow downward under the influence of gravity and that they grow around objects in the soil. Stems grow upward.

▶ *Teaching Background*

The roots will grow down (toward the earth), and the stems will grow up (away from the earth). The plant responses that cause this are called **tropisms. Geotropism** forces roots down as auxins (plant hormones) are concentrated by gravity along the bottom cells of stems and root tips. The bottom cells in the stem are stimulated by the hormones to grow faster than cells higher up; they get longer and curl upward. Root cells are more sensitive to these hormones than are stem cells, so the root cells inhibit cell growth. Root top cells elongate faster, and root tips curve downward.

C. INSECTS

▶ *Science Background*

Insects are the most successful group of animals on earth. Insects dominate the planet in terms of number of individuals and species. There are more kinds of insects than all other kinds of animals put together. All insects have six legs and three body parts: the head, thorax, and abdomen. Insects that may be familiar to children include dragonflies, crickets, lice, beetles, butterflies, flies, fleas, and ants.

Insects change in form through a process called metamorphosis as they grow and mature. Some insects progress from egg, to larva, to a pupal stage, and then to adults. Other insects look pretty much like adults when they hatch from eggs.[4]

NSES **Science Standards**

All students should develop an understanding of

- characteristics of organisms (K–4).
- structure and function in living systems (5–8).
- life cycles of organisms (K–4).
- organisms and their environments (K–4).

Objectives for Students

1. Recognize the wide variation in insects.
2. Identify and describe different parts/structures of insects.
3. Define *metamorphosis* and name the stages in the metamorphosis of a mealworm.
4. Describe the sequence of stages in the development of a mealworm.
5. Ask questions about ants that can be answered through investigations.
6. Design and carry out descriptive investigations to gather information and answer questions about ants.

NSES **Concepts and Principles**

Activity I addresses these fundamental concepts and principles related to the *Science Standards:*

- Plants and animals have life cycles that include being born, developing into adults, reproducing, and eventually dying. The details of this life cycle are different for different organisms (K–4).

---

[4]Adapted from FOSS (Full Option Science System), 1995. *Insects.* Lawrence Hall of Science, Berkeley, CA. (Published by Delta Education, Nashua, NH.)

1. WHAT STAGES DO INSECTS GO THROUGH? (K–5)

Materials

Jars with covers (clear plastic, if possible)
Mealworms (from pet shop)
Bran or other cereal flakes
Magnifying lenses
Spoons
Pictures of people and insects at different growing stages

ENGAGE: ASK A QUESTION ABOUT OBJECTS, ORGANISMS, OR EVENTS IN THE ENVIRONMENT.

a. Ask: *What are the stages people go through as they grow and change? Do insects, like mealworms, go through stages too? How could we find out?*

EXPLORE: PLAN AND CONDUCT SIMPLE INVESTIGATIONS TO COLLECT RELEVANT DATA.

b. Obtain some mealworms from a pet store, granary, or commercial supplier (see Appendix C). Introduce the mealworms and challenge students to predict how the mealworms will change as they grow. Using spoons, you or the students can transfer several mealworms and some bran or cereal flakes into a jar or other container with a lid. Provide a container for each student or group of two or three students. Punch several small holes in the lids for air.

c. Have students observe the mealworms several times a week and record on a chart or log any observed changes in appearance (color, length, stage, etc.) or behavior.

EXPLAIN: USE DATA TO GENERATE INTERPRETATIONS, INCLUDING DESCRIPTIONS, CLASSIFICATIONS, PREDICTIONS, AND EXPLANATIONS.

d. Using pictures of people and insects at different stages of growth, discuss how these living things grow. Help students make a chart comparing the stages of insects' lives with humans', like the one shown.

Stages	
People	*Insects*
Child	Larva
Teenager	Pupa
Adult	Adult

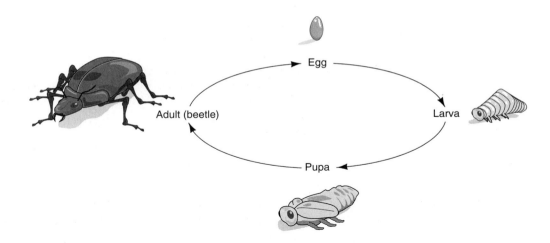

e. In addition, guide students to make a diagram, similar to the one shown, and include photos or drawings to visualize the stages of mealworm (and other insect) metamorphosis. Make the same kind of diagram for stages of human life (infant, child, teenager, and adult).

NSES **Concepts and Principles**

Activity 2 addresses these fundamental concepts and principles related to the *Science Standards:*

- Organisms have basic needs. Animals need air, water, and food (K–4).
- Organisms can survive only in environments in which their basic needs are met (K–4).
- Each plant or animal has different structures that serve different functions in growth, survival, and reproduction (K–4).

---

2. HOW DO ANTS LIVE? (K–2)

Materials

Widemouthed glass jar (commercial mayonnaise or pickle jar) with screw top punctured with very small holes
Empty washed soup can
Soil to fill the jar two-thirds full
Small sponge
Pan large enough to hold the widemouthed glass jar
Sheet of black construction paper
Crumbs and bits of food such as bread, cake, sugar, seeds
Colony of ants (from pet shop, home, or school grounds)

ENGAGE: ASK A QUESTION ABOUT OBJECTS, ORGANISMS, OR EVENTS IN THE ENVIRONMENT.

a. Ask: *What do ants look like? Are all ants alike, or are there different kinds of ants? Where do ants make their homes?* Lead children to draw pictures of ants and to describe and explain their pictures.

EXPLORE: PLAN
AND CONDUCT SIMPLE
INVESTIGATIONS TO
COLLECT RELEVANT DATA.

b. Set up an ant colony following these directions:
   1. Place the soup can in the center of the widemouthed glass jar as in the diagram.
   2. Fill the jar two-thirds full of soil.
   3. Punch several airholes in the screw cover.
   4. Place a sheet of black construction paper around the outside of the jar.
   5. Add a small sponge with water. Add crumbs and bits of food (bread, cake, sugar, and seeds).
   6. Add ants.
   7. Place a cloth over the top of the jar and screw the jar lid in place.
   8. Place the jar in a pan of water.

Safety Precautions

Caution children not to handle the ants. As a defense, ants bite and sting. Sometimes after biting an enemy, ants will spray a chemical into the open wound.

c. Ask: *What effect will a sheet of black paper placed around the jar have on the ants?* (This simulates the dark underground so ants will tunnel close to the sides of the glass jar.) *Why place the soup can in the center of the jar with soil around it?* (So ants will not burrow into the center but will tunnel out to the jar's sides and be more visible.) *What is the purpose of placing the jar in a pan of water?* (So the ants cannot escape.)

d. Guide children to observe ants, including observing with magnifying lenses. Instruct students to make records, including drawings, of what ants look like and what the ants do. Students should observe body characteristics such as are shown in the diagram.[5] Ask: *Are all ants in the ant colony alike?*
   How many pairs of legs do ants have?

---

[5]Adapted and modified from *Ant Homes Under the Ground*, one of more than 75 teacher's guides in the Great Explorations in Math and Science (GEMS) series, available from the Lawrence Hall of Science, University of California at Berkeley. For more information, visit their website at www.lhsgems.org.

What are the antennae on the head used for?
How do ants move?
What does the egg of an ant look like?

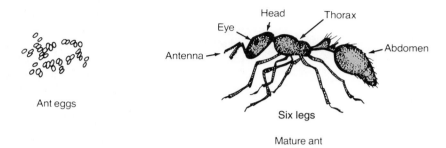

Ant eggs

Mature ant

e. Ask: *What do ants eat?*

Divide a paper plate into sections with a black marker. Place various food items on the plate (e.g., crackers, small seeds, sugar, lettuce). Set the plate outside near an ant trail on a nice warm day. Check back after 1 hour to see what has happened. Check back after 2 hours. What food have the ants taken? What is their favorite food?

EXPLAIN: USE DATA TO GENERATE INTERPRETATIONS, INCLUDING DESCRIPTIONS, CLASSIFICATIONS, PREDICTIONS, AND EXPLANATIONS.

f. Ask: *How do the ants connect their homes in the jar?*

What changes have the ants made in their environment since they were first placed in the jar?

In what ways are ants useful to people?
What are some other insects that live and work together?
What are some living things that are sometimes mistaken for insects?
What might happen if the ant colony were placed in a light, warm place?
How are ants different from spiders?
In what ways are ants social animals?

D. BIRDS

▶ *Science Background*

Birds are familiar animals in the child's environment. Birds differ in a variety of ways. Children can observe many different characteristics of birds, such as colors and sizes. Birds sing different songs, eat different kinds of food, and make different kinds of nests where they care for their young. The male bird may have a more colorful plumage than the female. Some birds change color with the season. Some birds migrate. Birds need trees and shrubs for protection from their predators, including small mammals, humans, and even other birds.

NSES   **Science Standards**

All students should develop an understanding of

- characteristics of organisms (K–4).
- structure and function in living systems (5–8).
- organisms and their environments (K–4).

Objectives for Students

1. Recognize the wide variation in birds.
2. Identify and describe different characteristics of birds.
3. Ask questions about birds that can be answered through investigations.
4. Design and carry out descriptive and classificatory investigations to gather information for answering questions about birds.

 NSES   Concepts and Principles

Activities 1–4 address these fundamental concepts and principles related to the *Science Standards* and *Benchmarks for Science Literacy:*

- Some animals and plants are alike in the way they look and the things they do, and others are very different from one another (K–2).
- A great variety of living things can be sorted into groups in many ways using various features to decide which things belong to which group (3–5).
- Organisms have basic needs. Animals need air, water, and food (K–4).
- Organisms can survive only in environments in which their basic needs are met (K–4).

1. WHAT DO YOU KNOW ABOUT THE BIRDS AROUND YOU? (K–6)

Materials

Bird book (showing local birds)
Pictures of birds
Bird feeders (commercial or made in class)

ENGAGE: ASK A QUESTION ABOUT OBJECTS, ORGANISMS, OR EVENTS IN THE ENVIRONMENT.

a. Lead children in a discussion of what they know about birds.
   Ask: *How are birds alike? How are birds different?*
   Where do some birds go during the winter?
   What kinds of homes do birds live in?
   What do birds do that is different from what other animals do?
   What kinds of foods do birds eat?
   What are the names of some local birds?
   What do these birds look like?

EXPLORE: PLAN AND CONDUCT SIMPLE INVESTIGATIONS TO COLLECT RELEVANT DATA.

b. If the natural environment lends itself to feeding and observing birds, have students observe birds on the way to and from school, or take a class field trip to a local area, park, or zoo. In a city, you will probably see sparrows or pigeons, jays in picnic areas, ducks in ponds, geese on golf courses, and seagulls at the seashore. In addition, you may want to provide pictures of different birds, nests, and eggs for students to handle, observe, and discuss.

c. Record students' responses to this question on the board: *How could we attract birds to our school grounds?*
   Ask: *Where could we make a good bird feeding and observing area?* (Tree and shrub shelter that is free from predators and visible from the classroom.)

d. Set up a bird feeding and observing area.
   1. With your students, survey your school grounds and pick the best spot for a bird feeding and observing area.
   2. Find out what kinds of birds are common in your area, what their food preferences are, how they eat (on the ground or from feeders), and any other information that will make your feeding and observing most useful for birds.

3. Put up a bird feeder(s) and a water tray.
4. Design an experiment or follow the suggestions provided to investigate birds.

2. WHAT KINDS OF FOODS DO DIFFERENT BIRDS PREFER? (K–6)

Materials

Bird food (bread, popcorn, commercial birdseed)
Plastic cups
Small pieces of cloth

ENGAGE: ASK A
QUESTION ABOUT OBJECTS,
ORGANISMS, OR EVENTS IN
THE ENVIRONMENT.

a. Ask: *What kinds of food do birds prefer?*

EXPLORE: PLAN
AND CONDUCT SIMPLE
INVESTIGATIONS TO
COLLECT RELEVANT DATA.

b. Try offering small equal amounts of two kinds of food (e.g., bread and birdseed) to the birds at the same time.

Safety Precautions

Do *not* feed birds directly from your hand; instead, put some food in such places as a bird feeder on a tree limb or a pole, on the ground, in a plastic cup, and so on.

EXPLAIN: USE
DATA TO GENERATE
INTERPRETATIONS,
INCLUDING DESCRIPTIONS,
CLASSIFICATIONS,
PREDICTIONS, AND
EXPLANATIONS.

c. Ask: *Which food do birds prefer? What is your evidence?*
   Where do birds prefer their food to be put?
   Did different birds like different places?
   What was the most popular feeding spot?

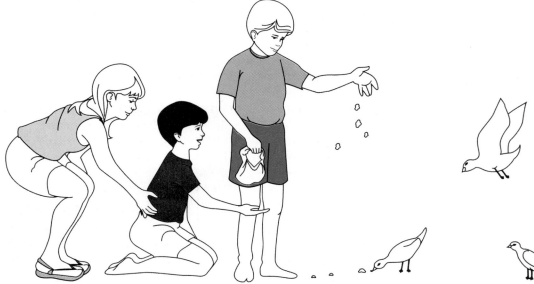

    d. Ask: *Does one individual bird or kind of bird get the most food?*
         How does the bird do it?
         What happens when you try to give food to the other birds?
         Why do you think this happens?

3. HOW DO BIRDS INTERACT WITH THEIR SURROUNDINGS? (3–6)

ENGAGE: ASK A QUESTION ABOUT OBJECTS, ORGANISMS, OR EVENTS IN THE ENVIRONMENT.

a. Ask: *How do loud noises and sudden movements affect birds?*

EXPLORE: PLAN AND CONDUCT SIMPLE INVESTIGATIONS TO COLLECT RELEVANT DATA.

b. While birds are gathered, make a really loud noise, but remain perfectly still. Observe what happens. Next, make a sudden dramatic movement, but be very quiet. Observe what the birds do.

EXPLAIN: USE DATA TO GENERATE INTERPRETATIONS, INCLUDING DESCRIPTIONS, CLASSIFICATIONS, PREDICTIONS, AND EXPLANATIONS.

c. Ask: *What did the birds do when you made a loud noise?*
    What did the birds do when you made a sudden movement?
    Did the loud noise or the sudden movement scare the birds more?
    How do you know?
    Why do you think this is so?

How could you help children understand what scientists do?

d. Explain that when they observed birds and investigated how birds responded to noise and movement, they were acting like scientists. The investigation was a controlled experiment. Discuss with the children why it was important to control for movement when they were testing the effects of noise and why it was important to control for noise when they were testing the effects of movement.

4. HOW CAN YOU FIND OUT MORE ABOUT BIRDS? (3–6)

ENGAGE: ASK A QUESTION ABOUT OBJECTS, ORGANISMS, OR EVENTS IN THE ENVIRONMENT.

a. Ask: *Why is it so important to continue feeding birds and supplying water once we begin?*
    How are these "wild birds" the same and different from domestic (pet) birds like parrots and canaries?
    How do birds help people?
    How might birds harm people?
    What are some different ways birds in our neighborhood build their nests?

EXPLORE: PLAN AND CONDUCT SIMPLE INVESTIGATIONS TO COLLECT RELEVANT DATA.

b. The following types of questions can be asked about any of the local birds. These questions may have to be modified, however, depending on the kinds of birds that are found in your region.

- **Redheaded Woodpecker.** *Where does the woodpecker build its nest? How does it build its nest? What kind of food does the woodpecker eat? How does the woodpecker benefit and harm our environment? How does a woodpecker's beak aid it in getting food?*

- **Hummingbird.** *How does the male hummingbird differ in color from the female? Where do hummingbirds get their food? Are hummingbirds as big as cardinals or sparrows? Why do you have difficulty finding their nests? How do hummingbirds help in the pollination of plants? How does a hummingbird's beak aid it in getting food?*

- **Starling.** *Why do many other birds prefer not to live near starlings? What color is the starling? How does the starling vary in color compared with the hummingbird and woodpecker? Why do farmers dislike starlings during fruit harvesting season?*

NSES   **Concepts and Principles**

Activity 5 addresses this fundamental principle related to the *Science Standards:*

- Each plant or animal has different structures that serve different functions in growth, survival, and reproduction (K–4).

5. HOW DO BIRD BONES DIFFER FROM MAMMAL BONES? (3–6)

Materials

Beef and chicken bones (one of each for every two students). If possible, these should be cut in half.

Wing bones of chickens (or any other bird).

ENGAGE: ASK A QUESTION ABOUT OBJECTS, ORGANISMS, OR EVENTS IN THE ENVIRONMENT.

a. Ask: *How do bird bones differ from the bones of mammals?*

EXPLORE: PLAN AND CONDUCT SIMPLE INVESTIGATIONS TO COLLECT RELEVANT DATA.

b. Allow students to help furnish beef and chicken bones.
   1. Obtain a cut chicken bone, a cut beef bone, and a wing bone of a chicken.
   2. *How did you know which bone was from a chicken and which was from a cow?*
   3. Examine the centers of the two bones and record how the structure of the beef bone differs from that of the chicken bone.
   4. Look at the chicken wing bone.
      How does its structure compare with the arm bones of a person?

EXPLAIN: USE DATA TO GENERATE INTERPRETATIONS, INCLUDING DESCRIPTIONS, CLASSIFICATIONS, PREDICTIONS, AND EXPLANATIONS.

c. Ask: *What advantages do you think bones of birds and mammals have for them?*
   What are some other structural differences between birds and mammals?

II. ORGANISMS AND THEIR ENVIRONMENTS

Organisms have basic needs. Animals need air, water, and food. Plants require air, water, nutrients, and light. Organisms can survive only in environments in which their basic needs are met.

A. AQUARIUM HABITATS

▶ *Science Background*

An aquarium is a wonderful context for studying aquatic life. There are many environmental factors important to life in aquarium habitats, including temperature, water transparency, nutrients, and concentrations of dissolved gases (oxygen and carbon dioxide).

Both plants and animals use oxygen and give off carbon dioxide through respiration. Plants also use carbon dioxide and give off oxygen in the process of photosynthesis. During daylight hours, aquatic plants produce more oxygen than plants and animals consume in respiration. At night, both plants and animals use accumulated oxygen.

When carbon dioxide dissolves in water, it makes the water acidic. Bromothymol blue (BTB) is a chemical indicator that can be used to monitor acid concentration in aquariums. BTB changes color, depending on the acidity of the water. A few drops of BTB in a container of water that is neutral produces a pale blue. If the water is acidic, its color shifts to green or yellow when BTB is added. If the water is basic, the color turns to deep blue.

NSES **Science Standards**

All students should develop an understanding of

- organisms and their environments (K–4).

Objectives for Students

1. Define *habitat* and *ecosystem*.
2. Identify and describe the parts of aquarium and terrarium habitats and describe how the parts in each system interact.
3. Construct aquarium and terrarium habitats.
4. Ask questions and design and carry out investigations about components and interactions within ecosystems.

NSES **Concepts and Principles**

Activities 1–3 address these fundamental concepts and principles related to the *Science Standards:*

- Organisms have basic needs. Animals need air, water, and food. Plants require air, water, nutrients, and light. Organisms can survive only in environments in which their basic needs are met (K–4).
- An organism's patterns of behavior are related to the nature of that organism's environment, including the kinds and numbers of other organisms present, the availability of food and resources, and the physical characteristics of the environment (K–4).
- When the environment changes, some plants and animals survive and reproduce, and others die or move to new locations (K–4).

1. HOW CAN I CONSTRUCT AN AQUARIUM HABITAT? (1–3)

Materials

A 6 liter, clear plastic basin (used as the aquarium)
Five small aquatic plants (approximately 3 to 4 inches or 10 cm in height)
Freshwater fantailed guppy
Two water snails

ENGAGE: ASK A QUESTION ABOUT OBJECTS, ORGANISMS, OR EVENTS IN THE ENVIRONMENT.

a. Ask: *What is an aquarium? What lives in an aquarium? What are some of the things fish, plants, and other organisms need to survive in an aquarium? How must an aquarium be constructed and maintained to support living things?*

EXPLORE: PLAN AND CONDUCT SIMPLE INVESTIGATIONS TO COLLECT RELEVANT DATA.

b. It is preferable for each group of students to have their own aquarium. Teachers should guide and work with students to construct and maintain a freshwater aquarium, following these instructions:
   1. *Container.* Obtain a 4 to 6 liter (1 to 1.5 gallons), rectangular clear plastic container with strong walls. The container should have a large surface area to allow gas exchange with the atmosphere, but should not be too shallow. Wash the container well with water, but not soap.

2. *Sand.* Obtain a supply of coarse white sand. Rinse the sand in a bucket to remove debris. Add white sand to a depth of about 4 cm to the bottom of the aquarium container.

3. *Water.* Age tap water in an open container for 24 to 48 hours to allow chlorine in the water to escape. You may choose to use bottled spring water (but not distilled water). Gently pour the water into the container, perhaps over clean paper to prevent disturbing the sand.

4. *Plants.* Obtain water plants from a pond or purchase them from a science supply company or a local pet shop (see Appendix C and D). Root about two sprigs of waterweed (elodea) and two sprigs of eelgrass in the sand. Add some duckweed as a floating plant. Overplanting is better for your aquarium than underplanting. Allow 1 to 2 weeks for the plants to become acclimated to the water before adding animals.

5. *Fish.* Purchase small fish from a pet store or obtain some free from an aquarium hobbyist. Obtain male and female guppies or goldfish. Place the plastic bag containing the fish in your aquarium water for a few hours for the water temperatures in the bag and the aquarium to become equal. Use a dip net to add three to four fish to the aquarium. A rule of thumb is not to have more than 1 cm of fish (excluding tail) per liter of water. Dispose of the plastic container and water the fish came in.

6. *Snails.* Add several small pond snails to your aquarium.

7. *Care.* Add a plastic lid to your aquarium. Lift the corners of the lid to allow exchange of gases between the water and the atmosphere. Thus, you will not need a pump for aeration. Keep a supply of aged tap water available to replace evaporated water as necessary, keeping the water in the aquarium at a predetermined level.

8. *Temperature.* Place your aquarium in the room so that it can get light, but not direct sunlight. Too much light will promote the growth of algae (which can, if you desire, be observed and studied by students). The aquarium should be maintained at room temperature (70° to 78°F or 21° to 25°C; see Appendix H for conversions). A gooseneck lamp with a 60 to 75 watt bulb can be used to warm the water if necessary. Adjust the lamp so the bulb is a few centimeters above the water, until the temperature is maintained at the desired level. Check with your principal about school regulations concerning leaving the lamp on over the weekend.

9. *Food.* Feed the fish a small amount (a pinch) of commercial fish food every other day (or as instructed on the package). Do not overfeed. Uneaten food will decay, polluting the water. Fish can go as long as 2 weeks without food. Fish may supplement their diet by eating from the water plants. Snails do not require any special food. They eat water plants or the debris that collects on the bottom of the aquarium.

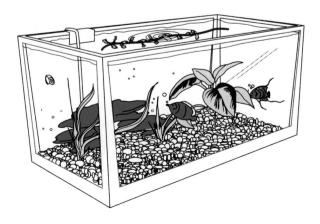

c. Two alternative containers for aquariums are shown in the following illustrations.

Food jar
aquarium

Soda bottle
aquarium

2. WHAT CAN I OBSERVE IN AN AQUARIUM? (1–3)

Materials

Aquarium
Plants
Fish
Snails

ENGAGE: ASK A
QUESTION ABOUT OBJECTS,
ORGANISMS, OR EVENTS IN
THE ENVIRONMENT.

a. Ask: *What happens to the living things within an aquarium? How can we find out?*

EXPLORE: PLAN AND
CONDUCT SIMPLE
INVESTIGATIONS TO
COLLECT RELEVANT DATA.

b. Let the children assist you in preparing one aquarium for each group of four students, following the instructions in Activity 1. Tell each group to observe their aquarium closely. Provide magnifying lenses to assist the students in their observations. Encourage them to talk freely about what they see. While the students are observing, move from group to group and listen to their discourse and questions. Do not answer their questions yet, but use them to help you plan class discussion.

c. Instruct the children to make records in their investigation journals of what they observe. Students might write about what they see and make labeled drawings with crayons, markers, pens, and pencils. Let children use their own terminology in their journals at first, gradually introducing (inventing) technical terms to supplement descriptions.

EXPLAIN: USE DATA TO GENERATE INTERPRETATIONS, INCLUDING DESCRIPTIONS, CLASSIFICATIONS, PREDICTIONS, AND EXPLANATIONS.

d. Take time on a regular basis to discuss with students what they are observing, changes they have noted, and questions they may have raised. Gather the students in a large group and ask such questions as: *What did you observe? Did anyone observe anything else? What is on the bottom of the aquarium?* (Sand.)

e. Explain that a **habitat** is a place where an animal or plant naturally lives or grows. A habitat provides the food, shelter, moisture, light, air, and protection the plants or animals need to survive. Ask: *Think of the aquarium as a habitat for fish; what components of the aquarium habitat support the fish and snails that live there?*

ELABORATE: EXTEND CONCEPTS, PRINCIPLES, AND STRATEGIES TO NEW SITUATIONS AND QUESTIONS.

f. Ask: *What do you wonder about fish and snails?* Lead the children to ask questions that can be answered through further observations or investigations. Children might ask such questions as: *What do the fish and snails eat? How much do they eat? Do the snails have mouths? What are those feelers on the snails?* (Antennae.) *What do they do?* (They contain the snails' eyes.) *What do the snails eat?* (Algae.) *Do the fish and snails sleep? Can they see me? What makes the water green? Will the fish have babies? Which is the mother fish and which is the daddy fish?* (The male guppies are more brightly colored than the females, plus, the females give birth to the baby guppies.) *What is the black stuff on the bottom of the aquarium?* (Detritus; waste products from fish.)

Do not answer the children's questions yet. Post their questions in the room for them to see, think about, and answer through further observation and investigation. Encourage them to observe carefully to try to answer the questions they have posed. Students should add to their journals and drawings regularly.

▶ *Teaching Suggestions*

Encourage children to look for changes in their aquariums. Point out that they will need their records to help them determine what is new in their aquariums.

- Children might observe clumps of transparent spheres on plants and the aquarium sides. These are eggs laid by the snails. Baby snails will hatch from the eggs. Mark the location of snail eggs on the outside of the aquarium with a marking pen. Ask students to observe the clumps regularly. Eventually, a small, black spot will appear in each sphere, becoming larger each day. After a week or 2 a small snail will hatch.

- If you are keeping guppies in your aquariums, children might also observe the birth of baby guppies. Female guppies carry their eggs in their bodies and deliver their young live. Children might note, with much amazement, that the baby guppies are eaten by the adults. To keep the young from being devoured, use a fish net to transfer the adults to another aquarium.

3. WHAT ENVIRONMENTAL FACTORS CAN AFFECT LIFE IN AN AQUARIUM HABITAT? (4–6)

Materials

Small container
BTB (bromothymol blue, obtained from science supply company, swimming pool supply company, or pharmacy)
Vinegar
Clean straws

ENGAGE: ASK A QUESTION ABOUT OBJECTS, ORGANISMS, OR EVENTS IN THE ENVIRONMENT.

a. Ask: *What environmental factors can affect life in an aquarium habitat?*

EXPLORE: PLAN AND CONDUCT SIMPLE INVESTIGATIONS TO COLLECT RELEVANT DATA.

b. Explain to students that the acidity of the water is one factor that needs to be controlled in an aquarium to support life. Explain that BTB is a chemical indicator, indicating whether a liquid is basic, neutral, or acidic. To demonstrate how BTB works, tell students to add two drops of BTB to 5 ml of water in a container. Ask: *What do you observe?* The water should be blue, indicating it is neutral.

Next, show your students a vial to which you have added 5 ml of water. Add two drops of BTB. Dip a straw in vinegar and then in the vial. Ask: *What do you observe?* Explain that the water turned green when the BTB was added because the vinegar was acidic.

Now, tell students to gently blow two or three breaths into the water in their own vials using a clean straw. Ask: *What do you observe now?* After a few breaths, the water usually turns yellow.

EXPLAIN: USE DATA TO GENERATE INTERPRETATIONS, INCLUDING DESCRIPTIONS, CLASSIFICATIONS, PREDICTIONS, AND EXPLANATIONS.

c. Ask: *What did you do? What did you see happen? Why do you think the water turned yellow when you breathed into it?* (The yellow color indicated that a weak acid formed from the interaction of the water in the vial and the carbon dioxide in your breath.)

ELABORATE: EXTEND CONCEPTS, PRINCIPLES, AND STRATEGIES TO NEW SITUATIONS AND QUESTIONS.

d. Explain to students that it is important to know the amount of acid in aquarium habitats because too much acid is harmful to the fish and other living organisms. Tell students to collect 5 ml of aged water and put it into a clean vial. Also tell them to add 5 ml of aquarium water to a second vial. Add two drops of BTB to each vial. Cap the vials and swirl the water in them. Usually the aquarium water will turn green or yellow, indicating acidity. Ask: *What do you think caused the acidity of the aquarium water?* Make a list of responses, such as something from the fish, too much food, chemicals from the air, something from the plants.

e. Ask how the students might investigate to find the source of the acid. Through discussion, allow the students to come up with the idea of running a controlled investigation. In the investigation, one factor is changed at a time, with everything else remaining the same.

B. TERRARIUM HABITATS

▶ *Science Background*

A terrarium is a habitat for plants and small animals, such as earthworms, pill bugs, and frogs. Terrariums must include everything a plant or animal needs to survive.

 Science Standards

All students should develop an understanding of

- organisms and their environments (K–4).

Objectives for Students

1. Define habitat and ecosystem.
2. Identify and describe the parts of aquarium and terrarium habitats and describe how the parts in each system interact.
3. Construct aquarium and terrarium habitats.
4. Ask questions and design and carry out investigations about components and interactions within ecosystems.

Concepts and Principles

Activities 1–5 address these fundamental concepts and principles related to the *Science Standards*:

- Organisms have basic needs. Animals need air, water, and food. Plants require air, water, nutrients, and light. Organisms can survive only in environments in which their basic needs are met (K–4).
- An organism's patterns of behavior are related to the nature of that organism's environment, including the kinds and numbers of other organisms present, the availability of food and resources, and the physical characteristics of the environment (K–4).
- When the environment changes, some plants and animals survive and reproduce, and others die or move to new locations (K–4).

1. WHAT IS IN SOIL? (K–5)

Materials

Soil
Magnifying lenses
Plastic spoons

ENGAGE: ASK A QUESTION ABOUT OBJECTS, ORGANISMS, OR EVENTS IN THE ENVIRONMENT.

a. Explain to students that soil is a very important natural resource that supports plant and animal life. Ask: *Where do you find soil? What do you think is in soil?*

EXPLORE: PLAN AND CONDUCT SIMPLE INVESTIGATIONS TO COLLECT RELEVANT DATA.

b. Instruct materials managers to pick up materials. Tell students to use the spoon to spread out their soil on a piece of white paper. Ask: *What do you observe about the soil?* Challenge students to use all of their senses except taste to observe the soil and to record at least three observations using each sense. To enhance the smell of soil, tell students to spray a bit of moisture on it.

EXPLAIN: USE DATA TO GENERATE INTERPRETATIONS, INCLUDING DESCRIPTIONS, CLASSIFICATIONS, PREDICTIONS, AND EXPLANATIONS.

c. Ask: *What did you observe? What was in your soil sample? Which senses was it easier to make observations with?*

2. WHAT IS AN EARTHWORM LIKE? (K–5)

Materials

Earthworms
Magnifying lenses

ENGAGE: ASK A QUESTION ABOUT OBJECTS, ORGANISMS, OR EVENTS IN THE ENVIRONMENT.

a. Ask: *What are earthworms like? How do they move? Where do they live? What do they eat? How could we find the answers to these questions?*

EXPLORE: PLAN AND CONDUCT SIMPLE INVESTIGATIONS TO COLLECT RELEVANT DATA.

b. Distribute an earthworm in a clear plastic cup to each group. Ask: *What do you observe about the earthworm?* Encourage students to use magnifying lenses to see details of the earthworms. If students wish, allow them to gently feel the earthworms or to hold them in their hands. Use the spoons to gently move the earthworms and see how they respond. Tell students to draw pictures of the earthworms in their investigation journals.

EXPLAIN: USE DATA TO GENERATE INTERPRETATIONS, INCLUDING DESCRIPTIONS, CLASSIFICATIONS, PREDICTIONS, AND EXPLANATIONS.

c. Ask: *What did you observe about the earthworm? What were its characteristics? Did your earthworm have eyes and ears? How do you think it senses things, finds food, and finds its way around? What did your earthworm tend to eat? What did it do?*

▶ *Teaching Background*

Worms are segmented and have bristles on each segment. Worms have no eyes or ears, but their pointed head and round body is sensitive to vibrations and chemicals. Earthworms absorb water and oxygen through their skin. Remind students to keep an earthworm moist at all times when observing or it can dry out and die.

Earthworms prefer to eat dried leaves and other organic matter, but will eat soil and extract the decomposing nutrients if nothing else is available. A worm's waste or casings contain nutrients that enrich the soil and provide the necessary nutrients for plant growth. An earthworm's tunneling mixes and aerates the soil.[6]

3. HOW CAN WE BUILD A TERRARIUM ENVIRONMENT FOR EARTHWORMS? (1–3)

Materials

Container for the terrarium (e.g., glass or plastic tanks, storage boxes, deli salad containers, fish bowls, plastic bottles, or jars)
Soil
Sand
Small plants
Birdseed or grass seeds
Spray bottle for water
Litter (twigs, bark, and leaves)
Earthworms (obtained from digging in moist soil, from bait shop, or from commercial supplier—see Appendix C)

[6]GEMS (Great Explorations in Math and Science), 1994. *Terrarium Habitats*. Lawrence Hall of Science, Berkeley, CA.

Safety Precautions

Collect soil from clean areas so that it is free from contaminants; wash your hands and have students wash their hands thoroughly after handling soil.

ENGAGE: ASK A QUESTION ABOUT OBJECTS, ORGANISMS, OR EVENTS IN THE ENVIRONMENT.

a. Explain that a **terrarium** is any enclosed container that has been set up to house plants and small animals. Terrariums must contain all the components the plants and animals need to survive.

b. Ask: *What do earthworms need to survive?* (Air, water, food, soil.) *Suppose we wanted to build a terrarium for earthworms. What components should the earthworm terrarium include?* (Soil with air and moisture, plants as a source of food.)

EXPLORE: PLAN AND CONDUCT SIMPLE INVESTIGATIONS TO COLLECT RELEVANT DATA.

c. Assist your students to construct a terrarium for each cooperative group in your classroom. To build a terrarium, follow these instructions:
   1. Obtain a container for your terrarium.
   2. Clean the container with water and rinse it well.
   3. Mix three parts soil with one part sand and fill the terrarium container one-third full of the mixture.
   4. Make small holes in the soil and plant two or three small plants in the holes. Cover the roots with soil and firmly press soil on all sides of the stems. Sprinkle some seeds over the soil.
   5. Add litter—twigs, bark, and leaves.
   6. Add moisture with a spray bottle. Limit the amount of moisture in a terrarium to about four squirts of water.
   Caution: Do not overwater the terrarium during this investigation.
   7. Carefully place an earthworm and a dry leaf for the earthworm to eat in the terrarium.
   8. Place a lid on the terrarium and put it in a cool place where it can get natural light, but no sunlight.
   9. Your terrarium should need no more than about two squirts of moisture per week.[7]

EXPLAIN: USE DATA TO GENERATE INTERPRETATIONS, INCLUDING DESCRIPTIONS, CLASSIFICATIONS, PREDICTIONS, AND EXPLANATIONS.

d. Ask: *What is a habitat?* Explain that a **habitat** is a place where an animal or plant naturally lives or grows. A habitat provides the food, shelter, moisture, light, air, and protection that the plants or animals need to survive. Your terrarium is a habitat for plants and earthworms. Ask: *How are the needs of earthworms met by the terrarium habitat? What other habitats do you observe regularly? What is the habitat for birds? fish? deer? humans?*

ELABORATE: EXTEND CONCEPTS, PRINCIPLES, AND STRATEGIES TO NEW SITUATIONS AND QUESTIONS.

e. Allow students to observe their terrarium habitats regularly for several weeks. Ask: *What changes have taken place in your terrarium? What do the earthworms do? What is your evidence about what earthworms eat? What happens to the plants? What happens to the seeds? Do you detect any moisture in your terrarium? How does the terrarium habitat supply the needs of the earthworms?*

Students should keep written or pictorial records of their observations in their investigation journals.

---

[7]Adapted and modified from *Terrarium Habitats*, one of more than 75 teacher's guides in the Great Explorations in Math and Science (GEMS) series, available from the Lawrence Hall of Science, University of California at Berkeley. For more information, visit their website at www.lhsgems.org.

4. HOW CAN WE BUILD A DESERT TERRARIUM? (3–5)

Materials

Terrarium container
Cactus plant
Twig
Bottle cap
Desert animal, such as a lizard or horned toad

ENGAGE: ASK A QUESTION ABOUT OBJECTS, ORGANISMS, OR EVENTS IN THE ENVIRONMENT.

a. Ask: *What is a desert terrarium? What animals and plants might live there?* How can we build desert terrariums?

EXPLORE: PLAN AND CONDUCT SIMPLE INVESTIGATIONS TO COLLECT RELEVANT DATA.

b. A desert terrarium can be built out of a large mayonnaise jar, soda bottle, or other container, as in the illustrations.
   1. Select and clean a container for the terrarium.
   2. Place about 2 cups of sand onto the bottom of the jar or bottle.
   3. Place a small cactus plant, a twig, and a small bottle cap filled with water in the terrarium.
   4. Place a small desert animal, such as a lizard or horned toad, in the desert terrarium habitat.
   5. Place the terrarium so that it receives sunlight every day.
   6. Feed the animals live mealworms (see Appendix F for feeding requirements). These can be obtained from a local pet shop.
   7. Keep the bottle cap filled with water.
   8. Spray one or two squirts of water into the terrarium every 2 weeks, only if the terrarium is dry.

c. Regularly observe and keep records on how the desert animals interact with their terrarium habitat.

EXPLAIN: USE DATA TO GENERATE INTERPRETATIONS, INCLUDING DESCRIPTIONS, CLASSIFICATIONS, PREDICTIONS, AND EXPLANATIONS.

d. Ask: *Why do dryland animals have such scaly skin?*
   Why do you think ferns or mosses would not survive in this habitat?
   Would frogs or turtles be able to live in this habitat? Why or why not?

Food jar terrarium

Soda bottle desert terrarium

5. HOW CAN WE BUILD A WETLAND TERRARIUM? (3–5)

Materials

Terrarium container with lid
Gravel
Ferns, mosses, lichens, and liverworts
Small water turtle or frog

ENGAGE: ASK A QUESTION ABOUT OBJECTS, ORGANISMS, OR EVENTS IN THE ENVIRONMENT.

a. Ask: *What is a wetland terrarium? What animals and plants might live there? How can we build wetland terrariums?*

EXPLORE: PLAN AND CONDUCT SIMPLE INVESTIGATIONS TO COLLECT RELEVANT DATA.

b. A wetland terrarium can be built in a large mayonnaise jar or other container, as in the illustrations.
   1. Select and clean a container for the terrarium.
   2. Spread gravel out on the bottom of the jar so it will be concentrated toward the back of the jar, as shown in the diagram.
   3. Place ferns, mosses, lichens, and liverworts over the gravel.
   4. Pour some water in the jar. (Do not put in so much that it covers the back portion of the arrangement.)
   5. Place a dried twig in the jar.
   6. Place a small water turtle or frog in the jar.
   7. Cover the jar with the punctured lid.
   8. Feed the turtle or frog insects or turtle food every other day (see Appendix F).
   9. Place the terrarium in an area where light is weak.

Lid

Gravel

Tape wood strips

Bog terrarium

c. Regularly observe and keep records on how the wetland animal interacts with its terrarium habitat.

EXPLAIN: USE DATA TO GENERATE INTERPRETATIONS, INCLUDING DESCRIPTIONS, CLASSIFICATIONS, PREDICTIONS, AND EXPLANATIONS.

d. Ask: *What kinds of conditions do the turtle, frog, or lizard need to survive in their particular habitats?*

What kinds of conditions do the bog plants require to grow well?

What kinds of food do the turtle, frog, or lizard eat?

What do you think would happen to the turtle if you left it in the desert habitat or to the lizard if you put it in the bog habitat?

What other kinds of environments or habitats could you make?

What does the environment have to do with the kinds of organisms found in it?

What might happen to a fern plant if it were transplanted to a desert region?

What might happen to a penguin if it were taken to live in a desert?

What would humans need to survive in an artic region?

ELABORATE: EXTEND CONCEPTS, PRINCIPLES, AND STRATEGIES TO NEW SITUATIONS AND QUESTIONS.

e. Complete the following chart for the aquarium and terrarium habitats you constructed, describing the food, water, shelter, and other conditions you provided for the organisms living there.

NAME OF HABITAT:	
Habitat Living Conditions	Description
Food	
Shelter	
Air	
Temperature	
Climate	
Water	
Others	

III. STRUCTURES AND FUNCTIONS OF HUMAN SYSTEMS

Each plant or animal has different structures that serve different functions in growth, survival, and reproduction. For example, animals, including humans, have body structures for respiration, protection from disease, and digestion of food. Warm-blooded animals have structures for regulating temperature. Humans have distinct body structures for walking, holding, seeing, and talking.

A. THE HUMAN SYSTEM FOR RESPIRATION

▶ *Science Background*

Humans, like other animals, need oxygen to survive. Oxygen is taken in through breathing. Breathing is controlled by movement of the diaphragm. When the diaphragm moves down, air is forced into the lungs. When the diaphragm moves up in the rib cage, air is forced out of the lungs. Gases and water vapor are exhaled from the lungs. When a person exercises, breathing rate increases. Breathing increases because more carbon dioxide is produced. Carbon dioxide causes the diaphragm to involuntarily work more rapidly. Lung capacity varies from person to person and can be increased by aerobic training.

Science Standards

All students should develop an understanding of

- characteristics of organisms (K–4).
- structure and function in living systems (5–8).

Objectives for Students

1. Define *system* and apply the term to human systems.
2. Ask questions and design and carry out investigations to answer questions about structure and function in the human respiratory system.
3. Describe the form and function of the human system for respiration.

Concepts and Principles

Activities 1–6 prepare students to understand these fundamental concepts and principles related to the *Science Standards*:

- Living systems at all levels of organization demonstrate the complementary nature of structure and function (5–8).
- The human organism has systems for digestion, respiration, reproduction, circulation, excretion, movement, control and coordination, and protection from disease. These systems interact with one another (5–8).

1. HOW DOES BREATHING CHANGE YOUR CHEST SIZE? (2–4)

Materials

Tape measure

ENGAGE: ASK A QUESTION ABOUT OBJECTS, ORGANISMS, OR EVENTS IN THE ENVIRONMENT.

a. Ask: *How does the size of your chest vary when you breathe? How might you find out?*

EXPLORE: PLAN AND CONDUCT SIMPLE INVESTIGATIONS TO COLLECT RELEVANT DATA.

b. Guide small cooperative groups of students to conduct this investigation.
    1. With a tape measure, check and record these measurements.

	Top of Chest	Lower Diaphragm
Inhale		
Exhale		

2. Construct a class graph to illustrate variations in measurement among students.

EXPLAIN: USE DATA TO GENERATE INTERPRETATIONS, INCLUDING DESCRIPTIONS, CLASSIFICATIONS, PREDICTIONS, AND EXPLANATIONS.

c. Ask: *How do inhale and exhale chest measurements vary for different students? for boys and girls? for tall and short students? Is there a pattern?*

....

2. WHAT IS IN OUR BREATH? (3–6)

Materials   Mirror (preferably metal)

ENGAGE: ASK A QUESTION ABOUT OBJECTS, ORGANISMS, OR EVENTS IN THE ENVIRONMENT.

a. Ask: *What do you see when you breathe outside on a very cold day?*
   Why do you think that happens?
   How might we find out?

EXPLORE: PLAN AND CONDUCT SIMPLE INVESTIGATIONS TO COLLECT RELEVANT DATA.

b. Assist students to do this activity:
   1. Obtain a mirror.
   2. Hold the mirror near your nose and mouth and exhale on it.
      What do you see on the mirror?

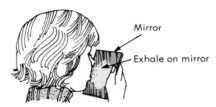

Mirror
—Exhale on mirror

EXPLAIN: USE DATA TO GENERATE INTERPRETATIONS, INCLUDING DESCRIPTIONS, CLASSIFICATIONS, PREDICTIONS, AND EXPLANATIONS.

c. Ask: *Why does moisture collect on the mirror?* (Water vapor is exhaled. When the warm moist exhaled air comes in contact with the cooler mirror, water condenses on the surface of the mirror.) Ask: *Where does the moisture come from?* (From the exhaled air.) *What kinds of gases do you think you exhale?*

....

3. HOW CAN WE TEST THE GASES IN OUR BREATH? (3–6)

Materials   Three plastic cups
                         Turkey baster or large syringe
                         Plastic drinking straws
                         Calcium hydroxide tablets (obtain from a drugstore)

ENGAGE: ASK A QUESTION ABOUT OBJECTS, ORGANISMS, OR EVENTS IN THE ENVIRONMENT.

a. Ask: *Is there a difference in the composition of the air around us and the air we exhale? How can we identify the gases contained in exhaled air?*

EXPLORE: PLAN AND CONDUCT SIMPLE INVESTIGATIONS TO COLLECT RELEVANT DATA.

b. This investigation can be done as a teacher demonstration or by students in cooperative groups:
1. Obtain two clear plastic cups, a turkey baster, a straw, and 100 cc of limewater made by dissolving a calcium hydroxide tablet in a large container of water. Mix half the limewater with regular water in each cup. Let the water settle.
2. Put a straw in one cup and a turkey baster or large syringe in the other. Describe how the limewater in the cups looks.

(a) Breath in limewater

(b) Baster in limewater

3. One student should blow through a straw into one cup of limewater while the other pumps the bulb of the turkey baster into the other cup of limewater.

EXPLAIN: USE DATA TO GENERATE INTERPRETATIONS, INCLUDING DESCRIPTIONS, CLASSIFICATIONS, PREDICTIONS, AND EXPLANATIONS.

c. Ask: *What happens to the limewater as you blow (exhale) through the straw into the water? Why does the water get "cloudy"?*
What happens to the limewater when you squeeze the turkey baster into it?
Why do you think the limewater did not change?
Why is this a controlled experiment? What condition is varied?
What is the responding variable? What do you think is controlled?

▶ *Teaching Background*

This investigation compares breathed air that is blown through a straw with regular air that is pumped from a turkey baster. The test results suggest that breathed air contains a significant amount of carbon dioxide gas. When carbon dioxide is added to limewater, the water changes to a milky color because the carbon dioxide combines with calcium hydroxide to form a white precipitate. You can see the white powder precipitate on the bottom of the cup. You can test the white powder that falls to the bottom by adding some vinegar; vinegar will cause calcium or carbonate to foam. Regular air may also contain carbon dioxide, but not enough to detect by this procedure.

....

4. WHAT MAKES YOU BREATHE FASTER? (3–8)

Materials

Stopwatch
Mirror

ENGAGE: ASK A QUESTION ABOUT OBJECTS, ORGANISMS, OR EVENTS IN THE ENVIRONMENT.

a. Ask: *How many times a minute do you breathe? How do you know? How would you go about finding out?*

EXPLORE: PLAN AND CONDUCT SIMPLE INVESTIGATIONS TO COLLECT RELEVANT DATA.

b. This activity should be done in groups of three: one student does the activity; the second student counts the number of breaths; the third student is the timekeeper. At the completion of each activity, the students should rotate in their tasks until all have completed the activity. Explain that students should count the number of exhaled breaths in a time interval. Students may use a mirror to see the exhaled breaths.

1. Student 1 should breathe normally. Student 2 should count the number of exhaled breaths in 15 seconds. Student 3 should use a stopwatch to start the count at an inhale phase and stop the count after 15 seconds. Do this three times, 1 minute apart.
2. Have the student being tested run in place for 1 minute and then repeat step 1.
3. Use this chart for recording your data.

Time	At Rest	After Exercise
1 minute		
2 minutes		
3 minutes		

4. When you finish three "at rest" and three "after exercise" data collections, rotate the jobs until all three of you have breathed, counted breaths, and kept time.
5. Graph your rest and exercise record on a diagram like the one shown.

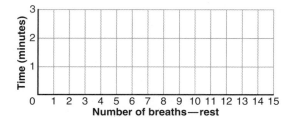

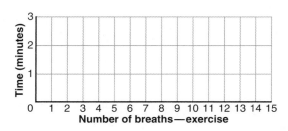

EXPLAIN: USE DATA TO GENERATE INTERPRETATIONS, INCLUDING DESCRIPTIONS, CLASSIFICATIONS, PREDICTIONS, AND EXPLANATIONS.

c. Ask: *What is the average number of times per minute a person breathes at rest? How would you figure that?* (Take the average of all nine readings, including three readings per person.)

What is the average number of times per minute a person breathes after exercise?

Why do you think exercise makes a person breathe faster?

What is your evidence that you exhale or breathe out water vapor?

5. HOW CAN WE MAKE A MODEL OF LUNGS? (3–8)

Materials

For each group:

- Plastic cup
- Drinking straw
- Small plastic bag
- Small balloon
- Rubber band
- Scissors

ENGAGE: ASK A QUESTION ABOUT OBJECTS, ORGANISMS, OR EVENTS IN THE ENVIRONMENT.

a. Ask: *How do your lungs work to inhale and exhale gases?*

EXPLORE: PLAN AND CONDUCT SIMPLE INVESTIGATIONS TO COLLECT RELEVANT DATA.

b. Guide students to conduct this activity. You may wish to punch a hole in the plastic cups (see step 3) before students begin the activity. The heated tip of an ice pick will pierce the plastic easily.

1. Obtain a plastic drinking straw, a small plastic bag, two rubber bands, a clear plastic cup, a small balloon, and scissors.
2. Cut the straw in half.
3. In the bottom of the cup, punch a hole the same width as the straw.
4. Stretch and blow up the balloon a few times.
5. Using a tightly wound rubber band, attach the balloon to the straw. Be sure the balloon does not come off when you blow into the straw, and that the rubber band does not crush the straw.

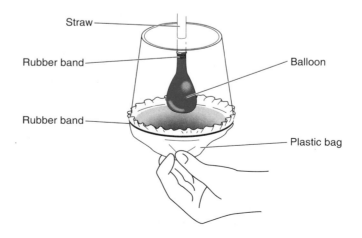

Straw

Rubber band

Balloon

Rubber band

Plastic bag

6. Push the free end of the straw through the cup's hole and pull until the balloon is in the middle of the cup. Seal the area around the hole and straw with modeling clay.

7. Place the open end of the cup into the small plastic bag and fold the bag around the cup, securing it tightly with a rubber band or masking tape. The plastic bag should be loose, not stretched taut, across the cup's opening.

8. Ask: *What do you think might happen to the balloon if you pull down on the plastic bag at the bottom of the cup?*

9. Pull down on the plastic bag. Record your observation. Ask: *What do you think might happen if you push up on the plastic bag?*

10. Push up on the plastic bag. Record your observation.

EXPLAIN: USE DATA TO GENERATE INTERPRETATIONS, INCLUDING DESCRIPTIONS, CLASSIFICATIONS, PREDICTIONS, AND EXPLANATIONS.

c. Ask: *What changes did you observe in the system? Why do these changes happen? Where in your body do you have something that works like this?*

Referring to a model or illustration of the chest cavity, guide students to identify the parts of the body used in breathing and describe how they function. Ask: *How is this physical model like the lungs?*

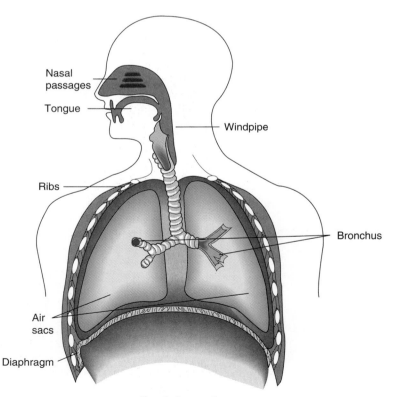

Respiratory system

6. HOW BIG ARE YOUR LUNGS? (3–5)

Materials

Dishpan
Drinking straws that are designed to bend (substitute plastic tubing obtained from
    aquarium shops)
Ruler
Measuring cup
Water
Gallon jug

ENGAGE: ASK A
QUESTION ABOUT OBJECTS,
ORGANISMS, OR EVENTS IN
THE ENVIRONMENT.

a. Ask: *How much air do your lungs hold? How could you measure the capacity of your lungs?*
   Do boys have bigger lungs than girls?

EXPLORE: PLAN
AND CONDUCT SIMPLE
INVESTIGATIONS TO
COLLECT RELEVANT DATA.

b. Fill the dishpan about one-quarter full of water. Fill the jug to the very top with water. Put your hand tightly over the mouth of the jug and invert it in the dishpan, making sure not to let any air get into the jug. Put one end of the drinking straw in your
mouth, bend the straw gently, and slip the other end into the mouth of the jug. With
one continuous breath, keep blowing until you are completely out of air, as shown in
diagram (a).

Important: Make sure the mouth of the jug remains below water level.

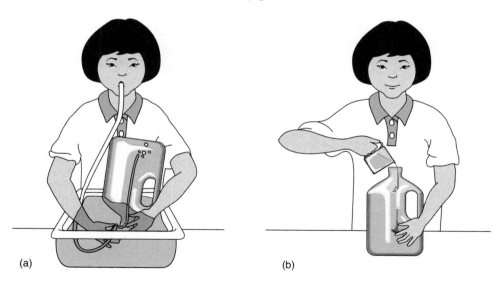

(a)   (b)

c. When you cannot blow any more water out of the jug, slide your hand over the jug's
mouth and turn it right side up. To measure how much air you exhaled, do this:
   1. Pour measuring cups filled with water into the jug until you have refilled the jug,
      as shown in diagram (b).
   2. The amount of water you use to refill the jug is the amount of air you exhaled.

Safety Precautions   For hygienic reasons, use separate drinking straws or plastic tubing for each student.

EXPLAIN: USE DATA TO GENERATE INTERPRETATIONS.

    d. Ask: *Why does the water leave the jug when you blow into it?* (Air is a real material substance that forces the water out of the jug.) *How does this investigation show the capacity of your lungs? Who had the larger lung capacity, boys or girls? What is your evidence?*

B. THE HUMAN SYSTEM FOR REGULATING TEMPERATURE

▶ *Science Background*

Normal body temperature is 98.6°F. To maintain this temperature, the body converts food energy to heat energy. When the environment is very warm or through exercise, the temperature of the body may exceed the normal level. The body then cools itself through perspiring. When perspiration evaporates from the body, the body is cooled.

NSES **Science Standards**

All students should develop an understanding of

• structure and function in living systems (5–8).

Objectives for Students

    1. Describe how the evaporation of perspiration cools the body.

NSES **Concepts and Principles**

Activity I addresses these fundamental concepts and principles related to the *Science Standards:*

• All organisms must be able to obtain and use resources, grow, reproduce, and maintain stable internal conditions while living in a constantly changing external environment (5–8).
• Regulation of an organism's internal environment involves sensing the internal environment and changing physiological activities to keep conditions within the range required to survive (5–8).

1. HOW DOES YOUR BODY COOL ITSELF? (K–5)

Materials   Two old socks (wool or cotton are best) for each student
Electric fan

ENGAGE: ASK A QUESTION ABOUT OBJECTS, ORGANISMS, OR EVENTS IN THE ENVIRONMENT.

    a. Using a medicine dropper, place a few drops of water on the back of the hand of each student. Tell the students to gently blow across the water drop. Ask: *What happened to the water drop?* (It disappeared—evaporated.) *How did your hand feel?* (It got cooler.) Explain that evaporation is a cooling process. When water evaporates, the surface from which it evaporated gets cooler.
        Ask: *How does your body use evaporation to cool itself?*

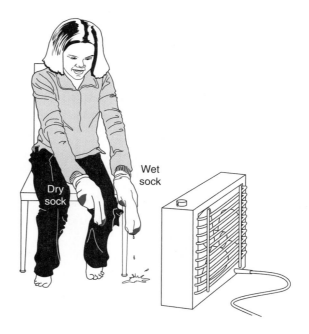

EXPLORE: PLAN AND CONDUCT SIMPLE INVESTIGATIONS TO COLLECT RELEVANT DATA.

b. Have students place a dry sock on one hand and wet sock on the other hand. To improve the cooling effect, use a fan to blow air over the students' hands.

EXPLAIN: USE DATA TO GENERATE INTERPRETATIONS, INCLUDING DESCRIPTIONS, CLASSIFICATIONS, PREDICTIONS, AND EXPLANATIONS.

c. Invite students to share their findings from the exploration phase. Ask: *Which hand felt cooler, the one with the wet sock or the one with the dry sock? Why? What is the role of the moisture in cooling? What do you think happens when perspiration evaporates? Why does a fan cool us even on a hot day? Why do you feel cool on a hot summer day when you come out of the water after swimming?*

C. THE HUMAN SKIN AND PROTECTION FROM DISEASE

▶ *Science Background*

Our skin serves to protect us from microorganisms that cause disease. A cut or wound in the skin can let microorganisms enter the body. Microorganisms sometimes cause infection and disease. Cuts and wounds should be properly treated immediately to prevent infection. Antiseptics kill microorganisms; thus, they can be used for the treatment of cuts or wounds. Heat can also kill microorganisms.

NSES   **Science Standards**

All students should develop an understanding of

- structure and function in living systems (5–8).
- regulation and behavior (5–8).

Objectives for Students

1. Describe how the skin functions to protect people.
2. Compare the human skin to skins on fruits.
3. Describe how cuts and wounds should be treated and why.

NSES

Concepts and Principles

Activity 1 addresses these fundamental concepts and principles related to the *Science Standards:*

- The human organism has systems for digestion, respiration, reproduction, circulation, excretion, movement, control and coordination, and protection from disease (5–8).
- Disease is a breakdown in structure or function of an organism. Some diseases are the result of intrinsic failure of the system. Others are the result of damage by infection by other organisms (5–8).

1. HOW DOES OUR SKIN PROTECT US? (3–8)

Materials

Four unblemished apples
Three sewing needles
Book of matches
Candle on a pie tin
Rotten apple
Small sample of soil
Five small pieces of cardboard for labels
Rubbing alcohol

ENGAGE: ASK A QUESTION ABOUT OBJECTS, ORGANISMS, OR EVENTS IN THE ENVIRONMENT.

a. Ask: *How is the covering of an apple or an orange like your skin? What are the advantages of the covering on apples, oranges, and other types of fruit? How does the covering of your body, the skin, protect you?*

EXPLORE: PLAN AND CONDUCT SIMPLE INVESTIGATIONS TO COLLECT RELEVANT DATA.

b. The teacher should demonstrate the following steps for the students:
   1. Obtain five pieces of cardboard for labels, a candle in a pie tin, a match, three needles, and one rotten and four unblemished apples.
   2. Put the labels (a), (b), (c), and (d) on the four unblemished apples.
   3. Sterilize three needles by heating them in the flame of a candle. Ask: *What does it mean when a person says he or she wants to sterilize something? What does heat do to sterilize the needles?* (Discuss harmful microorganisms and disease. Explain that heat kills the microorganisms.) *In what other ways might you sterilize something?*
   4. With a sterile needle, puncture apple (a) in three places. Apply rubbing alcohol over two of the punctures. Explain that rubbing alcohol is an antiseptic that can also kill microorganisms.
   5. Push the second sterilized needle into the soil and then into three places in apple (b).
   6. Puncture apple (c) in three places with the third sterile needle, but do not apply any rubbing alcohol to the three punctures.
   7. Do nothing to apple (d) or to the rotten apple.

8. Place all four labeled apples in a warm place for several days.

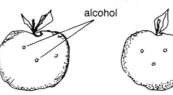

(a) Three punctures with sterile needle; alcohol applied on two punctures

(b) Puncture with needle stuck in soil

(c) Puncture with needle but no alcohol

(d) Control (no holes)

Rotten

c. Ask: *What do you think might happen if the apples stand for a few days? In what ways do you think they will look alike? How will they be different? Why?*

d. Instruct each cooperative group to observe the apples daily. Every other day, students should make a diagram or illustration of the changes taking place. Changes should be discussed within lab groups.

EXPLAIN: USE DATA TO GENERATE INTERPRETATIONS, INCLUDING DESCRIPTIONS, CLASSIFICATIONS, PREDICTIONS, AND EXPLANATIONS.

e. Ask: *What has happened to some of the apples?*
   How are the apples alike? How are they different?
   How does the appearance of each apple relate to what was done to it in the investigation?
   What do you conclude about the observed changes in the apples?

f. Ask: *The skin of an apple is similar to what part of your body? Why did the rotten spots seem to grow a little larger each day?* (Microorganisms have a fantastic growth rate. As long as there is a substantial amount of food present and space enough for growth, they will continue to reproduce.) *What do you think might happen if your skin were punctured? What might a person do to a wound or puncture if he or she did not want to get an infection?* (The wound should be cleaned, an antiseptic applied, and the wound covered with a sterile bandage.) *What is the role of the sterile bandage? Should we have covered the "wound" of the apple with a sterile bandage?*

g. Ask: *How is this experiment a controlled experiment?*
   Be sure that students understand why this is a controlled experiment. The manipulated variable is the condition of the needle puncturing the apples. The responding variable is what happens to the apple. Apple (d), the apple that is not punctured, is the control in the experiment.

D. FOOD AND THE HUMAN SYSTEM FOR DIGESTION

▶ *Science Background*

Food provides energy and nutrients for growth, development, and normal functioning. Good nutrition is essential for good health. Foods contain starches, sugars, fats, and proteins that the body needs. During digestion, our body breaks down starches into glucose, a type of sugar, and the glucose then supplies energy for our muscles. Rice, corn, and potatoes are major sources of starch. Glucose itself is another major source of energy. Grapes, raisins, and bananas are natural sources of glucose. Soft drinks are another source of glucose. Fatty foods, such as fried foods, candy bars, cookies, and chips, can supply a great deal

of energy per gram, but if the energy is not used, it is stored as fat within the body. During digestion, proteins are broken down into amino acids, substances our bodies need to build and repair tissues.

Specific chemical and physical tests can be conducted to determine which nutrients are in foods. Iodine can be used to test for starches. Tes-Tape can be used to test for glucose. Brown paper can be used to test for fats. Protein test papers (Coomassie blue test papers), purchased from a scientific supply company, can be used to test for proteins.

NSES **Science Standards**

All students should develop an understanding of

- structure and function in living systems (5–8).
- regulation and behavior (5–8).

Objectives for Students

1. Describe the structure and function of the human system for digestion.
2. Ask questions and design and carry out investigations about the contents of foods.
3. Describe and demonstrate tests of foods for water content, starch, sugars, fats, vitamins, and minerals.
4. Plan and commit to eating healthy diets that supply essential nutrients.

NSES **Concepts and Principles**

Activities 1–9 address these fundamental concepts and principles related to the *Science Standards:*

- The human organism has systems for digestion, respiration, reproduction, circulation, excretion, movement, control and coordination, and protection from disease (5–8).
- Behavior is one kind of response an organism can make to an internal or environmental stimulus (5–8).
- Behavioral response is a set of actions determined in part by heredity and in part from experience (5–8).

1. HOW MUCH WATER IS IN OUR FOODS? (5–8)

Materials

Blunt plastic knives
Scale for weighing
Lettuce, tomatoes, apples, oranges
Hand juicer
Paper plates
Small paper cups
Thick white bread
Bread toaster

ENGAGE: ASK A QUESTION ABOUT OBJECTS, ORGANISMS, OR EVENTS IN THE ENVIRONMENT.

a. Display a collection of foods. Ask: *How much water is in our foods? How could we find out?*

EXPLORE: PLAN AND CONDUCT SIMPLE INVESTIGATIONS TO COLLECT RELEVANT DATA.

b. As a class or in cooperative groups, guide students to carry out these activities:
  1. Weigh each of the foods individually on a scale and record their weights in the "before" column of the chart.

WATER CONTENT CHART

Food	Weight of Food in Grams or Paper Clips		
	Before	After	Weight of Water in Food
Lettuce			
Tomato			
Orange			
Apple			
Bread			

  2. Using a hand juicer, squeeze out all of the juice from the tomato. Weigh the tomato pulp (without the juice) and record the weight in the "after" column.
  3. Spread the lettuce leaves out on paper plates to dry overnight. The next day, weigh the lettuce leaves and record their weight in the after column.
  4. Repeat the previous step for the apple and the orange.
  5. Toast the bread in the toaster, weigh the bread, and record the number in the after column.
  6. Calculate the fractions of water in each food by dividing the weight of water in the food by the original weight of the food.

EXPLAIN: USE DATA TO GENERATE INTERPRETATIONS, INCLUDING DESCRIPTIONS, CLASSIFICATIONS, PREDICTIONS, AND EXPLANATIONS.

c. Ask: *What changes did you note in the foods? Why do you think the weight of each food changed? Which food initially had the highest fraction of water? Which food had the lowest fraction of water?*

ELABORATE: EXTEND CONCEPTS, PRINCIPLES, AND STRATEGIES TO NEW SITUATIONS AND QUESTIONS.

d. Ask: *What foods can you think of that are eaten in both fresh and dried form?* (Grapes/raisins, plums/prunes, and so on.) *What would you do to investigate what happens to raisins or prunes when they are soaked in water?* (Try it and see.)

▶ *Teaching Background*

Although water is not one of the basic nutrients, we must have it every day. We could not live without it. Besides drinking liquids, here are some common foods and the percentages of water by weight we get when we eat them. Students' test results may not agree with these. Even after students treat the various foods, they still will likely contain some water.

Lettuce	95%	Carrot	90%
Yogurt	90%	Apple	85%
Pizza	50%	Bread	35%

2. WHAT IS STARCH, AND HOW CAN WE TEST FOR IT? (5–8)

Materials

Paper plates
Dropper
Thin slices of banana, apple, potato, white bread, cheese, egg white, butter
Cracker
Cornstarch
Iodine solution
Granulated sugar

ENGAGE: ASK A QUESTION ABOUT OBJECTS, ORGANISMS, OR EVENTS IN THE ENVIRONMENT.

a. Some foods contain starch. Starch is a nutrient that provides energy for cells to use. Ask: *Which of these foods contains starch? How might we find out?*

EXPLORE: PLAN AND CONDUCT SIMPLE INVESTIGATIONS TO COLLECT RELEVANT DATA.

b. Explain that the chemical iodine can be used to test foods for starches. When iodine is placed on a starchy food, the food turns varying shades of purple-black in relation to the amount of starch present in it.

Safety Precautions

Iodine solution is poisonous, may cause burns if it is too strong, and can stain clothing. It must not be eaten. Because iodine is poisonous, do *not* eat any of the tested foods or give them to pets. Dispose of them properly.

c. Assist cooperative groups to carry out this investigation.
   1. On a paper plate, arrange and label each food sample as shown in the illustration.

   2. Look at the colors of each food and record them on a chart.
   3. Place a drop of iodine solution on each sample of food.
   4. Look at the color of each food where the iodine drop touched it.

EXPLAIN: USE DATA TO GENERATE INTERPRETATIONS, INCLUDING DESCRIPTIONS, CLASSIFICATIONS, PREDICTIONS, AND EXPLANATIONS.

d. Ask: *How have some of the food colors changed?*
    Which foods have something in common after getting an iodine drop?
    If starch turns blue-black in iodine, which of your sample foods would you say contain starch?
    Which do not have starch?

▶ *Teaching Background*

Starch provides energy for cells to use. Major sources of starch are rice, corn, and potatoes. Like most starchy foods, these foods also contain vitamins and minerals. During digestion, the body breaks down starch into glucose, and the glucose provides energy for cells.

Some starchy foods are also high in fiber, indigestible material that helps move matter through the digestive tract. Fruits, vegetables, and whole grains are some sources of fiber.

Because they contain large amounts of starch, rice and flour turn purple-black when iodine is added. Certain vegetables and fruits contain little starch and may turn only a very faint purple-black during an iodine test.[8]

3. WHAT ARE FATS, AND HOW DO WE TEST FOR THEM? (5–8)

Materials

Paper plates
Water
Butter
Vegetable oil
Samples of common snack foods: peanuts, bread, margarine, celery, carrots, mayonnaise, lettuce, bacon, corn or potato chips, pretzels, cheese, cookies, cake, apple, whole milk, yogurt, chocolate
Brown paper bags or brown paper towels cut into 2 inch squares (enough so that there is one square for each food sample)
Source of light: sunlight or lamp
Dropper

ENGAGE: ASK A QUESTION ABOUT OBJECTS, ORGANISMS, OR EVENTS IN THE ENVIRONMENT.

a. Fats also supply energy for the body.
    Ask: *How could we test to see if foods contain fat?*
b. Explain that fats leave greasy spots on brown paper, and this is a way to test for them. Assist students to carry out this test in cooperative groups:
    1. Put several drops of water on one square of brown paper, as in diagram (a). On a second square, put drops of oil as in diagram (b).

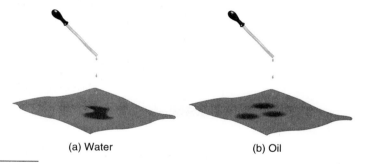

(a) Water   (b) Oil

[8]Science and Technology for Children (STC), *Food Chemistry*. Burlington, NC: Carolina Biological Supply Company, 1994.

2. Fats feel slippery when rubbed between the fingers.
   Ask: *How does the water stain feel? How does the oil stain feel?*
3. Ask: *How do the two stains look? What do you think will happen to the two stains after 10 minutes?*
4. After 10 minutes, check the two squares of paper.
   What happened to each stain?
   Where did the water drop go?
   How do the oil drops look?
   Explain that the water evaporated, but the oil stains remained shiny. This is the spot test for fats.

EXPLORE: PLAN AND CONDUCT SIMPLE INVESTIGATIONS TO COLLECT RELEVANT DATA.

c. Have groups of students conduct their own spot tests using the samples of snack foods.
   1. Get a paper plate containing samples of snack foods, squares of brown paper, and a copy of the lab sheet shown in the diagram.

FAT SPOT TEST LAB SHEET		
Food Samples	Predicted Fat	Contains Fat
Peanuts		
Bread		
Margarine		
Celery		
Carrots		
Mayonnaise		
Lettuce		
Bacon		
Corn/Potato chips		
Pretzels		
Cheese		
Cookies		
Cake		
Apple		
Whole milk		
Yogurt		
Chocolate		

2. Mark an X in the "predicted fat" column for foods you think contain fat.
3. Firmly rub each food sample 10 times on a separate square of brown paper, and label the paper with the food's name.
4. After 10 minutes, hold each paper square up to a source of light as in the illustration.

Safety Precautions   It is all right to use illumination from a window as a source of light, but caution children not to look directly into the sun.

5. Mark an X in the "contains fat" column of your chart for each food that left a greasy spot.

EXPLAIN: USE DATA TO GENERATE INTERPRETATIONS, INCLUDING DESCRIPTIONS, CLASSIFICATIONS, PREDICTIONS, AND EXPLANATIONS.

d. Ask: *How did your predictions compare with your findings?*
   How would you summarize your test findings as to which foods contained fat?
e. Discuss with students the importance of reading food labels for ingredients. Also discuss how they might select foods with less fat.
   Ask: *Why might it be healthier to eat such foods as skim milk, low-fat cottage cheese, and nonfat ice cream?*
   How could we have a party, serving good-tasting foods, and still cut down on the amount of fat we eat?

▶ *Teaching Background*

Some foods have a lot of fat, and others have little or no fat. Fats that are thick (solid) at room temperature usually come from animals like cows, pigs, and sheep. These fats are called **saturated fats**. Fats that are soft (semisolid) at room temperature usually are made from animals (e.g., lard and butter) or are manufactured (e.g., margarine). Fats that are liquid at room temperature usually come from plants (e.g., peanut oil, olive oil, corn oil).

4. WHAT IS GLUCOSE, AND HOW DO WE TEST FOR IT? (5–8)

Materials

Tes-Tape (get in drugstore)
Bananas (fairly ripe)
Milk
Different kinds of apples (McIntosh, Delicious, Rome)

Granular sugar, moistened with water
Oranges
Maple syrup
Honey
Paper plates
Small paper cups

Preparation

For efficiency in distribution, the teacher or designated students should prepare the following beforehand for each group of two to four students: paper plate containing cut samples of foods and small cups with very small samples of honey, milk, and maple syrup; 1 inch Tes-Tape strip for each food to be tested; data collection sheet.

ENGAGE: ASK A
QUESTION ABOUT OBJECTS,
ORGANISMS, OR EVENTS IN
THE ENVIRONMENT.

a. Explain that glucose is one kind of sugar. Many foods contain glucose. Glucose is a major source of energy for our bodies. Ask: *How can we test foods for glucose?*

EXPLORE: PLAN
AND CONDUCT SIMPLE
INVESTIGATIONS TO
COLLECT RELEVANT DATA.

b. Explain to students that they will use Tes-Tape to test different foods for glucose. Tes-Tape is a special chemically treated paper designed for use by people who have diabetes. Guide cooperative groups of students to conduct this investigation:
   1. Get a paper plate that contains food samples, Tes-Tape strips, and a data collection sheet.
   2. Assign one group member to each of the following tasks: tester, observer, and recorder.
   3. The tester should number each food, then write the numerals 1 through 10 on separate Tes-Tape strips.

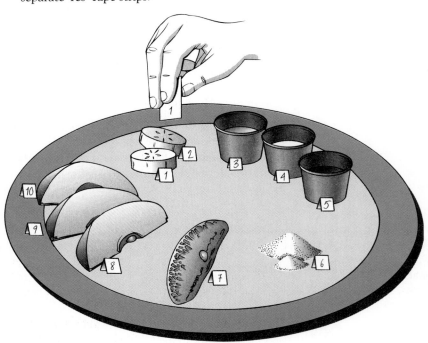

4. Using the appropriately numbered strip that corresponds to the food being tested, the tester should touch a 1 inch strip of the Tes-Tape to each food separately, until the strip is wet, and hand the Tes-Tape to the observer.
5. The observer should look at the wet end of the Tes-Tape to see *what color it is.*
6. The observer gives the following information to the recorder:
   a. Number of the sample Tes-Tape strip
   b. Name of the food sample
   c. Color of the wet end of the Tes-Tape strip
7. The students should repeat the preceding procedures with all of the food samples.
8. As each food is tested, the recorder notes on the Tes-Tape data collection sheet the data that the observer provides. The recorder attaches each Tes-Tape strip in the appropriate place on the chart.

TES-TAPE SUGAR TEST DATA COLLECTION SHEET		
Food Samples	Tape Color after Test	Tape Strip
Orange		
Banana, ripe		
Banana, green		
Maple syrup		
Milk		
Honey		
McIntosh apple		
Yellow Delicious apple		
Rome apple		
Granulated sugar		

EXPLAIN: USE DATA TO GENERATE INTERPRETATIONS, INCLUDING DESCRIPTIONS, CLASSIFICATIONS, PREDICTIONS, AND EXPLANATIONS.

c. Ask: *From the data collected, which foods contain glucose? What evidence do you have to support this?*

From the changes in the Tes-Tape color, which foods appear to have the most glucose? the least?

Which foods, if any, did not change the color of the Tes-Tape? Why do you think this happened?

ELABORATE: EXTEND CONCEPTS, PRINCIPLES, AND STRATEGIES TO NEW SITUATIONS AND QUESTIONS.

d. Have students bring in labels from food packages, read the ingredients list, and list all the forms of sugar each food contains, such as honey, brown sugar syrup, sweeteners, corn sugar, corn sweeteners, molasses, invert sugar, sucrose, fructose, dextrose, maltose, lactose, and so on.

Find out the amounts of sugar (both labeled and "hidden") in the common foods you eat. For example, soft drinks can contain about 8 teaspoons per 12 ounces, and many breakfast cereals contain about 2 1/2 teaspoons (10 g) of sugar plus 3 teaspoons (13 g) of other carbohydrates for a total of 5 1/2 teaspoons (23 g) per 1 ounce serving.

Ask: *What do you think might happen if you tested artificial sweeteners (saccharin, aspartame, etc.) with Tes-Tape?*

Why would it be healthier to eat fresh fruit as a snack rather than cakes, candy, and soft drinks, even though all of these contain sugar?

▶ *Teaching Background*

There are several types of sugars, including sucrose, lactose, fructose, and glucose. Glucose is a major source of energy for the body. Starches consist of long linked chains of glucose. Much of the glucose the body needs comes from the breakdown of starches. There are also natural sources of glucose, including apples, grapes, raisins, and bananas. Soft drinks are another source of glucose. Sweets ordinarily contain other types of sugars.[9]

··

5. HOW CAN YOU SEE WHICH SODA HAS MORE SUGAR? (5–8)

Materials

Three pairs of 12 ounce cans of soft drinks, unopened, assorted flavors and brands (each pair should contain one diet and one regular of same flavor and brand)
Aquarium filled with water
Scale for weighing

ENGAGE: ASK A QUESTION ABOUT OBJECTS, ORGANISMS, OR EVENTS IN THE ENVIRONMENT.

a. Place a can of regular cola and a can of diet cola in an aquarium filled with water. The regular can of cola sinks, but, surprisingly, the can of diet cola floats.

Ask: *Why do you think the can of diet cola floated while the can of regular cola sank?*

EXPLORE: PLAN AND CONDUCT SIMPLE INVESTIGATIONS TO COLLECT RELEVANT DATA.

b. When students suggest that the can of diet cola was lighter, ask: *How could we test this hypothesis?*

c. Instruct students to
   1. weigh each of the six cans of diet and regular soft drinks;
   2. record the weights in a table like the one illustrated;

---

[9]Science and Technology for Children (STC), *Food Chemistry*. Burlington, NC: Carolina Biological Supply Company, 1994.

3. test each of the six cans to determine if it floats or sinks; and
4. record their observations about floating or sinking in the table.

SUGAR CONTENT OF DIET AND REGULAR SOFT DRINKS

Pair	Brand	Diet Weight	Regular Weight	Float or Sink?
1				Diet
				Regular
2				Diet
				Regular
3				Diet
				Regular

EXPLAIN: USE DATA TO GENERATE INTERPRETATIONS, INCLUDING DESCRIPTIONS, CLASSIFICATIONS, PREDICTIONS, AND EXPLANATIONS.

d. Ask: *What did you determine in your tests? Did your data support the hypothesis that the cans of regular soft drinks were heavier than the cans of diet soft drinks?*

e. Ask: *Why do you think a can of diet cola is lighter than a can of regular cola of the same brand and flavor?* When students suggest that the cans of regular soft drink contain more liquid than the cans of diet soft drink, lead them to examine labels to compare the volumes of liquid in the regular and diet soft drink cans. Students might also open the cans and measure the volume using a graduated cylinder.

If students do not suggest it, also ask them to compare the ingredients of the regular and diet soft drinks. The weight of a diet soft drink is usually about 10 to 15 g less than the weight of a regular soft drink. The difference is usually sugar or corn syrup.

6. WHAT ARE PROTEINS, AND HOW DO WE TEST FOR THEM? (5–8)

Materials

For each group:

- Six Coomassie blue protein test strips in a clean envelope
- Test tray
- Forceps
- Petri dish
- Toothpicks
- Paper towels

(Protein test strips and other materials are available from Carolina Biological Supply—see Appendix C for address.)

For the class:

- Half liter (1 pint) white vinegar
- Half liter (1 pint) rubbing alcohol
- 1 liter plastic bottle to mix and store developing solution
- Medicine droppers
- Plastic spoons
- One carton skim milk, 237 ml (one-half pint)
- Unshelled peanuts
- Rice grains

Preparation

To test for proteins, students immerse a Coomassie blue test strip in a liquid or food, and then place the test strip in a developing solution for several minutes. To prepare the developing solution, mix together half a liter of white vinegar and half a liter of rubbing alcohol in a 1 liter plastic mixing bottle. Close the bottle and store the developing solution.

ENGAGE: ASK A QUESTION ABOUT OBJECTS, ORGANISMS, OR EVENTS IN THE ENVIRONMENT.

a. Ask: *What nutrients have we tested for so far?* Starch, fat, and glucose (sugar). *What do you know about proteins? What foods contain proteins? How can we test liquids and foods for proteins?*

EXPLORE: PLAN AND CONDUCT SIMPLE INVESTIGATIONS TO COLLECT RELEVANT DATA.

b. Hold up a strip of protein test paper. Handle the test strip only with forceps so as not to contaminate it with your hands. Explain to students that the strip has a special chemical—Coomassie blue—on it that reacts to proteins. During testing, the paper must be developed in a special solution. When developed, the color of the paper will stay deep blue if the protein content of the food being tested is high; the blue color will fade if there is a medium amount of protein in the food; and the blue color will disappear if the food contains little or no protein.

c. To test liquids or foods for proteins, have students follow these directions:
   1. Put three drops of milk in section 1 of the test tray.
   2. Put three drops of water in section 2 of the test tray.
   3. Using a spoon, put a few grains of rice in section 3 of the test tray. Put two or three drops of tap water on the rice and stir for about a minute with a toothpick.
   4. Shell a peanut (without touching the nut itself) and place it in section 4 of the test tray. Use a plastic spoon to crush the peanut. Add two or three drops of water and stir with a new toothpick.
   5. Using a spoon, put a small amount of crushed granola bar in section 5 of the test tray. Add two or three drops of water and stir with a new toothpick.
   6. Obtain six test strips and number them 1 to 6 on the white end of the strips. Be careful not to touch the test strips. Holding a test strip by its white end with forceps, immerse the blue end in the liquid or food just long enough to wet the strip—test strip 1 in the milk, test strip 2 in water, test strip 3 in the moistened rice, test strip 4 in the moistened peanut, and test strip 5 in the moistened granola bar. Place test strip 6 in the empty section 6 of the test tray as a control. Use clean toothpicks to make sure each food is in contact with the test paper. Be sure the white end of each test strip is not in contact with the liquid or food being tested.

7. Leave the test strips in the tray sections just long enough to wet the strips. Using forceps, remove each of the numbered test strips from the tray sections and place them on a paper towel. Use clean toothpicks to clean any food particles from them and use a paper towel to blot off any excess liquid.

8. Ask your teacher to pour a little developing solution in the bottom of your petri dish. Using forceps, transfer each of the test strips to the developing solution. Make sure the blue tip of the test strip is immersed.

9. Leave the test strips in the developing solution for about 5 minutes. Keep stirring the solution with a toothpick.

10. After 5 minutes, remove the protein test papers from the developing solution and place them on a paper towel.

11. Note and record the color of each test strip in the following chart. Based on the color observed, determine the protein content of each food—high, medium, or low.

PROTEIN TEST RESULTS

Liquid or Food	Color of Protein Test Strip	Protein Content (High, Medium, or Low)
1. Milk		
2. Tap water		
3. Rice		
4. Peanut		
5. Granola bar		
6. Control		

EXPLAIN: USE DATA TO GENERATE INTERPRETATIONS, INCLUDING DESCRIPTIONS, CLASSIFICATIONS, PREDICTIONS, AND EXPLANATIONS.

d. In a class-sized group, invite students to discuss their procedures and share their results.
Ask: *What happened to the protein test strips in each liquid or food? Which food or liquids were high in proteins? Which had a medium protein content? Which foods had a low amount or no proteins?* Share the following master chart of protein test results with students.

PROTEIN TEST RESULTS

Liquid or Food	Color of Protein Test Strip	Protein Content (High, Medium, or Low)
1. Milk	Remains blue	High
2. Tap water	Blue disappears	Low
3. Rice	Blue disappears	Low
4. Peanut	Remains blue	High
5. Granola bar	Blue almost disappears	Medium
6. Control	Blue disappears	Low or none

▶ *Teaching Background*

Protein is one group of food nutrients that the body uses for building tissues and repairing broken-down cells. Proteins are vital for children's proper physical and mental growth and development. Because protein cannot be made by or stored in the body, it must be eaten regularly to promote the repair of used body cells. Eggs, cheese, meat, fish, and legumes are some foods that contain large proportions of protein.

In a protein test, the chemical Coomassie blue actually binds to protein. Because of this chemical reaction, the protein and Coomassie blue will remain on the test paper after it has been in the developing solution. In the absence of protein, the Coomassie blue will dissolve in the developing solution.[10]

7. WHAT ARE MINERALS, AND HOW DO WE TEST FOR THEM? (5–8)

Materials

Two chicken leg bones stripped of all meat
Two covered jars large enough to hold the chicken bones
Soap
Water
Paper towels

ENGAGE: ASK A QUESTION ABOUT OBJECTS, ORGANISMS, OR EVENTS IN THE ENVIRONMENT.

a. Ask: *What do bones do for our bodies?*
    Why must bones be strong and hard?
    What do we eat that might make bones strong and hard?
    What might cause bones to get soft and weak?
    How might we test for calcium?

EXPLORE: PLAN AND CONDUCT SIMPLE INVESTIGATIONS TO COLLECT RELEVANT DATA.

b. Demonstrate this activity for your students:
    1. Wash both chicken leg bones and dry them with paper towels.
    2. Pass both chicken bones around the classroom.
    3. Ask: *How do the bones feel? Are they hard or soft?*
    4. Place a chicken bone in each jar.
    5. Pour vinegar in one jar only and water in the other, cover both jars, and let stand for several days.

---

[10]Activities on proteins are based on activities in *Food Chemistry*, Science and Technology for Children (STC), National Science Resources Center, Smithsonian Institution, Washington, D.C. STC guides and materials are available from Carolina Biological Supply (see Appendix C for address). Reprinted with permission from the National Science Resources Center, Washington, DC.

6. After several days, remove the bone from the jar of vinegar, rinse it thoroughly with water, and dry it well with a paper towel. Remove the other bone from its jar of water, and dry it with a paper towel.

7. Pass both bones around the classroom and ask: *Do both bones feel the same? If not, how are they different?*

Safety Precautions

Because vinegar is a mild acid, you should wash your hands with soap and water after conducting the activity.

EXPLAIN: USE DATA TO GENERATE INTERPRETATIONS, INCLUDING DESCRIPTIONS, CLASSIFICATIONS, PREDICTIONS, AND EXPLANATIONS.

c. Ask: *Why do you think the bone that was in vinegar is soft and rubbery?*

Lead students to understand that the bone that was in vinegar is soft and rubbery because its calcium has been removed. Vinegar (acetic acid) reacts with calcium and can be used as a test for it. Minerals make up a large part of bones and teeth, which is why minerals are so important for children. Although we need small amounts of many minerals (called *trace elements*), calcium is needed in larger quantities for bone and teeth formation.

Ask: *Why do you think it is so important for students to eat a lot of milk products?* (Calcium is found in large quantities in milk and milk products and in smaller quantities in green leafy vegetables and oranges.)

What might happen if you did not eat enough milk products?

8. WHAT ARE VITAMINS, AND HOW DO WE TEST FOR THEM? (5–8)

Materials

To make vitamin C indicator liquid for the class:

- Teaspoon
- Cornstarch
- Measuring cup
- Water
- Pan
- Hot plate
- Empty plastic gallon jug
- Iodine

For each group:

- Ruler
- Six clean baby food jars
- Variety of at least six different juices that are canned, frozen, or fresh (e.g., orange, apple, grape, pineapple, etc.)
- Six droppers
- Six wooden stirrers

Preparation

A simple vitamin C indicator liquid can be made ahead of time and will keep for several days. You will know when it is time to dispose of it, because it will lighten from its optimum color of royal blue to a very pale blue. To make 1 gallon of vitamin C indicator:

1. Boil 1 1/2 teaspoons (6 ml) of cornstarch in 1 cup (250 ml) of water for 2 minutes.

2. Put 10 full droppers of the cornstarch mixture into a gallon jug of water, use a clean dropper to add 1 dropper full of iodine, cover the jug, and shake it until you have a uniform blue color.

ENGAGE: ASK A QUESTION ABOUT OBJECTS, ORGANISMS, OR EVENTS IN THE ENVIRONMENT.

a. Ask: *What do you know about vitamins? What are vitamins? How can we test foods for vitamins?*

EXPLORE: PLAN AND CONDUCT SIMPLE INVESTIGATIONS TO COLLECT RELEVANT DATA.

b. Tell students that we can test for vitamin C by testing how it reacts with a special mixture of cornstarch, iodine, and water. Explain that the fewer drops of juice needed to make the blue color disappear, the more vitamin C that juice contains. Instruct students to follow these directions to test foods for vitamin C:
1. Using your ruler to measure, pour 1 cm of vitamin C indicator liquid into each of six clean baby food jars. Label each jar with the name of the juice you will test for vitamin C.
2. Using a clean dropper for each juice, add one kind of juice to each jar of indicator liquid, one drop at a time, and count the number of drops. (See the diagram.) Stir the liquid indicator with a clean wooden stirrer as you add drops.
3. When the indicator is no longer blue, the test is finished.
4. Record the number of drops of each juice needed to clear up the blue vitamin C indicator liquid.

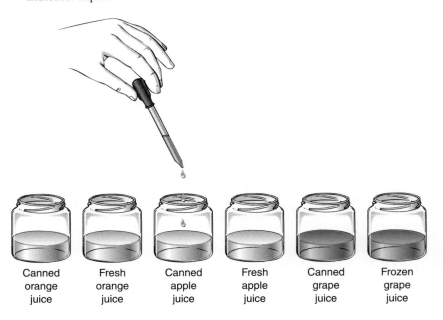

| Canned orange juice | Fresh orange juice | Canned apple juice | Fresh apple juice | Canned grape juice | Frozen grape juice |

EXPLAIN: USE DATA TO GENERATE INTERPRETATIONS, INCLUDING DESCRIPTIONS, CLASSIFICATIONS, PREDICTIONS, AND EXPLANATIONS.

c. Invite students to discuss their procedures and results.

Ask: *Which juice(s) caused the blue color to disappear with the least number of drops? Which juice(s) caused the blue color to disappear with the most drops?*

Explain that scientists have discovered more than 26 vitamins our bodies need. The lack of one vitamin could result in a vitamin deficiency disease. Vitamin C is probably the best known vitamin. It is found in citrus fruits, tomatoes, raw cabbage, strawberries, and cantaloupe.

Ask: *From these tests, which juice(s) had the most vitamin C?*

ELABORATE: EXTEND CONCEPTS, PRINCIPLES, AND STRATEGIES TO NEW SITUATIONS AND QUESTIONS.

d. Ask: *How do you think the following conditions could affect the vitamin C content of foods: heat, sunlight, air, age of food, and so on? How could you design experiments to test these variables?*

9. HOW MUCH OF EACH NUTRIENT DOES YOUR BODY NEED, AND HOW CAN YOU FIND OUT WHAT IS IN EACH FOOD? (5–8)

Materials

Food labels from a large variety of packaged foods. Collect food labels yourself, and ask students to collect and bring in empty food packages or labels from the packages. You will need at least one food label for each pair of students.

ENGAGE: ASK A QUESTION ABOUT OBJECTS, ORGANISMS, OR EVENTS IN THE ENVIRONMENT.

a. Ask: *Can you think of another way, besides testing, to determine the nutritional content of foods?* If students do not suggest reading food labels, raise the idea.

EXPLORE: PLAN AND CONDUCT SIMPLE INVESTIGATIONS TO COLLECT RELEVANT DATA.

b. Pass out food labels and a copy of the food label record sheet to pairs of students. Ask: *What kind of information is given on the food labels?* Discuss the information given on the food labels. Explain that starch and sugar are carbohydrates. The labels give the total amount of carbohydrates in one serving of the food, but not the specific amounts of starch or sugar. Also explain that people who study nutrients (called **nutritionists**) suggest the average amount of each nutrient a person should consume. This amount is called the recommended daily allowance, or RDA. Answer questions students might have, for example, about serving sizes or grams and milligrams.

```
┌─────────────────────────────────────────┐
│ Nutrition Facts                           │
│ Serving Size 2/3 cup (55g)                │
│ Servings Per Container 12                 │
├───────────────────────────────────────────┤
│ Amount Per Serving                        │
│ Calories 210                              │
│     Calories from Fat 25                  │
│                          % Daily Value*   │
│ Total Fat 3g                        5%    │
│     Saturated Fat 1g                4%    │
│     Polyunsaturated Fat 0.5g              │
│     Monounsaturated Fat 1.5g              │
│ Cholesterol 0mg                     0%    │
│ Sodium 140mg                        6%    │
│ Potassium 190mg                     5%    │
│ Total Carbohydrate 44g             15%    │
│     Other Carbohydrate 23g                │
│     Dietary Fiber 3g               13%    │
│     Sugars 18g                            │
│ Protein 5g                                │
│ Vitamin A                           0%    │
│ Vitamin C                           0%    │
│ Calcium                             2%    │
│ Iron                                6%    │
│ Thiamine                           10%    │
│ Phosphorus                         10%    │
│ Magnesium                          10%    │
└───────────────────────────────────────────┘
```

* Percent Daily Values are based on a 2000 calorie diet. Your daily values may be higher or lower depending on your calorie needs.

	Calories	2,000	2,500
Total Fat	Less than	65g	80g
Sat Fat	Less than	20g	25g
Cholesterol	Less than	300g	300g
Sodium	Less than	2400mg	2400mg
Potassium		3500mg	3500mg
Total Carbo		300g	300g
Dietary Fiber		25g	30g

Calories per gram:

Fat 9 • Carbohydrate 4 • Protein 4

c. Tell students to examine the food labels and record on their record sheet the information given about carbohydrates (starch and sugar), fats, proteins, calcium (a mineral they have tested), and vitamin C (the type of vitamin they have tested).

Food Label Record Sheet

Name of Food _____

Serving Size _____

Nutrient	Weight per Serving	Percentage of U.S. RDA
Carbohydrates		
Fats		
Proteins		
Minerals-calcium		
Vitamins-vitamin C		

EXPLAIN: USE DATA TO GENERATE INTERPRETATIONS, INCLUDING DESCRIPTIONS, CLASSIFICATIONS, PREDICTIONS, AND EXPLANATIONS.

d. Bring pairs of students together in groups of eight. Ask students to compare the nutrition facts from their food labels and record sheets and to complete the facts chart illustrated:

FOOD GROUP FACTS CHART

Calories	Food highest in calories per serving:	Food lowest in calories per serving:
Carbohydrates	Food highest in carbohydrates per serving:	Food lowest in carbohydrates per serving:
Fats	Food highest in fats per serving:	Food lowest in fats per serving:
Proteins	Food highest in proteins per serving:	Food lowest in proteins per serving:
Calcium	Food highest in calcium per serving:	Food lowest in calcium per serving:
Vitamin C	Food highest in vitamin C per serving:	Food lowest in vitamin C per serving:

e. Assemble the class as a whole and discuss which kinds of food are high and low in basic nutrients.

ELABORATE: EXTEND CONCEPTS, PRINCIPLES, AND STRATEGIES TO NEW SITUATIONS AND QUESTIONS.

f. Sometimes nutritionists recommend selecting foods from the basic food groups, such as meats, fruits, vegetables, breads and cereals, and dairy products. Introduce the *Food Guide Pyramid*. Ask:

> Which food group relates to carbohydrates?
> Which food group relates to proteins?
> Which food group relates to fats?
> Which food group relates to vitamin C?
> Which food group relates to calcium?
> Through discussion, develop a typical day's menu for students in your class.

Ask: *How close are the daily food choices in the menu to the recommendations of the pyramid? In the menu, is there more food in one group than is recommended? Is there less food than recommended for one group?*

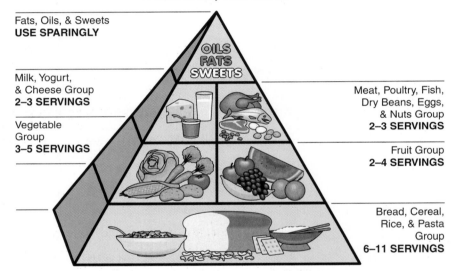

Food Guide Pyramid
A Guide to Daily Food Choices

IV

Earth and Space Science Activities

Earth is the home planet of human beings, the only planet in the universe known to support life. Life is possible on the earth largely because of a set of linked factors, including the earth's position within the solar system, its size and mass, its structure and resources, its range of temperatures, its atmosphere, and its abundance of water.

Students in grades K–8 can begin to develop understanding of the earth as a set of closely interrelated systems by studying the geological structure of the earth; the atmosphere, climate, and weather of the earth; the earth's oceans; and the earth in the solar system.

I. STRUCTURE OF THE EARTH

Children explore the complexities of the earth as they study the properties of rocks and minerals, the crystalline structure of minerals, and the structure of the earth's surface.

A. PROPERTIES OF ROCKS AND MINERALS

▶ *Science Background*

A mineral is a solid element or compound that has a specific composition and a crystalline structure. There are many different minerals in and on the earth—for example, talc, calcite, quartz, fluorite, and diamond. Minerals can be distinguished by such properties as hardness, texture, luster, streak color, cleavage, density, crystalline structure, and chemical properties.

Rocks are usually composed of minerals. Waves, wind, water, and ice cause erosion, transport, and deposit of earth materials. Sediments of sand and smaller particles are gradually buried and are cemented together with dissolved minerals to form solid rock. Rocks buried deep enough may be re-formed by pressure and heat, melting and recrystallizing into different kinds of rock. Layers of rock deep within the earth may be forced upward to become land surfaces and even mountains. Eventually, this new rock will erode under the relentless, dynamic processes of the earth.

Rocks bear evidence of the minerals, temperatures, and forces that created them. Through studies of thousands of layers of rocks, geologists have described the long history of the changing face of the earth.[1]

NSES Science Standards

All students should develop an understanding of

- properties of the earth's systems (K–4).
- structure of the earth's systems (5–8).

Objectives for Students

1. Describe properties of rocks and minerals, including texture, luster, color, cleavage, hardness, density, and crystalline structure.
2. Perform tests to determine the hardness of minerals and rocks.
3. Construct charts of the properties of a variety of minerals and rocks, and use the charts to identify specific minerals and rocks.

NSES Concepts and Principles

Activities 1–9 address these fundamental concepts and principles related to the *Science Standards*:

- The earth's materials are solid rocks and soils, water, and gases of the atmosphere (K–4).
- The varied materials have different physical and chemical properties (K–4).

1. WHAT ARE ROCKS AND MINERALS LIKE? (2–5)

Materials for Activities 1–9

Kits of rock samples, including such rocks as basalt, granite, limestone, marble, pumice, sandstone, shale, and slate

Kits of mineral samples, including such minerals as feldspar, calcite, fluorite, gypsum, graphite, hematite, hornblende, magnetite, mica, and quartz

Streak plates

Nails

Pennies

(Kits of rocks and minerals can be obtained from scientific supply houses such as Delta Education or Carolina Biological. For addresses, see Appendix C.)

ENGAGE: ASK A QUESTION ABOUT OBJECTS, ORGANISMS, OR EVENTS IN THE ENVIRONMENT.

a. Ask: *Where do you find different kinds of rocks?* (At home, on the school campus, on the way to school.) *How are the different rocks alike? How are they different? Where do you think the rocks originally came from?*

---

[1]American Association for the Advancement of Science (1993). *Benchmarks for Science Literacy* (New York: Oxford University Press); F. J. Rutherford and A. Ahlgren (1990). *Science for All Americans* (New York: Oxford University Press).

EXPLORE: PLAN
AND CONDUCT SIMPLE
INVESTIGATIONS TO
COLLECT RELEVANT DATA.

b. Initially refer to both rocks and minerals as "rocks." Provide each small group with a mixture of samples of several different rocks. For example, select large and small samples of calcite, quartz, feldspar, talc, granite, sandstone, and magnetite. Let each student in the cooperative groups examine each rock. Ask the groups to discuss what is the same and what is different about the rocks. Students often describe rocks in imaginative detail: "This rock weighs three and a half crayons. This rock is shiny and has little ripples. This one is shaped like a loaf of bread and you can stand it on its end."

c. Select four rocks that are similar in color, such as four black rocks. Place the rocks on a tray so that each student in the group can observe them. Tell each student to write down descriptions of the four rocks, without letting the other students in the group know which rocks they are describing. Ask them to take turns reading their description of one rock, while the other students try to determine which rock is being described.

EXPLAIN: USE
DATA TO GENERATE
INTERPRETATIONS,
INCLUDING DESCRIPTIONS,
CLASSIFICATIONS,
PREDICTIONS, AND
EXPLANATIONS.

d. Ask: *What were some of the property words you used to describe the rocks?* (Words related to color, texture, relative shininess, relative weight, shape, etc.)

e. Explain that rocks and minerals are different kinds of objects. A mineral has a specific composition and a *crystal* structure. Rocks are made up of minerals.

2. WHAT IS MEANT BY THE STREAK OF A MINERAL AND HOW CAN WE TEST FOR IT? (2–5)

ENGAGE: ASK A
QUESTION ABOUT OBJECTS,
ORGANISMS, OR EVENTS IN
THE ENVIRONMENT.

a. Ask: *How can we identify different minerals? What properties of minerals can we use to identify them?*

   When students suggest color as a property that can be used to identify minerals, provide this information:

   Color was probably one of the first properties you used to describe the minerals. Observable color of a mineral is not a conclusive clue to its identity, because different samples of the same mineral may have different colors. The color of the powdered form of the mineral is more consistent than its observable color. Geologists obtain powdered forms of minerals by wiping them across a *streak plate*.

EXPLORE: PLAN
AND CONDUCT SIMPLE
INVESTIGATIONS TO
COLLECT RELEVANT DATA.

b. Provide each small group with a mineral kit and two streak plates. Tape identifying numbers, 1–12, to each mineral. Do not reveal the names of the minerals yet.

c. Demonstrate how one stroke of the mineral across the porcelain plate will usually produce a streak.

d. Point out to students three or four similarly colored minerals. Tell them to test the streak of each one. Instruct students to note the streak color for each mineral and to compare it with the observable color of the mineral.

e. Have the students begin a mineral properties chart as in the illustration. Children should start with a blank chart and fill in all parts of it, including the labeling of each column, as they make observations and tests of each mineral. Use observed color and streak color as the first two properties on the chart.

f. Interact with cooperative groups to assess their color and streak descriptions of different minerals.

With the children in a class-sized group, ask: *Why should we record descriptions of rocks and minerals in a chart?* Explain that building a chart of mineral properties is a way to organize data. Charts of mineral properties help us to summarize observations and identify unknown minerals. Other ways to organize data and information include data tables, graphs, and classification systems.

MINERAL PROPERTIES CHART

Number of Mineral	Observed Color	Streak Color	Feel	Hardness	Luster		
1	green to white	grayish					
2			soapy	softer than a penny			
3					metallic		
4					dull		
5							
6							
7							
8							
9							
10							
11							
12							

3. HOW CAN MINERALS BE IDENTIFIED BY FEEL? (2–5)

a. Ask: *How can the feel of a mineral be used to identify the mineral? What are some words that describe the feel of a mineral?* (Smooth, rough, rounded edges, and soapy.)

b. Have students feel each mineral and record their descriptions in their charts.

c. As you work with groups, assess students' chart entries. With the whole class, review the meaning of *feel* and words they have used to describe the feel of each mineral.

4. WHAT IS MEANT BY THE HARDNESS OF A MINERAL AND HOW CAN WE TEST FOR IT? (2–5)

ENGAGE: ASK A QUESTION ABOUT OBJECTS, ORGANISMS, OR EVENTS IN THE ENVIRONMENT.

a. Ask: *Are the minerals in your kit equally hard? Which one seems hardest? Which one seems softest? How can you tell?*

Explain that the relative hardness of a mineral can be determined by a scratch test. The harder of two minerals will scratch the softer.

EXPLORE: PLAN AND CONDUCT SIMPLE INVESTIGATIONS TO COLLECT RELEVANT DATA.

b. Demonstrate how to use a penny to gently scratch a soft mineral and a nail to gently scratch a mineral of medium hardness. Explain that students will classify minerals as *soft*, *medium*, and *hard* using a copper penny and a steel nail as standards:
   • A soft mineral can be scratched by a penny.
   • A mineral of medium hardness can be scratched by a nail.
   • A hard mineral cannot be scratched by a nail.

To prevent damage to minerals, encourage students to scratch gently.

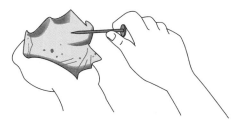

c. Have students test the hardness of each mineral in their charts. Tell students to add a "hardness" column to the mineral properties chart and to record the hardness of each mineral.

EXPLAIN: USE DATA TO GENERATE INTERPRETATIONS, INCLUDING DESCRIPTIONS, CLASSIFICATIONS, PREDICTIONS, AND EXPLANATIONS.

d. In a large group, ask students to report the results of their hardness tests. Work toward agreement in hardness test results. Students may have to retest some mineral samples.

5. WHAT IS MEANT BY LUSTER AND HOW CAN IT BE USED IN IDENTIFYING MINERALS? (2–5)

ENGAGE: ASK A QUESTION ABOUT OBJECTS, ORGANISMS, OR EVENTS IN THE ENVIRONMENT.

a. Tell students that *luster* refers to the way a mineral's surface reflects light.

Ask: *What are some words you can use to describe the luster of a mineral?*

Explain that some minerals have a metal-like luster and are called metallic. Other minerals are nonmetallic. Some terms you could use to describe the nonmetallic luster of a mineral might be *dull*, *glassy*, *waxy*, *pearly*, and *shiny*.

EXPLORE: PLAN AND CONDUCT SIMPLE INVESTIGATIONS TO COLLECT RELEVANT DATA.

b. Have students hold each of their minerals up to the light or shine a flashlight on each one and describe its luster. Tell them to add the luster descriptions to their mineral properties charts.

EXPLAIN: USE DATA TO GENERATE INTERPRETATIONS, INCLUDING DESCRIPTIONS, CLASSIFICATIONS, PREDICTIONS, AND EXPLANATIONS.

c. In a large group, ask students to report the results of their luster tests. Work toward agreement in test results. Students may have to retest some mineral samples.

1. Pick up mineral A. Shine the penlight on it.

2. Describe how the rock looks in the light. Dull? Shiny? Glassy?

3. Using the terms you have agreed on in class, record results in the space labeled "Light" on your mineral profile sheet.

4. Repeat steps 1, 2, and 3 for the other 11 minerals.

6. HOW CAN THE TRANSMISSION OF LIGHT THROUGH A MINERAL BE USED TO IDENTIFY THE MINERAL? (2–5)

ENGAGE: ASK A QUESTION ABOUT OBJECTS, ORGANISMS, OR EVENTS IN THE ENVIRONMENT.

a. Hold common transparent (e.g., clear plastic), translucent (e.g., wax paper), and opaque (e.g., aluminum foil) materials to the lens of an overhead projector or flashlight. Ask: *How do these materials differ in the way they transmit light?* Explain that materials can be *transparent*, with a lot of light shining through them; *translucent*, with a little light shining through; or *opaque*, with no light shining through. Ask: *How can the amount of light a mineral transmits help us in identifying it?*

EXPLORE: PLAN AND CONDUCT SIMPLE INVESTIGATIONS TO COLLECT RELEVANT DATA.

b. Have students shine a flashlight on each mineral and look to see how much light is transmitted. Students should record their findings for each of the numbered minerals in their mineral properties charts.

7. WHAT CAN THE SHAPE OF A MINERAL TELL US? (2–5)

ENGAGE: ASK A QUESTION ABOUT OBJECTS, ORGANISMS, OR EVENTS IN THE ENVIRONMENT.

a. Ask: *Do any of your minerals seem to have a characteristic shape?*
b. Tell students that the shape of a mineral is often a clue to its crystal-like structure. The shape of minerals might be described as like a cube, like a box that is bent over (calcite), having crystals, having masses that are not fully crystals, having thin layers (e.g., biotite), or having no special shape.

EXPLORE: PLAN AND CONDUCT SIMPLE INVESTIGATIONS TO COLLECT RELEVANT DATA.

c. Have students describe the shape of each mineral and add their descriptions to the mineral properties chart. Circulate among cooperative groups to assess the descriptions of shape entered in the chart.

EXPLAIN: USE DATA TO GENERATE INTERPRETATIONS, INCLUDING DESCRIPTIONS, CLASSIFICATIONS, PREDICTIONS, AND EXPLANATIONS.

d. Work with individuals and small groups to suggest procedures and answer questions related to the shape property. Spot-check their mineral charts to assess understanding.

8. WHAT SPECIAL PROPERTIES DO DIFFERENT MINERALS HAVE? (2–5)

ENGAGE: ASK A QUESTION ABOUT OBJECTS, ORGANISMS, OR EVENTS IN THE ENVIRONMENT.

a. Ask: *What other special properties of your minerals have you observed?*

EXPLORE: PLAN AND CONDUCT SIMPLE INVESTIGATIONS TO COLLECT RELEVANT DATA.

b. Have students list other special properties of each mineral on their mineral properties charts. For example, they should use a magnet to test each mineral for magnetic properties or use a batteries and bulb test circuit to see if the mineral conducts electricity.

EXPLAIN: USE DATA TO GENERATE INTERPRETATIONS, INCLUDING DESCRIPTIONS, CLASSIFICATIONS, PREDICTIONS, AND EXPLANATIONS.

c. Supply the name of each of the minerals numbered 1–12. Provide students with a master chart of mineral properties and have them compare their charts with the master chart. If discrepancies occur with any of the minerals, encourage students to make some fresh observations.

9. HOW CAN YOU IDENTIFY AN UNKNOWN MINERAL? (2–5)

ENGAGE: ASK A QUESTION ABOUT OBJECTS, ORGANISMS, OR EVENTS.

a. Ask: *How can you use your mineral properties chart to identify a mineral sample?*

EXPLORE: PLAN AND CONDUCT SIMPLE INVESTIGATIONS.

b. Give students one or more of minerals 1–12 with the identifying number labels removed. Have students use their mineral properties charts to identify each mineral.

c. Ask: *What have you concluded about the identity of your unknown samples? How did you use observation and your charts to identify the unknown samples?*

EXPLAIN: USE DATA TO GENERATE INTERPRETATIONS.

B. THE STRUCTURE OF MINERALS: CRYSTALS AND CRYSTAL FORMATION

▶ *Science Background*

Crystals are nonliving substances that form into rocklike bodies of various shapes. Crystals grow in size when more layers of the same substance are added on; the basic crystal shape, however, remains the same. The size of crystals is determined by differences in the rate of crystallization. If crystals are disturbed in the forming process, they will break apart into hundreds of microscopic pieces. Crystalline form is important in determining some of the properties of substances.

NSES Science Standards

All students should develop an understanding of

- properties of the earth's systems (K–4).
- structure of the earth's systems (5–8).

Objectives for Students

1. Demonstrate and describe different kinds of investigations to grow crystals.
2. Describe how crystal size is affected by conditions during formation.
3. Distinguish between and describe the formation of stalactites and stalagmites.

NSES **Concepts and Principles**

Activities 1–4 address these fundamental concepts and principles related to the *Science Standards:*

- Earth materials are solid rocks and soils, water, and gases of the atmosphere (K–4).
- The varied materials have different physical and chemical properties (K–4).

1. HOW CAN SALT CRYSTALS BE GROWN? (3–6)

Materials

Salt
Tablespoon
Jar lid
Small glass
Magnifying lens

ENGAGE: ASK A QUESTION ABOUT OBJECTS, ORGANISMS, OR EVENTS IN THE ENVIRONMENT.

a. Guide students to examine a grain of salt through a magnifying lens. Ask: *What do you see? What does a salt grain look like? What are crystals? How are crystals formed?*

EXPLORE: PLAN AND CONDUCT SIMPLE INVESTIGATIONS TO COLLECT RELEVANT DATA.

b. Guide students to conduct these activities within their cooperative groups:
1. Obtain a tablespoon of salt, a jar lid, and a small glass of water. Mix the salt into the glass of water. Stir the water well. Let the solution stand for a few minutes until it becomes clear.
    Ask: *What happens to the salt?*
2. Very gently pour some of the salt solution into the jar lid. Put a piece of string in the solution, letting one end hang out, as in diagram (a). Let the solution stand for several days where the lid will not be disturbed.
    Ask: *What do you predict will happen to the salt solution?*

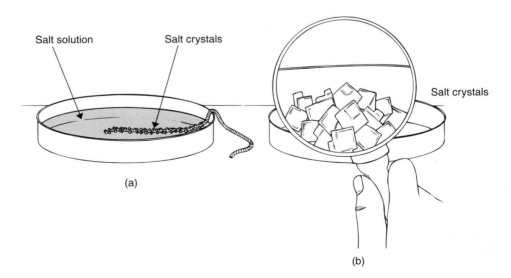

Salt solution   Salt crystals

Salt crystals

(a)

(b)

3. After several days have passed, use your magnifying lens to look at the materials in the lid. Lift the string out of the jar lid. Examine the string with your magnifying lens. Describe what you see with the hand lens. See diagram (b).

EXPLAIN: USE DATA TO GENERATE INTERPRETATIONS, INCLUDING DESCRIPTIONS, CLASSIFICATIONS, PREDICTIONS, AND EXPLANATIONS.

c. Ask: *How are the materials in the lid different from your original salt solution? Why do you now have a solid when you started out with a liquid? What name could you give to the formations in the lid?*

d. Explain to the students that the salt dissolved in the water. When the salt water stood for several days, the water evaporated, leaving behind crystals of salt. Crystals are non-living substances found in nature that are formed in various geometrical shapes.

2. HOW CAN SUGAR CRYSTALS BE GROWN? (3–6)

Materials

Tablespoon	Jar lid
Granulated sugar	Small glass

ENGAGE: ASK A QUESTION ABOUT OBJECTS, ORGANISMS, OR EVENTS IN THE ENVIRONMENT.

a. Instruct students to examine grains of sugar through a magnifying lens. Ask: *What do you observe? How are sugar crystals different from salt crystals? How can we grow crystals of sugar?*

EXPLORE: PLAN AND CONDUCT SIMPLE INVESTIGATIONS TO COLLECT RELEVANT DATA.

b. Students should conduct these activities in their cooperative groups:
   1. Obtain a tablespoon of sugar, a jar lid, and a small glass of water. Be sure the tablespoon is clean. Mix a tablespoon of sugar into the glass of water. Stir the water well. Let the solution stand for a few minutes until it becomes clear. Ask: *What happens to the sugar?*
      How is the sugar solution similar in appearance to the salt solution?
   2. Very gently pour some of the sugar solution into the lid and let the solution stand undisturbed for several days. Ask: *What do you think might happen to the sugar solution?*
   3. After several days have passed, use your magnifying lens to look at the materials in your lid.

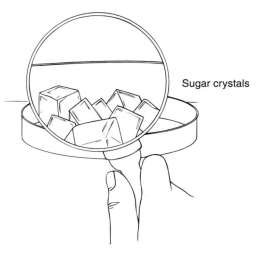

Sugar crystals

EXPLAIN: USE DATA TO GENERATE INTERPRETATIONS, INCLUDING DESCRIPTIONS, CLASSIFICATIONS, PREDICTIONS, AND EXPLANATIONS.

c. Ask: *How are the materials in this lid different from the salt crystals? How are they alike? What happened to the sugar solution?*

Explain that when the sugar water stood for several days, the water evaporated, leaving behind sugar crystals.

3. HOW DOES THE RATE OF COOLING DURING CRYSTAL FORMATION AFFECT CRYSTAL SIZE? (3–6)

Materials

Pyrex beaker
Alum
Tablespoon
Hot plate
Cooking mitt

Clean jar lid
String
One smooth, sanded washer
Pencil

ENGAGE: ASK A QUESTION ABOUT OBJECTS, ORGANISMS, OR EVENTS IN THE ENVIRONMENT.

a. Ask: *What determines how large a crystal is?*

EXPLORE: PLAN AND CONDUCT SIMPLE INVESTIGATIONS TO COLLECT RELEVANT DATA.

b. Demonstrate the following steps for your students:
   1. Heat 200 ml of water in a Pyrex beaker. Add 3 tablespoons of alum. Heat and stir the mixture until the alum fully dissolves, as in diagram (a).

(a)   (b)   (c)

2. Using an insulated cooking mitt, remove the beaker and put it on a solid surface where it cannot be moved or struck.
3. Carefully pour a small amount of the alum solution into a clean jar lid as in diagram (b). Place the lid in a secure, dry place away from heat sources or direct sunshine.
4. Sand a washer and tie it to one end of a piece of string. Wind and tie the other end to a pencil so that when the pencil is suspended across the top of a jar, the washer hangs down about 1 cm from the bottom of the jar as in diagram (c). Place the jar in a secure, dry place next to the jar lid.
5. Have students observe the jar and lid every day. Caution students not to shake or move the containers.

EXPLAIN: USE DATA TO GENERATE INTERPRETATIONS, INCLUDING DESCRIPTIONS, CLASSIFICATIONS, PREDICTIONS, AND EXPLANATIONS.

c. Have students record their observations and use their data to answer these questions:
Where did the first crystals form: bottom of jar, sides of jar, or string?
How does the size of crystals in the jar compare with that in the jar lid?
Why do some rocks have large crystals and some have small crystals?

d. Through discussion, explain that minerals are crystalline in structure. The form of the crystals is important in determining some of the properties of minerals. Differences in the rate of crystallization determine differences in crystal size. Crystals in the jar lid are smaller than those in the jar due to the differences in cooling times. Slower cooling (jar) produces larger crystals, whereas faster cooling (lid) produces smaller crystals.
Ask: *Why would the liquid in the jar cool slower than the liquid in the jar lid?*

4. WHAT ARE STALACTITES AND STALAGMITES, AND HOW ARE THEY FORMED? (3–6)

Materials

Paper towel
Epsom salt
Spoon
30 cm (1 ft) of thick string
Large tin can
Two small jars or clear plastic cups
Two heavy washers

ENGAGE: ASK A QUESTION ABOUT OBJECTS, ORGANISMS, OR EVENTS IN THE ENVIRONMENT.

a. Ask: *How are some rocks formed in caves?*
What is a stalactite, and how is it formed?
What is a stalagmite, and how is it formed?

EXPLORE: PLAN AND CONDUCT SIMPLE INVESTIGATIONS TO COLLECT RELEVANT DATA.

b. Allow students to carry out this investigation in cooperative groups:
1. Fill the large tin can about three-quarters full of water. Add Epsom salt one spoonful at a time, stirring vigorously after each addition, until no more will dissolve.

Note: Epsom salt crystals will fall to the bottom of the can when no more will dissolve.

2. Fill the two small jars or plastic cups with the Epsom salt solution and place the containers 5 cm (2 in.) apart on the paper towel. Tie a heavy washer to each end of the string. Place one washer in each of the small jars or paper cups.

Note: Arrange the string in the cups so that you have at least 5 cm (2 in.) between string and the paper towel.

3. Observe the jars or cups, the paper towel, the string, and the washer daily. Record the observations on a record sheet or in your science journals.

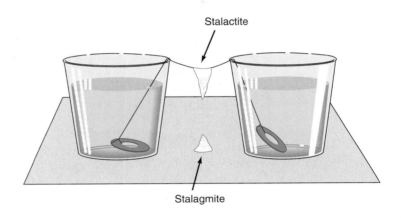

c. Ask: *What do you observe? What is the substance deposited on the string and on the paper towel? How did they get there? What is your evidence?*

d. Help students learn the difference between stalactites and stalagmites. Point out that the deposits that hang down are called **stalactites** (*c* for ceiling), while those that point up are called **stalagmites** (*g* for ground).

Ask: *Is the crystal formed on the string like a stalactite or a stalagmite? Why do you think so? Is the crystal formed on the paper towel like a stalactite or a stalagmite? Why do you think so?*

EXPLAIN: USE DATA TO GENERATE INTERPRETATIONS, INCLUDING DESCRIPTIONS, CLASSIFICATIONS, PREDICTIONS, AND EXPLANATIONS.

How could you help children understand what scientists do?

e. Children sometimes fail to understand the link between causes and effects because they think of an investigation in terms of its component parts rather than its interactions. Scientists use the notion of *system* to help them think in terms of components and interactions. Explain that a system is a collection of components that interact to perform some function. Examples of systems are a school system and the city water system.

Thinking of an investigation as a **system** made up of parts that interact with one another can help to broaden children's thinking. Ask: *What are the components of our investigation system?* (Containers, Epsom salt, water, string, washers, paper towels.) *How does each component interact with other components? What is your evidence?*

By observing small systems, we can draw inferences about what happens in larger systems of the world. Ask: *How is what we observed like what might happen in a cavern in the earth?*

Stalactites and stalagmites in Mammoth Cave, Mammoth Cave National Park, Kentucky.

C. STRUCTURE OF THE EARTH'S SURFACE

▶ *Science Background*

The earth's surface is always changing. Waves, wind, water, and ice shape and reshape the earth's land surface by eroding rock and soil in some areas and depositing it in other areas, sometimes forming seasonal layers. Smaller rocks come from the breaking and weathering of bedrock and larger rocks. Soil is made partly from weathered rock, partly from plant and animal remains. Soil also contains many living organisms.

Source: American Association for the Advancement of Science (1993). *Benchmarks for Science Literacy.* New York: Oxford University Press.

NSES   **Science Standards**

All students should develop an understanding of

- properties of the earth's systems (K–4).
- structure of the earth's systems (5–8).

Objectives for Students

1. Describe how germinating seeds and plants can naturally break up rocks and soil.
2. Demonstrate a procedure for determining the composition of soils.

3. Describe what might be found in soils.
4. Demonstrate a procedure to illustrate how the earth's surface forms layers.
5. Demonstrate, describe, and explain a procedure to illustrate how layers in the earth's surface might be observed.

NSES

Concepts and Principles

Activities 1–3 address these fundamental concepts and principles related to the *Science Standards:*

- Soils have properties of color and texture, capacity to retain water, and ability to support the growth of many kinds of plants (K–4).
- Soils consist of weathered rocks and decomposed organic material from dead plants, animals, and bacteria. Soils are often found in layers, with each having a different chemical composition and texture (5–8).
- The surface of the earth changes. Some changes are due to slow processes, such as erosion and weathering, and some changes are due to rapid processes, such as landslides, volcanic eruptions, and earthquakes (K–4).

1. HOW CAN LIVING THINGS PRODUCE FORCES THAT CAN CHANGE THE EARTH'S SURFACE? (K–2)

Materials

Two plastic vials or medicine bottles with snap lids
Dry bean seeds
Water

ENGAGE: ASK A QUESTION ABOUT OBJECTS, ORGANISMS, OR EVENTS IN THE ENVIRONMENT.

a. Ask: *How can germinating seeds produce forces that can change rocks and soil?*

EXPLORE: PLAN AND CONDUCT SIMPLE INVESTIGATIONS TO COLLECT RELEVANT DATA.

b. Fill both of the vials or medicine bottles with as many dry beans as will fit. Add as much water as you can to one vial of beans. Snap the lids on both vials.
   Ask: *What do you think might happen to the two vials?*

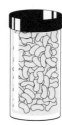

A Water   **B** No water

EXPLAIN: USE DATA TO GENERATE INTERPRETATIONS, INCLUDING DESCRIPTIONS, CLASSIFICATIONS, PREDICTIONS, AND EXPLANATIONS.

c. Observe both vials the next day.

Ask: *What do you observe? Why did it happen?*

Lead students to understand that in the container with water, the beans expanded and lifted the lid off. In the vial without water, there was no observable change. Ask: *How could the force of germinating seeds and growing plants produce changes in the earth's surface?* Help students infer that swelling and growing plants change the land by breaking up rocks and soil just as the swelling beans lifted the vial's lid off. Ask students to find places on the school grounds or on concrete walks where plants grow through and crack rocks like this:

2. WHAT IS IN SOIL? (3–6)

Materials

Soil (from backyard)
Alum
Clear plastic vial with lid

ENGAGE: ASK A QUESTION ABOUT OBJECTS, ORGANISMS, OR EVENTS IN THE ENVIRONMENT.

a. Ask: *What is in soil? How can we find out?*

EXPLORE: PLAN AND CONDUCT SIMPLE INVESTIGATIONS TO COLLECT RELEVANT DATA.

b. To observe different kinds of materials in backyard soil:

1. Add about 1 inch of soil to a clear plastic vial with a lid (approximately 1 inch in diameter and 3 inches high).
2. Add a pinch of alum to the soil. Tell the students that alum is a chemical used in making pickles. It is safe, but caution the students not to taste it.
3. Fill the vial to the top with water, cover it, and shake it vigorously.
4. Place the vial on the table and leave it there for the duration of the investigation.
5. After several minutes, observe and record observations. The alum acts as a dispersing agent, helping the soil particles to break into smaller parts and settle out into layers. Students should observe sand at the bottom of the vial, silt above the sand, clay above the silt, water, and organic matter floating on the water.

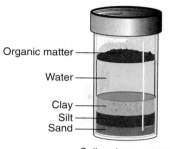

Organic matter
Water
Clay
Silt
Sand

Soil + alum + water

EXPLAIN: USE DATA TO GENERATE INTERPRETATIONS, INCLUDING DESCRIPTIONS, CLASSIFICATIONS, PREDICTIONS, AND EXPLANATIONS.

c. Ask: *From the results of your investigation, what do you conclude is in soil? Which particles do you think are larger: sand, clay, or silt? Why do you think so?*

Source: GEMS (Great Explorations in Math and Science), 1994. *Terrarium Habitats.* Lawrence Hall of Science. University of California at Berkeley.

3. WHAT IS CORE SAMPLING, AND HOW CAN WE USE IT TO INFER LAYERS IN THE EARTH? (K–5)

Materials

Cupcakes
Clear plastic straws
Plastic knives

Preparation

In this activity, straws will be used to take core samples of layered cupcakes. Layered cupcakes may be made by the teacher or a parent volunteer as follows:

1. Use either different flavors or white batter mixed with food coloring.
2. Put batter in four layers in foil or paper cups.
3. Bake the cupcakes. Add frosting if desired.

ENGAGE: ASK A QUESTION ABOUT OBJECTS, ORGANISMS, OR EVENTS IN THE ENVIRONMENT.

a. Ask: *How do geologists study what is below the earth's surface?*
Provide students this background information:
>   **Geologists** study the earth and use many devices to discover what is under the surface. **Core sampling** is done by putting hollow drilling tubes into the ground and extracting a sample of what the tubes went through.

b. Show students a cupcake. Ask: *What do you think is inside the cupcake? How could we find out without eating it or cutting into it? How can scientists learn what's underground?*

EXPLORE: PLAN AND CONDUCT SIMPLE INVESTIGATIONS TO COLLECT RELEVANT DATA.

c. Provide groups of students one cupcake on a paper plate, five clear plastic straws cut into thirds, a plastic knife, drawing paper, and markers. Do *not* remove the foil or paper cup from the cupcake.

d. Instruct students to draw what they think the inside of the cupcake looks like.

e. Explain and demonstrate to students how to take side "core samples," as in diagram (a):
   1. Carefully insert a straw into the side of the cupcake, rotate slightly, remove, and place sample on paper plate.
   2. Repeat with another straw.
f. Instruct students to take two side core samples of their cupcake. Ask: *Can you determine what the entire cupcake looks like with these two core samples? If not, what must you do?*
g. Instruct students to take three samples by inserting the straw straight down into the cupcake, as in diagram (b).

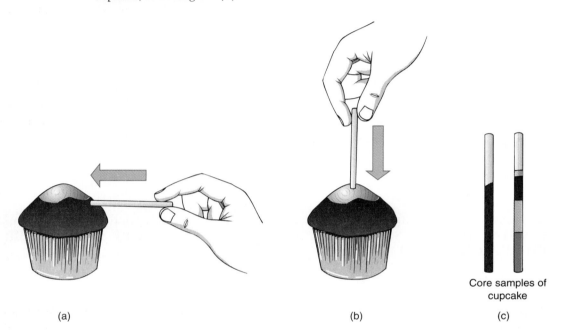

(a)   (b)   (c)

Core samples of cupcake

h. Compare these samples with those taken from the side, as in diagram (c).

EXPLAIN: USE DATA TO GENERATE INTERPRETATIONS, INCLUDING DESCRIPTIONS, CLASSIFICATIONS, PREDICTIONS, AND EXPLANATIONS.

i. Ask: *How are they different? Based on your core samples, what do you infer is inside the cupcake?*
   Instruct students to make drawings of what they now think the inside of the cupcake looks like.
j. Tell students to use the plastic knives to cut down and separate the cupcakes into halves. Ask: *How do your direct observations compare with your inferences and your drawings? How could geologists use core sampling to infer what is inside the earth?*

Source: Cupcake Geology activity in the Mesa Public Schools Curriculum Unit "Earthquakes" by JoAnne Vasquez.

II. THE ATMOSPHERE, WEATHER, AND CLIMATE OF THE EARTH

Our spherical earth consists mostly of rock, with three-fourths of the planet covered by a thin layer of water and the entire planet blanketed by a thin layer of air called the atmosphere. Weather (in the short run) and climate (in the long run) involve the transfer of heat energy from the sun in and out of the atmosphere. The earth has a variety of climatic patterns, which consist of different conditions of temperature, precipitation, humidity, wind, air pressure, and other atmospheric phenomena. Water continuously circulates in and out of the atmosphere—evaporating from the surface, rising and cooling, condensing into clouds and then rain or snow, and falling again to the surface. The water cycle plays an important part in determining climatic patterns.

Children can begin to understand the atmosphere, water cycle, weather, and climate by engaging in inquiry activities related to evaporation and condensation, and observing and recording the weather on a regular basis. Emphasis should be on developing observation and description skills and forming explanations based on observable evidence.[2]

A. THE WATER CYCLE

▶ *Science Background*

In the **water cycle**, water evaporates into the air as **water vapor**.

As the air becomes laden with water vapor, the **relative humidity** of the air increases. When warm, moist air cools, it condenses as liquid water on available surfaces such as an iced tea glass, a bathroom mirror, or dust particles in the air.

NSES   **Science Standards**

All students should develop an understanding of

- changes in the earth and sky (K–4).
- structure of the earth's systems (5–8).

Objectives for Students

1. Observe and describe the disappearance of water that is left uncovered.
2. Define *evaporation* and explain that evaporated water has not disappeared but has changed into water vapor (a gaseous state) and has gone into the air.
3. Use the cohesive bond model of water developed in previous activities to explain what happens when a liquid evaporates.
4. Explain how interactions between a liquid and its environment may affect evaporation.
5. Define *condensation* and *dew point*.
6. Describe and demonstrate the conditions for condensation.
7. Construct and explain a model of the water cycle.

NSES   **Concepts and Principles**

Activities 1–9 address these fundamental concepts and principles related to the *Science Standards:*

- Water, which covers the majority of the earth's surface, circulates through the crust, oceans, and atmosphere in what is known as the "water cycle" (5–8).
- Water evaporates from the earth's surface, rises and cools as it moves to higher elevations, condenses as rain or snow, and falls to the surface where it collects in lakes, oceans, soil, and rocks underground (5–8).

---

[2]*Science for All Americans, Benchmarks for Science Literacy,* and the *National Science Education Standards.*

....

1. HOW MUCH WATER EVAPORATES FROM AN OPEN AQUARIUM? (K–2)

Materials

Aquarium or other large, open container

Safety Precautions

When children work with water, cover their work tables, perhaps with newspapers. Have plenty of paper towels on hand to clean up water spills.

ENGAGE: ASK A
QUESTION ABOUT OBJECTS,
ORGANISMS, OR EVENTS IN
THE ENVIRONMENT.

a. Ask: *How can we determine the amount of water that evaporates from an aquarium?*

EXPLORE: PLAN
AND CONDUCT SIMPLE
INVESTIGATIONS TO
COLLECT RELEVANT DATA.

b. Assist students to conduct this investigation:
  1. Using masking tape or marking pens, mark the beginning water levels of a class-room aquarium.
  2. Check the water levels each morning. Using a measuring cup, add enough water to the containers to bring the water levels back up to the original marks you made. Be sure the water added to the aquarium sits in a large open container for at least 24 hours.
  3. Keep a record of how much water was added to your containers each week.

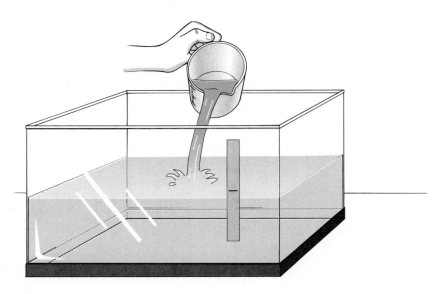

EXPLAIN: USE
DATA TO GENERATE
INTERPRETATIONS,
INCLUDING DESCRIPTIONS,
CLASSIFICATIONS,
PREDICTIONS, AND
EXPLANATIONS.

c. Ask: *How much water evaporated from the aquarium each day?*

2. WHERE DOES WATER GO WHEN IT EVAPORATES? (K–2)

Materials
Aquarium with water, fish, and sand
Empty aquarium container
Sand

ENGAGE: ASK A QUESTION ABOUT OBJECTS, ORGANISMS, OR EVENTS IN THE ENVIRONMENT.

a. Ask: *When water evaporates, where does it go?*

EXPLORE: PLAN AND CONDUCT SIMPLE INVESTIGATIONS TO COLLECT RELEVANT DATA.

b. Lead children to form hypotheses about where the water in an aquarium or other container went when it disappeared. Possible hypotheses include the following:
  * The missing water soaked into the sand.
  * The fish drank it.
  * The custodian spilled it.
  * It went into the air.

c. Help the children design and conduct controlled investigations to test each hypothesis. In a controlled investigation, all variables are kept the same except one.
  1. To test if the water soaked into the sand, observe two aquariums with water and fish, one with and one without sand.
  2. To test if the fish drank the water, compare one container with fish and one without (both containers should be identical in every other way except one has no fish).
  3. To test if the water went into the air, observe one container covered and one uncovered.

EXPLAIN: USE DATA TO GENERATE INTERPRETATIONS, INCLUDING DESCRIPTIONS, CLASSIFICATIONS, PREDICTIONS, AND EXPLANATIONS.

d. Ask: *What did you observe in your investigations? What can you conclude?* Discuss with the students how they can interpret the data from each of their experiments. For example, explain that the amount of the evaporated water was the same in aquariums with and without sand, so the water must not have soaked into the sand. There was a difference in the evaporated water only in the experiment in which one aquarium was covered and the other was not covered. Therefore, the cover must have prevented water from evaporating.

  Discuss with the children how these experiments provide evidence that the water went into the air. Explain that the missing water does not just disappear; it changes into water vapor (a gaseous state) and goes into the air.[3]

3. HOW CAN YOU PROMOTE THE EVAPORATION OF WATER? (K–2)

Materials
Shallow containers such as jar lids
Lamp with 60 watt bulb

Safety Precautions
Caution the children not to touch the light bulb and electrical connections. For safety reasons, you may choose to demonstrate that water evaporates more quickly when it is heated.

---

[3]Adapted from a variation of an SCIS activity developed by Herbert Thier.

ENGAGE: ASK A QUESTION ABOUT OBJECTS, ORGANISMS, OR EVENTS IN THE ENVIRONMENT.

a. Ask: *What can you do to speed up the evaporation of water?*

EXPLORE: PLAN AND CONDUCT SIMPLE INVESTIGATIONS TO COLLECT RELEVANT DATA.

b. Place water in two shallow containers, such as jar lids. Lead the students to try different things to promote evaporation. Eventually they should focus on (1) fanning the air above the liquid and (2) heating the liquid with the light from an unshaded 60 watt light bulb in a lamp. Emphasize that students should do something to the liquid in one jar lid and do nothing to the liquid in the other. For example, the liquid in one container is fanned; the other is not. The liquid in one container is heated by the light source; the other is not. This way, they can compare the water levels in the two containers and see whether evaporation is affected by fanning or heating.

EXPLAIN: USE DATA TO GENERATE INTERPRETATIONS, INCLUDING DESCRIPTIONS, CLASSIFICATIONS, PREDICTIONS, AND EXPLANATIONS.

c. Ask: *Does fanning water speed up its evaporation? What is your evidence? Does shining light on water speed up its evaporation? What is your evidence? Why do you think fanning the water or shining light on it speeded up the evaporation?*

4. WHICH EVAPORATES MORE QUICKLY, WATER OR RUBBING ALCOHOL? (4–6)

Materials

Rubbing alcohol
Droppers

Safety Precautions

Do not allow students to handle or touch the rubbing alcohol.

ENGAGE: ASK A QUESTION ABOUT OBJECTS, ORGANISMS, OR EVENTS IN THE ENVIRONMENT.

a. Ask: *Which evaporates more quickly, water or rubbing alcohol?*

EXPLORE: PLAN AND CONDUCT SIMPLE INVESTIGATIONS TO COLLECT RELEVANT DATA.

b. The teacher should place drops of water and drops of rubbing alcohol near one another on wax paper for each cooperative group. The students then observe the two liquids to determine what happens to them over time. (To speed up evaporation, children may gently fan both of the drops of liquid.)

EXPLAIN: USE DATA TO GENERATE INTERPRETATIONS, INCLUDING DESCRIPTIONS, CLASSIFICATIONS, PREDICTIONS, AND EXPLANATIONS.

c. Ask: *What happened to each liquid? Where did each liquid go when it disappeared? Which liquid evaporated more quickly? Using what you know of the bonding of drops in a liquid, why do you think the drops of alcohol evaporated more quickly?*

▶ *Teaching Background*

The cohesive force of drops for one another is greater in water than in alcohol. Thus, the alcohol drops can escape the cohesive forces holding them in the liquid more easily than the water can. That is the reason alcohol evaporates more quickly than water.

5. HOW FAST DOES WATER IN A WET SPONGE EVAPORATE? (3–6)

Materials

Meterstick or wire coat hanger
Paper clips
Sponge
Masking tape or marking pens

ENGAGE: ASK A QUESTION ABOUT OBJECTS, ORGANISMS, OR EVENTS IN THE ENVIRONMENT.

a. Ask: *How can we determine the rate of evaporation of water in a wet sponge?*

EXPLORE: PLAN AND CONDUCT SIMPLE INVESTIGATIONS TO COLLECT RELEVANT DATA.

b. Assist students to set up and conduct this investigation:
   1. Using a meterstick or wire coat hanger, and paper clips, build either of the balances shown.
   2. Soak a piece of sponge until it is very wet, but not dripping. Hang the sponge with an S-shaped paper clip or string to one end of the balance. Add paper clips to the other end until the balance is level.
      How many clips did it take?
   3. Every 15 minutes, check to see if the balance is level.
      What do you see happening after several observations?
      Why do you think the paper clip end of the balance is lower?
   4. Keep a written record of what happens.
   5. At each 15 minute observation, take off and record how many paper clips must be removed to keep the balance level.
   6. When the sponge is dry, take your written observations and plot a line graph with the data. Set up your graph like the one that follows.

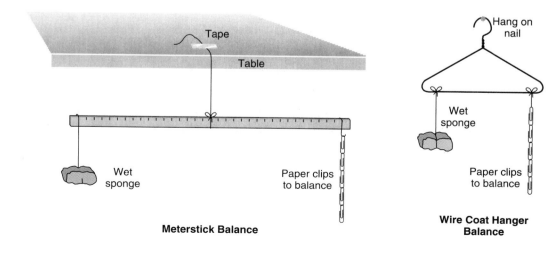

Meterstick Balance

Wire Coat Hanger Balance

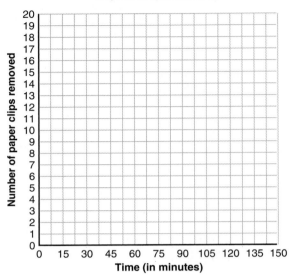

Graph of Evaporation Data

EXPLAIN: USE DATA TO GENERATE INTERPRETATIONS, INCLUDING DESCRIPTIONS, CLASSIFICATIONS, PREDICTIONS, AND EXPLANATIONS.

c. Ask: *What does the graph tell you about the rate of evaporation of the water in a wet sponge?*

6. WHAT VARIABLES AFFECT HOW QUICKLY WATER EVAPORATES IN A WET SPONGE? (3–6)

ENGAGE: ASK A QUESTION ABOUT OBJECTS, ORGANISMS, OR EVENTS IN THE ENVIRONMENT.

a. Ask: *What are some variables that might affect how quickly the water in the sponge of Activity 5 evaporates? How could you set up an experiment to test the effect of these variables on evaporation?*

EXPLORE: PLAN AND CONDUCT SIMPLE INVESTIGATIONS TO COLLECT RELEVANT DATA.

b. Some variables that might affect the rate of evaporation are type of liquid (water vs. alcohol), temperature of the liquid (hot vs. cold), air temperature (hot vs. cold), wind velocity (no wind, moderate wind, strong wind), and relative humidity (dry day vs. moist day). Guide students in designing investigations, gathering data, and recording and graphing the results in the same way as was done in the previous activity.

EXPLAIN: USE DATA TO GENERATE INTERPRETATIONS, INCLUDING DESCRIPTIONS, CLASSIFICATIONS, PREDICTIONS, AND EXPLANATIONS.

c. Ask: *What did you observe in your investigations? What do you conclude?*

ELABORATE: EXTEND CONCEPTS, PRINCIPLES, AND STRATEGIES TO NEW SITUATIONS AND QUESTIONS.

d. Ask: *How do your findings from your investigation relate to each of these situations?*
  * Water evaporates faster from your hands when you vigorously rub them together.
  * A blow dryer can be used to dry your hair faster.
  * Your hair dries faster on a dry day than on a wet one.
  * A wet towel dries faster if it is spread out rather than crumpled in a ball.

7. WHAT IS CONDENSATION? HOW DOES IT OCCUR? (3–6)

Materials

Clean, empty vegetable or fruit cans
Ice

ENGAGE: ASK A QUESTION ABOUT OBJECTS, ORGANISMS, OR EVENTS IN THE ENVIRONMENT.

a. Ask: *What is condensation? What conditions are needed for condensation?*

EXPLORE: PLAN AND CONDUCT SIMPLE INVESTIGATIONS TO COLLECT RELEVANT DATA.

b. Provide each group two identical, empty vegetable cans. Give students these instructions:
  1. Add the same amount of water to each can so that they are about three-fourths full.
  2. Place ice in one of the cans so that the water is almost to the top of the can.
  3. Stir the water in each can.
  4. Observe the outside of each can.

EXPLAIN: USE DATA TO GENERATE INTERPRETATIONS, INCLUDING DESCRIPTIONS, CLASSIFICATIONS, PREDICTIONS, AND EXPLANATIONS.

c. Ask: *What happened to the outside of each can as you stirred the water?* (Moisture collected on the outside of the container with ice water.) *What conditions were necessary for the water to appear on the outside of the can?* (The can had to be cool.) *Where did the water come from?*

d. If students suggest that cold water soaked through the can, ask: *How could we test this hypothesis?*

   Hint: You might put food dye in the water and then observe to see if any of the food coloring actually soaked through the can.

   Ask: *People often say that a glass of ice water is sweating; why is this explanation incorrect?*

e. Provide this explanation of condensation:
   When water evaporates, it goes into the air as water vapor. If moisture-laden air comes into contact with a surface that is cool enough, then water vapor condenses (changes from a gas to a liquid) from the air and collects on the cool surface.

ELABORATE: EXTEND CONCEPTS, PRINCIPLES, AND STRATEGIES TO NEW SITUATIONS AND QUESTIONS.

f. Ask: *What is the source of the warm, moist air in each of these examples of condensation? What is the surface on which water condenses in each case?*
  * *Formation of clouds.* (Warm, moist air in the atmosphere rises and cools. As the water vapor cools, it condenses on dust particles.)
  * *Dew.* (Warm, moist air is cooled as it mixes with cooler air near the surface of the earth. As the water vapor cools, it condenses on the grass and other surfaces.)
  * *Vapor trails.* (Warm, moist air from the exhaust of a jet mixes with cooler air high in the atmosphere. As the water vapor cools, it condenses on dust particles in the atmosphere.)
  * *Moisture on bathroom mirrors after a hot shower.* (Warm, moist air produced during the hot shower condenses on the cooler bathroom mirror.)

8. HOW CAN EVAPORATION AND CONDENSATION BE USED TO DESALINATE SALT WATER? (3–5)

Materials

Salt
Water
Tablespoon
Small weight (rock)
Large sheet of black construction paper
Large clear plastic bowl
Plastic wrap
Large rubber band
Small glass custard cup

ENGAGE: ASK A QUESTION ABOUT OBJECTS, ORGANISMS, OR EVENTS IN THE ENVIRONMENT.

a. Ask: *How can evaporation and condensation be used to remove the salt from salt water?*

EXPLORE: PLAN AND CONDUCT SIMPLE INVESTIGATIONS TO COLLECT RELEVANT DATA.

b. This activity may be done individually or in groups of two to four:
   1. Pour 3 tablespoons of salt into a large clear plastic bowl, add water to a depth of about 2 to 3 cm, and stir until all the salt is dissolved.
   2. Place the small glass cup in the water in the center of the bowl, as in the diagram.
   3. Cover the large bowl with plastic wrap and fasten the wrap with a large rubber band.
   4. Place a weight (small pebble) on top of the plastic wrap directly above the custard dish, as shown in the diagram.
   5. *Caution:* Make certain that the plastic wrap sticks tightly to the sides of the bowl and that the large rubber band keeps it sealed when the pebble is placed on the wrap.
   6. Carefully place the bowls in direct sunlight on a sheet of black construction paper, making sure the custard cup is directly under the weight pushing down on the plastic wrap.

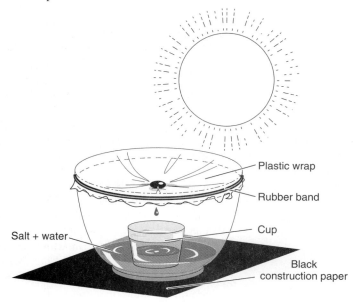

Plastic wrap
Rubber band
Cup
Salt + water
Black construction paper

7. *What do you think might happen to the salt water?*
8. *Why do you think you were told to cover the salt water with plastic wrap?*
9. *Why do you think you were told to put the bowl on black construction paper?*
10. Record your observations every day.
11. Take off the plastic wrap and taste the water in the custard cup.

EXPLAIN: USE DATA TO GENERATE INTERPRETATIONS, INCLUDING DESCRIPTIONS, CLASSIFICATIONS, PREDICTIONS, AND EXPLANATIONS.

c. Ask: *How does the water taste?*
   Where did the water in this dish come from?
   What happened to your salt solution?
   Where did the water in the bowl go?
   Why did the water "disappear"?
   What is left in the bottom of the large bowl?

▶ *Teaching Background*

Water in a saline solution absorbs the sun's energy and evaporates, leaving the salt behind.

9. WHAT IS THE TEMPERATURE AT WHICH CONDENSATION TAKES PLACE? (3–6)

Materials

Clean, empty cans
Ice
Thermometers

ENGAGE: ASK A QUESTION ABOUT OBJECTS, ORGANISMS, OR EVENTS IN THE ENVIRONMENT.

a. Ask: *How can we find out how cold a surface has to be before water vapor condenses on it?*

EXPLORE: PLAN AND CONDUCT SIMPLE INVESTIGATIONS TO COLLECT RELEVANT DATA.

b. Give students these instructions:
   1. Fill an empty can about three-fourths full of tap water at room temperature.
   2. Place a thermometer in the water and read the temperature.
   3. Add about one-fourth can of ice to the water.
   4. Stir the ice and water and read the temperature every 2 minutes.
   5. Carefully observe the outside of the can. At the first sign of condensation, read the temperature of the cold water. Wiping the outside of the can occasionally with a brown paper towel will aid in determining when condensation first forms on the can.

EXPLAIN: USE DATA TO GENERATE INTERPRETATIONS, INCLUDING DESCRIPTIONS, CLASSIFICATIONS, PREDICTIONS, AND EXPLANATIONS.

c. Instruct groups to record on the board the temperature at which condensation first occurred. Note discrepancies among the data collected. According to the *Benchmarks for Science Literacy*, when students arrive at very different measurements of the same thing, "it is usually a good idea to make some fresh observations instead of just arguing about who is right" (American Association for the Advancement of Science, 1993, *Benchmarks For Science Literacy*. New York: Oxford University Press, p. 10).

d. Explain that the temperature at which condensation will form on a cool surface is called the *dew point*. The dew point depends on the relative humidity of the air, that is, on the relative amount of moisture already in the air.

B. WEATHER

▶ *Science Background*

The components of weather are temperature, precipitation, humidity, wind, air pressure, clouds, and other atmospheric phenomena. These weather conditions can be readily observed and recorded by children. By keeping a weather journal during the year, students can discover weather patterns and trends, though they may not be consistent. Younger students can draw daily weather pictures of what they see; older students can make charts and graphs from the data they collect using simple weather instruments.

> **NSES**   **Science Standards**
>
> All students should develop an understanding of
>
> • properties of the earth's systems (K–4).
> • structure of the earth's systems (5–8).

Objectives for Students

1. Name and measure such components of weather as temperature, wind direction and speed, air pressure, and precipitation.
2. Describe patterns and trends in local weather conditions.
3. Construct a variety of weather instruments.
4. Name and describe different types of clouds, and explain how clouds are formed.

> **NSES**   **Concepts and Principles**
>
> Activities 1–7 address these fundamental concepts and principles related to the *Science Standards:*
>
> • Water circulates through the crust, oceans, and atmosphere in what is known as the water cycle (5–8).
> • The atmosphere is a mixture of gases that include water vapor (5–8).
> • Clouds, formed by the condensation of water vapor, affect weather and climate (5–8).
> • Global patterns of atmospheric movement influence local weather (5–8).

1. HOW CAN WE DESCRIBE THE WEATHER? (K–3)

Materials   Thermometers

ENGAGE: ASK A QUESTION ABOUT OBJECTS, ORGANISMS, OR EVENTS IN THE ENVIRONMENT.

a. Ask: *What is our weather like today?* Record the words students use to describe the weather (*cold, hot, warm, muggy, cloudy, rainy, windy,* etc.).

Ask: *If we wanted to compare the weather today with the weather on another day, what would we record about today's weather?* Most children see weather forecasts on television. They are beginning to learn that weather controls much of their lives, from the clothes they wear to the games they play. Through discussion, lead children to consider these variables related to weather: temperature, cloud cover, wind, humidity, and rain or snow (precipitation).

EXPLORE: PLAN AND CONDUCT SIMPLE INVESTIGATIONS TO COLLECT RELEVANT DATA.

b. Construct a bulletin board depicting a large weather chart similar to the one shown in the diagram on page A-248. Encourage children to make daily observations of weather conditions and to make entries on the class weather chart.

c. Examine the weather chart with the children. Discuss the kinds of things children might do that would be affected by the weather. If they play outside, what would they wear: warm clothes, rain gear? Discuss the weather conditions for several days in a row.

EXPLAIN: USE DATA TO GENERATE INTERPRETATIONS, INCLUDING DESCRIPTIONS, CLASSIFICATIONS, PREDICTIONS, AND EXPLANATIONS.

d. Ask: *What patterns in the weather do you see? How has the temperature changed from day to day? How is the weather today different from last summer? last winter?* Count the number of cool days, warm days, cloudy days, clear days, rainy days, and dry days to help find patterns in the weather.

ELABORATE: EXTEND CONCEPTS, PRINCIPLES, AND STRATEGIES TO NEW SITUATIONS AND QUESTIONS.

e. Ask: *What is the weather like in other regions? How would weather conditions affect life in other regions?* Using the Internet, find and chart daily weather conditions in other regions and countries around the globe.

2. HOW DOES OUTSIDE TEMPERATURE CHANGE THROUGHOUT A DAY AND FROM DAY TO DAY? (2–4)

Materials   Thermometers

ENGAGE: ASK A QUESTION ABOUT OBJECTS, ORGANISMS, OR EVENTS IN THE ENVIRONMENT.

a. Ask: *How does the temperature vary from place to place? Is the temperature the same inside and outside the classroom? Is the temperature the same everywhere on the school grounds? Is the temperature the same in the shade and the sun?*

EXPLORE: PLAN AND CONDUCT SIMPLE INVESTIGATIONS TO COLLECT RELEVANT DATA.

b. Guide students to measure and compare the temperature at various locations: inside and outside the classroom, in the sun and in the shade, and at different places on the school grounds. Discuss the differences in the temperatures at different locations and why the differences might occur.

	MON	TUES	WED	THURS	FRI	MON	TUES	WED	THURS	FRI	MON	TUES	WED	THURS	FRI
Day **Date**															
Temperature 🌡️															
Clouds ☁️	◯	◯	◯	◯	◯	◯	◯	◯	◯	◯	◯	◯	◯	◯	◯
Wind 🪁	—	—	—	—	—	—	—	—	—	—	—	—	—	—	—
Other	▭	▭	▭	▭	▭	▭	▭	▭	▭	▭	▭	▭	▭	▭	▭
Student's Name															

EXPLAIN: USE DATA TO GENERATE INTERPRETATIONS, INCLUDING DESCRIPTIONS, CLASSIFICATIONS, PREDICTIONS, AND EXPLANATIONS.

c. Ask: *Is the temperature the same throughout the day?* Allow students to measure the outside temperature every hour. Discuss the temperature differences that are observed. Emphasize that how the temperature changes is very important to judging the weather.

3. HOW ARE CLOUDS AND FOG FORMED? (3–6)

Materials

Ice cubes
Two clear, narrow-mouthed bottles
Hot and cold water
Matches

ENGAGE: ASK A QUESTION ABOUT OBJECTS, ORGANISMS, OR EVENTS IN THE ENVIRONMENT.

a. Ask: *What is a cloud and how is it formed?*
   What is fog and how is it formed?

EXPLORE: PLAN AND CONDUCT SIMPLE INVESTIGATIONS TO COLLECT RELEVANT DATA.

b. Fill a bottle with very hot water and let it sit for a few minutes. Then pour out most of the water, leaving about 2 cm of water in the bottom of the bottle. For comparison, set up an identical bottle with an equal amount of cold water. Place an ice cube on the top of each bottle as shown in the diagram.

EXPLAIN: USE DATA TO GENERATE INTERPRETATIONS, INCLUDING DESCRIPTIONS, CLASSIFICATIONS, PREDICTIONS, AND EXPLANATIONS.

c. As students observe the two bottles, ask:
   What do you see happening in each bottle?
   Why did the cloud or fog form in the bottle?
   Why do you think clouds or fog formed in the bottle with hot water and not in the bottle with cold water?

ELABORATE: EXTEND CONCEPTS, PRINCIPLES, AND STRATEGIES TO NEW SITUATIONS AND QUESTIONS.

d. Set up the bottle with hot water as in step *b.* Light a match, extinguish it, and blow some of the smoke from the match into the bottle. Place an ice cube on the bottle. Ask: *What differences do you observe with and without the smoke? What was the purpose of the smoke?* (To provide particles on which water vapor might condense.)

e. Ask: *How do clouds and fog form in nature?*

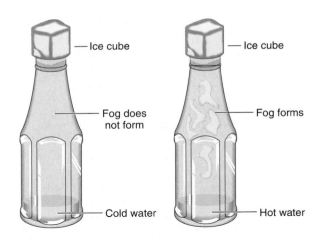

4. HOW CAN YOU MAKE A WIND VANE, AND HOW IS IT USED TO DETERMINE WIND DIRECTION? (3–6)

Materials

Scissors
Construction paper
Drinking straw
Pencil with eraser
Straight pin
Glass bead
Empty thread spool
A 30 cm square piece of corrugated cardboard

ENGAGE: ASK A QUESTION ABOUT OBJECTS, ORGANISMS, OR EVENTS IN THE ENVIRONMENT.

a. Ask: *How can you tell the direction the wind is blowing?*
    How does knowing wind direction help us understand weather and weather prediction?
    What instruments can be used to find wind direction and speed?
    How can we make and use these instruments?

EXPLORE: PLAN AND CONDUCT SIMPLE INVESTIGATIONS TO COLLECT RELEVANT DATA.

b. To make a wind vane, follow these directions:
    1. Cut an arrow-shaped point and tail fin from construction paper, as shown in the diagram.
    2. Attach the point and tail fin to the straw by cutting notches in both ends of the straw and gluing the cutouts in place.
    3. Attach the straw to a pencil by sticking the straight pin through the middle of the straw, through a glass bead, and into the pencil eraser. Make sure the straw can swing easily in all directions and is balanced.

    Note: Move the pin in the straw until it balances with arrow and tail attached.

    4. Glue the empty thread spool to the center of the corrugated cardboard. Mark north, south, east, and west on the cardboard as shown in the diagram.

5. When the glue has dried, push the pencil into the hole of the spool and check to see that the straw moves easily. You now have a wind vane.

c. Carefully take your wind vane outdoors and line up the north label on your wind vane with the north on a magnetic compass. If the wind is strong, tape the cardboard to a horizontal surface or weight it down with something heavy.

EXPLAIN: USE DATA TO GENERATE INTERPRETATIONS, INCLUDING DESCRIPTIONS, CLASSIFICATIONS, PREDICTIONS, AND EXPLANATIONS.

d. Ask: *What do you see happening to the arrow?*
   From which direction is the wind blowing? How do you know?
   How would you name this wind?
   The arrow will swing around until the point faces the direction from which the wind is blowing. This direction then becomes the wind's name.
      Ask: *Does the wind always blow from the same direction? How could we find out?*

e. Keep a record of wind observations three times a day for 1 week. Make sure to record the data on a chart.
      After 1 week, do you detect
   any pattern of winds during the day?
   any pattern of winds from day to day?
   any prevailing or consistent direction from which the wind blows?
   any correlation between wind direction and weather conditions, such as temperatures, humidity, clouds, and so on?

f. Check local TV weather and newspapers for wind direction. *How do your data compare? If they differ, why do you think so?*

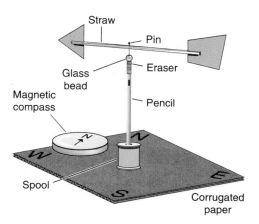

▶ *Teaching Background*

Wind, or moving air, brings about changing weather conditions. A **wind vane** is an instrument that shows the direction from which the wind is blowing. Winds are named for the direction from which they blow. For example, a north wind is blowing from the north to the south. An **anemometer** is an instrument that measures wind speed.

5. HOW CAN YOU MEASURE HOW FAST THE WIND BLOWS? HOW DOES WIND SPEED VARY WITH LOCATION AND TIME? (3–6)

Materials

Long sewing needle
30 cm of monofilament nylon line
Ping-Pong ball
Glue
Cardboard

Red marking pen
Protractor
Bubble level (hardware store)
Tongue depressor

Preparation

Thread a sewing needle with a 30 cm monofilament line, push the needle through the Ping-Pong ball, and knot and glue the end of the line to the Ping-Pong ball.

Safety Precautions

Use caution when pushing the needle through the Ping-Pong ball.

ENGAGE: ASK A QUESTION ABOUT OBJECTS, ORGANISMS, OR EVENTS IN THE ENVIRONMENT.

a. Ask: *How can we measure how fast the wind blows?*

EXPLORE: PLAN AND CONDUCT SIMPLE INVESTIGATIONS TO COLLECT RELEVANT DATA.

b. Either the teacher or students should follow these directions to make an anemometer:
   1. Glue the other end of the line that is attached to the Ping-Pong ball to the center of a protractor. With the marking pen, color the line red.
   2. Glue a bubble level to the protractor as shown in the diagram.
   3. Glue a tongue depressor to the protractor as a handle. You now have an anemometer to measure wind speed.
   4. When the glue is dry, carefully take your anemometer outside to test it in the wind.
c. To take readings of the wind's speed, follow these directions:
   1. In the wind, hold the protractor level using the tongue depressor handle.
   2. Keep the protractor level by making sure the bubble is centered in the bubble level.
   3. Observe any swing of the Ping-Pong ball and string and see what angle the string makes on the protractor. For instance, in the diagram the string moved to approximately 65 degrees.

Bubble level

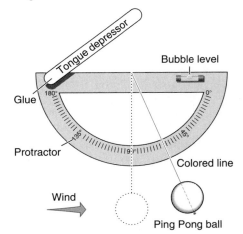

d. Use your anemometer in various spots on your school grounds, and then refer to the following chart to find the wind speed.

Protractor Anemometer Wind Speeds

String Angle	Wind Speed (Miles per Hour)	String Angle	Wind Speed (Miles per Hour)
90	0	50	18.0
85	5.8	45	19.6
80	8.2	40	21.9
75	10.1	35	23.4
70	11.8	30	25.8
65	13.4	25	28.7
60	14.9	20	32.5
55	16.4		

After you have tested the wind speed in different places on your school grounds, record the data on a chart like this one.

Date								
Time								
Protractor angle								
Wind speed								
Wind direction								

EXPLAIN: USE DATA TO GENERATE INTERPRETATIONS, INCLUDING DESCRIPTIONS, CLASSIFICATIONS, PREDICTIONS, AND EXPLANATIONS.

e. Invite students to describe their anemometers and explain how they work. Guide students to use their charts to answer these questions:
Where does the wind blow the fastest on your school grounds?
Does wind blow faster at ground level or at higher levels?
Is there a place where wind blows faster, such as between two buildings or at a corner of two wings of a building? Why?

6. HOW CAN YOU MEASURE AIR PRESSURE CHANGES, AND HOW DO AIR PRESSURE CHANGES AFFECT WEATHER? (3–6)

Materials

Large can (e.g., coffee can)
Large balloon and rubber band
Straw
Glue
Straight pin
Index card

a. Blow up a balloon.

Ask: *What is in the balloon?* (Air.) *How do you know there is air in the balloon?* (The air pushes back when we press on the balloon.)

Lead students to understand that we live at the bottom of an ocean of air that presses on us at all times. The pressure of the atmosphere (air pressure) is a variable that affects weather conditions. A barometer is an instrument that measures the pressure of the air.

b. To make a barometer, follow these directions:
   1. Obtain a can, such as a coffee can, a balloon, a rubber band, a straw, glue, a straight pin, and a card.
   2. Cover the can with a piece of a large balloon and use a tight rubber band to seal the can.
   3. Place a small amount of glue in the center of the balloon on the can and attach a straw, as shown in the diagram. Place another drop of glue on the other end of the straw and attach the pin.
   4. Mark an index card with lines that are the same distance apart. Tape the card on the wall as shown in the diagram. Set the can so the pin points to one of the middle lines on the card.

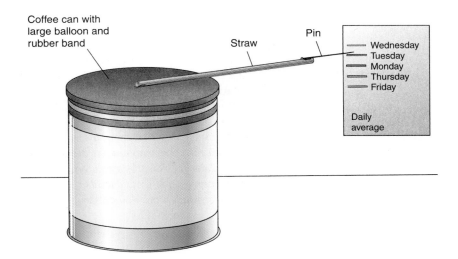

c. Ask: *What happens to the balloon on top of the can if the air pressure on it increases? What happens to the position of the pin on the end of the straw?*

What happens to the balloon if the air pressure outside the can decreases? What happens to the position of the pin on the end of the straw?

Lead students to understand that when air pressure increases, it pushes down on the balloon, causing the straw to indicate a high reading. When the air pressure is low, the opposite will happen. A falling barometer reading may indicate that a storm is approaching.

d. Record the readings of the barometer three times a day for a week. Observe and record the type of weather (temperature, cloud conditions, humidity, wind) that exists at the time of each barometer reading.

EXPLAIN: USE DATA TO GENERATE INTERPRETATIONS, INCLUDING DESCRIPTIONS, CLASSIFICATIONS, PREDICTIONS, AND EXPLANATIONS.

e. Ask: *How do the readings of the barometer differ during the day?*
  How do the readings differ from day to day?
  What might cause the readings to vary?
  What kind of air pressure generally existed during your fair-weather readings?
  What kind of air pressure generally existed during your stormy-weather readings?

Note: Room temperature will affect the barometer students make in this activity. This barometer does not, therefore, measure only air pressure differences. You may want to have some students keep their barometers outside class and then compare the readings from the different locations.

7. HOW CAN YOU MEASURE RELATIVE HUMIDITY AND HUMIDITY CHANGES? (3–6)

Materials

Two thermometers
Wide cotton shoelace
Small dish of water
Empty milk carton
Thread
Piece of cardboard

ENGAGE: ASK A QUESTION ABOUT OBJECTS, ORGANISMS, OR EVENTS IN THE ENVIRONMENT.

a. Ask: *What instrument is used to measure the amount of water, or humidity, in the atmosphere?*
  How can this instrument be made, and how does it work?
b. Give students these instructions:
  1. Obtain an empty milk carton, two identical thermometers, a cotton shoelace, and some thread.
  2. Cut a 10 cm section from the cotton shoelace and slip the section over the bulb of one of the thermometers. Tie the shoelace section with thread above and below the bulb to hold the shoelace in place. Thread the other end of the 10 cm section through a hole in the milk carton and allow it to rest in a small bottle or dish of water inside the milk carton.

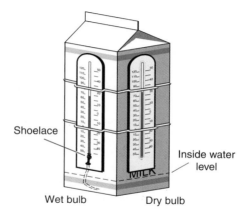

Shoelace

Inside water level

Wet bulb   Dry bulb

FINDING RELATIVE HUMIDITY IN PERCENT

Difference in degrees between wet-bulb and dry bulb thermometers

	1	2	3	4	5	6	7	8	9	10	11	12	13	14	15	16	17	18	19	20	21	22	23	24	25	26	27	28	29	30
30°	89	78	68	57	47	37	27	17	8																					
32°	90	79	69	60	50	41	31	22	13	4																				
34°	90	81	72	62	53	44	35	27	18	9	1																			
36°	91	82	73	65	56	48	39	31	23	14	6																			
38°	91	83	75	67	59	51	43	35	27	19	12	4																		
40°	92	84	76	68	61	53	46	38	31	23	16	9	2																	
42°	92	85	77	70	62	55	48	41	34	28	21	14	7																	
44°	93	85	78	71	64	57	51	44	37	31	24	18	12	5																
46°	93	86	79	72	65	59	53	46	40	34	28	22	16	10	4															
48°	93	87	80	73	67	60	54	48	42	36	31	25	19	14	8	3														
50°	93	87	81	74	68	62	56	50	44	39	33	28	22	17	12	7	2													
52°	94	88	81	75	69	63	58	52	46	41	36	30	25	20	15	10	6													
54°	94	88	82	76	70	65	59	54	48	43	38	33	28	23	18	14	9	5												
56°	94	88	82	77	71	66	61	55	50	45	40	35	31	26	21	17	12	8	4											
58°	94	89	83	77	72	67	62	57	52	47	42	38	33	28	24	20	15	11	7	3										
60°	94	89	84	78	73	68	63	58	53	49	44	40	35	31	27	22	18	14	10	6	2									
62°	94	89	84	79	74	69	64	60	55	50	46	41	37	33	29	25	21	17	13	9	6	2								
64°	95	90	85	79	75	70	66	61	56	52	48	43	39	35	31	27	23	20	16	12	9	5	2							
66°	95	90	85	80	76	71	66	62	58	53	49	45	41	37	33	29	26	22	18	15	11	8	5	1						
68°	95	90	85	81	76	72	67	63	59	55	51	47	43	39	35	31	28	24	21	17	14	11	8	4	1					
70°	95	90	86	81	77	72	68	64	60	56	52	48	44	40	37	33	30	26	23	20	17	13	10	7	4	1				
72°	95	91	86	82	78	73	69	65	61	57	53	49	46	42	39	35	32	28	25	22	19	16	13	10	7	4	1			
74°	95	91	86	82	78	74	70	66	62	58	54	51	47	44	40	37	34	30	27	24	21	18	15	12	9	7	4	1		
76°	96	91	87	83	78	74	70	67	63	59	55	52	48	45	42	38	35	32	29	26	23	20	17	14	12	9	6	4	1	
78°	96	91	87	83	79	75	71	67	64	60	57	53	50	46	43	40	37	34	31	28	25	22	19	16	14	11	9	6	4	1
80°	96	91	87	83	79	76	72	68	64	61	57	54	51	47	44	41	38	35	32	29	27	24	21	18	16	13	11	8	6	4
82°	96	91	87	83	79	76	72	69	65	62	58	55	52	49	46	43	40	37	34	31	28	25	23	20	18	15	13	10	8	6
84°	96	92	88	84	80	77	73	70	66	63	59	56	53	50	47	44	41	38	35	32	30	27	25	22	20	17	15	12	10	8
86°	96	92	88	84	80	77	73	70	66	63	60	57	54	51	48	45	42	39	37	34	31	29	26	24	21	19	17	14	12	10
88°	96	92	88	85	81	78	74	71	67	64	61	58	55	52	49	46	43	41	38	35	33	30	28	25	23	21	18	16	14	12
90°	96	92	88	85	81	78	74	71	68	64	61	58	56	53	50	47	44	42	39	37	34	32	29	27	24	22	20	18	16	14

Air temperature (reading of dry-bulb thermometer) in degrees fahrenheit

Example:
Temperature of dry-bulb thermometer 76°
Temperature of wet-bulb thermometer 68°
The difference is 8°

Find 76° in the dry-bulb column and 8° in the difference column. Where these two columns meet, you read the relative humidity. In this case, it is 67%.

3. Attach both thermometers to the milk carton as shown in the diagram. You now have a **hygrometer**—an instrument that measures the relative humidity in the atmosphere.

Note: The two thermometers should register the same temperature before the shoelace is placed over one of them; otherwise, the difference in readings must be considered a constant that is part of all computations.

4. When the shoelace is wet, fan it with a piece of cardboard for 1 minute.
5. Ask: *What do you think might happen to the thermometer with the wet shoelace? Why do you think so?*
6. Check the temperature readings of the two thermometers.
7. Ask: *How do you account for the difference in readings between the thermometer with the shoelace (called the "wet bulb") and the one without the shoelace (called the "dry bulb")?*
8. Explain that when the shoelace is wet, the evaporation of the water results in a cooling of the wet-bulb thermometer, whereas the dry-bulb thermometer will continue to read the temperature of the air around it.

Note: This is the same phenomenon that occurred in a previous activity where students placed one dry wool or cotton sock and one wet wool or cotton sock on their hands to show the cooling effect of evaporation.

9. Look at the relative humidity table provided. To locate the relative humidity on the table, find the temperature of the dry-bulb thermometer on the *y* axis (vertical axis) and the difference between the readings of the two thermometers on the *x* axis (horizontal axis). The example below the table shows a dry-bulb temperature of 76°F, a difference of 8°F (wet-bulb, 68°F), and a relative humidity of 67%.

10. Take readings on your hygrometer every day for 2 weeks and record your findings. Also try readings in different places.

EXPLAIN: USE DATA TO GENERATE INTERPRETATIONS, INCLUDING DESCRIPTIONS, CLASSIFICATIONS, PREDICTIONS, AND EXPLANATIONS.

c. Invite students to share their records from the exploration phase. Ask: *What reasons can you give for different readings?*

Using your hygrometer, can you predict which days are better for drying clothes outside?
How is relative humidity used by weather forecasters to predict weather?
Why were you asked to fan the wet-bulb thermometer?

▶ *Teaching Background*

Air contains moisture (from evaporated water from the ground, rivers, lakes, and oceans). Air pressure and temperature affect the amount of moisture air can hold at any given time. Relative humidity is the amount of water vapor actually contained in volume of air divided by the maximum amount that could be contained in the same volume.

III. THE EARTH'S OCEANS

Our earth has been called *the water planet.* Children are naturally drawn to water. "Whether they are playing in a pond, chasing waves at the beach, or splashing in a rain puddle on a city street, children are entranced by water" (Valerie Chase, 1997, *Living in Water.* Baltimore: National Aquarium in Baltimore, p. 1).

The earth's water is found in oceans, lakes, rivers, ponds, and streams; in ground water systems; and in ice and water vapor forms. Water circulates through the crust, atmosphere, and oceans of the earth in the *water cycle.* Rain falling on land collects in rivers and lakes, soil, and porous layers of rock, and much of it flows back to the oceans.

More than 97% of all the water on the earth is salt water in ocean basins. Oceans, as well as the land, are contained within the crust of the earth. Oceans cover 71% of the earth's surface, with land covering 29%. There are four oceans on the earth: Pacific Ocean, Atlantic Ocean, Indian Ocean, and Arctic Ocean. The Antarctic Ocean is included with the Pacific, Atlantic, and Indian Oceans. Seas, gulfs, and bays are all parts of oceans that are partially enclosed by land.

Ocean floors are typically 2 to 3 miles deep in the Pacific, Atlantic, and Indian Oceans. The Mariana Trench, stretching in the western Pacific from New Guinea toward the sea of Japan, reaches depths of 6.5 miles below sea level and about 3 miles below the level of the sea floor flanking it. In comparison, the Grand Canyon is about 1 mile deep and Mount Everest is about 5.5 miles above sea level.

Shores are places where land and sea meet, where we can take quiet walks and lose ourselves in thought or search for shells, driftwood, and strange creatures.

For plants and animals to survive in the ocean, on the ocean floor and ocean trenches, or on rocky shores they need to be able to adapt to tremendously varied conditions. For example, plants and animals on the seashore must resist battering ocean waves or find security in crevices and fissures. Most of the animals on sandy shores live below the surface. A sandy beach may appear lifeless, but when the tide rolls in, the inhabitants spring into action and an astounding variety of life is revealed.

NSES **Science Standards**

All students should develop an understanding of

- structure of the earth's systems (5–8).

Objectives for Students

1. Demonstrate that the water pressure in a body of water increases with depth.
2. Demonstrate and explain that the buoyant force of salt water is greater than the buoyant force of fresh water.
3. Compare the surface area of the earth that is ocean with that which is land.
4. Compare the amount of water in the oceans with the total amount of water in the earth system.
5. Identify a variety of foods that contain nutrients from ocean organisms.
6. Describe and explain the effects of pollution on life in water.

NSES **Concepts and Principles**

Fundamental concepts and principles that underlie the standards and relate to oceans include the following:

- In the course of the water cycle, water evaporates from the earth's surface, rises and cools as it moves to higher elevations, condenses as rain or snow, and falls to the surface where it collects in lakes, oceans, soils, and underground (5–8).
- Water is a solvent. As it passes through the water cycle it dissolves minerals and gases and carries them to the oceans (5–8).
- Oceans have a major effect on climate, because water in the ocean holds a large amount of heat (5–8).

1. WHAT PART OF THE EARTH'S SURFACE IS COVERED BY OCEANS? (3–6)

Materials

Inflatable globe (preferably showing natural land features rather than political boundaries)

ENGAGE: ASK A QUESTION ABOUT OBJECTS, ORGANISMS, OR EVENTS IN THE ENVIRONMENT.

a. Hold up the inflatable globe. Ask: *What is this globe a model of?* (Earth.) *How is it like the real earth and how is it different? What is shown on the globe's surface?* (Land and oceans.) *About how much of the earth is covered by oceans? How could we use the globe to find out?*

EXPLORE: PLAN AND CONDUCT SIMPLE INVESTIGATIONS TO COLLECT RELEVANT DATA.

b. Tell the class we need to collect data by using a sampling method. Help the student follow these steps:
   1. Show the class a two-column table with the headings "Ocean" and "Land."
   2. Select a student to be the record keeper.
   3. Instruct one student to toss the inflatable globe to another student.
   4. The person who catches the globe will look to see if his or her right thumb is on an ocean or land part of the globe's surface and report this information to the record keeper.
   5. The record keeper will make a tally mark in the appropriate column on the table.
   6. Then the inflatable globe should be tossed to another student and the process repeated.
   7. Continue for a total of 100 tosses.

EXPLAIN: USE THE DATA TO GENERATE INTERPRETATIONS, INCLUDING DESCRIPTIONS, CLASSIFICATIONS, AND EXPLANATIONS.

c. Ask: *How many times out of 100 tosses was the catcher's right thumb on an ocean area?* (Approximately 70 times.) *How many times out of 100 tosses was the catcher's right thumb on a land area?* (Approximately 30 times.)

d. Ask: *Why do you think the catcher's right thumb was on an ocean area more often than on a land area?* (Because more of the surface of the inflatable globe is ocean area so there is more chance of the catcher's right thumb being on an ocean.) Discuss the term *percent* with the class. *What percent of the times was the catcher's thumb on an ocean area?* (The answer should be close to 70%.) *What percent of the times was the catcher's thumb on a land area?* (Answer should be close to 30%.)

e. Challenge the class to find out what percent of the earth's surface is covered by oceans using their textbook or other references. (70%.) Ask the class to explain how well and why this sampling technique worked to estimate the relative amount of land and ocean on the earth's surface.

2. WHAT PART OF THE EARTH'S WATER IS IN THE OCEANS? (3–8)

Materials

Six 2-liter bottles
Graduated cylinders
Permanent marker
Colored water

ENGAGE: ASK A QUESTION ABOUT OBJECTS, ORGANISMS, OR EVENTS IN THE ENVIRONMENT.

a. Ask: *What part of the earth's water is in the oceans? How could we make a model to show this?*

b. Conduct this teacher demonstration:
   1. Show the class a 2-liter bottle labeled "All Earth's Water" filled with 2,000 ml of colored water. Tell them this represents all the water on the earth.
   2. Then display five other 2-liter bottles containing the following volumes of colored water on a table in front of a sheet of chart paper: Bottle A, 1,944 ml; Bottle B, 1,750 ml; Bottle C, 1,400 ml; Bottle D, 1,000 ml; Bottle E, 700 ml.
   3. Tell the students that one of these bottles represents the amount of water in the earth's oceans.
   4. Ask students to vote for the one they think represents the water in the earth's oceans by writing the letter of their choice on a Post-it note. Have the students stick their Post-it in a column above the bottle that matches the letter they chose.
   The class has just created a histogram of their ideas.

EXPLORE: PLAN AND CONDUCT SIMPLE INVESTIGATIONS TO COLLECT RELEVANT DATA.

c. Ask: *How could we find out which bottle best represents the amount of water in the earth's oceans?*

d. Ask groups of students to decide what information they would need and how they would make the bottle that represents the water in the earth's oceans. After they have had some discussion time, provide the information that 97.2% of the earth's water is in the oceans. You might also reveal that the bottle labeled "All Earth's Water" contains 2,000 ml of colored water. Allow groups to use colored water, graduated cylinders, and a 2-liter bottle to create a model that represents the amount of water in the oceans.

EXPLAIN: USE THE DATA TO GENERATE INTERPRETATIONS, INCLUDING DESCRIPTIONS, CLASSIFICATIONS, AND EXPLANATIONS.

e. Encourage groups to compare their completed model with the "All Earth's Water" bottle. Ask each group to explain to the class how they decided how much water to put in the bottle and how they carried out their idea.

f. Based on the models constructed by the groups, ask them to vote again (this time by a show of hands) for the lettered bottle that they think best represents the amount of water in the earth's oceans. (They should select bottle A.) Ask: *Are you surprised by how much of the earth's water is in the oceans? Do you think that the oceans are an important part of our planet? Why?*

ELABORATE: EXTEND CONCEPTS, PRINCIPLES, AND STRATEGIES TO NEW PROBLEMS AND QUESTIONS.

g. Ask students to list the places that water is found in the earth's system. Answers might include lakes, rivers, ponds, oceans, puddles, in the soil, underground, in the air as water vapor, in clouds as water droplets, frozen in ice caps and glaciers, and so on. Challenge them to find out how much of the earth's water is found in each and to create a visual representation of their findings. They might make a model or a circle graph.[4]

3. DO OBJECTS FLOAT DIFFERENTLY IN SALT WATER THAN IN FRESH WATER? (4–6)

Materials

Two raw eggs
Two clear glass containers
Box of Kosher or pickling salt, which can be purchased in many supermarkets. When dissolved in water, this salt produces a clear solution. Table salt can be substituted, but it makes a cloudy rather than a clear solution
Large container for mixing concentrated salt water

ENGAGE: ASK A QUESTION ABOUT OBJECTS, ORGANISMS, OR EVENTS IN THE ENVIRONMENT.

a. For this teacher demonstration you will need a mixture of concentrated salt water for one container and an equal amount of fresh water for the other container. Then follow these steps:
   1. Prepare the salt water by mixing one part salt with four parts cool water in a large container. For example, if you use 300 ml cups (10 oz), add half a cup of salt to 2 cups of water. Stir the salt-water mixture thoroughly until the salt dissolves.
   2. Pour concentrated salt water into one container and put an equal amount of fresh water in the other container.

b. Show the students the two containers of water without discussing their contents. Ask: *Do you think an egg will float in water?*

[4]Data relating to this investigation is available at http://www.sea.edu/k12lessonplans/ K12WatersEarth.htm.

EXPLORE: PLAN AND CONDUCT SIMPLE INVESTIGATIONS TO COLLECT RELEVANT DATA.

c. Put an egg in each container and ask: *What did you observe?* Discuss students observations with them.

EXPLAIN: USE DATA TO GENERATE INTERPRETATIONS, INCLUDING DESCRIPTIONS, CLASSIFICATIONS, PREDICTIONS, AND EXPLANATIONS.

d. Ask: *Why do you think the egg floated in one container of water and sank in the other one?* Through questioning and discussion, lead students to understand that salt water is denser than fresh water. The denser salt water was able to support the egg. Ask: *Would it be easier for you to float in a fresh water lake or in the ocean? Why?*

ELABORATE: EXTEND CONCEPTS, PRINCIPLES, AND STRATEGIES TO NEW SITUATIONS AND QUESTIONS.

e. Ask: *How much salt will need to be added to fresh water to increase its density so that it will support an egg?*

f. Place an egg in the fresh water. Add salt a spoonful at a time, stirring the water, until the egg rises and floats. Count the number of spoonfuls of salt needed. Measure the volume of salt added and compare it to the original volume of the water.[5]

4. WHAT AFFECTS THE PRESSURE OF A STREAM OF WATER? (3–5)

Materials

Plastic gallon milk jug

ENGAGE: ASK A QUESTION ABOUT OBJECT, ORGANISMS, OR EVENTS IN THE ENVIRONMENT.

a. Ask: *If the side of a plastic milk jug were punctured with very small holes (one above another) and the jug were then filled with water, what do you think would happen to the water? How would the water pour out of the holes?*

EXPLORE: PLAN AND CONDUCT SIMPLE INVESTIGATIONS TO COLLECT RELEVANT DATA.

b. Prepare and perform this teacher demonstration for students:
   1. Obtain a clean, plastic, 1-gallon milk jug.
   2. About 4 cm from the bottom of the milk jug, puncture a *very small hole* with a pencil or nail. Puncture three additional small holes 1 cm apart, vertically, above the first hole as in the diagram. Put masking tape over the holes.

   Note: Do not make the holes too large.

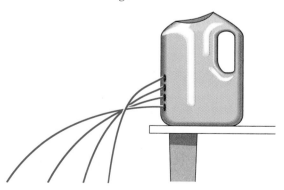

---

[5]For additional information on this activity, see Science and Technology for Children. (1995). *Floating and Sinking: Teacher's Guide*. Burlington, NC: Carolina Biological Supply.

3. Fill the container half full with water. Hold the plastic jug over a sink, large basin, or tub, and remove the masking tape as shown.

c. Ask: *What do you notice about the way the water comes out of the holes? Which stream went the greatest distance? Which stream went the least distance?*

EXPLAIN: USE DATA TO GENERATE INTERPRETATIONS, INCLUDING DESCRIPTIONS, CLASSIFICATIONS, PREDICTIONS, AND EXPLANATIONS.

d. Ask: *Why do you think the water comes out of the holes like this?*

e. Ask: *If the jug were filled closer to the top with water, do you think there would be a difference in the way the water comes out? Tape over the holes, refill the jug until the water is within a centimeter of the top, and remove the tape. Ask: What do you notice about the way the water comes out of the holes? What difference did you notice in the way the water came from the holes of the jug when there was less water and when there was more water in it?*

f. Ask: *What can you conclude about how water pressure varies with depth?*

ELABORATE: EXTEND CONCEPTS, PRINCIPLES, AND STRATEGIES TO NEW SITUATIONS AND QUESTIONS.

g. Ask: *What results do you think you would get if you used a quart, half-gallon, or 2-gallon container?* Try it and record your findings.

5. WHAT FOODS CONTAIN PRODUCTS FROM THE OCEAN? (4–6)

Materials

Food product labels
Grocery store advertisements
Sorting mats and transparency with a Venn diagram as shown

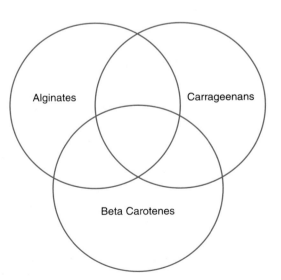

Preparation

Several weeks before this lesson, ask your students and colleagues to collect the ingredient lists from the following products they might use at home: brownie mix, cheese, chocolate milk, coffee creamer, cottage cheese, egg substitute, evaporated milk, frozen foods and desserts, frozen yogurt, ice cream, infant formula, margarine, mayonnaise, multiple vitamins, pet food, pudding, relishes, salad dressing, sauces and gravies, sour cream, toothpaste, whipped topping, whipping cream, and yogurt. Provide a box for collection of the labels and containers in your classroom.

ENGAGE: ASK A QUESTION ABOUT OBJECTS, ORGANISMS, OR EVENTS IN THE ENVIRONMENT.

a. Distribute the grocery store advertisements to the class and encourage them to look them over. Ask: *Do you eat anything that comes from the ocean?* (Students will probably suggest fish, shrimp, clams, etc.) *What do these products eat?* (Students will probably say other smaller animals in the ocean.) *Are there plants in the ocean?* (Students will probably say seaweed or algae.) *Do some of the animals in the ocean eat the ocean plants? Do you eat any of the ocean plants?* (Some students may know that seaweed is used to wrap sushi.)

EXPLORE: PLAN AND CONDUCT SIMPLE INVESTIGATIONS TO COLLECT RELEVANT DATA.

b. Guide students to collect data following these procedures:
   1. With students working in small groups (4 students per group is best), distribute to each group at least 10 ingredient lists from different products from the collection box. The groups do not need to have the same assortment of ingredient lists.
   2. Provide each group with a copy of the Venn diagram. Give the students a few minutes to look at their materials. Suggest that they use the Venn diagram to organize their ingredient lists based on the presence of alginates, carrageenans, and beta-carotenes.
   3. If students need assistance, display the transparency of the Venn diagram on the overhead projector and model the procedure. Ask a student to read an ingredient list to look for any or all of these ingredients. Then write the name of the product in the appropriate segment of the Venn diagram. Do several more examples if necessary.
   4. Each group should write the names of each of the products for which they have an ingredients list on their Venn diagram. If you want them to include more product names, they can switch label sets with another group.

EXPLAIN: USE DATA TO GENERATE INTERPRETATIONS, INCLUDING DESCRIPTIONS, CLASSIFICATIONS, AND EXPLANATIONS.

c. Ask the groups to share their findings with the class. Have them describe what the product names in each segment of the Venn diagram have in common.
d. Ask if anyone knows what these ingredients are. Then tell the students that each of these ingredients comes from seaweeds, which are large forms of marine algae that grow in coastal waters around the world. The three terms on the Venn diagram refer to compounds extracted from each of the three main kinds of marine algae: brown, red, and green. Alginates come from brown algae. They make water-based products thicker, creamier, and more stable. In ice cream, they prevent the formation of ice crystals. Carrageenans come from red algae. They are used in stabilizing and gelling foods, cosmetics, pharmaceuticals, and industrial products. Beta-carotene comes from green algae. It is a natural pigment that is used as yellow-orange food coloring and may help prevent certain types of cancers.

ELABORATE: EXTEND CONCEPTS, PRINCIPLES, AND STRATEGIES TO NEW PROBLEMS AND QUESTIONS.

e. Challenge students to find other products that contain these ingredients in their pantries or at the grocery store. Bring samples of edible seaweed such as nori, kombu, dulse, and kelp to class for students to observe. Explain that these marine algae are used in many Asian cuisines, often as wrappers for rice, meat, and vegetables (sushi). Using proper sanitation precautions, offer samples of the edible seaweed to students who wish to try it.

Source: This activity is based on two lessons from the internet: "There Are Algae in Your House!" from the Ocean Planet Website of the Smithsonian (http://seawifs. gsfc.nasa.gov/OCEAN_PLANET/HTML/education-lesson . . .) and "Is there Seaweed/Algae in your food?" from Neptune's Website: Oceanography lesson plans (http://pao.cnmoc. navy.mil/educate/Neptune/lesson/social/algae.htm).

6. WHAT ARE SOME EFFECTS OF WATER POLLUTION? (3–8)

Materials

For each group, 4 quart-sized or 2-liter clear containers (plastic soda bottles, food jars with covers, etc.)
Tap water aged for 3 to 4 days
Soil and/or gravel from an aquarium or pond
Water with algae and other aquatic microorganisms from a freshwater aquarium or a pond
Measuring cups and spoons
Plant fertilizer
Hand lenses for each group
Liquid laundry detergent (not green)
Motor oil
Vinegar

Preparation

Two weeks in advance of conducting this activity, four jars should be set up by you and designated student helpers for each cooperative group of students:
1. Fill four containers one-third full with aged tap water, add 4 cm of pond soil or aquarium gravel, and then fill the rest of the jar with pond water and algae.
2. Add 1 teaspoon of plant fertilizer to each jar, stir well, and loosely screw on the jar covers.
3. Put the jars near the window in good, indirect light or under a strong artificial light.
4. Label the jars A, B, C, and D.

ENGAGE: ASK A QUESTION ABOUT OBJECTS, ORGANISMS, OR EVENTS IN THE ENVIRONMENT.

a. Ask: *What things do people do, sometimes unknowingly, that result in water pollution? How can water pollution affect water environments in ways that are detrimental to the organisms that live in or depend on the water?*

EXPLORE: PLAN AND CONDUCT SIMPLE INVESTIGATIONS TO COLLECT RELEVANT DATA.

b. Guide students to conduct this investigation:
1. Provide each group of students the four jars that were set up 2 weeks earlier. The jars contain pond water, algae, pond soil or aquarium gravel, and fertilizer.
2. Instruct the groups to observe and describe on their record sheets how each jar looks. Make sure students use hand lenses.

RECORDING OBSERVATIONS		
Date _____ Observers'/Recorders' Names _____		
Jar	Observation Before Additive	Observation after Additive
A		
B		
C		
D		

3. Students should add 2 tablespoons of detergent to jar A; enough motor oil to cover the surface of jar B; and 1/4 to 1/2 cup (250 mL) of vinegar to jar C. Jar D will not have any additive and will be the control. See the diagram.

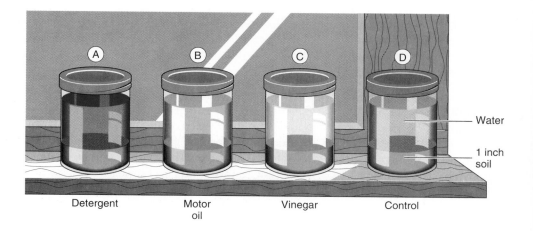

Detergent   Motor oil   Vinegar   Control   Water   1 inch soil

4. Students should loosely cover the jars and return them to the light as before.
5. Ask: *What do you think might happen in each of the jars?*
6. Provide time for students to observe and record their observations two to three times a week. After 4 weeks, groups should summarize their observations.

EXPLAIN: USE DATA TO GENERATE INTERPRETATIONS, INCLUDING DESCRIPTIONS, CLASSIFICATIONS, PREDICTIONS, AND EXPLANATIONS.

c. Ask: *What changes did each jar go through? Why do you think jars A, B, and C went through such changes?*

ELABORATE: EXTEND CONCEPTS, PRINCIPLES, AND STRATEGIES TO NEW SITUATIONS AND QUESTIONS.

    d. Ask: *How could you apply these findings?*
How might you set up activities to try to reverse the effects of the pollutants used in jars A, B, and C?
Where in everyday life do we see the effects of water pollution like that in jars A, B, and C?
How could these effects be prevented?

7. HOW CAN WE TRY TO REVERSE THE EFFECTS OF AN OIL SPILL? (3–8)

Materials

Aluminum pan
Motor oil
Feathers
Paper towels
Dishwashing liquid
Four hard-boiled eggs
Paper plate
Very large rubber band
Turkey baster

ENGAGE: ASK A QUESTION ABOUT OBJECTS, ORGANISMS, OR EVENTS IN THE ENVIRONMENT.

    a. Ask: *How difficult do you think it is to clean up an oil spill? How do you think it could be done?*
What is the most effective way to clean up an oil spill?
What devastating effects does an oil spill have on the environment?

EXPLORE: PLAN AND CONDUCT SIMPLE INVESTIGATIONS TO COLLECT RELEVANT DATA.

    b. Fill an aluminum pan half full of water, cover the water surface with motor oil, and use it for the following parts of the activity.

    c. Feathers in an oil–water mix. Leave feathers in the oil–water mix for several minutes. Remove the feathers. Ask: *How do you think we might remove oil from the feathers?* Try wiping the feathers with paper towels. Ask: *Did wiping with paper towels remove all the oil?* Try cleaning the feathers with dishwashing liquid. Ask: *Which method of cleaning the oil off the feathers was better? What other ways might we try to remove the oil from feathers?* Try them.

    d. Eggs in an oil–water mix. Put four hard-boiled eggs (with shells on) into the oil–water mix and then remove one egg at a time after each of these intervals: 15 minutes, 30 minutes, 60 minutes, and 120 minutes. Ask: *What happens to the eggs?* Try removing the oil from the eggs with the methods you used for the feathers. After cleaning the oil off the eggs, crack and remove the shells. Ask: *Did the oil get inside the egg that was in the oil for 15 minutes? the one for 30 minutes? the one for 60 minutes? the one for 120 minutes?* Record your findings. Ask: *If oil did get into the egg, can it be removed?*

    e. Removing or containing oil. Using the following materials, how might you remove or keep the oil from spreading: paper towel, dishwashing liquid, turkey baster, large rubber band? Lay a paper towel on the surface of the oil and let it stay for 3 minutes. Remove the paper towel and put it on the paper plate. Ask: *What do you see happening to the paper towel and oil?* Add more motor oil, if needed, and spread a very large rubber band on the top of the oil. Ask: *What happens to the oil?* Using the turkey baster, try to remove the oil. Ask: *What happens to the oil?* Replace the oil into the pan of water. Add several drops of dishwashing liquid. Ask: *What happens to the oil? Ask: Which method was best for removing the oil? Which method was best for keeping the oil together in one place?*

EXPLAIN: USE DATA TO GENERATE INTERPRETATIONS, INCLUDING DESCRIPTIONS, CLASSIFICATIONS, PREDICTIONS, AND EXPLANATIONS.

f. Ask: *What possible problems and adverse effects might result when chemicals are used to remove oil from animals in a real oil spill? How might an oil spill in Alaska affect people in the continental United States? Sometimes oil spills are purposely set on fire. What adverse effects might this have on the environment?* Lead students to understand that oil spills adversely affect land and water plants and animals directly by coating them with oil, often leading to their deaths. In addition, an oil spill affects future plant and animal life by destroying eggs and interfering with plant reproduction. Sometimes, the procedures used to reverse oil spills can interfere with environmental interrelationships, especially when chemicals are used.

Additional Activities Related to Oceans

Scientific study of the oceans bridges many science disciplines. Marine biologists monitor animals and plants that live in ocean habitats. Some chemists investigate mineral content and salinity levels of oceans. Physical oceanographers study wave and tidal action. Meteorologists observe weather systems affected by ocean currents. Therefore, many of the activities from previous sections could be included in a study of the oceans.

- Activities on the water cycle, such as "How Much Water Evaporates from an Open Aquarium?" (p. A-238), "Where Does Water Go When It Evaporates?" (p. A-239), "How Can You Promote the Evaporation of Water?" (p. A-239), and "What Is Condensation? How Does It Occur?" (p. A-243) can contribute to an understanding of how water circulates between land, the atmosphere, and bodies of water.
- Activities on aquariums, including "How Can I Construct an Aquarium Habitat?" (p. A-178), "What Can I Observe in an Aquarium?" (p. A-180), and "What Environmental Factors Affect Life in an Aquarium Habitat?" (p. A-181) involve simulations of marine environments.
- "How Can Salt Crystals Be Grown?" (p. A-227) could help to explain formation of sea salt and the increased salinity of some tidal pools. "How Can Evaporation and Condensation Be Used to Desalinate Salt Water?" (p. A-244) further explores the nature of salt water.

IV. VIEWING THE SKY FROM EARTH

A. POSITIONS AND MOTIONS OF THE SUN, MOON, AND STARS

▶ *Science Background*

Beyond the earth's atmosphere, other objects are visible in the earth's sky. The brightest and most noticeable of these is our sun, the star at the center of our solar system. Energy from the sun heats both the ocean and land, drives the process of photosynthesis enabling plants to produce food, and illuminates our world during the daytime. Our moon appears about the size of the sun in our sky, though it does not shine as brightly. Rather than producing its own light, the moon is visible because of reflected sunlight. Other planets in our solar system are also visible in the earth's sky. Mercury, Venus, Mars,

Jupiter, and Saturn appear at times in the night sky, looking like bright, non-twinkling stars. The other, more distant planets can be viewed through telescopes, but cannot be located with just the naked-eye. A clear night sky also reveals patterns of stars, known as constellations.

Objects in our sky appear to move because the earth rotates on its axis once every 24 hours, the period known as 1 day. Though it appears that the sun, moon, planets, and most of the stars rise in the east and set in the west, it is really the earth's turning that is responsible for this apparent motion. Polaris, the North Star, because of its unique location directly above the earth's north pole, appears to remain stationary in the sky for viewers in the northern hemisphere.

Through the following activities, discussion, and expository teaching you will help the students begin to develop an understanding of these fundamental principles about distant objects in the sky:

1. The sun, moon, and stars all have properties, locations, and movements that can be observed and described.
2. The sun has a pattern of movement through the sky. It appears to move across the sky in the same way every day, but its path slowly changes during the seasons.
3. The moon appears to move across the sky much like the sun.
4. The observable shape of the moon changes from day to day in a cycle that lasts about a month.
5. Stars, in their constellations, appear to move in the sky during the night.
6. Most objects in the solar system are in regular and predictable motion. Those motions explain such phenomena as the day and the phases of the moon.

Understanding of these principles can be developed from an early age, beginning with observations over time, and progress at higher grade levels to the development of explanations for the observed phenomena.

NSES **Science Standards**

As a result of their science activities, all students should develop an understanding of

- objects in the sky (K–4).
- changes in the earth and sky (K–4).
- the earth in the solar system (5–8).

Objectives for Students

1. Observe and describe properties, locations, and movements of the sun, moon, and stars in the sky.
2. Describe the apparent daily motion of the sun across the sky and discuss how this motion varies during the year.
3. Compare and contrast the apparent motion of the sun across the sky with the apparent motion of the moon across the sky.
4. Observe, describe, and name the moon's phases as they change during the month, and explain why this happens.
5. Use compass directions and angles to describe the position of objects in the sky.

NSES

Concepts and Principles

Activities 1–4 are daytime astronomy activities involving the observation of shadows. They address these fundamental concepts and principles related to the *Science Standards:*

- The sun, moon, and stars all have properties, locations, and movements that can be observed and described (K–4).
- The sun has a pattern of movement through the sky. It appears to move across the sky in the same way every day, but its path slowly changes during the season (K–4).

1. WHAT CAUSES SHADOWS? (K–2)

Materials   Overhead projector
Projection screen or blank wall

ENGAGE: ASK A QUESTION ABOUT OBJECTS, ORGANISMS, OR EVENTS IN THE ENVIRONMENT.

a. Turn on the overhead projector so that it illuminates the projection screen or blank wall. Select several students to stand between the projector and the screen (facing the screen). Ask: *What do you see on the screen?* (Shadows.) *What causes these shadows?*

EXPLORE: PLAN AND CONDUCT SIMPLE INVESTIGATIONS TO COLLECT RELEVANT DATA.

b. Ask: *What is necessary for a shadow to form? If we didn't have the light from the overhead or the students standing here would there be a shadow on the screen? How could we find out?* Students may suggest having the volunteer students move out of the light, or turning off the overhead. Try these things and other suggestions they may come up with.

EXPLAIN: USE DATA TO GENERATE INTERPRETATIONS, INCLUDING DESCRIPTIONS, CLASSIFICATIONS, AND EXPLANATIONS.

c. Ask: *When were shadows produced? What did they look like? What two things must you have to create a shadow?* Lead the children to the realization that in order to have a shadow there must be a light source and an object to block the light. Encourage them to develop an operational definition of a shadow. (A dark area caused by the blocking of light.)

2. HOW CAN SHADOWS BE CHANGED? (K–2)

Materials   Flashlight
Two large sheets of white paper
Scissors
Plastic funnel
Pencil or crayon

ENGAGE: ASK A QUESTION ABOUT OBJECTS, ORGANISMS, OR EVENTS IN THE ENVIRONMENT.

a. Ask: *Are shadows of the same object always the same size and shape?* Encourage students to share their ideas.

EXPLORE: PLAN AND CONDUCT SIMPLE INVESTIGATIONS TO COLLECT RELEVANT DATA.

b. Working with a partner, students should put a funnel on a large sheet of white paper. Suggest that they use the flashlight to make a shadow of the funnel on the paper. Encourage them to try shining the flashlight from different positions. Ask: *How does the shadow change?*

c. Suggest that students do the following to record the size and shape of two shadows. One student should shine the flashlight on the funnel while the other one traces and cuts the shadow shape out with the scissors, in this sequence:

   1. First, while holding the flashlight low and to the side, trace and cut out the shadow of the funnel. Label it "low."

   2. Next, switch roles with your partner. Put a new piece of white paper under the funnel, hold the flashlight high, and then trace and cut out the shadow of the funnel. Label it "high."

   3. Compare the size and shape of the two cutout shadows.

EXPLAIN: USE DATA TO GENERATE INTERPRETATIONS, INCLUDING DESCRIPTIONS, CLASSIFICATIONS, AND EXPLANATIONS.

d. Ask: *Are both of your shadow shapes the same?* (No.) *How are they different?* (They are different sizes and shapes.) *Which one is longer?* (The one labeled "low" is longer.) *Which one is shorter?* (The one labeled "high" is shorter.) *What caused the difference in shapes?* (The position of the light source.) Try to lead the students to the conclusion that the position of the light source affects the shadow's size and shape. When the light source is low, shining on the object from the side, the shadow is long and when the light source is high, shining down on the object from above, the shadow is short.

ELABORATE: EXTEND CONCEPTS, PRINCIPLES, AND STRATEGIES TO NEW PROBLEMS AND QUESTIONS.

e. Ask: *What happens to the shadow if you move the light source in an arc from one side of the object, over it, and to the other side of the object?* This simulates the apparent motion of the sun in the sky and provides background experience for future activities.

3. HOW DO SHADOWS CAUSED BY THE SUN CHANGE DURING THE DAY? (K–4)

Materials

Flagpole or fence post
Sidewalk chalk
Paint stirrers (to use as stakes in the lawn)

ENGAGE: ASK A QUESTION ABOUT OBJECTS, ORGANISMS, OR EVENTS IN THE ENVIRONMENT.

a. Ask: *Do you think that shadows outdoors change during the day? How might we find out?*

EXPLORE: PLAN AND CONDUCT SIMPLE INVESTIGATIONS TO COLLECT RELEVANT DATA.

b. On a sunny day, take the class outside to the flagpole or a fence post early in the morning. Ask: *Does the flagpole or fence post have a shadow? How could we mark the position of this shadow?*

c. Show the students the sidewalk chalk and paint stirrers if they need a hint. Have the students identify the "end" of the shadow, that is, the part cast by the top of the flagpole or the fence post. If the end of the shadow falls on concrete, sidewalk chalk can be used to mark its position. If the end of the shadow falls on grass, a paint stirrer can be used as a stake to mark its position. Record the time of the observation either in chalk on the concrete or with pencil on the paint stirrer. Throughout the day, about once each hour if possible, return to the flagpole or fence post with the class to mark the shadow's current position.

EXPLAIN: USE DATA TO GENERATE INTERPRETATIONS, INCLUDING DESCRIPTIONS, CLASSIFICATIONS, AND EXPLANATIONS.

d. After making the final afternoon observation, ask: *What did you find out about how the shadow changed during the day?* (It started out long on that side, then got shorter, then got longer on the other side.) *Why do you think the shadow changed in this way?* (Because the sun seemed to move across the sky.) *How did the position of the sun change during our observations today?* (Indicating directions, lead students to understand that it started out low over there in the morning, moved higher in the sky around noon, then kept moving that way in the afternoon.) Develop the concept that the sun appeared to move from east to west in the sky during the day and that caused the size, shape, and direction of the shadow to change over time.

ELABORATE: EXTEND CONCEPTS, PRINCIPLES, AND STRATEGIES TO NEW PROBLEMS AND QUESTIONS.

e. Ask: *Do you think the flagpole or fence post shadow will change the same way tomorrow? next week? next month? How could we find out?* Assist the students in continuing their investigation of shadow positions throughout the school year and help them look for patterns in their findings.

4. HOW CAN SHADOWS TELL YOU WHEN IT IS LOCAL NOON? (4–6)

Materials (For each small group of students)

Long nail
Hammer
Sheets of white paper (8.5 × 11 inches)
Rectangular board big enough to hold the paper
Pencil
Clock or watch
Metric ruler

ENGAGE: ASK A QUESTION ABOUT OBJECTS, ORGANISMS, OR EVENTS IN THE ENVIRONMENT.

a. Ask: *On a sunny day, at what time are shadows the shortest? How could we find out? How does the position of the sun in the sky relate to the length of the shadow cast by an object?*

b. Put a piece of paper in the middle of the board. Hammer the nail into the board and paper as shown, making sure the nail will not easily come out of the board.

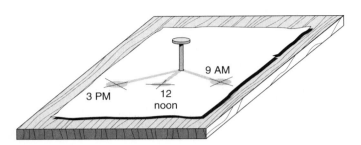

c. Late in the morning about 10:30, place the board where it will get sunlight until about 2:00 in the afternoon. Do not move the board during your observations. Every half hour or at shorter intervals, draw an X at the end of the shadow cast by the nail. Beside the X, note the time of each observation.

d. Upon returning to the classroom, carefully measure the distance between each X and the nail to the nearest millimeter. Create a data table that shows the time of the observation and the length of the corresponding shadow. Construct a line graph to represent these data. The manipulated or independent variable, "time of observation," should be plotted on the x axis; the responding or dependent variable, "shadow length," should be plotted on the y axis.

EXPLAIN: USE
DATA TO GENERATE
INTERPRETATIONS,
INCLUDING DESCRIPTIONS,
CLASSIFICATIONS, AND
EXPLANATIONS.

e. Ask: *Did the shadow length change during your observation period? When was it shortest? When would you expect to have the shortest shadow?* (When the sun was highest in the sky.) Explain that "local noon" occurs when the sun is at its highest point above the horizon for a given day. Local noon does occur in the middle of the day at a given location, but because time zones cover large geographic areas, local noon probably does not occur exactly at 12:00 noon according to your accurately set clock. Daylight savings time, which shifts the time by 1 hour during certain months of the year, also affects the clock time that local noon occurs. Ask: *Is local noon exactly at 12:00 noon on the clock at our location? How do you know?*

ELABORATE: EXTEND
CONCEPTS, PRINCIPLES,
AND STRATEGIES TO NEW
PROBLEMS AND
QUESTIONS.

f. Ask: *Do you think local noon will occur at the same time tomorrow at this location? How could we find out? How could you modify your observations to be more certain of the actual time of local noon? Do you expect students in other towns to find the same time for local noon at their location? Why or why not? How could you find out?* (Students might suggest sharing data electronically with schools in other geographic areas.)

NSES   Concepts and Principles

Activities 5–7 relate to the relative positions and motions of the sun, earth, and moon. They address these fundamental concepts and principles related to the *Science Standards:*

- The sun, moon, and stars all have properties, locations, and movements that can be observed and described (K–4).
- The sun has a pattern of movement through the sky. It appears to move across the sky in the same way every day, but its path slowly changes during the season (K–4).

5. WHY IS THERE DAY AND NIGHT? (2–4)

Materials

Styrofoam ball (about the size of a baseball)
Craft stick and brad for each small group
Lamp with a bright bulb (at least 100 watts)
Globe
Room that can be darkened
Small lump of sticky tack

ENGAGE: ASK A QUESTION ABOUT OBJECTS, ORGANISMS, OR EVENTS IN THE ENVIRONMENT.

a. Ask: *What do you think causes day and night? Does every place on earth have daytime or nighttime at the same time?*

EXPLORE: PLAN AND CONDUCT SIMPLE INVESTIGATIONS TO COLLECT RELEVANT DATA.

b. Distribute a ball, craft stick, and brad to each small group. Demonstrate how to assemble these parts as shown.

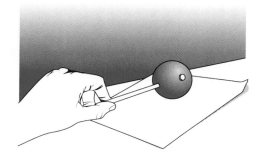

c. Have the students hold the ball by the craft stick. Then darken the room lights and turn on the bright light. Tell students to discover what they can about the way the ball is lit and record observations about their ball. The following questions might guide their thinking: *How much of the ball is lit up? Is the brad in the lit part? If not, what can you do to the ball to move the brad to the lit part? If you became tiny and were on the brad on the lit side of the ball, would you be able to see the bright light bulb? If you were tiny and were on the brad on the unlit side of the ball, would you be able to see the bright light bulb?*

EXPLAIN: USE DATA TO GENERATE INTERPRETATIONS, INCLUDING DESCRIPTIONS, CLASSIFICATIONS, AND EXPLANATIONS.

d. Ask the class to share their observations of the balls in the bright light.

e. Show the globe to the class. Ask: *What is the globe a model of?* (earth.) *How is the globe like the earth? How is it different?* Place the lamp several meters from the globe and darken the room. Then, turn on the bright bulb. Ask: *What do you think the bright bulb is a model of?* (The sun.) *How is the bright bulb like the sun? How is it different? Is the entire globe lit by the bright light? How much of it is lit?* (One half.) *Which half?* (The half toward the bright light.) *How does this model now show day and night?* (The lit side of the earth is having daytime, and the unlit side is having nighttime.) *What happens when I turn the globe?* (The places that are lit change.) *Are the same places on the earth having daytime when the globe is turned?* (No.)

f. Stick the small lump of sticky tack on the globe to mark the location of your school. Ask: *Is it day or night where the sticky tack is? What could I do to the globe so that the sticky tack is having daytime, then nighttime, then daytime, and so on?*

g. Slowly spin the globe on its axis in a counterclockwise direction as viewed from above the north pole. As the sticky tack moves from darkness into the light, explain to the students that this is sunrise for the people at that location. When the sticky tack is in the center of the lit side of the globe, with the light shining directly onto it, it is noon for the people at that location. When the sticky tack moves from the lit to the unlit area, it is sunset. When the sticky tack is in the center of the unlit area, on the side of the earth away from the sun, it is midnight.

6. HOW DOES THE APPEARANCE OF THE MOON'S SHAPE CHANGE OVER TIME? (2–4)

Materials

Black construction paper
Soft white chalk

ENGAGE: ASK A QUESTION ABOUT OBJECTS, ORGANISMS, OR EVENTS IN THE ENVIRONMENT.

a. Distribute materials to the students. Give them 5 minutes to draw the shape of the moon. Post the pictures for all to see. Ask: *Are all the drawings the same shape?* (No.) Sort them so that similar shapes are grouped together. Ask representatives from each group to tell why they drew the moon the way they did. Ask: *Can everyone's drawing be correct even if they are different shapes?* (Yes.) *How can this be?* (The moon doesn't always appear the same shape.) *How could we find out how the appearance of the moon's shape changes over time?* (Hopefully, someone will suggest observing and recording the moon's appearance in the sky for a week or so.)

EXPLORE: PLAN AND CONDUCT SIMPLE INVESTIGATIONS TO COLLECT RELEVANT DATA.

b. Have the students take home a large sheet of black construction paper and some white chalk, then observe the moon daily for a week. They should divide their paper into eight equal rectangles as shown.

Moon Calendar by Suzy	11/5	11/6	11/7
11/8	11/9	11/10	11/11

Students can use the first rectangle for the title and their name and the remaining seven spaces for their daily observations. It is best to begin this assignment several days after new moon when fair weather is expected—the waxing crescent moon should be visible in the western sky shortly after sunset. Assuming it is clear, the moon should be visible in the evening sky for the next week. If there is an overcast night, students should indicate on their chart that the sky was cloudy.

EXPLAIN: USE DATA TO GENERATE INTERPRETATIONS, INCLUDING DESCRIPTIONS, CLASSIFICATIONS, AND EXPLANATIONS.

c. At the end of the observation period, students should bring their moon calendars to class to share and compare. Ask: *How did the moon's shape seem to change during the week?* Have them see if everyone's observations supported the same conclusions. Ask: *Did more of the moon appear to be illuminated each night?* Tell the students that the apparent shape of the moon is known as its phase. Use a chart like this to introduce the names of the phases. Challenge the students to identify which phases they observed.

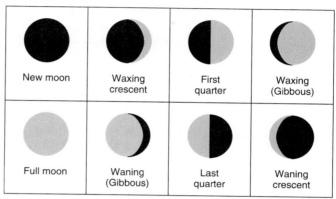

Phases of the Moon as Seen from the Earth

ELABORATE: EXTEND CONCEPTS, PRINCIPLES, AND STRATEGIES TO NEW PROBLEMS AND QUESTIONS.

d. Ask students to predict what the moon will look like for the next few days, then make observations to check their predictions.

An ongoing Moonwatch Bulletin Board[6] could be maintained in your classroom. Each night, have three students draw the shape of the moon on an index card. Have the three students compare their drawings and arrive at one drawing that represents their observations. Post the drawing on the appropriate month/date cell on the bulletin board calendar. As a pattern develops, have the class predict the next day's moon phase.

7. WHY DOES IT APPEAR THAT THERE ARE PHASES OF THE MOON? (4–6)

Materials

Styrofoam ball (about the size of a baseball) and a craft stick for each student
Lamp with a bright bulb (at least 100 watts)
A room that can be darkened

ENGAGE: ASK A QUESTION ABOUT OBJECTS, ORGANISMS, OR EVENTS IN THE ENVIRONMENT.

a. Ask: *What are moon phases? Why does the moon have phases?*

EXPLORE: PLAN AND CONDUCT SIMPLE INVESTIGATIONS TO COLLECT RELEVANT DATA.

b. Use some simple objects to create a model that shows the cause of the moon's phases as viewed from the earth. In this model a styrofoam ball represents the moon, a bright light bulb represents the sun, and your head represents the earth. Your eyes will see the view of the moon phase from the earth.

---

[6]For additional details on moon watches, see G. Robert Moore, "Revisiting Science Concepts," *Science and Children* 32(3), November/December 1994, 31–32, 60.

c. Insert the craft stick into the styrofoam ball to act as a handle. Hold the moon ball in your left hand with your arm outstretched. Ask: *How much of the moon ball can you see at one time?* Darken the room. Ask: *Is it easy to see the moon ball? Is any part of it illuminated?* Turn on the bright light bulb to represent the sun. Look at the moon ball from several angles. Ask: *Is part of it illuminated now? How much of the moon ball is illuminated at the same time?* Describe the location of the lit part in relation to the bright light.

d. The moon orbits around the earth each month. To simulate this in your model, stand facing the bright light, hold the moon ball in your left hand so that the moon ball appears to be a little to the left of the light bulb. Ask: *Is a lit area visible on the moon ball when it is in this position?* Describe it. (The right edge of the moon ball is illuminated in a narrow crescent shape.) Slowly turn to your left, keeping your arm holding the moon ball outstretched. Watch how the illuminated part of the moon ball varies as its position changes. If the moon ball goes into the shadow cast by your head, just lift the moon ball a little higher so the light can reach it. Move the moon ball around its orbit several times. Look for patterns in the way it is illuminated.

EXPLAIN: USE DATA TO GENERATE INTERPRETATIONS, INCLUDING DESCRIPTIONS, CLASSIFICATIONS, AND EXPLANATIONS.

e. Have a class discussion about the questions posed in the explore phase of the lesson. Lead the students to an understanding of the following concepts.
   1. The moon does not produce its own light, it reflects light from the sun.
   2. Half of the moon, that half facing the sun, is illuminated at any given time.
   3. We can only see half of the moon's surface at any given time, the half that is facing the earth.
   4. Depending on the relative positions of the earth, sun, and moon, only part of the illuminated moon's surface may be facing the earth, so we see phases of the moon.

ELABORATE: EXTEND CONCEPTS, PRINCIPLES, AND STRATEGIES TO NEW PROBLEMS AND QUESTIONS.

f. Have the students complete an illustration showing the apparent moon phase when the moon is at various positions in its orbit around the earth. This illustration is really a two-dimensional model to explain why the moon appears to have phases. A completed illustration might look something like the following diagram.

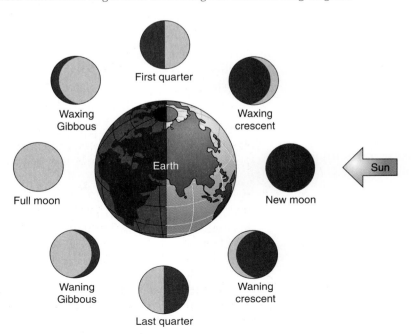

Concepts and Principles

Activity 8 introduces an easy way for students to describe the location in the sky of celestial objects. It addresses this fundamental principle related to the Science Standards:

- The sun, moon, and stars all have properties, locations, and movements that can be observed and described.

8. HOW CAN WE DESCRIBE POSITIONS OF OBJECTS IN THE SKY? (4–6)

Materials

Cardinal direction signs
Ten index cards each labeled with a large number from 1 to 10
Masking tape or sticky tack
Adding machine tape
"Handy Angle Measurements" sheet

ENGAGE: ASK A QUESTION ABOUT OBJECTS, ORGANISMS, OR EVENTS IN THE ENVIRONMENT.

a. Post cardinal directions—north, south, east, and west—on the classroom walls. Post the 10 index cards at various locations on the walls and ceiling of the classroom. Put a strip of adding machine tape all the way around the room at the students' seated eye level. This represents the horizon.

b. Ask: *How could you explain to someone where to look for a particular object in the sky? What kinds of measurements and units might be helpful?* Ask several students to describe the location of something in the classroom. Discuss alternative approaches.

EXPLORE: PLAN AND CONDUCT SIMPLE INVESTIGATIONS TO COLLECT RELEVANT DATA.

c. Point out the cardinal directions signs posted in the room. Distribute copies of the "Handy Angle Measurements" sheet shown in the diagram on page A-278. Demonstrate how to extend your arm, and discuss the angles represented by the different parts of the hand. Mention that the adding machine tape around the room represents the horizon, the starting point for their angle measurements. Ask the students to try to measure the angle from the horizon line to the point straight overhead using an outstretched arm and clenched fist. It should take approximately nine fists, since the angle from the horizon to the point overhead (zenith) is 90 degrees and each fist represents about 10 degrees.

d. Have the students number from one to ten on a sheet of paper. Ask them to use cardinal directions and angle measurements to describe the position of each index card number posted in the room, from their seat.

Note: Because the cards are relatively close to the observers, the observing position will affect the results. Do not expect students in different parts of the room to have the same direction and angle measurement for each card.

EXPLAIN: USE DATA TO GENERATE INTERPRETATIONS, INCLUDING DESCRIPTIONS, CLASSIFICATIONS, AND EXPLANATIONS.

e. Ask: *How were you able to describe the positions of the index cards?* (By finding the direction to look and measuring how high above the horizon with my outstretched hand.)
   Could you use this same technique to describe the position of objects in the sky? What would you need to know to be successful? (Cardinal directions.)

Safety Precautions

Caution students to never look directly at the sun. The sun is very bright. Looking at it could cause blindness. Only use this technique to describe the location of the moon, stars, planets, and so on.

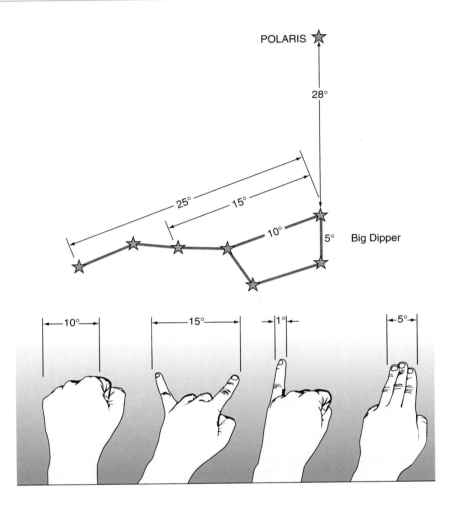

f. Apply this measuring technique to describing the position of the moon in the sky. Find out how the moon moves across the sky during the night. Determine the cardinal directions around your observation point. A compass, street map, or locating Polaris (the North Star) should help.

g. Record your observations in a data table like the one shown.

ELABORATE: EXTEND CONCEPTS, PRINCIPLES, AND STRATEGIES TO NEW PROBLEMS AND QUESTIONS.

Time of Observation	Direction	Angle above the Horizon
7:30 PM		
8:00 PM		
8:30 PM		
9:00 PM		
9:30 PM		
10:00 PM		

Observe and record the position of the moon at half-hour intervals. Describe how the moon moves during the night. Develop an investigation to determine how the position of the moon at a given hour changes from night to night. Ask: *What did you find?*

h. If you live in the northern hemisphere, you can determine your latitude by measuring the position of Polaris above the horizon. Polaris is the end star in the handle of the Little Dipper. The pointer stars of the Big Dipper are helpful in finding Polaris. Polaris is *not* the brightest star in the sky. To find it, face the northern horizon. Look for the patterns shown in the handy angle measurement diagram. The orientation of the Big Dipper will vary, but its pointer stars always point toward Polaris. Decide which star is Polaris. Determine how many degrees it is above the horizon using the Handy Angle Measurement technique. That number of degrees should be the same as the latitude of your observation position. Note the position of Polaris relative to objects on the ground (trees, houses, etc.). Try finding Polaris several hours later. Ask: *Is it still in the same angle above the horizon? Is it still in the same place relative to the objects on the ground?*

You might notice that while Polaris is in the same location, the nearby star patterns have seemed to move in a counterclockwise direction around Polaris. Activity 5, Making a Star Clock in the GEMS (Great Explorations in Math and Science) Module *Earth, Moon, and Stars*, is a very good activity related to the motion of the circumpolar constellations (those around the pole).[7]

B. MODELS OF THE SOLAR SYSTEM AND THE EARTH-MOON SYSTEM

▶ *Science Background*

Our solar system includes the sun (our star), nine planets, and numerous smaller bodies including asteroids and comets that orbit around the sun. The four planets closest to the Sun—Mercury, Venus, Earth, and Mars—are known as the inner planets. They are relatively small, rocky bodies. The other five planets—Jupiter, Saturn, Uranus, Neptune, and Pluto—are known as the outer planets. All of the outer planets except Pluto are large and gaseous. Pluto is small and believed to be icy. The orbits of the planets lie roughly in the same plane and are elliptical in shape.

The earth-moon system is unique in the solar system. Other planets have moons, but the earth is the only planet with just one very large moon. Although much smaller than the sun, our moon appears about the same size in our sky. This is because it is much closer to the earth.

Scale models are an obvious strategy for helping students develop the concepts of relative sizes and distances in space.

Through the following activities, discussion, and expository teaching, you will help the students begin to develop an understanding of the relative sizes and distances in our solar system and in the earth-moon system.

NSES **Science Standards**

All students should develop an understanding of

• the earth in the solar system (5–8).

---

[7]For many good astronomy activities see Sneider, Cary I. (1986). *Earth, Moon, and Stars*. Great Explorations in Math and Science (GEMS). Berkeley: Lawrence Hall of Science, University of California.

Objectives for Students

1. Demonstrate and describe a scale model of our solar system.
2. Name the planets in order of size.
3. Name the planets in order of distance from the sun.
4. Demonstrate and describe a model of the earth-moon system.

 NSES Concepts and Principles

Activities 1–3 relate to the use of models to represent the vast sizes and distances found within our solar system. The activities address these fundamental concepts and principles that support the *Science Standards:*

- The earth is the third planet from the sun in a system that includes the moon, the sun, eight other planets and their moons, and smaller objects, such as asteroids and comets (5–8).
- The sun, an average star, is the central and largest body in the solar system (5–8).
- Models can represent the real world, making abstract concepts more concrete (5–8).

1. HOW SPREAD OUT ARE THE PLANETS IN OUR SOLAR SYSTEM? (3–6)

Materials

Ten sentence strips, each labeled with one of the solar system bodies (Sun, Mercury, Venus, Earth, Mars, Jupiter, Saturn, Uranus, Neptune, Pluto)

ENGAGE: ASK A QUESTION ABOUT OBJECTS, ORGANISMS, OR EVENTS IN THE ENVIRONMENT.

a. Ask students to draw a picture showing what they know about the orbits of the planets around the sun in our solar system. To assess students' prior knowledge, ask: *How many planets did you include? Could you name the planets? Do you think you placed the planets in the right order from the sun? Are the orbits of the planets all the same distance apart? What is a scale model? Was your drawing a scale model? Why or why not?*

EXPLORE: PLAN AND CONDUCT SIMPLE INVESTIGATIONS TO COLLECT RELEVANT DATA.

b. Select 10 students to represent the major bodies in the solar system. Give each of them a labeled sentence strip to hold.

Select a starting place at one edge of the playground or at the end of a very long hall. Instruct the sign holding students to follow these instructions for constructing the model solar system.

1. The "sun" stands at one end of the area.
2. Mercury takes 4 small steps from the sun.
3. Venus takes 3 small steps outward from Mercury.
4. Earth takes 2 small steps beyond Venus.
5. Mars takes 5 small steps beyond Earth.
6. Jupiter takes 34 small steps beyond Mars.
7. Saturn takes 40 small steps beyond Jupiter.
8. Uranus takes 90 small steps beyond Saturn.
9. Neptune takes 100 small steps beyond Uranus.
10. Pluto takes 88 small steps beyond Neptune.

c. Tell the class that the positions of the students with the signs represent the average distance between the planets' orbits. With the holders remaining in their places and holding up their signs all the students should observe the spacing and think about these questions: *Which planets' orbits are closest together? Which ones are really spread out? Are the planets' orbits spaced at equal distances from the sun?*

EXPLAIN: USE DATA TO GENERATE INTERPRETATIONS, INCLUDING DESCRIPTIONS, CLASSIFICATIONS, AND EXPLANATIONS.

d. Upon returning to the classroom, discuss the students' responses to the questions. Important ideas to emerge from the discussion include the following:
  - The first four planets—Mercury, Venus, Earth, and Mars—do not have much distance between their orbits. These planets are known as the inner planets.
  - The rest of the planets—Jupiter, Saturn, Uranus, Neptune, and Pluto—have rather large distances between their orbits. These planets are known as the outer planets.

Explain that the planets are not usually lined up as in our model. The model does not show the actual positions of the planets, but the relative spacing of their orbits.

2. HOW DO THE PLANETS IN OUR SOLAR SYSTEM COMPARE IN SIZE? (5–8)

Materials

Butcher paper
Pencils
Markers
Scissors
Metersticks
Metric rulers or metric tapes

ENGAGE: ASK A QUESTION ABOUT OBJECTS, ORGANISMS, OR EVENTS IN THE ENVIRONMENT.

a. Cut out a circle with a diameter of 5.6 cm to represent Earth. Show the circle to the class. Ask: *If we made a scale model of the planets in our solar system, how big would each planet be if Earth was this big?*

b. Have the class count off by eights. Tell each of the "ones" to draw a circle to represent Mercury in this model. Each of the "twos" should draw Venus to this scale, and so on. When the models showing student's prior knowledge are cut out, ask all the "ones" to bring their Mercury circles to the front of the room. Compare the range of sizes represented and how these circles compare with the Earth circle. Ask: *What does this tell us about what these people know about the size of Mercury compared to Earth?* Repeat this procedure with each of the other number groups and their cutout planets. You will probably be able to conclude that as a class we really are not sure how the planets compare in size.

EXPLORE: PLAN AND CONDUCT SIMPLE INVESTIGATIONS TO COLLECT RELEVANT DATA.

c. Tell the class that the diameter of the Earth circle in our model is 5.6 cm. Measure its diameter so they can confirm its size. Tell them that you will give each person the diameter measurement of their planet, so that they can make an accurate scale model for our solar system models. The following table includes the data:

Group Number from Counting Off	Planet	Diameter in Centimeters
Ones	Mercury	2.1
Twos	Venus	5.3
Threes	Mars	3.0
Fours	Jupiter	62.6
Fives	Saturn	52.8
Sixes	Uranus	22.4
Sevens	Neptune	21.7
Eights	Pluto	1.0

It may be necessary to review the meaning of the term *diameter*—the distance across the circle through the center. If students are reminded that diameter = 2 × radius, they might realize that if they find the radius (half of the diameter) of their circle and swing the radius around a center point, they will get a circle of the proper diameter. This technique is especially useful for the big planet circles.

d. After each circle is cut out, it should be labeled with the name of the planet it represents. Students should have the diameter of their planet circle checked for accuracy by at least two other students and make any necessary corrections.

e. Encourage students to get into solar system groups of eight so that there is one model of each planet in their group. Provide each group with a 5.6 cm diameter Earth circle. Challenge the groups to use their models to make a list of the planets in order of size from smallest to largest.

EXPLAIN: USE DATA TO GENERATE INTERPRETATIONS, INCLUDING DESCRIPTIONS, CLASSIFICATIONS, AND EXPLANATIONS.

f. Ask: *How did you compare the planets' sizes?* (We made scale models.) *Are our models the actual sizes of the planets?* (No. They are much smaller, but are "to scale" so they can be compared.) You may want to explain that in our model 1 cm = approximately 2,285 km. At this scale, the diameter of the sun would be approximately 6 meters. Perhaps you could draw a circle with a diameter of 6 meters on the playground so they could see how big the sun is compared to the planets. Ask: *Do our models show the actual shapes of the planets?* (No. Planets are spheres, not circles. We made a two-dimensional rather than a three-dimensional model.)

g. Ask: *What did you learn about the relative sizes of planets?* (They vary greatly in size.) *What was the order of the planets from smallest to largest diameter?* (Pluto, Mercury, Mars, Venus, Earth, Neptune, Uranus, Saturn, Jupiter.)

ELABORATE: EXTEND CONCEPTS, PRINCIPLES, AND STRATEGIES TO NEW PROBLEMS AND QUESTIONS.

h. Ask students to make up comparison questions about the relative diameters of the planets, for example: *Which planet has a diameter about half Earth's diameter?* (Mars.) *How many Earth diameters would fit in one Jupiter diameter?* (Eleven.) Have them challenge each other to find the answers using the scale models as an aid.

3. HOW COULD YOU MAKE A SCALE MODEL OF THE EARTH AND MOON? (5–8)

Materials

Basketball
Volleyball
Softball
Baseball
Tennis ball
Golf ball
Ping-Pong ball
Piece of rope 7.28 meters long
Metric rulers

ENGAGE: ASK A QUESTION ABOUT OBJECTS, ORGANISMS, OR EVENTS IN THE ENVIRONMENT.

a. Hold up the basketball. Tell the class that in our model of the earth and moon, it will represent Earth. Display the other balls. Ask: *Which ball would you select to represent the size of the moon in our model?* Record responses on a histogram on the board. *What would we need to know to determine which ball best represents the size of the moon when the earth is the size of a basketball?* (The actual diameter of the earth and the moon.)

EXPLORE: PLAN AND CONDUCT SIMPLE INVESTIGATIONS TO COLLECT RELEVANT DATA.

b. The diameter of the earth is 12,756 km and the diameter of the moon is 3,475 km. Ask: *What information do we need to collect about the balls to select the best ball to represent the moon?* Have the students get into small groups to come up with a plan to determine which ball would represent the moon. Carry out your plan.

EXPLAIN: USE DATA TO GENERATE INTERPRETATIONS, INCLUDING DESCRIPTIONS, CLASSIFICATIONS, AND EXPLANATIONS.

c. Ask: *Which ball did your group select to be the best moon ball if the earth is the size of the basketball?* (The tennis ball is best, because the earth's diameter is about 3.7 times the diameter of the moon, and the basketball's diameter is about 3.7 times the diameter of the tennis ball.)

Ask: *What procedures did your group use to solve this problem?* (Measured the balls, used ratios, etc.) This might be an appropriate time for a review about ratios and proportions. *What is the scale of this model?* (1 cm on this model = approximately 530 km in reality.)

ELABORATE: EXTEND CONCEPTS, PRINCIPLES, AND STRATEGIES TO NEW PROBLEMS AND QUESTIONS.

d. Ask: *If we use the basketball to represent the earth and the tennis ball to represent the moon, how far apart should they be held to represent the actual distance between the earth and the moon?* Ask a student to hold the basketball to represent the earth. Start with the tennis ball close to the basketball and slowly walk away. Ask the students to tell you when you should stop. As different groups of students or individuals tell you the distance is right, stick a piece of tape on the wall or floor to show the distance they predicted. After all have expressed their ideas, move back close to the basketball. Give the student holding the basketball one end of the 7.28 meter rope. Slowly unwrap the rope as you retrace your steps away from the basketball. When you get to the end of the rope, hold up the tennis ball. Now the model represents the relative sizes of the earth and the moon and how far they are apart. The actual distance from the earth to the moon is approximately 384,000 km. The moon is approximately 30 Earth-diameters from the earth.

Appendixes

Sixty Years of Elementary School Science: A Guided Tour

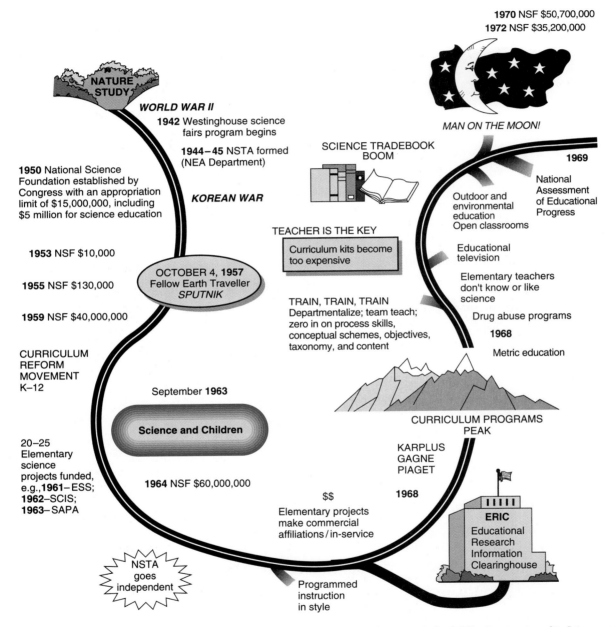

1970 NSF $50,700,000
1972 NSF $35,200,000

NATURE STUDY

MAN ON THE MOON!

WORLD WAR II

1942 Westinghouse science fairs program begins

1944–45 NSTA formed (NEA Department)

SCIENCE TRADEBOOK BOOM

1969

1950 National Science Foundation established by Congress with an appropriation limit of $15,000,000, including $5 million for science education

KOREAN WAR

National Assessment of Educational Progress

Outdoor and environmental education Open classrooms

TEACHER IS THE KEY

Educational television

1953 NSF $10,000

Curriculum kits become too expensive

OCTOBER 4, 1957 Fellow Earth Traveller *SPUTNIK*

Elementary teachers don't know or like science

1955 NSF $130,000

TRAIN, TRAIN, TRAIN Departmentalize; team teach; zero in on process skills, conceptual schemes, objectives, taxonomy, and content

Drug abuse programs

1968

1959 NSF $40,000,000

Metric education

CURRICULUM REFORM MOVEMENT K–12

September 1963

Science and Children

CURRICULUM PROGRAMS PEAK

KARPLUS GAGNE PIAGET

20–25 Elementary science projects funded, e.g., 1961–ESS; 1962–SCIS; 1963–SAPA

1964 NSF $60,000,000

$$ Elementary projects make commercial affiliations / in-service

1968

ERIC Educational Research Information Clearinghouse

NSTA goes independent

Programmed instruction in style

Source: Modified from Phyllis R. Marcuccio "Forty-Five Years of Elementary School Science: A Guided Tour" as it appeared in *Science and Children 24,* no. 4 (January 1987): 12-14. Copyright 1987 by the National Science Teachers Association. Reproduced with permission.

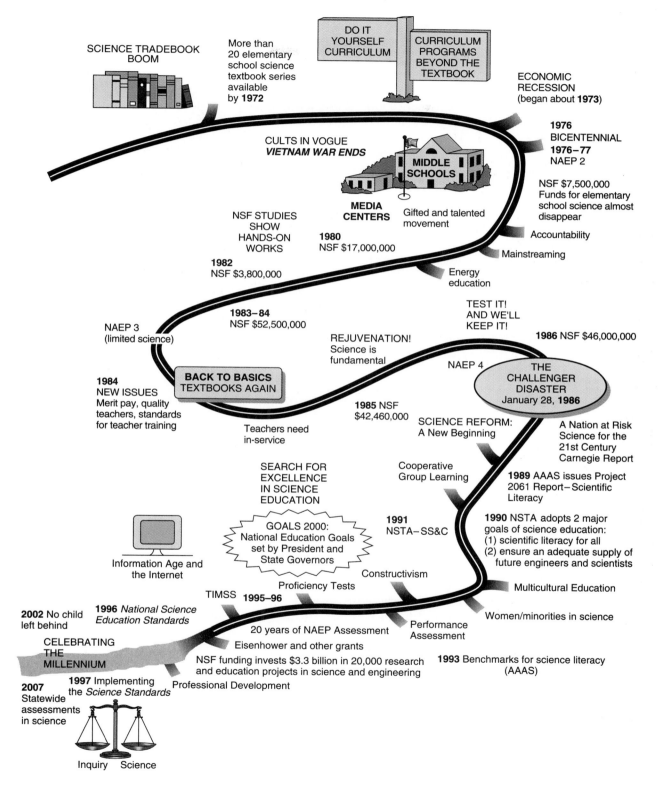

SCIENCE TRADEBOOK BOOM

More than 20 elementary school science textbook series available by **1972**

DO IT YOURSELF CURRICULUM

CURRICULUM PROGRAMS BEYOND THE TEXTBOOK

ECONOMIC RECESSION (began about **1973**)

CULTS IN VOGUE *VIETNAM WAR ENDS*

MIDDLE SCHOOLS

MEDIA CENTERS

Gifted and talented movement

1976 BICENTENNIAL **1976–77** NAEP 2

NSF $7,500,000 Funds for elementary school science almost disappear

Accountability

Mainstreaming

NSF STUDIES SHOW HANDS-ON WORKS

1980 NSF $17,000,000

1982 NSF $3,800,000

Energy education

1983–84 NSF $52,500,000

TEST IT! AND WE'LL KEEP IT!

1986 NSF $46,000,000

NAEP 3 (limited science)

REJUVENATION! Science is fundamental

NAEP 4

THE CHALLENGER DISASTER January 28, **1986**

1984 NEW ISSUES Merit pay, quality teachers, standards for teacher training

BACK TO BASICS TEXTBOOKS AGAIN

1985 NSF $42,460,000

SCIENCE REFORM: A New Beginning

A Nation at Risk Science for the 21st Century Carnegie Report

Teachers need in-service

Cooperative Group Learning

1989 AAAS issues Project 2061 Report–Scientific Literacy

SEARCH FOR EXCELLENCE IN SCIENCE EDUCATION

Information Age and the Internet

GOALS 2000: National Education Goals set by President and State Governors

1991 NSTA–SS&C

Constructivism

1990 NSTA adopts 2 major goals of science education: (1) scientific literacy for all (2) ensure an adequate supply of future engineers and scientists

Multicultural Education

Proficiency Tests

TIMSS **1995–96**

2002 No child left behind

1996 *National Science Education Standards*

CELEBRATING THE MILLENNIUM

2007 Statewide assessments in science

1997 Implementing the *Science Standards*

20 years of NAEP Assessment

Eisenhower and other grants

NSF funding invests $3.3 billion in 20,000 research and education projects in science and engineering

Professional Development

Performance Assessment

Women/minorities in science

1993 Benchmarks for science literacy (AAAS)

Inquiry   Science

AP-3

Notes on the Guided Tour

Notable Achievements

- Elementary school science now has a niche in elementary schools: It is accepted as important for all students, it is integrated with other subjects in the curriculum, and it is supported by principals and other administrators led by a government that expects all of its citizens to be scientifically literate.
- There is a new breed of elementary science specialists.
- Hands-on teaching is giving rise to inquiry and technology to foster creativity, intuition, and problem-solving skills. (Hands-on teachers are "guides" rather than "tellers.") The popularity of hands-on inquiry teaching is also creating a need for more in-service training and for more science centers and labs.
- Nonschool settings, such as outdoor education centers and museums, have increased their support, often introducing subject matter that includes issues of social concern like pollution, ecology, and energy education.
- Teaching tools—books, software, videos, and other multimedia products—drive the changing curricula.
- Up-to-date research in science education is readily available through the Eisenhower Clearinghouse.
- Recent and projected certification programs subject teachers to more rigorous standards.
- Studies and testing, forums and conferences exist to deal specifically with the concerns of elementary science.
- The business and industry communities, concerned about the interrelationships of science, technology, and society, have sought a role in science education. Organizations like the American Chemical Society, the National Academy of Science, and the American Association for the Advancement of Science have also cooperated to forward the cause of science education.
- SI metric measure has been generally adopted to in science education.
- A teamwork approach to curriculum building now exists among teachers, scientists, administrators, community, and government.
- There are established pockets of commitment to science, and programs have been developed to point out excellent science teaching throughout the country.

Familiar Road Signs

- Surges in National Science Foundation funding
- Efforts following crisis situations
- The continuing presence of textbooks
- National Assessment of Educational Progress reports
- Calls for new curricula
- Calls for in-service programs

Some Remaining Problems

- Teachers continue to be educated in the same way.
- No comprehensive, agreed-upon scope and sequence has been established.
- Progress depends on funds from the National Science Foundation.

- The pool of students interested in science is shrinking—nearly half the current ninth grade class in urban high schools will not even graduate, let alone seek science-related careers.
- Despite millions of dollars spent on curriculum studies, teachers still depend on textbooks.
- The United States continues to lag behind other countries in the amount of science being taught to children.
- The best science students are not attracted to science teaching careers.
- Average Americans care more for pseudoscience than science.
- Teachers do not apply educational research.
- Attaining proficiency for all students on statewide assessments in science is a continuing challenge for students, teachers, and schools.

Science Supplies, Equipment, and Materials Obtainable from Community Sources

This is only a partial list of possible community sources for science program materials in elementary and middle schools. Other sources that should not be overlooked include parents, the janitor or custodian of the school, the school cafeteria, radio and television repair shops, florists' shops, other teachers in the school, junior and senior high school science teachers, and so on. The materials are there; it just takes a little looking.

There are times, though, when in spite of the most careful searching, certain pieces of equipment or supplies are not obtainable from local sources; there are also many things that schools should buy from scientific supply houses. A partial list of some selected, reliable scientific supply houses is provided in Appendix C.

Dollar Store or Department Store

balloons
balls
compasses (magnetic)
cotton (absorbent)
flashlights
food coloring
glues and paste
inks
magnifying glasses
marbles
mechanical toys
mirrors
mousetraps
paper towels
scissors
sponges
staples
thermometers

Drugstore

adhesive tape
alcohol (rubbing)
bottles
cigar boxes
cold cream
corks
cotton
dilute acids, preferably 1–5%
dilute H_2O_2 (1.5%)
forceps or tweezers
limewater
medicine droppers
pipe cleaners
rubber stoppers
soda bicarbonate

spatulas
straws
sulfur
Tes-Tape™
tincture of iodine, diluted to straw color

Electrical Appliance Shop

bell wire
dry cells
electric fans
flashlight bulbs
flashlights
friction tape
magnets (from old appliances)
soldering iron

Fabric Shop

cardboard tubes
cheesecloth
flannel
knitting needles
leather
needles
netting
scraps of different kinds of fabrics
silk thread
spools

Farm or Dairy

birds' nests
bottles
clay
containers
gravel

hay or straw
humus
insects
leaves
loam
lodestone
rocks
sand
seeds

Fire Department

samples of materials used to extinguish various types of fires
water pumping equipment

Plant Nursery or Garden Supply Store

bulbs (tulips, etc.)
fertilizers
flowerpots
garden hose
garden twine
growing plants
labels
lime
peat pots
seed catalogs
seeds
spray guns
sprinkling cans
trowels and other garden tools

Service Station

ball bearings
cans
copper tubing

gears
gear transmissions
grease
inner tubes
jacks
maps
pulleys
tools
valves from tires
wheels

Grocery Store

aluminum foil
aluminum pie tins
ammonia
baking soda
borax
cellophane
clothespins
cornstarch
corrugated cardboard boxes
food storage bags
fruits
granulated sugar
paper bags
paper towels
paraffin
plastic wrap
salt
sandwich bags
sealable plastic bags
sponges
vegetables
vinegar
wax
wax paper

Hardware Store

brace and bits
cement
chisels
clocks
corks
dry-cell batteries
electric push buttons, lamps, and
    sockets
extension cords
files

flashlights
fruit jars
glass cutters
glass friction rods
glass funnels
glass tubing
hammers
hard rubber rods
insulated copper wire
lamp chimneys
metal and metal scraps
metersticks
nails
nuts and bolts
paints and varnishes
plaster of paris
pulleys
sandpaper
saws
scales
scrap lumber
screening
screwdrivers
screws
steel wool
thermometers (indoor and outdoor)
3–6 volt toy electric motors
tin snips
turpentine
wheelbarrow
window glass (broken pieces will do)
wire
yardsticks

Machine Shop

ball bearings
iron filings
iron rods
magnets
nuts and bolts
scrap metals
screws
wire

**Medical Centers, Dental Offices,
or Hospitals**

corks
flasks

funnels
glass tubing
lenses
litmus paper
microscopes
models, such as teeth
rubber sheeting
rubber stoppers
rubber tubing
test tube holders
test tubes
thermometers
tongue depressors

Music Shop

broken string and drumheads
musical instruments
pitch pipes
tuning forks

Pet Shop

air pumps
animal cages
ant houses
aquariums
cages
fish
insects
nets (butterfly, fish, etc.)
plastic tubing
strainers
terrariums

Restaurant or Fast-Food Outlet

beverage stirrers
bones (chicken, etc.)
bottles
cans (coffee, 5-gallon size)
drums (ice cream)
five-gallon cans (oil)
food coloring
gallon jars (widemouthed, pickles, mayon-
    naise, etc.)
gallon jugs (vinegar)
pie tins
plastic spoons
plastic trays
soda straws

Note: For additional sources of common, easily obtained supplies and apparatus suitable for your elementary or middle school science program, see *The NSTA Guide: Science Education Suppliers* (Arlington, VA: National Science Teachers Association, published annually).

Selected Sources of Scientific Supplies, Models, Living Things, Kits, and Software

Brock Optical

Microscopes—rugged enough for small children
E-mail: magiscope@aol.com
URL: http://www.magiscope.com

Carolina Biological Supply Company

Instructional materials for all sciences; Science and Technology for Children (STC) guides and materials
E-mail: carolina@carolina.com
URL: http://www.carolina.com

Delta Education

Materials, kits, and activities for hands-on science programs, including FOSS, SCIS 3 + , and DSMII (Delta Science Modules)
E-mail: ecurran@delta-edu.com
URL: http://www.delta-education.com

Discovery Scope

Small, hand-held microscopes
E-mail: dscopes@aol.com
URL: http://www.discoveryscope.net

Educational Innovations

Heat-sensitive paper, UV-detecting beads, Cartesian diver, super-absorbent polymers, and other science supplies
E-mail: info@teachersource.com
URL: http://www.teachersource.com

Educational Products, Inc.

Science fair display boards and materials
E-mail: kdavis@educationalproducts.com
URL: http://www.educationalproducts.com

Estes Industries

Model rockets
E-mail: agrimm@centurims.com
URL: http://www.esteseducator.com

ETA/Cuisenaire

Hands-on science materials
E-mail: info@etacuisenaire.com
URL: http://www.etacuisenaire.com

Fisher Science Education

Instructional materials for all sciences
E-mail: info@fisheredu.com
URL: http://www.fisheredu.com

Forestry Suppliers, Inc.

Orienteering compasses, water, soil, and biological test kits, tree borers, soil sieves, rock picks, weather instruments, and other materials for interdisciplinary science teaching
E-mail: fsi@forestry-suppliers.com
URL: http://www.forestry-suppliers.com

Ken-A-Vision Manufacturing Co., Inc.

Microscopes
E-mail: info@ken-a-vision.com
URL: http://www.ken-a-vision.com

Lab-Aids, Inc.

Single-concept hands-on kits for chemistry, biology, environmental science, and earth science
E-mail: customerservice@lab-aids.com
URL: http://www.lab-aids.com

Learning Technologies, Inc.

Portable planetariums and other materials for astronomy teaching
E-mail: starlab@starlab.com
URL: http://www.starlab.com

Mountain Home Biological

Living materials, barn owl pellets, skull sets
E-mail: mtnhome@gorge.net
URL: http://www.pelletlab.com

NASCO

Science, materials and supplies
E-mail: info@enasco.com
URL: http://www.nascofa.com

National Gardening Association

GrowLab guides for kids' gardening, professional development materials on plant science
E-mail: MK@garden.org
URL: http://www.kidsgardening.com

NSTA Science Store

Books, posters, software, CD-ROMs
URL: http://www.nsta.org

Ohaus Corporation

Balances and measurement aids
E-mail: cs@ohaus.com
URL: http://www.ohaus.com

Pitsco LEGO Educational Division

LEGO construction kits, model hot air balloons, educational technology products
E-mail: pitsco@pitsco.com
URL: http://www.pitsco-legodacta.com

Rainbow Symphony, Inc.

Lesson kits for the study of light and color, specialty optics materials, diffraction gratings, 3-D lenses, solar eclipse safe-viewing glasses
E-mail: kathy@rainbowsymphony.com
URL: http://www.rainbowsymphony.com

Sargent-Welch

GEMS materials, materials for all sciences
E-mail: Sarwel@Sargentwelch.com
URL: http://www.Sargentwelch.com

TOPS Learning Systems

Science lessons using simple available materials
E-mail: tops@canby.com
URL: http://www.topsscience.org

Source: Compiled from advertisements and Web searches.

Noncommercial Sources and Containers for Living Things

Organisms	Noncommercial Source	Culture Containers
POND SNAILS	Freshwater ponds, creeks	Aquaria, large battery jars, gallon glass jars
LAND SNAILS	Mature hardwood forests: on rocks, fallen logs, damp foliage	Terraria, large battery jars
DAPHNIA	Freshwater ponds: at water's edge, and associated with algae	Gallon glass or plastic jars
ISOPODS AND CRICKETS	Under rocks, bricks, and boards that have lain on the ground for some time; between grass and base of brick buildings	Glass or plastic terraria, plastic sweater boxes (Provide vents in cover.)
MEALWORM BEETLES	Corn cribs, around granaries	Gallon glass jars with cheesecloth
FRUIT FLIES	Trap with bananas or apple slices. (Place fruit in a jar with a funnel for a top.)	Tall baby food jars, plastic vials (Punch hole in jar lids, cover with masking tape, and then prick tiny holes in tape with a pin.)
WINGLESS PEA APHIDS*	Search on garden vegetables (e.g., English peas)	On pea plants potted in plastic pots, milk cartons (keep aphids in a large terrarium so they cannot wander to other plants in the school.)
GUPPIES	Obtain free from persons who raise guppies as a hobby. (They are usually glad to reduce the population when they clean tanks.)	Aquaria, large battery jars
CHAMELEONS*	Dense foliage along river banks or railroad tracks. (Catch with net or large tea strainer.)	Prepare a cage using a broken aquarium. (Broken glass can be replaced by taping cloth screening along sides.)
FROGS*	Along edges of ponds, ditches, creeks (Catch with large scoop net.)	Large plastic ice chest (Set near a sink so a constant water supply can be provided.)
CHLAMYDOMONAS AND EUGLENA	Freshwater pond	Gallon glass jars, aquaria, battery jars
ELODEA (ANARCHARIS)*	Ponds, creeks: usually along edge or in shallows	Aquaria, large battery jars
EELGRASS*	Wading zone or brackish water	Aquaria, large battery jars

| DUCKWEED | Edge of ponds or freshwater swamps | Aquaria, large battery jars |
| COLEUS AND GERANIUM | Persons who raise them (Start by rooting cuttings in 1 part sand, 1 part vermiculite, in plastic bags.) | Clay pots, milk cartons, tin cans |

Source: Carolyn H. Hampton and Carol D. Hampton. "The Establishment of a Life Science Center." Reproduced with permission by *Science and Children* 15 (7), (April 1978), 9. Copyright 1978 by The National Science Teachers Association, 1840 Wilson Blvd., Arlington, VA 22201–3000.

*These species are difficult to obtain from their natural habitats. Unless you have a convenient source, it is better to buy them commercially. Try a local aquarium, pet shop, or science supply house.

Note: For additional excellent articles on raising and using living things in elementary school classrooms, see Carol Hampton, Carolyn H. Hampton, and David Kramer, *Classroom Creature Culture: Algae to Anoles,* rev. ed., 1994, Arlington, VA: National Science Teachers Association.

Constructing Storage Areas for Supplies and Houses for Living Things

Your classroom has unused space that can be used for storage, such as spaces below window ledges, countertops, sinks, above and around heating units (radiators), and even under student desks.

You can purchase excellent commercially made cabinets that fit any of these spaces, or your students and/or your custodian and you can construct them. With some creativity, you and your students can arrange these cabinets in a variety of ways.

Small Items Storage

With an inquiry-based science program, you will constantly need to store many small items. Shoe, corrugated cardboard, cigar, and other small boxes provide space for collecting, organizing, and storing small, readily available materials for particular science areas. The following diagrams illustrate how to construct and store shoe boxes for small science items. Cardboard or clear plastic shoe boxes may be used. You may also use large cardboard boxes for storage, placing them in easily obtained wood or steel shelving units especially designed for this purpose. Your custodian can help with this.

SHOE BOX COLLECTION

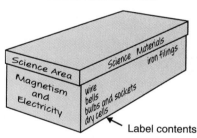

Living Things Storage

Encourage your students to bring small animals (including insects) and plants into your classroom. To be well prepared, have the following kinds of containers available:

- Insect cages
- Small animal cages
- Aquariums
- Terrariums

Insect Cages.[1]

Use small cake pans, coffee can lids, or covers from ice cream cartons for the cage cover and base. Roll wire screening into a cylinder to fit the base and then lace the screening together with a strand of wire.

---

[1] For additional information about insects in the classroom, see: Laurel D. Hansen, Roger D. Akre, and Elizabeth A. Myhre, "Homes Away from Home: Observe Insects Indoors with These Creature Containers," *Science and Children* 31(1), September 1993, 28–31; Rebecca Olien, "Worm Your Way Into Science—Experiments with These Familiar Creatures Promote a Better Understanding of the Natural World," *Science and Children* 31(1), September 1993, 25–27.

STORAGE OF SHOE BOX COLLECTIONS

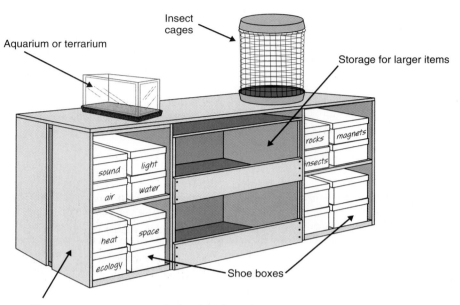

Insect cages

Aquarium or terrarium

Storage for larger items

rocks   magnets

insects

sound   light

air   water

heat   space

ecology

Shoe boxes

Four orange crates, two vertical, two horizontal

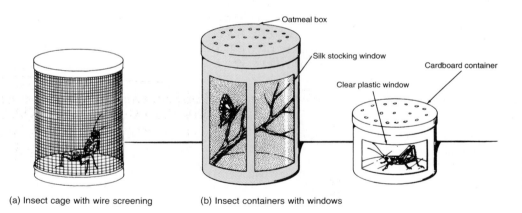

Oatmeal box

Silk stocking window

Cardboard container

Clear plastic window

(a) Insect cage with wire screening

(b) Insect containers with windows

You can cut windows in a paper coffee container, oatmeal box, or another suitable cardboard or Styrofoam container. Cut out the window and glue clear plastic wrap, cellophane, silk, a nylon stocking, or some other thin fabric over the opening as shown.

Another home for insects such as ants that live in the soil can be made by filling a widemouthed quart or gallon pickle or mayonnaise jar with soil up to 2 inches from the top. Cover the jar with a nylon stocking and place it in a pan of water. Put the insects in and cover the jar with black construction paper to simulate the darkness of being underground.

Small Animal Cages.

You can also use some of the insect cages for other small animals. Larger animals can be housed in cages that you and your students construct from window screening. Cut and fold the screening as shown in the diagram. Use nylon screening or be very careful of the sharp edges of wire screening. Tack or staple three sides of the screening to a wooden base and hook the other side for a door.

For housing *nongnawing* animals, you will need a wooden box and sleeping materials such as wood shavings. *Gnawing* animals need a wire cage. A bottle with a one-hole stopper and tubing hung on the side of the cage will supply water. Before proceeding, consult publications such as *Science and Children* and read some of the articles on the care and maintenance of various animals.

Terrariums.

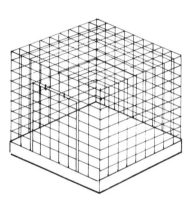

The word *terrarium* means "little world." In setting up a terrarium for any animal, you should try to duplicate in miniature the environment in which the animal originally lived. You can make a terrarium with five pieces of glass (four sides and bottom) taped together. The top should be made of glass as well, but should have a section cut out to allow for access to the terrarium. Place the finished glass terrarium in a large cookie or cake pan. Commercially made terrariums are also available.

Another simple terrarium can be made from a 2-liter plastic pop bottle, charcoal, pebbles, topsoil, small plants, and scissors (see the diagram).

Constructing a 2-liter bottle terrarium

Soak the bottle in warm water to remove labels and glue. Carefully pry the bottom (a) from the bottle (b) so the bottom remains intact. Turn the bottle on its side. Rub your hand over it to find the ridge. With scissors, make a slit about 1.5 cm above the ridge. Cut all the way around the bottle at that level, staying above the ridge. Discard the top of the bottle and the cap.

Put layers of charcoal, pebbles, and topsoil into part (a). Select and arrange the plants in the soil. You can add moss, bark, or small ornaments to your terrarium. Moisten, but do not saturate, the soil. Invert bottle (b) upside down into (a). Push down gently to seal. Your terrarium is ready!

Source: Virginia Gilmore, "Helpful Hints—Coca-Cola® Bottle Terrarium." Reproduced with permission by *Science and Children* 16(7), April 1979, 47. Copyright 1979 by the National Science Teachers Association, 1840 Wilson Blvd., Arlington, VA 22201.

Food Requirements for Various Animals

Food and Water	Guinea Pigs	Hamsters	Mice	Rats
Daily				
pellets		large dog pellets:		
or		1 or 2		
grain	corn, wheat, or oats		canary seeds or oats	
green or leafy vegetables, lettuce, cabbage, and celery tops	2 leaves	1 1/2 T	2 tsp	3–4 tsp
		1 leaf	1/8–1/4 leaf	1/4 leaf
or				
grass, plantain, lambs' quarters, clover, alfalfa	1 handful	1/2 handful	—	—
or				
hay, if water is also given				
carrots	1 medium			
Twice a week				
apple (medium)	1/4 apple	1/8 apple	1/2 core and seeds	1 core
iodized salt (if not contained in pellets)		sprinkle over lettuce or greens		
corn, canned or fresh, once or twice a week		1 T or	1/4 T	1/2 T or
		1/3 ear	or end of ear	end of ear
water	1/4 ear	necessary only if lettuce or greens are not provided		

Food and Water	Water Turtles	Land Turtles	Small Turtles
Daily			
worms or night crawlers	1 or 2	1 or 2	1/4 inch of tiny earthworm
or			
tubifex or bloodworms			enough to cover half the area of a dime
and/or			
raw chopped beef or meat and fish-flavored			
dog or cat food	1/2 tsp	1/2 tsp	
fresh fruit and vegetables		1/4 leaf lettuce or 6–10 berries or 1–2 slices peach, apple, tomato, melon or 1 T corn, peas, beans	
dry ant eggs, insects or other commercial turtle food			1 small pinch
water	always available at room temperature; should be ample for swimming and submersion		
	3/4 of container	large enough for shell	1/2 to 3/4 of container

Food and Water Plants (for Fish)	Goldfish	Guppies
Daily		
dry commercial food	1 small pinch	1 very small pinch; medium-size food for adults; fine-size food for babies
Twice a week		
shrimp—dry—or another kind of dry fish food	4 shrimp pellets or 1 small pinch	dry shrimp food or other dry food: 1 very small pinch
Two or three times a week		
tubifex worms	enough to cover 1/2 area of a dime	enough to cover 1/8 area of a dime
add enough "conditioned" water to keep tank at required level	allow 1 gallon per inch of fish; add water of same temperature as that in tank—at least 65°F	allow 1/4–1/2 gallon per adult fish; add water of same temperature as that in tank —about 70° to 80°F
Plants:		
cabomba, anarcharis, etc.	should always be available	

Food and Water	Newts	Frogs
Daily		
small earthworms or mealworms or	1–2 worms	2–3 worms
tubifex worms or	enough to cover 1/2 area of a dime	enough to cover 3/4 area of a dime
raw chopped beef	enough to cover a dime	enough to cover a dime
water	should always be available at same temperature as that in tank or at room temperature	

Note: See also: *Using Live Insects in Elementary Classrooms for Early Lessons in Life,* available from Center for Insect Science, Education Outreach, 800 E. University Blvd., Suite 300, Tucson, AZ 85721.

Source: Grace K. Pratt, *How to . . . Care for Living Things in the Classroom,* Arlington, VA: National Science Teachers Association, 11.

Safety Suggestions for Elementary and Middle School Inquiry Activities

1. Review science activities carefully for possible safety hazards.
2. Eliminate or be prepared to address all anticipated hazards.
3. Post appropriate safety rules in the classroom, review specific applicable safety rules before each activity, and provide occasional safety reminders during the activity.
4. Do not allow students to handle equipment, supplies, and chemicals until they have been given specific information on their use.
5. Maintain fair, consistent, and strictly enforced discipline during science activities.
6. Be particularly aware of possible eye injuries from chemical reactions, sharp objects, small objects such as iron filings, and flying objects such as rubber bands.
7. Require students to wear American National Standards Institute approved safety goggles (with Z87 printed on the goggles) whenever they do activities in which there is a potential risk to eye safety.
8. Consider eliminating open flames; use hot plates where possible as heat sources.
9. Prevent loose clothing and hair from coming into contact with any chemicals, equipment, flame, or other sources of heat.
10. Consider eliminating activities in which students taste substances; do not allow students to touch or inhale unknown substances.
11. Warn students of the dangers of handling glassware; be sure proper devices for handling hot objects are available.
12. Warn students of the dangers of electrical shock; use small dry cells in electrical activities; be aware of potential problems with the placement of extension cords.
13. Instruct students in the location and proper use of specialized safety equipment, such as fire extinguishers, fire blankets, or eye baths, when that equipment might be required by the science activity.
14. Instruct students in the proper care and handling of classroom pets, fish, or other live organisms used as part of science activities.
15. For students with disabilities, ensure safe access and use of equipment and materials.
16. Instruct students to report immediately to the teacher
    - any equipment in the classroom that appears to be in an unusual or improper condition,
    - any chemical reactions that appear to be proceeding in an improper way, or
    - any personal injury or damage to clothing caused by a science activity, no matter how trivial it may appear.
17. Provide practice sessions for safety procedures.

Sources: The University of the State of New York, *Elementary Science Syllabus*, 49, 1985, Albany, NY: The State Education Department, Division of Program Development; Ralph E. Martin, Colleen Sexton, Kay Wagner, and Jack Gerlovich, *Teaching Science for All Children*, 1994, Boston: Allyn & Bacon.

Measuring Tools, Measuring Skills

In elementary and middle school science and mathematics, students should have many opportunities to

- use a variety of types of measuring instruments;
- measure length, area, volume, mass, and temperature; and
- make comparisons using different systems of units.

Metric Prefixes

milli = .001 (one thousandth)
centi = .01 (one hundredth)
kilo = 1000 (one thousand)

Measuring Length
Length is a linear measure.

Metric Units

millimeter = 0.001 meter (one-thousandth of a meter; the thickness of about 20 pages)
centimeter = 0.01 meter (one-hundredth of a meter; width of a little fingernail)
kilometer = 1000 meters (about 10 city blocks)

Some Conversions

1 inch = 2.54 centimeters
1 centimeter = 10 millimeters
100 centimeters = 1000 millimeters = 1 meter
1 meter = 39.37 inches = 3.28 feet
1000 meters = 1 kilometer = 0.621 mile
100 meters = 109 yards
1 yard = 3 feet

Use the ruler to convert lengths between units.

1 in.	= _____ cm	= _____ mm
3 in.	= _____ cm	= _____ mm
10 cm	= _____ mm	= _____ in.
140 mm	= _____ cm	= _____ in.

Use the ruler to measure lengths.

Length of dollar bill = _____ in. = _____ cm = _____ mm
Diameter of quarter = _____ in. = _____ cm = _____ mm
Thickness of quarter = _____ in. = _____ cm = _____ mm

Measuring Area
Area is a surface measure.

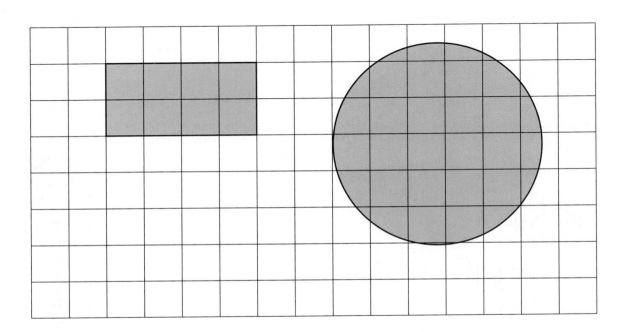

The area of each small square in the figure is 1 square centimeter = 1 cm^2.

Determine the area of the shaded rectangle

- by counting squares. _____
- by formula ($A = L \times W$). _____

Determine the area of the shaded circle

- by counting squares. _____
- by formula ($A = \pi r^2$). _____

Measuring Volume
Volume is three-dimensional.

1 cubic centimeter (cm^3 or cc) is the volume of a cube that is 1 centimeter on each side.

Some Conversions

$1 \text{ cm}^3 = 1 \text{ cc} = 1 \text{ milliliter (ml)}$
$1000 \text{ cm}^3 = 1000 \text{ ml} = 1 \text{ liter}$
$1 \text{ liter} = 1.06 \text{ quarts}$

Determine the volume of the large solid in the figure

- by counting unit cubes.
- by using the formula, $V = L \times W \times H$._____

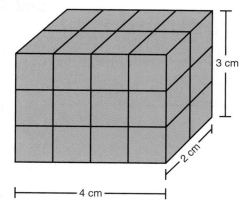

Estimate the volume of a golf ball in cubic centimeters. A golf ball has a diameter
of about 4 cm.

[*Answer:* Estimate how many unit cubes (1 cm³) might fit inside a golf ball if it were
hollow. A good estimate of its volume might be between 25 and 40 unit cubes. By formula, the volume of a golf ball is about 33.5 cm³.]

Measuring Mass and Weight

Mass is a measure of the amount of matter in an object and, also, a measure of the inertia of an object. Mass is measured in grams, milligrams, or kilograms using a balance. Weight is a measure of the
gravitational pull on an object, measured with a spring scale. Mass and weight are not the same thing,
but the weight of an object can be found from its mass.

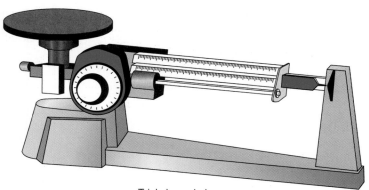

Triple beam balance

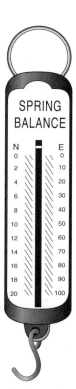

Spring scale

Some Conversions

1000 grams (g) = 1 kilogram (kg)
1 milligram = 0.001 gram (one-thousandth of a gram)
1 gram = 1000 milligrams (mg)
1 kg-mass weighs 2.2 pounds on the surface of the earth

Nutrition Facts

Serving Size 2/3 cup (55g)
Servings Per Container 12

Amount Per Serving

Calories 210
    Calories from Fat 25

% Daily Value*

Total Fat 3g	**5%**
Saturated Fat 1g	**4%**
Polyunsaturated Fat 0.5g	
Monounsaturated Fat 1.5g	
Cholesterol 0mg	**0%**
Sodium 140mg	**6%**
Potassium 190mg	**5%**
Total Carbohydrate 44g	**15%**
Other Carbohydrate 23g	
Dietary Fiber 3g	**13%**
Sugars 18g	
Protein 5g	
Vitamin A	0%
Vitamin C	0%
Calcium	2%
Iron	6%
Thiamine	10%
Phosphorus	10%
Magnesium	10%

* Percent Daily Values are based on a 2000 calorie diet. Your daily values may be higher or lower depending on your calorie needs.

	Calories	2,000	2,500
Total Fat	Less than	65g	80g
Sat Fat	Less than	20g	25g
Cholesterol	Less than	300g	300g
Sodium	Less than	2400mg	2400mg
Potassium		3500mg	3500mg
Total Carbo		300g	300g
Dietary Fiber		25g	30g

Calories per gram:
Fat 9   •   Carbohydrate 4   •   Protein 4

Some Masses and Weights

Mass of nickel = 5 g

Mass of small child weighing about 60 pounds on earth = 27.3 kg (divide 60 by 2.2)

Weight on moon of small child of mass 27.3 kg = 10 pounds (1/6 of weight on earth)

Food labels tell how many grams and milligrams of different substances are in a food product.

Measuring Temperature

Temperature is a measure of how hot or cold a substance is. Temperature is measured with a thermometer in degrees Celsius or degrees Fahrenheit.

Some Equivalent Temperatures: Use the Fahrenheit/Celsius thermometer to convert from one temperature unit to the other.

Boiling point of water	100°C =	°F
Normal body temperature	°C =	98.6 °F
Room temperature	22°C =	°F
Freezing point of water	0°C =	°F
Slush of crushed ice, water, and ice cream salt	°C =	10°F
A really cold day in Alaska	°C =	−15°F

Temperature in °C and °F

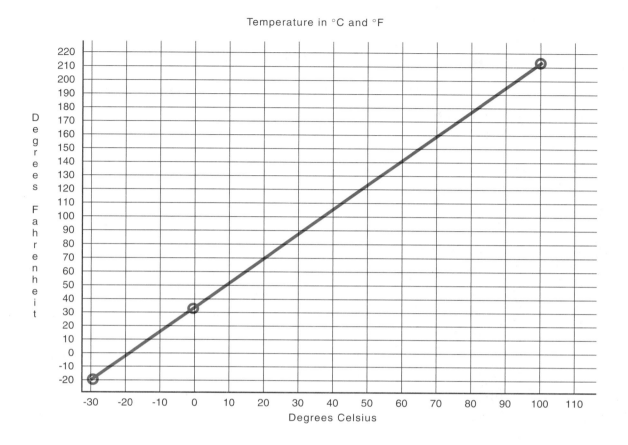

Use the graph to find equivalent temperatures.

0°C   = _____ °F
212°F = _____ °C
40°F   = _____ °C
180°F = _____ °C
50°C   = _____ °F

Selected Science Education Periodicals for Teachers and Children

American Biology Teachers

National Association of Biology Teachers
http://www.nabt.org/

Audubon Magazine

National Audubon Society
http://www.Audubon.org/nas/

Discover Magazine

http://www.discover.com/

Journal of Research in Science Teaching

National Association for Research in Science Teaching
http://www.narst.org

National Geographic

National Geographic Society
http://www.nationalgeographic.com/

National Geographic Kids

National Geographic Society
http://www.nationalgeographic.com/kids/

Natural History

American Museum of Natural History
http://www.amnh.org/naturalhistory/

Ranger Rick

National Wildlife Federation
http://www.nwf.org

School Science and Mathematics

School Science and Mathematics Association
http://www.ssma.org

Science

American Association for the Advancement of Science
http://www.aaas.org

Science and Children

National Science Teachers Association
http://www.nsta.org

Science Education

John Wiley & Sons
http://www.wiley.com

Science Scope

National Science Teachers Association
http://www.nsta.org

Scientific American

http://www.sciam.com

Sky and Telescope

Sky Publishing Corp.
http://www.skyandtelescope.com

Super Science (for grades 3–6)

Scholastic
http://teacher.scholastic.com

The Science Teacher

National Science Teachers Association
http://www.nsta.org

Your Big Backyard

National Wildlife Federation
http://www.nwf.yourbigbackyard.com/

Professional Societies for Teachers, Supervisors, and Science Educators

American Association for the Advancement of Science (AAAS)

http://www.aaas.org

American Association of Physics Teachers (AAPT)

http://www.aapt.org/

American Chemical Society (ACS)

http://www.acs.org/

Association for Educators of Teachers of Science (AETS)

http://www.aets.chem.pitt.edu/

Association for Supervision and Curriculum Development (ASCD)

http://www.ascd.org/

Council for Elementary Science International (CESI)

http://unr.edu/homepage/crowther/
    cesi.html

International Society for Technology in Education (ISTE)

http://www.iste.org/

National Association of Biology Teachers (NABT)

http://www.nabt.org/

National Association of Geoscience Teachers (NAGT)

http://www.nabt.org/

National Geographic Society (NGS)

http://www.nationalgeographic.com

National Science Teachers Association (NSTA)

http://www.nsta.org

National Wildlife Federation (NWF)

http://www.nwf.com/

School Science and Mathematics Association (SSMA)

http://www.ssma.org

Contemporary Elementary Science Projects and Programs

Name	Grades	Address	Characteristics
AIMS	K–10	AIMS Educational Foundation http://www.aimsedu.org/	*Activities for Integrating Math and Science Project:* Integration of math skills with science processes into a series of enjoyable investigatory activities; accompanying teacher booklets.
Bottle Biology	K–8	Department of Plant Pathology College of Agricultural and Life Sciences, University of Wisconsin, Madison. Available from NSTA Science Store http://www.nsta.org	*Bottle Biology* is an ideas book for exploring the world through soda bottles and other recyclable materials. The book contains over 20 scientific investigations using bottle constructions, including the Ecocolumn, the Predator-Prey Column, the Niche Kit, and the TerrAqua Column.
BSCS	K–6	BSCS http://www.bscs.org/	*Biological Science Curriculum Study:* Name of project, "Science for Living: Integrating Science, Technology, and Health." Integrated curriculum designed to relate what children know with their exploration and evaluation of new knowledge. Designed around concepts and skills for each grade level: order and organization (grade 1); change and measurement (grade 2); patterns and prediction (grade 3); systems and analysis (grade 4); transformation and investigation (grade 5); balance and decisions (grade 6). Each investigatory lesson has five sequenced phases: engagement, exploration, explanation, elaboration, and evaluation.
ESS	K–6	Available from: Delta Education http://www.delta-education.com	*Elementary Science Study:* A program of 56 nonsequential, open-ended exploratory activities that are not grade-level specific. Student worksheets, booklets, and teacher's guides. Most units are accompanied by kits of materials. Films and film loops also available. Although designed for regular students, ESS units have been shown to be useful in teaching science to children who have language deficiencies, learning difficulties, or other learning disadvantages.
FOSS	K–6	Lawrence Hall of Science http://www.lhs.Berkeley.edu/ Available from: Delta Education http://www.delta-education.com	*Full Option Science System:* Designed for both regular and special education students, 12 modules with lab kits are available. Lessons are in earth, life, and physical sciences with extension activities in language, computer, and math. Can be integrated with textbook programs and state frameworks.

Name	Grades	Address	Characteristics
GEMS	1–10	Lawrence Hall of Science http://www.lhs.Berkeley.edu/	*Great Explorations in Math and Science:* Developed at the Lawrence Hall of Science, this is a series of more than 30 teacher's guides for activities using easily obtained materials.
GrowLab	K–8	National Gardening Association http://www.kidsgardening.com	*GrowLab: Activities for Growing Minds* is a K–8 curriculum guide for use with an indoor classroom garden. Many delightful activities with catchy titles and graphics are included.
PEACHES	Preschool	Lawrence Hall of Science http://www.lhs.Berkeley.edu/	*Preschool Explorations for Adults, Children, and Educators in Science.* The PEACHES program consists of 10 teacher's guides for children's activities and teacher workshops. Teacher's guides on such topics as *Ant Homes under the Ground, Homes in a Pond, Ladybugs,* and *Elephants and Their Young* are available.
SAVI/SELPH (Designed for students with disabilities)	2–10	Available from: Sargent-Welch http://www.Sargentwelch.com Lawrence Hall of Science http://www.lhs.Berkeley.edu/	*Science Activities for the Visually Impaired/Science Enrichment Learning for the Physically Handicapped:* Teacher activity guides in nine modules, student equipment kits.
SCIS 3+	K–6	Available from: Delta Education http://www.delta-education.com	*Science Curriculum Improvement Study:* Originally developed by a team at the University of California, Berkeley, there have been several generations of SCIS developed, with the most recent being SCIS 3+. The SCIS programs are built around a hierarchy of science concepts. Science process skills are integrated into the materials-centered programs, which use an inductive instructional approach and a three-phase learning cycle: (1) student exploration, (2) teacher explanation of concepts, and (3) student application of the old with new.
STC	1–6	National Science Resources Center Smithsonian Institution Available from: Carolina Biological Supply Co. http://www.carolina.com	*Science and Technology for Children:* This program consists of units of hands-on instruction that integrate science and mathematics with other disciplines. A primary focus of program developers is to interest more females and minority children in science.

Source: Modified from Richard D. Kellough, *Integrating Mathematics and Science for Kindergarten and Primary Children*, 1996, Upper Saddle River, NJ: Merrill/Prentice Hall, 396–397.

Index